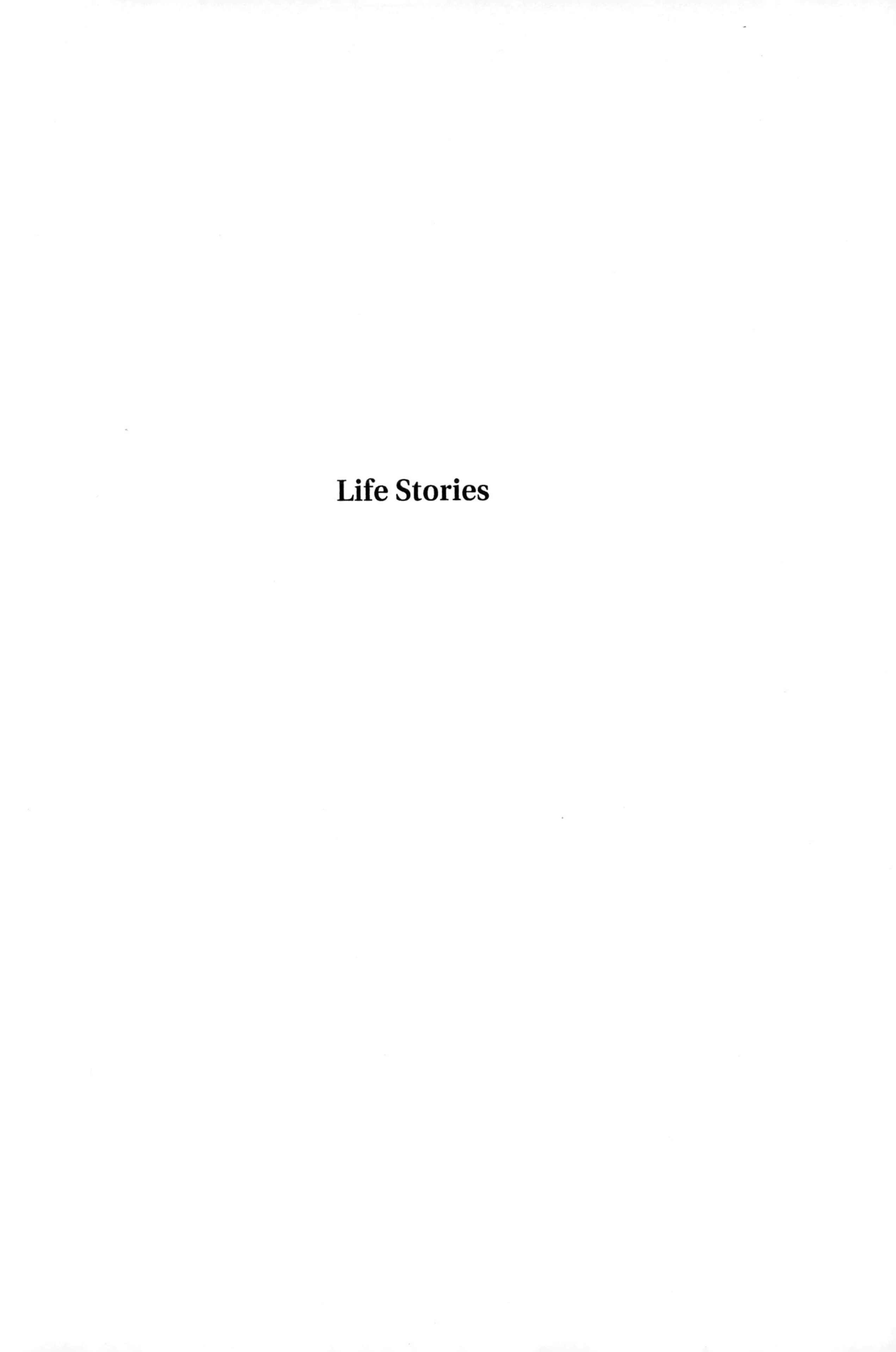

Life Stories

Recent Titles in the Libraries Unlimited Real Stories Series
Robert Burgin, Series Editor

The Inside Scoop: A Guide to Nonfiction Investigative Writing and Exposés
Sarah Statz Cords

Real Lives Revealed: A Guide to Reading Interests in Biography
Rick Roche

Women's Nonfiction: A Guide to Reading Interests
Jessica Zellers

Life Stories

A Guide to Reading Interests in Memoirs, Autobiographies, and Diaries

Maureen O'Connor

Real Stories
Robert Burgin, Series Editor

AN IMPRINT OF ABC-CLIO, LLC
Santa Barbara, California • Denver, Colorado • Oxford, England

Library of Congress Cataloging-in-Publication Data

O'Connor, Maureen, 1947-
Life stories : a guide to reading interests in memoirs, autobiographies, and diaries / Maureen O'Connor.
p. cm. -- (Real stories)
Includes bibliographical references and indexes.
ISBN 978-1-59158-527-5 (acid-free paper)
1. Autobiography--Bibliography. 2. Readers' advisory services--United States. 3. Public libraries--United States--Book lists. I. Title.
Z5301.O27 2011
[CT25]
016.92--dc23 2011017225

ISBN: 978-1-59158-527-5

15 14 13 12 2 3 4 5

Libraries Unlimited
An Imprint of ABC-CLIO, LLC

ABC-CLIO, LLC
130 Cremona Drive, P.O. Box 1911
Santa Barbara, California 93116-1911

This book is printed on acid-free paper ∞
Manufactured in the United States of America

To my three remarkable children, Geoff, Kate, and Beth O'Connor,
who will all one day be able to write their own notable memoirs.

Contents

Series Foreword

In my foreword to Sarah Statz Cords's *The Real Story: A Guide to Nonfiction Reading Interests,* I noted that her book provided a much-needed map to "the rich and varied world of nonfiction."

The titles in the Real Stories series flesh out the map that Sarah drew and take us even deeper into the exciting worlds of nonfiction genres—Investigative Writing, Biography, Autobiography and Memoir, Women's Nonfiction, True Adventure, Travel Literature, Environmental Writing, True Crime, Sports Stories, and many others.

The titles in this series are designed to assist librarians and other professionals who work with readers in identifying nonfiction books that their patrons or customers will enjoy reading. The titles in the series will also help libraries evaluate and build their collections in the various nonfiction genres.

Similar to the titles in Libraries Unlimited's Genreflecting Advisory Series, each of the volumes in the Real Stories series focuses on a popular genre in the nonfiction arena. Individual guides organize and describe hundreds of books each and include definitions of each genre and its subgenres, as well as a discussion of the appeal of the genre and its subgenres. Because readers' advisory is ultimately about making connections, recommendations of other nonfiction books and fiction read-alikes are also provided for each book highlighted.

With *The Real Story,* nonfiction lovers gained the equivalent of general guidebooks to fiction genres, such as Herald's *Genreflecting* or Saricks's *Readers' Advisory Guide to Genre Fiction.* With the titles in the Real Stories series, we now have even more specific guidebooks, similar to the fiction guides *Make Mine a Mystery* and *Hooked on Horror*.

As twentieth-century architect Mies van der Rohe reminded us, God is in the details. The titles in the Real Stories series help us to better understand the details of nonfiction and thereby to better serve our users who read nonfiction for pleasure.

On a final, personal note, this is the last title in the series that I will be editing. It has been my pleasure to work with four excellent authors—Sarah Statz Cords, Maureen O'Connor, Rick Roche, and Jessica Zellers—and a very fine editor—Barbara Ittner—to put together the first volumes in the Real Stories series. Sarah Statz Cords will now take over the work of editing future titles in the series, and I hope that she has the good fortune to work with authors as talented as those with whom I have worked.

Robert Burgin

Acknowledgments

One happy task in writing a book like this is remembering all the people who helped make it possible, either by moral support or by actual real help. As I am not shy about asking for help, I have several people to thank, beginning with Reuven Martin and his parents, Pam and Steve. Reuven spent many hours setting up the bones of an Access database for me at the beginning, and I was most grateful to him and his parents for their support. For other technical support I would like to thank Gabe O'Neill, Kevin O'Reilly, and Rajas Sambhare. My librarian friends, Chanda Gilpin and Sarah Hart, provided reference help and continuing encouragement, not to mention patience at my lack of availability for social gatherings. Agnes Garvey, also at Brampton Library at the time, was always her cheerful and accommodating self in acquiring books for me through interlibrary loan, while Marcia Aronson at Ottawa Public Library was very encouraging and sent me suggestions of memoirs to include. My friend Lin Billingsley in Kentucky went to great lengths to try to unearth some local information for me; it's always more difficult when the information is not to be found.

Many thanks, too, to Duncan Smith of EBSCO Publishing for so generously providing me with home access to *NoveList Plus*.

Of course many thanks go to Robert Burgin, whose patience, encouragement, and help with all the details have kept me going and have greatly enhanced the final product. Thanks as well to Barbara Ittner for her continuing patience and support and for her hard work in producing this series.

To Sharon DeJohn, the final editor in this endeavor, I say thank you for applying your considerable and varied skills to make this a better book, all the while keeping your calm and patience through all my questions and concerns.

My children (Geoff, Kate, and Beth) have always been at my back, ready to help, to listen, to encourage, and to answer questions that fall in their areas of expertise. Special thanks to my daughter Beth, who helped me on my way to my final draft with her consummate editing skills, her diligence, and her eagle eye.

Introduction

Purpose and Scope of This Book

In keeping with the other books in the Real Stories series published by Libraries Unlimited, this volume is a genre guide to memoirs and autobiographies in their varying formats. Divided into categories that will appeal to a variety of readers, it offers a broad range of possibilities for both the reader and the library staff helping the reader find not only a good book to read, but also a follow-up to that book, something else to capture the reader's interest once the first book has been read. Given the great popularity of memoirs these days and the profusion in publishing, it is always useful to have a guide helping one decide where to start and what to choose. Suggestions for help in using this book are detailed below.

This book is meant to be a popular introduction to the memoir and autobiography, a sampling of the titles available, rather than an in-depth, scholarly work. There have been countless books and articles written on the topic, covering the autobiography or memoir in general, specific formats of autobiography or memoir, and specific groups of autobiographers or memoirists. There are also courses in the field, for both researchers and writers. It was not, however, my mandate to add to that academic field. Although I have offered some historical touchstones, this is not a history of the memoir. (Those interested in that aspect of the memoir may read Ben Yagoda's accessible ***Memoir: A History*** for a popular history of the genre.) For those interested in greater analysis of the memoir/autobiography genre, or in how to write a memoir, I have created a list of resources in Appendix D.

Selection Process

Library Web sites were one of the main sources I used to gather titles for possible inclusion as main entries in this book. Many libraries offer lists of biographies that might also include memoirs and autobiographies or lists that are specifically autobiographical. Some libraries also offer the always interesting "Nonfiction That Reads Like Fiction" list, which usually includes at least some memoirs and autobiographies. The incomparable Molly Williams, a library volunteer in Maine, has developed a Web site that lists library booklists (http://librarybooklists.org/index.html). Her site, Library Booklists, includes a link to the libraries that have booklists with that very title, "Nonfiction That Reads Like Fiction." Other useful sources, excluding libraries, are listed below:

- Adult Reading Round Table (ARRT) Nonfiction Genre Study (http://www.arrtreads.org/nonfictiongenrestudy.htm). You can also check out ARRT for other lists.
- BiblioTravel (http://www.bibliotravel.com/)
- *Booklist Online* (requires a subscription)
- Fiction_L booklists (http://www.webrary.org/rs/flbklistmenu.html)
- Lists of Bests, a Web site that includes, among others, the Modern Library's "100 Best Books of the 20th Century," the *Hungry Mind Review*'s "100 Best 20th-Century American Books of Fiction and Nonfiction," the *Guardian*'s list of "100 Best Books of All Time," and the New York Public Library's "Books of the Century" (http://www.listsofbests.com/lists/home/books)
- Longitude Books—Recommended Reading for Travelers (http://www.longitudebooks.com/home.html)
- *NoveList Plus* (requires a subscription)
- *Outside* Online, "The Outside Canon" (http://outsideonline.com/magazine/0596/9605feo.html?rf_region_dd=5&rf_state_dd=&price=4)
- overbooked.com: a resource for readers (http://www.overbooked.org/)
- *The Reader's Advisor Online* (http://www.readersadvisoronline.com/blog/)
- ReadingGroupGuides (http://www.readinggroupguides.com/findaguide/biography.asp)
- *Sports Illustrated*, "The Top 100 Sports Books of All Time" (http://sportsillustrated.cnn.com/si_online/features/2002/top_sports_books/1/)

In addition to booklists generated by libraries and other Web sites, I also made use of lists provided by a number of award-granting organizations. If the organizations offered awards for nonfiction in general, I combed those lists; if they offered awards for biography, autobiography, and/or memoir, so much the better. Many of the awards' Web sites list finalists as well as winners, which was very useful. Appendix C details the major awards I have included in my annotations, although I also consulted lists by regional award-granting organizations.

Once I had amassed a significant number of autobiographical titles (4,000 or so), I then needed to cull them, which I initially did by determining their availability in North America through WorldCat (http://www.worldcat.org/). Unless it had won a major award, I established early on that a title had to be in at least 1,200 libraries to qualify as a main entry. Using this criterion, it became clear that a common element among many of these titles was that they were older, and of those, many were out-of-print. I then set new criteria, namely that the title had to be in print and in at least 500 libraries. Many of the original titles that were pulled to make way for more current titles can be found in the classics sections or in Appendix A.

Because I know there will be a significant Canadian audience for this book as well, I had slightly different criteria for the inclusion of Canadian memoirs. I checked Library and Archives Canada, the Toronto Public Library, and the Vancouver Public Library for availability in Canadian libraries. Because my professional career has been spent in Canada, I felt that I had an empirical knowledge of the types of memoirs that would interest Canadian (and other) readers and made my choices accordingly.

Using various online resources for information, I was able to keep up-to-date with new publications, so that titles published as late as the fall of 2010 are also included.

The end result is that there are 655 main entries, with over 2,800 distinct read-alikes and other titles. The nature of these works ranges from seminal in the field to ephemeral but current, from literary to pedestrian in style. There should be something among them to appeal to most readers. The books also cross disciplines, sometimes creating a conundrum for placing them. Readers may expect to find a specific author in a specific chapter, but an overriding feature of that author or memoir may have convinced me to put it elsewhere—thus one benefit of the Author/Title Index. Readers will be reminded throughout that many of the memoirs found in one chapter could easily fit in another.

How to Use This Book

Organization of the Chapters

There are thirteen chapters in this book, each focusing on a specific topic. The book starts on a primarily upbeat note, featuring the excitement of "Travel and Adventure"; as the reader moves through the next chapters, "Celebrities," "The Creative Life," "The Working Life," and "Place and Time," the tone starts to become more serious, with such topics as "Life Away from Home," "Life with Others," and "The Inner Life." "The Political Life" begins the segue into the darker and more turbulent section of the book, as we see just how difficult people's lives have been in "Changing Lives in History," "Life on the Dark Side of History," "Life at War," and "Surviving Life." While the writers' lives have been downright dreadful at times, their spirit of hope often comes through, so that what might seem to be a book of despair is actually a book of inspiration.

Each of the chapters has the same basic setup. They all begin with an introduction to that category of memoir, sometimes with a bit of history given, when known. The appeal of the category follows, along with a brief explanation of how the chapter is organized.

The entries begin with five "Classics," titles that may be out of print but are still widely available and widely read. They represent people who have made history in their fields, blazed trails, or otherwise contributed to society. Some of the titles in these sections may appear too new to be called classics. Elaine Showalter, a professor of English at Princeton, defines what she refers to as an "instant classic," referring specifically to fiction, but her definition applies to nonfiction as well: "An instant classic is a contemporary novel that immediately dazzles readers, influences other writers, attracts the interest of academics, wins prizes and enters the literary curriculum" (Showalter, 2000). So it is with the memoirs that I have labeled "classic." They made a big splash when they were originally published, and they continue to be read by many. There is more on the classics in Appendix A.

Then each chapter is divided into subsections, broken down into categories that relate to the chapter as a whole. Following the entries with their annotations is "Consider Starting With . . . ," a list of suggested titles, taken from that chapter, with which to begin. "Fiction Read-Alikes" come next, again based on the topic of that particular chapter. The sources of any quotes that have been used in the chapter are at the end, under "Works Cited."

The Main Entries, Annotations and "Now Try" Sections

Each of the main entries has four parts. The first is the bibliographic or publishing information. The authors' names, with their birth and death dates where known, are given, followed by any authorial help the author may have had, whether it was in the writing or the editing of the work. Next is the title, followed by edition and new introduction, preface, etc., if applicable, then the publisher—not necessarily the original one, as the dates that follow the publisher are the most recent American publication dates, along with the original copyright date. Following are such facts as number of pages and whether or not there are illustrations or maps. The ISBN of the latest publication date follows that, and then the various formats in which the title is available. At times an abridged audiobook is read by the author, whereas the full-text is read by a freelance audiobook reader. Whenever authors were involved in any way in the reading of their books, that was indicated in this part of the entry. To add one more descriptive characteristic to the title to aid potential browsers, the Dewey decimal number has been provided. If the book is a translation, the translator's name is included at the end in square brackets.

The book's annotation tells a little about the author and a little about the book itself. Sometimes the annotation recounts a bit of the author's story and sometimes a little about the publishing history of the book, if that seems germane. This is the feature that may help readers decide whether or not to pick up that memoir. If the author has won specific personal awards, they are mentioned here, and if the book has been a finalist for or won a book award, that is also mentioned here. Because the worlds that individual memoirists travel in can be small, their work and writings may at times intersect with others. Where memoirists are mentioned in annotations for titles other than their own or in text and there are main entries for those authors elsewhere in this book, their names have been underscored. "Subjects" follow, providing another access point. Occasionally subject headings may not seem to apply, based on the annotation, but that is because there was more to the book than could be described in the annotation. In addition, if the book won an award that is listed in Appendix C, there will be a subject heading for that award. Because readers are often interested in reading about people who have lived a long time, I have added the subject headings "Octogenarians," "Nonagenarians," and "Centenarians." (Yes, there are indeed a few of those!)

The final section, "Now Try," is a major feature of good readers' advisory service. These titles are meant to offer something else to the reader who has enjoyed the main entry. The titles in the "Now Try" section are a mix. To begin with, if there are other interesting or relevant titles by the memoirist, I have made mention of them. If there are interesting or relevant titles about the memoirist, I have often mentioned them as well. I then selected three other titles, what readers' advisors call "read-alikes." These choices follow two separate theories of readers' advisory. One is to find something that "feels" like the book, in terms of tone, writing style, or mood. It can sometimes be difficult to find a good match based on those criteria, because although the style or mood may match, the book may still be quite different overall from the original memoir and not at all what the reader is looking for. The other theory is to follow a reading path (usually referred to as a reading map). In this case, the idea is to find something salient in the original work that sparks the curiosity or interest of the reader and offer other titles to help the reader pursue that idea or information. For example, if readers enjoyed reading in ***An American Childhood*** about Annie Dillard's interest in the natural life she found in her city, Pittsburgh, they might also enjoy reading about another young girl who had a similar interest, but in her rural home, in Mary Lawson's ***Crow Lake***. Another example might be Sheila Munro's memoir, ***Lives of Mothers & Daughters: Growing Up with Alice Munro***, about her and her mother. Readers may then want to read about other mother–daughter relationships, perhaps even as specific as mother–daughter writers as in Linda Gray Sexton's ***Searching for Mercy Street: My Journey Back to My Mother, Anne Sexton***. As I wrote each "Now Try" section, I felt that I was back in the library, having a conversation with you, the reader, about what books you might enjoy after reading the original memoir, so that the selections in this book are based on my own style of readers' advisory. Anyone else writing this same book would likely offer quite different suggestions; while readers' advisory is based on theory, it still is an art and therefore subjective. My goal in writing this section was not to repeat read-alikes, thus offering as broad a range of titles overall as possible. Except for fourteen repeated titles, I managed to do that.

Although the majority of the read-alikes are nonfiction, over 300 are fiction, not counting the "Fiction Read-Alikes" sections. I urge readers to look closely at these read-alikes; many of the authors are award winners in their own right, whether for their writing or for work in their field. There may even be more MacArthur Fellows among the read-alikes than among the main entries, yet those awards are rarely alluded to in the "Now Try" section.

"Consider Starting With . . ." and "Fiction Read-Alike" Sections

Following the annotated entries is a list drawn from them, "Consider Starting With . . ." Most of the chapters have titles numbering in the thirties and forties, but three have titles numbering in the eighties. Sometimes it's difficult to know where to begin, so I have picked ten from each chapter as a possible start, pulling from each of the sections titles that are either seminal to the literature or of particular interest for one reason or another. The "Fiction Read-Alikes" that follow that list are ten suggestions of novels to read based on the subject matter of the chapter.

Works Cited

Each chapter ends with a list of sources consulted that I have quoted from directly. Those interested in the subject of memoirs may find here some signposts for further reading.

Appendices and Indexes

Following the thirteen chapters are four appendices. The first is a list of classics that I felt it necessary to at least mention and include in the Author/Title Index. As I mentioned earlier in the Introduction, these may be older titles and even out of print, but they are important in the canon of memoirs and autobiographies, and their writers are important for their contributions during their lifetimes. If a classic title was used as a read-alike, however, it will not be listed in this appendix.

Appendix B is "Controversial Titles." Truth is a significant issue in memoir writing, and the titles in this section do not meet the basic criterion of telling the truth to the best of one's memory. Many of these titles created a furor when the deceptions were discovered; James Frey does not hold the monopoly on this kind of controversy. While they are not included as main entries in the book, I felt they needed to be mentioned.

The third appendix lists the relevant major national and international awards that many of the writers have won, detailing what the award recognizes. There are no awards specific to memoir only, but memoir/autobiography is now recognized as a legitimate category for book awards. In looking at various awards, it is often plain to see that initially a book award might have been given for biography, and then autobiography was added, often coupled with the biography award; finally memoir was added, often with autobiography being severed from biography and included now with memoir. This change in focus reflects the increasing popularity of the memoir genre. As yet, however, no one has created an individual book award solely for the memoir. In this book, as much as possible, all the awards granted to a book have been indicated in the annotations, whether the book was a finalist or a winner. However, in the subject headings, and in Appendix C, only major national and international awards have been highlighted.

The final appendix is a list of resources for the person who has a keen interest in the genre of memoir/autobiography. They are either analyses of the genre or books designed to help the budding memoir writer. The list is by no means inclusive.

The book ends with two indexes, the first of the authors and titles referred to throughout the book. The other, a subject index derived from the subject headings provided with each entry, also includes the names of people referred to in the annotations who are not the memoirists. Including these names in the index adds access to over 500 more people.

Suggestions for Use

Those who use this book should find several access points, whether the user is a readers' advisory staff person or an interested reader. The Table of Contents might be the first place to start, if one is interested in a particular kind of memoir, because it breaks down the chapters into their various sections. In the Author/Title Index, the page numbers of the main entries for the memoirists and their titles are in boldface type. If readers have a favorite author, or a particular title in mind that they have enjoyed, they can look it up in the index, then consult that page to find other titles that might appeal. By the same token, if readers are interested in a specific topic that may cross chapter categories (African-American women, for example), or a format such as graphic narratives, they can look those up in the Subject Index and see where that leads them. There are more than 2,800 subject headings, offering a broad range for readers. Simply browsing can also be fun; as I was writing this book I found of interest any number of titles in areas that I normally wouldn't even think about reading and am excited to share them with potential readers.

The Autobiographical Genre

Definitions

Autobiographical writing has been around for centuries, represented by autobiography, memoir, personal essays, journals, diaries, letters, novels, and even poetry. But the memoir has taken hold and leapt out in front of all the autobiographical formats and for that reason is largely represented throughout this book.

Although at times the words "memoir" and "autobiography" are used interchangeably, there really is a difference between the two. The autobiography is generally seen as the purview of a person who has been in the public eye and who, toward the end of an illustrious life, sets that life down, generally in chronological order, for posterity. The memoir, in contrast, tends to be shortened in time and focuses more on the writer as an individual. "Unlike autobiography, which moves in a dutiful line from birth to fame, memoir narrows the lens, focusing on a time in the writer's life that was unusually vivid, such as childhood or adolescence, or that was framed by war or travel or public service or some other special circumstance" (Zinsser, 1998). Judith Barrington, a poet, memoirist, and creative-writing teacher, makes an excellent distinction between the two: "A quick key to understanding the difference between the two lies in the choice of a preposition: autobiography is a story *of* a life; memoir is a story *from* a life. The latter makes no pretense of capturing the whole span from birth to the time of writing; in fact, one of the important skills of memoir writing is the selection of the theme that will bind the work together and set boundaries around it" (Barrington, 2007). As readers will see, this theme can cover almost the entire range of knowledge and can be written in tones ranging from light and hopeful to dark and despairing.

Journals and diaries, along with letters, are perhaps the most personal of the autobiographical writings. Apart from being a recounting of daily activities, people seen, and events attended, they can also be the source of the most honest thoughts of the writer. Most diaries or journals were written for the writer alone: "The book, carefully hidden, is both friend and confidant, one from whom neither criticism nor treachery need be feared. The daily words comfort, justify, absolve" (James, 2000). That said, however, there are some writers who planned to make their diaries and journals public, offering to the world at large insights into their thinking as well as the political and social history of the day.

Letters are often the most honest reflection of writers' thoughts and deeds, unless the writers assume that their letters will be published. Although autobiographical writing for publication was not very common among women before the twentieth century, some women did narrate their lives for publication, and a sharp contrast was noted between what they may have written in their letters to friends and relatives and what they wrote in their autobiographies. The real person came through in the letters; the autobiography was a whitewashed version. Because of the volume of collections of letters available, and because the nature of the format is significantly different from the autobiographical narrative, with very few exceptions, letters have not been included in this book.

Personal essays also provide a way for writers to share themselves with their readers, but in quite a different manner. The personal essay is generally seen as the way writers work through their own thoughts and ideas about events or issues, so that the reader is almost watching the writer thinking. Alfred Kazin, a noted essayist, describes his format "'as an open form—as a way of thinking things out for himself, as a way of discovering what he thinks . . . it is not the thought that counts but the experience we get of the writer's thought; not the self, but the self thinking'" (quoted in Steinberg, 2003).

As we will see in a later discussion of the history of the genre, autobiographical novels were chosen by many authors as the way to tell their story, a path chosen to diminish the vulnerability of the writer. Poetry too has been used, most notably by Walt Whitman in ***Leaves of Grass***, as a means of telling the writer's story.

For our purposes, however, the focus here is on the memoir, a format that has come into its own in the last fifty years and shows no signs of disappearing.

Traits of the Memoir

Style

Memoirs "are the traces of a life: memories of others, of situations, and of one's own self. . . . Stories of having lived, in the best words the writer can capture to tell them, are shaped from these traces" (Carr, 2008). They are the most democratic form of the autobiographical genre, in that anyone can write a memoir, whether famous or not, regardless of race, color, creed, gender, or sexual orientation. But there are expectations: memoirs should combine an honest rendering of the writer's experience with a readable story. And writers must engage in a contract with their readers: "The way it is represented here is, to the best of our knowledge, the way it happened" (Clark, 2007).

How writers honor that contract is a major issue in any discussion of the memoir. The memoir is known today to be part of the larger genre of "creative nonfiction," a label that would appear to be an oxymoron. But the expectation is that writers will use the techniques of creative writing to create a gripping story of their experience, an experience that is real and therefore not fiction. The tools used in crafting fiction—plot, character development, setting, and language—when used in a memoir, enhance the writer's story. Jill Ker Conway describes it this way: "In order to construct a lively narrative you have to select—just the way a novelist does—what events to highlight, what characters to develop, which ones to leave just in an outline. You have to build up tension in a narrative and resolve it. And those are all the art of the novelist" (Conway, 1998a). Conway refers to the notion of selecting, a real conundrum for the memoirist. By selecting what one includes or excludes, where to start and to end, the story shifts its focus; it is incumbent on the writer, then, to keep faith with the contract and remain true to the story being told. The tone should be intimate, as though one were having a conversation over coffee or in a bar, but as Annie Dillard says, the writer mustn't "'hang on the reader's arm, like a drunk, and say, 'And then I did this and it was so interesting'" (quoted in Zinsser, 1998). There must be judicious selection to keep the story moving.

Vivian Gornick offers a theory about memoir writing that is quite apt. She distinguishes between a situation and a story, and it is that distinction that makes writing a memoir so challenging. The writer lives through a situation, but must make the telling of that situation a story, must put herself back there, remembering who she was then and what she was thinking and feeling then. This becomes a process of self-definition, as presumably the purpose in writing is to interpret the situation and what it meant to the writer in her personal development and growth. As Bernard Cooper puts it, "'The chief privilege of writing a memoir was the opportunity to go back and make sense of events that left me dumbstruck, mired in confusion, unarmed with the luminous power of words'" (quoted in Drager, 2007). Gornick sums up thus: "Every work of literature has both a situation and a story. The situation is the context or circumstance, sometimes the plot; the story is the emotional experience that preoccupies the writer: the insight, the wisdom, the thing one has come to say"

(Gornick, 2001). (Ironically Gornick, prolific in the field of creative writing and memoir, stunned an audience of creative writers when she admitted to the use of "literary license" in her memoir about her mother, creating characters and situations that were not true. That is why her book, ***Fierce Attachments: A Memoir,*** is listed in Appendix B, among the controversial titles.)

Critics today laud what they refer to as the "literary memoir" and usually hail writers such as Mary Karr and Frank McCourt for their excellence in that regard: "The literary memoir is not lies packaged as truth, but truth told as a conscious act of construction" (Hetzel, 2006). Mary Karr's first memoir, ***The Liars' Club: A Memoir,*** is a prime example of this. The story opens with a highly dramatic scene in which she, the young child, refuses to talk, creating suspense in the reader: What happened? Why won't she say anything? The reader does not learn for quite some time what actually happened before the opening scene. This "construction" is a reflection of how the author herself felt when writing about that situation: she needed to approach it slowly, introducing it and then drawing back. By using this construction, she succeeds in gripping the reader and at the same time illustrating how it actually was for her in living the situation.

Culture

It is difficult to talk about the influence of culture on the memoir without bringing in the history of autobiographical writing, so there may be some overlap here with the history that follows. The issue of culture is a circular one: the memoirist describes the way we live now (or the way he lived then), but that way is formed by the culture of the day; yet the telling of it influences the culture. "In short, we live in an auto/biographical age that uses the personal narrative as a lens onto history and the contemporary world. In every medium, cultures are permeated and increasingly transformed by auto-biographical narratives, productions, and performances of identity." At the same time, "the role and function of auto-biographical genres are . . . closely connected to our understanding of the times and places in which we live" (Egan and Helms, 2002). One source of the furor over memoir, in conjunction with the question of style, is how memoirists present themselves: Are they placing themselves "within the context of a vital historical moment," or are they presenting their lives as that vital historical moment (Clarke, 1999)? If the latter, the memoir generally loses credibility, as writers thus appear to be "navel-gazing" narcissists. The phrase "the personal is political" became almost a mantra of the twentieth century, but in fact, the truth of it has long been evident in autobiographical writing, as writers place themselves in the context of their historical time, either as witnesses to or participants in major events.

What writers reveal about themselves and their situations and how they do so is also a significant part of the cultural context. Jean-Jacques Rousseau broke away from the "powerful taboos and social covenants" (Zinsser, 1998) of his day when he wrote his revolutionary autobiography, ***Confessions***. But Janet Mason Ellerby didn't/couldn't write the story of her situation for almost fifty years. In ***Following the Tambourine Man: A Birthmother's Memoir,*** she tells her story of being unwed and pregnant in the 1960s, sent to a home for unwed mothers, and forced to give up her baby for adoption.

In today's culture, young women reading that story might be shocked: not that she was pregnant "out of wedlock," but that she was treated in such a manner. They will recognize how different their world is from Ellerby's, a world in which Ellerby would not have been able to tell her story publicly by writing a memoir.

Issues in Autobiographical Writing

Truth

It seems as though one cannot talk about the memoir these days without invoking the name of James Frey as the exemplar of the "problem" of the memoir. Much ink was spilled over the fact that he lied in his memoir. The fact is, though, that he first presented that book to his publisher as a novel; it was the publisher who changed it to a memoir and who should really bear the brunt of the blame. There are other writers more guilty of tarring the memoir genre with the brush of untruth, and they can be found in Appendix B. In writing about memoir and the issue of truth, writers take two sides. On the one hand are those for whom "emotional truth" is the core, and it doesn't really matter how the writer achieves it. Even as far back as the first century BCE, Cicero said that "it is the strength of the argument that matters most, . . . not the precision of its evidence" (D'Agata, 2003). On the other hand are those for whom the contract between the writer and the reader is sacred, who hold that the measures often taken to achieve emotional truth belong in fiction, not in memoirs. What Frey had done was create a character in his story that helped him cope with his situation and come to an understanding of it; it was not the real James Frey in that story. This is why he was right to present it to the publisher as a novel, as many autobiographical novelists do.

Several factors influence the issue of truth in a memoir, one of them being style. As discussed previously, the memoirist is encouraged to use novelistic techniques in bringing the story to life, using character, setting, plot, language, and other stylistic devices to enhance the storytelling. Writers often use actual dialogue in their memoirs, a fact that causes great concern among critics, disbelieving that one could accurately remember actual conversations. The poet Molly Peacock has an interesting take on that. She refers to it as a "mimicking." When she sat down to write her memoir, ***Paradise, Piece by Piece***, she took herself back in memory, sitting on the floor under the kitchen table, listening to the adults talk: "I could 'hear' them speak. I could mimic them the way only a child mimics a parent or a teacher, with . . . appalling accuracy. Thus, as I remembered each situation and reinserted myself into it, remaking myself small, retuning myself to the feelings of being in that place and at that time, I reheard their voices, now coming out of my own heart, that is, my own mouth" (Peacock, 1999). Using such techniques is quite acceptable in the eyes of most critics; what is not acceptable is adding to the story characters, places, and events that did not exist, simply to make a better story. The question of truth is intertwined in the following issues as well.

Memory

One cannot talk about truth and the memoir without talking about memory. Critics of the memoir ask how anything in the memoir can be trusted, given the untrustworthiness of memory. Proponents of emotional truth as opposed to accuracy agree with Maureen Murdock, who refers to "'the fragmented and selective nature of memory, which, though not always factually accurate, conveys an emotional truth that is crucial in identity development'" (quoted in Bannan, 2005). But other authors, recognizing the difficulties presented by memory, still adhere to the idea that it is their memory and therefore the truth of their situation and their story. We have all experienced retelling a family story only to be contradicted by another family member. Yet the memory is clear in our minds as the way we are telling the story. Wayson Choy said of his memoir, ***Paper Shadows: Memoir of a Past Lost and Found,*** "'No doubt, other views and opinions exist about the same persons and events. This book is, however, about the people and stories as I remember them—from my own life'" (quoted in Fetherling, 2001). W. B. Yeats recognizes a basic problem with memory when discussing his memoir, ***Reveries over Childhood and Youth***: "'I have changed nothing of my memories to my knowledge; and yet it must be that I have changed many things without my knowledge'" (quoted in Yagoda, 2009).

Author and writing instructor William Loizeaux offers a theory on various degrees of memory and remembering in the memoir. The most accurate is the memory based on written fact: a diary entry, a document, research discovered. Alice Sebold's ***Lucky*** is a good case in point: she used police reports and trial transcripts to tell much of the story of her rape. The next most accurate is an actual memory retrieved by the writer, deemed as a sharp memory, full of details and therefore believable. Following that is not so much a memory as what Loizeaux refers to as "informed imagination." Mary Karr describes a scene that must have happened, although she doesn't actually remember it; it did need to have happened, though, in view of what followed, and it was logical that it happened as she described it. She also says that her family must have wept at a certain point because they were "a family of inveterate weepers" (***The Liars' Club: A Memoir***, p. 258). And then there is the absence of memory, the fact of which, when admitted to by the writer, adds greatly to the credibility of the memoir. Alice Sebold often points out a detail that she doesn't remember, something as small as who lived next door to her. These memoirists tell their story as we would tell a friend our stories, interrupting ourselves to explain the level of veracity in our tales (Loizeaux, 2006).

Ethics

One of the questions about truth in the memoir is, "Who is looking over the writer's shoulder?" Whose familial voice is in the writer's head saying, "You can't tell that story!" If there is someone psychologically looking over the writer's shoulder, is that influencing the story? the angle? the truth? One of the reasons writers might choose to write their stories late in life is to avoid hurting people or invading their privacy, hoping that most people will no longer be around to read the work. Other authors ask specifically not to have their stories published until after their own deaths. Lucille Ball hid her manuscript, not to be found until after her death; the note she left on it stated that she didn't want to hurt her first husband, Desi Arnaz. What are the ethics involved in telling tales on others while telling your own tale? For some writers, it is all about the writing, and everything else becomes secondary. An interesting situation arose in the Hendra family. Tony Hendra, a satirist and former editor of the *National Lampoon*, wrote a "confessional" memoir entitled ***Father Joe: The Man Who Saved My Soul***. The following year his daughter, Jessica, wrote her own memoir, with the help of Blake Morrison, ***How to Cook Your Daughter: A Memoir***, detailing what her father had left out in his "confession": his sexual abuse of her. She did this knowing that she was now violating her father, although not to the extent to which he had violated her, and that she would thus sever any hope of reconciliation with him. One can sense in this the importance to her of coming to grips with the abuse she had suffered.

Particularly since the James Frey incident, publishers ask their writers to change people's names in the interests of preserving the subjects' privacy, and at times authors will do it themselves. They may also change telling details to protect someone's privacy, but this starts to beg the issue of truth. If the author changes the location of an event, the spot where he chooses to place it could create a set of expectations in the reader, expectations that cannot truthfully be met. For example, if the writer grew up in a number of towns, but for simplicity's sake described his life events as taking place in one town only, the reader has the expectation that the culture of that town may have formed the writer, when such is not necessarily the case. The writer may also change names of schools, for example, creating fictitious names. What happens to researchers who are using that memoir as a primary source for a topic they are working on?

Voice and Authorship

The question of voice is an interesting one in the memoir, and again truth and memory are large players here. William Gass offers a tongue-twisting rendition of the issue: autobiography divides the self "into the-one-who-was and the-one-who-is. The-one-who-is has the advantage of having been the-one-who-was. Once." (Gass, 1994). Thus there are two personae involved in the memoir: the one who is telling the story and the one who lived the story. But whose truth is it? Does it belong to the-one-who-is (as an adult, with many years' experience and perspective to add to the mix) or to the-one-who-was, who has only a child's-eye view of the situation? If the writer follows Gornick's theory of looking at the situation and, remembering who the-one-who-was was, the-one-who-is should be able to write a creditable story. When writing about earlier days, particularly childhood days, the danger for the memoirist is in losing empathy and understanding for that younger child. Despite knowing what the adult knows, the writer should not disdain the child's fears, disappointments, or joys at small pleasures.

Throughout this book, the reader will find entries that begin with the memoirist's name, often followed on a second line by a coauthor's name. In the read-alikes section of the entries, after citing a memoirist's name, the phrase "with the help of" often appears. This is known as *collaborative autobiography*, and it comes in various "packages." Although a significant number of the memoirists in this book are writers by trade, an equally significant number are not. For them to write their own stories seems almost inconceivable in some cases. There are writers whose names reappear throughout this book as coauthors of several memoirs, because this is how they earn their living: writing others' life stories as told to them by the subjects. This differs from biography in the following ways: the biographer may never meet the subject, particularly if the subject is dead; and the biographer usually gathers information for the book from other books, documents, and interviews with the subject's associates, although in the case of an authorized biography, the writer may also have personal access to the subject. The difference for the reader is "that one reads an autobiography to see how the writer experienced and evaluates his or her life and a biography to find a more objective view" (Hudgins, 1996).

The coauthor of a memoir usually spends many hours with the subject, listening to the stories, pulling out details, trying to correct inconsistencies, persuading the subject to open up to the feelings and thoughts that went along with the situations. The really skilled coauthors will be able not only to write the story, but to do so in the voice of the subject as well, so that those who personally know the subject will believe that it is indeed a legitimate telling. But what if the coauthor knows that the subject is skewing the true version of events, a skewing that can be verified through research? Wherein does the coauthor's loyalty lie? To the truth of the historical record or to the story of the memoirist? In many cases the subject has the opportunity to read what the coauthor has written, making corrections, deleting sections, etc. Discrepancies between what the subject has said and what the coauthor has written should certainly come out at this point. On the other side of that coin, however, is an infamous story about Ronald Reagan's coauthored memoir, ***An American Life***, of which he apparently said, "'I hear it's a terrific book! One of these days I'm going to read it myself'" (Green, 2009).

Not all writers acknowledge their coauthors in their books. Sarah Palin's ***Going Rogue: An American Life*** is a case in point. Nowhere on her title page or copyright page is there a suggestion that anyone but Palin wrote her story. But with today's technological networking, it became widely known that Lynn Vincent helped her with the story. This is what is referred to as ghostwriting, since the coauthor is not visible, and it raises some ethical questions. Is this plagiarism, suggesting that the writer is taking credit for work—and no one knows what percentage of the work—done by someone else? And if we cannot trust the authorship, can we trust the content? It also suggests a false image of the memoirist: that he or she is capable of writing a coherent book when, in fact, that may not be the case.

Another form of collaborative autobiography is ethnographic autobiography; one could write a book on that topic alone. Briefly, we can look at the story of Black Elk to illustrate the problems of ethics, voice, and truth in collaborative ethnographic autobiography. To begin with, Black Elk welcomed John G. Neihardt onto the reservation and after several meetings with him finally agreed to tell Neihardt his story. He told it in Lakota. Neihardt also spoke to Black Elk's family and other members of the Oglala Nation. Neihardt translated the Lakota into English, adding his own perspective. Not wanting to admit to Black Elk's acculturation and conversion to Roman Catholicism, he left that out; Neihardt wanted to tell a story of an American Indian shaman who stayed true to his heritage. But that was not Black Elk's story. This situation raises issues of both truth and ethics, particularly if the coauthor has an agenda separate from the subject's. Despite this co-opting of Black Elk's story, I decided to keep the entry, ***Black Elk Speaks,*** in the book for its overall significance.

Appeal of the Autobiographical Genre

The appeal of the autobiographical genre for the reader may be closely aligned to the appeal for the writer. Very often writers need to write their stories, to understand who they are and what their place is in this world, often to lay to rest ghosts that won't let them move on. For the same reason, readers may also need to read these stories, to understand who they are and what their place is in this world, often to lay to rest ghosts that won't let them move on.

Experiential

Perhaps the most important appeal of the memoir is the experiential one. Several authors have weighed in on this, saying why they have written at least one memoir. Their motives for writing often become an appeal factor for the reader. If we look at why an author wants to write a memoir, we will see a positive outcome for the reader. The writer writes to pass on a learning experience to the reader, and the reader then learns and benefits from the writer's experience. St. Augustine, whose ***The Confessions*** dates from 397 CE, felt that his story of sin, suffering, and redemption could encourage and inspire other sinners to recognize how they too could be redeemed. Peter Abelard, a medieval philosopher and author of ***The Story of My Misfortunes; the Autobiography of Peter Abelard,*** said "'In comparing your sorrows with mine you may discover that yours are in truth nought, or at the most but of small account, and so shall you come to bear them more easily'" (quoted in Yagoda, 2009). Henry Louis Gates Jr., a twentieth-century African-American academic and author of a childhood memoir, ***Colored People: A Memoir,*** said: "'I wanted to write a book that imitated the specialness of black culture when no white people are around. . . . If you ask me what the legacy of my book will be . . . I would like it to make younger people feel freer to tell their own stories'" (quoted in Zinsser, 1998). Jill Ker Conway, a twentieth-century academic, feminist, and author of several memoirs, including ***The Road from Coorain,*** said "'I thought it was important . . . to relate the story of a young woman taking charge of her own life in an unromantic way, in which it's perfectly clear that she arrives at a moment of choice'" (quoted in Zinsser, 1998). Bobbie Ann Mason, a twentieth-century novelist and author of ***Clear Springs: A Memoir,*** speaks for many writers and readers when she says, "'I think it's a natural impulse to want to find some kind of coherence and meaning in your life, to find that it has a narrative, and that there are patterns. There are themes in your life, and themes that connect back to previous generations. You can see where you fit into the puzzle'" (Mason, 1999). The main idea in the experiential appeal is that readers can look at someone else's story through their own lens, seeing what others make of the world, how others have coped with trauma, and what other families are like, and make informed judgments about their own views of the world, see how they can now cope with trauma, perhaps look at their own families differently. Even stories that should be inherently different—for example, a young Christian girl from the Midwest living with an authoritarian father, reading the story of a young Muslim girl from Saudi Arabia living with an authoritarian father—can bridge cultural and geographical gaps, helping that young girl from the Midwest recognize that she is one of millions in the same plight.

Character

Readers who do not like character-driven stories should never read memoirs, as that is what they are all about. They feature the writer and the friends and family of the writer, and if the personality of the writer is not appealing to that reader, the reader will move on. If however, the reader is taken with the character, a relationship develops wherein the reader then shares the experience with the writer and takes from the reading perhaps all that the writer had planned. Character is not just the personality, however. Character can also be the career of the writer. Some people may want to read everything they can about scientists, or chefs, or dancers, or politicians because whatever goes into the makeup of those professions is something that appeals to them. Because memoirs cross all disciplines of knowledge, there is a broad range for readers to choose from.

Story

Not all memoirs have a story as such, but most do. Sometimes the nature writers, or the spiritual memoirists, may have a more contemplative, more reflective aspect to their narratives. Others, though, have whopping stories to tell, whether climbing to the top of a mountain, running the Iditarod, waging war on the battlefield, escaping captivity, or doing humanitarian work. The story grips and the reader is satisfied, often coming away with new ideas to ponder and digest.

Setting

Because memoirs are being written from various corners of North America and from various corners of the world and are often translated, the opportunities for traveling to other parts of the country, the continent, or the world are rich. Even if the setting is just a different household in a different culture, the chance to steep oneself in a different world is there. Richard Rodriguez, a twentieth-century writer and author of the memoir ***Hunger of Memory: The Education of Richard Rodriguez; an Autobiography***, put it nicely, "'There was Spanish in my house, not Yiddish. But in that wonderful way that books allow, one life sharing with another, I walked with Alfred Kazin through Brooklyn,'" speaking of Kazin's ***A Walker in the City*** ("Cultural Legacy," 1998).

Learning

For all the reasons mentioned above, learning is a strong appeal of the memoir. Readers can learn about professions, scientific theories, life in other countries, other religions, relationships with animals, military lives, and medical conditions, to suggest just a few subjects. Apart from the technical knowledge that readers can absorb, however, is something more intangible, ideas and philosophies that might provide new inspirations in living one's own life. Perhaps the idea of doing humanitarian work had never occurred to a reader. Reading about Craig Kielburger or Muhammad Yunus could change that. Perhaps one had always held a prejudice against a particular ethnic group or a particular religion. Reading about those groups or those religions, becoming informed, could make all the difference in readers' lives.

Because of both the experiential and the learning appeals of memoirs, the issue of truth is especially important. Readers, accepting the unspoken contract with writers, engage with their books, trusting in their veracity, involving themselves in the writers' stories, assimilating any lessons learned. There is no wonder that the outrage at having been deceived can be so strong and so loud: the writer has betrayed the reader.

History of the Autobiographical Genre

The history and development of the autobiographical genre are closely connected to the history and development of world culture. Changes in the genre either reflect changes in the culture, or, in some cases, help precipitate those changes.

The earliest Western writings that we know about deal with exploits and travel, by such people as Herodotus, who started writing his ***Histories*** around 557 BCE, describing his travels to report on the Persian wars. Xenophon's ***Anabasis*** (ca. 421 BCE) also dealt with war, as did Julius Caesar's ***"De Bello Gallico" & Other Commentaries of Caius Julius Caesar*** (ca. 46 BCE). These stories all reflect the archetypal image of the journeying hero, accomplishing great deeds. History and travel are again reflected in ***The Jewish War*** (ca. 77 CE) by Flavius Josephus.

This trend underwent a major change in ***The Confessions*** (397 CE) by Saint Augustine, a man who traced a journey, but an inner, spiritual one, toward God. This is the first memoir to reveal the inner life of the writer. Peter Abelard's ***The Story of My Misfortunes; The Autobiography of Peter Abelard*** (1134) has been referred to as the first "misery memoir," as he recounts all the trials and tribulations he suffered in his life, particularly as a result of falling in love with Heloise.

Still continuing with spiritual autobiographies, we have the first known works by women: ***The Revelation of Divine Love in Sixteen Showings Made to Dame Julian of Norwich*** (1393) and ***The Book of Margery Kempe*** (1437). This latter work, almost a female version of Augustine's ***The Confessions,*** is the first-known "as-told-to" work, since Margery was illiterate and she was asked to dictate her story of conversion to two scribes. While this is referred to as the first English-language autobiography, if we accept the autobiographical genre as including time-limited narratives, then Julian of Norwich's ***Revelations*** should make that claim.

Benvenuto Cellini's ***The Autobiography of Benvenuto Cellini*** (written in 1558, published in 1728) set the genre on its ear. His was considered the first memoir, one that could be called "The Life and Times of Benvenuto Cellini," which painted a detailed picture of his Renaissance Florentine world and its people. He soon got tired of writing it himself, however, and dictated the remainder of his story while he worked on his sculptures. The "as-told-to" memoir has a long and noble tradition.

Moving over to France, we come upon Michel de Montaigne, initiator of the personal essay (***Essays***, 1580), a writer who not only created a new form but also added a new element in the content. While he was open about reflecting on his weaknesses, he also wrote of his strengths, something not normally found in a spiritual reflection. (Michel de Montaigne's essays had a great influence on the writing of Gore Vidal.) Jean-Jacques Rousseau took this flaunting of one's strengths one step further in his ***Confessions***, a memoir ironically named, as he was not "confessing" for purposes of conversion. His form of memoir is also referred to as an "apology," "a personal self-defense or justification. The author of the apology accepts no guilt for his or her thoughts or actions, seeking only vindication through honest disclosure of the self" (Kappel, 2001). Rousseau told of his inner-life journey toward fame, particularly his secular inner life, his private and unseemly behavior. As mentioned previously, by openly describing his transgressions, Rousseau flew in the face of his culture and its moral codes.

In England the Puritans were calling for what the sixteenth-century theologian William Perkins referred to as "'a narrow examination of thy selfe and the course of thy life'" (quoted in Mendelsohn, 2010). The most famous autobiography resulting from this call is John Bunyan's ***Grace Abounding to the Chief of Sinners*** (1666). The Puritans then brought this habit of "negative self-examination" with them to America when they immigrated.

Two eighteenth-century revolutions, one in America and one in France, created the climate for a major change in the autobiographical genre. Both wars featured the common man rising up against established authorities, and "the common man triumphed, overthrowing the old aristocratic order and therefore making the potential significance of each unique life unlimited, regardless of class or status. Ordinary people were suddenly empowered with the newfound notion that their own lives and ideas were meaningful" (Kappel, 2001). This gave rise to a democracy in autobiographical writing, where anyone could try his or her hand at it. The first major autobiography to follow this, to symbolize the democratic life of a self-made man, was ***The Autobiography of Benjamin Franklin*** (1793), a precursor to the rags-to-riches memoir of the celebrity.

Stendhal's memoir, ***The Life of Henry Brulard*** (written 1835–1836, published 1890), is particularly notable for the fact that it is a memoir of childhood and not a happy one. Around the same time as Stendhal, Goethe wrote ***The Autobiography of Johann Wolfgang von Goethe*** (1833), considered to be the first literary memoir, not surprising, given that he was a poet. He is also said to have written the first autobiographical novel, ***The Sorrows of Young Werther*** (1774).

The nineteenth century in the United States saw a variety of autobiographical works. Writers like Henry David Thoreau (***Walden***, 1854) and Walt Whitman (***Leaves of Grass***, 1881) continued with the introspective reflection, although Whitman added to his by writing it in poetry and by celebrating himself, too. In contrast, Ulysses S. Grant wrote what is considered to be one of the finest military memoirs ever written, ***Personal Memoirs of U. S. Grant*** (1885-1886).

The nineteenth century also saw the rise of the slave narrative, a form that had already been in circulation with the publication of Olaudah Equiano's ***The Interesting Narrative of the Life of Olaudah Equiano or Gustavus Vassa, the African/Written by Himself*** (1789). The ***Narrative of the Life of Frederick Douglass, an American Slave, Written by Himself*** and Harriet A. Jacobs's ***Incidents in the Life of a Slave Girl: Written by Herself*** are two seminal works in the history of the slave narrative. This form of autobiographical writing marked a new direction in autobiography, as the writers were speaking not only for themselves, but also for a group who could not do so. The narratives "are largely shaped by the ideas they are trying to convey through the lives they describe. Although they are written by individuals about their own experience, they are also works that speak about and for an entire group of people, giving them a communal voice" (Kappel, 2001). This tradition carried on, not just in African-American writing, but also in writing from other groups—most notably survivors of genocides and other forms of oppression.

The turn of the century in America saw a new form of writing, as world-weariness and cynicism set in, with writers wanting to depict life as they really saw it. The culture of the day was such, however, that they could not tell their stories openly. Autobiographical fiction came into its own at this point. Perhaps the most renowned is Marcel Proust's seven-volume work, currently referred to as ***In Search of Lost Time*** (the title's original translation was ***Remembrance of Things Past***), and published in English between 1922 and 1931. Writers such as John Dos Passos, Ernest Hemingway, F. Scott Fitzgerald, and Sherwood Anderson all drew on their personal experiences for their fiction, but did not feel that the culture of the day would allow them to blatantly air their personal lives. What Upton Sinclair wrote as fiction (novels such as ***The Jungle*** about the meatpacking industry) would now be written as investigative journalism. (Despite its being fiction, however, that novel made a remarkable difference in the world he was describing, as laws were passed to improve the industry.) Writers like Siegfried Sassoon and Wilfred Owen used their poetry to depict the grim nature of war. As James Atlas put it, "The history of American literature is a history of private experience enacted on a public stage" (1996). Another factor regarding the autobiographical novel is that it can be less taxing for the writer. Writing a memoir, though therapeutic for writers, can also be extremely painful as they situate themselves in their past and try to find the story; they may have to ask questions and face answers that are just too difficult. The novel doesn't require the same commitment, although it can still be difficult to face the reality of their situations. John Irving's ***Until I Find You: A Novel***, is his most autobiographical fiction to date (2005); his story of a father and son is too painful for Irving to write as memoir. Writing it as a novel allows him some therapeutic release but does not force him to open the door completely.

The Second World War and the Holocaust broke down many cultural barriers to what could be said out loud, presented as fact in the form of nonfiction. The last half of the twentieth century saw a flood of books by Holocaust survivors and their children as well, since they too suffered generationally from what their parents had undergone. Genocide didn't start or stop with the Holocaust, however, and survivors from various parts of the world have told their stories, not so much to celebrate themselves for surviving, but largely to inform the world about what has been happening in their countries:

> [They are] both witness literature and survival epic . . . documenting the suffering self but also, necessarily, recording the tormenting other . . . . Each of these witness memoirs had to bear an awful burden, standing in for the thousands of memoirs that would never be written. As the "I" became "we," the personal journey that had begun in the fourth century was transformed . . . into a highly political one. The conversation between one's self and God had become a conversation with, and about, the whole world. (Mendelsohn, 2010)

There was another revolution in the 1960s, with outrage against the Vietnam War building up, students striking in their colleges, the civil rights movement heating up. Just as the eighteenth-century revolutions had, this rising up of the common man and woman brought great changes to autobiographical writing. Citizens were enjoined to "make love, not war," and took that call seriously, making love openly and bringing onto the public stage what used to be reserved for private spaces. The culture was changing, and autobiographical writing changed with it. Groups who had normally been marginalized started to find their voice, and those who already had a voice brought their personal stories into the public forum in the form of nonfiction rather than autobiographical fiction. Women started to tell their stories, as well as African-Americans, Latino-Americans, Asian-Americans, and gay and lesbian writers in greater and greater numbers. "Like many other things in American life, autobiography broke loose in the middle and late 1960s" (Yagoda, 2009).

Along with this grassroots political revolution was another taking place in the field of journalism. Referred to as the "New Journalism," it involved a change in the journalistic culture whereby reporters or journalists inserted themselves into the story. Rather than objectively reporting, they told stories from their points of view; they were either witnesses or participants, but they were there and so they appeared in their stories. Norman Mailer was one of the first to do this, reporting on the revolt against the Vietnam War: "Mailer acts out a nation's inner conflict over its participation in an unpopular war in Asia by acting out his own inner conflicts that bedevil him as he records the demonstration" (Kappel, 2001).

Along with this change came a related change in nonfiction writing, exemplified by Truman Capote's ***In Cold Blood: A True Account of Multiple Murder and Its Consequences*** (1965). The term "creative nonfiction" was coined to describe Capote's kind of writing, a real story told using the stylistic elements of fiction and presented as fact. This kind of writing became a standard style for the autobiographical genre, giving rise to the issue of truth in memoir, as many critics find it hard to believe in the reality of a story that reads like a novel.

Cultural changes in television programming have been responsible for a new trend in autobiographical writing. Reality television, particularly in the form of talk shows, displays "ordinary" people facing the camera and telling their deepest secrets about shocking behavior in their lives to millions of viewers. This seems to allow writers to do the same (Susanna Kaysen's latest memoir, ***The Camera My Mother Gave Me***, about her vaginal pain, is a case in point), and along with the rash of "tell-all" memoirs has come a backlash against the genre as a whole. Michiko Kakutani, a senior critic for *The New York Times*, weighs in against this new trend in memoir writing, saying that it

> is just one step removed from the willful self-absorption and shameless self-promotion embraced by the "Me Generation" and its culture of narcissism . . . the memoir craze . . . reflects our obsession with navel gazing and the first person singular . . . . [This genre] also coincided with our culture's enshrinement of subjectivity—"moi" as a modus operandi for processing the world. (Kakutani, 2006)

Very telling in this discussion is the fact that in the list of classics in Appendix A, there are only fourteen titles related to Chapter 13, the final chapter that focuses on this type of memoir. The chapter itself contains eighty-three titles.

Another publishing phenomenon in the twenty-first century has been the increasing proliferation of the political memoir. These books appear in good time for presidential elections, with candidates beginning their campaigns early by publishing their stories to date. They also come after the end of an administration, with participants in that administration rushing to tell their sides of the story, either to set the record straight or to say "I was there."

This history seems to be ending on a negative note, but the contents of this book will illustrate to the reader that there are still excellent memoirs being written. In fact, Jill Ker Conway believes that autobiographical writing is almost the only recourse these days for readers who are interested in "the entire span of humanistic inquiry about what it means to be human, how the individual is shaped by society, whether she or he ever has free will, what shapes the imagination, what talents are valued and what misunderstood, how great political figures are formed and how they resonate with their followers" (1998) as she believes most nonfiction writing has become inaccessible to the general populace, being written by and for specialists.

Chronology of Significant Memoirs Before the Twentieth Century

557 BCE ff.	Herodotus (b. ca. 484 BCE), *Histories*
ca. 421 BCE	Xenophon (ca. 430–ca. 354 BCE), *Anabasis*
ca. 46 BCE	Caesar, Julius (100–144 BCE), *"De Bello Gallico" & Other Commentaries of Caius Julius Caesar*
ca. 77 CE	Josephus, Flavius (37–100), *The Jewish War*
167 CE	Aurelius, Marcus, Emperor of Rome (121–180), *The Meditations of Marcus Aurelius Antoninus*
397 CE	Augustine, Saint, Bishop of Hippo (354–430), *The Confessions*
1002	Sei Shōnagon (ca. 967–?), *The Pillow-Book of Sei Shōnagon*
1134	Abelard, Peter (1079–1142), *The Story of My Misfortunes; The Autobiography of Peter Abelard* [*Historia Calamitatum*]
1393	Dame Julian of Norwich (b. 1343), *The Revelation of Divine Love in Sixteen Showings Made to Dame Julian of Norwich*
1437	Kempe, Margery (ca. 1373–ca. 1440), *The Book of Margery Kempe*
1558	Cellini, Benvenuto (1500–1571), *The Autobiography of Benvenuto Cellini* (first published 1728)
1565	Teresa of Ávila, Saint (1515–1582), *Teresa of Ávila: The Book of My Life* (1562–1565)
ca. 1568	Díaz del Castillo, Bernal (1496–1584), *The History of the Conquest of New Spain* (first published around 1803)
ca. 1570	Cardano, Girolamo (1501–1576), *The Book of My Life (De Vita Propria Liber)*
1580	Montaigne, Michel de (1533–1592), *Essays*
1585	Paré, Ambroise (ca. 1510–1590), *The Apologie and Treatise of Ambroise Paré, Containing the Voyages Made into Divers Places, with Many of His Writings upon Surgery*
1594	Carvajal, Luis de (ca. 1567–1596), *The Enlightened; the Writings of Luis de Carvajal, el Mozo*
1666	Bunyan, John (1628–1688), *Grace Abounding to the Chief of Sinners*

1731	Ignatius, of Loyola, Saint (1491–1556), *A Pilgrim's Journey: The Autobiography of Ignatius of Loyola*
1740–1746	Saint-Simon, Louis de Rouvroy, duc de (1675–1755), *Historical Memoirs of the Duc de Saint-Simon*
1740–1789	Wesley, John (1703–1791), *The Journal of the Reverend John Wesley*
1782	Rousseau, Jean-Jacques (1712–1778), *Confessions*
1789	Equiano, Olaudah (ca. 1745–1797), *The Interesting Narrative of the Life of Olaudah Equiano or Gustavus Vassa, the African / Written by Himself*
1789–1798	Casanova, Giacomo (1725–1798), *History of My Life* (published 1826–1838)
1793	Franklin, Benjamin (1706–1790), *The Autobiography of Benjamin Franklin*
1796	Gibbon, Edward (1737–1794), *Memoirs of My Life*
1796	The *Oxford English Dictionary* cites this date as the first use of the term "autobiography," by the book reviewer William Taylor
1798–1805	Wordsworth, William (1770–1850), *The Fourteen-Book Prelude*
1822	De Quincey, Thomas (1785–1859), *Confessions of an English Opium-Eater*
1833	Goethe, Johann Wolfgang von (1749–1832), *The Autobiography of Johann Wolfgang von Goethe*
1835–1836	Stendhal (1783–1842), *The Life of Henry Brulard* (published in 1890)
1845	Douglass, Frederick (1818–1895), *Narrative of the Life of Frederick Douglass, an American Slave, Written by Himself*
1854	Thoreau, Henry David (1817–1862), *Walden*
1855	Whitman, Walt (1819–1892), *Leaves of Grass*
1861	Jacobs, Harriet A. (1813–1897), *Incidents in the Life of a Slave Girl: Written by Herself*
1864	Newman, John Henry (1801–1890), *Apologia Pro Vita Sua*
1873	Mill, John Stuart (1806–1873), *The Autobiography of John Stuart Mill*
1885–1886	Grant, Ulysses S. (1822–1885), *Personal Memoirs of U. S. Grant*

Works Cited

Atlas, James. 1996. "Confessing for Voyeurs; the Age of the Literary Memoir Is Now." *The New York Times on the Web*, May 12. Accessed July 22, 2010. http://www.nytimes.com/1996/05/12/magazine/confessing-for-voyeurs-the-age-of-the-literary-memoir-is-now.html.

Bannan, Helen M. 2005. "Writing and Reading Memoir as Consciousness-Raising: If the Personal Is Political, Is the Memoir Feminist?" *Feminist Collections* 26 (2–3) (Winter–Spring): 1–4. Accessed June 18, 2007. http://minds.wisconsin.edu/bitstream/handle/1793/22242/fcBannan.htm?sequence=2.

Barrington, Judith. 2007. "Writing the Memoir." In *The Handbook of Creative Writing*, edited by Steven Earnshaw, 109–15. Edinburgh: The University of Edinburgh Press.

Carr, David. 2008. "Reading Memoirs, Remembering Ourselves." *NoveList* (March). EBSCO*host*. Accessed May 2, 2009.

Clark, Roy Peter. 2007. "The Line Between Fact and Fiction." *Creative Nonfiction* 16. Accessed January 10, 2008. https://www.creativenonfiction.org/thejournal/articles/issue%2016/16clark_theline.htm.

Clarke, Brock. 1999. "Why Memoir Isn't Always Art." *The Chronicle of Higher Education* 45 (10) (October 29): B9 *MasterFILE Premier*, EBSCO*host*. Accessed January 29, 2009.

Conway, Jill Ker. 1998a. "Reflections on Autobiography: Interview with Jill Ker Conway by David Gergen." *Online NewsHour*, June 1. Accessed July 11, 2007. http://www.pbs.org/newshour/gergen/june98/conway_6-1.html.

Conway, Jill Ker. 1998b. *When Memory Speaks: Exploring the Art of Autobiography*. New York: Vintage Books.

"Cultural Legacy." 1998. *The NewsHour with Jim Lehrer*, August 30. Accessed October 31, 2010. http://www.pbs.org/newshour/essays/august98/rodriguez_8-28.html.

D'Agata, John. 2003. "Joan Didion's Formal Experience of Confusion." *Believer* (October). Accessed July 5, 2007. http://www.believermag.com/issues/200310/?read=article_dagata.

Drager, Lindsey. 2007. "Significance of the Term 'Literary' in the Literary Memoir." Analytical essay written at Grand Valley State University, no longer available.

Egan, Susanna, and Gabriele Helms. 2002. "Auto/biography? Yes. But Canadian?" *Canadian Literature* 172 (Spring): 5–16.

Fetherling, George, ed. 2001. "Preface." In *The Vintage Book of Canadian Memoirs*. Toronto: Vintage Canada.

Gass, William H. 1994. "The Art of Self: Autobiography in an Age of Narcissism." *Harper's Magazine* (May): 43–52. Accessed July 23, 2010. http://www.proquest.com.ezproxy.library.wisc.edu/.

Gornick, Vivian. 2001. *The Situation and the Story: The Art of Personal Narrative*. New York: Farrar, Straus & Giroux.

Green, Erin. 2009. "Palin's Book, Others Feature a Ghostwriter's Touch." *The Newsroom*, September 30. Accessed October 30, 2010. http://news.yahoo.com/s/ynews/20090930/ts_ynews/ynews_ts933.

Hetzel, Ellen. 2006. "Lies and Literary Memoirs." Book Babes, *PoynterOnline*, January 17. Accessed January 29, 2009. http://www.poynter.org/column.asp?id=57&aid=95321.

Hudgins, Andrew. 1996. "An Autobiographer's Lies." *The American Scholar* 65 (Autumn): 541–53. Library Lit & Inf Full Text, *WilsonWeb*. Accessed July 22, 2010.

James, P. D. 2000. "Prologue." In *Time to Be in Earnest: A Fragment of Autobiography*, xi–xiv. New York: Knopf.

Kakutani, Michiko. 2006. "Bending the Truth in a Million Little Ways." Critic's Notebook, *The New York Times*, January 17. Accessed July 22, 2009. http://www.nytimes.com/2006/01/17/books/17kaku.html.

Kappel, Lawrence. 2001. "A Historical Overview of the Autobiography." In *Autobiography*, edited by Lawrence Kappel, 14–31. San Diego, CA: Greenhaven Press.

Loizeaux, William. 2006. "In Memoirs, Varieties of Truth." *csmonitor.com*, February 8. Accessed May 2, 2007. http://www.csmonitor.com/2006/0208/p09s02-coop.html.

Mason, Bobbie Ann. 1999. "Facing Toward Home: Interview with Bobbie Ann Mason by Michael Sims." *BookPage* (May). Accessed August 22, 2010. http://www.bookpage.com/9905bp/bobbie_ann_mason.html.

Mendelsohn, Daniel. 2010. "But Enough About Me: What Does the Popularity of Memoirs Tell Us About Ourselves?" *The New Yorker*, January 25. Accessed October 19, 2010. http://www.newyorker.com/arts/critics/books/2010/01/25/100125crbo_books_mendelsohn.

Peacock, Molly. 1999. "The Poet as Hybrid Memoirist." *Writer* 112 (2) (February): 20. *MasterFILE Premier*, EBSCO*host*. Accessed January 29, 2009.

Showalter, Elaine. 2000. "Showalter Defines 'Instant Classics'." *Princeton Weekly Bulletin*, November 20. Accessed December 4, 2010. http://www.princeton.edu/pr/pwb/00/1120/8b.shtml.

Steinberg, Michael. 2003. "Finding the Inner Story in Memoirs and Personal Essays." *Fourth Genre: Explorations in Nonfiction* 5 (1): 185–88.

Yagoda, Ben. 2009. *Memoir: A History*. New York: Riverhead Books.

Zinsser, William, ed. 1998. *Inventing the Truth: The Art and Craft of Memoir*. New York: Houghton Mifflin.

Chapter 1

Travel and Adventure

Description

This first chapter combines both travel and adventure memoirs, as the two go naturally hand-in-hand. For the reader who loves to travel, even if the vehicle is a book and an armchair, there are many lands here to be explored, and not just in the traditional manner. The memoirists in this chapter have adventurous souls and have taken to the roads, to the skies, to the water, to the mountains, and even to outer space and, by writing their stories they have invited all those interested to come along.

Adventure and travel writing date back to the earliest days of civilization, not long after the invention of writing in 3500 BCE; fragments of travel accounts have been found in Mesopotamia and Egypt (Bentley, 2004). Perhaps the earliest-known travel-adventure story is one that was etched into clay tablets around 2000 BCE: the *Epic of Gilgamesh,* is a poem that combined elements of myth and folklore and that was immensely popular for centuries. Including quests and journeys, it was a forerunner to many of our adventure stories today, fiction and nonfiction. The first "complete" narratives we know of begin with Exodus, the story of Moses and his journey with the Israelites out of Egypt, sometime between 1440 and 1400 BCE, followed by Homer's *The Odyssey* (ninth century BCE), another epic poem, which combines several elements of today's adventure story, along with the journey. Also important in the history of travel writing are the travels of Herodotus (484–425 BCE), the historian who was researching the history of the Persian Wars, a study that took him through Egypt and Anatolia, described in great detail in his ***Histories***. On the Eastern front Zhang Qian, a Chinese envoy in the first century BCE, traveled far and wide through central Asia as far west as modern-day Afghanistan, to search for allies for the Han dynasty.

Initially travel was undertaken for political goals such as Qian's, for commerce, for determining who had what to trade (or pillage), or for territorial expansion. Then many travelers began undertaking pilgrimages, or Hajjes, depending on their religion, which provided another form of travel account. Perhaps the best-known and most valuable is the narrative of Ibn Battūta (***The Travels of Ibn Battūta, A.D. 1325–1354***), who began his travels from Morocco with a Hajj to Mecca, but then continued to central Asia, India, China, sub-Saharan Africa, and parts of Mediterranean Europe before returning home. His is a remarkable documentation of the Islamic world in the fourteenth century.

From the Middle Ages until the twentieth century, travel that was not for pilgrimage was largely undertaken for the purposes of imperialistic expansion, and many of the memoirs about these travels took the form of logs or journals of explorers. But once the new land was "discovered," scientists then made their way to document the flora and fauna of the new territory. Missionaries also headed out, for the purpose of changing the indigenous populations' religious beliefs.

With the technological advances that began in the late nineteenth century, however, the modes of travel began to change, as did the nature of travel. Now people could travel more quickly (via airplane) to farther destinations, or they could choose to travel in a more leisurely fashion, via ocean liner. Of course the people doing this were largely of the moneyed class. In the latter half of the twentieth century, travel opened up even more widely to the middle class and to young people who didn't need much money to travel, as long as they were innovative and adventurous. The reasons for travel, then, expanded to include personal self-discovery; a desire to understand other cultures, with a view to better understanding one's own; and an opportunity for employment or education elsewhere. Other people often traveled expressly for adventure. If one lived in Texas and wanted to mush dogs, one had to travel. Often travel memoirs mirror the adventurous spirit of the memoirist, one not content to stay at home.

This combination of daring spirit and restlessness reflects the characteristics of the traditional adventure tales, such as those of Gilgamesh and Odysseus, wherein the protagonist leaves his home, family, and friends to embark on a venture whose risks are known to be high. The protagonist often makes detailed preparations for the journey, knowing the dangers for which he must be prepared. Or the protagonist may begin an adventurous journey that turns into a disaster, requiring strength, ingenuity, and courage on his part to survive. There is usually more physical action in these memoirs than in many others, whether it's piloting a boat or climbing a mountain.

The question of gender in the adventure story is an important one. Traditionally, the woman stayed at home and, because of her enforced domesticity, never learned the kinds of skills that may be required in undertaking an adventurous journey. It was often a need to escape this very domesticity that motivated men to challenge themselves, to forge new frontiers (Baker, 2005). With some exceptions, until recently the adventure story has been the domain "of men—and usually, White, Western men at that" (Brandt, 2004). By extension, because these adventures were written by men, they were assumed to be for men, thus imparting to men the qualities inherent in the protagonist/hero. For women to have left home and taken part in adventurous activities then was quite remarkable, a real breaking of the expected mold. In the "Classics" section of this chapter, one woman is represented (Isabella L. Bird), although she was certainly not the only woman to break gender barriers. Of the remaining thirty memoirists, only five are women. Are there fewer women traveling and being adventuresome? Or might there be fewer writing their stories? Perhaps the audience for women's adventure writing isn't as great as it is for men's, so that the distribution of such writings may not be so great. In Appendix A the reader can find the stories of more women adventurers to read.

Setting is also a primary characteristic of the travel adventure tale. It is usually exotic, or at least unknown to the protagonist and the general reader. Because the setting is foreign to most, "the action itself must necessarily occur outside of everyday life" (Baker, 2005), another element of the adventure story.

Thus far, most of this discussion of travel and adventure stories could apply to either fiction or nonfiction. The primary difference between the two is characterization. Earlier adventure novels usually featured cardboard, single-dimension characters (Saricks, 2001). The action was of import; the character mattered less, except in his formulaic strength, courage, and ingenuity, although he was usually depicted as likable and "good." Women were rarely featured, or if they were, they were even more formulaic than the men and were there primarily to create a foil for the male hero. By contrast, the character in the adventure memoir is a real person, multidimensional and complex, and not necessarily always likable or "good." This person often has a need to push the envelope of danger or endurance, sometimes just to say it can be done.

As in memoir in general, the travel-adventure narrative crosses over many other genres and subjects, including history, exploration, nature, anthropology, spirituality, and geography. Classifying these works is largely subjective. For example, Michael J. Novacek's memoir, ***Time Traveler: In Search of Dinosaurs and Ancient Mammals from Montana to Mongolia,*** could easily go in Chapter 4, "The Working Life," with the other scientists, but the nature of his work is such that it fits quite nicely in adventure and travel. By the same token, Frances Mayes's series is usually found in the travel section, but in this book you will find her in Chapter 6, "Life Away from Home," as she has made Tuscany her second home. None of these categorizations is cast in stone—they simply illustrate the versatile nature of the memoir genre, thus enabling the readers' advisor to have a broad spectrum to offer the nonfiction reader.

Travel and adventure memoirs are stories about adventurous people who often undergo adverse conditions far afield to travel, to search for answers, to learn about themselves or about other peoples, and sometimes to advance the field of knowledge.These travelers often thrive on their adrenaline-producing adventures and have every expectation of returning home with exotic tales to tell.

Appeal

People read travel and adventure memoirs for a variety of reasons. The vicarious experience is very important here. Some readers may be homebound, whether because of physical, lifestyle, or economic limitations, or because of a reluctance to venture afar. These are people who might never want to climb a mountain, go to either of the poles, or live in a country where they don't speak the language or can't get a burger. But these same people may love to sit in the comfort of their homes and read about other people doing what they might never do. They can still sit on the edge of their seats or stay up until the middle of the night, reading to see what happens next, how dire are the circumstances, how clever is the protagonist, and how they all survive. In fact, it is more likely to be the reader who could/would never participate in such activities who will read these stories, to be transported to a different life, to have a new experience without actually having to face the risks. The fact that the character in the book is a real person, the memoirist, enhances the excitement. We know that the person lived to tell this particular tale, but the incidents described can still be spine-tingling, as the reader imagines the writer having experienced those dangers and thrills.

Experience and learning are almost co-appeal factors in this chapter. The reader has a chance to take that car ride, that boat ride, that walk, and learn about the landscape, the people, the customs, the history, the politics of the area, without suffering from the blisters, the dust, the cold, the heat, or the fear. Furthermore, the reader can vicariously feel the joy, the wonder, the amazement, or the sorrow. And in some cases, the reader then may be inspired to take the same or a similar trip. If the memoirist is engaging in unusual activity in a country, there is more learning to acquire. What preparations must be made? How does one actually carry out that activity? What does one do if things go wrong? In the face of unexpected disaster, the survival skills of the protagonist can be fascinating for the reader to learn firsthand how necessity can truly be the mother of invention.

This moves us right into another major appeal: setting. People often pick up books simply because they are about a particular country, part of the world, or biome. The books that closely describe the environs, the landscape, the people, or the food of that particular spot appeal to those who want to learn more about that area. On the other hand, there are also readers who may be planning to do something similar to what our memoirists have done, or at least to travel to one of the countries where these activities occur. Readers may want to get a "feel" for the place(s) they are going to visit. Certain works can very strongly evoke a sense of place that heightens not only the reader's feelings of anticipation, but also the actual experience itself if the writer has been true to the locale. Readers about to travel may also find themselves learning important information about the countries in their itinerary. The setting itself—whether mountain, sea, or outer space—is an area to learn about, particularly since it is usually in an exotic locale.

The nature of the action story usually dictates a faster-paced tale. But an interesting outcome of the travel and adventure memoir is that the protagonist often learns much about himself or herself, an enlightenment that may come with reflection.

Thus the story itself, while very gripping, may include at times a slower pace as the writer describes his reflections and beliefs as they relate to the experience he's undergoing. The tone of a travel book can make a great difference to a reader. In the books that follow, the tones range from harrowing and edge-of-the-seat to quiet and reflective, and the style of writing enhances that tone. In some cases there is much action and dialogue, in others more description and introspective thought.

All of this leads to a primary appeal factor of the memoir itself, which is character. Adversity brings out unknown traits in people—good or bad traits, as the case may be. Whether the story concerns a spiritual quest, cultural experience, risky venture, or journey just for the sake of the journey, the reader often has an opportunity to learn about the writer, as the memoirist learns more about himself or herself in facing hardships, unusual or difficult travel or living situations, or even strangers. Some travelers are also very good at engaging new people in conversation, so the reader has a chance to meet these people too and, in some cases, gain new perspectives on situations the reader had had no prior knowledge or experience of. For those who enjoy character-based stories, this revelation and/or development of character is an added appeal.

Organization of This Chapter

The chapter begins with five classics encompassing both travel and adventure and moves on to "Journeyers," wherein it is the trip itself that is important. In some cases, though, the traveler makes the journey for a specific purpose: to land in a new place and stay there for a while. These stories are featured in the third section, "Visitors." The fourth category, "In Search Of . . . ," is a bit of a combination of the first two. Sometimes people travel for a very specific reason, often in search of something personal for themselves (as in Peter Matthiessen's ***The Snow Leopard***), to learn something new, or to accomplish something specific. So they make their journeys, and often the journey is peripatetic, but they may also stay for a while in a specific place while they try to accomplish their goals. We then come to "Adventurers," containing books about those people who need excitement in their lives, an added zest that often requires traveling to attain. These people are usually greater risk-takers than the normal traveler. The final section, "Heroes," focuses on those who are forced to prove their mettle as their journeys go terribly wrong. The true courage of these memoirists is plain for all to see.

Classics

The five titles here are long-standing favorites of readers, stories of intrepid and interesting people. They range from domestic to unusual in locale and represent a number of forms of transportation: feet, horse, ship, airplane, and car.

Although she was not the only woman to seek adventure, Isabella L. Bird is the only woman represented here, and her story does not rest solely in the Rocky Mountains. In reading these classic stories, the reader can get a real sense of adventure when comparing the conveniences in travel we have today with the rigors of earlier travel.

> Classic travel and adventure stories illustrate the indomitable spirit of writers in days gone by, their tales revealing their courage in striking out for new territory, unaided by today's technological advances. Their works and, often their deeds, have remained in the public eye for decades or even longer.

Bird, Isabella L. (1831–1904)

A Lady's Life in the Rocky Mountains. Introduction by Stephanie Nikolopoulos. Barnes & Noble Books, 2005, 1879. 206pp. ill. 9780760763131. Also available in e-book. 978.02092

Isabella Bird's letters to her sister Henrietta, recounting her travels through the Rocky Mountains, represent the tip of the iceberg in her adventures around the world; despite the brace she wore for her spine, she traveled tens of thousands of miles on horseback. She stopped in the Rockies for several months on her way home to England from the Sandwich Islands. Because of her love of adventure, she was able to travel far and wide, learn how local people lived, and write about her scientific findings, thus becoming the first woman to be named a fellow of the Royal Geographical Society.

Subjects: 19th Century; American West; Classics; Colorado; Explorers; Firsts; Frontier and Pioneer Life; Letters; Overland Travel; Rocky Mountains; Solo Travel; Victorian Women

Now Try: Bird's life was so full and fascinating that you will want to read more about her: Evelyn Kaye has written a well-received biography, ***Amazing Traveler, Isabella Bird: The Biography of a Victorian Adventurer***. But you can also read more by Bird herself, as she describes other journeys; of particular interest is ***Unbeaten Tracks in Japan***. Another nineteenth-century woman traveling across the Rocky Mountains was Nancy Kelsey, whose story Cecelia Holland re-created in her novel, ***An Ordinary Woman: A Dramatized Biography of Nancy Kelsey***. Reminiscent of Isabella Bird is Dervla Murphy, who traveled through the Himalayas on horseback, but in the twentieth century. She recounts this trip with her five-year-old daughter in ***Where the Indus Is Young: A Winter in Baltistan***. If you like reading letters, you may want to look at ***Queen Victoria in Her Letters and Journals: A Selection***, edited by Christopher Hibbert, which would also give you a sense of Bird's time.

Dana, Richard Henry (1815–1882)

Two Years Before the Mast: A Personal Narrative of Life at Sea. Introduction by Gary Kinder. Notes by Duncan Hasell. Modern Library, 2001, 1840. 516pp. ill. 9780375757945. Also available in large print, audiobook, and e-book. 910.45

Richard Henry Dana's retelling of his trip as a Harvard-graduate deckhand on a brig going round Cape Horn to California has been immensely popular from the time of its publication in 1840. Dana was able to recapture in great detail the rigors of sea life, the beauties of the sights he saw, the brutal working conditions of the sailors, and the mechanics of the brig itself. He also captured the level of courage and endurance exhibited by the sailors on the brig, including his own, as a safe return was never a given. Of particular interest to his readers, aside from the cruel life of the deckhands, is the information imparted about the coast of California, as yet undiscovered. Although Dana's income from the book sales was a pittance (his publisher removed his copyright, so that all he earned from the book was $250.00), he did garner a large clientele of sailors for his law practice because of the book; he became an expert and author in maritime law because of his experience. His primary purpose in writing this book was not to make money but to tell what life was like from the forecastle, hoping to improve sailors' working conditions.

Subjects: 19th Century; *Alert* (Brig); Boat Travel; Classics; *Pilgrim* (Brig); Sailors; Seafaring Life; Travel; Working Conditions

Now Try: Paul Watson wrote his lively adventure story/memoir for a purpose as well: to advocate for animals who could not speak for themselves, as we see in ***Seal Wars: Twenty-Five Years on the Front Lines with the Harp Seals.*** Captain James Cook was a seaman and explorer, whose journals (***The Journals of Captain Cook***) of his travels in the Pacific Islands also provided very detailed descriptions of newfound territories. If you'd like to read a novel set in Dana's time in Massachusetts, Robert J. Begiebing has written ***The Adventures of Allegra Fullerton; or, a Memoir of Startling and Amusing Episodes from Itinerant Life: A Novel,*** in which the title character is rescued by Dana.

Lindbergh, Charles A. (1902–1974)

***The* Spirit of St. Louis.** Scribner, 2003, 1953. 562pp. ill. 9780743237055. Also available in large print, audiobook, and video. 629.13092

Best known for the record-breaking transcontinental flight that he details in this memoir, Charles Lindbergh was also an important scientist/inventor and conservationist. Despite the title, this memoir covers much more than his 3,600-mile solo trip from New York to Paris in 1927. Lindbergh also treats the reader to stories of his childhood in Minnesota and Washington, D.C., his aviation training, his stunt flying, and his career as an airmail carrier. He then gives an exhaustive accounting of all the preparations necessary for his solo flight, including finding investors, building the plane, and planning his route. The account of his actual flight is told in great detail, and we learn just how agonizing it was to stay awake the entire time.

***The* Spirit of St. Louis** was awarded the Pulitzer Prize for Biography or Autobiography. Lindbergh was named one of *Time*'s People of the Century in the Heroes & Icons category and was awarded the National Geographic Hubbard Medal for aviation exploits.

Subjects: Aviation; Classics; Firsts; Pilots; Pulitzer Prize for Biography or Autobiography; Solo Travel; *Spirit of St. Louis* (Airplane); Transatlantic Flights

Now Try: A. Scott Berg won a Pulitzer Prize for his depiction of this complicated and controversial man in his biography, ***Lindbergh.*** While he was writing ***The*** **Spirit of St. Louis**, Lindbergh had difficulty with the tone and finally decided to write it in the present tense, to bring an immediacy and excitement to it. This unusual style was also used by Hans Küng in ***My Struggle for Freedom: Memoirs.*** Thomas Fleming has written a novel that covers several decades of aviation history in the twentieth century and includes such real characters as Lindbergh, in ***Conquerors of the Sky.*** The decade in which Lindbergh made his historic flight was a decade of firsts in a variety of fields and disciplines; Nathan Miller brings it all together in ***New World Coming: The 1920s and the Making of Modern America.***

Matthiessen, Peter (1927–)

The Snow Leopard. Introduction by Pico Iyer. Penguin Books, 2008, 1978. 336pp. ill. maps. 9780143105510. Also available in audiobook. 915.4

Peter Matthiessen agreed to accompany field biologist George Schaller on a trek to observe the Himalayan blue sheep, also hoping to spot at some point in their arduous journey the elusive snow leopard. At the same time, however, Matthiessen was on a spiritual pilgrimage. He had begun studying Zen Buddhism at home and, having recently suffered the death of his wife, was in search of the Lama of Shey at an ancient shrine on Crystal Mountain, looking for some personal quietude and deeper meaning in his own life. Matthiessen offers the reader a tour of the Tibetan plateau just before the winter winds begin to blow, as well as a very personal and candid look at himself.

The Snow Leopard was selected as a Notable Book by the American Library Association, it was number eleven in World Hum's top thirty travel books of all time, it was a finalist for the National Book Critics Circle Award in General Nonfiction, and it won the National Book Award for Contemporary Thought.

Subjects: ALA Notable Books; Americans in Tibet; Biologists; Classics; Himalayas; National Book Award for Contemporary Thought; Nature Writers; Octogenarians; Overland Travel; Schaller, George; Tibet; Zen Buddhism

Now Try: Matthiessen, a naturalist and conservationist, has been described as a visionary; this same visionary quality can be found in the person of Ed Ricketts, a little-known naturalist and ecologist. Eric Enno Tamm tells Ricketts's story in ***Beyond the Outer Shores: The Untold Odyssey of Ed Ricketts, the Pioneering Ecologist Who Inspired John Steinbeck and Joseph Campbell.*** Not surprising, given the awards won and the description as a "visionary," Matthiessen's writing has been described as luminous, similar in style to Sharman Apt Russell's ***An Obsession with Butterflies: Our Long Love Affair with a Singular Insect.*** But Matthiessen is not just a dreamer: he looks at reality with a clear eye and presents his findings with candor. A rather esoteric yet accessible book combining Buddhism and science, ***The Quantum and the Lotus: A Journey to the Frontiers Where Science and Buddhism Meet,*** is structured in the form of a conversation between a Buddhist monk (Matthieu Ricard) who is a molecular scientist and an astrophysicist (Trinh Xuan Thuan) raised as a Buddhist.

Steinbeck, John (1902–1968)

Travels with Charley: In Search of America. (John Steinbeck Centennial Edition). Penguin Books, 2002, 1962. 214pp. map. 9780142000700. Also available in large print, Braille, audiobook, e-audiobook, and e-book. 917.3

Nobel Prize laureate and inveterate traveler John Steinbeck was amazed when he realized he had not explored his own country firsthand for over twenty years. He made preparations to do just that, planning a 10,000-mile journey in an innovative, custom-made truck with a cabin built on the back where he could eat and sleep. While he called this truck Rocinante, after Don Quixote's horse, he actually thought of it more as a turtle shell, as he was carrying his house on his back. Traveling in the early 1960s on the back roads of thirty-eight states with Charley, his poodle, Steinbeck revels in the people he meets, but shudders at the racism he encounters. He recounts his various adventures as they occur, so that the book reads anecdotally, a story one can pick up and put down, enjoying at leisure, just as Steinbeck does, the traveling and the sightseeing.

Steinbeck was awarded the Nobel Prize in Literature and in 1964, the Presidential Medal of Freedom by President Johnson.

Subjects: Classics; Nobel Prize Laureates; Overland Travel; Road Trips; Social History, United States; Solo Travel; Travel, United States; Writers

Now Try: Steinbeck's wife, Elaine, named this work in honor of a book much-loved by them both: Robert Louis Stevenson's ***Travels with a Donkey in the Cevennes***. Steinbeck's is a book to be read slowly, to be savored, much like Roger Angell's collection of autobiographical essays, ***Let Me Finish***. Richard Grant is another traveler, but he was interested in other travelers; he describes his findings in ***American Nomads: Travels with Lost Conquistadors, Mountain Men, Cowboys, Indians, Hoboes, and Bullriders***. If you'd like to read more about Steinbeck, always a controversial figure, try ***The True Adventures of John Steinbeck, Writer*** by Jackson J. Benson or ***Steinbeck: A Life in Letters***, edited by Steinbeck's wife, Elaine, and Robert Wallsten.

Journeyers

Ted Bishop finds a real similarity between research and motorcycle riding: each "takes you places you never expected to go, and in many ways the journey is more important than the destination" (McMaster, 2004). This is particularly true for the travelers in this section. Here you will see people using various means of transportation—motorcycles, cars, boats, feet—that enable them to have a wide range of experiences, meet new people, and often see at a more leisurely pace the world around them as they travel. Or they have the flexibility to stray from the itinerary and explore the unbeaten path. For most of these writers, the journey is paramount, not just for the landscapes, but also for the

people they meet along the way, and it is often these people who provide the greatest delight for the reader.

> Journey stories focus on those who, using a variety of modes of transportation, love to travel for the sake of the journey itself and the people they meet along the way. Because they often travel the unbeaten path, they encounter adventures and people that the guided-tour traveler might never experience.

Bishop, Edward (1949–)

Riding with Rilke: Reflections on Motorcycles and Books. W. W. Norton, 2006, 2005. 261pp. map. 9780393062618. 378.712334

Ted Bishop headed out on his academic sabbatical for Austin, Texas, to do some research on Virginia Woolf, leaving Edmonton, Alberta, on his Ducati motorcycle (nicknamed il Mostro). His research in the archives at the University of Texas, Austin, sent him to New York and then to England, but he flew back to Austin to pick up his Ducati and ride back home. On the ride home he wiped out, breaking his back in two places. Bishop's convalescence enabled him to write this memoir, detailing his love of the journey and the people he met as he took the back roads and ate in "mom-and-pop" diners. But he also loved the research he did and communicates this with a *joie de vivre* that makes his book appealing to both riders and readers.

Riding with Rilke won the province of Alberta's Wilfred Eggleston Award for Non-Fiction and was nominated for the Governor General's Literary Award for Non-Fiction.

Subjects: Accident Victims; Austin, TX; Books and Reading; College Professors, Canada; Motorcycle Travel; Reflections; Road Trips; Solo Travel; Travel, United States; Woolf, Virginia

Now Try: The unusual aspect of Bishop's book is his combination of literary research and analysis with reflections on riding and the actual journey he is taking. Amitav Ghosh also combines research and travel in his story of a journey through Egypt, ***In an Antique Land.*** For more *joie de vivre,* you may want to read the story of the lover of another member of the literati, told by Kathi Diamant in ***Kafka's Last Love: The Mystery of Dora Diamant.*** A darker but healing motorcycle trip around America was taken by Neil Peart after the deaths of his wife and daughter, a trip he describes in ***Ghost Rider: Travels on the Healing Road.***

Elliot, Jason (1965–)

An Unexpected Light: Travels in Afghanistan. Picador USA, 2001, 1999. 473pp. maps. 9780312274597. Also available in audiobook. 915.81

When he was nineteen, Jason Elliot left Britain to fight in Afghanistan with the mujahideen against the Soviets. Thoroughly taken with the country, he returned ten years later to travel through Afghanistan, to look beyond its wars and conflicts. He was provided with hospitality by countless Afghans as he made his journey, enabling him to see the unexpected light, the beauty of the country, and the culture and kindness of the people. While traveling, Elliot harks back to his time with the mujahideen, so that there is a back-and-forth of currency and reminiscence. Adding to the mix is his reflective thought as he closely observes his surroundings, with a view to portraying them honestly but sensitively for others.

An Unexpected Light was selected as a Notable Book by the American Library Association and won the Thomas Cook Travel Book Award.

Subjects: Afghanistan; Afghanistan Civil War (1979–); ALA Notable Books; English in Afghanistan; Mujahideen; Overland Travel; Social Life and Customs, Afghanistan; Thomas Cook Travel Book Award

Now Try: Fluent in Farsi, Elliot made a trip to Iran several years later, which he describes in ***Mirrors of the Unseen: Journeys in Iran***. His writing has been compared to that of Robert Byron, author of ***The Road to Oxiana***, a classic travel book written about the same geographical area as Elliot's books. Elliot displays a great cultural sensitivity in his depiction of the Afghan people, a sensitivity also to be found in Thomas Cahill's ***Sailing the Wine-Dark Sea: Why the Greeks Matter***. Jamaica Kincaid offers a new view of the Himalayas as she describes "the walk" she took, particularly interested in the flora growing there, but encountering a variety of people too, writing about them with candor in ***Among Flowers: A Walk in the Himalaya***.

Heat Moon, William Least (1939–)

River-Horse: The Logbook of a Boat Across America. Penguin Books, 2001, 1999. 506pp. ill. 9780140298604. Also available in large print, audiobook, and e-audiobook. 917.3049

This is the third of a travel trilogy by William Least Heat Moon. The first, ***Blue Highways: A Journey into America***, takes the reader with the author along the blue highways of America, those marked in blue on the map, not the red, divided highways, traveling 13,000 miles around the perimeter of the United States. His second, ***PrairyErth: (A Deep Map)***, is by contrast a very close look at one place in Kansas, Chase County. He finishes his trilogy with this narrative of his trip from New York City to Oregon along the waterways that formed so much of American history. Just reading the table of contents provides a bird's-eye view of not only Heat Moon's travels, but also the geography of the United States, as we travel from east to west. His journey in the boat he named *Nikawa*, Osage for "river-horse," is arduous but still a worthy challenge as he meets people along the way who enhance the trip. As might be expected, he remarks at certain points that the early explorers would never recognize the routes they had taken, yet at others he is mindful of how it seems as though nothing has changed. Through his trilogy Heat Moon offers an in-depth and close-up view of America in its history and its diversity.

Subjects: American Indians; Boat Travel; History, United States; Inland Navigation; *Nikawa* (Boat); Osage Nation; River Travel; Solo Travel; Travel, United States; Writers

Now Try: Heat Moon didn't stop here with his traveling. He recently went back to his journeying among the small towns of America in ***Roads to Quoz: An American Mosey***. A classic river adventure was John Wesley Powell's journey down the Colorado River. Using Powell's diaries of that trip, Edward Dolnick has written ***Down the Great Unknown: John Wesley Powell's 1869 Journey of Discovery and Tragedy Through the Grand Canyon***. John Graves tells his story of traveling a river he knew would disappear once the dams destined for the Brazos River were put in place. His lyrical and meditative book about that journey is entitled ***Goodbye to a River: A Narrative***. Perhaps the greatest American classic of life on the water is Mark Twain's ***Life on the Mississippi***, a typical Twain recounting of boating on the great river.

Paterniti, Michael

Driving Mr. Albert: A Trip Across America with Einstein's Brain. Dial Press, 2001, 2000. 211pp. 9780385333009. Also available in large print, Braille, and audiobook. 616.07

The quest of Michael Paterniti and pathologist Thomas Harvey is to deliver Albert Einstein's brain, kept in formaldehyde for forty-two years, to Einstein's adopted granddaughter, necessitating a trip from New Jersey to California. During that trip, the bloom comes somewhat off the rose in the relationship between the driver (Paterniti) and the doctor (Harvey), but we are treated to knowledgeable comments on Einstein, the man and scientist; thoughts on death; and Paterniti's reactions to his first look at the various regions that make up America. One of the author's unusual experiences is a visit with William S. Burroughs, a former neighbor of Thomas Harvey, whom they stop to visit.

When Paterniti first wrote up this story for *Harper's Magazine*, he won a National Magazine Award for it.

Subjects: Brain; Burroughs, William S.; Einstein, Albert; Harvey, Thomas Stoltz; Pathologists; Road Trips; Travel, United States

Now Try: To learn why Dr. Harvey had Einstein's brain to begin with and what kind of controversy that stirred up, the reader may want to look at ***Possessing Genius: The Bizarre Odyssey of Einstein's Brain*** by the medical journalist Carolyn Abraham. Studying the brain to determine genius is an occupation that dates back to the nineteenth century; Brian Burrell takes an interesting look at this in ***Postcards from the Brain Museum: The Improbable Search for Meaning in the Matter of Famous Minds***. Two Canadian writers take a road trip together, but the bloom does not come off the rose in their travels, as this married couple, Wayne Grady and Merilyn Simonds, describe in ***Breakfast at the Exit Café: Travels Through America***.

Stewart, Rory (1973–)

The Places in Between. Harcourt, Inc., 2006, 2004. 299pp. ill. maps. 9780156031561. Also available in large print, audiobook (read by the author), and e-audiobook. 915.8104

Rory Stewart (ex-military and a foreign services officer) decided after his diplomatic stints in Indonesia, Yugoslavia, and Afghanistan to go for a walk—across a 6,000-mile stretch of territory in Asia, traveling in Nepal, India, Pakistan, Turkey, Bangladesh, and Afghanistan. It is the latter part of his difficult journey that he describes in this award-winning tale. Knowledgeable in Persian dialects and understanding Muslim customs, Stewart and his canine companion Babur (named after the first Mogul emperor of Afghanistan) traveled through snow-deep mountains and villages, depending on the hospitality of the local people to survive and hoping at the same time to survive the teenage soldiers, the Taliban, and other outlaws they encountered. He narrates his harrowing experiences while at the same time offering his views on the disparate nature and beliefs among the Afghans.

The Places in Between was short-listed for the John Llewellyn Rhys Prize and the *Guardian* First Book Award and won the Royal Society of Literature Ondaatje Prize.

Subjects: Afghanistan; English in Afghanistan; Overland Travel; Social Life and Customs, Afghanistan

Now Try: After Stewart went home to Scotland for a break, he was asked by the British government to return to Iraq to be a provincial governor and help in the Coalition. This almost fatal task he describes in ***The Prince of the Marshes: And Other Occupational Hazards of a Year in Iraq***. Comparable to Stewart's, John McPhee's prose style is also lean, particularly in ***Looking for a Ship***, McPhee's story of accompanying a merchant marine on a journey with the ever-shrinking U.S. Merchant Marine. When he is not recounting a hair-raising tale, Stewart is often meditative, reflecting on the stories he has heard from a variety of people. This same meditative nature is found in another quite different walking story. Peter Jenkins's walk was also very long, but not in such potentially hostile territory as Stewart's. In his classic ***A Walk Across America***, Peter discovered both his country and his life's *métier*. The NPR radio journalist Rob Gifford took a trip to China, for much the same reasons as Stewart, but Gifford's mode of transportation was quite different; he drove the 3,000-mile Route 312, a journey he describes in ***China Road: A Journey into the Future of a Rising Power***.

Theroux, Paul (1941–)

Dark Star Safari: Overland from Cairo to Cape Town. With a new postscript. Houghton Mifflin, 2004, 2003. 485pp. maps. 9780618446872. Also available in audiobook and e-book. 916.04329

When he was young, Paul Theroux spent time in Malawi with the Peace Corps (1963–1965) teaching, until he was kicked out for writing an anti-

Vietnam War editorial and participating in a failed *coup d'état*. He went from Malawi to Uganda to teach at the Makerere University, where he stayed until the violence became too threatening for him and his family. Now Theroux is back, hitching a ride via train, canoe, "chicken bus," and cattle truck, along the route from Cairo to Cape Town, looking again at the continent he had loved so much as a young man. He brackets his trip with visits to two authors, Naguib Mahfouz and Nadine Gordimer, and in between visits his old schools in Malawi and Uganda and talks to political prisoners, prime ministers, former students, and farmers. He is distressed by the negative changes but sees hope in individual situations and in the continuing natural beauty of the continent.

Subjects: Africa; Malawi; Overland Travel; Peace Corps; Uganda

Now Try: ***My Secret History*** by Theroux is a semiautobiographical novel about a young man, born in Massachusetts, who makes his way to Africa. A new writer who has been compared favorably to Theroux is Eddy L. Harris, who also journeyed to Africa, as he recounts in ***Native Stranger: A Black American's Journey into the Heart of Africa***. Theroux's observations in his travels are eye-opening, just as journalist Lynne Duke's are in ***Mandela, Mobutu, and Me: A Newswoman's African Journey***. Many writers have come out of the Peace Corps, including Bob Shacochis, winner of the National Book Award for First Fiction for his collection, ***Easy in the Islands: Stories***.

Visitors

People travel far and wide for many reasons: sometimes they are asked by another agency to make a fact-finding trip; sometimes they want to experience a country for themselves; sometimes they procure teaching jobs or join the Peace Corps; and at other times they go in the company of a spouse or close personal friend, a visit that results in being worth writing about. The stories in this section are not those of people who went for a whirlwind "If-this-is-Tuesday-it-must-be-Belgium" kind of tour. These people went and stayed for a while, whether traveling throughout the country (M. G. Vassanji), or staying put (Peter Hessler). And then they went home, to write about their experiences and perhaps to set out once again to travel further.

The travel and adventure memoirs about visitors comprise stories of writers who have traveled for an extended stay in one particular country—not to live permanently—but to visit long enough to get to know the country well, whether it is completely new to them or is the country of their family heritage. It is not the journey that they describe so much as the life they encounter once they have arrived.

Bauer, Gabrielle (1957–)

Tokyo, My Everest: A Canadian Woman in Japan. Hounslow Press, 1995. 223pp. 9780888821812. Also available in e-book. 953.135

Because she already knew Japanese when she traveled to Japan to teach English, Gabrielle Bauer had a distinct advantage in getting to know her host country: she understood the nuances of what they said to her and the whys of what the people would do. Which isn't to say that she understood everything; she was baffled at their penchant for self-humiliation, as witnessed on their karaoke nights and in their televised game shows. Nor could Bauer understand, after she had fallen in love with a Japanese man (an affair she describes with candor), why she suddenly left the country, her adopted homeland, and the man she loved. Was it something in herself, or in the man she took as her lover?

Tokyo, My Everest was cowinner of the Canada-Japan Literary Award.

Subjects: Canada-Japan Literary Award; Canadians in Japan; Japan; Love Affairs; Social Life and Customs, Japan; Tokyo, Japan

Now Try: In this book, Bauer describes for the reader quite a bit about Japan's popular culture, much as Japanese expert Donald Richie did in his ***Introducing Japan.*** Bauer's candor about her life in Japan is also seen as a major feature in other titles set in the Far East: Victoria Armour-Hileman's ***Singing to the Dead: A Missioner's Life Among Refugees from Burma,*** and Tiziano Terzani's amazing story ***A Fortune-Teller Told Me: Earthbound Travels in the Far East.*** Several years after her return to Canada, Bauer wrote another memoir, ***Waltzing the Tango: Confessions of an Out-of-Step Boomer.***

Bellow, Saul (1915–2005)

To Jerusalem and Back: A Personal Account. Penguin Books, 1998, 1976. 182pp. 9780670717293. Also available in large print and e-book. 915.694

After Saul Bellow married his fourth wife, Alexandra Ionescu Tulcea, he accompanied her to Jerusalem, where she had contracted to teach mathematics at Hebrew University for three months. He spent his time talking to people from all walks of life, trying to come to terms with the Arab–Israeli question. Bellow's book is a combination of the sights he saw and the meals he ate, the conversations he had with luminaries and the man in the street, some fiction, some reflection on the issues. He returned home to Chicago and, like his fictional characters, was no more settled in his mind about the situation than he was when he started out.

Bellow received the Nobel Prize in Literature just at the time that he was writing this personal account. He was also the recipient of the National Medal of Arts and the American Academy of Arts and Letters Gold Medal.

Subjects: Americans in Israel; Arab–Israeli Conflict; Israel; Jerusalem, Israel; Jewish Men; Jews, History; Nobel Prize Laureates; Nonagenarians; Writers

Now Try: Bellow did not write any personal accounts apart from this, but critics say that his fiction, in particular ***The Adventures of Augie March,*** is very autobiographical. However, to learn more about the man, you may want to try ***Bellow: A Biography*** by James Atlas. Bellow came away from Jerusalem almost more confused about the conflict than when he had arrived there; a recent novel by Richard North Patterson, ***Exile: A Novel,*** though primarily a thriller, still goes into the Arab–Israeli conflict in great depth, presenting views from just about every side there is, illustrating just how complex the issues are. Despite the many facets of Bellow's book, or perhaps because of them, ***To Jerusalem and Back*** has been described as honest and engrossing. Fern Schumer Chapman also wrote an honest, engrossing book, retelling the story of her mother's return to a different country, the country where Chapman's grandparents had died in the Holocaust: ***Motherland: Beyond the Holocaust; A Daughter's Journey to Reclaim the Past***. Another American writer, William Golding, traveled to the Nile River Valley and also wrote an insightful account on his return home, ***An Egyptian Journal***.

Connelly, Karen (1969–)

Burmese Lessons: A True Love Story. Nan A. Talese/Doubleday, 2010, 2009. 382pp. 9780385528009. Also available in e-book. 959.1053

After traveling to and living in Thailand, the poet Karen Connelly set her sights on Burma. Sponsored by PEN Canada, she lived in Greece, and made trips to Burma in the late 1990s to interview political prisoners, including Aung San Suu Kyi, the embattled politician trying to wrest her country back from dictatorship; this takes place before Suu Kyi's house arrest. Connelly is able to interview a number of people, trying to capture the culture of the country as well as its political upheavals and troubled history, all the while aware of her Western perspective. She gets involved in some of the actual uprisings and then meets Maung, a revolutionary, and falls completely in love. Now her writing is laced with musings about him and about a decision she must face: whether to make her life in Burma or to continue as before, visiting various countries to learn and write about them.

Subjects: Burma; Canadians in Burma; Dissidents; Politics, Burma; Social Life and Customs, Burma; Writers, Canada

Now Try: Connelly's account of her stay in Thailand is the award-winning ***Dream of a Thousand Lives: A Sojourn in Thailand***. Before writing this memoir of her time in Burma, Connelly wrote the novel ***The Lizard Cage,*** about a political prisoner there. Since Connelly's time in Burma, the country suffered through cyclone Nargis while continuing to bear the weight of the military dictatorship. Emma Larkin writes about both in ***Everything Is Broken: A Tale of Catastrophe in Burma***. Another honest look at Southeast Asia comes from the Danish writer Carsten Jensen (translated by Barbara Haveland), ***I Have Seen the World Begin***. When a poet writes prose, it is usually easy to tell that the writer is a poet, and such is definitely the case with Karen Connelly. Another poetically written story is ***The Whale Rider*** by Witi Tame Ihimaera, a story familiar to many through the movie of the same name.

Hessler, Peter (1969–)

River Town: Two Years on the Yangtze. H. Holt, 1996. 410pp. maps. 9780805038880. Also available in audiobook. 915.1

Imagine teaching in a classroom where your every word is reported back to Communist Party leaders at the school where you are teaching. This was Peter

Hessler's experience as a Peace Corps volunteer in Sichuan Province, China, in the late 1990s. But that didn't seem to prevent his immersing himself in the culture of the town and getting to know and appreciate his students, most of whom were children of peasants and very serious about their education. Already able to speak Mandarin, Hessler still spent time with a Chinese tutor, trying to learn Sichuanese and further enhancing his understanding of the world in which he found himself, a world that was undergoing many changes, including the culture clash between old and new. Despite the hardships he encountered, he is able to describe his two years with humor and sensitivity.

River Town was selected as a Notable Book by the American Library Association and awarded the Kiriyama Prize.

Subjects: ALA Notable Books; Americans in China; China; Education; Fuling, Sichuan Sheng, China; Kiriyama Prize; Peace Corps; Social Life and Customs, China

Now Try: After his Peace Corps stint, Hessler returned to China (where he makes his home) and subsequently wrote ***Oracle Bones: A Journey Between China's Past and Present***, another award-winning book. As the title ***River Town*** indicates, the town where Hessler was living is along the mighty Yangtze, a river thoroughly explored by Simon Winchester in ***The River at the Center of the World: A Journey up the Yangtze and Back in Chinese Time***. During his summer vacation, Hessler went off by himself to travel the Silk Road, a journey also taken by Colin Thubron, recounted in ***Shadow of the Silk Road***. Hessler's account of his two years is an impressionistic portrayal of that time, much as Merrill Gilfillan's description of his beloved prairies is in ***Magpie Rising: Sketches from the Great Plains***.

Vassanji, M. G. (1950–)

A Place Within: Rediscovering India. Anchor Canada, 2009, 2008. 440pp. ill. map. 9780385661799. 819.32

Kenyan-born M. G. Vassanji was asked by a writer in India, "What's so special about returning to India?" Vassanji's answer is this book, his first work of nonfiction. His grandparents were born and raised in India, and Vassanji traveled to the country several times to recognize his own place in it. Conducting his research in various places and at various times, Vassanji has created a portrait of the country and his place within it as diversified as the country itself, his journeys almost as haphazard as the country itself. Invited to various conferences or to meet with different writers, he moves all over the country, providing a history, discoursing on the violence, and presenting a sympathetic view of this country that is part of his roots.

A Place Within was awarded the Governor General's Literary Award for Non-Fiction.

Subjects: Canadians in India; Family; Governor General's Literary Award for Non-Fiction; History, India, History; India; Social Life and Customs, India; Writers, Canada

Now Try: V. S. Naipaul, born in Trinidad, also visited his heritage country and presented his collage in ***India: A Million Mutinies Now***. Vassanji's horror at the violence, particularly between Muslims and Hindus, is also felt by Amitava Kumar, who explores the issue of sectarian violence in ***Husband of a Fanatic: A Personal Journey Through India, Pakistan, Love and Hate.*** Vassanji's writing in ***A Place Within*** has been referred to as "striking," much like John Julius Norwich's in ***The Paradise of Cities: Venice in the 19th Century***, a work comprising a collage of writers' reactions to the city.

In Search Of . . .

People are often in search of something—knowledge, another person, a home, or a prize of some sort—and the quest has a long tradition in literature. In this section, the quest embarked upon is usually something more material than spiritual (spiritual quests are covered in Chapter 8, "The Inner Life"). In this section you will find a myriad of stories depicting travel for a purpose: to retrace steps already taken, to learn more about family history, or to achieve greater understanding. The participants come away with more knowledge, although their mysteries may not have been solved; for many of them, however, the experience has been life-changing. An interesting side note is that Charles Montgomery (***The Shark God***) and J. B. MacKinnon (***Dead Man in Paradise***) are colleagues, members of FCC, a small narrative nonfiction coalition in Vancouver, and are back-to-back winners of the Charles Taylor Literary Prize for Nonfiction. Their books both concern a quest to learn more about a missionary relative in a far-off setting.

> The travelers in this section are in search of something specific, giving their travels a defined purpose. Their quest might be to prove a theory, to learn a skill from an expert in the field, or to determine the truth of a family-history story. The writers have all traveled long distances, and though they may not always have found a happy resolution, their quests are what remain important.

Feiler, Bruce S. (1964–)

Walking the Bible: A Journey by Land Through the Five Books of Moses. Harper Perennial, 2005, 2001. 451pp. maps. 9780060838638. Also available in large print, audiobook (read by the author), e-audiobook, e-book, and video. 915.60454

Bruce Feiler has sand in his shoes, as his personal bibliography can attest to. After living in and writing about Cambridge, England, Japan, and the United States, he decided to take his curious mind and restless feet to the land of the Bible, joining up with Avner Goren, an archaeologist, in a quest to find archaeological evidence for the Pentateuch, the first five books of the Bible. Feiler's pilgrimage began in Turkey (Mount Ararat), continued through Palestine, Israel, and Egypt,

1 2 3 4 5 6 7 8

and finally ended in Mount Nebo, Jordan. He consulted archaeological documents; spoke to people of the three main religions of the area; and found at the end that not only had he confirmed his original notions, he had also strengthened his own faith.

Subjects: Arab–Israeli Conflict; Archaeology; Bible, Geography; Deserts; Goren, Avner; Middle East; Pentateuch; Pilgrimage

Now Try: Feiler was so taken with his travels in biblical lands that he continued to pursue his research, the results of which can be found in ***Abraham: A Journey to the Heart of Three Faiths*** and ***Where God Was Born: A Journey by Land to the Roots of Religion***. Karen Armstrong also spent much time in Israel, researching the roots of three great religions; one of her many titles is ***A History of God: The 4000-Year Quest of Judaism, Christianity, and Islam***. But there is more to Feiler's book than religion: there is the evidence of his intellectual curiosity, a trait that was a major characteristic of Joseph Needham, as depicted by Simon Winchester in ***The Man Who Loved China: The Fantastic Story of the Eccentric Scientist Who Unlocked the Mysteries of the Middle Kingdom***. Feiler's book is also meditative, as he travels far and wide on his pilgrimage; a similar quality is evident in Marjorie Agosín's own personal quest: ***Cartographies: Meditations on Travel*** (translated by Nancy Abraham Hall).

Heyerdahl, Thor (1914–2002)

Kon-Tiki*: Across the Pacific by Raft.* Tess Press, 2004, 1950. 255pp. ill. 9781579124403. Also available in large print, Braille, audiobook, e-book, and video. 910.4 [Trans. by F. H. Lyon]

Thor Heyerdahl is often thought of as an adventurer who made several voyages and wrote about them, but he really was a very serious scientist (anthropologist) with a theory of cultural diffusion that he spent his lifetime trying to prove. He believed (as opposed to the isolationists) that ancient man traveled the world and populated various regions. His voyage on the *Kon-Tiki* was to prove that early peoples living in South America were not only able to, but actually did, travel from the western coast of South America to Polynesia. In his lifetime of travels he became an ardent conservationist, particularly in the realm of ocean pollution. To accompany this book, readers should pick up Heyerdahl's ***Green Was the Earth on the Seventh Day***, the story of his living with his new wife in the Marquesas Islands in 1937–1938. It was here that he formed many of the ideas espoused in **Kon-Tiki**.

Kon-Tiki was selected as a Notable Book by the American Library Association.

Subjects: ALA Notable Books; Explorers; Norwegians; Octogenarians; Pacific Ocean; Polynesia; Sailors; Seafaring Life; Translations

Now Try: For a very different adventure, but still a classic spine-tingler, try ***Skeletons on the Zahara: A True Story of Survival*** by Dean King. Heyerdahl is well-known for his explorations of Easter Island (***Aku-Aku, the Secret of***

Easter Island), but he was not the only person to explore it. JoAnne Van Tilburg has written the biography of archaeologist and ethnographer Katherine Routledge and her explorations in 1914–1915: ***Among Stone Giants: The Life of Katherine Routledge and Her Remarkable Expedition to Easter Island***. Novelist T. R. Pearson tells the true story of a Heyerdahl imitator who embarked on a Pacific voyage in a raft, inadequately outfitted, but equipped with an indomitable spirit, in ***Seaworthy: Adrift with William Willis in the Golden Age of Rafting***.

Horwitz, Tony (1958–)

Confederates in the Attic: Dispatches from the Unfinished Civil War. Vintage Books, 1999, 1998. 406pp. map. 9780679758334. Also available in large print and audiobook. 973.7

After investigating a war halfway across the world in the Middle East (***Baghdad Without a Map, and Other Misadventures in Arabia***), Pulitzer Prize–winning journalist Tony Horwitz decided to investigate a war in his own backyard, the American Civil War. Growing up in Virginia, he had always had a fascination with this war, so he finally decided to travel the "Confederate States" to search out the reasons for the war's continuing attraction to himself and countless others, more than a century after its passing. He met a large variety of eccentric characters, including Shelby Foote, the renowned Civil War historian. But what Horwitz discovered was that the war really wasn't over—at least not in the minds and hearts of Black and White Southerners.

Subjects: American South; Civil War, United States (1861–1865), Influence; Foote, Shelby; Historical Reenactments; History, United States; Hodges, Robert; Journalists

Now Try: Horwitz tackles another American iconic issue, the discovery of America, in ***A Voyage Long and Strange: Rediscovering the New World***. His penchant for joining obsessive participants is shared by Mark Svenvold, who joined a group of storm chasers, subsequently writing ***Big Weather: Chasing Tornadoes in the Heart of America***. A picaresque tale, told with a combination of comedy and sobriety, ***Confederates*** is similar to Nick Thorpe's ***8 Men and a Duck: An Improbable Voyage by Reed Boat to Easter Island***. Readers who find ***Confederates*** an engaging portrait of contemporary people involved in the Civil War may want to read an equally engaging memoir from the actual time period: ***Fighting for the Confederacy: The Personal Recollections of General Edward Porter Alexander***, edited by Gary W. Gallagher.

MacKinnon, J. B. (1970–)

Dead Man in Paradise. New Press, 2007, 2005. 261pp. map. 9781595581815. Also available in audiobook. 364.152

James MacKinnon was born five years after the murder of his uncle in the Dominican Republic during the 1965 Revolution, but he grew up hearing about that uncle, a missionary priest with a passion for social justice. Forty years after the murder, MacKinnon went down to the island to determine for himself just what happened, as no one had ever been brought to justice for the assassination of Father Art and two policemen. What he found surprised him, as the issue was still alive and people were still in fear of just talking about it. But MacKinnon eventually did find people willing to talk to him, others who came to warn him, and even an ally in the National Palace who handed documents over to him. He was able to name the shooter, but there is still a mystery about exactly why and under whose orders the killing was carried out.

Dead Man in Paradise was a finalist for the BC National Award for Canadian Non-fiction, the Hubert Evans Non-fiction Prize (BC Book Prizes), and the Pearson Writers' Trust Non-Fiction Prize; it won the Charles Taylor Prize for Literary Non-fiction.

Subjects: Charles Taylor Prize for Literary Non-fiction; Dominican Republic, History; MacKinnon, Art; Missionaries; Murder; Writers, Canada

Now Try: MacKinnon's writing style is to alternate chapters between the milieu of his uncle's life in the 1960s and MacKinnon's own current efforts to determine what really happened then. This same structure is used by Barry Clifford and Paul Perry as they describe their search for Captain Kidd's pirate ship. In ***Return to Treasure Island and the Search for Captain Kidd***, they alternate the story of Kidd's piracy with their own story of search and discovery. The other structural element in MacKinnon's book comes from his basically writing a true crime story, but layering it with memoir and a travelogue. Similar layering is done in Pulitzer Prize–winning Samantha Power's biography of a diplomat, ***Chasing the Flame: Sergio Vieira de Mello and the Fight to Save the World***. In addition to all that, MacKinnon has written a fascinating history of the unrest (and American occupation) in the Dominican Republic at the time. Nobel Laureate Mario Vargas Llosa's award-winning novel, ***The Feast of the Goat*** (translated by Edith Grossman), portrays the Dominican Republic just before this time, before the dictator Rafael Trujillo's assassination.

Mendelsohn, Daniel Adam (1960–)

The Lost: A Search for Six of Six Million. Photographs by Matt Mendelsohn. HarperCollins, 2006. 516pp. ill. 9780060542993. Also available in large print and e-book. 973.049240092

As he was growing up, Daniel Mendelsohn often heard tales of his grandfather's brother in Ukraine, but when he asked what happened to the granduncle and his family, he was told only that "they were killed by the Nazis." Greatly interested in family and family history, Mendelsohn decided to find out for himself just what had happened to his grand-uncle, his wife, and their four daughters. He traveled far and wide over a period of five years, going from the family's town of Bolechow (now Bolekhiv), Ukraine, to Australia, Israel, and Sweden. His brother Matt often accompanied him, taking photographs that were eventually displayed in an exhibition at the French Holocaust museum, the Shoah Memorial, in Paris.

The Lost has been met with much acclaim, being awarded the National Book Critics Circle Award in Autobiography/Memoir, the National Jewish

Book Award, the Salon Book Award, the American Library Association Sophie Brody Award, and the *Prix Médicis étranger* for the French translation.

Subjects: Family History; Holocaust, Jewish (1939–1945); Holocaust Survivors; Jaeger Family; Jewish Men; National Book Critics Circle Award in Autobiography/Memoir; National Jewish Book Award; Ukraine; Writers

Now Try: Prior to this, Mendelsohn had already expressed his interest in family history in his memoir, ***The Elusive Embrace: Desire and the Riddle of Identity***. Another family memoir is one by C. K. Williams, ***Misgivings: My Mother, My Father, Myself***, also meditative in tone. Not just meditative, ***The Lost*** is also empathic in its treatment of Mendelsohn's family history, similar to Christopher A. Bohjalian's novel, ***Skeletons at the Feast: A Novel***, about three young Jews trying to cross the Third Reich to Allied lines. Elie Wiesel referred to ***The Lost*** as a "highly colored tapestry" (Wiesel, 2006), much like Mark Mazower's ***Salonica, City of Ghosts: Christians, Muslims, and Jews, 1430–1950***.

Montgomery, Charles (1968–)

The Shark God: Encounters with Ghosts and Ancestors in the South Pacific. HarperCollins, 2006, 2004. 370pp. maps. 9780060765163. Also available in audiobook and e-book. 919.504

Charles Montgomery happened upon a book, ***The Light of Melanesia: A Record of Fifty Years Mission Work in the South Seas; Written After a Personal Visitation Made by Request of the Right Rev. John Selwyn, D.D., Late Bishop of Melanesia***, written by his great-grandfather, H. H. Montgomery, an Anglican missionary working in the South Pacific. Already an award-winning travel writer, Charles Montgomery decided to follow his great-grandfather's footsteps, to learn what his ancestor's South Pacific was like now and see who had won out, the shamans or the missionaries. He traveled across the Solomon Islands, the Reef Islands, and Vanuatu (formerly the New Hebrides), speaking to indigenous peoples, Christians, and shamans, and discovered that the inhabitants had basically created a new religion, one that combined their shark spirits with a Western, Christian God.

The Last Heathen (the original Canadian title) won the Hubert Evans Non-fiction Prize (BC Book Prizes) and the Charles Taylor Prize for Literary Non-fiction.

Subjects: Charles Taylor Prize for Literary Non-fiction; Culture Clash; Indigenous Peoples, Melanesia; Melanesia; Missionaries; Montgomery, H. H.; Shamanism; Social Life and Customs, Melanesia; South Pacific; Writers, Canada

Now Try: The shamans are a large part of Melanesian culture and a major topic of investigation for Montgomery. To find out more about them, the reader may want to look at Nevill Drury's ***The Shaman's Quest: Journeys in an Ancient Spiritual Practice***. Montgomery took with him on his travels a large dose of skepticism; this same skepticism is evident in Lee Strobel when he set out to investigate the truth behind the claims about Jesus in ***The Case for Christ: A Journalist's Personal Investigation of the Evidence for Jesus***. Montgomery's recounting of his travels is breathtaking, as are Moritz Thomsen's descriptions of Ecuador in ***Living Poor: A Peace Corps Chronicle***.

Polly, Matthew

American Shaolin: Flying Kicks, Buddhist Monks, and the Legend of Iron Crotch; An Odyssey in the New China. Gotham Books, 2008, 2007. 366pp. ill. 16pp. of plates. 9781592403370. Also available in e-book. 796.8155

Matthew Polly was a Rhodes scholar, a self-proclaimed geek, and a ninety-pound weakling when he decided to do something about his self-image. That something involved traveling to China to fulfill a long-held dream of learning martial arts from the experts: the fighting monks at the Shaolin Temple in Henan Province. As he tells in his humorous style, what he initially found was a far cry from his anticipations. He found a communistic and tacky tourist trap. Once he saw the monks, however, he realized that they still adhered to the age-old traditions Polly had expected to find. Polly describes how he became transformed through the work of the monks and his own determination to change from a skinny geek to a champion kick-boxing fighter who can hold his own with the best. Along with the training, we are also treated to his view of life there and the people he encounters, as we watch his metamorphosis.

Subjects: Athletes; China; Henan Province, China; Kick-Boxing; Martial Arts; Self-Discovery; Shaolin Monastery, China

Now Try: David Carradine, who was Polly's childhood hero, wrote his own memoir, particularly about the Kung-Fu movies he made—more about those, really, than the philosophy suggested by his title, ***Spirit of Shaolin***. Readers who would like to hear more from the man who made the martial arts so popular would enjoy Bruce Lee's ***Words of the Dragon: Interviews 1958–1973***, edited by John Little. Tim Clissold is an Englishman who traveled to China and in ***Mr. China: A Memoir*** describes how he wound up learning much about and from the Chinese that he had never expected to learn.

Adventurers

The memoirists here reflect a real range of risk-takers. Some are willing to face the elements and human nature to further their knowledge; others have a need to push themselves, to prove themselves capable of going beyond the norm; still others do what they do because they can, or because the opportunity lends itself. In this section we travel the world from Antarctica to the Arctic, from the Himalayas to Alaska to outer space. We have men and women, scientists, journalists, and athletes.

Although all of the writers in this chapter are adventurers of one sort or another, the characters in this section could often be referred to as extreme adventurers. They take on incredible risks—mountain climbing, cold-water swimming, white-water rafting, traveling in outer space—for the sheer pleasure of it (and occasionally to advance knowledge), and they often need to travel far afield to accomplish their goals.

Clapp, Nicholas (1936–)

The Road to Ubar: Finding the Atlantis of the Sands. Houghton Mifflin, 1999, 1998. 342pp. ill. maps. 9780395957868. Also available in audiobook. 939.49

Nicholas Clapp is a documentary filmmaker who heard about the lost city of Ubar when he was looking for a new project after a stint in southern Arabia. After reading Bertram Thomas's ***Arabia Felix: Across the "Empty Quarter" of Arabia,*** he became fascinated with the notion of Ubar and how it could never be found. Discovering an error in an atlas by Ptolemy, he then asked for help from NASA in providing satellite photos of the area that Clapp thought could contain Ubar. His riveting story goes on from there to discuss how he and his team succeed in their adventurous quest.

The Road to Ubar was selected as a Notable Book by the American Library Association.

Subjects: 1980s; ALA Notable Books; Arabia; Excavations (Archaeology); Filmmakers; Oman; Ubar (Extinct City)

Now Try: Wilfred Thesiger, the author of the classic adventure and travel story ***Arabian Sands,*** is one of several people who had unsuccessfully searched for Ubar. While excavations are back-breaking and often tedious, they also offer the opportunity for adventure and the excitement of discovery. Such is the case for William M. Kelso, whose archaeological team successfully excavated Jamestown, Virginia, described in ***Jamestown, the Buried Truth***. David Grann is an adventurer who went looking for Percy Fawcett, another adventurer who disappeared in his search for a lost city in the Amazon. Grann recounts his story in ***The Lost City of Z: A Tale of Deadly Obsession in the Amazon.***

Cox, Lynne (1957–)

Swimming to Antarctica: Tales of a Long-Distance Swimmer. Knopf, 2004. 323pp. 9780375415074. Also available in large print and e-book. 797.21092

Swimming in a pool during a hailstorm in July when she was nine changed Lynne Cox's life. She was so exhilarated by the sensations she experienced that she wanted nothing more than to search out similar experiences throughout her life. This memoir is a collection of twenty-four essays that recount her early days as a chubby swimmer; her record-breaking swims in adverse conditions (including the English Channel when she was fifteen); and her unusual physiology, which allows her to perform such feats as swimming across the Bering Strait and in Antarctic waters. Cox's swim across the Bering Strait, from Alaska to the Soviet Union, was something she wanted to do as a symbol of peace, bridging the gap between the two countries during the Cold War. As she says, it took "2 hours, 6 minutes, and 11 years," since it took her that long simply to get permission to do the swim.

Cox was inducted into the International Swimming Hall of Fame in 2002.

Subjects: Bering Strait; Firsts; Long-Distance Swimming; Personal Essays; Record-Breakers; Spirituality; Swimming

Now Try: Cox broke the record for time in swimming the English Channel, but she was not the first woman to do so—that record goes to Gertrude Ederle, who was competing against three other women in 1926. Reading ***The Great Swim*** by Gavin Mortimer will also highlight the difference in the media hype generated by Ederle's swim and the low profile of Cox's swim. Christopher A. Bohjalian has written a novel that is reminiscent in its refreshing style of Cox's memoir, also accenting environmental issues surrounding water, in this case in Vermont, ***Water Witches***. If you enjoy reading about intrepid women, you may also like Julia Whitty's story of life in the water on the other side of the world. The poetic language in her memoir, ***The Fragile Edge: Diving and Other Adventures in the South Pacific***, matches that of Cox, particularly in her memoir ***Grayson***, about Cox's experience with a baby whale separated from its mother in the Pacific Ocean.

Flowers, Pam (1946–)
Dixon, Ann (1954–), coauthor

Alone Across the Arctic: One Woman's Epic Journey by Dog Team. Alaska Northwest Books, 2001. 120pp. ill. map. 9780882405476. 919.804

At the age of forty-six, Pam Flowers embarked on an adventure to retrace the steps of the explorer Knud Rasmussen, going in reverse from Barrow, Alaska, to Resolution Bay in Canada, a trip of 2,500 miles that she accomplished with eight sled dogs. They began in February1993 and reached their goal almost a year later. Ironically, the most hazardous time for them was in the summer, when the ice was unsafe. Flowers offers descriptions of each of her dogs so that the reader comes to know them as characters; they were as integral to her success as food, water, and shelter. She gives credit to her lead dog, Douggie, who seemed to know the way when the weather was too inclement to see far. Flowers felt by the end of the trip that she and her eight dogs had all gained a sense of true self-respect for their accomplishment.

Subjects: Alaska; Arctic Regions; Dogsledding; Endurance Sports; Explorers; Firsts; Mushers; Northern Canada; Overland Travel; Rasmussen, Knud; Sled Dogs; Solo Travel

Now Try: Faith Conlon, Ingrid Emerick, and Christina Henry de Tessan have collected a number of stories about women who have traveled alone in their aptly titled collection, ***A Woman Alone: Travel Tales from Around the Globe***. Liv Arnesen and Ann Bancroft embarked on a walking trek across Antarctica, a feat they describe, with the help of Cheryl Dahle, in ***No Horizon Is So Far: Two Women and Their Extraordinary Journey Across Antarctica***. Polly Evans, a woman who needs to travel everywhere to learn as she goes, decided to learn about sled dogs, an experience she describes in ***Mad Dogs and an Englishwoman: Travels with Sled Dogs in Canada's Frozen North***.

Glenn, John (1921–)
Taylor, Nick (1945–) coauthor

John Glenn: A Memoir. Bantam Books, 2000, 1999. 564pp. ill. 16pp. of plates. 9780553110746. Also available in large print, audiobook, and e-book. 973.927092

The first American to orbit the earth, the oldest person to fly into space, a war hero, and a record-setter as a politician in Ohio, John Glenn is a bona fide hero; however, he refuses to refer to himself as such. His memoir, written after he declined to run for a fifth term in the Senate and after he had made his final trip into space, details in a down-to-earth yet gripping fashion his life and its times, from his early-childhood friendship with the girl, Annie, who would become his wife, through his careers as a Marine pilot, an astronaut, and a politician.

Glenn was awarded the National Geographic Hubbard Medal, and ***John Glenn*** was a Book-of-the-Month main selection when it was first published.

Subjects: 20th Century; Astronauts; Courage; Discovery Mission; Fighter Pilots; Firsts; Legislators; Nonagenarians; Project Mercury

Now Try: Christopher C. Kraft gives us a view of another side of space flight with his memoir, ***Flight: My Life in Mission Control***. Moving from the military to politics is not an unusual path, as we see in ***John F. Kerry: The Complete Biography by the* Boston Globe *Reporters Who Know Him Best***, by Michael Kranish, Brian C. Mooney, and Nina J. Easton; the biography tells another story of a life lived serving the public. And if you like Glenn's plainspoken style, you may want to read another plainspoken adventure story set in a much humbler venue: Nathaniel Stone's ***On the Water: Discovering America in a Rowboat***, a story in which Stone follows his dream of traveling on water.

Hawk, Tony (1968–)
Mortimer, Sean (1971–), coauthor

Hawk: Occupation, Skateboarder. ReganBooks, 2000. 289pp. ill. 9780060198602. 796.22092

Until he was six years old and his brother gave him an old skateboard, Tony Hawk was a miserable and challenging child. He became much happier with the skateboard, but as he describes his early childhood, it is obvious that he still felt very out-of-place, particularly during the period when the sport of skateboarding was at its most unpopular. By the time he was sixteen, however, he was a professional and had various scars to prove it. When Hawk retired from professional skateboarding in 1999, after finally completing the legendary 900-degree aerial turn, he was named the Alternative Athlete of the Year by ESPN. He pays homage to his father, Frank, who supported him throughout his childhood, driving him to contests, building skateboard ramps, and founding the National Skateboarding Association. Hawk himself has created the Tony Hawk Foundation (http://www.tonyhawkfoundation.org), a nonprofit that promotes and gives financial support to skateboard parks in low-income neighborhoods. Hawk has subsequently written a journal of life on the road, making commercials, performing demos, opening stores, and signing autographs, ***Between Boardslides and Burnout: My Notes from the Road.***

Subjects: Athletes; Childhood and Youth; Competitions; Extreme Sports; Fathers and Sons; Hawk, Frank; Skateboarding; Tony Hawk Foundation

Now Try: Jocko Weyland is a skating journalist who offers a history of skateboarding in various parts of the world, along with anecdotes of his own skating adventures, in ***The Answer Is Never: A Skateboarder's History of the World.*** Extending the world of "boards" is Jamie Brisick, who has written a history of three board-sports: ***Have Board, Will Travel: The Definitive History of Surf, Skate, and Snow.*** Kevin Michael Connolly, who was born without legs, found another constructive use for a skateboard as his primary means of transportation when he toured Europe for the first time. This photographer and champion skier offers his story along with accompanying photographs in ***Double Take: A Memoir.***

Hays, David (1930–), and Daniel Hays (1960–)

My Old Man and the Sea: A Father and Son Sail Around Cape Horn. Harper Perennial, 1996, 1995. 227pp. ill. maps. 9780060976965. Also available in large print, Braille, and audiobook. 910.45

Winners of the Feller Trophy for crossing the Gulf Stream in a nine-foot dinghy, David (father) and Daniel (son) Hays embarked on another journey, again in a small boat, aiming to round Cape Horn. And so they did, furnished with compass, sextant, two-way radio, and a kitten. Along the way they weathered not only climatic storms, but personal ones as well, cementing their relationship as father and son. Once again they set a record, being the first Americans to round the Cape in such a small boat.

Subjects: Boat Travel; Cape Horn, Chile; Fathers and Sons; Firsts; Sailors; Seafaring Life; *Sparrow* (Yacht); Travel

Now Try: One reason Daniel agreed to this trip was that he was not ready to settle down. Once he decided he was ready, he made an attempt to do so, but as he tells in his second adventuresome book, ***On Whale Island: Notes from a Place I Never Meant to Leave,*** that didn't quite work out. His father David, winner of the Harvard Arts Medal for his National Theatre of the Deaf, also wrote about a new chapter in his life. ***Today I Am a Boy*** describes his joining at age sixty-seven a class of twelve-year-olds to learn Hebrew and study for his bar mitzvah. Another father-son duo endured a canoe trip to Brazil, to the mouth of the Amazon, in Don Starkell's ***Paddle to the Amazon,*** edited by Charles Wilkins. Sailing around Cape Horn or canoeing to the Amazon are not the usual means for parent-child bonding; another unusual venture was captured in John Marchese's ***Renovations: A Father and Son Rebuild a House and Rediscover Each Other.*** Mark Kingwell bonds with his father and brothers in an annual fishing trip, as he recounts in ***Catch & Release: Trout Fishing and the Meaning of Life.***

Heller, Peter

Hell or High Water: Surviving Tibet's Tsangpo River. Rodale. 2004. 278pp. 9781579548728. Also available in audiobook, e-audiobook, and e-book. 797.122409515

Peter Heller, a seasoned kayaker, was asked by *Outside* magazine to cover the trip a group of extreme kayakers were making down the Yarlung Tsangpo River. Rushing through a deep gorge in Tibet, this river had never been successfully navigated, the effort being compared to snowboarding down Mount Everest. Scott Lindgren was determined, however, and he assembled a group of like-minded kayakers to form an expedition. Because he hadn't invited Heller, who was more or less foisted on them by *Outside*, their sponsor, he bore a noticeable hostility against Heller, a challenge that Heller had to deal with in addition to trying to stay alive on the trip. Apart from discussing the group dynamics and the trip itself, Heller also provides a history of the area as well as descriptions of the flora and fauna they pass through.

Subjects: Athletes; Extreme Sports; Journalists; Kayaking; *Outside* (Magazine); River Travel; Tibet; Yarlung Tsangpo River, Tibet

Now Try: Scott Lindgren wrote and directed a video documentary about the expedition, ***Into the Tsangpo Gorge***, before Heller's book was published. Putting the dangers of the Tsangpo River in proper perspective is the story of a previous expedition, abandoned when one of the members was killed. The exciting but tragic story is told by Todd Balf in ***The Last River: The Tragic Race for Shangri-la***. To add to the reader's knowledge of Tibet, particularly the spiritual aspects of the gorge through which the river flows, is Ian Baker's account of finding its legendary waterfall, ***The Heart of the World: A Journey to the Last Secret Place***. Not all kayaking is extreme, as Paul Theroux illustrates in his story of a kayaking trip through the islands of Oceania, ***The Happy Isles of Oceania: Paddling the Pacific***.

Hill, Lynn (1961–)
Child, Greg (1959–), coauthor

Climbing Free: My Life in the Vertical World. Foreword by John Long. W. W. Norton & Co., 2003, 2002. 270pp. ill. 9780393324334. 796.522092

"Climbing free" is the sport of rock or mountain climbing without the aid of any equipment except one's own body. According to Lynn Hill, whose memoir describes the sport as well as her own life in it, there is meant to be no effect on the rocks climbed, no holes or chips created by pitons, for example. Hill has been referred to as the greatest female athlete of the 1980s and 1990s for her rock-climbing exploits, including her successful ascent of "The Nose" on El Capitan in Yosemite National Park. She was not only the first woman to achieve that feat, but also the first person. In her memoir she tells how she first became interested in rock climbing at the age of fourteen, when she accompanied her older sister to the Joshua Tree National Park in California. Hill shares with her readers the path of her legendary career and also paints a picture of the rock-climbing culture, the people who are brilliant in the air, but less so on the ground. Her memoir reveals her personal life as well, her romantic relationships and her failed marriage, presenting her as both a climber and a woman.

Subjects: Extreme Sports; Firsts; Mountaineering; Rock Climbing; Yosemite National Park, CA

Now Try: Arlene Blum has also made history for women in mountaineering, as she describes in her memoir, ***Breaking Trail: A Climbing Life.*** If you would like to read more about Yosemite National Park as a climber's mecca, you might be interested in Galen A. Rowell's ***The Vertical World of Yosemite; A Collection of Photographs and Writings on Rock Climbing in Yosemite.*** Rachael Scdoris is yet another woman who has made her mark on a sport, in her case sled-dog racing: legally blind, she nevertheless was able to complete her dream of racing in the Iditarod, a 1,000-mile race in Alaska. With the help of Rick Steber, she has told her story in ***No End in Sight: My Life as a Blind Iditarod Racer.***

Karnazes, Dean (1962–)

Ultramarathon Man: Confessions of an All-Night Runner. J. P. Tarcher/Penguin, 2005. 280pp. ill. 9781585422784. Also available in audiobook, e-audiobook, e-book, and video. 796.42092

When Dean Karnazes was in high school, he was on the track-and-field team for a while, but quit when his favorite coach retired. He didn't run again until his thirtieth birthday, when facing a midlife crisis, spurred in part by the death of his sister, he decided out of the blue to run from San Francisco to Half Moon Bay, a jaunt of thirty miles. By definition, this run was an ultramarathon, because it was more than 26.2 miles and, as he tells it, that is a short ultramarathon for him. Apart from the length of the ultramarathons he runs, for Karnazes the location is also of importance, as it can significantly add to the challenge of his running. He has run in weathers of two extremes: a marathon in sneakers at the South Pole and a 135-mile run through Death Valley. He has also run fifty marathons in fifty days, one in each state. His run on his birthday was obviously a life-changing event, a realization that there was more to him than his business image would suggest. In his memoir he offers his ideas on why he runs and also provides great detail about the ups and downs of running, the types of pain and injuries, and the ultimate glory of it all. ***50/50: Secrets I Learned Running 50 Marathons in 50 Days—and How You Too Can Achieve Super Endurance!*** is his subsequent story of those fifty runs.

Subjects: Athletes; Competitions; Endurance Sports; Marathons; Runners; Ultramarathons

Now Try: Kirk Johnson also ran the Death Valley ultramarathon, and much like Karnazes, his interest in running seems to have been sparked somewhat by the death of a loved one. He tells his story in ***To the Edge: A Man, Death Valley, and the Mystery of Endurance.*** Christopher McDougall has opened a new world of running for the reader, the world of the Tarahumara indigenous peoples in Mexico. In ***Born to Run: A Hidden Tribe, Superathletes, and the Greatest Race the World Has Never Seen,*** he reveals how a race was created to pit the legendary

2 3 4 5 6 7 8

athletic Tarahumara peoples against American ultramarathon runners. John L. Parker Jr.'s novel, ***Once a Runner: A Novel,*** was originally self-published and sold out of his car at running races; it is now almost a cult classic among runners, a must-read for the serious runner.

Krakauer, Jon (1954–)

Into Thin Air: A Personal Account of the Mount Everest Disaster. Anchor Books, 2009, 1997. 404pp. ill. 9780307475251. Also available in large print, Braille, audiobook, e-audiobook, and e-book. 796.012

Jon Krakauer's book is perhaps the best known of the many stories written about the disastrous climb of Everest in May1996. Because he had done some mountain climbing, Krakauer was asked by *Outside* magazine to participate in a climb to write a story on the commercialization of Everest. The irony of his assignment to this particular climb is that it was in part due to the growing commercialization that so many people died in that event. Weather was indeed a factor, as a freak blizzard came up unexpectedly, but there were so many people climbing at the same time that there were literally traffic jams, and climbers had to wait for inordinately long periods to climb—up or down. In his memoir Krakauer paints a clear picture not only of the various personalities among the climbers, but also of what a strenuous climb is really like. Krakauer creates an immediacy in his writing so that even those unfamiliar with mountain climbing come away with a much more accurate idea of what it entails.

Into Thin Air was selected as a Notable Book by the American Library Association and was winner of the Pacific Northwest Booksellers Association Award; it was also a finalist for several awards, including the Pulitzer Prize for General Nonfiction and the National Book Critics Circle Award in General Nonfiction.

Subjects: ALA Notable Books; Himalayas; Journalists; Mount Everest; Mountaineering; Mountaineering Accidents; *Outside* (Magazine)

Now Try: Another incredible story of a much more successful climb of Everest at that same time is Göran Kropp's tale, written with David Lagercrantz, of his 7,000-mile bicycle ride from Stockholm to the foot of Everest, and his two attempts (the second, successful one a few days after the tragic blizzard) at climbing Everest, told in ***Ultimate High: My Everest Odyssey***. Another epic tale of unexpected disaster is told in Sebastian Junger's ***The Perfect Storm: A True Story of Men Against the Sea***. Many readers wonder why anyone would undertake such incredible risks. Maria Coffey asks that very question, from the point of view of a family member left behind forever, in ***Where the Mountain Casts Its Shadow: The Dark Side of Extreme Adventure***. Another profession that often defies understanding is the smoke jumper, a forest firefighter who parachutes into areas that are otherwise difficult to reach. Murry A. Taylor tries to explain the attraction in ***Jumping Fire: A Smokejumper's Memoir of Fighting Wildfire***.

Novacek, Michael J.

Time Traveler: In Search of Dinosaurs and Ancient Mammals from Montana to Mongolia. Farrar, Straus & Giroux, 2003, 2002. 368pp. ill. 9780374528768. 560.92

For most children the early keen interest in dinosaurs gives way to other things and dinosaurs become forgotten. Not so for paleontologists, those who study fossils. Michael Novacek is the curator of fossil mammals in the division of paleontology at the American Museum of Natural History in New York. While his title may sound dry to some, his memoir will put paid to that notion. Often referred to as the Indiana Jones of paleontology, he draws a clear picture in his memoir of what is actually required to gain the knowledge that fills our books and museums. His memoir begins with a fairly normal childhood exploring backyards in Los Angeles and moves from there to his education as a novice digger, to his gradual move up the knowledge chain until he is in charge of expeditions himself. These expeditions provide the excitement in the memoir—the natural dangers, the weather, the food, but also the unexpected dangers created by people and events. Mixed in with the adventure are scientific explanations, written for the layperson and made interesting by the author's writing skill and understanding of what can still enthrall that young dinosaur-loving person inside the reader.

Subjects: American Museum of Natural History, NY; Archaeology; Baja California; Chile; Dinosaurs; Fossils; Mongolia; Paleontologists; Patagonia; Scientists; Travel; Yemen

Now Try: John R. Horner is another respected paleontologist who has written books explaining paleontology to the layperson. His latest work, written with James Gorman, is based on the notion that birds are the descendants of dinosaurs, and their DNA can be used to build a dinosaur: ***How to Build a Dinosaur: Extinction Doesn't Have to Be Forever***. Allied to paleontology is evolutionary biology. Geerat J. Vermeij, a renowned evolutionary biologist, believes that he has an advantage over others because he is blind and can feel on shells and mollusks things that sighted people would not see and would overlook. He explains this in ***Privileged Hands: A Scientific Life***. Where Novacek would venture into the extreme heat, Bill Streever takes his scientific quests into the extreme cold. The Alaskan biologist tells his story in ***Cold: Adventures in the World's Frozen Places***.

Paulsen, Gary (1939–)

Winterdance: The Fine Madness of Running the Iditarod. Harcourt Brace, 1996, 1995. 256pp. ill. 8 pp. of plates. map. 9780156001458. Also available in Braille. 798.8

People seek adventure in all manner of ways, and young-adult writer Gary Paulsen is no exception. Having run dogs in Minnesota, he thought he might go for the big one: the Iditarod, the dogsled race in Alaska that stretches from Anchorage to Nome, a distance of 1,180 miles. He begins inauspiciously, getting lost in Anchorage itself with his team of fifteen dogs. Battling winds, cold, and snow such as he'd never imagined, getting lost again to the tune of an extra 120 miles, Paulsen still manages to finish in seventeen days, with the normal time anywhere between two and three weeks. Stopped after his second race by a heart condition, he then turned to motorcycles, detailing another long-distance trek in ***Pilgrimage on a Steel Ride: A Memoir About Men and Motorcycles***.

Subjects: Alaska; Dogsledding; Endurance Sports; Iditarod (Race), AK; Mushers; Sled Dogs; Writers

Now Try: The titles mentioned above are not the only ones that Paulsen has written about his life. Two others detail the years of his childhood and of his adolescence, respectively: ***Eastern Sun, Winter Moon: An Autobiographical Odyssey*** and ***The Beet Fields: Memories of a Sixteenth Summer***. The Iditarod Trail commemorates various elements of Alaskan history, including the journey taken to bring serum in a blizzard from Nome to a small community threatened by an outbreak of diphtheria. Gay and Laney Salisbury recount this harrowing drama in ***The Cruelest Miles: The Heroic Story of Dogs and Men in a Race Against an Epidemic***. Farley Mowat has been compared in style to Paulsen, with Mowat sharing Paulsen's love of the outdoors and the northern climes. ***Never Cry Wolf*** may be an appropriate title of his to try here. The first novel in Sue Henry's **Alex Jensen and Jessie Arnold Alaska Mystery** series is ***Murder on the Iditarod Trail***.

Weihenmayer, Erik (1968–)

Touch the Top of the World: A Blind Man's Journey to Climb Farther Than the Eye Can See. Includes a new Afterword, "On Everest." Plume, 2002, 2001. 342pp. 9780452282940. Also available in large print, Braille, audiobook, e-audiobook, and video. 796.522092

Erik Weihenmayer knew from an early age that he would develop blindness, as he was born with a congenital eye disease. He talks about his childhood and his mother, who supported him in his efforts to deal with the knowledge of his ever-increasing loss of sight. His father supported his interests in stretching his boundaries. By the time Weihenmayer was an adolescent he had lost both his sight and his mother, who died in a car accident. His parents had already laid the groundwork, however, for him to cope with both of these issues. His mother's death was a tragedy; his blindness was just something he would have to manage. He had learned to climb in a rock-climbing gym in a school for the blind, and the treacherous climb up Mount McKinley put the seal on his love for the sport. Apart from recounting his adventures in his memoir, Weihenmayer also talks about his blindness and how what he finds most limiting is the limitations that others place on him; he is trying to change the public attitude toward people with blindness.

Subjects: Athletes; Blind; Death of a Parent; Extreme Sports; Fathers and Sons; Mountaineering; Teachers

Now Try: With the help of Sally Jenkins, Marla Runyan describes in her memoir, ***No Finish Line: My Life as I See It***, how running races, breaking records, and qualifying for the Olympics all contributed to her developing a more accepting attitude toward herself and a recognition of what she could do regardless of her deteriorating eyesight. A nineteenth-century man of courage and charisma was James Holman, a blind man who traveled, who fought against the African slave trade, and who hunted rogue elephants.

Jason Roberts has brought this forgotten man back into public notice with ***A Sense of the World: How a Blind Man Became History's Greatest Traveler***. Not a mountaineer, Graham Bowley was not keen to write about the mountain-climbing disaster on K2 in 2008 for *The New York Times*. He changed his mind, however, once he met the survivors, and, as he says in the afterword of his book, ***No Way Down: Life and Death on K2***, he had his own set of adventures meeting the various people involved.

Heroes

In his story about landing a plane on the Hudson River, Captain Sullenberger agrees with what others have said; namely, that he is not a hero, he was just responding to a crisis. He didn't put himself in harm's way to save anyone, which was their definition of a hero. There will be others who will disagree with this definition, that heroes come in various guises, and the fact that he did respond, and calmly and capably at that, suggests that he acted in a heroic way. The same is true of the other memoirists in this section. While they have taken on activities that do have risk involved, none of them actually expected to face what they describe in their stories. They all have had very difficult choices to make, some of which they may originally have thought would be beyond them, but they did what needed to be done to save themselves or others and lived to tell about it, developing character as they went.

> The heroes featured in this section are adventurers, like the other memoirists in the chapter. Their stories are distinguished by the unexpected turn their adventures took, placing them, and sometimes others with them, in perilous danger. The courage and determination of the writers saved the day for themselves and others, either in the immediate situation or in the work they took up after the disaster.

Nielsen, Jerri (1952–2009)
Vollers, Maryanne, coauthor

Ice Bound: A Doctor's Incredible Battle for Survival at the South Pole. Talk Miramax Books/Hyperion, 2001. 362pp. 9780786866847. Also available in large print, audiobook (read by the author), and e-audiobook. 362.19699449092

Hoping to find an escape from her difficult life—a bitter divorce and estrangement from her teenage children—Dr. Jerri Nielsen applied for and won a position as team physician for a research team in the Antarctic in 1999. The first part of Nielsen's memoir covers her time as an emergency doctor prior to her heading south, as well as the difficulty of life with her husband and the bitterness of their divorce. When she reaches the point where she finds a lump on her breast while working in Antarctica, she begins her journey into resourcefulness, fear, depression, bravery, and an amazing amount of teamwork. A courageous airdrop is executed to provide her with chemotherapy, but it soon becomes apparent that she needs more care than she can provide for herself. The alternatives are surgery on herself or a dangerous trip to the South Pole Station to pick her up. An Air National Guard unit from upstate New York, the reserve component of the U.S. Air Force, made the risky flight in, sat for twenty minutes on the ground to drop off her replacement and pick her up, and then took off. Perhaps one of the contributing factors to the success of this whole story is a combination of Nielsen herself, becoming one with her icy, thin-air environment, accepting the limitations placed on her, and the people surrounding her, who were heroic themselves in the parts they played.

Subjects: Abuse (Spousal); Air National Guard; Amundsen Scott South Pole Station (Antarctica); Antarctica; Breast Cancer; Courage; Divorce; Physicians; Polar Regions

Now Try: Kenneth Kamler was a doctor and climber on the fateful Mount Everest climb in 1996. He describes what it is like to provide medical care under the kinds of conditions he faced in ***Doctor on Everest: Emergency Medicine at the Top of the World: A Personal Account Including the 1996 Disaster.*** Each Air National Guard unit has its own levels of risk to encounter. In Alaska, they are often called out to rescue would-be mountain climbers. Bob Drury catalogues one season in the life of the 210th Pararescue Squadron, ***The Rescue Season: The Heroic Story of Parajumpers on the Edge of the World.*** Shelley Lewis has an iconoclastic yet comforting view of breast cancer based on her own experience with it. Even her title intrigues: ***Five Lessons I Didn't Learn from Breast Cancer (and One Big One I Did).***

Parrado, Nando (1949–)
Rause, Vince, coauthor

Miracle in the Andes: 72 Days on the Mountain and My Long Trek Home. Three Rivers Press, 2007, 2006. 291pp. ill. 32pp. of plates. 9781400097678. Also available in large print, audiobook, e-audiobook, and e-book. 982.6

Young rugby players traveling to Chile from Uruguay for a game had their lives irrevocably altered when their plane crashed in the Andes: some of the travelers died on impact; others were seriously wounded. The story of this accident was told shortly afterward in 1972 by Piers Paul Read (***Alive***) with input from Nando Parrado, but Parrado is adding a very personal touch to the story more than thirty years later. When Parrado awoke from a three-day coma due to a fractured skull, he found his mother already dead and his sister dying. The thought of his father and his father's grief propelled him into going for help, along with a fellow traveler, Roberto Canessa. Seventy days after the crash, these two men found a peasant across the river, and the rescue began. This story is about more than the logistics of survival, although that does represent an astounding part of it. It is about the human spirit: how everyone came together for each other as well as for themselves. The fact that Parrado waited so long to tell his story allows him to reflect on its meaning and illustrate how it changed his life.

Subjects: 1970s; Accidents; Airplane Accidents; Andes Mountains; Canessa, Roberto; Cannibalism; Courage; Death of a Parent; Loss; Survival

Now Try: Norman Ollestad's father was also the moving spirit behind Norman's survival of a tragic plane crash, as he describes in ***Crazy for the Storm: A Memoir of Survival***. William W. Prochnau and Laura Parker asked the survivors of the emergency landing on the Hudson about their thoughts on what averting that tragedy has meant to them in their lives since. Their reflections are to be found in ***Miracle on the Hudson: The Survivors of Flight 1549 Tell Their Extraordinary Stories of Courage, Faith, and Determination***. Peter DeLeo also waited many years before writing his story, ***Survive!: My Fight for Life in the High Sierras,*** the story of piloting a small-engine plane that crashed and of walking out of the area to look for rescuers for his passengers.

Picciotto, Richard
Paisner, Daniel (1960–), coauthor

Last Man Down: A Firefighter's Story of Survival and Escape from the World Trade Center. New Afterword. Berkley Books, 2003, 2002. 243pp. 9780425289887. Also available in large print and e-book. 364.1097471

Chief of a battalion of seven companies in the New York City Fire Department, Richard Picciotto was used to being in command. The day he saw on television two airplanes fly into the towers of the World Trade Center, he told central dispatch that he and his men were on their way, even though the disaster was over 300 blocks away. Picciotto had been involved in the terrorist attack on the Center in 1993 and knew the building. Besides, how could anyone stay away? His account is somewhat different from many because he was there, right in the midst, experiencing the terror and the chaos. He was also there when the second tower collapsed, and he and several others were buried in the rubble. They had the good fortune of landing in a vacuum created by the twisted steel around them and were fairly unscathed when the rescuers got through to them about four hours later. Picciotto is the type of leader who is forthright and direct and doesn't tolerate bureaucracy. In the midst of his narration he directs barbs at the bureaucrats who had limited their budgets with the result that their equipment wasn't as it should have been. He's clear about those who helped and those who didn't. The book starts gravely, listing the names of every firefighter who died from the attack. This goes on for several pages.

Subjects: Fire Departments; Firefighters; Heroism; New York, NY; Rescue Work; September 11 Terrorist Attacks, 2001; World Trade Center, NY

Now Try: David Halberstam took one small group's story, that of Engine 40, Ladder 35, and described the tragedy that encompassed them on September 11, 2001, in ***Firehouse***. Dennis Smith, already long retired from firefighting, joined his former colleagues at the World Trade Center that day and then wrote the story of those he worked alongside in ***Report from Ground Zero: The Story of the Rescue Efforts at the World Trade Center***. There are many, many other stories to be told from that September 11. Jim Dwyer and Kevin Flynn are two journalists who interviewed countless people who had gone to work that day in the World Trade Center; the authors went through e-mails, emergency radio transcripts, and reams of pages of oral histories to bring together an account of what these people did when they realized their lives were at stake: ***102 Minutes: The Untold Story of the Fight to Survive Inside the Twin Towers.***

Ralston, Aron (1975–)

Between a Rock and a Hard Place. Atria Books, 2004. 354pp ill. maps. 9780743495806. Also available in large print, Braille, audiobook (read by the author), e-audiobook, e-book, and video. 796.52230289

Aron Ralston set out to establish certain things when he chose to write the story of his hiking accident and the action he took to save himself. Ralston was an experienced hiker and climber in Utah, where his misadventure befell him. But he broke a major rule one afternoon when he set out on his own, a rule that he urges others to keep in mind whenever they head out into the wilds: let someone else know where you're going. As he recalls his fall, with his right arm caught behind a boulder, and details everything that occurs during the six days he is trapped, he also remembers specific fear-inducing incidents from earlier climbs. These incidents he chose deliberately, as he uses lessons he learned from each of them to help him in his current predicament. This is one of the messages that Ralston wants to pass on: we all make mistakes; we all encounter fearful situations. It is what we learn from them that counts, and it is important to use what we learn the next time we are faced with challenges. His memoir is full of detail, due in part to his training as a mechanical engineer, but some of the detail is very grisly, hard for some to read. It is also full of ingenuity: how he managed to survive for six days without succumbing to dehydration or hypothermia, to say nothing of surviving what he did to himself to escape from behind that rock and find help. The reciprocal love of family and friends that enabled Ralston to survive in the park also sustained him in the months to come through his recovery.

Subjects: Accidents; Blue John Canyon, UT; Canyonlands National Park, UT; Courage; Deserts; Rock Climbing; Survival; Utah

Now Try: The title of the movie made from Ralston's book is ***127 Hours.*** Joe Simpson has a harrowing story to tell as well: climbing in the Andes with a friend, breaking his leg, and falling into a crevasse, while his friend makes his arduous way back to camp, thinking Joe is dead. In Simpson's memoir ***Touching the Void,*** the reader learns about the trauma of both men and about their strong friendship. Two other friends, David Shaw and Don Shirley, also participated in a disastrous undertaking, this time in cave diving, another extreme sport. Phillip Finch recounts in ***Diving into Darkness: A True Story of Death and Survival*** the story of these two men who dive more than 800 feet underwater to try to retrieve the body of a diver who had died there ten years earlier. Disaster also befell five hikers who went up the Half Dome in Yosemite and encountered Mother Nature in the form of a thunderstorm. As revealed in ***Shattered Air: A True Account of Catastrophe and Courage on Yosemite's Half Dome*** by Bob Madgic and Adrian Esteban, in this case the real heroes were the rescue workers who went in at midnight by helicopter to bring all the hikers home—those who survived and those who didn't.

Reeve, Christopher (1952–2004)

Still Me. Ballantine Books, 1999, 1998. 324pp. ill. 9780345432414. Also available in large print, Braille, audiobook (read by the author), and e-book. 791.43028092

In this first memoir, Christopher Reeve goes into great detail about the accident that changed his life and the ensuing treatments. But he also describes his life before the accident as well, his family (parents), children from an earlier relationship, his movie work, and his relationship with his wife and their little boy, who was three when Reeve had his riding accident. He is very honest about his feelings, about the shock of changing in one day from being a sailor, a skier, a rider, and an action-figure actor to being a quadriplegic, confined to a wheelchair, requiring a vent to help him breathe. He doesn't take a lot of time for self-pity, however. Reeve had been a social activist before he became a quadriplegic, but he became even more active once he was able to function again. Four years after writing this memoir, he wrote a book that was more deliberately motivational, ***Nothing Is Impossible: Reflections on a New Life***. His wife, Dana, published a collection of the letters that he received after his accident: ***Care Packages: Letters to Christopher Reeve from Strangers and Other Friends***. The couple also started the Christopher & Dana Reeve Foundation (http://www.christopherreeve.org), which continues their work today.

Subjects: Accidents; Actors; Christopher & Dana Reeve Foundation; Equestrian Accidents; Paralysis; Quadriplegics; Spinal-Cord Injury

Now Try: Dana Reeve died of lung cancer not even two years after her husband, Christopher, died of heart failure. Christopher Andersen has written the story of their life together: ***Somewhere in Heaven: The Remarkable Love Story of Dana and Christopher Reeve***. After he felt he was able to work again, Christopher Reeve directed a movie about Brooke Ellison, a young woman who was the first quadriplegic to graduate from Harvard. She and her mother Jean have written the story, ***Miracles Happen: One Mother, One Daughter, One Journey***, of how they worked together to ensure that Brooke could have as normal a life as possible. Harriet McBryde Johnson, a controversial and outspoken lawyer and activist for people with disabilities, was born with a neuromuscular disease that put her in a wheelchair. Her memoir, ***Too Late to Die Young: Nearly True Tales from a Life***, teaches readers to regard people in wheelchairs as real, fully dimensional persons. Joni Eareckson Tada is another activist for persons with disabilities, but because she found spiritual inspiration in her healing process from a diving accident, her activism has a Christian perspective. Her original memoir was entitled ***Joni: An Unforgettable Story***, written with Joe Musser.

Sullenberger, Chesley (1951–)
Zaslow, Jeffrey, coauthor

Highest Duty: My Search for What Really Matters. William Morrow, 2009. 340pp. ill. 16pp. of plates. 9780061924682. Also available in large print, audiobook (some sections read by the author), e-audiobook, and e-book. 629.13092

The flight that made Captain "Sully" Sullenberger famous actually lasted only five minutes. He had been in the air ninety-five seconds when his plane ran into a flock of geese, killing the engines. Four minutes later the plane was sitting on the Hudson River, everyone safe and intact. The captain is modest about his accomplishment, saying that it was his training that helped, along with his first officer, Jeff Skiles, and his three flight attendants. He traces his life back to his childhood and his early fascination with planes, lessons learned from his parents, his wife, and their adopted daughters. Sullenberger also describes his life in the U.S. Air Force and his peacetime military career before he became a commercial pilot. As a commercial pilot he took on the subject of piloting safety and trained flight crews in safety practices during emergencies. In his memoir the captain also talks about the instant fame that he and his family underwent. He believes that much was made of his accomplishment because of the national climate at the time, with people suffering economically and needing a lift. (Librarians who read this book will enjoy a particular story in it about a library book.)

The flight crew was given a rare award, the Master's Medal from the Guild of Air Pilots & Air Navigators, and they were also given the keys to the city by New York City Mayor Michael Bloomberg.

Subjects: Accidents; Air Safety; Airplane Accidents; Aviation; Courage; Heroism; Hudson River, NY; New York, NY; Pilots; United States Air Force; US Airways Flight 1549

Now Try: Richard Phillips, captain of a Merchant Marine ship, also proved heroic in saving his men from four Somali pirates, never sure that he himself would get out alive. That he was able to tell his story with the help of Stephan Talty, ***A Captain's Duty: Somali Pirates, Navy SEALs, and Dangerous Days at Sea***, obviously confirms that he did, but not without much suffering. Unsung heroes were those in the Coast Guard until David Helvarg wrote his history of that organization, ***Rescue Warriors: The U.S. Coast Guard, America's Forgotten Heroes***, focusing on several remarkable rescue efforts. In a completely different vein is the story of a young woman, Ashley Smith, trying to recover from drug addiction. As she and Stacy Mattingly relate in ***Unlikely Angel: The Untold Story of the Atlanta Hostage Hero***, Ashley became the hostage of a killer and convinced him to turn himself in, proving that heroes and heroic behavior can be found anywhere.

Consider Starting With . . .

Elliot, Jason. *An Unexpected Light: Travels in Afghanistan*

Glenn, John. *John Glenn: A Memoir*

Heat Moon, William Least. *River-Horse: The Logbook of a Boat Across America*

Hessler, Peter. *River Town: Two Years on the Yangtze*

Krakauer, Jon. *Into Thin Air: A Personal Account of the Mount Everest Disaster*

Matthiessen, Peter. *The Snow Leopard*

Mendelsohn, Daniel Adam. *The Lost: A Search for Six of Six Million*

Novacek, Michael J. *Time Traveler: In Search of Dinosaurs and Ancient Mammals from Montana to Mongolia*

Picciotto, Richard. *Last Man Down: A Firefighter's Story of Survival and Escape from the World Trade Center*

Steinbeck, John. *Travels with Charley: In Search of America*

Fiction Read-Alikes

Baricco, Alessandro. *Silk.* Hervé Joncour travels to Japan on several occasions for silkworms, unexpectedly falling in love as he does so.

Coelho, Paulo. *The Zahir: A Novel of Obsession.* The narrator travels from Paris to Kazakhstan in search of his wife, a journalist who has gone missing.

Elphinstone, Margaret. *Voyageurs: A Novel.* A brother leaves England for Canada in search of his sister, traveling while the War of 1812 rages.

Greene, Graham. *Travels with My Aunt.* Taking early retirement, Henry Pulling is convinced to travel with his aunt on the Orient Express.

Kirshenbaum, Binnie. *The Scenic Route: A Novel.* Traveling by car through Europe gives Sylvia Landsman the opportunity to regale her traveling companion with the stories of her life.

McCrumb, Sharyn. *St. Dale.* A NASCAR star is the reason for a memorial tour of racetracks, a bus trip through seven Southern states.

McMurtry, Larry. *Loop Group.* Maggie Clary, a sound dubber for B-grade movies, goes on a road trip with her best friend in the hope of rejuvenating her life.

Radish, Kris. *Annie Freeman's Fabulous Traveling Funeral.* Annie Freeman's final request to her best friend is to travel the United States with other friends, sprinkling her ashes in specific spots ranging from Sonoma, California, to Manhattan, New York.

Tan, Amy. *Saving Fish from Drowning.* An art expedition to Burma turns dire as the members of the group get lost in the jungle.

Wu, Cheng'en. *Journey to the West.* This four-volume novel details a sixteen-year pilgrimage from China to India, with the goal of returning to China a multitude of Buddhist scriptures.

Works Cited

Baker, Jackie. 2005. "Pam Houston: Redefining the Adventure Story." *Associated Content,* October 27. Accessed October 2008. http://www.associatedcontent.com/article/11928/pam_houston_redefining_the_adventure.html?cat=38.

Bentley, Jerry. 2004. "Travel Narratives." *World History Sources,* January 12. Accessed November 19, 2008. http://chnm.gmu.edu/worldhistorysources/unpacking/travelmain.html.

Brandt, Anthony. 2004. "Extreme Classics: The 100 Greatest Adventure Books of All Time." *National Geographic Adventure Magazine* (May). Accessed October 2006. http://www.nationalgeographic.com/adventure/0404/adventure_books.html.

McMaster, Geoff. 2004. "Motorcycle Riding Fuels the Art of Archival Research." *ExpressNews* University of Alberta, May 28. Accessed October 2008. http://www.expressnews.ualberta.ca/article.cfm?id=5844.

Saricks, Joyce G. 2001. *The Readers' Advisory Guide to Genre Fiction.* Chicago: American Library Association.

Wiesel, Elie. 2006. "Bearing Witness." *The Washington Post,* October 8, T01. Accessed November 2008. http://www.washingtonpost.com/wp-dyn/content/article/2006/10/05/AR2006100501336.html.

Chapter 2

Celebrities

Let me tell you about the very rich. They are different from you and me.
—Fitzgerald (1996)

Description

And so it would seem. Television programs such as *Lifestyles of the Rich and Famous* have created an image of celebrities: beautiful people with extravagantly furnished homes, boats, and closets, and glamorous, easy living and luxury. It is that very difference that pulls the reader into a book about the rich and famous, as celebrity memoirs seem to deal in the stuff dreams are made of—our dreams. We dream of fame, recognition, accolades, beautiful possessions. And if we can't achieve our dreams on our own, we may capture the feeling vicariously through the lives of those who have.

This is the celebrity memoir's initial attraction to the reader. In this chapter the memoirists all have one thing in common besides money: the reader has likely heard of them. And that is because they are famous. Not all rich people are famous, and not all famous people are rich, but in this chapter, just about everyone is, or has been, both. Reading the stories that they themselves have told lets us into their homes and lives, to see where the truth really lies. And so, expecting glamour, gossip about other famous people, insights into their personal lives that we can gossip about with others, we dive in.

But after one reads their stories, the real truth comes out: they are not so different from you and me after all. They suffer heartache, illness, disappointment, fear, and insecurity, just as we do. In fact, many of the celebrity memoirs here could just as easily fit in Chapter 13, "Surviving Life."

In today's culture of movies, television, radio, magazines (especially the ones at the grocery checkouts), Internet, blogging, PDAs, etc., it's almost impossible not to keep up with the famous and the latest developments in their lives.

Of course it wasn't always thus. Not only have the methods of creating and spreading fame changed over the centuries, but so also have the reasons for doing so. People like the Caesars and Alexander the Great were famous because of their military prowess and ability to take over lands and peoples. They spread their fame by having coins struck with their likenesses on them and by naming cities and/or months after themselves (Epstein, 2005). As time moved on, patrons of the arts had music composed in their names (who would know of the Margrave of Brandenburg-Schwedt except for Bach?) and portraits painted of themselves and their families.

After the invention of the printing press, newspapers and books could then tell the tales of the world's heroes (or of the people who considered themselves heroes). But it wasn't until the twentieth century, with Walter Winchell's gossip column in the *New York Evening Graphic* (1924 and later), that a new form of journalism and celebrity writing arrived. Winchell called himself a maverick, foregoing the requirement of journalists to confirm their news stories; his currency was innuendo, rumor, and gossip, anything he felt he could write about the "stars" of the day. *Rolling Stone* came on the scene in 1967, but it differed from the early gossip tabloids in that the magazine hired top writers to write about the celebrity scene, and it wasn't just gossip, but also opinion that they were offering (Shenk, 1996).

Many of the books in this chapter, particularly about those involved in the entertainment world, were written "to set the record straight." Tired of what they had been reading about themselves in newspapers, tabloids, and magazines, some celebrities felt obliged to tell their own stories. Others told their stories because they'd been asked to, particularly the more "serious" entertainers, to set down their thoughts about their art and how they learned their craft. And some apparently told their stories because they were offered generous advances by a publisher.

What the reader will find in this chapter is a range of stories, as diverse as the characters in them. People come from all backgrounds, some very rich, some very poor. What they all seem to have in common, however, is a determination and perseverance to fulfill their dreams, no matter how far-fetched those dreams may initially appear. Many of these stories reflect the American Dream in action.

Celebrity memoirs are the stories told by people generally famous in the world of pop culture. The memoirists may have help writing their stories, but they often bare their souls to tell the world what their lives are really like, and how different they may be from what the media have described.

Appeal

Memoirs, being about people, are usually character driven, and it is the characters in this chapter who are paramount. Because of our already established feeling about some of these people, we approach their stories with a certain expectation and anticipation. We read their stories and find ourselves amazed, angered, saddened, excited, and disappointed, just as we would if we heard a friend telling these stories. Our emotions are engaged if the storyteller has done a good job.

We have a dichotomy in attitude toward the rich and famous: we want to know all about the brightness and wonder in their lives, so different from our own, but we also want to see them fall, to know that they are human, that they are no better than we (and sometimes much worse). That is another appeal of these books: that despite the differences, we can see ourselves in their stories. If we've been turned down for a job, had marriage difficulties, suffered the death of a loved one, had financial difficulties, we can see that these things happen as well to those we might consider heroes, and we compare how they have handled their problems to how we have.

Another appeal of the celebrity memoir is setting and the vicarious experience of sharing the limelight. We feel the triumph of success, of renown. We stand on that stage, hear the applause, and bask in the glow of reflected glory. We ride alongside celebrities in their limos and marvel at their mansions. The settings of their lives are exotic and fascinating.

Learning is also an appeal here. Because of the detail provided, we learn how records are produced in recording studios, how actors develop their skills, what it takes to become a tennis legend, etc.

Organization of This Chapter

The environment here is largely the entertainment and popular-culture world: sports, music, stage, and screen. The chapter begins with classic memoirs, stories of people who have been significant in their field and will be long remembered. From there we move to those born in greatly straitened circumstances, whose stories are Horatio Alger tales, of climbing out of poverty into an entirely new world. Some of the people in the "From Rags to Riches" section could easily have been put in other sections, as they are athletes, singers, or actors. But their origins were such that they needed to be put in a category of their own. The final section, "In the Limelight," features the athletes, the singers, and the actors who have "made it" and who have written their own (or have had ghostwritten) stories.

Classics

The five memoirists in this section offer a wide range of experience and personalities. They are well-known for their professional skills and the new ideas they have brought to their craft. Through their talents and dedication to their professions, they have advanced the fields in which they worked.

The celebrities in the classics section are all known for pushing the envelope in their chosen fields and creating a name for themselves as outstanding practitioners of their professions. Through reading these memoirs, we learn more about the memoirist's craft, whether in sports, music, or theater.

Abdul-Jabbar, Kareem (1947–)
McCarthy, Mignon, coauthor

Kareem. Random House, 1990. 233pp. ill. 9780394559278. 796.323

This memoir, unlike Abdul-Jabbar's earlier one, ***Giant Steps***, written with the help of Peter Knobler, is in the form of a diary that he kept during his last season in professional basketball. He knew it would be his last season, and the entire year was more or less a way of saying good-bye to all his fans. He was known for being aloof and made an effort in this book to reveal his philosophies of life and the game even as he recounted his days at home and away on the court. A man who may never be surpassed in his record-breaking achievements, Kareem Abdul-Jabbar was more than just a basketball machine, which comes out loud and clear in this book.

Abdul-Jabbar was inducted into the Naismith Memorial Basketball Hall of Fame. He was also inducted into the Academy of Achievement, and when asked which book was of the greatest import to him, he cited ***The Autobiography of Malcolm X***, by Malcolm X and Alex Haley.

Subjects: African-American Men; Athletes; Basketball; Black Muslims; Conversion; Diaries; Los Angeles Lakers (Basketball Team); Muslim Men; National Basketball Association; Record-Breakers; Writers

Now Try: Kareem Abdul-Jabbar, a Muslim who converted from Catholicism and changed his name from Lew Alcindor, is a bit of a Renaissance man, as evidenced by both his interests and concerns outside basketball and the books he writes about those interests. He spent a year on a reservation, coaching basketball in a high school there, and wrote of that experience, with the help of Stephen Singular, in ***A Season on the Reservation: My Sojourn with the White Mountain Apache***. He also wanted to highlight the accomplishments of a Black battalion in the Second World War, which he did with Anthony Walton in ***Brothers in Arms: The Epic Story of the 761st Tank Battalion, WWII's Forgotten Heroes***. Born and raised in Harlem and an avid jazz fan, Abdul-Jabbar was greatly influenced by the rich culture in which he grew up, the telling of which he and Raymond Obstfeld recently published in ***On the Shoulders of Giants: My Journey Through the Harlem Renaissance***. If you'd like to read a fictional account of the Harlem Renaissance, you can try Len Riley's ***Harlem: A Novel***. Those who would like to read more about sports may enjoy Roland Lazenby's "oral history," ***The Show: The Inside Story of the Spectacular Los Angeles Lakers in the Words of Those Who Lived It***. Pete Maravich was another record-breaking basketball player for whom religion became very important. Mark Kriegel has portrayed his short-lived and difficult life in ***Pistol: The Life of Pete Maravich***.

Ashe, Arthur (1943–1993)
Rampersad, Arnold (1941–), coauthor

Days of Grace: A Memoir. Ballantine, 1994, 1993. 352pp. ill. 9780345386816. Also available in large print and audiobook. 796.342092

Prior to this memoir, Arthur Ashe had written others: ***Advantage Ashe*** (with Clifford George Gewecke Jr.); ***Arthur Ashe, Portrait in Motion*** (with Frank Deford, a diary of 1973–1974, detailing the life of a professional tennis player); and ***Off the Court*** (with Neil Amdur). Each of these memoirs offers various aspects of his life in detail. This final memoir is more reflective and introspective, revealing Ashe's thoughts about race relations, AIDS, prejudice in all its guises, and politics. He discusses the death of his mother when he was a young boy of six and the positive and strong influence his father had on him. He also describes his illness with AIDS and talks about privacy. Involved in a number of causes, namely apartheid in South Africa, AIDS education, gay rights, and Black youth, Ashe discourses on these topics throughout his memoir. He also mentions specific tennis players, most notably Jimmy Connors and John McEnroe. Knowing he is dying, he ends the book with a letter to his daughter, Camera.

Ashe was given the Presidential Medal of Freedom by President Clinton in 1993.

Subjects: African-American Men; Athletes; Death of a Parent; Fathers and Sons; Firsts; HIV/AIDS; Political Activists; Race Relations; Reflections; Social Activists; South Africa; Tennis

Now Try: After his heart surgery, forced to retire from active play, Ashe turned his interests toward research and writing and with the assistance of several others, wrote a three-volume work, ***A Hard Road to Glory: A History of the African-American Athlete***. Arthur Ashe was the first African-American tennis player to win the men's singles at Wimbledon, the U.S. Open, and the Australian Open. Cecil Harris and Larryette Kyle-DeBose have written a history of Black tennis players, ***Charging the Net: A History of Blacks in Tennis from Althea Gibson and Arthur Ashe to the Williams Sisters***. Both Arthur Ashe and Nat King Cole had much in common in the way they handled race issues and in what each of them did for his profession. Daniel Mark Epstein has written a highly acclaimed biography of the singer, simply titled ***Nat King Cole***. Ashe's memoir is inspirational; if you enjoy reading inspirational stories, you may want to read the collection by Jay Allison and others, ***This I Believe: The Personal Philosophies of Remarkable Men and Women***.

Davis, Miles (1926–1991)
Troupe, Quincy (1943–), coauthor

Miles, the Autobiography. Simon & Schuster Paperbacks, 2005, 1989. 441pp. ill. 32pp. of plates. 9780671725822. Also available in audiobook and e-book. 788.92092

Although this autobiography was given the American Book Award from the Before Columbus Foundation, it is not for the faint of heart. Miles Davis illustrates the accuracy of his earned epithet, "bad man," in his use of language and display of attitude in this book. But he also demonstrates the accuracy of his earned reputation as one of the most influential and original musicians of his time, changing the course of jazz music from bebop to cool to modal to fusion, often basing his improvisations on what he was feeling from his audience.

It is no surprise that Davis was inducted into the Nesuhi Ertegun Jazz Hall of Fame, but it is a testament to his influence that he was also inducted into the Rock and Roll Hall of Fame.

Subjects: African-American Men; American Book Award; Bebop; Drug Abuse; Fusion Music; Jazz Musicians; Racism; Trailblazers; Trumpet Players

Now Try: To get a perspective on Davis and his music from a distance and to understand his place in the music of his time, you may want to look at Richard Cook's ***It's About That Time: Miles Davis on and off Record***. The definitive biography written about Davis was published even before his autobiography, but it is still cited: ***Miles Davis: A Biography*** by Ian Carr. Davis was world-renowned for his musical art, but he also turned his hand to painting. George Wein, founder of the Newport Jazz Festival, and his wife, Joyce, collected African-American art (Davis's work among others); Patricia Hills and Melissa Renn created a book exhibition of the Weins' art collection, connecting it to music: ***Syncopated Rhythms: 20th-Century African-American Art from the George and Joyce Wein Collection***. Clive James has included Davis in a collection of essays in which he discusses the important cultural figures of the twentieth century, ***Cultural Amnesia: Necessary Memories from History and the Arts***. For something a little lighter, you may want to try Bill Moody's **Evan Horne Mysteries**, Evan being a jazz pianist; the third in the series is ***The Sound of the Trumpet: An Evan Horne Mystery***.

Gielgud, John (1904–2000)
Miller, John (1937–), and John Powell (1931–), coauthors

Gielgud, an Actor and His Time. Applause, 1997, 1979. 233pp. ill. 16pp. of plates. 9781557832993. Also available in Braille, audiobook (read by the author), and e-book. 792.028092

Grandnephew of Dame Ellen Terry, England's greatest nineteenth-century actress, John Gielgud learned his love for the theater at an early age. Although he appeared in a silent movie in the 1920s, he was initially reluctant to embrace the film world, much preferring the stage, where he shone. Apart from his stellar career as a stage actor, Gielgud also produced plays and in fact had his own stage company. When his method of acting started to become unpopular in Britain, he finally embraced the screen world. When in his eighties Gielgud's memory began to fail him in learning large portions of dialogue at a time, he gave himself over entirely to film. The same year that he was knighted (1953), Gielgud suffered a humiliating setback when he was arrested for homosexual soliciting, a crime in England at the time. His case became so notorious (almost leading him to commit suicide) that it is thought to have begun the slow journey to banning the witch hunts against gay people and changing English legislation.

Gielgud subsequently received two more honors from the queen of England: the Order of the Companion of Honour and the Order of Merit.

Subjects: Acting; Actors, England; Broadway; Filmmaking; Gay Men; Nonagenarians; Shakespearean Actors, England; Stage Actors, England; Theater

Now Try: Gielgud actually wrote six autobiographical works, the most unusual being ***Acting Shakespeare,*** written with the help of John Miller, in which he recounts anecdotes from his life as they relate to his countless performances in Shakespeare's plays. Gielgud's memoir is written with empathy, particularly for aspiring young actors; self-effacing, he ascribes much of his success to being in the right place at the right time, being offered the right script, etc. Jane Hamilton treats her main character in ***The Short History of a Prince: A Novel*** with the same kind of empathy. As one would expect, Gielgud is genteel in his writing, as is Kenneth Clark in ***Another Part of the Wood: A Self Portrait***. Those interested in other aspects of the theater, particularly in England, may want to read a book for which Gielgud wrote the foreword: ***Design by Motley,*** by Michael Mullin, a look at costumes and sets as designed by a group of three women.

Hepburn, Katharine (1907–2003)

Me: Stories of My Life. Ballantine, 1996, 1991. 420pp. ill. 9780345410092. Also available in large print, Braille, audiobook (read by the author), e-audiobook, and e-book. 791.43028092

Katharine Hepburn was raised in an affluent household by a warm and loving family that withstood the tragic death of a child and instilled in her values that she carried throughout her life, values, including independence, that often got her in trouble, as her iconoclastic behavior was not always happily received. This lack of acceptance climaxed in the thirties when her rebellious behavior, coupled with her still-burgeoning development as an actor, caused her to be labeled "box-office poison." At this point Hepburn returned to Broadway, where she starred in a play written for her by Philip Barry, ***The Philadelphia Story,*** and overcame her detractors. She subsequently starred in the movie of the same name. Her memoir is just what she says: "stories," including anecdotes about working with directors like George Cukor and her long-standing affair with Spencer Tracy.

Hepburn has a star on the Hollywood Walk of Fame and received four Academy Awards along with the Kennedy Center Honors.

Subjects: Actors; Broadway; Golden Age of Hollywood; Hollywood, CA; Love Affairs; Nonagenarians; Stage Actors; Theater; Tracy, Spencer; Trailblazers; Women in Film

Now Try: In addition to this memoir, Hepburn also wrote about the film that gave her credence as a serious actor: ***The Making of "The African Queen," or, How I Went to Africa with Bogart, Bacall, and Huston and Almost Lost My Mind***. People have regarded Hepburn as more than an actress; they see her as having provided an important role model for women. Karen Karbo's ***How to Hepburn: Lessons on Living from Kate the Great*** bears witness to that. Dorothy Thompson was another remarkable woman, a journalist who carved a niche in her own field. Readers may enjoy Peter Kurth's biography, ***American Cassandra: The Life of Dorothy Thompson***. Another American iconoclast of patrician upbringing was Peggy Guggenheim, whose story Mary V. Dearborn has written: ***Mistress of Modernism: The Life of Peggy Guggenheim***. Given the rejection of Hepburn because of her behavior and her subsequent comeback, readers may be interested in looking behind the scenes in Jeanine Basinger's ***The Star Machine***.

From Rags to Riches

The stories that follow deal with people who were born into poverty and disadvantage, some with innate talent, some not, but all determined to make something of themselves, to rise above the station they were born into. For some their poverty continued into their young adulthood, but perseverance and the drive for the American Dream finally resulted in success and, in most cases, world renown. These people could have been placed elsewhere in this book, but their rise from disadvantage to success takes precedence here.

Rags-to-riches stories focus on coming up from poverty to a life of fame and wealth. Through determination, hard work, and sometimes a little luck, the people here managed to rise from poverty and otherwise difficult childhoods to create their own career success as adults.

Charles, Ray (1930–2004)
Ritz, David (1943–), coauthor

Brother Ray: Ray Charles' Own Story. Da Capo Press, 2004, 1978. 364pp. ill. 9780306814310. Also available in Braille, audiobook, e-audiobook, and e-book. 784.092

Known as "The Genius," Ray Charles was the first to sing in a musical style that became known as "soul," with his hit song "I Got a Woman." He overcame early poverty, tragedy, blindness, racism, drug addiction, and womanizing to become a legend in the world of popular music, blending gospel, blues, jazz, and country into his own influential style. Once Charles crossed over into integrated audiences, he then refused to perform in front of segregated audiences. He was a determined musician and businessman and always stood up for himself and his rights, owning his own masters, for example.

Among Charles's many awards are the National Medal of Arts, the Kennedy Center Honors, a Grammy Lifetime Achievement Award, induction into the Rock and Roll Hall of Fame, and induction into the Blues Hall of Fame.

Subjects: African-American Men; American South; Blind; Blues Music; Businessmen; Child Prodigies; Drug Abuse; Jazz Musicians; Soul Musicians

Now Try: David Ritz, the ghostwriter for this memoir, listened to Charles's voice and let it speak, resulting in a musical, soulful style. ***Blue Bossa*** by Bart Schneider is a soulful novel, telling the tale of a jazz great who has been sidelined by drugs and is trying to restore himself. Another real-life musician who also battled addiction is Chet Baker, as James Gavin recounts in ***Deep in a Dream: The Long Night of Chet Baker***. The language and import of music sing out in the story of a homeless violinist, Nathaniel Ayers, told by Steve Lopez and subsequently made into a movie of the same name: ***The Soloist: A Lost Dream, an Unlikely Friendship, and the Redemptive Power of Music***. Charles's memoir was originally written in 1978, when he still had decades of musical success ahead of him; this updated version does not capture everything, so you may want to pick up Michael Lydon's ***Ray Charles: Man and Music*** for a more definitive record.

Dion, Céline (1968–)
Germain, Georges-Hébert, coauthor

Céline Dion: My Story, My Dream. With a new Epilogue, "The Birth of Céline's First Child." HarperCollins, 2002, 2000. 385pp. ill. 9780002000611. Also available in large print. 781.57 [Trans. by Bruce Benderson]

Céline Dion was the youngest of fourteen children, growing up in a household that was economically poor but musically rich. When she was five, she sang at her brother's wedding, and when she was twelve, she began the fulfillment of a dream by making a demo tape for a new record producer, René Angélil, who promised to make her a star. He mortgaged his house and cashed in his own savings to produce her first album, and together they traveled the road from rags to riches, becoming partners in life as well as in music.

Dion was awarded the Order of Canada in 1998 and promoted to Companion of the Order of Canada in 2008.

Subjects: Angélil, René; French-Canadians; Pop Singers, Canada; Poverty, Canada; Québec; Singers, Canada; Translations

Now Try: The man who helped Dion write her memoir (Georges-Hébert Germain) also wrote an authorized biography of her, entitled ***Céline: The Authorized Biography of Céline Dion***. Dion's story is an uplifting one, as is the story of Barbara Corcoran, another woman who grew up with a dream in a large family. Barbara's story, written with the help of Bruce Littlefield, can be found in ***Use What You've Got: And Other Business Lessons I Learned from My Mom***. Another legend who came out of a life of poverty is David Beckham, who, with the help of Tom Watt, has written his own story, ***Beckham: Both Feet on the Ground***. Kathi Kamen Goldmark, the founder of The Rock Bottom Remainders (a band solely comprised of authors) has written a rather offbeat rags-to-riches novel, ***And My Shoes Keep Walking Back to You: A Novel***, about a backup singer who makes good.

1 2 3 4 5 6 7 8

Gardner, Chris (1954–)
Troupe, Quincy, and Mim Eichler Rivas, coauthors

The Pursuit of Happyness. Amistad, 2006. 302pp. ill. 9780060744861. Also available in large print, audiobook, video, and e-book. 323.6

Chris Gardner had a difficult childhood, alternating between foster homes and abuse from a stepfather when he was with his mother, but his mother instilled some important traits in him that propelled him to where he is today: a very successful stockbroker and a philanthropist giving back to the community that helped him along the way. At what may have been the lowest point in his life, he was living homeless with a toddler, often sleeping in subway restrooms or shelters and eating from soup kitchens.

Gardner has been the recipient of many awards, including the NAACP Image Award.

Subjects: African-American Men; Businessmen; California; Fathers and Sons; Homelessness; Philanthropists; San Francisco, CA; Spirituality; Stockbrokers; Triumph over Adversity

Now Try: Reginald F. Lewis is a man who has many things in common with Gardner, and before he died of brain cancer at age fifty, he had achieved his own successful combination of business and philanthropy. Blair S. Walker, who finished the book after Lewis's death, tells Lewis's story in ***"Why Should White Guys Have All the Fun?" How Reginald Lewis Created a Billion-Dollar Business Empire.*** Homelessness is a situation that can strike anyone; former publisher Richard LeMieux has his own motivational story to tell in ***Breakfast at Sally's: One Homeless Man's Inspirational Journey.*** Another heartwarming, coming-from-behind story is that of a group of kids from an underprivileged school who beat all odds to win an electric-car-building competition, a story told by Caroline Kettlewell in ***Electric Dreams: One Unlikely Team of Kids and the Race to Build the Car of the Future.***

Joyner-Kersee, Jacqueline (1962–)
Steptoe, Sonja, coauthor

A Kind of Grace: The Autobiography of the World's Greatest Female Athlete. Warner Books, 1997. 310pp. ill. 9780446522489. Also available in audiobook and e-book. 796.42

Jackie Joyner was born into abject poverty in East St. Louis, Illinois, but found her niche as a young teenager in track and field. Inspired by both her grandmother and her mother to do well and make a name for herself, she persevered in developing her athletic skills, so that by the time she retired from athletics (due to exercise-induced asthma), she had broken many records and had won six Olympic medals, three of them gold. Joyner-Kersee's specialty was the heptathlon, in which she set several records, earning herself the description "the world's greatest female athlete."

Joyner-Kersee has been inducted into the USA Track & Field Hall of Fame.

Subjects: African-American Women; Athletes; Grandmothers; Olympic Gold Medalists; Poverty; Record-Breakers; Track and Field

Now Try: Joyner-Kersee's story is an inspiring one, particularly for women. Kim Doren and Charlie Jones have collected a number of anecdotes and inspirational messages from a group of successful women in ***You Go Girl! Winning the Woman's Way***. Rachel Toor also developed a love of running, which she convincingly conveys with a view to inspiring her readers in ***Personal Record: A Love Affair with Running***. Those looking for a good read about the Olympics may want to try Maynard F. Thomson's novel, ***Dreams of Gold,*** about the aspirations of a figure skater.

Osbourne, Ozzy (1948–)
Ayres, Chris (1975–), coauthor

I Am Ozzy. Grand Central Publishing, 2010, 2009. 391pp. ill. 32pp. of plates. 9780446569897. Also available in large print, audiobook, e-audiobook, and e-book. 782.42166

John Osbourne was a working-class son of the Midlands, eighteen years old, and in prison. In this gritty, scatological memoir he recounts the changes in his life that led him from prison to working in a slaughterhouse to being a member of what became a very successful heavy-metal band, Black Sabbath. Perhaps in keeping with the kind of music he created, perhaps harking back to his cut-up days as a young boy in Aston, his antics as a performer became only more notorious. Osbourne recounts his various drug addictions, his close encounters with death, his marriage to Sharon, and how he almost sabotaged that through his drinking. His memoir is raw, but with a conversational style. He doesn't apologize for his behavior, but rather marvels that that poor kid in Aston with no evident potential now owns two houses and has five children and four grandchildren. He even wonders at the fact that he has managed to live this long.

Subjects: Alcoholics; Black Sabbath (Musical Group); Drug Abuse; English-Americans; Musicians, England; Osbourne, Sharon; *The Osbournes* (Television Program); Rock Musicians; Singers

Now Try: Readers who have enjoyed the MTV program *The Osbournes* will enjoy reading Sharon Osbourne's autobiography, written with the help of Penelope Dening, ***Sharon Osbourne Extreme: My Autobiography***. David Bowie, born in the suburb of Brixton, shares a similar background with Osbourne. Marc Spitz has recently written a biography of the man and his music, ***Bowie: A Biography***. Ian Christe traces the history of heavy metal music from its beginning with Black Sabbath to today in ***Sound of the Beast: The Complete Headbanging History of Heavy Metal***. George Carlin was an iconoclastic comedian who would say whatever he wanted in whatever medium. He too had a hard-knocks childhood; although he had been dictating his autobiography to Tony Hendra, he didn't live long enough to finish it, a task Hendra assumed and published as ***Last Words***.

Sheldon, Sidney (1917–2007)

The Other Side of Me. Warner, 2006, 2005. 412pp. ill. 16pp. of plates. 9780446617505. Also available in large print, audiobook, and e-book. 813.54

Sidney Sheldon uses the metaphor of an elevator to describe his life, always going up and down; his memoir is also much like that. Sheldon lived with bipolar disorder for most of his years, a fact that contributed to the ups and downs, the highs and lows. He injects his memoir more with the manic side of him, but then that may have also been due to the nature of his life. Growing up in an immigrant family that was always moving, either to flee debts or to chase a job, he knew that the one constant in his childhood was poverty. His memoir describes his early, disruptive days and then moves on through his first efforts at writing, his successes in Hollywood and New York (with anecdotes about his many Hollywood friends), and finally his books. Sheldon didn't start writing fiction until he was fifty, so he had a lot of non-book-related stories to tell. Readers who have enjoyed his novels will find the vintage Sheldon stamp on his memoir.

One award that readers may not associate with Sidney Sheldon is his star on the Hollywood Walk of Fame.

Subjects: Children of Immigrants; Jewish Men; Nonagenarians; Novelists; Poverty; Russian-Americans; Screenwriters; Television Writers

Now Try: Sheldon's memoir's title is a reference to his second novel, the best-selling ***The Other Side of Midnight***. Sam Wyly grew up in the Great Depression on a poor cotton farm in Louisiana. In his memoir about his successes, ***1,000 Dollars and an Idea: Entrepreneur to Billionaire***, he also describes all the lessons he has learned, even those from when he was a little boy. Jeff Henderson's success story is quite a bit different: jailed for doing drugs, he learned to cook in the kitchen of a federal prison. As he relates in ***Cooked: From the Streets to the Stove, from Cocaine to Foie Gras***, he is now an executive chef. Lillian Lincoln Lambert broke not only economic barriers, but race and gender barriers too, being the first African-American woman to graduate from the Harvard Business School with an MBA. After twenty-five years as CEO of a multi-million-dollar business that she founded, she has written her memoir with the help of Rosemary Brutico: ***The Road to Someplace Better: From the Segregated South to Harvard Business School and Beyond***.

In the Limelight

While several of the memoirists in the previous section could have been placed in this one, the reverse is also true of some of the people found in this section. Many of the celebrities featured here have also had to overcome adversity to achieve their dreams, but that is not the real focus of their stories.

The three subsections in this section—sports, music, and stage and screen—focus on popular culture more than on what is known as "serious" entertainment. For classical musicians and dancers, please see Chapter 3, "The Creative Life." In this section readers will not only discover the lives of celebrities and their colleagues, but in many instances, will also learn what those celebrities did to advance their art and why they received the accolades they did.

In the limelight is where most of the memoirists in this chapter have basked, and this section is the core of the chapter, focusing on the lives and careers of people known to sports, music, and acting buffs. Readers will learn about the lives of the stars but have the added bonus of learning more about their career fields as well.

Sports Stars

One of the interesting thoughts about this subgenre is that usually athletes are people of action, not prone to sit down and write. Even so, the athlete gave not only his or her permission, but also his or her time to the writer, talking into tape recorders, handing over journals, and telling his or her version of his or her story. In some cases, the focus may be as much on the sport, the personalities in it, and the rivalries, as on the life story of the athlete. Thus the sports aficionado can look forward to learning more detail about a favorite sport or about a sport as yet unfamiliar. There is often more to these stories than sports, however, so readers who care more about people than sport may still find something of interest here.

Memoirs of sports stars are generally as-told-to stories, given that writing is not the usual avocation of the athlete. The memoirists describe how they have arrived where they are, often at the top or very close to the top of their game, and what they had to overcome in order to get there. They sometimes offer their own philosophies of sportsmanship or of life, which they have developed through their experiences. Sometimes, too, they describe life after their career heyday, a life that doesn't necessarily match up with their athletic careers.

Agassi, Andre (1970–)

Open: An Autobiography. Vintage Books, 2010, 2009. 385pp. ill. 9780307388407. Also available in audiobook, e-audiobook, and e-book. 796.342092

Readers who are surprised by the content of this memoir, the story of a tennis star who hated tennis, will find it clearer when they learn about Andre Agassi's father, Mike, a Golden Gloves fighter who could never make it professionally and who therefore set his hopes on his son in another sport he considered as pugilistic as boxing. Agassi is as honest as a reader might hope to find, describing the agony of a childhood pushed into pain for tennis, his successes in the sport as an adult that brought him no satisfaction except the knowledge that he would have mollified his father, his drug use, and his lies about it. He also talks about his relationships, bad and good, with well-known women like Brooke Shields and his wife, Steffi Graf. Agassi left school at fourteen, and he and his wife have opened a charter school for underprivileged children, using the Andre Agassi Foundation for Education (http://www.agassifoundation.org/) to foster quality education. Since he retired from professional tennis in 2006, he is now able to lead a life according to his own choosing. While J. R. Moehringer collaborated with Agassi on the writing of this book, he insisted that his name not be anywhere on it; he believed that it really was Agassi's work and Agassi's voice. As Moehringer so creatively put it: " 'The midwife doesn't go home with the baby' " (McGrath, 2009).

Subjects: Agassi, Mike; Andre Agassi Foundation for Education; Athletes; Education; Fathers and Sons; Graf, Steffi; Self-Acceptance; Shields, Brooke; Tennis

Now Try: With the help of Peter Bodo, Pete Sampras tells his story of tennis and his rivalry with Agassi in ***A Champion's Mind: Lessons from a Life in Tennis***. Roger Angell spent a season with David Cone, another athlete who suffered from a domineering father. Angell tells Cone's story in ***A Pitcher's Story: Innings with David Cone***. Another man who is giving back to his community is Twesigye Jackson Kaguri, a Ugandan living in the United States who has built a school in Uganda for AIDS orphans; he explains why, with the help of Susan Urbanek Linville, in ***The Price of Stones: Building a School for My Village***.

Gordeeva, Ekaterina (1971–)
Swift, E. M. (1951–), coauthor

My Sergei: A Love Story. Warner Books, 1997, 1996. 340pp. ill. 16pp. of plates. 9780446605335. Also available in large print, Braille, and audiobook. 796.91

A child of the Soviet system, where her skating prowess was identified and fostered through the sports establishment, Gordeeva was paired at the age of eleven with a young man four years her senior. Together they trained and competed for thirteen years, winning international championships, Olympic gold medals, and the hearts of their audience. They gradually fell in love themselves and married when Gordeeva was twenty. And then three years after the birth of their daughter, Sergei died suddenly of a heart attack while practicing. Gordeeva's story recounts all of this, including her depression and world-weariness after Sergei's death.

Subjects: Athletes, Soviet Union; Death of a Spouse; Depression; Figure Skating; Grinkov, Sergei; Married Couples; Olympic Gold Medalists

Now Try: Joy Goodwin provides an inside view of Olympic skating and three specific paired teams; her book, ***The Second Mark: Courage, Corruption, and the Battle for Olympic Gold***, also tells the story of one night's competition among these three pairs when corruption almost won the day. Ekaterina Gordeeva had many things come to her early in life; young widowhood would have been completely unexpected, though.

Katherine Ashenburg addresses this very situation in her look at death and bereavement, ***The Mourner's Dance: What We Do When People Die***. On a cheerier note, if you love figure skating, you may want to delve into the **Figure Skating Mystery Series** by Alina Adams, featuring figure-skating researcher Rebecca "Bex" Levy; the first in the series is ***Murder on Ice***.

Hamill, Dorothy (1956–)
Amelon, Deborah, coauthor

A Skating Life. Hyperion, 2007. 238pp. ill. 9780101303280. Also available in large print and e-book. 796.912092

One of the issues that Dorothy Hamill raises in this memoir is what to do after you've won the Olympic Gold Medal. Perhaps it's different now, but thirty years ago life was difficult for a woman Olympic athlete—in the training and in the life afterward. Unprepared for a future beyond the Olympics and suffering from a genetic depression, a condition she wasn't initially aware of, Hamill had a very difficult life off the skating rink. She matter-of-factly discusses her problems—her mental health, her relationships, and her finances—with a view to helping others who might be in similar circumstances.

Hamill has been inducted into both the U.S. Figure Skating Hall of Fame and the Academy of Achievement.

Subjects: Athletes; Bankruptcy; Depression; Figure Skating; Marriage; Olympic Gold Medalists

Now Try: If you'd like to see an overall look at the grueling sport of figure skating, you might find of interest Christine Brennan's ***Inside Edge: A Revealing Journey into the Secret World of Figure Skating***. Dorothy Hamill's mother was usually the one to travel and take her to the various rinks where Hamill would practice and compete. Her mother also spent much of her time fighting the old boys' network on behalf of her daughter. The issue of women in sports is looked at from one specific perspective by Michael Y. Sokolove in ***Warrior Girls: Protecting Our Daughters Against the Injury Epidemic in Women's Sports***. Katarina Witt is also a figure-skating gold medalist; she wrote her story, with E. M. Swift: ***Only with Passion: Figure Skating's Most Winning Champion on Competition and Life***.

Jordan, Michael (1963–)
Vancil, Mark (1958–), ed.

For the Love of the Game: My Story. Crown Publishers, 1998. 156pp. ill. 9780609602065. 796.323

Michael Jordan has enhanced this story of his career on and off the basketball court with 200 glossy photos, providing both a verbal and a visual memoir. He has been called the greatest basketball player ever, although he renounces that title, saying that all great players evolve from the great players before them. Jordan seems to succeed wherever he tries—

in basketball, in business, and in writing—so he and Mark Vancil put their writing skills to use once again in ***Driven from Within*** to share with others how Jordan has achieved his successes.

Subjects: African-American Men; Athletes; Basketball; Businessmen; Chicago Bulls (Basketball Team); Olympic Gold Medalists; Record-Breakers

Now Try: Bill Bradley, a former basketball star, has also taken a philosophical look at the sport, to draw parallels between it and success in life, in ***Values of the Game***. Michael Jordan has not only written his own books on basketball and on his life; he has inspired other writers to do so as well. David Halberstam's book, ***Playing for Keeps: Michael Jordan and the World He Made***, was published at the same time as Jordan's ***For the Love of the Game***. Scott Simon, a noted reporter and broadcaster, has written about his love of the game, particularly as played by the Chicago Bulls, in ***Home and Away: Memoir of a Fan***. Alonzo Mourning is another basketball-playing Olympic Gold Medalist, another man who has an inspiring story to tell, which he does with the help of Dan Wetzel in ***Resilience: Faith, Focus, Triumph***.

Louganis, Greg (1960–)
Marcus, Eric (1958–), coauthor

Breaking the Surface. Sourcebooks, 2006, 1995. 306pp. ill. 32pp. of plates. 9781402206665. Also available in e-book and video. 797.24092

At the 1988 Summer Olympics, Greg Louganis won not only two gold medals, but also the Maxwell House/United States Olympic Committee Spirit Award for his embodiment of the Olympic spirit and his courage. He received this latter award in light of the fact that he had hit his head on the diving board, had four stitches and a waterproof patch put on his head, and went back to execute his best dive yet. It was after the stitches that he won the gold medals. What the presenters of the award didn't know, however, was that he was battling more than that, as he'd been diagnosed HIV-positive several months earlier. Louganis's memoir recounts the challenges in his childhood, along with his successful diving competitions, his later problems with drug abuse, some of his relationships, and his coming out. He concludes with his presence at the Gay Games in 1994.

Subjects: Adoptees; Adoption; Athletes; Diving; Dyslexia; Gay Men; HIV/AIDS; Olympic Gold Medalists; Triumph over Adversity

Now Try: Rudy Galindo suffered similar difficulties to Louganis, but managed to overcome them in his ice-skating career. With the help of Eric Marcus, he told his story in ***Icebreaker: The Autobiography of Rudy Galindo***. Katie Hnida exhibits great courage too in her challenging story of trying to break a gender barrier in sports and what it cost her, ***Still Kicking: My Journey as the First Woman to Play Division I College Football***. With the help of Brian Cazeneuve, Olympic swimming medalist Michael Phelps tells his story in ***Michael Phelps: Beneath the Surface***.

McEnroe, John (1959–)
Kaplan, James (1951–), coauthor

You Cannot Be Serious. Berkley Books, 2003, 2002. 342pp. ill. 9780425190081. Also available in e-book. 796.342

Known by the media as "SuperBrat," John McEnroe made a name for himself for his outstanding prowess on the tennis court as well as for his frequent and petulant outbursts of temper. His behavior often got in his way, but he still managed to excel at major games and was a frequent participant and winner in the Davis Cup competitions. He was a star off the court as well, a jet-setter married for a while to Tatum O'Neal, and he includes all of these aspects of his life in his memoir.

John McEnroe was inducted into the International Tennis Hall of Fame.

Subjects: Athletes; Davis Cup (Tennis); Jet Set; O'Neal, Tatum; Temper; Tennis

Now Try: In this memoir, McEnroe shows a maturity that allows him to look back on his life on the courts with some chagrin and self-deprecating humor. Mickey McDermott is another athlete who made a name for himself, in his case through alcohol abuse, and the same self-deprecating humor comes out in his story, written with the help of Howard Eisenberg: ***A Funny Thing Happened on the Way to Cooperstown***. McEnroe is very honest in his story, particularly in relating how he regards his earlier behavior and in his discussion of his private life, making this a no-holds-barred kind of story. Stuart Evey has written a similar kind of story, with Irv Broughton, about the cable station that McEnroe announces for: ***ESPN: The No-Holds-Barred Story of Power, Ego, Money, and Vision That Transformed a Culture***. McEnroe's honesty reflects a mature self-awareness, a quality we also see in William Shatner's ***Up till Now: The Autobiography***, written with the help of David Fisher.

Palmer, Arnold (1929–)
Dodson, James (1953–), coauthor

A Golfer's Life. Ballantine Books, 2000, 1999. 420pp. ill. 9780345414823. Also available in large print and audiobook (read by James Dodson). 796.35209

Arnold Palmer's friendships—with his parents, his wife, other golfers such as Jack Nicklaus, and father figures like Dwight Eisenhower—were as important to him as his golf career. This memoir, then, includes not only play-by-play descriptions of games lost and won, but also anecdotes and reflections on the important and influential people in his life. He began his golf life playing in his hometown, Latrobe, Pennsylvania, on the course where his father was head groundskeeper, playing at dawn before any of the members would be on the course. He now owns that golf course.

After a stunning decade in the 1960s, Palmer was inducted into the World Golf Hall of Fame in 1974. He also received a Presidential Medal of Freedom in 2004 from President George W. Bush.

Subjects: Athletes; British Open Golf Tournament; Friendships; Golf; Masters Golf Tournament; Reflections; U.S. Open Golf Tournament

Now Try: Palmer's story of his victories and disappointments and of his relationships with others is deeply moving, as is his coauthor Dodson's own story, ***Final Rounds: A Father, a Son, the Golf Journey of a Lifetime.*** Palmer writes about his relationships with candor, as does Richard Ford in his collection of stories about relationships, ***A Multitude of Sins.*** A different perspective on the game of golf is given by Catherine M. Lewis in ***"Don't Ask What I Shot": How Eisenhower's Love of Golf Helped Shape 1950s America.***

Payton, Walter (1954–1999)
Yaeger, Don, coauthor

Never Die Easy: The Autobiography of Walter Payton. Villard, 2000. 268pp. ill. 9780679463313. Also available in large print, audiobook, and e-book. 796.332

Walter Payton was an American hero on and off the football field. He died of liver cancer before this book could be finished, so that what began as an "as-told-to" autobiography finished as a combined memoir/eulogy. The title of his autobiography comes from an exhortation from his college coach: never die easy in a game—make your opponent work for your defeat. Payton always gave it his best, even if his best proved not quite good enough. His coauthor, Yaeger, elicited comments and stories from Payton's family, friends, and sports associates, creating a *mélange* of tales about a man who gave his all both on the football field and, in the larger world, to the Walter & Connie Payton Foundation, their charitable foundation helping needy children (http://www.payton34.com/). Payton's request to Yaeger was that the book be inspirational, and all those who read it agree that Yaeger succeeded well in his mandate.

Walter Payton was inducted into the Pro Football Hall of Fame.

Subjects: African-American Men; Athletes; Chicago Bears (Football Team); Football; Liver Cancer; Philanthropists; Walter & Connie Payton Foundation

Now Try: Readers who enjoy learning about the lives of football greats may also be interested in the memoirs of Tom Landry, football coach of both the New York Giants and the Dallas Cowboys, ***Tom Landry: An Autobiography,*** written with Gregg Lewis. Payton was a selfless and spiritual man who not only did not ask to be moved ahead on the organ-donor list for a new liver, but actually donated his own organs when he died. This same selflessness is evident in David Hilfiker's ***Not All of Us Are Saints: A Doctor's Journey with the Poor.*** Payton's memoir is really an oral history, a collage of multiple voices; Peter Golenbock uses the same technique in ***In the Country of Brooklyn: Inspiration to the World.***

Rodman, Dennis (1961–)
Keown, Tim, coauthor

Bad as I Wanna Be. Dell, 1997, 1996. 323pp. ill. 9780440222668. Also available in audiobook, e-audiobook, and e-book. 796.323092

One of the best rebounders in National Basketball Association (NBA) history, Dennis Rodman has also established a reputation for himself off the court, a reputation that is furthered by this memoir. Believing that his personal unhappiness was due to his not expressing his true self, Rodman decided to change all that, to begin acting in a way that represented the real Dennis Rodman. He covers much of these thoughts and the activities that demonstrate them in his memoir, from his early childhood to his athletic accomplishments, from his love for his daughter to his highly public affair with Madonna. He criticizes the administration of the NBA as well as his teammates, and he elaborates on his views about his sexuality, cross-dressing, drugs, and marriage. The text of the book is in multiple fonts, various type sizes, and a mixture of bold and italic typography, perhaps to resemble his various tattoos and piercings and his multicolored hair. The rough language is also in keeping with what one might expect from someone who marches in Rodman-like style to his own drummer. He followed this memoir with another the next year, ***Walk on the Wild Side,*** aided by Michael Silver.

Subjects: African-American Men; Athletes; Basketball; Cross-Dressing; Love Affairs; Madonna; Promiscuity; Sexuality

Now Try: Jayson Williams is another outspoken professional basketball player who writes his own brash story with the help of Steve Friedman: ***Loose Balls: Easy Money, Hard Fouls, Cheap Laughs, and True Love in the NBA***. Men and women cross-dress for any number of reasons; Josh Kilmer-Purcell relates his double life posing as a drag queen in ***I Am Not Myself These Days: A Memoir.*** Despite, or perhaps because of, his iconoclasm, Rodman has injected humor into his memoir, the same kind of humor one can find in the essays in Tony Kornheiser's ***Bald as I Wanna Be***.

Stringer, C. Vivian (1948–)
Tucker, Laura (1973–), coauthor

Standing Tall: A Memoir of Tragedy and Triumph. Crown, 2008. 291pp. ill. 16pp. of plates. 9780307406095. Also available in audiobook, e-audiobook, and e-book. 796.323092

On the court Vivian Stringer's life has been full of triumph, leading three separate collegiate teams to the NCAA Final Four (the only coach to have done so) and turning these teams around in the process. She has won awards and been inducted into the Women's Basketball Hall of Fame. Off the court, however, she has dealt with the disabling illness of her infant daughter, the sudden death of her husband when he was in his forties, and her own breast cancer. Her childhood as the daughter of loving and inspiring parents (her father was a coalminer) gave her the background and fortitude to withstand the racism, sexism, and life events that could easily have felled her. In her memoir she reveals all of this and makes a brief mention of the controversy sparked by Don Imus with his racist and

1 2 3 4 5 6 7 8

sexist remarks against Stringer's Rutgers team. She reveals, too, how she regards her role as a basketball coach—not just to teach the young women how to excel at the sport, but also to teach them how to excel in life. The title comes from something her father said to her at a pivotal point in her adolescence: "If you don't stand for something, you'll fall for anything."

Subjects: African-American Women; Basketball; Basketball Coaches; Breast Cancer; College Sports; Courage; Death of a Spouse; Family Relationships; Firsts; Illness in Children

Now Try: Young women have been playing basketball since the beginning of the twentieth century; Linda S. Peavy and Ursula Smith have written the story of an unusual group of girls who learned this new game of basketball when they were sent from their reservation to a government school: ***Full-Court Quest: The Girls from Fort Shaw Indian School, Basketball Champions of the World***. Stringer was also assistant coach to the team that won the Olympic gold medal in 2004. From the other side of the court is a story by an Olympic basketball player who then went professional, ***Don't Let the Lipstick Fool You*** by Lisa Leslie, with Larry Burnett. The emotional ups and downs in Stringer's memoir are not unlike the emotions the reader will find in a novel like Helen Dunmore's ***Mourning Ruby***.

Torre, Joe (1940–)
Verducci, Tom, coauthor

The Yankee Years. With a new Afterword. Anchor Books, 2010, 2009. 516pp. ill. 24pp. of plates. 9780767930420. Also available in large print, audiobook, e-audiobook, and e-book. 796.352092

Joe Torre discusses his twelve-year stint managing the New York Yankees, but does so in a slightly different fashion from the standard memoir. Working with *Sports Illustrated* senior writer Tom Verducci, Torre decided to have the memoir told as a third-person narrative, although it is his story as told to Verducci. In the book he describes how he brought the Yankees into post-season play for the first time in fifteen years, winning the Championship four years running. He also talks about specific players and creates some controversy in doing so, but his take on owner George Steinbrenner is a large part of the book. The issue of trust and the use of steroids are also major topics. Torre felt betrayed by the general manager, Brian Cashman, when it came to his final contract, a contract he wouldn't accept. Torre then went on to manage the Los Angeles Dodgers, leading them to their first post-season victory since 1988.

Subjects: Baseball; Baseball Managers; Drugs in Sports; New York Yankees (Baseball Team); Steinbrenner, George; World Series (Baseball)

Now Try: In ***Chasing the Dream: My Lifelong Journey to the World Series: An Autobiography***, also written with Tom Verducci, Torre tells his story about his baseball years prior to managing the Yankees. George Steinbrenner was perhaps one of the most controversial figures in professional baseball. Readers can find out more about him in a biography by Peter Golenbock, ***George: The Poor Little Rich Boy Who Built the Yankee Empire***. If you'd like a different perspective on Torre's reign with the Yankees, you may enjoy newspaper columnist Joel Sherman's ***Birth of a Dynasty: Behind the Pinstripes***

with the 1996 Yankees. Another memoir told with third-person narration is Frankie Saggio and Fred Rosen's ***Born to the Mob: The True-Life Story of the Only Man to Work for All Five of New York's Mafia Families***.

Music Stars

The stories in this section involve musicians of many stripes: folk, jazz, blues, country, pop, rock, even children's. Classical music does not enter into this section—it is in Chapter 3, "The Creative Life." In this section you will learn about the business of music making as well as the performing of it. And you will see how the vagaries of life are part of anyone's story. What you will really see, though, are the remarkable people who made significant changes in an important art and industry.

Memoirs of music stars provide an interesting view of the popular culture of the time, as these musicians describe not only their personal lives, but the musical worlds they have traveled in. Some of these musicians have been trailblazers, creating new styles of music, offering insights into that particular musical genre. They also have stories to tell of overcoming hardships to achieve their dreams, or perhaps the hardships, particularly in the form of addictions, have come as a result of achieving their dreams.

Buffett, Jimmy (1946–)

A Pirate Looks at Fifty. Ballantine, 2000, 1998. 420pp. map. 9780449005866. Also available in large print and e-book. 782.42164

When Jimmy Buffett, singer, songwriter, novelist, and conservationist, turned fifty, he decided to do it in style. He gathered his family and, starting out from Key West, spent three weeks over Christmas (his birthday is Christmas Day) heading south to the Caribbean and Central and South America. Between the tales of their trip he provides details of his preceding years, how he started in music in New Orleans, how he loves to fly and nearly killed himself in a crash in Nantucket, and how hedonistic he used to be. He is a born storyteller, as listeners can hear in his music, and that same rhythm comes through in his writing.

Both this memoir and Buffett's ***Where Is Joe Merchant? A Novel Tale*** were number one on *The New York Times* best-seller lists, making him one of a select few to have been number one on both the fiction and nonfiction best-seller lists of *The New York Times*.

Subjects: Adventurers; Personal Essays; Pilots; Rock Musicians; Singers; Songwriters; Travel; Writers

Now Try: Buffett's memoir is rambling and ruminating, much in the same style as Frank Conroy's collection of essays as he too expresses his thoughts about life in ***Dogs Bark, but the Caravan Rolls On: Observations Then and Now***. Jimmy Buffett, although he may be serious at times, prefers to take a humorous look at life around him; Dave Barry does much the same in an amusing look at fifty: ***Dave Barry Turns 50***. An island lover like Buffett, Thurston Clarke gives us a look at a variety of islands in ***Searching for Crusoe: A Journey Among the Last Real Islands***.

Cash, Johnny (1932–2003)
Carr, Patrick, coauthor

Cash: The Autobiography. Harper, 2007, 1997. 432pp. ill. 16pp. of plates. 9780061013577. Also available in large print and e-book. 782.421642

This second memoir by Johnny Cash is much more reflective than the first, ***Man in Black***, written more than twenty years earlier, as he looks over his life with regrets for the demons that plagued him and with joy for the successes that were his. Much of his success he attributes to his wife, June Carter, who helped him recover from drug addiction. Cash is legendary for his *mélange* of musical styles and roots, combining country, rock, folk, and spiritual music to create his own personal style.

His musical successes are also legion, ranging from several Grammy Awards to induction into the Country Music Hall of Fame, the Rock and Roll Hall of Fame, and the Academy of Achievement, as well as the awarding of the Kennedy Center Honors and the National Medal of Arts, the highest national honor bestowed on an artist.

Subjects: Carter, June; Conversion; Country Musicians; Drug Abuse; Imprisonment; Rock Musicians; Singers; Songwriters; Spirituality

Now Try: June Carter and Johnny Cash had one son, John Carter Cash, who wrote his mother's story: ***Anchored in Love: An Intimate Portrait of June Carter Cash***. But Johnny Cash had a daughter from a previous marriage; Rosanne Cash has recently written her story, ***Composed: A Memoir***. Cash's influence was felt as far north as New Hampshire, to hear Dana Andrew Jennings tell it. Jennings was weaned on Johnny Cash, as he relates in ***Sing Me Back Home: Love, Death, and Country Music***. This story of Johnny Cash's life, with its lows of addiction and prison and its highs of spiritual conversion and a happy life with June Carter, is straight from the heart. So too is Dr. Gabor Maté's work on why addiction is so prevalent in today's society, ***In the Realm of Hungry Ghosts: Close Encounters with Addiction***. For fun you may want to pick up a fictional debut by one of Cash's musical contemporaries, Willie Nelson, whose western, written with Mike Blakely, is entitled ***A Tale out of Luck***.

Dylan, Bob (1941–)

Chronicles. Simon & Schuster, 2005, 2004. 320pp. ill. 9780743244589. Also available in large print, Braille, audiobook, and e-book. 782.42164

Dylan's award-winning memoir is both fascinating and frustrating. Because it is only the first volume, much is left out, leading the reader to hope that the promised volumes two and three will materialize and fill in the blanks. At the same time, however, the reader is invited into the mind and some very detailed memories of the iconic musicologist, Bob Dylan, "voice of a generation." In addition, Jack Kerouac's presence is strongly felt throughout Dylan's rambles in this work. A chronicle though it may be, the book is not chronological, as Dylan begins with the signing of his first record contract and much later returns to his roots in northern Minnesota, where he was born Robert Zimmerman. Dylan claimed he could not be the voice of a generation when he himself did not understand that generation. Wherever that truth lies, there is no denying that Bob Dylan has been a major force in popular culture in the twentieth century.

Dylan has been inducted into both the Rock and Roll Hall of Fame and the Songwriters Hall of Fame and has been awarded both the Kennedy Center Honors and a Grammy Lifetime Achievement Award. He was also named one of *Time*'s People of the Century in the Artists & Entertainers category. ***Chronicles*** was a finalist for the National Book Critics Circle Award in Biography and the winner of the Quill Award for Biography/Memoir.

Subjects: Folk Singers; Kerouac, Jack; Minnesota; New York, NY; Rock Musicians; Songwriters

Now Try: The cover of Dylan's album ***The Freewheelin' Bob Dylan*** features Dylan walking toward 4th Street with a relatively unknown woman. That woman, Suze Rotolo, has finally written her story in ***A Freewheelin' Time: A Memoir of Greenwich Village in the Sixties***, a chronicle that may fill in some of the blanks left by Dylan himself. Greil Marcus takes a look at the songwriting culture of the sixties through one song: ***Like a Rolling Stone: Bob Dylan at the Crossroads***. Despite the title, Marcus's book is not so much about Bob Dylan as it is about American popular culture. Another musical icon of the time was Janis Joplin, a singer whose story Alice Echols tells in ***Scars of Sweet Paradise: The Life and Times of Janis Joplin***. Pete Seeger used his music to convey his social messages as well. Alec Wilkinson has had many conversations with this nonagenarian, to provide a rounded look at the man in ***The Protest Singer: An Intimate Portrait of Pete Seeger***.

Jackson, Michael (1958–2009)

Moonwalk. Original Foreword by Jacqueline Kennedy Onassis; New Foreword by Berry Gordy; Afterword by Shaye Areheart. Harmony Books, 2009, 1988. 300pp. ill. 20pp. of plates. 9780307716989. Also available in e-book. 782.42166

Michael Jackson was twenty-nine when he wrote this, his only memoir. Yet he had accomplished much by that point, offering enough background to his later, stranger life to suit many readers. He describes what it was like to be part of a family singing group and how their fortunes changed once the Jackson 5 were discovered by Motown producers. He was a child at the time and got up to childish antics. Jackson also talks about what inspired him to create the music he did and how he learned to become the outstanding dancer he was, with unusual, intricate moves. He talks about good friends, friends like *Quincy Jones* and Marlon Brando, and about his hard times with the rumor mills always spreading stories. He even discusses plastic surgery, which he had already begun by that stage in his life.

Jackson was inducted into the Rock and Roll Hall of Fame twice: once with the Jackson 5 and once as a solo performer. He was also inducted into the Songwriters Hall of Fame.

Subjects: Childhood and Youth, African-American; Dancers; Family Relationships; Jackson 5 (Musical Group); Motown; Rhythm and Blues Singers; Rock Musicians; Songwriters

Now Try: Robert Sullivan has edited a *Life* magazine commemorative edition of a photograph "album" of Michael Jackson entitled ***Michael***, including pictures never before released. Alissa Quart looks at the issue of pushing children too much in their childhood in her study, ***Hothouse Kids: The Dilemma of the Gifted Child***. Another musical icon was Elvis Presley (and coincidentally the father of Michael Jackson's wife, Lisa Marie), a man who also seemed to have more than he could properly handle as his life progressed. Peter Guralnick has written a two-volume biography of Presley. The first is ***Last Train to Memphis: The Rise of Elvis Presley***; the second is ***Careless Love: The Unmaking of Elvis Presley***. Also following a difficult personal path despite his musical success was James Brown, who published his autobiography, ***I Feel Good: A Memoir of a Life of Soul***, not long before his death.

Jones, Quincy (1933–)

Q: The Autobiography of Quincy Jones. Harlem Moon, 2002, 2001. 412pp. ill. 40pp. of plates. discography. filmography. 9780385488969. Also available in large print, audiobook, and e-book. 781.64

Quincy Jones's first major gig as a young performer was as back-up trumpeter for Billie Holiday. From there he went on to become a big name as a musician, composer, arranger, businessman, and producer, bringing out such singles as "We Are the World," and such albums as Michael Jackson's ***Thriller***. To read his autobiography is to get a snapshot view of the entertainment industry in the second half of the twentieth century. This book is a combination of Jones's reminiscences in his own hand and essays written by people close to him, people like Ray Charles, Peggy Lipton (one of his wives), and his children.

Jones has been awarded the Kennedy Center Honors, was inducted into the Academy of Achievement, and was honored with a Horatio Alger Award. ***Q*** was given the Anisfield-Wolf Book Award, an award that recognizes books on issues of race and culture.

Subjects: African-American Men; Anisfield-Wolf Book Award; Arrangers (Musicians); Businessmen; Entertainment Industry; Jazz Musicians; Music Producers; Trumpet Players

Now Try: In addition to the formats mentioned above, there is a four-CD set entitled ***Q: The Musical Biography of Quincy Jones*** that may interest the reader who would like to listen to his music while learning about his life. Jones has written forewords to several books, but perhaps one of the more interesting for readers of his autobiography would be in ***Temples of Sound: Inside the Great Recording Studios*** by Jim Cogan and William Clark. Jones also contributed to a book edited by Henry Louis Gates entitled

In Search of Our Roots: How 19 Extraordinary African-Americans Reclaimed Their Past. Jones's technique of alternating chapters can also be found in a poignant memoir by Laurence Shames and Peter Barton, in which Shames writes chapters connecting Barton's chapters about his shortened life, ***Not Fade Away: A Short Life Well Lived.*** But perhaps the overriding feature of Jones's autobiography is the eloquence of his writing, as he translates his musical talent into a literary talent. Eloquence is also the hallmark of Robert Ford's novel, ***The Student Conductor.***

Judd, Wynonna (1964–)
Cox, Patsi Bale, coauthor

Coming Home to Myself. Signet, 2007, 2005. 321pp. ill. 9780451218087. Also available in large print, audiobook, e-audiobook, and e-book. 782.421642092

Wynonna Judd's memoir is more about her own personal growth and triumph over adversity than about her musical career, although her singing is certainly a major part of her life. In her memoir, though, she speaks honestly about the difficulties she has had, particularly with self-image and self-esteem. She describes her mother, Naomi, as very controlling, made more difficult, perhaps, because they were a singing duo for quite a while. Despite her huge professional success, both with her mother and in singing solo, Judd has had serious financial troubles. Because of her lack of self-confidence she became an emotional eater, so that she also has to contend with weight issues. Perhaps the biggest trial for her was discovering as an adult that her mother had lied to her all her life about the true identity of her father. Her memoir, despite all its woes, is inspiring for others who share similar difficulties, as she also reveals how she is trying to overcome her personal issues of self-acceptance so that the other problems will recede.

Subjects: Country Musicians; Divorce; Empowerment of Women; Judd, Ashley; Judd, Naomi; The Judds (Musical Group); Mothers and Daughters; Self-Acceptance; Singers

Now Try: Loretta Lynn, a record-breaking country singer, wrote a second memoir, also with Patsi Bale Cox, ***Still Woman Enough,*** following her classic ***Loretta Lynn: Coal Miner's Daughter,*** which she wrote with George Vecsey. Judd's relationships with her mother and her younger sister are reflected in the humorous memoir, ***Girls Only: Sleepovers, Squabbles, Tuna Fish and Other Facts of Family Life,*** of the journalist Alex Witchel. Reba McEntire is a successful businesswoman as well as a record-breaking country singer; but after her tour manager and several of her band members were killed in a plane crash, she wrote a more spiritual memoir sharing her life experiences and what she has learned from them: ***Comfort from a Country Quilt.***

Raffi (1948–)

The Life of a Children's Troubadour: An Autobiography. Homeland Press, 2000, 1999. 316pp. ill. 9781896943503. 782.42

A children's entertainer and advocate, Raffi tells his story of moving from Egypt (where his family had been exiled from Armenia) to Canada when he was an adolescent and the difficulties that entailed for him. Although he began his musical career as a hopeful folk singer, he soon realized that children were his preferred audience, a recognition that set him on a path he had never expected to travel. Now a renowned child advocate and environmentalist, Raffi has used his music and his spin-off books to promote his messages of respect for the child, for peace, and for the planet.

Raffi is the recipient of numerous awards in both the recording world and the humanitarian world, including the Order of Canada. His books have been printed on recycled and chlorine-free paper.

Subjects: Armenian-Canadians; Child Advocates, Canada; Children's Musicians, Canada; Environmental Activists, Canada; Immigrants, Canada; Singers, Canada; Toronto, ON

Now Try: The novelist Gay Courter is a volunteer child advocate in the Florida legal system, sharing her stories in ***I Speak for This Child: True Stories of a Child Advocate***. Another children's entertainer, although one not so publicly visible as Raffi, is Kevin Clash, who talks about his life entertaining children in ***My Life as a Furry Red Monster: What Being Elmo Has Taught Me About Life, Love, and Laughing out Loud,*** written with Gary Brozek. Some readers may be intrigued by the notion of a troubadour and his life. W. S. Merwin has elegantly provided such a story in his exploration of southwest France and the troubadour tradition in ***The Mays of Ventadorn***.

Sting (1951–)

Broken Music: A Memoir. Dell, 2009, 2003. 440pp. 9780440241157. Also available in large print and e-book. 782.42166092

By learning the source of his professional name and his memoir title, we also learn something of the childhood and adolescence of Gordon Sumner, lead guitarist and vocalist for the punk band The Police. Initially playing in jazz bands to learn more about music, Sumner often wore black sweaters with wide yellow strips (as seen on the book cover), leading someone to tell him he resembled a wasp; thus the name. The book title has a more unhappy provenance. Sting found his relationship with his parents problematic, particularly when one day he walked in on his mother with one of her lovers. He went to his grandmother's, to bang on her piano, creating what she called "broken music." Reaching his fifties, Sting began to feel the compulsion to write his childhood story, to "try to understand the child I was, and the man I became." Thus his memoir, written in the present tense, has the feel of a diary to it; its language also represents the intelligent, articulate singer-composer. The memoir weaves stories of his parents in and out as he recounts his childhood and adolescence up to the formation of The Police.

Subjects: Childhood and Youth; Composers, England; England; Fathers and Sons; Mothers and Sons; Musicians, England; The Police (Musical Group); Rock Musicians

Now Try: A musician who has the same cachet as Sting is Bono, a singer and social activist whose story, a collection of conversations with Michka Assayas, is simply titled ***Bono***. One of Sting's coguitarists in The Police was Andy Summers, a musician who has also written his memoir in the present tense: ***One Train Later: A Memoir***. Sting's reaching out to music was in large part a result of the difficult relationship between his parents. Stewart O'Nan's fifteen-year-old protagonist in his novel, ***Snow Angels***, also suffers from the bitter relationship between his parents.

Stage and Screen Stars

This section might be one of the most popular, in bookstores and libraries, for readers of memoirs and biographies. Here the reader will find the stories of people they see larger than life on the big screen or on the stage. The reader might also look for a "tell-all" or for enlightenment into the art of acting. The reader might also like to get the writer's version of a scandal written about in entertainment magazines and tabloids or learn more about the film or stage industry in its early days. All of that and more are here in this section. There are some book award winners, some ghostwritten titles, and even one story found posthumously.

> Memoirs of stage and screen stars are stories of celebrities who have been successful in their careers in television and film as well as on the stage in live theater. They are often written by themselves and provide insights into the craft of their profession and how the business changes and evolves. They also invite the reader into their own personal lives, recounting their early lives and the struggles they had to overcome to become the celebrities that they are.

Andrews, Julie (1935–)

Home: A Memoir of My Early Years. Hyperion, 2008. 339pp. ill. 32pp. of plates. 9780786865659. Also available in large print, audiobook, and e-book. 792.4020892

In this memoir Julie Andrews takes us from her childhood to her arrival in Los Angeles for the making of the movie ***Mary Poppins***. When she arrived there, she was with her first husband, Tony Walton, and her baby, Emma. She offers a bit of family history, describing her parents' background, especially the particularly difficult childhood her own mother, Barbara, had had. There is much in her memoir about the war and their poverty. When Ted Andrews, her stepfather and a Canadian tenor, decided to have Andrews's voice tested, they were amazed to discover the adult quality and range of it. She was a star at the age of twelve and the youngest person yet to perform for the Royal Family. By the time she was fifteen, she had left school and was supporting her family, as both her mother and her stepfather had become alcoholics. Andrews goes on to describe her transition from vaudeville in England, to her debut on Broadway in Sandy Wilson's ***The Boy Friend,*** to being recognized by Walt Disney.

Julie Andrews was inducted into the Academy of Achievement, citing as her recommended book a childhood favorite, the Carnegie Medal winner ***The Little Grey Men: A Story for the Young in Heart*** by "BB." She was also awarded the Kennedy Center Honors.

Subjects: Actors, England; Broadway; Childhood and Youth; Children of Alcoholics; Divorce; Singers, England; Vaudeville; Women in Film; World War II (1939-1945)

Now Try: The same conversational, chatty tone in Andrews's memoir can be found in the memoir of another Broadway singer, Carol Channing's ***Just Lucky I Guess: A Memoir of Sorts***. Mary Martin is another singer whose fame was made with a child's story (***Peter Pan***); she also played the role of Maria Trapp on Broadway. Ronald L. Davis has told her story in ***Mary Martin, Broadway Legend***. The humor and warmth in Andrews's memoir add to the charm of the book; Jean Ritchie writes her musical story with warmth as well, although her background is very different from that of Andrews. ***Singing Family of the Cumberlands*** (illustrated by Maurice Sendak) is about the folk songs and singers of the Appalachian Region.

Bacall, Lauren (1924–)

By Myself and Then Some. Rev. ed. HarperEntertainment, 2006, 2005. 506pp. ill. 9780061127915. Also available in large print and audiobook (read by the author). 791.43028092

This volume is a revised edition of Lauren Bacall's first book, ***Lauren Bacall by Myself,*** a memoir that won the National Book Award for Autobiography. In that one she detailed her start in Hollywood, thanks to a photograph of her by Diana Vreeland on the cover of *Harper's Bazaar*. She started off running, starring opposite Humphrey Bogart in the movie ***To Have and Have Not***. Bacall's memoir sensitively portrayed her relationship with Bogie, a love that was never equaled for the rest of her life. Born in the Bronx, raised in Brooklyn by her mother and two uncles (having been deserted by her father), she remained true to her roots and her Jewish heritage. While the current memoir adds to the original, the new material, as the title suggests, is largely Bacall's reflections on many of those friends and loved ones who are no longer with her.

Bacall won the Kennedy Center Honors, has a star on the Hollywood Walk of Fame, and has two Tony Awards to her credit, but says that her National Book Award for her first memoir is the most precious of her awards.

Subjects: Actors; Bogart, Humphrey; Golden Age of Hollywood; Hollywood, CA; Love Affairs; National Book Award for Autobiography; Octogenarians; Reflections; Women in Film

Now Try: Readers may like to look at Ernest Hemingway's novel that started Bacall on her way: ***To Have and Have Not***. Bacall writes with an emotional clarity and an immediacy that can also be found in Elizabeth Maguire's novel ***The Open Door,*** a story about a relationship between Henry James and the niece of James Fenimore Cooper. In her memoir Lauren Bacall provides snapshots of her life and the people in it, but of course Bogie has central stage. Readers may enjoy reading Stephen Humphrey Bogart's memoir of his father, ***Bogart: In Search of My Father***.

Ball, Lucille (1911–1989)
Hoffman, Betty Hannah, coauthor

Love, Lucy. Foreword by Lucie Arnaz. Boulevard Books, 1997, 1996. 235pp. ill. 32pp. of plates. 9781572973237. Also available in large print and e-book. 791.45028092

Though written in the mid-1960s, this book was not discovered until after Lucille Ball's death in 1989, found among her papers with a note saying she hadn't published it because she didn't want to hurt her first husband, Desi Arnaz. The book covers her life from her formative childhood in Celoron, New York, through her success as "Queen of Comedy," to her marriage with Gary Morton and the reestablishment of a cordial relationship with Arnaz. She also talks extensively about her love for and marriage to Arnaz.

Before she died, Ball had been awarded two stars on the Hollywood Walk of Fame, one for television and one for movies; the Kennedy Center Honors; and membership in both the National Women's Hall of Fame and the Broadcasting & Cable Hall of Fame. She was posthumously awarded the Presidential Medal of Freedom by President George H. W. Bush in 1989 and was named one of *Time*'s People of the Century in the Artists & Entertainers category.

Subjects: Actors; Arnaz, Desi; Comediennes; Hollywood, CA; *I Love Lucy* (Television Program); New York (State); Television Actors; Women in Film

Now Try: Lucille Ball's success was due in large part to her own comic genius, but it was helped along by her writers, Madelyn Pugh Davis and Bob Carroll Jr., who have written their own perspective on the comedienne, ***Laughing with Lucy: My Life with America's Leading Lady of Comedy***. A comedienne whose humor is different from Ball's has written collections of her own reflections. You may want to have a look at ***My Point—And I Do Have One*** or ***The Funny Thing Is—*** by Ellen DeGeneres. Lucille Ball has written her memoir in her own voice with poignancy and vitality. Such is the style of Jeanne Ray's love story, ***Julie and Romeo: A Novel***. Ball was greatly influenced by Norman Vincent Peale, imbuing her writing with his positive spirit. His landmark book, ***The Power of Positive Thinking***, is still available for people to read.

Crystal, Billy (1947–)

700 Sundays. Warner Books, 2006, 2005. 182pp. ill. 9780446698511. Also available in large print and e-book. 792.7028092

The first incarnation of this title was a solo Broadway show that Billy Crystal wrote and starred in, winning a Tony Award for Best Special Theatrical Event. The book is a paean to his parents, particularly his father, with whom Billy calculates he may have spent 700 Sundays. Crystal's dad,

Jack, worked two jobs and was therefore home on Sundays only, and he died when Crystal was fifteen. But the years before he died were full, and Crystal recounts many anecdotes that reveal the fabric of his family and his upbringing. Of particular importance in his formation was the jazz world they were immersed in, Jack running a jazz record store and Crystal's Uncle Milt Gabler starting up Commodore Records, the label that recorded Billie Holiday's "Strange Fruit" when no one else would. Crystal says that being on stage is like a jazz riff to him. The other major influence was the encouragement he received from his parents to watch and perform comedy, as he obviously had a bent for it from early on.

Subjects: Actors; Comedians; Crystal, Jack; Death of a Parent; Family Relationships; Fathers and Sons; Jazz; Long Island, NY; Theater; Uncles

Now Try: Billy Crystal wrote a children's picture book when he learned he was to become a grandfather: ***I Already Know I Love You***, illustrated by Elizabeth Sayles. Crystal's memoir, as one might expect, is like a stand-up comic's monologue and laugh-out-loud funny. It reminds one of Sarah Vowell's collection of essays, ***The Partly Cloudy Patriot***. In addition to all he has accomplished as a writer and as an actor on Broadway and on screen, Billy Crystal has also made a name for himself as a frequent host of the Academy Awards. Steve Pond talks about Crystal (and many others) in ***The Big Show: High Times and Dirty Dealings Backstage at the Academy Awards***, a book that includes the work of several photographers. Obviously Crystal's family was very helpful to Billie Holiday, an important figure in jazz. William Dufty worked with her on her memoir, ***Lady Sings the Blues***.

Farrow, Mia (1945–)

What Falls Away: A Memoir. Bantam, 1998, 1997. 341pp. ill. 32 pp. of plates. 9780553564662. Also available in large print and audiobook (read by the author). 791.43028092

Mia Farrow, daughter of writer and director John Farrow and actress Maureen O'Sullivan, has roughly divided her memoir into three parts. The first, seen through a gauzy prism, is of her childhood, the fairy-tale childhood that ended when she was nine, stricken with polio and confined to an iron lung in a sanatorium for a year. The second section deals with her years as a young adult, including her marriage at the age of nineteen to Frank Sinatra, who was thirty years her senior. She left that marriage for an ashram in India, which may have been the start of her long spiritual journey. The final section of the book is devoted to the many children she has, biological and adopted, and the disastrous end to her relationship with Woody Allen, after he seduced (and eventually married) Farrow's adopted daughter. Frightened that he had also abused another of her children, Farrow took Allen to court and has included as a postscript the judge's ruling on the custody battle. One reviewer felt that Farrow did not show appropriate anger in the last part of her book, that it seemed part of her spiritual journey to work through her troubles.

Subjects: Actors; Allen, Woody; Child Custody; Courage; Incest; O'Sullivan, Maureen; Previn, André; Sinatra, Frank; Spirituality; Women in Film

Now Try: Mia Farrow had hired a college student to help her out with her children. Kristi Groteke happened to be working with the family during all the controversy and has offered (with writing help from Marjorie Rosen) an objective view of her experience in ***Mia & Woody: Love and Betrayal***. Larry King, with the help of Rabbi Irwin Katsof, interviewed a number of celebrities about their views on spirituality, specifically praying. He published these interviews in a book called ***Powerful Prayers***. Perhaps because of the journey she has taken in this book, Farrow's writing has been described as beautifully crafted, just as Kate Morton's prose has been described in her novel about family dramas, ***The House at Riverton: A Novel***. Helen Grigsby Doss adopted several children of various ethnic backgrounds in the 1950s. She wrote about the experience at the time and then recently updated the story in ***The Family Nobody Wanted***.

Fonda, Jane (1937–)

My Life So Far. Random House, 2006, 2005. 599pp. ill. 9780812975765. Also available in large print, audiobook (read by the author), e-audiobook, e-book, and video. 791.43028092

Jane Fonda has written her memoir in Three Acts. Act One, "Gathering," is her formative childhood, where she lived with a cold father and a manic-depressive mother who committed suicide when Fonda was a young teen, although Fonda was told that her mother had had a heart attack. Act Two, "Seeking," concerns her three marriages to three very different men, her children, her political activism (when she earned the epithet "Hanoi Jane"), her fitness business, and her long-term eating disorder. Act Three, "Beginning," is Fonda's current quest for self-discovery, living single as a born-again Christian but fighting against the conservative right, advocating for adolescent sexual health.

Fonda focuses very little on the films she made, although she has won two Academy Awards and several Golden Globe Awards.

Subjects: Actors; Death of a Parent; Eating Disorders; Fathers and Daughters; Fitness; Fonda, Henry; Political Activists; Social Activists; Turner, Ted; Women in Film

Now Try: Fonda's book is articulate and honest, and readers of her story may appreciate the same honesty and articulation in Katha Pollitt's collection of essays, ***Subject to Debate: Sense and Dissents on Women, Politics, and Culture***. Fonda, of course, is not alone in suffering from an eating disorder. In a collection edited by Kate Taylor, several writers offer their own personal experiences on one disorder in particular, ***Going Hungry: Writers on Desire, Self-Denial, and Overcoming Anorexia***. One of Fonda's greatest regrets is not having had a chance to understand her mother and make peace with her. Iris Krasnow talks about Fonda's situation and that of many others in ***I Am My Mother's Daughter: Making Peace with Mom—Before It's Too Late***. If you'd like a perspective of Fonda's marriage to Ted Turner from his point of view, you may want to read his ***Call Me Ted***, written with Bill Burke.

Gilbert, Melissa (1964–)

Prairie Tale: A Memoir. Foreword by Patty Duke. Gallery Books, 2010, 2009. 367pp. ill. 9781416599173. Also available in large print and e-book. 792.02809

Children growing up watching Melissa Gilbert as Laura Ingalls Wilder on *Little House on the Prairie* believed that Melissa was Laura and that their lives must have been the same off and on the screen. Gilbert puts paid to that notion in this memoir of her childhood with her adopted family and her life after leaving the family home. Because of the goal of perfectionism that her mother set for her, and with her father dying when she was a preteen, Gilbert had a hard time defining herself. She turned to destructive relationships, some drugs, and alcohol. Now a regular member of Alcoholics Anonymous, she has changed her priorities and has begun to recognize her own self-worth, happy with her husband, Bruce Boxleitner, and their blended families.

Melissa Gilbert is the youngest actor to have a star on the Hollywood Walk of Fame.

Subjects: Actors; Alcoholics Anonymous; Boxleitner, Bruce; Identity (Psychology); Landon, Michael; *Little House on the Prairie* (Television Program); Self-Destructive Behavior; Self-Discovery; Sobriety; Television Actors

Now Try: The daughter of John Phillips and stepdaughter of Michelle Phillips, members of the musical group The Mamas and the Papas, Mackenzie Phillips tells a story with Hilary Liftin in ***High on Arrival*** of decades of self-destructive behavior, particularly involving drugs. Another television star, Valerie Bertinelli, had weight and other issues to deal with, which she discussed in ***Losing It: And Gaining My Life Back One Pound at a Time***. Many child actors have sad tales to tell, including Tatum O'Neal, whose ***A Paper Life*** details many of the negatives that grew out of her early stardom.

Hawn, Goldie (1945–)
Holden, Wendy (1961–), coauthor

A Lotus Grows in the Mud. Berkley Books, 2006, 2005. 433pp. ill. 16pp. of plates. 9780425207888. Also available in large print, audiobook (read by the author), e-audiobook, and e-book. 791.43028092

Goldie Hawn always wanted to be a dancer while she was growing up in suburban Maryland, but the closest she got was go-go dancing in the sixties, as she came to realize that she just wasn't good enough. But along the way she discovered her comic talent and made a big start in Dan Rowan and Dick Martin's ***Laugh-In***. Hawn suffered through two failed marriages before she settled down with Kurt Russell. Between making films and being with her children (she is now a grandmother), she has traveled in search of spiritual enlightenment. This memoir is more about that search than about her life as an actress.

Hawn has won an Academy Award for Best Supporting Actress.

Subjects: Actors; Comediennes; Family Relationships; *Laugh-In* (Television Program); Reflections; Russell, Kurt; Spirituality; Women in Film

Now Try: Goldie Hawn said that she has continued to develop her spirituality through learning from her own experiences. Nevada Barr, author of the **Anna Pigeon Mysteries**, says much the same thing in ***Seeking Enlightenment—Hat by Hat: A Skeptic's Path to Religion.*** Another woman who has traveled for purposes of personal enlightenment is June Callwood's daughter, Jill Frayne, whose ***Starting Out in the Afternoon: A Mid-Life Journey into Wild Land*** contains her own personal reflections, as does Goldie's book. As one would expect, Hawn's book is full of her effervescent humor. A character similar to hers is the heroine (Aletta Honor) of two novels by Dayna Dunbar, the first being ***The Saints and Sinners of Okay County: A Novel.***

Jewison, Norman (1926–)

This Terrible Business Has Been Good to Me: An Autobiography. Key Porter, 2006, 2004. 304pp. ill. 9781552632116. 791.4302

Referred to as a "Canadian pinko" by John Wayne, Norman Jewison chooses to make movies that will speak to an issue, movies such as ***In the Heat of the Night*** (based on John Dudley Ball's book of the same name) or ***The Hurricane*** (based on Rubin Carter's own story, ***The Sixteenth Round: From Number 1 Contender to #45472***). But he also likes movies to speak to the heart of the common man, movies like ***Moonstruck*** and ***Fiddler on the Roof*** (***Tevye's Daughters*** by Sholem Aleichem), which some people doubted a Christian, which Jewison is, could do well. He began his directing career in university and took advantage of a work/study program in London with the BBC; then it was back home to work with the Canadian Broadcasting Corporation until he was noticed by CBS and asked to work for the show *Your Hit Parade.*

Jewison has a star on the Hollywood Walk of Fame and one on the Canada Walk of Fame (in front of the Royal Alexandra Theatre in Toronto) and has been awarded both the Irving Thalberg Award for Lifetime Achievement by the Academy of Motion Pictures and the Companion to the Order of Canada.

Subjects: Acting; Directors, Canada; Filmmakers, Canada; Octogenarians; Screenwriters, Canada

Now Try: Jewison hadn't planned to write an autobiography, although he does have writing experience from screenwriting. His intended biographer, Jay Scott, died prematurely, but before his death extracted a promise from Jewison to finish the work that he had started. Jewison did so, but not in a linear fashion. His style is elliptical, since he jumps around as associations come to him. Ward S. Just's style in the novel ***Echo House*** is also elliptical, in the same manner as Jewison's. Another well-known Canadian filmmaker is James Cameron, whose biography Rebecca Keegan has written: ***The Futurist: The Life and Films of James Cameron.*** To hear what other directors have to say about the directing business, you might want to look at Peter Bogdanovich's interviews with directors in ***Who the Devil***

Made It: Conversations with Robert Aldrich, George Cukor, Allan Dwan, Howard Hawks, Alfred Hitchcock, Chuck Jones, Fritz Lang, Joseph H. Lewis, Sidney Lumet, Leo McCarey, Otto Preminger, Don Siegel, Josef von Sternberg, Frank Tashlin, Edgar G. Ulmer, Raoul Walsh.

Jones, James Earl (1931–)
Niven, Penelope (1939–), coauthor

Voices and Silences: With a New Epilogue. Limelight Editions, 2002, 1993. 423pp. ill. 9780879109691. 792.028092

When one sees how many of James Earl Jones's credits include being "the voice" of a character, it's amazing to read that he had a serious stutter that rendered him psychologically mute when he was growing up. He had been separated from his parents and moved from Mississippi to Michigan to be raised by his grandparents, and it was at this point that his stutter began. Thanks to an inspired teacher in high school, he began once again to speak and to learn to control his stutter. Jones took a degree in acting at the University of Michigan and cut his acting teeth Off Broadway, a more ethnically inclusive venue. This particular edition of his autobiography is an update from the original publication in 1993. It also includes a foreword by Penelope Niven, who had written this story after hours of taped conversations with Jones. Her writing is transparent, so that Jones's real voice comes through.

Jones has received the Kennedy Center Honors, a Horatio Alger Award, and the National Medal of Arts. He was also inducted into the Academy of Achievement, and when asked what was a significant book for him, he cited Henry Wadsworth Longfellow's ***The Song of Hiawatha,*** because its rhythm helped him to start speaking again.

Subjects: Acting; Actors; African-American Men; Broadway; Multiracial Heritage; Stuttering; Theater; Voice Actors

Now Try: Jones's autobiography is considered to be an excellent text on acting as well as a window into his own life. Simon Callow, having been told he was not a born actor, went on to disprove that and discusses the art of acting in his own memoir, ***Being an Actor***. One of the most important events in Jones's life was to have an inspired teacher who changed his life. Gloria Wade Gayles interviewed a number of well-known people about teachers who inspired them and collected those interviews in ***In Praise of Our Teachers: A Multicultural Tribute to Those Who Inspired Us.*** If readers would like to pursue further the subject of stuttering, Benson Bobrick's ***Knotted Tongues: Stuttering in History and the Quest for a Cure*** might be a good place to start.

MacLaine, Shirley (1934–)

My Lucky Stars: A Hollywood Memoir. Bantam Books, 1996, 1995. 378pp. ill. 9780553072339. Also available in large print. 791.43028092

Shirley MacLaine has written several memoirs, many of them focusing on her keen interest in the metaphysical. This particular title speaks largely of both her acting career and her political activism. Since earlier memoirs spoke about her middle-class upbringing in Virginia, this one begins with her second movie, ***Artists and Models***, which was the beginning of her role as mascot in the Rat Pack. MacLaine goes on to discuss her unusual open marriage with Scott Parker, who usually lived in Japan, raising their daughter there, and she candidly talks about her affairs. She describes her difficulties on the set of Larry McMurtry's ***Terms of Endearment*** (the only movie for which she won an Academy Award). She also speaks plainly about Hollywood, its nastiness, and the unsatisfactory roles available for women.

In addition to her Academy Award, MacLaine has also won an Emmy and several Golden Globes as well as a star on the Hollywood Walk of Fame.

Subjects: Acting; Actors; Hollywood, CA; Love Affairs; Parker, Scott; Political Activists; Rat Pack; Women in Film

Now Try: Two more recent books of MacLaine's, published after this one, are ***Out on a Leash: Exploring the Nature of Reality and Love***, in which she talks about newly discovering how important to one a pet can be, and ***Sage-ing While Age-ing***, a book whose theme has been addressed by others: how one's experiences enhance one's aging and how one's aging enhances one's experience. MacLaine writes with humor, and her memoir is a bit of romp, much in the same way as Finola Hughes and Digby Diehl's novel, ***Soapsuds*** (about a daytime soap opera actress). MacLaine is not the only actress to turn activist. Among several others is Susan Sarandon, about whom Marc Shapiro has written ***Susan Sarandon: Actress-Activist***. The Rat Pack has always fascinated movie aficionados, and in Shawn Levy's story, we find Shirley MacLaine right in there with them (the only woman allowed): ***Rat Pack Confidential: Frank, Dean, Sammy, Peter, Joey & the Last Great Showbiz Party***.

O'Donnell, Rosie (1962–)

Find Me. Warner Books, 2002. 213pp. 9780446530071. Also available in large print, audiobook (read by the author), and e-book. 792.7028092

This memoir by Rosie O'Donnell deals primarily with her encounter, through an adoption agency that O'Donnell supports, with a disturbed young adolescent whose original call claimed that she was a pregnant rape victim. Something in this girl's story resonated deeply with O'Donnell, causing her to look at her own life and the causes of her ongoing depression. In her story O'Donnell looks back at her childhood, her mother's early death, and her father's emotional abandonment of the family, entwining that story with her near-obsession with this young teen in New Jersey. Perhaps because of her own upbringing, O'Donnell has become a child advocate, founding the For All Kids Foundation (http://www.forallkids.org) and writing children's books as fund-raisers. She also used this memoir to come out publicly, hoping to bring out into the open discussions of sexual orientation and gay parenting.

Subjects: Actors; Adoption; Comediennes; Depression; Dissociative Identity Disorder; For All Kids Foundation; Fund-Raisers; Lesbians; Queer Parents; Women in Film

Now Try: Five years and much controversy after ***Find Me***, O'Donnell wrote another memoir, ***Celebrity Detox: The Fame Game***, in which she discusses her career from her early ambitions to her current (at the time of the book) withdrawal from television. She has also cowritten, with Deborah Axelrod and Tracy Chutorian Semler, a book for women entitled ***Bosom Buddies: Lessons and Laughter on Breast Health and Cancer***. Rosie's profile has been included in Robert Bernstein's ***Families of Value: Personal Profiles of Pioneering Lesbian and Gay Parents***. One of the controversies surrounding O'Donnell was her involvement with *McCall's* magazine, which she took over when it was floundering. The relationship did not go well, and former editor-in-chief of *McCall's*, Sally Koslow, has written a *roman à clef*, ***Little Pink Slips***. O'Donnell's show was very similar in format to Mike Douglas's show, and she wrote the introduction to his memoir of that show, ***I'll Be Right Back: Memories of TV's Greatest Talk Show***, written with Thomas Kelly and Michael Heaton.

O'Hara, Maureen (1920–)
Nicoletti, John (1962–), coauthor

'Tis Herself: A Memoir. Simon & Schuster, 2004. 323pp. 9780743246934. Also available in large print, Braille, audiobook, and e-book. 791.43028092

"The Queen of Technicolor," so called because of her bright-red hair and green eyes, grew up as a tomboy, a feature that served her well in her career. Mentored by Charles Laughton, Maureen O'Hara started young and was brought from the United Kingdom to Hollywood to star opposite him in ***The Hunchback of Notre Dame*** (Victor Hugo) in 1939. She went on to star in five films with John Wayne, because she was the only woman strong enough to play opposite him. O'Hara's personal life proved less successful than her professional life, particularly when her third husband, Charles F. Blair Jr., died mysteriously in a plane crash. Her husband had owned a commercial airline in the Antilles, one of their domiciles, and on his death she became president of the company, the first woman president of any American commercial airline.

Never nominated for an Academy Award (because the studios were more interested in her face than her talent), O'Hara has, however, been given a star on the Hollywood Walk of Fame.

Subjects: Actors; Businesswomen; Firsts; Golden Age of Hollywood; Hollywood, CA; Irish-Americans; Laughton, Charles; Nonagenarians; Wayne, John; Women in Film

Now Try: Maureen O'Hara was feisty both on and off the set. In 1957 she and Liberace together took a tabloid magazine, *Confidential*, to court for lying about her and for saying he was homosexual. They won their cases, and the magazine was eventually put out of business. This trial and others are covered by the journalist who reported on them, Theo Wilson, in ***Headline Justice: Inside the Courtroom: The Country's Most Controversial Trials***. O'Hara's account, as one might expect, has a no-nonsense tone in her frankness. This is the same tone to be found in the life story of another strong-minded, feisty woman like Maureen O'Hara, ***Kate Field: The Many Lives of a Nineteenth-Century American Journalist*** by Gary Scharnhorst. A powerful personality, one could compare O'Hara to another strong woman, depicted by Alison Weir in ***The Life of Elizabeth I***.

Plummer, Christopher (1929–)

In Spite of Myself: A Memoir. Vintage Canada, 2009, 2008. 648pp. ill. 9780307396808. Also available in e-book. 791.43028092

Perhaps because of his reputation as a Shakespearean actor, one might not expect the ebullience found in Christopher Plummer's autobiography. He has done more than Shakespeare, however, in his long career as an actor, having acted since his teens in Montréal. Plummer fills his memoir with stories of growing up in a privileged family (his great-grandfather was Sir John Abbott, the third prime minister of Canada), making his way through theater in Canada and the United States and into film as well. He also confesses to affairs, drinking, bad marriages, and ignoring his daughter, Amanda, until she was an adult. For those interested in the stage and screen world as a *métier*, Plummer also offers his views on stagecraft and introduces the reader to many of the actors who peopled his world.

Christopher Plummer has won many awards, among them Tonys, Emmys, and a place on the Canada Walk of Fame. He was also named Companion of the Order of Canada.

Subjects: Actors, Canada; Fathers and Daughters; Filmmaking; Octogenarians; Plummer, Amanda; Shakespearean Actors, Canada; Stage Actors, Canada; Theater

Now Try: Helen Mirren, who has had the same type of acting experience as Plummer, has recently written a memoir, ***In the Frame: My Life in Words and Pictures***. For those interested in New York theater, Theodore Mann has written a history of one theater, the venue that launched the career of several actors. ***Journeys in the Night: Creating a New American Theatre with Circle in the Square: A Memoir*** includes a video documentary of the theater, done in 1977. Sir Tyrone Guthrie was instrumental in creating the Stratford Shakespeare Festival in Stratford, Ontario, a theater where Plummer has often acted (including during the 2010 season). Guthrie wrote about his own career in ***A Life in the Theatre***.

Poitier, Sidney (1927–)

The Measure of a Man: A Spiritual Autobiography. HarperSanFrancisco, 2007, 2000. 255pp. ill. 9780061357909. Also available in large print, Braille, audiobook (read by the author), e-audiobook, and e-book. 791.43028092

Sidney Poitier is taking his own measure in this book, looking back and reflecting on his values and his comportment, judging whether or not his behavior has measured up to his values. He wrote in much greater detail about his life in ***This Life*** (1980), and here he updates the information and looks back at the various elements that have shaped his life. Poitier's persistence and determination are noteworthy. With only four years of schooling, he could hardly read and therefore could not properly audition; with a thick Caribbean accent (he was from the Bahamas), he could barely make himself understood in New York.

From that low point Poitier persevered to the point where he won Academy Awards (one as Best Actor and an honorary one to recognize his overall achievements), received the Kennedy Center Honors, and was knighted. He received the Presidential Medal of Freedom in 2009 from President Obama.

Subjects: Actors; Bahamian-Americans; Broadway; Directors; Illiteracy; Octogenarians; Racism; Reflections; Stage Actors; Theater; Triumph over Adversity

Now Try: Poitier wrote a book for his great-grandchild, ***Life Beyond Measure: Letters to My Great-Granddaughter***. In 1967 Poitier was in two significant movies, ***In the Heat of the Night*** (John Dudley Ball), directed by Norman Jewison, and ***Guess Who's Coming to Dinner***. They were two of the five movies nominated for Best Picture in 1967, all reflecting significant societal and cinematic changes in Hollywood. Mark Harris looks at this phenomenon in ***Pictures at a Revolution: Five Movies and the Birth of the New Hollywood***. Two other successful African-Americans who have written reflective memoirs are Robert Guillaume, with the help of David Ritz (***Guillaume: A Life***) and Thomas Sowell (***A Personal Odyssey***). And for an outsider's thoughtful look at Poitier's life, you may want to pick up Aram Goudsouzian's ***Sidney Poitier: Man, Actor, Icon***.

Radner, Gilda (1946–1989)

It's Always Something. 20th anniversary ed. Simon & Schuster, 2009, 1989. 286pp. ill. 16pp. of plates. 9781439148860. Also available in audiobook (read by the author) and e-audiobook. 792.7

Professionally, Gilda Radner was best known for her personae created on the television show *Saturday Night Live*, but personally she is best known as the comedienne who died so young of cancer and whose legacy lives on. Her memoir is somewhat about her life, describing her childhood and her marriage to Gene Wilder and her unsuccessful efforts to bear a child with him, leading to the discovery of her ovarian cancer. But the book is mainly about Radner's cancer journey, the fear, the pain, the ugliness of it, and her determination to fight it with humor and hope. The book was published the same year as her death. Gene Wilder, along with three other friends, established an organization, Gilda's Club (http://www.gildasclub.org), for cancer patients and their families.

Radner was inducted into the Broadcasting & Cable Hall of Fame.

Subjects: Actors; Comediennes; Coping in Women; Gilda's Club; Married Couples; Ovarian Cancer; *Saturday Night Live* (Television Program); The Wellness Community, CA; Wilder, Gene

Now Try: If you'd like to read more about Radner and Gene Wilder, he wrote his own memoir, ***Kiss Me Like a Stranger: My Search for Love and Art***. Radner's book has been an inspiration for many cancer patients as they read it; Barbara Abercrombie discusses how writing about your experience can prove therapeutic in ***Writing Out the Storm: Reading and Writing Your Way Through Serious Illness or Injury***. Radner's humor was often outrageously funny and irreverent, and it still is in her book. If you would like something else outrageously funny, try Jill Conner Browne's first novel, written with Karin Gillespie, ***The Sweet Potato Queens' First Big-Ass Novel: Stuff We Didn't Actually Do, but Could Have, and May Yet***. Radner's indomitable spirit can also be seen in Cybill Shepherd through her memoir, ***Cybill Disobedience: How I Survived Beauty***

Pageants, Elvis, Sex, Bruce Willis, Lies, Marriage, Motherhood, Hollywood, and the Irrepressible Urge to Say What I Think.

Swayze, Patrick (1959–2009), and Lisa Niemi (1956–)

The Time of My Life. Atria Books, 2010, 2009. 247pp. ill. 9781439158616. Also available in large print, audiobook (read by the author), e-audiobook, and e-book. 791.43028092

Patrick Swayze and Lisa Niemi had that rare element in their celebrity lives: a first marriage that lasted for almost thirty-five years. Together they wrote a memoir of Swayze's life, a story that necessarily includes his wife, Lisa. They talk of his childhood and how he learned to dance from his mother, a dance teacher. They struggled together as they tried to map out their careers, but Swayze's career didn't really take off until 1987, with his role in ***Dirty Dancing***. He describes how he practiced all his dance moves for that film with Lisa, as she was also a dancer. He also had a great interest in flying, a fact that might have saved him from self-destruction through alcohol, as he couldn't drink if he wanted to fly. They had two properties, one of which is a ranch that they turned into a wildlife preserve, trying to save the animals and regenerate the trees. A good part of the book, however, talks about Swayze's diagnosis with stage-four cancer, his treatments, and his attitude toward it.

Patrick Swayze was given a star on the Hollywood Walk of Fame.

Subjects: Actors; Alcoholics; Choreographers; Dancers; Film Industry; Los Angeles, CA; Married Couples; Pancreatic Cancer; Sobriety

Now Try: Farrah Fawcett is another actor who succumbed early to cancer. Her best friend of thirty years, Alana Stewart, shares her diary entries about her friend in ***My Journey with Farrah: A Story of Life, Love, and Friendship***. The dance that Swayze did in ***Dirty Dancing*** was quite different from that of Michael Flatley, a dancer who became a household name with his Celtic dance routine, Riverdance. With the help of Douglas Thompson, he has written his autobiography, ***Lord of the Dance***. Cleveland Amory also turned his ranch into a sanctuary, although his was more for domestic animals. He describes his work there in ***Ranch of Dreams: The Heartwarming Story of America's Most Unusual Animal Sanctuary***.

Wagner, Robert (1930–)
Eyman, Scott (1951–), coauthor

Pieces of My Heart: A Life. It Books, 2009, 2008. 329pp. ill. 9780061373329. Also available in audiobook (read by the author), e-audiobook, and e-book. 791.43028092

Robert Wagner has six decades of acting work to his credit, and his recounting of his career is like a who's who of filmmaking. He describes how he got the acting bug and what his father thought of it. Wagner was old-school in his beliefs about stagecraft, which meant that sometimes he was passed over for more modern-style actors. After his film career seemed to be dwindling, he became successful in a television series. He talks about his friendships with a large number of well-known people and his affairs with several women, including a much older Barbara Stanwyck. But it is Wagner's love affair and two marriages with Natalie Wood that seem to be at the core of who he was for many years, particularly after her puzzling death. Here he describes the events surrounding her death and the ensuing investigation. He describes his long-term marriage with Jill St. John, the woman he married once he felt he was over Natalie Wood's death. One of the differences between Wagner's memoir and many other celebrity memoirs is his description of the movie studio world and system in the early days, providing some history for movie buffs.

Subjects: Actors; Film Industry; *Hart to Hart* (Television Program); Hollywood, CA; Love Affairs; Marriage; Promiscuity; St. John, Jill; Television Actors; Wood, Natalie

Now Try: Tony Curtis was a good friend of Wagner's, as they had started out together. Curtis wrote a memoir also: ***American Prince: A Memoir***. Suzanne Finstad delves into Natalie Wood's family, her Russian heritage, and her relationship with her mother in interviews with many who knew her for an in-depth biography of the actress, ***Natasha: The Biography of Natalie Wood***. Of the same vintage as Wagner was Paul Newman, also very tied to method acting and a member of the Actors Studio, all of which Shawn Levy discusses in a recent biography, ***Paul Newman: A Life***.

Consider Starting With . . .

Agassi, Andre. *Open: An Autobiography*

Bacall, Lauren. *By Myself and Then Some*

Charles, Ray. *Brother Ray: Ray Charles' Own Story*

Crystal, Billy. *700 Sundays*

Dylan, Bob. *Chronicles*

Gielgud, John. *Gielgud, an Actor and His Time*

Jones, Quincy. *Q: The Autobiography of Quincy Jones*

Jordan, Michael. *For the Love of the Game: My Story*

Poitier, Sidney. *The Measure of a Man: A Spiritual Autobiography*

Torre, Joe. *The Yankee Years*

Fiction Read-Alikes

Binchy, Maeve. *Quentins*. Ella Brady helps create a documentary film about the famous restaurant, Quentins, in Dublin.

Haeger, Diane. *The Perfect Royal Mistress: A Novel*. Actress Nell Gwynne rises from a life of poverty to a successful acting career and then becomes mistress to King Charles II.

Harris, E. Lynn. *Basketball Jones*. When an NBA star gets married to protect his image, his gay lover finds their lives complicated by threats of blackmail and intrigue.

Hough, Robert. *The Final Confession of Mabel Stark: A Novel.* Famed circus tiger trainer Mabel Stark looks over her life from the vantage point of eighty years.

King, Kevin. *All the Stars Came out That Night: A Novel.* An amalgam of unlikely celebrities come together in this novel about the 1934 World Series.

Mosley, Walter. *Fortunate Son*. The son of an impoverished single mother is raised with the son of a wealthy heart surgeon in a novel in which the doctor's son takes his privilege for granted.

Ray, Junior Michael, and Corinne Joy Brown. *Sanctuary Ranch*. Wanting to succeed as a country music singer, Amelia Talbot agrees to go to Wyoming for a makeover.

Smiley, Jane. *Ten Days in the Hills*. A group of friends in the movie business gather after the Academy Awards in a home in the Hollywood Hills.

Spencer, Scott. *The Rich Man's Table*. The ignored son of a famous rock musician decides to write his father's biography.

Wagner, Bruce. *The Chrysanthemum Palace*. Three children of successful actors have difficulty finding their own place in the world.

Works Cited

Epstein, Joseph. 2005. "The Culture of Celebrity: Let Us Now Praise Famous Airheads." *The Weekly Standard*, October 7. Accessed January 19, 2009. http://www.weeklystandard.com/Content/Public/Articles/000/000/006/187rmfyj.asp?pg=1.

Fitzgerald, F. Scott. 1996. "The Rich Boy." In *Babylon Revisited and Other Stories*, 152–87. New York: Simon & Schuster.

McGrath, Charles. 2009. "A Team, but Watch How You Put It." *The New York Times*, November 11. Accessed December 7, 2010. http://www.nytimes.com/2009/11/12/books/12agassi.html.

Shenk, Joshua Wolf. 1996. "Star Struck—High-End Periodicals' Obsession with Celebrities." *Washington Monthly* 28 (6) (June): 12. *MasterFILE Premier*, EBSCO*host*. Accessed January 19, 2009. http://search.ebscohost.com/login.aspx?direct=true&db=f5h&AN=9606215226&site=ehost-li.

Chapter 3

The Creative Life

Description

"Every writer is a writer first" (Atwood, 2005). The same could be said for musicians, dancers, visual artists, and other creators. In the creative person resides a compulsion to create: pianists' fingers will play on any surface; artists will doodle whenever they are away from their medium; writers will compose and edit in their heads, even away from their writing utensils. There are always challenges, perhaps political, perhaps practical; there may be no opportunity to develop the talent, no audience for an artist's type of creativity, no way of broadcasting or marketing that talent. In the case of the successful ones, however, the artists' compulsions were so strong, and in many cases their talents so great, that they broke through the barriers and succeeded, not only in expressing themselves creatively, but also in having their art shown widely enough to gain significant notice.

To what end all this creativity? There are universal themes in the created product (good vs. evil, the place of the self within a larger community), and these artists use their own medium to work out for themselves and to communicate to others what their views are on these universal themes.

Our concern here, though, is to read about these creative efforts. And herein lies a difficulty. Even going back in history there is not much precedent. The sculptor Benvenuto Cellini wrote ***The Autobiography of Benvenuto Cellini***, a work that is generally considered to be the first real literary autobiography in the Western world. It is a masterpiece of vivacity that opens a large window onto the cultural world of sixteenth-century Italy and France (and an equally large window on the accomplishments of one Benvenuto Cellini). In the same century in France, Michel de Montaigne published his ***Essays***, a philosophical exercise in trying to understand humankind, using himself as his subject. Thus we learn about him and his life as he discusses the large questions of the day. His autobiography has had a great influence on subsequent writers, including Gore Vidal, whose second volume of autobiography (***Point to Point Navigation: A Memoir, 1964–2004***) follows the format of Montaigne's essays. Not much later is Jean-Jacques Rousseau's ***Confessions***, a candid challenge to eighteenth-century morals and the social mores of Europe.

In nineteenth- and twentieth-century autobiographical writing we have many exemplars from people whose vocation is that of writer. This should not be surprising, given that writing is their mode of creative expression and their world. In addition, until current technology became so prevalent, authors "wrote in a world where print was still king, and literature was at the center of a nation's culture" (Menand, 2005).

For the other creative artists, however, it is a different story. The other artists—the dancers, the musicians, the visual artists—usually express themselves creatively in their own world, through the art they create from their talents, so that having their memoirs is more the exception than the rule. There have been several exceptions to this rule, however: a number of renowned ballerinas and choreographers did write their stories, but with the intended audience so small, their books are no longer in print. Fewer classical musicians seem to have written their memoirs, but for those who did, the same situation exists. As we will see with the visual artists, of those whose memoirs are in print and available in enough libraries to warrant including here, some have used their artwork rather than a monograph to tell their stories.

Those who are disappointed at the small number of memoirists among the nonwriters may consider biographies. Rick Roche's ***Real Lives Revealed: A Guide to Reading Interests in Biography*** (Libraries Unlimited, 2009) offers some good choices. There is also a wonderful PBS Web site, *American Masters* (http://www.pbs.org/wnet/americanmasters/), which sheds light on a variety of artists in their creative fields, artists that you will find in this chapter, and many more.

The creative life stories here focus on those *artistes* involved in the worlds of classical dance and music; of the visual arts, specifically photography and painting; of creative humor, both writing and performing; and of writing, primarily fiction. In the case of the artists in particular, the reader also learns the difficulties and joys of the creative profession.

Appeal

As with memoirs in general, the primary appeal in this chapter is character. Who are these people who have such talent? What drives them to hone their craft, to develop such artistry? We hear stories of the creative temperament—often difficult to deal with—and now we have a chance to find out what that temperament is really like.

This chapter is also high in the learning/experiencing appeal factor. Several of these artists trod new paths to better not only their own artistic expression, but also the world in which they and others express that artistic view. This is particularly noticeable in the section on the artists.

Another appeal of this section is the chance of discovery—a new medium, a new artist—whose field or work you may want to explore further. The tones will vary, from ebullient to bleak, largely depending on the temperament of the artist.

Organization of This Chapter

The chapter begins with classic representations of various arts, stories of people well-known to most and outstanding in their fields. It continues with stories of artists whose field of entertainment may appeal to a more select group of people: the classical dancer, the classical musician, the visual artist. Bridging these artists with the writer is the humorist. The humorist could be an entertainer—a stand-up comic or a television performer—or a writer. From there we segue to the major portion of the chapter: the writer. Here you will find an eclectic group of writers of both serious literature and popular fiction: novelists, poets, short-story writers, playwrights, and literary critics.

Classics

In this section you will find classic examples of memoirs from the various arts: a classical singer, a writer, a dancer, an artist, and a photographer. These people have all created lasting works or, as in the case of the singer (Marian Anderson), have blazed trails for others to follow. They all represent the determination of the human spirit to follow the passion of their innate talents. And in the creation of their works they have also had to overcome different barriers placed in their way.

> The "Classics" section of "The Creative Life" encompasses the breadth of the arts represented in this chapter, with the classic memoirists blazing trails in their fields, establishing new benchmarks for their art, or showing great courage in moving forward in their work.

Anderson, Marian (1897–1993)

My Lord, What a Morning: An Autobiography. Foreword by James Anderson DePreist. University of Illinois Press, 2002, 1956. 319pp. ill. 9780252070532. Also available in large print and e-book. 782.1092

Marian Anderson was a groundbreaking classical singer, beginning her career in her father's church, singing gospel music, and making her way through the world of classical music to Carnegie Hall. In Europe she was recognized for the remarkable contralto that she was; in the United States, she was seen first as a Black woman and then as a classical performer. Anderson's legend was established, however, when she was refused permission to sing at Constitutional Hall in 1939. Eleanor Roosevelt was so outraged that she dropped her membership in the Daughters of the American Revolution, the owners of the building. Roosevelt, along with Anderson's then-manager Sol Hurok, arranged for her to sing Easter Sunday at the Lincoln Memorial, where 75,000 people came out to hear her sing.

Anderson was inducted into the National Women's Hall of Fame, awarded the National Medal of Arts and the Kennedy Center Honors, and given the Presidential Medal of Freedom in 1963 by President Johnson. ***My Lord, What a Morning*** was selected as a Notable Book by the American Library Association.

Subjects: African-American Women; ALA Notable Books; Classical Musicians; Classics; Contraltos; Nonagenarians; Racism; Singers; Trailblazers

Now Try: Anderson's family gave Allan Keiler permission to write her definitive biography: ***Marian Anderson: A Singer's Journey***. The concert at Lincoln Memorial creates an interesting backdrop in a novel about a mixed-race couple and their musical children in Richard Powers's ***The Time of Our Singing***. Both Marian Anderson and Eleanor Roosevelt are featured in a book by Susan Ware, ***Letter to the World: Seven Women Who Shaped the American Century***. Mahalia Jackson is another great African-American singer, although she stayed primarily with gospel music; her story can be found in ***Got to Tell It: Mahalia Jackson, Queen of Gospel*** by Jules Victor Schwerin. Another groundbreaking African-American woman is Zora Neale Hurston; a recent biography of her is ***Wrapped in Rainbows: The Life of Zora Neale Hurston*** by Valerie Boyd.

Angelou, Maya (1928–)

I Know Why the Caged Bird Sings. Random House Trade Paperbacks, 2009, 1969. 289pp. 9780812980028. Also available in large print, Braille, audiobook (read by the author), e-audiobook, e-book, and video. 818.5409

To read Maya Angelou's full autobiography (or at least the first seventy-four years of it) is to read six volumes: ***I Know Why the Caged Bird Sings, Gather Together in My Name, Singin' and Swingin' and Gettin' Merry Like Christmas, The Heart of a Woman, All God's Children Need Traveling Shoes,*** and ***A Song Flung up to Heaven***. In the first of those six volumes, the title featured here, she describes her early childhood in Stamps, Arkansas, raised largely by her grandmother, Annie Johnson Henderson, being raped as a young child, and her teenage pregnancy (Guy Johnson is her son). The reason that she and her brother are in Stamps with her grandmother is that her parents sent them there, as the children were cramping their style. In Stamps, then, although Angelou has the strength and support of her grandmother, she still feels abandoned and, given the flagrant racism in the town at the time, that she belongs nowhere. Racism is a continuous thread throughout this volume, but despite the challenges she faces, her faith in God is strong, and she maintains a hope that she can overcome the restrictions placed on her.

Proving that she did overcome the restrictions placed on her was President Clinton's invitation to Angelou to write and deliver a poem at his inauguration. She was also inducted into the Academy of Achievement and the National Women's Hall of Fame and is a recipient of the National Medal of Arts and the Horatio Alger Award. ***I Know Why the Caged Bird Sings*** was selected as a Notable Book by the American Library Association.

Subjects: African-American Women; ALA Notable Books; American South; Classics; Grandmothers; Henderson, Annie Johnson; Johnson, Guy; Octogenarians; Poets; Rape; Stamps, AK; Teenage Mothers; Writers

Now Try: Angelou has often said that it was her grandmother who put her on solid footing and grounded her in a good moral stance. Dennis Kimbro has addressed the richness of grandmothers from one perspective in ***What Keeps Me Standing: A Black Grandmother's Guide to Peace, Hope & Inspiration***. Adam Fairclough offers an extensive history of the Black struggle in the American South in ***Better Day Coming: Blacks and Equality, 1890–2000***. Teenage pregnancy is a challenge to many young women, a challenge that the writer Meredith Hall wrote about in ***Without a Map: A Memoir***.

Duncan, Isadora (1877–1927)

My Life. Liveright, 1996, 1927. 255pp. 9780871401588. Also available in large print. 792.8092

Isadora Duncan's first memory was of being thrown out of a burning building: thus was her life. Her personal life was so dramatic that it threatened to overtake the importance of her creative life, a life known for pioneering modern dance, wherein she laid the groundwork for dancers and choreographers like Ruth St. Denis, Agnes De Mille, and Martha Graham, all contributors to the creation of modern dance. She describes the foundations of her own education, with a childhood interest in classical music and poetry, and a great interest in Greek art. Duncan translated her personal experience with education into a passion about the education of children, believing that their regular curriculum should incorporate music, dance, the classics, and self-expression, as well as regular academics. To this end she founded several schools in Europe, where she was much better received than in her native America, and her legacy was handed down by some of her school *protégés*, the Isadorables. This memoir was published just after Duncan's tragic and freakish death when the long scarf she was wearing became caught in the wheels of a new car she had finally been able to afford.

Subjects: Choreographers; Classics; Dancers; Death of a Child; Education; Modern Dance; Trailblazers; Women's Rights Activists

Now Try: To gain a more objective view of Duncan's life, you may want to read what is considered to be a definitive biography of Duncan by Peter Kurth, ***Isadora: A Sensational Life***. Duncan's contribution to the theory of modern dance was gauzy clothing and draping, along with bare feet and emotional body movements; Loie Fuller used lighting to enhance the body movements of modern dancers, as described by Richard Nelson Current and Marcia Ewing Current in ***Loie Fuller, Goddess of Light***. Although it is out of print, Martha Graham's story of her late entry into dance and the changes she made to the art is still widely available: ***Blood Memory***. Modern dance figures importantly in the story of three women who are trying to break out of their straitened lives in the novel ***The Dance of the Mothers*** by Millicent Dillon.

O'Keeffe, Georgia (1887–1986)

Georgia O'Keeffe. Black Dog & Levanthal Publishers, 1995, 1976. 216pp. ill. 9781884822292. 759.13

This memoir looks like anything but. In the 1930s, an artist advised Georgia O'Keeffe to write about her paintings, which she did. When O'Keeffe writes about her paintings it is with reference to her life, and this is how we get her memoir. The book itself is oversized, to enhance the 108 color plates of various reproductions, all selected by O'Keeffe, some never having been reproduced before. The paintings themselves provide a memoir of sorts as they range from the beginning of her career to the point of this publication. Some of the notes have been taken from a small work previously published, ***Some Memories of Drawings***. O'Keeffe brings the reader along on her journey from Wisconsin to New York City to New Mexico and to the summer home in Lake George, New York, owned by the Stieglitz family, her in-laws.

Georgia O'Keeffe was a recipient of the National Medal of Arts and was given the Presidential Medal of Freedom in 1977 by President Ford and the Gold Medal of Painting by the National Institute of Arts and Letters; she was also inducted into the National Women's Hall of Fame.

Subjects: Artists; Classics; New Mexico; New York (State); Nonagenarians; Stieglitz, Alfred

Now Try: O'Keeffe's autobiography consists of illustrations of her work combined with commentary about those pieces as they remind her of various aspects of, and events in, her life. The art director for *The New York Times*, Jerelle Kraus, does something similar in ***All the Art That's Fit to Print (and Some That Wasn't): Inside "The New York Times" Op-Ed Page***, gathering a range of editorial cartoons over the years. Nature was obviously very important to O'Keeffe as she worked to illustrate its generative character. Elizabeth Dodd investigates the meeting of art and nature in ***In the Mind's Eye: Essays Across the Animate World***. Judy Chicago is another artist who makes use of the flower to strengthen her feminist statements. Her memoir, with photography coordinated by Douglas Woodman, is entitled ***Beyond the Flower: The Autobiography of a Feminist Artist***. It's true that O'Keeffe's memoir is a tease for those interested in her. To garner a more complete view of both O'Keeffe and her renowned husband, Alfred Stieglitz, the best options are ***Full Bloom: The Art and Life of Georgia O'Keeffe*** by Hunter Drohojowska-Philp and ***Alfred Stieglitz: A Biography*** by Richard Whelan.

Parks, Gordon (1912–2006)

Voices in the Mirror: An Autobiography. Introduction by Melvin Van Peebles. Harlem Moon, 2005, 1990. 422pp. ill. 24pp. of plates. 9780385266987. 770.92

A Renaissance man, Gordon Parks was foremost a photographer, but he also wrote fiction, poetry, nonfiction, and screenplays; in addition, he composed music and directed films during his long life. This autobiography isn't his first—***To Smile in Autumn: A Memoir*** precedes this—but it is the most inclusive up to his late seventies. He recounts his comforting childhood in Kansas, his difficult and poverty-stricken adolescence after the death of his mother, and his decision to buy a camera when he was young in order to document the sights he saw, reflecting the poverty and racism that so embittered him. Parks became the first Black photographer for both *Vogue* magazine and *Life* and the first Black film director; among his films is the highly acclaimed ***Shaft***. Apart from his narrative, however, he also includes his thoughts and reflections on what he has seen and experienced. Shortly before his death Parks published a third work: ***A Hungry Heart: A Memoir***.

Parks was inducted into the International Photography Hall of Fame and was awarded the National Medal of Arts.

Subjects: African-American Men; Classics; Death of a Parent; Directors; Firsts; Nonagenarians; Photographers; Poverty; Racism; Reflections; Screenwriters

Now Try: Though he may have been cited as the first Black photographer to work for specific magazines, Parks was definitely not the first African-American photographer of renown, as demonstrated by ***Reflections in Black: A History of Black Photographers, 1840 to the Present*** by Deborah Willis. Parks's autobiography is a powerful one, in which he details how he used a camera to fight where others might have used guns. In a similar fashion, the poet Don Mattera, after having been a gang leader, began to use his creative talents in drama and poetry to rail against the injustices in his South African society; his compelling memoir is entitled ***Sophiatown: Coming of Age in South Africa***. Parks recounts in his poignant memoir having to drop out of school to take various jobs in his teens, just trying to stay alive. Novelist Paul Auster had similar experiences, as he also poignantly writes in ***Hand to Mouth: A Chronicle of Early Failure***.

Artists

This section gathers together a representation of artists in their various *métiers*: dance, music, and visual art—paintings and photography.

Dance may be one of the most esoteric of the creative arts. It is found in the musical—on Broadway or in movies—but is primarily found on stage in the form of either modern dance "concerts" or ballet, which can also include modern dance. The type of dance under discussion here is classical, rather than street or folk. Its audience is fairly select in numbers, and for this reason the demand for books by its artists is less than in most of the other fields. Memoirs by trailblazers in the art, people like Martha Graham and Agnes De Mille, are no longer in print. Other greats, like George Balanchine and Jerome Robbins, have not written memoirs. To read their stories, you will have to look for biographies, not autobiographies. Robert Gottlieb was an editor at Knopf who was responsible for much of the dance literature that did get published. He has recently gathered a sizable number of excerpts from the literature (1,330 pages) into a work entitled ***Reading Dance: A Gathering of Memoirs, Reportage, Criticism, Profiles, Interviews, and Some Uncategorizable Extras***. In the few titles here the dancers discuss their personal lives as well as their art, so that the reader who dips into these books will have a greater understanding and appreciation of the art.

As with dance, serious music has a limited audience, and therefore so does publishing in the field. One of the interesting features of what is here, however, is that we can see music from a variety of artistic facets—we have a singer, instrumentalists, and a conductor. By reading the stories of these artists we also gain a view of the social history of their time.

The same holds true of visual arts as for the other classic art forms: there are relatively few memoirs, and they are either out of print or very sparsely distributed in libraries across the country. In this section we have a photographer and a painter representing the field. An interesting element of some of the artists' memoirs is that they are not necessarily in a traditional format; the artistry comes out even in their memoirs.

The artists here describe how they discovered their talent and how they arrived where they did. They also share stories from their particular arenas of creative achievement, so that the reader is able to learn about the life of a photographer, of a pianist, or of a ballerina. Since most of these artists do not work alone, the reader is also treated to vignettes about others who share similar talents.

Adams, Ansel (1902–1984)
Alinder, Mary Street (1946–), coauthor

Ansel Adams, an Autobiography. Little, Brown, 1996, 1985. 339pp. ill. 9780821222416. 770.92

Ansel Adams spent five years writing this autobiography, but had selected illustrations for the first chapter only by the time he died. His assistant and curator, Mary Street Alinder, finished the project for him. She included 270 illustrations, not just of his oeuvre, but also of his family and friends. Although he'd always been drawn to the wilderness and photography, Adams initially thought he would make his career as a concert pianist (he was self-taught). But after spending time with the Sierra Club and photographing Yosemite and the Sierras for them, he realized that his real passion and art lay in photography. He believed in the craft as well as the art of photography and has written and taught extensively on both aspects. Adams developed a "Zone System" for composition that is widely used by professional photographers. He also became an avid conservationist, arguing boldly for various ecological systems throughout North America. In fact, his book written with Nancy Newhall, ***This Is the American Earth***, along with Rachel Carson's ***Silent Spring*** (illustrated by Lois and Louis Darling), initiated the first grassroots environmental movement.

Adams was awarded the Presidential Medal of Freedom in 1980 by President Carter. ***Ansel Adams, an Autobiography*** was selected as a Notable Book by the American Library Association.

Subjects: ALA Notable Books; *Aperture* (Magazine); California; Environmental Activists; Octogenarians; Photographers; Photography, Artistic; Sierra Club; Sierra Nevada Mountains, CA; Trailblazers; Yosemite National Park, CA

Now Try: A little more than a decade after Adams died, Mary Street Alinder wrote a much more complete biography of him than he had offered: ***Ansel Adams: A Biography***. Adams was instrumental in founding a photography magazine in 1952. Richard H. Cravens wrote a history of that magazine when it turned fifty: ***Photography Past Forward: "Aperture" at 50, with a History***. To see another beautiful collection of photographs of America, taken by a variety of photographers, look at Robert Sullivan's ***America the Beautiful: A Photographic Journey, Coast to Coast—and Beyond***. Adams's style in telling his story is fragmentary, speaking of people and events almost as they pop into his head. The artist Mary Pratt exhibits that same stylistic trait in her memoir, ***A Personal Calligraphy***.

Ailey, Alvin (1931–1989)
Bailey, A. Peter, coauthor

Revelations: The Autobiography of Alvin Ailey. Replica Books, 2000, 1995. 183pp. ill. 16pp. of plates. 9780735100800. 792.8028

The title of Alvin Ailey's autobiography comes from one of his most popular ballets. He dictated his life story to A. Peter Bailey, who finished it after Ailey's death, with a chapter added at the end comprised of interviews Bailey conducted with people close to Ailey. He was born poor in Texas to a single mother who traveled a lot looking for work. When his mother moved to Los Angeles, a good friend, Carmen De Lavallade, encouraged him—a skilled gymnast—to join the classes at Lester Horton's dance studio, the only school open to multiethnic groups. Ailey later joined De Lavallade on Broadway in New York and began his stellar career. Despite his struggles with a sense of self-worth along with chronic depression, he still managed to make an international name for himself for his dance, his choreography, and the Alvin Ailey American Dance Theater (http://www.alvinailey.org/).

Ailey was a recipient of the Kennedy Center Honors.

Subjects: African-American Men; Alvin Ailey American Dance Theater, NY; Ballet Dancers; Choreographers; Fatherless Children; Gay Men; Poverty; Racism; Texas

Now Try: It is suggested that readers of Ailey's autobiography also read Judith Jamison's story, written with Howard Kaplan, ***Dancing Spirit: An Autobiography,*** to provide a rounder picture of both dance in the United States in mid-century and the dance scene for African-American dancers. Jerome Robbins also had a rocky personal life, yet managed to make his own mark in American ballet. Dance critic Deborah Jowitt has written a very well-received biography, ***Jerome Robbins: His Life, His Theater, His Dance.*** Carlos Acosta shared some of Ailey's difficulties because of the color of his skin. Now an international star, he tells his story in ***No Way Home: A Dancer's Journey from the Streets of Havana to the Stages of the World.*** To provide more information specifically on African-American dancers, John O. Perpener has made an extensive study of eight, placing them in historical and cultural context in American dance in ***African-American Concert Dance: The Harlem Renaissance and Beyond.***

Farrell, Suzanne (1945–)
Bentley, Toni, coauthor

Holding on to the Air: An Autobiography. University Press of Florida, 2002, 1990. 322pp. ill. 9780813025933. 792.8092

This ballet dancer, who was sent for ballet classes to cure both her behavior as a tomboy and her career goal to be a clown, came to the early notice of George Balanchine, thus changing the direction of her life. Suzanne Farrell's memoir begins with her early childhood escapades in Cincinnati. Diana Adams, who became Farrell's source of inspiration for her personal diary, saw Farrell dance and brought her to New York for an audition, an event that resulted in Farrell's obtaining a scholarship to Balanchine's School of American Ballet. Balanchine saw something special in her, both creatively and personally, fell in love with her, and made her his muse. He choreographed many dances on her and by the time she was twenty, she was a principal dancer. Her memoir includes the story of her marriage to a younger dancer, Paul Mejia, which caused their expulsion from New York ballet; her later return to New York; her forced retirement because of hip surgery; and her subsequent career overseeing Balanchine's creative output.

Farrell was inducted into the Academy of Achievement and awarded both the Kennedy Center Honors and the National Medal of Arts.

Subjects: Arthritis; Balanchine, George; Ballet Dancers; Childhood and Youth; Cincinnati, OH; Love Affairs; Mejia, Paul; School of American Ballet, NY

Now Try: One of the first major works that Farrell danced in, when she was only seventeen, was composed by Igor Stravinsky, a composer who often worked with Balanchine. Music professor Charles M. Joseph has written of the collaboration between these two twentieth-century giants: ***Stravinsky & Balanchine: A Journey of Invention.*** Twyla Tharp is another noted choreographer who has also placed her stamp on American dance. Dance critic Marcia B. Siegel describes how she did this in ***Howling Near Heaven: Twyla Tharp and the Reinvention of Modern Dance.*** Providing an excellent overview of dance in the twentieth century, Nancy Reynolds and Malcolm

McCormick have written a highly acclaimed work, ***No Fixed Points: Dance in the Twentieth Century***, covering various facets of the art.

Fleming, Renée

The Inner Voice: The Making of a Singer. Penguin Books, 2005, 2004. 222pp. 9780143035947. 782.1092

Renée Fleming calls this book the autobiography of her voice, and it is true that she shares less about her personal life than about her road from singing at home to starring on stage at the Metropolitan Opera. Her parents were both voice teachers and felt that nurturing the gift of the voice was as important as nurturing the health of the body and mind. In this environment Fleming developed the talent and determination to overcome her stage fright and to succeed, first in gaining acceptance at the Juilliard School of Music and later in gaining acceptance in the professional world of classical singing. She briefly refers to her failed marriage and her loving relationship with her two daughters, describing life as a single mother and a traveling professional and the changes she had to make to her singing schedule to accommodate her children's needs. Fleming offers much advice to singers and would-be singers, particularly in the care of the voice, but also in choosing a voice coach, scheduling concerts, marketing oneself, and other such elements that make up a singer's life. She also describes life backstage at the Metropolitan Opera House, a treat for opera lovers.

Subjects: The Juilliard School; Metropolitan Opera, NY; Opera; Rochester, NY; Singers; Single Mothers; Sopranos

Now Try: Rudolf Bing was the general manager of the Metropolitan Opera for twenty-two years and wrote an immensely popular memoir of his time there, ***5,000 Nights at the Opera***. Luciano Pavarotti was one of the many great stars Fleming came into contact with. He wrote two memoirs with the help of William Wright, ***Pavarotti, My Own Story*** and ***Pavarotti, My World,*** describing not only his singing career but his personal life as well. One of the only criticisms Fleming levies in her book is against what she calls "divadom," and she doesn't exclude herself from that company. One diva who attracts a lot of attention is Cecilia Bartoli, the subject of Manuela Hoelterhoff's ***Cinderella & Company: Backstage at the Opera with Cecilia Bartoli***.

Kahlo, Frida (1907–1954)
Freeman, Phyllis, ed.

The Diary of Frida Kahlo: An Intimate Self-Portrait. Introduction by Carlos Fuentes. Essays and commentaries by Sarah M. Lowe. H. N. Abrams, 2005, 1995. 295pp. ill. facsimile. 9780810959545. 759.972092 [Trans. by Barbara Crow de Toledo and Ricardo Pohlenz]

Frida Kahlo's diary was kept under lock and key in the Kahlo Museum in Mexico for forty years. This publication is a facsimile of her diary, written in various colors of inks, crayons, pencil crayons, and gouaches, accompanied by over 300 drawings, a fulsome introduction by the Mexican novelist Carlos Fuentes, and a clarifying essay and commentaries by art historian Sarah Lowe. The diary covers only Kahlo's last ten years, yet manages to encompass the dominating motifs in her life: her ill health from a very serious bus/trolley accident when she was eighteen; her solitude and loneliness; her obsessive love for her husband, Diego Rivera, despite infidelity on both sides; and her identification with the Mexican Revolution in 1910 and all that it stood for. Through it all comes her keen desire to keep her sense of humor and joy in life.

Subjects: Accident Victims; Artists; Love Affairs; Married Couples; Mexican Revolution (1910); Mexicans; Mexico; Pain; Rivera, Diego; Solitude; Surrealists; Translations

Now Try: Because this diary covers ten years only of Kahlo's short but full life, you may want to read a well-regarded biography of her, ***Frida, a Biography of Frida Kahlo*** by Hayden Herrera. To learn more about Kahlo's famous artist husband, you can try Patrick Marnham's biography, ***Dreaming with His Eyes Open: A Life of Diego Rivera***. Kahlo's diary is an intimate one, broken open for the public to see. Nancy Milford plumbed Edna St. Vincent Millay's intimate diary to write a biography of that sensual poet, ***Savage Beauty: The Life of Edna St. Vincent Millay***. Some of the writing in the various colors in Kahlo's diary is referred to as "automatic writing"; the fictional novel *Lady Oracle*, in Margaret Atwood's novel of the same name, was accomplished when the fictional author received the gift of automatic writing. Pain, a constant companion, is a recurring theme in Kahlo's diary, as it is in poet Sarah Manguso's short memoir, ***The Two Kinds of Decay***.

Lang, Lang (1982–)
Ritz, David (1943–), coauthor

Journey of a Thousand Miles: My Story. Spiegel & Grau, 2009, 2008. 239pp. 9780385524575. Also available in audiobook, e-audiobook, and e-book. 786.2092

To read Lang Lang's memoir is to have an inside peek at life in China after Mao's Cultural Revolution. Lang Lang is a product of the one-child-family policy, and his parents were musicians *manqués* because of the Cultural Revolution. This combination, along with Lang Lang's own prodigious talent, joined together to create a high-pressure system in his family and his early life. He heard a composition by Franz Liszt in a Tom and Jerry cartoon when he was two and fell in love with classical music at that point. Reading musical notes before he could read writing, Lang Lang won a competition for children under ten when he was five. His parents were then determined that he would be Number One and sacrificed just about everything to achieve that goal. Some of the anecdotes Lang Lang tells in describing the arc of his career to this point are rather horrifying. Yet his talent and accomplishments speak for themselves and are as remarkable as the sacrifices made to get him where he is today.

Subjects: Childhood and Youth; China; Classical Musicians; Coming of Age; Cultural Revolution, China (1966–1976); Curtis Institute of Music, PA; Family Relationships; Fathers and Sons; Pianists

Now Try: Hao Jiang Tian is older than Lang Lang and therefore suffered different political trials; he and Lois B. Morris tell how he managed to succeed as an opera singer in both China and the United States in ***Along the Roaring River: My Wild Ride from Mao to the Met***. Ha Jin reveals various aspects of life in the Cultural Revolution in his collection, ***Under the Red Flag: Stories***. If you'd like to read about a very different classical pianist, you might enjoy the memoir of Hélène Grimaud, translated by Ellen Hinsey, ***Wild Harmonies: A Life of Music and Wolves***.

Leibovitz, Annie (1949–)
DeLano, Sharon, ed.

Annie Leibovitz at Work. Random House, 2008. 237pp. ill. 9780375505102. 779.2092

This memoir is very similar in concept to Georgia O'Keeffe's. Annie Leibovitz includes photographs spanning her career from the 1970s to the Obama campaign in 2008, and with each photograph she describes her technique and what went into the making of that picture. For Leibovitz her work is such an integral part of her life, that to see the various subjects she has shot and where is to have a narrative of her life. She began shooting for *Rolling Stone* magazine at the beginning of her illustrious career, a position that gave her entry into many otherwise closed doors. The progression of her pictures also incorporates changes in technology, including digital photography, something she was initially reluctant to begin using. Because of her penchant for conceptual photographs, however, she quickly saw the advantages of using digital cameras. The year after publishing this book, Leibovitz published ***A Photographer's Life, 1990–2005***, a memoir that was even more personal, chronicling in photographs the dying and deaths of both her father and her partner, Susan Sontag.

Subjects: Lesbians; Photographers; Photojournalists; Portrait Photography; *Rolling Stone* (Magazine); Sontag, Susan

Now Try: Margaret Bourke-White was a remarkable photographer in her time, making her name with *Life* magazine; her story is entitled ***Portrait of Myself***. Where Leibovitz photographed a wide assortment of people, Lee Miller focuses primarily on models. Carolyn Burke has told the story of her life—with and without a camera—in ***Lee Miller: A Life***. Photography often provides thought-provoking images and can be used quite successfully to make a point. David Elliot Cohen offers a range of photographs that speak to the various social ills of our world in ***What Matters: The World's Preeminent Photojournalists and Thinkers Depict Essential Issues of Our Time***.

Li, Cunxin (1961–)

Mao's Last Dancer. Putnam, 2003. 451pp. 8pp. of plates. geneal. table. 9780399150968. Also available in large print, Braille, audiobook, e-audiobook, and video. 792.8092

Born into dire poverty during Mao's Great Leap Forward, Cunxin Li's life changed in a remarkable fashion the day a delegation from Madame Mao came to his school looking for dancers, and Li's teacher unaccountably pointed him out as a candidate. Initially, the major benefit for Li of being taken away to ballet school was the fact that he had three meals a day—no longer did he have to endure a steady diet of dried yams. After experiencing two years of uninspired teaching, Li was finally given a ballet teacher who changed his life by teaching him the beauty of the dance and instilling in him a desire to excel beyond all others. The end result of this dedication was an unheard-of opportunity to dance in Houston for a year; close to his departure time from Houston, Li announced he would be defecting. His story does not end there, but what it includes, apart from the drama in his life, is the stark contrast between China and the United States. Although he achieved great success with the Houston Ballet, Li eventually moved to Australia, where he lives with his wife, Mary McKendry, whom he met in Houston.

Mao's Last Dancer was awarded a Christopher Award.

Subjects: Ballet Dancers; China; Chinese in America; Christopher Awards; Culture Clash; Defectors; Houston, TX; Social Conditions, China; Texas

Now Try: Memoirist Jung Chang and her husband Jon Halliday spent ten years researching the truth behind the myth of Mao Zedong, publishing their findings in ***Mao: The Unknown Story***. Ballet dancers come from all over the world; some of them have been profiled in a collection by Toba Singer, ***First Position: A Century of Ballet Artists***. Fan Shen also did what he had to do to survive the Cultural Revolution, but it wasn't pretty, as he describes in ***Gang of One: Memoirs of a Red Guard***.

Solti, Georg (1912–1997)
Sachs, Harvey (1946–)

Memoirs. Chicago Review Press, 1998, 1997. 288pp. ill. 9781556523373. Also available in e-book. 784.2092

The first six chapters of Georg Solti's memoir are titled with the names of cities that played a significant role in his life, from his birth in Budapest; continuing on to Zurich, where he, a Jew, sought refuge during the war; to Munich and Frankfurt, when the Americans asked him to come after the war to restore the German classical music scene. He moves on from there to London and his first conducting gig with the Royal Opera at Covent Garden and then to Chicago and a twenty-two-year tenure conducting the Chicago Symphony Orchestra, creating a standard for orchestras everywhere. The seventh chapter is entitled "The World," reflecting Solti's international status, and he ends with "Music, First and Last," in which he offers his perspectives on music and his favorite composers. Throughout the memoir we are treated to little vignettes about musicians he has worked with, and we get an inside view of the conductor's world.

Solti was the recipient of the Kennedy Center Honors, and at the time of his death had received more Grammy Awards than any other artist.

Subjects: Chicago Symphony Orchestra, IL; Classical Musicians; Conductors (Music); Jewish Men; Octogenarians; Symphony Orchestras

Now Try: The renowned conductor Zubin Mehta has just recently published his own memoir, with the help of Renate Gräfin Matuschka (and translated from the German by Anu Pande): ***Zubin Mehta: The Score of My Life***. Daniel Barenboim had toured with Solti and took his place in Chicago; he too has written his story, with the help of Michael Lewin: ***Daniel Barenboim: A Life in Music***. Donald Peck worked with Solti in the Chicago Symphony Orchestra as principal flutist, a story he tells in ***The Right Place, the Right Time! Tales of Chicago Symphony Days***.

Stern, Isaac (1920–2001)
Potok, Chaim (1929–2002), coauthor

My First 79 Years. Da Capo Press, 2000, 1999. 317pp. ill. 9780306810060. Also available in e-book. 787.2092

Isaac Stern began playing the violin because his friend did; there was initially no driving passion that led him to his lifelong career. In this memoir, as he tells his stories to the preeminent Jewish writer, Chaim Potok, he describes life as an internationally known and respected violinist and relates how he slowly got started on that path. But he was also an activist in various venues. Stern refused to play in either Germany or Austria because of their roles in the Holocaust, he played at Carnegie Hall in a successful effort to keep it from being torn down, and he often lobbied in favor of the state of Israel. In fact, he often played for patients in hospitals in Israel. He was well-known for mentoring young musicians and played himself in the movie ***Music of the Heart*** doing just that. Apart from the events and causes in his life, Stern also describes important friendships with several people, many of them well-known musicians such as Leonard Bernstein.

Stern was the recipient of the Kennedy Center Honors.

Subjects: Carnegie Hall, NY; Classical Musicians; Humanitarians; Israel; Jewish Musicians; Octogenarians; Russian-Americans; Violinists

Now Try: Isaac Stern and Artur Rubinstein had something in common apart from the entertaining nature of their memoirs: they both were encouraged to practice more. Rubinstein was notorious for playing the wrong notes, as he ruefully describes in his memoirs, ***My Young Years*** and ***My Many Years***. Pablo Casals was a good friend of Isaac Stern, as we see him remembered in Stern's book. Casals's memoir, ***Joys and Sorrows: Reflections,*** written with the help of Albert Eugene Kahn, offers not only his life story but a social history of his time as well. Arnold Steinhardt is the first violinist for the Guarneri String Quartet; in his memoir, ***Violin Dreams,*** he not only recounts his life story but also provides much information on the violin itself as he describes his quest for the perfect violin.

Tallchief, Maria (1925–)
Kaplan, Larry, coauthor

Maria Tallchief: America's Prima Ballerina. University Press of Florida, 2005, 1997. 351pp. ill. 9780805033021. 792.8028092

When the available ballet instruction on her reservation in Oklahoma was no longer enough for Maria Tallchief and her sister Marjorie, their mother, Ruth, took them to Los Angeles, where they studied with Bronislava Nijinska. Her childhood is part of Tallchief's memoir, along with her instant success in New York at the age of seventeen; her marriage to George Balanchine, who created several important roles for her; and her long-standing career that led to her title as "America's Prima Ballerina." She also discusses the toll that ballet dancing takes on the body, the long hours every day, and the perennial exhaustion. But her love for the art comes through as she describes her roles, the choreographers she worked with, and the dancers who accompanied her.

Tallchief has been awarded the Kennedy Center Honors and the National Medal of Arts and was inducted into the National Women's Hall of Fame.

Subjects: American Indian Women; Balanchine, George; Ballet Dancers; *Ballets Russes*; Nijinska, Bronislava; Octogenarians; Osage Nation; Tallchief, Marjorie

Now Try: Many women have danced for Balanchine, including Barbara M. Fisher. She has told her story in ***In Balanchine's Company: A Dancer's Memoir***. Maria and Marjorie were not the only American Indian ballet dancers. Lili Cockerille Livingston knew them all and wrote about them in ***American Indian Ballerinas***. Shortly before her death, Tallchief's teacher Bronislava Nijinska handed the manuscript of a long autobiography to her daughter, Irina, asking her to publish it in two parts, the first part largely reflecting the life and talent of her brother, Waslaw Nijinsky. Irina did as she was asked, with the help of Jean Rawlinson, and published the first part, ***Bronislava Nijinska—Early Memoirs***, but died before she could finish the second.

Humorists

Humor is a very delicate ingredient in a book. There are varying kinds of humor, varying tones, and varying audiences. What is hilarious to one person can be offensive to another. What is boring or "not funny" to one may be cheerily uplifting to another. In this section we have a broad range, from deadpan (Bob Newhart) to witty (Neil Simon) to whimsical (David Sedaris). What is also interesting about these selections is the variety of formats in which the comedians appear: television shows, record albums, magazines, radio, and books. Most of the situations are domestic, as humorists like to speak to the everyday detail in one's life.

The humorists here are known for their comedic performances and/or writing. Some have started off in one field, perhaps performing and moving to writing, and some have done the reverse. Or they may simply be comedic writers who have a special talent for humor. Readers have the added bonus of gaining insights into the world of comedy from some of the performers.

Alda, Alan (1936–)

Never Have Your Dog Stuffed: And Other Things I've Learned. With a new Afterword. Random House Trade Paperbacks, 2006, 2005. 235pp. ill. 9780812974409. Also available in large print, Braille, audiobook (read by the author), e-audiobook, and e-book. 792.028092

Alan Alda grew up with an actor father (Robert Alda) and a schizophrenic mother, although her illness was not diagnosed in his childhood. He performed in burlesque and vaudeville with his father and then went on to Broadway, television, and film. When he was quite young he developed polio and credits his mother with diagnosing it early and Sister Elizabeth Kenny for developing a way to treat it. Partly because of his respect for and debt to these two women, he became an impassioned feminist and a staunch supporter of the Equal Rights Amendment. Another side interest of Alda's is science: he was host of the PBS *Scientific American Frontiers* for eleven years. It is still possible to see these episodes online at http://www.pbs.org/saf/. Alda's memoir is not so much about his acting career, as it is about lessons learned growing up. The title comes from a real story about a dog who was important to him during his illness. It was taken to a taxidermist after its death and returned with a grimace on its face. That image has stuck with Alda, teaching him about the permanence of death and other life lessons.

Subjects: Actors; Alda, Robert; Comedians; Coming of Age; Directors; Equal Rights Amendment; *M*A*S*H* (Television Program); Mothers and Sons; *Scientific American Frontiers* (Television Program)

Now Try: Bill Murray writes his golf-related memoir, with the help of George Peper, ***Cinderella Story: My Life in Golf,*** with the same gentle humor that Alda uses. If you'd like to know more about Sister Elizabeth Kenny, the woman whose persistence in gaining acceptance for her treatment of polio greatly aided Alda, try her own story, written with the help of Martha Ostenso: ***And They Shall Walk: The Life Story of Sister Elizabeth Kenny.*** Alda wrote his book with a sense of wonderment at what the world has to offer, much as Timothy Ferris did in ***Seeing in the Dark: How Backyard Stargazers Are Probing Deep Space and Guarding Earth from Interplanetary Peril,*** an engaging look at the constellations and the amateurs who have advanced science by their own backyard discoveries. While in Chile filming for *Scientific American Frontiers,* Alda became seriously ill—close to dying—with an intestinal obstruction. His recovery led him to write a more spiritual look at himself and his life, ***Things I Overheard While Talking to Myself.***

Jacobs, A. J. (1968–)

The Know-It-All: One Man's Humble Quest to Become the Smartest Person in the World. Simon & Schuster, 2005, 2004. 388pp. 9780743250627. Also available in large print, audiobook, e-audiobook, and e-book. 031

In Chapter 1, "Travel and Adventure," we met some extreme adventurers who set almost impossible goals for themselves. Perhaps we should have

1 2 3 4 5 6 7 8

included A. J. Jacobs there, as his goal was such that it is truly remarkable he accomplished it: to read the 2002 edition of the *Encyclopedia Britannica* in a year, all 33,000 pages of it. His father had once tried, but gave out somewhere in the Bs; the rest of his family and friends thought at first that Jacobs was certifiable but later decided he was simply a bore to be avoided. He recounts his adventure with laugh-out-loud humor, describing how he flamed out on *Who Wants to Be a Millionaire?* and how he tried to join Mensa. Along with his hilarious stories, however, this editor for *Esquire* magazine does weigh in on the differences between knowledge and wisdom and between learning by reading and learning by living. While he is undergoing this mental-growth project, his wife is pregnant, a fact that Jacobs, in his fear of new fatherhood, tries to hide from as he reads page after page.

Subjects: Books and Reading; Editors; *Encyclopedia Britannica;* Expectant Fathers; Family Relationships; Intellectual Life; Marriage; Self-Education

Now Try: Jacobs stretches his wife's patience even further with the adventures/experiments he describes in a later memoir, ***The Guinea Pig Diaries: My Life as an Experiment***. Using humor and wit to (sort of) further education is the ploy of Thomas Cathcart and Daniel Klein in their book, ***Plato and a Platypus Walk into a Bar—: Understanding Philosophy Through Jokes***. Cathy Alter also set herself a mission; since she hadn't been too successful in creating a good life for herself, she decided to follow what all the women's magazines were advocating, without questioning anything. She describes her humorous experiment in ***Up for Renewal: What Magazines Taught Me About Love, Sex, and Starting Over***. The magazine *National Lampoon* has long been a source of humor for many intellectuals and some who are not so intellectual. The journalist Josh Karp offers a history of that magazine in ***A Futile and Stupid Gesture: How Doug Kenney and "National Lampoon" Changed Comedy Forever***.

Martin, Steve (1945–)

Born Standing Up: A Comic's Life. Scribner, 2008, 2007. 208pp. ill. 9781416553656. Also available in large print and audiobook (read by the author), e-audiobook, and e-book. 792.7028092

This memoir of Steve Martin takes him through his formative years, when he was still trying to find his professional persona, although he does have a number of successes within that time frame. He says that it is not an autobiography but a biography, since he was writing it about someone else he used to know. He describes living with a difficult father and escaping to Disneyland. There he sold guidebooks and magic tricks (which he then learned to perform) and then eventually did little theatrical performances himself. Martin describes the difficult years in stand-up comedy, wherein he tried to break the pattern of the political sixties, wanting to give the audience nothing to think about, but just make them laugh. At the same time he pursued an education, initially in philosophy, which informed his comedy, but more particularly his writing. His start in Hollywood began with his scriptwriting for a number of shows, most notably *The Smothers Brothers Comedy Hour*. He also had a number of appearances on such shows as *The Tonight Show* (with Johnny Carson) and *Saturday Night Live.*

Martin is a recipient of the Kennedy Center Honors.

Subjects: Actors; Comedians; Disneyland, CA; Fathers and Sons; Magicians; *Saturday Night Live* (Television Program); Screenwriters; *The Smothers Brothers Comedy Hour* (Television Program); Television Writers; *The Tonight Show* (Television Program); Writers

Now Try: Steve Martin has extended his creative energies to writing articles for *The New Yorker,* which have been collected into ***Pure Drivel;*** he has also written plays, novellas, and short stories. His comedic writing has been compared to that of S. J. Perelman, whose ***The Most of S. J. Perelman*** might prove interesting to the reader. One of the programs Martin watched with a budding professional interest was *The Steve Allen Show*. Steve Allen has written several books, including a mystery series starring himself and his wife Jayne Meadows, but of particular import here is ***How to Be Funny: Discovering the Comic You,*** written with Jane Wollman. Jerry Seinfeld, another popular television comic who got his start in stand-up comedy, has written a number of humorous reflections in ***SeinLanguage.***

Newhart, Bob (1929–)

I Shouldn't Even Be Doing This! And Other Things That Strike Me as Funny. Hyperion, 2007, 2006. 239pp. 9781401309152. Also available in large print, audiobook (read by the author), e-audiobook, and e-book. 792.7028092

Bob Newhart started out as an accountant and then moved to advertising copywriting. His first love was comedy, though, and he and a coworker at the advertising agency were always doing routines on the phone to each other. When his friend decided not to pursue his own comedy career, Newhart continued with the telephone routine by himself, speaking with a fictitious person on the other end. When he was thirty, he was introduced to the head of talent at Warner Brothers, and from that meeting came his first record album, ***The Button-Down Mind of Bob Newhart.*** This album was the first comedy album ever to hit Number One on the Billboard chart, and it won a Grammy Award for Album of the Year. From there Newhart went on to do stand-up comedy, movies (e.g., ***Elf***) and television, most notably two sitcoms, *The Bob Newhart Show* and *Newhart*. A special treat in this book is that he interweaves some of his comedy routines among the memories.

Newhart has a star on the Hollywood Walk of Fame.

Subjects: Actors; Advertising Copywriters; *The Bob Newhart Show* (Television Program); Comedians; *Newhart* (Television Program); Rickles, Don; Television Actors

Now Try: Newhart believes that Richard Pryor is one of the most important comedians of his time; Pryor wrote his own story, with the help of Todd Gold, ***Pryor Convictions, and Other Life Sentences.*** One of the classic comedians who influenced Newhart was Robert Benchley; you may want to read a collection of his writing, selected by his son, in ***The Benchley Roundup; A Selection by Nathaniel Benchley of His Favorites,*** with drawings by Gluyas Williams. One of the writers for Bob Newhart was Gary David Goldberg, who has written his own humorous memoir, ***Sit, Ubu, Sit: How I Went from Brooklyn to Hollywood with the Same Woman, the Same Dog, and a Lot Less Hair.***

Sedaris, David (1956–)

Dress Your Family in Corduroy and Denim. Back Bay Books, 2005, 2004. 257pp. 9780316010795. Also available in large print, Braille, audiobook (read by the author), e-audiobook, and e-book. 814.54

This collection of essays follows upon ***Me Talk Pretty One Day,*** winner of both the Lambda Literary Award for Humor and the Thurber Prize for American Humor. It focuses for the first half on Sedaris's childhood, on life with Mom and Dad, and the normal events in a child's life, with highlights such as snow days from school. In his own humorous style, Sedaris also talks about what it is like to grow up knowing that you are gay. The second half of the book sees him as an adult, interacting more with his siblings than with his parents and finding his partner, Hugh Hamrick. Sedaris's four other essay collections (thus far) are ***Barrel Fever: Stories and Essays***; ***Naked***; ***Holidays on Ice***; and ***When You Are Engulfed in Flames***. He has also written collections of short stories, and he and his sister Amy won an Obie Award for their play, ***One Woman Shoe***.

Dress Your Family in Corduroy and Denim was both a Stonewall Honor Book (American Library Association) and the winner of the Lambda Literary Award for Humor.

Subjects: Domestic Life; Family Relationships; Gay Men; Hamrick, Hugh; Humorists; Lambda Literary Award for Humor; National Public Radio; Personal Essays; Writers

Now Try: Another comic gay writer is Dan Savage, who also deals with the human condition in ***The Commitment: Love, Sex, Marriage, and My Family***. Ian Ferguson finds humor in his family too, although it is situated in a very different place from David Sedaris's. Ferguson's story is set in Fort Vermilion, Alberta; ***Village of the Small Houses: A Memoir of Sorts*** won The Stephen Leacock Memorial Medal for Humour. Paul Feig's writing is also reminiscent of Sedaris's absurdist, self-deprecating humor, as demonstrated in ***Kick Me: Adventures in Adolescence***.

Simon, Neil (1927–)

Rewrites: A Memoir. Touchstone, 1998, 1996. 397pp. ill. 16pp. of plates. 9780684835624. Also available in audiobook (read by the author) and e-book. 812.54

Neil Simon uses the writing of his plays (up to 1970) to tell the story of his life to that point. While the plays are dealt with in chronological order of their having been written, the personal stories are episodic, triggered as they are by memories created when discussing the plays. Simon dips into his childhood; his relationship with his brother Danny, with whom he had initially created a comedy-writing team; and his sexual initiation. He talks about the business of writing, agents, network businessmen, and writing block. And of course we meet a panoply of people in the theater world (Jerry Lewis, Mike Nichols, etc.). Simon also talks about his first wife of twenty years, Joan Baim, who died too early and whose death injected a serious tone into what had previously been straight comedy.

Apart from a Pulitzer Prize for his play ***Lost in Yonkers*** and various theatrical awards, Simon has also been awarded the Kennedy Center Honors.

Subjects: Baim, Joan; City Life; Death of a Spouse; Humorists; Mason, Marsha; New York, NY; Octogenarians; Playwrights; Radio Plays; Television Writers

Now Try: This first volume of Simon's memoirs takes the reader up to the death of his wife Joan in 1973. He wrote a second volume, ***The Play Goes On: A Memoir***, which takes the reader up to the present, through his marriage to and divorce from Marsha Mason plus others, his creative slumps, and his creative triumphs. Nancy C. Andreasen, with a doctorate in Renaissance literature, has studied Simon and others in trying to determine the nature of creativity: ***The Creating Brain: The Neuroscience of Genius***. If you'd like a closer look at the making of the film of Simon's prize-winning play, pick up Anne Hoy's edition of ***Neil Simon's "Lost in Yonkers": The Illustrated Screenplay of the Film***, with photographs by Zade Rosenthal. Marsha Mason, who has acted in five of Simon's plays, has written her own story, ***Journey: A Personal Odyssey***. A novel that has been compared to Simon's play ***Biloxi Blues*** in its atmosphere and content is *Pete Hamill's* ***Loving Women: A Novel of the Fifties***. Simon's memoirs read as though told by a raconteur, as does Peter Taylor's Pulitzer Prize–winning novel, ***A Summons to Memphis***.

Writers

Writers write their memoirs for a variety of reasons and in a number of formats. Some, like Maya Angelou, set out deliberately to write their stories, often as a way to find meaning in a life or to exorcise demons. Others simply write—journals, diaries—because that is part of their compulsion as a writer, to find their place in the world through such writing. In many cases, without these journals there would be no autobiographical work, as the writing life for the diarist is often more focused on the novel, the poem, or the play, rather than on the memoir. In this section, as one would expect, there are no ghostwritten or "as-told-to" memoirs. Readers who delve into these memoirs will often learn not only about the life of the writer, but also about the art of the writer or the art of writing.

The writers in this section differ from most of the writers throughout the book in that their talents lie in creative writing, both fiction and nonfiction, rather than journalistic or technical writing, for example. They have all written their own memoirs, as one would expect, and they share their life stories, often reflecting on personal philosophies as they do so.

Amis, Martin (1949–)

Experience: A Memoir. Vintage Books, 2001, 2000. 406pp. ill. 9780375726835. 823.914

Robertson Davies talked about the freedom one has as a writer after the writer's father has died, a freedom to articulate and make public thoughts and notions that would have been difficult beforehand (Davis, 1989). Such would seem to be the case with Martin Amis. Son of the award-winning writer Kingsley Amis, Martin too became an award-winning writer. In fact, his first novel, ***The Rachel Papers***, won the Somerset Maugham Award nineteen years after his father's ***Lucky Jim*** had won the same award. Five years after his father died, Amis wrote this memoir. Despite his father's debilitating alcoholism and divorce from his mother, Martin Amis still regards his father with respect and affection. His fiction is often vitriolic—certainly satiric and biting—but his memoir is more affectionate in tone, particularly when he is discussing those in his life who are important to him, especially his stepmother, the novelist Elizabeth Jane Howard. She encouraged him to read serious literature and to go to a "cram school" to pass the university entrance exams. After graduating from Oxford with honors, Amis became an editor for various reviewing journals and by 1980 felt he could concentrate full-time on writing.

Experience won the James Tait Black Memorial Prize for Biography.

Subjects: Amis, Kingsley; Children of Alcoholics; Essayists; Family Relationships; Fathers and Sons; Howard, Elizabeth Jane; James Tait Black Memorial Prize for Biography; Novelists, England; Stepmothers; Writers in the Family

Now Try: V. S. Naipaul's father, Seepersad, was a writer too, although not nearly so successful as his son. After Naipaul left Trinidad for England, where he worked to become a serious writer, he exchanged many letters with his father, which have been collected by Gillon Aitken in ***Between Father and Son: Family Letters***. Amis's writing style is both bitter and funny, similar to Jonathan Miles in his novel, ***Dear American Airlines***. Zoë Heller has that same penchant for being a critic of contemporary culture, as seen in her satiric first novel, ***Everything You Know***. Amis wrote a loose trilogy of London, and Anna Quindlen has included some of his writing in ***Imagined London: A Tour of the World's Greatest Fictional City***.

Atwood, Margaret (1939–)

Negotiating with the Dead: A Writer on Writing. Anchor Books, 2003, 2002. 219pp. 9781400032600. 808.3

This book is not a traditional memoir; rather, it intertwines Margaret Atwood's views on writing with bits and pieces of her life to illustrate how she developed her writing style and philosophies. Her childhood was formative for her, and she draws on it quite a bit for this book. Her father was a scientist, an entomologist and academic, resulting in the family's spending months every year in the Northern Ontario woods. In this environment Atwood learned about scientific method and the natural life surrounding her. Homeschooled for the first several years by her parents, she read voraciously and widely and knew at the start of high school in Toronto that she wanted to be a writer. By the time she had finished her undergraduate degree at the University of Toronto, she had published a prize-winning collection of poetry, ***Double Persephone***. She has been very involved with PEN, particularly PEN Canada.

Atwood has been named a Companion of the Order of Canada and was the winner of the Man Booker Prize for ***The Blind Assassin***.

> **Subjects:** Human Rights Activists, Canada; Literature; Northern Ontario; Novelists, Canada; PEN Canada; Poets, Canada; Writing
>
> **Now Try:** To learn more about Atwood and her perspectives, you could try two other books by her: ***Writing with Intent: Essays, Reviews, Personal Prose, 1983–2005*** and ***Morning in the Burned House***, a collection of her personal reflections and winner of the Trillium Award. Rosemary Sullivan provides more information about Atwood the person in ***The Red Shoes: Margaret Atwood Starting Out***. Carolyn Anthony collected the writings of a number of authors who wrote specific essays on the influence of family on their writing in ***Family Portraits: Remembrances***. Atwood writes with sly humor, a humor also visible in Margaret Drabble's novel, ***The Seven Sisters***. Another Canadian author who draws unusual character portraits in her fiction is Anne Fleming. Those who enjoy Atwood might enjoy Fleming's ***Anomaly***.

Barnes, Julian (1946–)

Nothing to Be Frightened Of. Vintage Canada, 2009, 2008. 250pp. 9780307356994. Also available in e-book. 823.914

Julian Barnes offers autobiographical tidbits in this treatise on death and faith. He was born of an agnostic father and an atheist mother, so religious faith was not part of his upbringing. He now wonders what difference having or not having faith makes in how one regards one's impending death. This sounds morbid and dreary, but Barnes actually addresses the topic with dry humor. In the midst of his musings he brings to life his now-dead parents; he also invokes his older brother, Jonathan, so that the reader is invited to meet the family of the child Julian Barnes. To help him with his philosophical look at death, something he feels compelled to consider now that he is getting closer himself, he calls on sages of the past, writers whose work he has long admired. Barnes says that this book is not his autobiography, but it is the closest the reader will come at this point to having anything autobiographical of his to read.

> **Subjects:** Aging; Death; Dying; Faith; Family Relationships; Mortality; Religion
>
> **Now Try:** The nonagenarian novelist and editor Diana Athill is not afraid of death, as she joyfully announces in her award-winning memoir ***Somewhere Towards the End***. David Eagleman is a neuroscientist who proffers with a bit of humor a number of pithy essays in ***Sum: Forty Tales from the Afterlives*** that speculate about what death will actually be like. If Julian Barnes were actually dying, he might write a book like the playwright Simon Gray's ***Coda***, looking frankly at his own mortality.

Berton, Pierre (1920–2004)

My Times: Living with History, 1947–1995. McClelland-Bantam, 1996, 1995 534pp. 24 pp. of plates. 9780770427290. 971.007202

Pierre Berton was a journalist, broadcaster, popular historian, prolific writer, and Canadian icon. He has written other memoirs, beginning with ***Adventures of a Columnist***, published when he was forty. In that book, he focuses on being a newspaper columnist, describing how one actually does it and using some of his best columns to illustrate the point. Following that is ***Starting Out, 1920–1947***, which covers the time from when Berton was a child in the Yukon to his working in the Klondike mining camps while attending university and then being hired as the youngest city editor on a Canadian daily. ***My Times*** takes him from his formal work as a journalist to his life as a popular historian, writing books for children and adults on topics covering Canada's history and culture. He was also an iconoclast and shocked the country by writing in 1966 ***The Comfortable Pew; A Critical Look at Christianity and the Religious Establishment in the New Age***.

Berton was named a Companion of the Order of Canada.

Subjects: Canada; Historians, Canada; Journalists, Canada; Octogenarians; Writers, Canada

Now Try: Jules Verne also wrote about the Klondike and the Arctic in ***The Golden Volcano***, said volcano supposedly being somewhere in the Arctic. An American popular historian who has covered similar territory to Berton is H. W. Brands, author of a lively account, ***The Age of Gold: The California Gold Rush and the New American Dream***. Stephen E. Ambrose is another well-known popular historian who, like Berton, has written about his own country's national railway, in ***Nothing Like It in the World: The Men Who Built the Transcontinental Railroad, 1863–1869***. A. B. McKillop, chair of the history department at Carleton University in Ottawa, has recently written a 791-page-biography of Berton in Berton's own lively style, ***Pierre Berton: A Biography***.

Clark, Mary Higgins (1929–)

Kitchen Privileges: A Memoir. Pocket Books, 2003, 2002. 207pp. ill. 9780743412612. Also available in large print and audiobook (read by the author), e-audiobook, and e-book. 813.54

The title of Mary Higgins Clark's memoir refers to the sign her mother posted outside their front door after Clark's father died when she was eleven. The sign said, "Furnished Rooms. Kitchen Privileges." Taking in boarders was the only way, during the Great Depression years, that Clark's mother could keep her children fed, clothed, and housed. She talks about some of the eccentric boarders they had, but she then moves on with her own life as she gets married and also loses her husband early. He died fifteen years after they were married, leaving her with five children to raise. She had a job writing radio scripts, but wanted to write novels. After six years of trying and being rejected, Clark's first novel (then entitled ***Aspire to the Heavens; A Portrait of George Washington***) was accepted, but it didn't really go anywhere. (In 2002 it was re-released as ***Mount Vernon***

Love Story: A Novel of George and Martha Washington and became a best seller.) Finally, in 1975, her first winning novel was published (***Where Are the Children?***), and her best-selling future was secured.

Kitchen Privileges was nominated for an Agatha Award for Best Nonfiction, and Clark has been given a Horatio Alger Award.

Subjects: Boarding Houses; Bronx (New York, NY); Childhood and Youth; Depression (Economic); Mystery Writers; Novelists; Octogenarians; Poverty; Widows; Working-Class Families

Now Try: Sema Wilkes also kept a boarding house, in Georgia, and has written a warm culinary memoir of her fifty-five plus years running it, including a history by John T. Edge: ***Mrs. Wilkes' Boardinghouse Cookbook: Recipes and Recollections from Her Savannah Table***. Mary Higgins Clark has very fond memories of her Irish father and contributed to a book put out by Karyn McLaughlin Frist, ***"Love You, Daddy Boy": Daughters Honor the Fathers They Love***. In many of Clark's books her innocent heroines have to get themselves out of dire trouble, much as Nancy Drew often had to do. Melanie Rehak has taken a look at that female character in ***Girl Sleuth: Nancy Drew and the Women Who Created Her***. The novelist Jerome Charyn honors his mother in ***The Dark Lady from Belorusse: A Memoir***, as she coped with life in a new country during his childhood, also in the Bronx.

Findley, Timothy (1930–2002)

Inside Memory: Pages from a Writer's Workbook. Commemorative ed. HarperFlamingoCanada, 2002. 308pp. 9780002005500. 819.354

The pages Timothy Findley refers to in his title are taken from his journals and notebooks spanning a period of thirty years. In his collection of memories Findley discusses the writing of each of his novels, so that the reader garners insights into his writing process as well as on the people who featured in his life. Bill Whitehead was his life partner, with whom he cowrote award-winning scripts for the Canadian Broadcasting Corporation. Also among those he admired and wrote about were a cast of characters ranging from Glenn Gould to Margaret Laurence to Ken Adachi.

Findley was made an Officer of the Order of Canada and awarded the *Chevalier de l'ordre des arts et des lettres* from France, where he and Bill lived part-time. ***Inside Memory*** won the Canadian Authors Association Literary Award for Non-fiction.

Subjects: Actors, Canada; Canadian Authors Association Literary Award for Non-fiction; Cannington, ON; Gay Men; Intellectual Life, Canada; Novelists, Canada; Ontario; Theater; Whitehead, William

Now Try: "Tiff" and Bill moved at one point to the small town of Cannington, Ontario, into a farmhouse they named Stone Orchard. This generated another memoir type of book, ***From Stone Orchard: A Collection of Memories***, which is not just his articles about life on a nineteenth-century farm, but other writings as well. Christopher A. Bohjalian is another writer who set out to live a more rural life and wrote for the local newspaper. His pieces were published in

Idyll Banter: Weekly Excursions to a Very Small Town. One of Findley's ploys is to borrow characters from other books to people his own. For example, the narrator of ***Famous Last Words: A Novel*** is Ezra Pound's character Hugh Selwyn Mauberley, from Pound's poem of the same name. Lin Haire-Sargeant does this and adds a little fillip; in *H.—: **The Story of Heathcliff's Journey Back to Wuthering Heights***, she uses not only the character from ***Wuthering Heights***, but also its author, Emily Brontë. Perhaps because of his acting experience, Findley's nonfiction writing is both dramatic and exuberant, much like the storytelling of Bella Bathurst in her biography of Robert Louis Stevenson's family, ***The Lighthouse Stevensons: The Extraordinary Story of the Building of the Scottish Lighthouses by the Ancestors of Robert Louis Stevenson.***

Franzen, Jonathan (1959–)

The Discomfort Zone: A Personal History. Picador, 2007, 2006. 195pp. 9780374299194. Also available in large print, audiobook (read by the author), and e-audiobook. 813.54

Much of the material in this collection of six essays had been previously published in *The New Yorker*, but Jonathan Franzen has pulled it all together to create an anecdotal memoir. Although each of the six essays has a central theme, throughout the book Franzen is taking a close and honest look at himself through the prism of each of these themes. In talking about the death of his mother and the resulting need to sell his childhood home, he reflects back on specific memories brought on by items throughout the house. Another essay revolves around his fascination with Charles Schulz's comic strip ***Peanuts*** and his preference for Snoopy. He ranges from his childhood through his adolescence, often unsuccessfully trying to belong, carrying out pranks, and getting involved with a counterculture group, to his failing marriage and his newfound fascination with birding.

Subjects: 1970s; 1980s; Adolescence; Death of a Parent; Marriage; Novelists; Personal Essays; Schulz, Charles

Now Try: The acuity with which Franzen can zero in on details is a trait of Adam Haslett in his short-story collection, ***You Are Not a Stranger Here.*** Franzen felt that he shared a number of common bonds with Charles Schulz; you may be interested in reading more about that cartoonist, to see for yourself where the similarities lie. A highly acclaimed biography by David Michaelis is simply titled ***Schulz and Peanuts: A Biography.*** In his book Franzen focuses heavily on the image of the nerd, which is how he saw himself as a teenager. Benjamin Nugent takes a close look at nerds in ***American Nerd: The Story of My People.***

Harris, E. Lynn (1955–2009)

What Becomes of the Brokenhearted: A Memoir. Anchor Books, 2004, 2003. 266pp. 9780385495066. Also available in large print, audiobook, e-audiobook, and e-book. 813.54

Lynn Harris sets out to tell his readers what can become of the brokenhearted, as that was how he grew up in Arkansas: beaten regularly by his stepfather (believed by Harris to be his father); feeling out of place and unworthy because of his homosexual feelings; and unsuccessful in finding someone to love him. Despite a successful undergraduate career he was jobless; homeless; bereft of many friends, who had died of AIDS; and suicidal. When a friend suggested he try to write something about how he was feeling, Harris wrote his first novel, which he then self-published. With the therapeutic nature of that exercise, along with his success as a novelist and his discovering God, he was able finally to find some happiness of his own. Knowing that many African-American gay men actually get married and have gay liaisons on the side, Harris believed that the African-American community should be honest about the homosexuals in their midst to avoid this practice, and that was what he tried to do with his novels. He began a genre of African-American fiction that speaks not only to African-American men but also to all readers, encouraging both honesty to oneself and self-acceptance. A particular irony of his title is that he died of heart failure when he was fifty-four.

Subjects: Abuse (Parental); African-American Men; Arkansas; Bisexuals; Gay Men; Loneliness; Novelists; Self-Acceptance

Now Try: Kenji Yoshino, a Japanese-American gay man, wrote his memoir, ***Covering: The Hidden Assault on Our Civil Rights,*** as a call for all to allow individuals the ability to express themselves and reveal their true identities. The commentator Keith Boykin takes on in nonfiction what Harris was trying to illustrate in his fiction: ***Beyond the Down Low: Sex, Lies, and Denial in Black America*** (with Harris writing the foreword to the book). The journalist John W. Fountain grew up in inner-city Chicago, but with the guidance of his grandparents, who opened a church there, True Vine, he found hope to make something of himself. He tells his story in ***True Vine: A Young Black Man's Journey of Faith, Hope, and Clarity.***

Hillerman, Tony (1925– 2008)

Seldom Disappointed: A Memoir. Perennial, 2002, 2001. 341pp. ill. photos. 9780060505868. Also available in large print, audiobook (read by the author), and e-audiobook. 813.54

Tony Hillerman's most satisfying award came from the Navajo people when they gave him the status of Special Friend of the Dineh in 1987. As a child growing up in Oklahoma, he had attended St. Mary's Academy, a local school for girls, populated largely by children in the Potawatomi Nation. After he'd returned home from World War II, Hillerman had witnessed a healing ceremony for two Navajo Marines. When he decided in the late sixties that he wanted to try his hand at writing fiction, he recalled that ceremony and felt it important to write about Navajo peoples and their traditions, to teach non-Navajo the truth about Navajo cultures. His first novel, ***The Blessing Way,*** was published in 1970, the first also in his **Joe Leaphorn and Jim Chee Mysteries** series featuring Navajo tribal policemen; its success was such that he was then able to leave his career as a journalist to devote his time to writing. His mother had a saying: "Blessed are those who expect little, for they are seldom disappointed." Hillerman turned that around to say that he was seldom disappointed because he always had good things happen to him; with that phrase the reader can appreciate the positive spirit in Hillerman's memoir.

Seldom Disappointed was awarded the Anthony Award for Nonfiction and the Agatha Award for Best Nonfiction.

Subjects: American Indians; American Southwest; Journalists; Mothers and Sons; Mystery Writers; Navajo Nation; Octogenarians; Oklahoma; Potawatomi Nation; World War II (1939-1945)

Now Try: In addition to his many novels, Hillerman has also written a guide to his favorite part of the country, accompanied by photographs taken by his brother Barney: ***Hillerman Country: A Journey Through the Southwest with Tony Hillerman***. One of the most notable aspects of Hillerman's writing is his evocation of place; the same can be said of Charles Frazier, whose "place" in ***Thirteen Moons: A Novel*** is the Smoky Mountains. Another writer who has a deep love for the Southwest is Ellen Meloy, who writes about that region in ***The Anthropology of Turquoise: Meditations on Landscape, Art, and Spirit***. Readers who would like to immerse themselves further in the Navajo world may enjoy the **Ella Clah Mysteries** by Aimée and David Thurlo, the first of which is ***Blackening Song***.

James, P. D. (1920–)

Time to Be in Earnest: A Fragment of Autobiography. Knopf, 2000, 1999. 269pp. 9780375410666. Also available in large print, audiobook, and e-book. 823.914

Taking to heart Samuel Johnson's dictum that it is "time to be in earnest" when one is seventy-seven, P. D. James decided at that point to keep a diary for one year, not so much to write down what she had for breakfast, but more to record the goings-on in her life and to see what anecdotes in her memory such events would recall. She chose to gloss over the difficulties, such as her husband's postwar mental illness, which gave her the role as family breadwinner. To her credit, after having had to leave school at the age of sixteen because of her family's financial woes, James created an admirable career path, advancing from hospital clerk to hospital administrator in charge of five psychiatric hospitals. While working with the hospitals she began to write fiction and published her first novel, ***Cover Her Face***, when she was in her early forties. She then became a manager in the criminal policy department of the British Home Office, whence she developed the knowledge required for her crime fiction. In her autobiography, she talks not only about her life, but also about her writing, her views on it, and her processes, and she includes a paper she gave on Jane Austen—her view of ***Emma*** as a detective novel.

Among James's many honors are the Grand Master Award for lifetime achievement from the Mystery Writers of America, the Order of the British Empire, and a seat in the House of Lords (Baroness James of Holland Park).

Subjects: Austen, Jane; Diaries; England; Mystery Writers, England; Nonagenarians

Now Try: A fun book to pick up, to find out the provenance of James's character Adam Dalgliesh, is André Bernard's ***Madame Bovary, C'est Moi!: The Great Characters of Literature and Where They Came From***. Before it closed its doors as an independent publisher, Scribner's was James's publisher. Charles Scribner Jr. has written the story of his tenure as publisher, ***In the Company of Writers: A Life in Publishing***, based on the oral history by Joel R. Gardner. If you'd like to read a crime writer similar to P. D. James who used to have almost the same cachet, you might enjoy Ngaio Marsh's **Roderick Alleyn Series**, the first one entitled ***A Man Lay Dead***.

Jong, Erica (1942–)

Fear of Fifty: A Midlife Memoir. With a new Foreword. Jeremy P. Tarcher/Penguin, 2006, 1994. 329pp. ill. 9781585425242. Also available in large print, audiobook (read by the author), e-audiobook, and e-book. 813.54

Erica Jong was an English professor and poet before her startling novel ***Fear of Flying; A Novel*** was published in 1973. That novel, coming as it did during the sexual revolution, made Jong's name a household word, both for its sexual explicitness and daring and for its call to women to admit to and allow their own sexuality. She wrote several more novels, some of which continued with Isadora Wing, the character in ***Fear of Flying***. It's hard not to think of her fiction as somewhat autobiographical, because Jong herself believed in sexual freedom and has married several times. ***Fear of Fifty*** begins with Jong's fiftieth birthday and removes the veil of fiction from her life story. It really is a coming-of-age story, as she offers vignettes of her marriages, her love affairs, her writing career and its celebrity, her motherhood, and her family relationships, all through the prism of gender roles and feminism as they have changed over her first fifty years.

Subjects: Aging; Family Relationships; Feminists; Gender Roles; Love Affairs; Marriage; Novelists; Poets; Sexuality; Single Mothers

Now Try: In her sixties Jong wrote another memoir, ***Seducing the Demon: Writing for My Life***, in which she adds more autobiographical details and muses on specific women poets who took their own lives. She also discusses how important writing is to her mental health. Before Erica Jong was Helen Gurley Brown, with her nonfiction work ***Sex and the Single Girl***, originally published in 1962 and recently re-released, offering women the notion that being single need not be a blight. Not surprisingly, Jong has contributed an essay to Jeffrey Escoffier's collection, ***Sexual Revolution***, with photographs by Fred W. McDarrah. Taking Jong's call for sexual freedom and openness one step further, Eve Ensler has put out a call to women to be more open about their bodies. She does this in tandem with raising awareness of violence against women, in her play ***The Vagina Monologues***. Jane Juska demonstrates how women in their later years not only have an interest in sex, but don't mind making it known, as she does in ***Unaccompanied Women: Late-Life Adventures in Love, Sex, and Real Estate***.

King, Stephen (1947–)

On Writing: A Memoir of the Craft. Scribner, 2010, 2000. 291pp. 9781439156810. Also available in large print, audiobook (read by the author), e-audiobook, and e-book. 813.54

In this book Stephen King sandwiches his thoughts on writing between two sections of memoir. In the first section we read about his childhood poverty, his misbehaving-but-always-writing youth, his university education on scholarship, his early jobs as a laborer in an industrial laundry and as an English teacher, and his success with the paperback edition of ***Carrie***, its best-seller status allowing him to write full-time. His section on writing is in the same conversational and blunt style as his memoir sections. King talks about the writer's toolbox, which includes the development of language through both reading and writing, but also includes real tools such as William Strunk and E. B. White's ***The Elements of Style***. (This tenth-anniversary edition of ***On Writing*** includes an updated reading list.) The final section is the story of his horrific accident, when he was hit by a car while he was out walking. The months of surgeries, physiotherapy, and pain led him to realize that if he couldn't write, he would be lost.

On Writing has won both the Bram Stoker Award for Nonfiction and the Locus Award for Best Nonfiction/Related/Reference Book.

Subjects: Accident Victims; Horror-Fiction Writers; King, Tabitha; Maine; Novelists; Short-Story Writers; Writing

Now Try: If you'd like to see Stephen King among his non-horror-writing colleagues, he is included in ***The Best American Essays, 2001***, edited by Kathleen Norris (series editor, Robert Atwan). Stan Wiater has collected a number of interviews with horror writers in ***Dark Dreamers: Conversations with the Masters of Horror***. Stephen King readers who want to find a new author who moves his story along in Stephen King style may want to read Scott Sigler's ***Infected: A Novel***. King's conversational tone can also be found in Michael Korda's ***Making the List: A Cultural History of the American Bestseller, 1900–1999***, a title that naturally includes Stephen King. A new biography of Stephen King has been written by Lisa Rogak: ***Haunted Heart: The Life and Times of Stephen King***.

L'Amour, Louis (1908–1988)

Education of a Wandering Man. Bantam, 2008, 1989. 232pp. ill. 16pp. of plates. 9780553057034. Also available in large print, Braille, and e-book. 813.52

Louis L'Amour's title nicely encapsulates his life. He left school at fifteen, believing that he could get a better education by traveling the world and reading the kind of books he'd already been devouring, than by sitting in the classroom. He subsequently published a collection of stories describing many of his adventures around the world, ***Yondering***. L'Amour was determined to be a writer and contributed to pulp magazines until they were no longer published. Hearing that Saul David, editorial director of Bantam Books, was in Los Angeles looking for a replacement for the deceased Luke Short, L'Amour made an appointment to see him, asked David to read a manuscript he'd brought along (***Hondo***), and signed a long-term contract on the spot. L'Amour had very definite ideas about his audience (the working people), his style (the action would start on the first page), and his objective (to share the notion of frontier with his audience). Those ideas obviously paid off, as Bantam distributes more than ten million of his books each year.

L'Amour was awarded both the Presidential Medal of Freedom by President Reagan (a fan) in 1984 and the Congressional Gold Medal, the first novelist ever to garner both awards.

Subjects: Firsts; Novelists; Octogenarians; Short-Story Writers; Travel; Western Writers

Now Try: L'Amour himself felt that his later work was finally at its peak, so that if you are new to his writing, you may want to begin with ***The Haunted Mesa,*** although others may suggest the **Sackett** series, the first of which is ***Sackett's Land***. And if you've read all of L'Amour, you might like to try a similar writer, Stephen Bly, whose **Code of the West Series** begins with ***It's Your Misfortune and None of My Own***. L'Amour wrote beyond the Western lands, however, as seen in a collection by Stephen Coonts, ***On Glorious Wings: The Best Flying Stories of the Century***. If you'd like a picture of L'Amour's Western world, you might want to pick up Bruce Wexler's ***The Wild, Wild West of Louis L'Amour: The Illustrated Guide to Cowboys, Indians, Gunslingers, Outlaws and Texas Rangers***. Dee Alexander Brown has gathered a collection of frontier stories, but it focuses on the humor people found in their frontier escapades: ***Wondrous Times on the Frontier***.

Lessing, Doris May (1919–)

Walking in the Shade: Volume Two of My Autobiography, 1949–1962. Harper Perennial, 1998, 1997. 404pp. ill. 9780060929565. Also available in e-book. 823.914

Novelist, essayist, short-story writer, polemicist, former Communist, feminist, science-fiction writer, and Nobel Prize laureate are all labels one can assign to Doris May Lessing. She has written two major volumes of autobiography, the first of which is ***Under My Skin: My Autobiography to 1949,*** which takes her up to 1949, when she arrived in London with a manuscript in one hand and a child from her second marriage in the other (she was thirty and was leaving behind her two children from her first marriage). ***Walking in the Shade*** takes her to the year (1962) in which her groundbreaking feminist novel, ***The Golden Notebook,*** was published. In this, her second volume of memoir, Lessing pits the responsibilities of her public life—single mother, lover, friend, member of the Communist Party—against her need for solitude and isolation in order to write. She also looks back at herself as she matures and often recoils in horror at what she perceives as a younger Doris Lessing, a reflection that illustrates the honesty with which she approaches her autobiography.

Doris Lessing is the recipient of a Nobel Prize in Literature.

Subjects: Communism; England; Feminists; Mothers and Daughters; Nobel Prize Laureates; Nonagenarians; Novelists, England; Single Mothers; Social History, England; Zimbabwe

1 2 3 4 5 6 7 8

Now Try: Lessing's final book (she says) is ***Alfred and Emily***, a two-part work about her parents: the first part is an imaginary story of what their lives and the world might have been like if World War I had not occurred, and the second part is a biography of them and their relationship. A young South African novelist, Pamela Gien, who may be following in Lessing's footsteps, has written a debut novel, ***The Syringa Tree: A Novel***, with many of the same perceptions that Lessing has revealed. One of the trademarks of Lessing's writing is her brutal honesty. Theodore Dreiser was so brutally honest in his autobiography that he delayed the publication of the first volume, ***Dawn: An Autobiography of Early Youth***, edited by T. D. Nostwich, for fifteen years to protect his family. Edna O'Brien shares with Lessing the theme of the trapped woman; her ***August Is a Wicked Month, a Novel*** is a good exemplar of that.

McMurtry, Larry (1936–)

Walter Benjamin at the Dairy Queen: Reflections at Sixty and Beyond. Simon & Schuster, 2001, 1999. 204pp. ill. 9780684870199. Also available in large print, audiobook (read by the author), and e-book. 813.54

Walter Benjamin was an early twentieth-century literary critic whose essay, "The Storyteller: Observations on the Works of Nikolai Leskov," Larry McMurtry happened to be reading in his local Dairy Queen in Archer City, Texas. The essay got McMurtry to thinking, and the cited title is the result. In this book he has written a collection of essays, some autobiographical and some on writers and his reflections on them and on writing in general. He focuses primarily both on place and how it relates to him and on literature and his relationship with that. Place for him is West Texas, where his grandparents settled as pioneers and his parents continued the family practice of ranching. McMurtry broke that tradition by moving into the world of literature, which he discusses at various points throughout his book. He manages to meld the two worlds by bringing his love of books and storytelling (a lost art, according to him) to his small town of Archer City, Texas, in the form of his antiquarian book collection and bookstore.

Subjects: Archer City, TX; Books and Reading; Booksellers; McMurtry Family; Novelists; Personal Essays; Reflections; Screenwriters; South Pacific; Texas; Travel

Now Try: Since writing this set of reflections, McMurtry set out to write what he refers to as a memoir trilogy, despite other memoirs he has written about specific activities. The first of the three is ***Books: A Memoir***; following that is ***Literary Life: A Second Memoir***; and recently released is ***Hollywood: A Third Memoir***. McMurtry has won Academy Awards for his screenplays and screenplay adaptations, most notably for the adaptation (coauthored by longtime friend Diana Ossana) of Annie Proulx's short story, "Brokeback Mountain." These three writers collaborated on a story about the making of the movie, ***"Brokeback Mountain": Story to Screenplay***. Jim Black has written quite a different story set in Archer City, ***River Season***, a coming-of-age story in which a Black man becomes a father figure for a young fatherless White boy. Writers such as Wallace Stegner have contributed to a collection of memories in ***Growing Up Western: Recollections***, by Dee Alexander Brown et al. and edited by Clarus Backes, with McMurtry writing the foreword. One of McMurtry's great writing strengths is his evocation of place. Elizabeth Hay has the same talent, as she portrays Western Canada in ***A Student of Weather***.

Mowat, Farley (1921–)

Otherwise. Emblem, 2009, 2008. 351pp. 9780771064906. 819.5409

In 1992 Farley Mowat said, referring to his just-published memoir, ***My Father's Son: Memories of War and Peace,*** " 'This is part of my autobiography, which I've been writing in bits and pieces. I've been doing it all my life. I write about what I know best' " (Shepstone, 1992). So many of Mowat's books are autobiographical, set in such places as the Arctic; Siberia; Saint-Pierre et Miquelon, France; and southern Ontario; and about such varied topics as wolves; war; birds; the Inuit; his father, Angus; cruise missiles; and his wife, Claire. He lived in those places and discovered his passions, which led to the experiences he writes about. He is an impassioned conservationist who has ruffled many feathers. There are times Mowat doesn't let facts get in the way of his story, but there is no denying the truth of his convictions about what humankind is doing to the environment and its peoples. This final memoir is his real coming-of-age story (1937–1948), when he describes his unfettered time as a youth commingling with the wildlife in his local environment and leaving that innocent world for the war in Italy, an event that made him lose faith in humanity and soured him for the conventional world he returned to. Accepting a job with a scientific expedition to the Barrenlands (Northwest Territories), he found his life's vocation there.

Mowat was awarded the Order of Canada in 1981.

Subjects: Arctic Regions; Canada; Children's Writers, Canada; Conservationists; Environmental Activists; Fathers and Sons; Mowat, Claire; Newfoundland; Nonagenarians; World War II (1939-1945); Writers, Canada

Now Try: Because none of Mowat's memoirs is a linear chronology of his whole life, you may want to read James King's authorized biography, ***Farley: The Life of Farley Mowat.*** Farley's wife Claire also wrote their story in ***Travels with Farley.*** Mowat's name has often been linked with Paul Watson, an early member of Greenpeace and founder of the Sea Shepherd Conservation Society. Peter Heller tells the story of one of Sea Shepherd's conservation efforts in ***The Whale Warriors: The Battle at the Bottom of the World to Save the Planet's Largest Mammals.*** If you like Mowat's writing about wolves, you may want to read Jiang Rong's ***Wolf Totem: A Novel,*** set in the Mongolian steppes (translated by Howard Goldblatt). James A. Houston, another Canadian who shares many themes with Mowat, has written more than one memoir as well, one of them being ***Confessions of an Igloo Dweller.***

Roth, Philip (1933–)

The Facts: A Novelist's Autobiography. Vintage, 1997, 1988. 195pp. 978067974-9059. Also available in audiobook, e-audiobook, and e-book. 813.54

Philip Roth adds a twist to this unconventional autobiography. He includes his fictional alter ego, Nathan Zuckerman, in this book—in fact, he asks Zuckerman to read and comment on it. Zuckerman's critique is an integral part of the book. Apart from that, however, it is an actual memoir, recounting anecdotes from various parts of Roth's life. He talks about growing up Jewish in Newark, New Jersey, and his college days at Bucknell. He met Margaret Martinson, his first wife, while teaching at the University of Chicago. He also talks about his early writing life and the controversies his writing has stirred up, particularly in the Jewish community. Roth takes the reader up to the publication of ***Portnoy's Complaint***, thus including his life in the 1960s. Given Roth's reputation as a writer, it is no wonder that he should discuss the essence of memoir as he is writing one, nor that he should "review" the work in the guise of Nathan Zuckerman.

Among his many awards Roth received the Gold Medal in Fiction by the American Academy of Arts and Letters and the National Medal of Arts.

Subjects: 1960s; Jewish Men; New Jersey; Newark, NJ; Novelists; Writing; Zuckerman, Nathan

Now Try: Edmund White is another novelist who writes autobiographical fiction and who has written a memoir as well, entitled ***My Lives***. John Barth's so-called memoir is actually a novel, ***Once upon a Time: A Floating Opera***. Readers who enjoy Roth's memories of growing up Jewish may enjoy the collection by Alan King and friends, ***Matzo Balls for Breakfast: And Other Memories of Growing Up Jewish***.

Schwartz, Lynne Sharon (1939–)

Ruined by Reading: A Life in Books. Beacon Press, 1996. 119pp. 9780807070826. Also available in e-book. 813.54

Lynne Schwartz heard a Chinese scholar say that one shouldn't read books, in order to keep the mind free from outside influences, causing her to write this memoir of her life with books. She would admit that books are an outside influence, but a very important one, helping to form a sense of self and to shape one's perception of one's world. An early reader, Schwartz had the advantage of having a library in her home in Brooklyn to explore. She was free to pick whatever she wanted, leading to an eclectic mix of the Grimm brothers' fairy tales, ***Heidi*** by Johanna Spyri, and Edgar Allan Poe's writings. The memoir is more of an essay than a chronological narrative, with the author using specific books and memories as touchstones for her thoughts on reading—how one chooses, where one reads, attitudes to the physical object. Schwartz focuses largely on her childhood and her teens, but she does take the reader up to the point of her first success as a novelist.

Subjects: Books and Reading; Brooklyn (New York, NY); Childhood and Youth; Novelists

Now Try: The author who immediately comes to mind here is Anne Fadiman, whose charming collection of essays on reading, ***Ex Libris: Confessions of a Common Reader***, would resonate with readers of this memoir. Schwartz said that the most important book from her childhood was Frances Hodgson Burnett's ***A Little Princess***, for substantiating her own thought that the life within was as valid as the life without. Betsy Hearne and Roberta Seelinger Trites have collected a variety of stories like that in *A Narrative Compass: Stories That Guide Women's Lives*. Barbara Feinberg offers an interesting corollary to what Schwartz is saying, decrying some of the books children are encouraged (or forced) to read and pointing out the flaws in today's elementary school curriculum vis-à-vis reading and writing. She would prefer a more imaginative and creative approach, as evidenced by her title, ***Welcome to Lizard Motel: Children, Stories, and the Mystery of Making Things Up; A Memoir***. Lynne Schwartz has followed up her reading memoir with a travel memoir, in which she also harks back to her Brooklyn days: ***Not Now, Voyager***.

Twain, Mark (1835–1910)
Smith, Harriet Elinor, et al., eds.

Autobiography of Mark Twain. Volume I. University of California Press, 2010. 736pp. ill. 16pp. of plates. 9780520267190. Also available in audiobook and e-book. 818.409

Mark Twain had instructed that his autobiography not be published for 100 years after his death, but that didn't stop publishers from issuing various versions of his life story as he had written it. He had originally released twenty-five chapters of an autobiography for the *North American Review*, and in 1924 Albert Bigelow Paine had those chapters published in two volumes under the title ***Mark Twain's Autobiography***. With the centenary of Twain's death in 2010, the University of Wisconsin Press released ***Mark Twain's Own Autobiography: The Chapters from the "North American Review"***. Following that release, however, came the work that the Mark Twain Project, out of the University of California (http://www.marktwainproject.org), has issued, the one annotated here. Twain decided just six years before he died to try an entirely new system for his autobiography, almost conversing with his stenographer and his secretary each day about whatever came into his head as they took notes. He was experimenting with a form of stream-of-consciousness style along with free association. This volume offers his edited dictations over a period of three months, along with biographies of his family members and some of the speeches he gave. It also provides manuscripts and dictations from the years 1870–1905. The actual autobiography doesn't start until page 201, but it is an enlightening picture of the man. The book is available online at the Mark Twain Project.

Subjects: 19th Century; Classics; Family Relationships; Journalists; Lecturers; Mark Twain Project; Mississippi River; Novelists; Social Commentary; Travel

Now Try: There have been several biographies written about Twain, but one of the most recent ones, ***Mark Twain: A Life***, by Pulitzer Prize–winning author Ron Powers, has been getting a lot of critical attention for its depiction of Mark Twain as a real person and as not only a product of his time, but also a chronicler of his time. One of Twain's good friends was the writer William Dean Howells; one of Howells's most popular novels is ***The Rise of Silas Lapham***. Twain's heritage is Scots-Irish, and he is included in novelist James H. Webb's first foray into nonfiction, ***Born Fighting: How the Scots-Irish Shaped America***. Another good friend of Twain's was the influential Henry Ward Beecher. You can read his story in Debby Applegate's Pulitzer Prize–winning ***The Most Famous Man in America: The Biography of Henry Ward Beecher***.

Updike, John (1932–2009)

Self-Consciousness: Memoirs. Knopf, 1998, 1989. 257pp. 9780394572222. 813.54

A collection of six essays, this is John Updike's reflections on various aspects of his life that have formed him. He initially decided to write them in protest against a would-be biographer. His title has a double meaning: there are woes he has suffered (psoriasis, asthma, stuttering) that have made him very self-conscious, but he is also a self-conscious writer. He is aware of himself as loving the "middle," so that his novels are primarily about middle-class people and situations. Given Updike's world renown, he is not perceived by others as middle class, yet he pursues middle-class activities in his way of life: participation in the community—on the spiritual level and on the civic level—learning to play golf, living in a small town, having four children with his first wife, Mary. He has created a representative of this middle class in Harold "Rabbit" Angstrom, featured in four novels, which have been collected into ***Rabbit Angstrom: A Tetralogy***. (He won the National Book Award, the Pulitzer Prize for Fiction, and the American Book Award for ***Rabbit Is Rich***.)

Besides all his literary awards, Updike was also inducted into the Academy of Achievement and awarded the National Medal of Arts.

Subjects: Asthma; Childhood and Youth; Family Relationships; Middle Class; Novelists; Pennsylvania; Personal Essays; Psoriasis; Reflections; Stuttering; Vietnam War (1961–1975)

Now Try: When he was inducted into the Academy of Achievement, Updike offered as his recommended read T. S. Eliot's ***The Waste Land***. Returning to the United States after a stay in England, Updike procured a job at *The New Yorker*, writing for the column, "Talk of the Town." David Remnick has collected a number of essays written by *The New Yorker* writers, including Updike: ***Life Stories: Profiles from "The New Yorker"***. Richard Yates also wrote a novel of a middle-class couple resembling Updike's fictional lives: ***Revolutionary Road***, made into a movie of the same name. Updike created fictional towns along with his fictional characters, one of which is Olinger, PA. Wendell Berry did the same thing, but his **Port William** stories are set in Kentucky. The first in that series is ***Nathan Coulter***. If you'd like to sample Updike's short-story writing and others of its quality, you might like ***50 Great American Short Stories***, edited by Milton Crane.

Vidal, Gore (1925–)

Palimpsest: A Memoir. Penguin, 1996, 1995. 435pp. ill. 32pp. of plates. 9780140260892. Also available in e-book. 818.5409

Palimpsest covers the years of Gore Vidal's life up to 1964, and his second memoir, ***Point to Point Navigation: A Memoir, 1964 to 2006***, brings his life pretty much up-to-date. As the reviewer in *Publishers Weekly* so aptly put it, "readers' reactions [to the memoirs] will be determined by how they already feel about him" (2006). There seem to be two camps of readers of Vidal's memoirs: those who see them as self-serving efforts to seek revenge on enemies, disseminating nasty gossip, and those who tolerate or excuse the sarcasm, seeing it as wit and trenchant observation. For those who respect Vidal's significant output of political and cultural writings—whether as fiction, essay, screenplay, or prose—his memoirs are a welcome overview of a life lived among the rich and famous. For those who are on the other side of the fence, his memoirs are backbiting and unfortunate. Perhaps when all is said and done, however, Vidal will be most noted for his historical and political writing, as politics runs through both his fiction and his nonfiction.

Vidal won a National Book Award for Nonfiction for ***United States: Essays: 1952–1992***, and he was inducted into the Academy of Achievement in 2006.

Subjects: Austen, Howard; Essayists; Gay Men; Mothers and Sons; Novelists; Octogenarians; Politics; Screenwriters; Social History, United States; Trimble, Jim

Now Try: Before ***Palimpsest***, Vidal had written a memoir of his early years, ***Screening History***, set primarily in Hollywood (where he was briefly engaged to Joanne Woodward). Fred Kaplan had access to much of Vidal's materials and had free editorial rein in writing ***Gore Vidal: A Biography***. Vidal's only complaints about the biography seemed to be that it was dull and had too much sex in it. For another writer whose elegant prose is tinged with searing candor, you may want to try composer Ned Rorem's diaries, the first one being ***The Paris Diary of Ned Rorem***. Noël Coward traveled in similar circles to Vidal. Graham Payn and Sheridan Morley have edited his diaries: ***The Noël Coward Diaries***. Dominick Dunne wittily portrays New York society in his novel, ***Too Much Money: A Novel***.

Vonnegut, Kurt (1922–2007)
Simon, Daniel, ed.

A Man Without a Country. Random House Trade Paperbacks, 2007, 2005. 145pp. ill. 9780812977363. Also available in audiobook and e-audiobook. 813.54

All of Kurt Vonnegut's autobiographical writing is set up as a collage, and there are repetitions in all three books. The first is ***Palm Sunday: An Autobiographical Collage***, and the second is ***Fates Worse Than Death: An Autobiographical Collage of the 1980s***. Reading his "collages" is like listening to an old, curmudgeonly storyteller sitting around the cracker barrel and telling his tales, with digressions and editorial comments thrown in. This third collage, however, does contain new material, lamenting the government of George W. Bush. But Vonnegut's was not an ordinary life, and perhaps some of the tales bear repeating. One of the most formative events in his life was being a POW in Germany, housed at night in the basement of a slaughterhouse in Dresden and thereby spared during the bombing raids on Dresden. This event (for which he won the Purple Heart) was the provenance of one of his best-loved novels, ***Slaughterhouse-Five; or, the Children's Crusade, a Duty-Dance with Death***. A victim of hereditary depression, in the 1980s Vonnegut tried to commit suicide. His death, when it did come, was from a brain injury due to a fall.

Subjects: Bush, George W.; Essayists; Humanists; Novelists; Octogenarians; Politics; War; World War II (1939–1945)

Now Try: The novelist Günter Grass also spent the war years in Germany, but fighting on the German side. In a translation by Michael Henry Heim, Grass recounts his boyhood and his time as a member of the Waffen-SS in ***Peeling the Onion***. Mark Dunn adopts Vonnegut's tone about the encroaching powers of government in his novel ***Ella Minnow Pea: A Progressively Lipogrammatic Epistolary Fable***. And Barbara Ehrenreich carries Vonnegut's views into the twenty-first century in ***This Land Is Their Land: Reports from a Divided Nation***.

Wright, Eric (1929–)

Always Give a Penny to a Blind Man: A Memoir. Key Porter Books, 1999. 216pp. 9781552630679. Also available in large print. 819.354

Almost two-thirds of this memoir deals with Eric Wright's life in England before he emigrated to Canada. He grew up in working-class London during the Great Depression and World War II, and the privations of that life turned him into a socialist. He was the ninth of ten children and grew up sharing a bed with several others and living hand-to-mouth. Apart from the poverty, what sorely rankled with Wright was the lack of encouragement for anything educational. His mother didn't trust education, and most teachers, with the exception of the one who encouraged him to try for a scholarship to a grammar school, couldn't be bothered with him. He departed for Canada in 1951, and the leave-taking with his parents was illustrative of the lack of warmth in which he grew up. The last few chapters in the book relate his early days as an immigrant in Canada, working in the north and getting a university degree. Those who are familiar with Wright's fictional protagonist, the policeman Charlie Salter, will recognize in him Wright's own background.

Subjects: Depression (Economic); England; London, England; Mystery Writers, Canada; Octogenarians; Poverty, England; Social History, England; Working-Class Families

Now Try: If you're not familiar with Wright's police procedurals, you might enjoy his award-winning **Inspector Charlie Salter** series, the first one being ***The Night the Gods Smiled: Introducing Inspector Charlie Salter***. Wright's lucid prose style can also be found in Mark Salzman's story of conducting writing workshops with young inmates in Los Angeles, ***True Notebooks***. Raymond Briggs is an author who also comes from a British working-class background. Instead of writing his own story, he has written a graphic novel about his parents, ***Ethel & Ernest***. Wright's mother was all about respectability, and Alan Bennett's (in working-class Leeds, rather than London) was all about not being pretentious. Bennett recalls his parents and his upbringing in ***Untold Stories***.

Consider Starting With . . .

Adams, Ansel. *Ansel Adams, an Autobiography*

Angelou, Maya. *I Know Why the Caged Bird Sings*

Clark, Mary Higgins. *Kitchen Privileges: A Memoir*

Duncan, Isadora. *My Life*

Hillerman, Tony. *Seldom Disappointed: A Memoir*

King, Stephen. *On Writing: A Memoir of the Craft*

Sedaris, David. *Dress Your Family in Corduroy and Denim*

Solti, Georg. *Memoirs*

Tallchief, Maria. *Maria Tallchief: America's Prima Ballerina*

Twain, Mark. *Autobiography of Mark Twain, Volume I*

Fiction Read-Alikes

Chevalier, Tracy. *The Lady and the Unicorn* is not just about the artist who created The Lady and the Unicorn Tapestries, but also about the man who commissioned them and his wife's desire to add to the original design.

Godden, Rumer. *Pippa Passes*. An English ballerina visiting Venice falls in love with an Italian gondolier.

Hellenga, Robert. *The Sixteen Pleasures* is the story of a woman who writes a screenplay based on her earlier discovery of a piece of Renaissance erotica.

Pears, Iain. *The Dream of Scipio*. A manuscript written in the fifth century is discovered by a poet in the fourteenth century and then rediscovered in the twentieth century by a classical scholar involved with a painter.

Ridley, John. *A Conversation with the Mann*. During the days of the civil rights movement; Jackie Mann is determined to become a successful stand-up comic.

Salzman, Mark. *The Soloist*. A child prodigy with the cello, Reinhart Sundheimer has lost the magic of music until he is asked to teach another child prodigy, a young Korean boy.

Seth, Vikram. *An Equal Music.* A violinist in a chamber group meets up with his lost love, a classical pianist, in Vienna.

Tremain, Rose. *Music & Silence.* Peter Claire is the court lutanist for the king in seventeenth-century Denmark.

Vreeland, Susan. *Luncheon of the Boating Party* is the story of Pierre Renoir and his friends, who are the subject of Renoir's famous painting of the same name.

Weber, Katharine. *The Little Women* is a modernistic, twentieth-century tale of the three remaining March sisters and their reaction to a modern situation, an unfaithful mother.

Works Cited

Atwood, Margaret. 2005. "On First Reading Gabrielle Roy." *Revista Mexicana de Estudios Canadienses (nueva época)* (diciembre). Accessed December 7, 2010. http://redalyc.uaemex.mx/pdf/739/73901002.pdf.

Davis, J. Madison, ed. 1989. *Conversations with Robertson Davies.* Jackson: University Press of Mississippi.

Menand, Louis. 2005. "Missionary; Edmund Wilson and American Culture." A Critic at Large, *The New Yorker,* August 8. Accessed December 7, 2010. http://www.newyorker.com/archive/2005/08/08/050808crat_atlarge.

Publishers Weekly. 2006. Review of *Point to Point Navigation: A Memoir, 1964–2006. Book Index with Reviews,* April 9. *EBSCOhost.* Accessed March 10, 2009.

Shepstone, Joe. 1992. "Farley Mowat: On Writing Fiction, Non-fiction & Autobiography." *cm archive* (November). Accessed March 4, 2009. http://www.umanitoba.ca/cm/cmarchive/vol20no6/farleymowat.html.

Chapter 4

The Working Life

Description

How often have you asked a friend, or even a new acquaintance, what that person's workday looks like? If you have asked and the person has answered in full, have you not been amazed at what makes up that job, have you not learned how much more complex the job is than you would ever have thought, looking in from the outside? In this chapter you will get an inside view of a variety of jobs, professions, or occupations that you may have no access to otherwise. And you will find in most of these narratives that the job is not just a job; as the people interviewed by Studs Terkel said, it is important to find a meaning, even a calling, in that job. It's the only activity that people spend eight hours or more doing at one stretch, and if it has no meaning, if it is "too small for our spirit," the spirit will only shrink (Terkel, 1974). Not all of the people in this chapter came away happy from their jobs, but there was definitely enough in their daily routine and outcomes to warrant writing about it. One major omission from this chapter is a career in the military; that occupation is covered in Chapter 12, "Life at War."

Given the nature of memoirs, it could be said that many entries in this entire book are work-related. Certainly that is true of athletes, singers, actors, politicians, writers, etc. But as I explained in the Introduction, any number of these memoirs could be slotted into an assortment of categories. Those in this chapter are here because of the emphasis on work as a major theme in life and as a way of drawing together similar occupations. Though the occupations may be similar, there are enough differences among them to provide for some interesting and varied reading.

By the same token, paths do cross within the disciplines, and that will also be obvious in certain cases, as some people in this chapter overlap with each other—not an unexpected outcome when people share a profession in a similar time period. Many of their names will be well-known to you; others were well-known in their day but slipped into anonymity and are known now only by people of a certain age or with a presiding interest in that field. Their lives were of interest and of import, however, so it is good to have them here with the better-known names. And of course the hope is that the reader will find something of interest, particularly in the unknown memoirists.

> Working-life memoirs tell the stories of people whose lives have been spent working in a wide variety of disciplines: commercial, academic and communication-related, blue collar, sociological, and scientific. The writers focus on their work lives, providing insights for the reader into what that particular job actually looks like.

Appeal

Apart from character, which is the main appeal of all memoirs, the primary appeal in this chapter is the learning/experience factor. You, the reader, have the opportunity to visit corporations, computer labs, jungles, neuroscience labs, elementary schools, and universities; the opportunity to travel to Barbados, Burma, Australia, and the Antarctic; and the opportunity to learn how so many discoveries were made in a variety of disciplines. You will see what life is like in a nursing home, an office, a classroom, or a restaurant. The learning that may come out of your reading may be more than just understanding processes that you'd never thought of before. It may also help expand your own vocational horizons, leading to a better understanding of how to lead, how to conduct research, how to think outside the box and solve a hitherto insoluble problem.

Detail is another appeal factor that enhances the learning/experience appeal. In order for the reader to understand what the writer is working at, it is important that the memoirist include fine detail to clarify his or her environment and work. And of course the details will vary, depending on the nature of the work. The particulars in Esmé Raji Codell's teaching day will be quite different from those at William M. Bass's forensic farm.

Character is another appeal, as many of the memoirists here have found a niche in which to make a difference. How did they find their niches? What makes them able to pursue their dreams in the face of the setbacks they must have encountered? Many of these people have more courage than the average person, more perseverance, more intelligence, perhaps even more luck. A number of these people have also translated their successes into giving back, creating foundations or other organizations to help others.

Organization of This Chapter

The organization of this chapter is topical and somewhat arbitrary, but it begins, as all the chapters do, with some classic titles representing various career worlds. We then continue with the commercial world in a very broad sense: "Businesspeople," followed by "Foodies"—the food world being a business unto itself—and then followed by "Working-Class People." Book- and writing-related fields follow, namely, "Educators" and "Media Personalities." The "Crime Fighters" section includes lawyers, a profession that involves much reading and writing, but also includes some science, so that it bridges "Media Personalities" and "Scientists." The "Health Scientists" section follows "Scientists," being a subset of that field.

Classics

As with the classics in other chapters, this section includes people very well-known and some not so well-known, although the latter have also made their mark in their field. Lincoln Steffens was the first investigative journalist to effect societal changes through his work, and Jesse Stuart is studied in education classes and continues to inspire incoming and current teachers. The other three are much better known: Lee Iacocca is widely acclaimed in the automobile industry; Dian Fossey's work to save the gorillas continues, carried on by those who have come after; and Charles Darwin's ideas remain the subject of hot debate nationwide.

> The classic memoirists in this section have furthered knowledge or practices in their fields and for that have become legendary in those fields. Although not every reader will know Lincoln Steffens, for example, most journalists will know the man for whom the term "muckraking" was coined.

Darwin, Charles (1809–1882)

The Voyage of the **Beagle.** National Geographic, 2009, 1839. 459pp. ill. maps. 9781426203916. Also available in Braille, audiobook, e-audiobook, and e-book. 574.9

When Charles Darwin was offered the opportunity to travel as a naturalist on a scientific expedition with Captain Robert Fitzroy, he leapt at the chance. He spent five years on the H.M.S. *Beagle,* visiting countless areas in the Southern Hemisphere. Because he had a tendency to seasickness, he often traveled overland, meeting the ship at ports. This form of travel enabled him to further his research on land as well as in coastal and marine environments. It was near Bahía Blanca in Argentina that he found the bones of "numerous gigantic extinct Quadrupeds" (***Voyage,*** Chapter V), covered in seashells, which finally solidified his theory that creatures do mutate and evolve. Darwin completed the trip in 1836, having sent reports back to England throughout the voyage, which were then published in scientific and popular journals. But it was not until 1859 that he published his revolutionary ***On the Origin of Species,*** which has pitted evolutionists against creationists ever since.

Darwin was awarded the Royal Society's prestigious Copley Medal.

Subjects: 19th Century; *Beagle* Expedition (1831–1836); Botanists, England; Classics; Evolution; Explorers; Galápagos Islands, Ecuador; Geology; Scientists; Seafaring Life; South America; Travel; Zoologists, England

Now Try: If you'd like a biography of Darwin, from among the many available you may want to choose the very well-received title by David Quammen, ***The Reluctant Mr. Darwin: An Intimate Portrait of Charles Darwin and the Making of His Theory of Evolution***. Another man who made revolutionary changes in his lifetime was Abraham Lincoln, born on exactly the same day as Charles Darwin. Adam Gopnik has written a fascinating comparison of the two men and their effects on society, ***Angels and Ages: A Short Book About Darwin, Lincoln, and Modern Life***. Darwin's thoughts on birds are included in Graeme Gibson's beautifully illustrated ***The Bedside Book of Birds: An Avian Miscellany***. If you are interested in twentieth-century ramifications of Darwin's work, two completely different books may be relevant. Michael D'Orso looks at the ravages of human contact with the sensitive ecosystem of the Galápagos Islands in ***Plundering Paradise: The Hand of Man on the Galápagos Islands,*** and Edward Humes chronicles a recent debate in the Pennsylvania courts on evolution versus creationism (or intelligent design, as it's now called) in the schools in ***Monkey Girl: Evolution, Education, Religion, and the Battle for America's Soul***.

Fossey, Dian (1932–1985)

Gorillas in the Mist. Houghton Mifflin, 2000, 1983. 326pp. ill. 80pp. of plates. 9780395489284. Also available in Braille, e-book, and video. 599.88

The main purpose for Dian Fossey in writing this memoir was to alert the world to the plight of the dying mountain gorilla species in the hope of stemming the rampant plundering that she was constantly battling. Originally published in 1983, the book helped, but didn't have nearly the effect that her murder, two years later, did. With the help of Louis Leakey, Fossey had established the Karisoke Research Center in Rwanda, where she set about observing the mountain gorilla. Already decreasing in number, the species was under threat of extinction, largely from local poachers, and Fossey became increasingly bitter in her fight against these people. After her death and the establishment of the Dian Fossey Gorilla Fund International (http://gorillafund.org/, originally the Digit Fund), the Rwandans came to understand that they could make more money by saving the gorillas and charging people to visit the perimeter of the reserve, than they could ever make by killing and/or capturing them.

Gorillas in the Mist was selected as a Notable Book by the American Library Association.

Subjects: ALA Notable Books; Animal Conservation; Animal Rights Activists; Classics; Environmental Activists; Gorillas; Karisoke Research Center, Rwanda; Leakey, Louis; Murder; Primates; Primatologists; Rwanda; Virunga Mountains, Rwanda

Now Try: Nature writer Camilla de la Bédoyère, in conjunction with photographer Bob Campbell, used Fossey's letters to forge a biography in ***No One Loved Gorillas More: Dian Fossey; Letters from the Mist***. The people who helped the Rwandans see the economic benefit of preserving the gorillas were Bill Weber and Amy Vedder, a married couple who enlisted the Rwandans to help themselves turn this conflict around. They have told their story in ***In the Kingdom of Gorillas: Fragile Species in a Dangerous Land***. F. B. M. de Waal has written several books on animals, particularly primates. In ***The Ape and the Sushi Master: Cultural Reflections by a Primatologist*** he explains how much more similar humans and animals are than humans want to think. Biruté Marija Filomena Galdikas, one of the Louis Leakey "Trimates" (Seaman, 2005), wrote ***Great Ape Odyssey***, in which she explores in words, with photographs by Karl Ammann, the four species of apes.

Iacocca, Lee A. (1924–)
Novak, William (1948–), coauthor

Iacocca: An Autobiography. Bantam Books, 2007, 1984. 365pp. ill. 16pp. of plates. 9780553384970. Also available in large print, Braille, audiobook, and e-book. 338.7

First-generation American Lee Iacocca learned about hard work and entrepreneurship from his Italian-born father. He rose from a childhood in which his father lost all his money at the beginning of the Great Depression to a career, first as president of the Ford Motor Company and then as record-setting president and chief operating officer of the Chrysler Corporation. Already a folk hero for his rescue of Chrysler, Iacocca's autobiography only adds to that reputation, setting a sales record for hardcover creative nonfiction. His book is a combination of life story and business philosophy, describing not only what he did at Ford (e.g., creating the Ford Mustang) and at Chrysler, but also his theories about what works in business management and, by extension, in government.

Subjects: Automobile Industry; Businessmen; Chrysler Corporation; Classics; Executives; Ford Motor Company; Iacocca Foundation; Italian-Americans; Management; Octogenarians; Philanthropists; Record-Breakers

Now Try: Iacocca continues to talk about his life and offer new ideas about management in a subsequent book, ***Talking Straight***, written with the help of Sonny Kleinfield. Straight and hard-hitting talk characterizes his autobiography, as is also the case with ***Deluxe: How Luxury Lost Its Luster*** by Dana Thomas. Although cowritten with a journalist, ***Iacocca*** rings with Iacocca's voice, a narrative told in his own vernacular, often racy and colorful. Jimmy Breslin makes use of the vernacular as well in his collection of Mafia-related stories, ***The Good Rat: A True Story***. Iacocca does not mince words about his treatment at the hands of Henry Ford II, including his being fired from Ford; Sparky Lyle received similar treatment at the hands of the New York Yankees and is also very frank in his tale of his time with them, ***The Bronx Zoo***, written with the assistance of Peter Golenbock.

Steffens, Lincoln (1866–1936)

The Autobiography of Lincoln Steffens. Heyday Books, 2005, 1931. 882pp. ill. 9781597140164. Also available in e-book. 070.92

After traveling and studying in Europe, Lincoln Steffens arrived back in New York with no particular career in mind, but managed to secure a position with the *New-York Evening Post*. Gradually, by trial and error and sometimes a little luck in being pointed in the right direction, he developed his own theories about what a reporter should be doing and what journalism should look like. He investigated corruption in municipalities and in the police force, and at one point he turned his eye on the state of New Jersey. Theodore Roosevelt coined the term "muckraker" expressly because of the work that Lincoln Steffens did as a journalist. Steffens believed that a journalist should understand both sides of an issue, to find the causes of the problem and then try to negotiate a settlement with both sides. He brokered an agreement between the United States and Mexico to prevent a war between them, but he was not successful in a dreadful labor dispute in California when one side broke faith. Disillusioned, he looked to Russia and began to feel that perhaps revolution really was the only way to go.

Subjects: Anticorruption Activists; California; Classics; Journalism; Journalists; Mexico; Muckrakers; New Jersey; Political Activists; Social History, United States; St. Louis, MO; Travel

Now Try: One of the people Steffens mentored was Walter Lippmann, who became a renowned political columnist. Ronald Steel has written Lippmann's story in the context of his time, ***Walter Lippmann and the American Century***. Ida M. Tarbell was a muckraker right up there with Steffens. He worked with her at *McClure's Magazine*, and then she joined him to take over the ailing *The American Magazine*. Tarbell has written her own version of the muckraking life in ***All in the Day's Work: An Autobiography***. If you'd like to read a history of investigative journalism, with writings from each journalist plus a brief biography, have a look at Bruce Shapiro's anthology, ***Shaking the Foundations: 200 Years of Investigative Journalism in America***.

Stuart, Jesse (1907–1984)

The Thread That Runs So True. Foreword by James M. Gifford. Afterword by J. R. LeMaster. Jesse Stuart Foundation, 2006, 1949. 331pp. ill. 9781931672429. Also available in e-book. 370.92

Jesse Stuart's parents were illiterate, but because his farming father strongly believed in education, he allowed Stuart to go to school as much as possible when he could be spared from farm work. His father's belief came to be Stuart's own guiding principle as he tried to effect changes in the Kentucky school system. It also informed his opinion of teaching and teachers: "Good teaching is forever and the teacher is immortal." This memoir of his days in education, first in a one-room schoolhouse and later as the principal of a city high school, has inspired generations of teachers. Stuart believed in educating not only his students, but also their parents, convinced that without appropriate behavior and cooperation from the parents, there would be no education for the children. And education, he thought, was the single most important commodity one could give a child. Stuart's legacy lives on in the Jesse Stuart Foundation (http://www.jsfbooks.com/), set up to support teachers in Kentucky and Appalachia, to carry on Stuart's work, and to publish regional and educational books.

Subjects: Appalachian Region; Classics; Education; Educators; Kentucky; Mountain Life; Teachers; Writers

Now Try: Apart from being an educator, Stuart was also a writer; one of his novels, ***Taps for Private Tussie,*** won the Thomas Jefferson Southern Award and was a Book-of-the-Month Club selection. He also wrote other memoirs: another one on education, ***To Teach, To Love***; a more personal one, with six woodcuts by Ishmael, ***Beyond Dark Hills, a Personal Story***; and one after his heart attack, in which he started a whole new way of life: ***The Year of My Rebirth,*** illustrated by Barry Martin. Another novelist who lived in the Kentucky hills and wrote a memoir, ***40 Acres and No Mule,*** was Janice Holt Giles. The story of teaching in hardscrabble situations is a common one, which Pat Conroy tells in ***The Water Is Wide,*** with photographs by William Keyserling and Paul Keyserling, about teaching on the island Yamacraw, off the coast of South Carolina. One of the most vocal current advocates for improved education is Jonathan Kozol, who has written a heartwarming collection of letters in which he not only supports a first-year teacher, but also expounds on some of his theories about current education: ***Letters to a Young Teacher.***

Businesspeople

In this section you will find the expected kind of business memoir, that of the CEO of a large company, as well as of some of the most successful entrepreneurs. You will see women breaking the glass ceiling and a successful business built on humanitarianism. The computer industry is represented here, starting with its early history and touching on current technology. The memoirists also offer theories on the sources of their successes and on how corporations should be run, although the reader might find conflicting ideas in that arena. The field in this section is relatively small, but it is broad, and there are several reactions one could have to these books, from an interest in seeing how the work is done or the results achieved, to the wonder of the creative mind.

> The businesspeople here all rose to the top of their game and have used the medium of the memoir to describe what that actually means and how they achieved such success. Not all started out to be businesspeople, however, which makes their success stories even more interesting, reflecting both strength and courage, to say nothing of ingenuity.

1 2 3 4 5 6 7 8

Fiorina, Carly (1954–)

Tough Choices: A Memoir. With a new Afterword. Portfolio, 2007, 2006. 336pp. ill. 8 pp. of plates. 9781591841814. Also available in audiobook (read by the author) and e-audiobook. 338.761004165092

A major in philosophy and a student of Latin and Greek, Carly Fiorina started out as a secretary in a brokerage firm. In this memoir she documents her career path from there to an executive position with AT&T, during which time she and two others created the marketing identity for Lucent Technologies. By the time she became CEO of Hewlett-Packard she was a recognizable face on the covers of business journals. Fiorina's memoir tells these stories and more, offering her take on management strategies, on women in the workforce, and on her business philosophies. Just at the time that her memoir was published, news was breaking about the kinds of behavior in the Hewlett-Packard boardroom that had led to her being fired, so that she was able at the same time to tell her own story.

Subjects: Businesswomen; Electronic Industries; Executives; Hewlett-Packard Company; Lucent Technologies; Management

Now Try: Although she talks about women in the workforce, Fiorina doesn't want to be looked at as "a woman in the workforce"; she prefers to be thought of first as an executive. Robin Wolaner, a publishing CEO, shares the same concern in her book, ***Naked in the Boardroom: A CEO Bares Her Secrets So You Can Transform Your Career.*** Fiorina's firing by the Hewlett-Packard board was not an isolated boardroom incident, as Alan S. Murray explains in ***Revolt in the Boardroom: The New Rules of Power in Corporate America.*** Women who are interested in the business world may enjoy the collection of stories of successful businesswomen in ***On Our Own Terms: Portraits of Women Business Leaders*** by Liane Enkelis, Karen Olsen, and Marion Lewenstein.

Graham, Katharine (1917–2001)

Personal History. Knopf, 2002, 1997. 642pp. ill. 32pp. of plates. 9780394585857. Also available in audiobook, e-audiobook, and e-book. 070.5092

At age seventy-nine Katharine Meyer Graham decided to write her memoirs, looking back over her long life, covering major historical events in the United States, and paying tribute to those who had been so influential in the development of *The Washington Post*. She interviewed over 200 people and along with her researcher, Evelyn Small, combed through countless files. She wrote her story and Evelyn edited it, creating this autobiography of a long and productive life. The book deals with three major themes: Graham's wealthy childhood; her marriage to Philip Graham; and her management of *The Washington Post*, made necessary by the suicide of her husband. In the final section she speaks of three incidents in particular: Watergate; the *Pentagon Papers* and Daniel Ellsberg; and the pressmen's strike, the handling of which showed her grit and courage and demonstrated how far she had come in her own personal development.

Katharine Graham was inducted into the National Women's Hall of Fame and the Broadcasting & Cable Hall of Fame. She also posthumously received the Presidential Medal of Freedom from President George W. Bush in 2002. ***Personal History*** was awarded the Pulitzer Prize for Biography or Autobiography.

Subjects: Bipolar Disorder; Businesswomen; Graham, Philip; Management; Newspaper Publishing; Octogenarians; *The Pentagon Papers*; Pulitzer Prize for Biography or Autobiography; Strikes and Lockouts; Suicide; Washington, DC; *The Washington Post* (Newspaper); Watergate Affair

Now Try: Graham subsequently edited a collection of writings by notable Washingtonians illustrating the social and political life of the District in ***Katharine Graham's Washington***. She was good friends with Janet Langhart Cohen, another strong woman who also had to learn to juggle family and leadership; Janet has written a memoir with Alexander Kopelman, ***From Rage to Reason: My Life in Two Americas***. Another honest and revealing memoir of the Washington scene is ***Inside: A Public and Private Life*** by Joseph A. Califano, a lawyer who represented the *Post* during the Watergate affair. Graham's autobiography is not the kind to breeze through, but rather one to read thoughtfully, much in the same way that David G. McCullough's ***Truman*** should be read.

Lawrence, Mary Wells (1928–)

A Big Life in Advertising. Simon & Schuster, 2003, 2002. 307pp. ill. 9780743245869. 659.1092

Mary Lawrence wanted to be an actor, but instead became a copywriter for an advertising agency, writing copy for a department store. The agency was Doyle Dane Bernbach, and under the tutelage of Bill Bernbach she found her life's passion. Always interested in theater, she found that advertising could be an intersection between business and theater. She started her own advertising agency, Wells Rich Greene, the first American woman to do so, and achieved one success after another. Lawrence is the person who created the "I Love New York" campaign and many others that have become part of the American cultural lexicon. In her memoir she focuses more on her advertising life—the highs and lows—than on her personal life, although she does give glimpses of that as well. She also talks about what is necessary to be successful in business. When she put her company on the stock market, she became the first woman CEO to have a company on the New York Stock Exchange. And finally, she talks about stepping down and what happened to the company after she left.

Subjects: Advertising Executives; Businesswomen; Executives; Firsts; Management; New York, NY; Octogenarians; Trailblazers; Wells Rich Greene, Inc.

Now Try: Sandra L. Kurtzig is another woman who built her own successful business, a computer software company called ASK Computer Systems, all of which she describes with the help of Tom Parker in ***CEO: Building a $400 Million Company from the Ground Up***. The advertising-executive population seems to be male dominated, but another woman, Jane Maas, also made it to the top of an agency, which she describes in ***Adventures of an Advertising Woman***. Kim Lavine had an idea about how she could work successfully from home, and in ***Mommy Millionaire: How I Turned My Kitchen Table Idea into a Million Dollars and How You Can, Too!***, she now offers advice to other women who would like to do the same.

Newman, Paul (1925–2008), and A. E. Hotchner (1920–)

In Pursuit of the Common Good. Broadway Books, 2008. 247pp. ill. 9780767929974. Also available in e-book. 338.76645

This saga, originally entitled ***Shameless Exploitation in Pursuit of the Common Good***, is almost an antibusiness book, as Paul Newman and A. E. Hotchner succeeded despite themselves. Not that they would say that. After giving his own homemade version of salad dressing to friends for Christmas over several years, Newman and his good friend Hotchner (a successful author) decided to sell some to local restaurants. That was the start of what became a multi-million-dollar business, which broke or ignored most of the rules of big business. They had two noticeably different attributes from other businesses at the time: their products were all made of natural ingredients, and their after-tax profits all went to a charity they founded: the Association of Hole in the Wall Camps (http://www.holeinthewallcamps.org/), which creates and supports camps for very sick kids to attend. The first half of the book is a bit of a romp, describing how they got into business; the second half is more subdued as they describe the founding of the charity and the building of each camp, including letters from some of the campers.

Subjects: Children; Children's Camps; Foodies; Friendships; Humanitarians; Illness in Children; Newman's Own; Nonprofit Organizations; Octogenarians; Philanthropists

Now Try: A. E. Hotchner is also the author of several biographies and memoirs, the latest of which is ***Paul and Me: Fifty-Three Years of Adventures and Misadventures with My Pal Paul Newman***. When we go into the grocery store we rarely give much thought to how what we're purchasing actually got there, how it was created and manufactured. One such product is Tabasco sauce, still made by its original owning family. Jeffrey Rothfeder tells the story in ***McIlhenny's Gold: How a Louisiana Family Built the Tabasco Empire***. Small business, which is what Newman and Hotchner's business started out being, is becoming a mainstay of the American economy and a major benefit to millions of families. Martha Shirk and Anna S. Wadia tell the stories of a number of women who pulled themselves and their families out of poverty by starting their own businesses in ***Kitchen Table Entrepreneurs: How Eleven Women Escaped Poverty and Became Their Own Bosses***. Hotchner and Newman were friends for over fifty years. The historian Stephen E. Ambrose looks at friendships between and among men, some related by blood, some not, in ***Comrades: Brothers, Fathers, Heroes, Sons, Pals***, illustrated by Jon Friedman.

Rockefeller, David (1915–)

Memoirs. Random House Trade Paperbacks, 2003, 2002. 521pp. ill. 16pp. of plates. 9780812969733. Also available in e-book. 332.1

David Rockefeller has worn many hats in his long life: politician, intelligence analyst, financier, philanthropist, foreign-affairs consultant, to name but a few. He describes all of these hats in this memoir of his first eighty years. While maintaining a low emotional profile, Rockefeller has been at the center of many controversies, especially related to the company he kept for the purposes of furthering economic or political ties. He often left his workplace at the Chase Manhattan Bank to travel in order to foster these ties and found himself the subject of much criticism for doing so. In his own view, it was important that the private sector find its role in world affairs, and he worked assiduously to this end. He also takes a great interest in philanthropy towards the arts, particularly the Museum of Modern Art, founded by his mother, Abby Aldrich Rockefeller.

David Rockefeller was awarded the Presidential Medal of Freedom in 1998 by President Clinton.

Subjects: Bankers; Businessmen; Chase Manhattan Bank; Nonagenarians; Philanthropists; Rockefeller Family; Upper Class

Now Try: Rockefeller's views regarding the role of the private sector in world affairs are shared by many of the people referred to in David J. Rothkopf's book, ***Superclass: The Global Power Elite and the World They Are Making***. In his autobiography Rockefeller gives a very thorough history of the Chase Manhattan Bank, such as has not been provided elsewhere. Ron Chernow did the same for the Morgan Stanley bank in ***The House of Morgan: An American Banking Dynasty and the Rise of Modern Finance***. Despite his low-key narrative, David Rockefeller is candid about life with his siblings, his parents, his larger family, and his business and political associates. This same candid nature is evident in another New Yorker's memoir, that of Max Frankel (journalist for and then editor of *The New York Times*), in ***The Times of My Life and My Life with "The Times"***.

Watson, Thomas J. (1914–1993)
Petre, Peter, coauthor

Father, Son & Co.: My Life at IBM and Beyond. Bantam Books, 2000, 1990. 468pp. ill. 32pp. of plates. 9780553380835. Also available in large print and audiobook. 338.7092

This is a classic father-and-son story, wherein the son feels inferior to the father for a long time, and it is not until he is far removed from the father that he is able to find his own talents and capabilities. When Watson Jr. was growing up, his father was running a large company that he had changed from the small Computer-Tabulating-Recording (CTR) Company into the very successful International Business Machines (IBM) Corporation. Watson Jr. persuaded his father—not without ferocious arguments—to hire engineers to help IBM get into the computer business. His father was still not convinced, even by the time he was handing the reins over to his son, but there was no denying the numbers, as Watson Jr. took the company from millions to billions in sales.

Watson Jr. was inducted into the U.S. Business Hall of Fame, was named one of *Time*'s People of the Century in the Builders & Titans category, and was awarded the Presidential Medal of Freedom in 1964 by President Johnson.

Subjects: Businessmen; Executives; Fathers and Sons; International Business Machines Corporation; Leadership; Pilots; Watson, Thomas J., Sr.

Now Try: Watson Sr. had an interesting story to tell as well, rising from a farmer's son to the head of a multinational corporation. Kevin Maney has told his story in ***The Maverick and His Machine: Thomas Watson, Sr., and the Making of IBM.*** The punch cards that formed the core of the business the senior Watson first started, and that he thought would never be replaced, have a fascinating history, dating back to the nineteenth century. This story can be found in ***Jacquard's Web: How a Hand-Loom Led to the Birth of the Information Age,*** by James Essinger. It's often interesting to see a successful person in context, and Richard S. Tedlow provides that in ***Giants of Enterprise: Seven Business Innovators and the Empires They Built.*** The story of fathers and sons is universal and can be found in any environment. In ***The Given Day: A Novel,*** Dennis Lehane tells the story of two policemen, father and son, in Boston during a time of great change.

Welch, Jack (1935–)
Byrne, John A., coauthor

Jack: Straight from the Gut. With a new Afterword. Warner Books, 2003, 2001. 480pp. ill. 9780446690683. Also available in large print, audiobook (read by the author), e-audiobook, and e-book. 338.7092

This memoir pays tribute to Jack Welch's mother, Grace, who shaped his life, particularly by encouraging him to get an education, which he did, attaining a doctorate in chemical engineering. Welch details his life at General Electric, from his starting position as a junior engineer to CEO. Making it to the top as the youngest CEO ever to head GE, he set about making radical changes in both the business end and the corporate culture. He was responsible for bringing the Six Sigma business method to GE. His memoir is a personal story, full of his triumphs and mistakes and peopled throughout by those who had a great influence on him.

Welch has been inducted into the U.S. Business Hall of Fame.

Subjects: Businessmen; Executives; General Electric Company; Leadership; Management; Mothers and Sons; Six Sigma (Quality Control Standard)

Now Try: Welch credits his mother and their relationship with some of the important life lessons he learned that led to his success. Colm Tóibín has written a collection of short stories, ***Mothers and Sons,*** dealing with that important relationship. There are various attitudes toward what constitutes great leadership; readers may be interested in reading ***It's Not About the Coffee: Leadership Principles from a Life at Starbucks*** by a senior executive with the company, Howard Behar and his coauthor, Janet Goldstein. If you'd like to read about another very successful businessman, one a little more altruistic, you might want to pick up Michael D'Antonio's ***Hershey: Milton***

S. Hershey's Extraordinary Life of Wealth, Empire, and Utopian Dreams. Not everyone likes Jack Welch and what he did to GE. Thomas F. O'Boyle has given the contrary view in ***At Any Cost: Jack Welch, General Electric, and the Pursuit of Profit.***

Foodies

Most of the people in this section are not professional cooks, but all have a relationship with food in some way. What they all have in common is a love of food and a desire to cook it well, even if that cooking doesn't turn professional. Among others, you will find here the restaurateur, the cookbook writer, the food writer, the television host, and the expatriate who becomes enamored of his new country's food.

> Foodies could be chefs, food writers, food network people, or simply lovers of food. Most of the people featured here began with a love of food and the art of making it. Many moved on to make food the focus of their working lives. In some cases, however, food has been an avocation, and the interest in it such that the writers simply had to tell others about the importance of food in their lives.

Bourdain, Anthony (1956–)

Kitchen Confidential: Adventures in the Culinary Underbelly. Harper Perennial, 2007, 2000. 312pp. 9780060899226. Also available in large print, audiobook (read by the author), and e-audiobook 641.5092

Before he started writing about real life in the kitchen, Anthony Bourdain wrote two crime novels, ***Bone in the Throat*** and ***Gone Bamboo***. Then he wrote an article for *The New Yorker*, "Don't Eat Before Reading This," and quickly jumped into the public consciousness. The response to that article, which discussed what really goes on in kitchens, was so favorable that it prompted Bourdain to write ***Kitchen Confidential***, an elaboration of the article. Bourdain refers to his book as a "horror story," so the weak of stomach may not want to read it. The memoir is full of stories, in very colorful language, about the types of people who populate kitchens: in Bourdain's words, "drunks, sneak thieves, sluts, and psychopaths." He also describes what happens in the kitchen and how the food is prepared, not always a pretty picture. But he offers more than that: he gives glimpses into his own life as well. In the twenty-five years covered in this memoir, he acquired a drug habit, opened a restaurant in Tokyo, and gradually worked his way up to high-end cooking with gigs at such restaurants as the Rainbow Room in the Rockefeller Center. He provides gossipy details

1 2 3 4 5 6 7 8

of the various restaurants he has worked in and even has a chapter of advice for the home cook.

Subjects: Chefs; Cooking; Drug Abuse; Foodies; New York, NY; Restaurants; Travel; Work Relationships

Now Try: Bourdain has since written several memoirs; the most recent is similar in style to his first, ***Medium Raw: A Bloody Valentine to the World of Food and the People Who Cook***. His writing is not for the weak of heart, as he likes extreme food and extreme language. The edginess of his style can be found in ***The Devil in the Kitchen: Sex, Pain, Madness, and the Making of a Great Chef*** by Marco Pierre White and James Steen or in Gordon Ramsay's ***Roasting in Hell's Kitchen: Temper Tantrums, F Words, and the Pursuit of Perfection***. The Culinary Institute of America (or CIA, as it's called) is a renowned culinary training center that Michael Ruhlman, an immersion journalist, attended, fast-tracking his way through the program. He tells the tale in ***The Making of a Chef: Mastering Heat at the Culinary Institute of America***.

Buford, Bill (1954–)

Heat: An Amateur's Adventures as Kitchen Slave, Line Cook, Pasta Maker, and Apprentice to a Dante-Quoting Butcher in Tuscany. Knopf, 2006. 318pp. 9781582340821. Also available in large print, audiobook, e-audiobook, and e-book. 641.59455

A journalist for *The New York Times*, Bill Buford initially wrote an article about Mario Batali, the owner of Babbo Ristorante e Enoteca in New York. Buford's interest in cooking then led him to try his hand at apprenticing in Batali's kitchen, with a view to writing about life in the restaurant trenches. What he found there, however, engendered a passion he didn't realize he had, and after three years in the Babbo kitchen, he set out for Italy to learn the arts of butchery and making pasta. The storytelling in ***Heat*** is done along two paths: the even-numbered chapters are Batali's story; the odd-numbered are Buford's. Along both paths, however, the reader is treated to the hectic, crazy world of the restaurant kitchen, where most of the line cooks want to be promoted to sous-chef and then chef and finally be able to open their own restaurants, creating fierce competition. It is into this environment that Buford, a journalist who doesn't know how to sharpen knives or dice carrots, unwittingly steps. The world he encounters in Italy is also a revelation. How many butchers play classical music and offer wine to their customers?

Subjects: Babbo (Restaurant), NY; Batali, Mario; Cecchini, Dario; Cooking; Italy; Journalists; New York, NY; Restaurants; Restaurateurs

Now Try: If you'd like to read another kitchen story, you may enjoy Jason Sheehan's ***Cooking Dirty: A Story of Life, Sex, Love and Death in the Kitchen***. Batali's mantra is "wretched excess is barely enough." That would also seem the mantra of Jeffrey Steingarten, author of, among other books, the memoir ***The Man Who Ate Everything: And Other Gastronomic Feats, Disputes, and Pleasurable Pursuits***. Dario Cecchini, the butcher, has his shop in Chianti; another view of Chianti is provided by tour guide Dario Castagno in ***Too Much Tuscan Sun: Confessions of a Chianti Tour Guide***, written with the help of Robert Rodi.

Child, Julia (1912–2004)
Prud'homme, Alex, coauthor

My Life in France. Photographs by Paul Child. Anchor Books, 2009, 2006. 414pp. ill. 9780307475015. Also available in large print, audiobook, e-audiobook, and e-book. 641.5092

Julia Child's first career was in the OSS (Office of Strategic Services), where she met her husband, Paul. After they married, Paul was transferred to France, and Child's very first meal in France, on their way to Paris, was a revelation to her: never before had she tasted food that was "exciting." This meal sparked her, in a strange country where she had no friends, couldn't cook, and didn't know the language, to attend cooking classes at the Cordon Bleu, a decision that changed both her life and the culinary world. This memoir largely tells the story of the six years she and her husband spent in France, years in which she would master her own art of French cooking and take up with two women who were in the midst of writing a cookbook. The result of that collaboration was that Child became the principal author of ***Mastering the Art of French Cooking,*** a book intended for an American audience, and originally developed by Simone Beck and Louisette Bertholle. Readers will find interesting insights into the world of publishing and the world of American cooking in the 1950s.

Julia Child was inducted into the National Women's Hall of Fame and given the Presidential Medal of Freedom in 2003 by President George W. Bush.

Subjects:1950s; Americans in France; Beck, Simone; Bertholle, Louisette; Book Publishing; Chefs; Child, Paul; Cookbooks; Food, France; France; Gastronomy; *Mastering the Art of French Cooking*; Nonagenarians; Paris, France; Provence, France

Now Try: While discussing the making of the cookbook and the reasons she was so keen to do so, Child describes the American cuisine of the time, a theme elaborated on by Laura Shapiro in ***Something from the Oven: Reinventing Dinner in 1950's America***. But Irma Rombauer and her daughter, Marion Rombauer Becker, were also around to help the American housewife; Anne Mendelson tells their story in ***Stand Facing the Stove: The Story of the Women Who Gave America "The Joy of Cooking"***. The French Culinary Institute in New York City is the scene of the chaotic cooking lessons taken by Katherine Darling, which she describes in ***Under the Table: Saucy Tales from Culinary School***. Noël Riley Fitch was given access to Child's diaries and correspondence, so a fuller picture of her life is available in ***Appetite for Life: The Biography of Julia Child***.

Clarke, Austin (1934–)

Pig Tails 'n Breadfruit: A Culinary Memoir. New Press, 2000, 1999. 248pp. 9781565845800. 641.5972981

Fiction writer Austin Clarke's collection of personal essays takes the reader back to the late 1930s and early 1940s, to St. Matthias in colonial Barbados, to the kitchens of his mother and her friends, where no one measured anything, but threw in a dash of this and a splash of that, to season and to taste. As Clarke describes the cooking of a dish, something about an ingredient triggers a story, as in the chapter on baking, where he remembers what an insult it would have been to suggest that someone was wearing a flour bag. Most of the text is in Barbadian dialect, easy to understand and lulling to the reader, as though you were there in the kitchen while the food is being prepared, and the talk flows all around you.

Pig Tails 'n Breadfruit was nominated for the James Beard Foundation Writing on Food Book Award.

Subjects: Barbadian-Canadians; Barbados; Childhood and Youth; Coming of Age; Cooking; Family Portraits; Food, Barbados; Novelists, Canada; Personal Essays; West Indies

Now Try: Melinda and Robert Blanchard, who had a specialty food shop in Vermont, took a vacation to Barbados. This trip changed their lives, and they describe how they set up a restaurant on another Caribbean island, Anguilla, in ***A Trip to the Beach***. Diana Abu-Jaber, an Arab-American, also knows how cooking and culture go hand in hand; readers of Clarke's memoir may enjoy her novel ***Crescent***. For another perspective of growing up in Barbados, again with the dialect a part of the writing, you may want to read George Lamming's ***In the Castle of My Skin***.

Deen, Paula H. (1947–)
Cohen, Sherry Suib (1934–), coauthor

Paula Deen: It Ain't All About the Cookin'. Simon & Schuster, 2009, 2007. 287pp. ill. 9781439163351. Available in large print and audiobook (read by the author). 641.5092

Food Network star Paula Deen has made her own way, from marriage to an alcoholic husband, through a long bout with agoraphobia, and fending off poverty, to a career with her own restaurant, her own television show, and her own magazine (*Cooking with Paula Deen*). In her down-home Southern-style language and exuberance she tells it all, from her childhood in her grandmother's kitchen to her happy second marriage in her late fifties. Deen describes how she spent so much time in the kitchen during her days of agoraphobia and how she started a brown-bag lunch service to help her family stay afloat when her alcoholic husband had lost yet another job. In between stories she disperses recipes, many of which are new.

Subjects: Agoraphobia; Alcoholism in the Family; American South; Businesswomen; Chefs; *Cooking with Paula Deen* (Magazine); Food Shows; Food, Southern; Mothers and Sons

Now Try: Cooking shows started with people like *Julia Child* and Dione Lucas and have grown into big business. Kathleen Collins offers a history of this form of entertainment in ***Watching What We Eat: The Evolution of Television Cooking Shows***. The flavor of Southern cooking is also captured in Pat Conroy's culinary memoir, the story of how he started cooking and discovered a new passion, which he relates, with the help of

Suzanne Williamson Pollak, in ***The Pat Conroy Cookbook: Recipes of My Life***. If you enjoy the good humor and salty language of Deen's memoir, you may also enjoy Kathleen Turner's storytelling in ***Send Yourself Roses: Thoughts on My Life, Love, and Leading Roles,*** written with the help of Gloria Feldt.

Jones, Judith (1924–)

The Tenth Muse: My Life in Food. Anchor Books, 2008, 2007. 290pp. ill. 9780307277442. Also available in e-book. 641.59

When ***Mastering the Art of French Cooking*** came across the desk of Judith Jones, an editor at Knopf, she took it to an editorial meeting, where Alfred Knopf himself said that if anyone bought a book with such a title, he would eat his hat (Grimes, 2006). Jones prevailed, however, and became Julia Child's editor for that and her subsequent books. In her memoir she talks about her various friends in the publishing and writing and cooking worlds in New York. She also describes the editing business (how she urged Doubleday, her employer at the time, to publish the English version of Anne Frank's ***The Diary of a Young Girl,*** for example). After taking on Julia Child's book, Jones started to focus more on food writers and their cookbooks and gradually developed a personal interest in food herself. She shared this interest with her husband, Evan, so that eventually he too joined her in the kitchen as they prepared meals together. When Evan got sick and died after their marriage of almost fifty years, her kitchen became a lonely spot for her. In due course she came to terms with her new life, though, and just recently wrote ***The Pleasures of Cooking for One.***

Subjects: Alfred A. Knopf, Inc.; Book Publishing; Child, Julia; Cookbooks; Cooking, International; Cooks; Death of a Spouse; Editors; Food Writing; Gastronomy; Jones, Evan; Married Couples; *Mastering the Art of French Cooking*

Now Try: Nancy Verde Barr also worked with Julia Child, but in the kitchen. Barr has written about their years together in ***Backstage with Julia: My Years with Julia Child.*** Judith Jones was very interested in bringing international cookery to the American table. She would appreciate the work of Cecilia Chiang, who brought real Chinese food to San Francisco; her memoir, written with the help of Lisa Weiss, ***The Seventh Daughter: My Culinary Journey from Beijing to San Francisco,*** mixes family memories with food memories. For readers who are interested in the publishing side of Jones's story, Al Silverman has written a fascinating history, ***The Time of Their Lives: The Golden Age of Great American Book Publishers, Their Editors, and Authors.***

Mayle, Peter (1939–)

French Lessons: Adventures with Knife, Fork, and Corkscrew. Vintage, 2002, 2001. 227pp. ill. 9780375705618. Also available in large print, audiobook, and e-book. 641.013

Once he had settled into his expatriate life in France (see p. 243 for ***Encore Provence: New Adventures in the South of France***), Peter Mayle set out to see the rest of the country through its gastronomic culture. Different locales meant different food: Martigny-les-Bains specialized in snails, while in Richerenches a Mass was offered to give thanks for the truffle, followed by a lunch featuring that delicacy. In Bourgogne marathoners running through were offered Médoc wine as a restorative, and Vittel highlights a festival for frogs' legs. In addition to the tour of the country and its culinary specialties, Mayle also presents a tour of the Michelin guide. Throughout the entire collection of essays, he portrays the love and enthusiasm the French people have for their food culture.

Subjects: English in France; Food, France; France; Gastronomy; Personal Essays; Social Life and Customs, France; Travel, France

Now Try: One of the elements of French dining that so impresses Mayle is the level of professionalism of the waiters. Swiss author Alain Claude Sulzer presents such a waiter in *A Perfect Waiter: A Novel* (translated from the German by John Brownjohn). Another cultural export of France is its impressionistic painters. In the same unpretentious writing style that Mayle uses, Jeffrey Meyers discusses the ***Impressionist Quartet: The Intimate Genius of Manet and Morisot, Degas and Cassatt***. Another gastronome who traveled far and wide is Bob Spitz, a writer who wanted to learn to cook, as he recounts in ***The Saucier's Apprentice: One Long Strange Trip Through the Great Cooking Schools of Europe***.

Powell, Julie (1973–)

Julie and Julia: 365 Days, 524 Recipes, 1 Tiny Apartment Kitchen . . . . Back Bay Books, 2009, 2005. 309pp. 9780316044271. Also available in large print, audiobook (read by the author), e-audiobook, and video. 641.5092

Disgruntled with her secretarial job in New York City, hearing her biological clock ticking loudly, and basically fed up with most aspects of her life except her husband, Julie Powell decided to distract herself with a project. She had always been fascinated by her mother's cookbook, ***Mastering the Art of French Cooking*** by Julia Child, and decided to borrow it when she was visiting her mother in Texas. She embarked on the project of cooking everything in the book in the space of one year, in a tiny apartment kitchen, progressing chapter by chapter. Powell's husband added an idea to the pot: he suggested she blog about it. It was the blogging that changed her life: her "bleaders" (blog readers) loved it and cheered her on so that she eventually came to the notice of the media. The Julie/Julia Project, as her blog was called, eventually became this book, which has also become a movie, ***Julie & Julia***.

Powell's book won the Quill Debut Author of the Year Award.

Subjects: Blogs; Child, Julia; Cookbooks; Cooking; Gastronomy; The Julie/Julia Project; *Mastering the Art of French Cooking*; New York, NY; Self-Discovery; Writers

Now Try: Julie Powell's life has changed since the publication of her book, a change she details in ***Cleaving: A Story of Marriage, Meat, and Obsession***. One of the difficulties one might have with such a project is the actual food the cook and guests are obliged to eat; sometimes the scheduled dish might not be to everyone's liking (sweetbreads come to mind). Robb Walsh doesn't seem to mind such challenges, as he relates in ***Are***

You Really Going to Eat That? Reflections of a Culinary Thrill Seeker. Nigel Slater is a British food writer whom Powell cites as one of her favorite writers, particularly enjoying ***The Kitchen Diaries: A Year in the Kitchen with Nigel Slater***, in which he details his eating life day by day for a year. Molly Wizenberg went to Paris to get over the death of her father and while there began a blog, Orangette. She, like Julie Powell, gained an audience (and a husband) from that blog, as well as a book, illustrated by Camilla Engman: ***A Homemade Life: Stories and Recipes from My Kitchen Table***.

Reichl, Ruth (1948–)

Tender at the Bone: Growing Up at the Table. Random House, 2010, 1998. 289pp. ill. 9780812981117. Also available in large print and audiobook (read by the author). 641.5092

This is the first of four memoirs by food writer and restaurant critic Ruth Reichl. In this debut memoir she recounts her childhood memories of food and people, particularly her mother, whose determination to waste no food led to various incidents of food poisoning. At the age of ten, it became Reichl's self-appointed mission to ensure that her mother didn't kill anyone at their dinner parties. She starts the book by mentioning how important storytelling was in her family and how they often didn't let the facts get in the way. She admits that while her stories are true, they may not be factual, that she conflated some people and embroidered some stories. This memoir takes us into the 1970s, when Reichl gets her first food-writing job in San Francisco. ***Comfort Me with Apples: More Adventures at the Table*** follows, focusing on her food writing. She then becomes a restaurant food critic in New York, which she details in ***Garlic and Sapphires: The Secret Life of a Critic in Disguise***. Her fourth book is more a mother–daughter memoir; Reichl goes through her mother's papers, putting her mother's writing into context vis-à-vis herself. This book is entitled ***Not Becoming My Mother: And Other Things She Taught Me Along the Way***.

Subjects: Coming of Age; Cooks; Food Habits; Food Writers; Mothers and Daughters; Reichl, Miriam B.

Now Try: Frank Bruni, a restaurant critic for *The New York Times*, has a bit of a weight problem. His memoir is candid about his struggles with food: ***Born Round: The Secret History of a Full-Time Eater***. Betty Fussell was a combination of Reichl and her mother, frustrated at the roles expected of women after the war, but determined to do something about it for herself, becoming a food writer and author, including her memoir, ***My Kitchen Wars***. Food and mystery lovers can have fun with both in Peter King's **Gourmet Detective Mysteries**, the first of which is ***The Gourmet Detective***.

Working-Class People

People who work in blue-collar jobs are less likely to write their memoirs, and for some unknown reason, those who do write them do not necessarily have the commercial success that others do. That having been said, however, we do have a broad sampling of occupations. The jobs represented here run the gamut from bicycle messenger to library assistant to undertaker to wait staff and everything in between. Reading these books will give you interesting insights into jobs we perhaps take for granted or never even think about.

The working-class stories here offer the reader a broad swath of jobs to learn about. Some of the writers took on a new job almost willy-nilly; others chose their jobs and found the experience so interesting they wanted to share their stories. Readers have no idea what kinds of situations people in other jobs might encounter and thus have the opportunity here of peeking inside someone else's work world to gain some new insights.

Borchert, Don (1949–)

Free for All: Oddballs, Geeks, and Gangstas in the Public Library. Virgin Books, 2008, 2007. 223pp. 9780753515013. 027.47949

In this memoir of his twelve years working as a library assistant in a small public library near Los Angeles, Don Borchert offers comic and not-so-comic stories of how the library as an institution has changed, particularly in its patronage. Borchert tells about the latchkey kids, a given in any public library, some of whom are out of control and some of whom are there for their own protection. He tells of the patron whose books must be stacked in alphabetical order after being checked out, of the police coming to raid the restroom where drug deals are going down, of the woman who bakes for the staff since she has no one else to bake for. Borchert also talks about the operations of a library—trying to stretch an already tight budget to provide programming for children, what a library does with discarded books, how staff are hired and trained. There is some personal information as well, discussions about Borchert's early knockabout jobs and his decision to take this job once he had a family. It is all done with a wry sense of humor.

Subjects: Adolescents; California; Library Assistants; Library Users; Public Libraries

Now Try: People who just pop into the library to pick up a few books and leave again might be very surprised to read Borchert's book, not expecting such behavior in a public library. The same could be said of many workplaces, including a cruise liner. Brian David Bruns has taken a comical look at the working side of the cruise ship in ***Cruise Confidential: A Hit Below the Waterline.*** Around the same time that Borchert's book came out, a librarian, Scott Douglas, also published a book, ***Quiet, Please: Dispatches from a Public Librarian,*** about his experiences in another California library system. And readers who think this unusual behavior in a public library is a product of the twenty-first century may find themselves surprised to read the anecdotes of Betty Vogel in ***A Librarian Is to Read,*** about her experiences in the 1970s.

Conover, Ted (1958–)

Newjack: Guarding Sing Sing. Vintage Books, 2001, 2000. 331pp. ill. 9780375726620. Also available in audiobook (read by the author), e-audiobook, and e-book. 365.92

"Newjack" is the inmates' term for a rookie corrections officer. When Ted Conover was refused admittance as a journalist to cover the life of a rookie, he realized the only way he could study the prison system was to become a rookie himself. Hiding his journalist persona, he successfully applied for admittance to the program, went through seven weeks of training in Albany and on-the-job training in Sing Sing, and then fended for himself in his assignment day by day. Conover found himself working in the gallery (the main area where the cells are); the mess hall; transportation detail; or "The Box," the isolation unit. He tried to have himself placed most often where he would have daily contact with the inmates, but it is really the officers themselves whose work lives he depicts in this memoir of a year in a prison. Conover soon learned that the daily grind, the constant underpinning of violence and fear, effected an unsettling change in himself. He details his own internal changes from a liberal and empathic man to one who felt that the inmates deserved the beatings they got. What he came out with ultimately, though, was a recognition that America has failed miserably in its concept of criminal punishment and that those who have the power to make significant changes should stand up and take notice.

Newjack was a finalist for the Pulitzer Prize for General Nonfiction and won the National Book Critics Circle Award in General Nonfiction.

Subjects: Journalists; National Book Critics Circle Award in General Nonfiction; Ossining Correctional Facility, NY; Prison Guards; Prisons, United States; Sing Sing Prison, NY; Writers

Now Try: During his journalistic career, Conover has immersed himself in a number of worlds. Another writer who immersed himself in a law-related world is Steve Bogira, author of ***Courtroom 302: A Year Behind the Scenes in an American Criminal Courthouse***. Joseph T. Hallinan tries to do what Conover did—illustrate the problems with incarceration in America—in ***Going up the River: Travels in a Prison Nation***. Jeffrey Archer, noted British novelist and peer, provides a view of prison from the other side of the bars, where he was sentenced to four years' imprisonment, serving two of those years and writing a three-volume memoir, **A Prison Diary**, the first volume of which bears the same name as the trilogy.

Culley, Travis Hugh

The Immortal Class: Bike Messengers and the Cult of Human Power. Random House Trade Paperbacks, 2002, 2001. 324pp. ill. 9780375760242. Also available in e-book. 384

Travis Hugh Culley moved from Florida to Chicago in the hope of setting up a theater as a vehicle for his playwriting. The theater he was able to set up, but the audience didn't come; looking for a way to stay alive, he answered an ad for bicycle courier. When a friend took him to a Critical Mass event, he became a convert to bike activism. This memoir, then, is a combination of many things: Culley's views on the car culture versus the bike culture, his take on Chicago, and his description of the life of the bike messenger. Although he doesn't go into it profoundly, he recognizes that there's a bit of a disconnect between his views about the car culture and the fact that he's couriering documents from one corporation to another. While he's doing this, however, he's also getting a close-up view of Chicago, a city he's come to love; because of his unusual perspective, he is able to give the reader unexpected and unusual glimpses of Chicago. Most exciting, however, is the actual job; with a writer's skill, Culley keeps the reader breathless as he tears through the traffic, occasionally jumping red lights, occasionally getting into accidents and breaking bones, but usually making his deadline and therefore making a living.

Subjects: Bicycle Messengers; Bike Culture; Chicago, IL; Critical Mass; Playwrights

Now Try: Bicycle couriers have been part of various countries' cultures for a long time. Restaurateur G. Franco Romagnoli was one as a young man during the war in Italy, using his bike as a vehicle of resistance, as he recounts in ***The Bicycle Runner: A Memoir of Love, Loyalty, and the Italian Resistance***. Jiro Adachi has written a novel about the bike-messenger subculture in New York City, ***The Island of Bicycle Dancers***. Another method of couriering is on rollerblades, a world that Joe Quirk writes about in his novel, ***The Ultimate Rush***.

Damrosch, Phoebe (1978–)

Service Included: Four-Star Secrets of an Eavesdropping Waiter. Harper, 2008, 2007. 228pp. 9780061228155. Also available in e-book. 647.95092

With a degree from Barnard College and some courses in a master's in fine arts behind her, Phoebe Damrosch was at loose ends, taking a variety of jobs, including one as a busgirl in a café. This led her to move upward in the restaurant chain and apply for an interview with Thomas Keller for a position in his soon-to-be-opened restaurant in New York City. She had tried to eat at his California restaurant, The French Laundry, but couldn't get a reservation, so she had some idea of the significance of what she was trying to do. Damrosch was given a position as a backserver, and in her memoir, describing with humor her nervousness and missteps, details how she still managed to move up in the serving-staff hierarchy to become the first female captain at Per Se. Readers learn initially about what is involved in opening a new restaurant, and once that has been accomplished, about how the front of the house works, how the staff are trained, and what is required of them. Damrosch also provides tips for diners and what is expected of them, such as not to send back your entrée with a complaint after you've eaten most of it. There is a subplot in Damrosch's restaurant story, as she falls in love with the sommelier, André Mack, and the reader is treated to the progress of that relationship.

Subjects: Food Service; Keller, Thomas; Love Affairs; Mack, André; New York, NY; Per Se (Restaurant), NY; Servers

Now Try: Another area of the kitchen that has not seen much publicity is the dessert station. Dalia Jurgensen describes her career change from office worker to pastry chef in ***Spiced: A Pastry Chef's True Stories of Trials by Fire, After-Hours Exploits, and What Really Goes on in the Kitchen.*** For the reader who is interested in Thomas Keller and his creative approach to food, ***The French Laundry Cookbook,*** written by Keller, Susie Heller, and Michael Ruhlman, and with photographs by Deborah Jones, might be an interesting choice; despite its title, it is more than a cookbook. Isadore Sharp is another entrepreneur who has very definite standards of style and customer service. Founder of Four Seasons Hotels, Inc., he shares his philosophy and his story (with the help of Alan Phillips) in ***Four Seasons: The Story of a Business Philosophy.***

Gass, Thomas Edward

Nobody's Home: Candid Reflections of a Nursing Home Aide. Foreword by Bruce C. Vladeck. ILR Press, 2005, 2004. 224pp. 9780801472619. 362.16092

Thomas Gass had a degree in psychology and had been a teacher for several years when his mother's health began to fail and she needed to go into a nursing home, a for-profit home in the Midwest. He tended to her while she was there and, after her death, applied there for a job as a nursing-home aide. Working in that home for three-and-a-half years, he kept a diary of his days and eventually wrote his story. His account is different from that of a social scientist, because those who purport to study nursing homes are usually allowed only into the ritzy homes. This is the first account from the front lines of the nursing-home aide, and it is very graphic in describing a typical day of the rushed and harried life of these workers. (He calculated that he and his coworker had 17.3 minutes each day they could give to each client.) While helping his clients in the bathroom, cleaning up after them, lifting and turning them, feeding them, and taking their temperature and blood pressure, Gass tried to keep in mind that these people used to have lives of interest, so he would try to show a personal interest in each one. The book is not a study of nursing homes; it is a poignant account of one frontline worker, but it does have an informative foreword by Bruce C. Vladeck, the former director of Medicare and Medicaid programs at the U.S. Department of Health and Human Services. One salient point he makes is that the fastest-growing job in the United States is that of health care aide, usually slated as a minimum-wage, unskilled-labor position.

Subjects: Aging; Health Care Aides; Institutions; Long-Term Care; Nurses' Aides; Nursing Homes; Reflections; Seniors

Now Try: Although the patients in ***Awakenings*** by Oliver W. Sacks have a specific health problem, they resemble the men and women in a nursing home who have become senile, losing their identity and personality, and becoming just another body to be warehoused. Tracy Kidder has written about a nursing home, but from the perspective of two residents, Joe Torchio and Lou Freed, who form a friendship in the home, in ***Old Friends***. In his collection of stories ***Tales of the Jazz Age***, F. Scott Fitzgerald included a poignant one entitled "The Curious Case of Benjamin Button," about a baby who gets younger as he grows older. This story (apart from being made into a movie of the same name) has been adapted into a graphic novel, ***The Curious Case of Benjamin Button: A Graphic Novel***, written by Nunzio DeFilippis and Christina Weir and illustrated by Kevin Cornell.

Gill, Michael Gates (1940–)

How Starbucks Saved My Life: A Son of Privilege Learns to Live Like Everyone Else. Gotham Books, 2008, 2007. 268pp. 9781592404049. Also available in large print, audiobook, e-audiobook, and e-book. 647.95092

In this riches-to-rags story, we learn what life is like as a barista for Starbucks. But in Michael Gill's memoir, it's really a rags-to-riches story in terms of quality of life and self-esteem. Gill had reached bottom in his professional and personal lives and just happened into a Starbucks during a job fair. The young manager asked him if he wanted a job, so he filled out an application, desperate for an income and work-provided health insurance. When he walked into work on the first day, he realized that he was the oldest employee there and the only White person. He details a year in his life at Starbuck's, learning how to clean restrooms, use the cash register, and make complicated beverages. He also learns about commuting to work, about living in a rented apartment, and about working with others whose lives have always been harder than his. In other words, he learns about life among the working class. An executive for an ad agency and the son of Brendan Gill, a longtime writer for *The New Yorker*, Michael Gill had been used to traveling among the *haute monde*, full of a sense of entitlement and ignorant of the way most people live. His gratitude to Starbucks shines throughout the book as he becomes a different person, delighted to have mastered the art of the barista.

Subjects: Advertising Executives; Baristas; Coffee; Divorce; Family Relationships; New York, NY; Starbucks Coffee Company

Now Try: If you'd like to read more about Starbucks as a company, Joseph A. Michelli has written an accessible book on the topic, ***The Starbucks Experience: 5 Principles for Turning Ordinary into Extraordinary***. Some companies seem more appealing to work for than others, making the reader more curious about what the working life there is like. David A. Vise and Mark Malseed have written a book that should prove of general interest: ***The Google Story***. For a bit of fun, you might like to pick up the first in Cleo Coyle's <u>Coffeehouse Mysteries</u>, ***On What Grounds***.

Greenlaw, Linda (1960–)

The Hungry Ocean: A Swordboat Captain's Journey. Hyperion, 1999. 265 pp. map. 9780786864515. Also available in large print, Braille, audiobook (read by the author), e-audiobook, and e-book. 639.2778

It was Linda Greenlaw's sister ship, *Andrea Gail*, that went down in the storm described in Sebastian Junger's ***The Perfect Storm: A True Story of Men Against the Sea***; Greenlaw, captain of the *Hannah Boden*, was Junger's technical consultant in his writing of the book. She then turned to writing herself, initially in this book, to tell the story of one typical fishing trip: a thirty-day outing from Gloucester, Massachusetts, to the Grand Banks of Newfoundland in search of swordfish. She describes the preparations necessary before even setting sail and lets the reader in on the characters who share a small space together over a period of thirty days. The work is backbreaking, and suspense is always part of it, because the fishermen won't know until they arrive back in dock what price their catch will bring. Junger said of Greenlaw that she was one of the best sea captains on the East Coast. Then Greenlaw decided to give up the long hauls and returned home to the tiny island of Isle au Haut, off the coast of Maine, to try her hand at lobster fishing. She tells about her year back with her parents in ***The Lobster Chronicles: Life on a Very Small Island***.

Subjects: Fishing Industry; *Hannah Boden* (Ship); Saltwater Fishing; Sea Captains; Swordfish Fishing; Work Relationships

Now Try: Greenlaw has found a second avocation: writing. She has written a collection of anecdotes "from the dry dock"; two mystery stories; a collection of recipes with her mother; and a sequel to ***The Hungry Ocean***, having decided to go back to swordfish fishing: ***Seaworthy: A Swordboat Captain Returns to the Sea***. The obvious title that Greenlaw's writing invokes is Herman Melville's ***Moby Dick***, as she has been referred to as a female Ahab. Peter Matthiessen has applied his storytelling talents to a tale of fishermen from Long Island in ***Men's Lives: The Surfmen and Baymen of the South Fork***. Greenlaw's profession is not largely populated by women; Barbara Holland has collected stories of other women who have stepped outside their expected gender role in search of adventure and change in ***They Went Whistling: Women Wayfarers, Warriors, Runaways, and Renegades***.

Jordan, Pete (1967–)

Dishwasher: One Man's Quest to Wash Dishes in All Fifty States. Harper Perennial, 2007. 358pp. ill. 9780060896423. Also available in e-book. 647.95092

Dishwashing is considered to be the lowliest job in the restaurant, but Pete Jordan chose to do it because it afforded him a freedom very few jobs did. Never highly ambitious, he dropped out of college and took a job dishwashing to pay the rent and then traveled a bit, dishwashing wherever he went. When he was in Alaska he got the idea of dishwashing his way around the country, and he almost made it. During his twelve years of travel, in which he washed dishes in almost every conceivable commercial kitchen, including on an oil rig and in a dining car on a train, Jordan also wrote an e-zine, *Dishwasher*, which developed almost a cult following. He was interviewed on NPR's *This American Life* several times and invited to appear on David Letterman (but he sent his friend to do that interview instead). While recounting his travels, the habits and lore of dishwashing, and the people he meets, Jordan also talks about the working conditions, the importance of dishwashers in the labor movement, and the famous people who had been "suds busters" in their youth.

Subjects: Blue-Collar Workers; *Dishwasher* (E-Zine); Dishwashers; E-Zines; Restaurants; Solo Travel; Travel, United States

Now Try: Jordan's book is a humorous travelogue of sorts, part of a genre of stories told by people traveling the country with a specific goal in mind. For Mike Walsh, an advertising executive, it was to fulfill his father's never-realized dream: ***Bowling Across America: 50 States in Rented Shoes***. Susan Orlean also uses the search for subcultures as her traveling theme in her witty memoir, ***My Kind of Place: Travel Stories from a Woman Who's Been Everywhere***. Another job that definitely enables travel is that of flight attendant. Rene Foss shares some of her stories in ***Around the World in a Bad Mood: Confessions of a Flight Attendant***.

Lynch, Thomas (1948–)

The Undertaking: Life Studies from the Dismal Trade. W. W. Norton, 2009, 1997. 199pp. ill. 9780393334876. 814.54

This is a collection of personal essays by poet and undertaker Thomas Lynch, not so much a traditional memoir as musings on a variety of topics, most of which concern his profession. One of several in the family who provide funeral services for the town of Milford, Michigan, Lynch describes the various aspects of life as an undertaker: getting called out in the middle of the night for a "collection," meeting with future clients for prearranged services, reminding clients to pick up their unclaimed ashes, and even embalming his own father. Lynch has definite opinions that he shares: their services are for the living, not the dead; he decries Jessica Mitford's book ***The American Way of Death***; and he actually disagrees with prearranging funerals.

The Undertaking won the *Chicago Tribune* Heartland Prize for Nonfiction and the American Book Award from the Before Columbus Foundation.

Subjects: American Book Award; Death; Funeral Homes; Funerals; Grief; Milford, MI; Personal Essays; Small Towns; Undertakers

Now Try: Perhaps the best-known story of undertakers these days is the television show ***Six Feet Under***, currently available on DVD. Marcus Galloway offers a look at undertaking in the days of the Wild West in his **Man from Boot Hill** series, the first in the series entitled ***The Man from Boot Hill***. If you'd like an alternative look at this industry, you might want to read ***Grave Matters: A Journey Through the Modern Funeral Industry to a Natural Way of Burial*** by Mark Harris.

Stern, Jane (1946–)

Ambulance Girl: How I Saved Myself by Becoming an EMT. Three Rivers Press, 2004, 2003. 231pp. 9781400048694. Also available in Braille, e-book, and video. 616.02509

Jane Stern may be better known to people as the cowriter of the **Roadfood** books, the contributor to *The Splendid Table* on NPR, or the author of articles in *Gourmet* magazine. In her early fifties her life came crashing down as she experienced clinical depression, claustrophobia, and almost agoraphobia. She decided to apply for training as an emergency medical technician, feeling that if she could face all her fears, most of which surrounded illness and death, she would either come out well at the other end or wind up in psychiatric care. Stern describes the training—more like boot camp, with an ex-Marine for a trainer, a man disdainful of the blue-collar town she lives in—and her surprise at how she excels in her studies. She describes the calls she makes and her fear at each one, fear that she overcomes each time. She also talks about the impact that being on call has on her marriage; no matter what she's doing, if her police radio goes off, she's there to respond. After several years Stern began to fall into depression again, primarily because of seeing someone she knew end up in a vegetative state after an EMT rescue. It made her doubt the worthiness of what they were doing. Witnessing the effects of rescue workers on the disaster of the September 11 attacks in New York, however, gave her a sense of community with emergency workers across the country and helped her to see them in a new light. Despite the seriousness of her topic, Stern is wry and self-deprecating, creating a humorous yet gripping read.

Subjects: Connecticut; Depression; Emergency Medical Technicians; Food Writers; Medical Assistance; Mental Health

Now Try: If you'd like to sample Stern's more traditional writing, you could pick up the culinary memoir that she and her then-husband, Michael, wrote together: ***Two for the Road: Our Love Affair with American Food***. Stern was not a paramedic; she didn't have the training for that. Peter Canning started out as an EMT and went back to school to become a paramedic. His emergency stories can be found in ***Paramedic: On the Front Lines of Medicine***. While Jane Stern couldn't be at Ground Zero, many women rescue workers were. Susan Hagen and Mary Carouba have collected a number of their stories in ***Women at Ground Zero: Stories of Courage and Compassion***. Frank Pierce is an EMS paramedic in New York City in Joe Connelly's novel, ***Bringing out the Dead***.

Educators

Education is the main thrust of this section, whether it be in an inner-city school in Los Angeles or an ivy-covered, prestigious university in Canada. From the various people in this chapter we learn not only about the importance of education, but also about differing methods of teaching, usually derived from experience in the classroom. We also see how influential these teachers can be, from the standpoint both of the students in their midst and of the writings they often published in their fields. For example, educators like Stephen Ambrose and Jill Ker Conway have been prolific in writing for journals and in writing monographs, so their various theories have been spread widely.

The educators here are practitioners in the field at all levels of education, sharing their experiences with small children, high school adolescents, or young adults in college. From their experiences they have derived philosophies of teaching and education that they share with the reader.

Ambrose, Stephen E. (1936–2002)

To America: Personal Reflections of an Historian. Simon & Schuster International, 2004, 2002. 288pp. 9780743252126. Also available in large print, Braille, audiobook, e-audiobook, and e-book. 973

To America is Stephen E. Ambrose's story of his life as seen through the history of America and his own changing views on various people and events, from Thomas Jefferson to now. Ambrose was so taken by the notion of " 'adding to the sum of the world's knowledge' " (Ambrose, 1998) that he decided to get his doctorate in history. He taught in the history department at the University of New Orleans (with a brief stop in Kansas, where, as a member of the faculty, both he and his wife heckled the visiting President Nixon) and has written a number of popular history books, telling America's story for the general public. One critic refers to him as a "triumphalist" (Ambrose, 1998) because of the way he usually celebrates America in his history books.

Ambrose was inducted into the Academy of Achievement in 1998.

Subjects: Biographers; College Professors; Historians; Historiography; History, United States; Reflections; Writers

Now Try: Stephen Ambrose founded the National D-Day Museum in New Orleans, which has been designated by Congress as the country's official World War II Museum (http://www.nationalww2museum.org/). Ambrose had written about D-Day in ***Pegasus Bridge: June 6, 1944*** and ***D-Day, June 6, 1944: The Climactic Battle of WWII*** and was then asked to consult on the making of the movie ***Saving Private Ryan***. When asked who his biggest influence was, apart from William B. Hesseltine, his history professor, Ambrose cited Douglas Southall Freeman and his technique of storytelling in his biography, ***R. E. Lee, a Biography***. Explaining history through storytelling is Ambrose's forte, a talent shared by Charles Bracelen Flood in ***Grant and Sherman: The Friendship That Won the Civil War***. Ambrose has had to field several charges of plagiarism, particularly when he does not enclose within quotation marks verbatim quotes from others in his text. His own view is that he footnotes the sources, so he is not stealing. Thomas Mallon addresses this issue in ***Stolen Words: Forays into the Origins and Ravages of Plagiarism***.

Codell, Esmé Raji (1968–)

Educating Esmé: Diary of a Teacher's First Year. Expanded ed. Algonquin Books of Chapel Hill, 2009, 1999. 262pp. 9781565129351. Also available in audiobook, e-audiobook, and e-book. 372.110092

The difficulties that Esmé Raji Codell had during her first year teaching fifth graders in inner-city Chicago were more from the adults around her than they were from the thirty-one children in the classroom. From the beginning one of her major tenets was the importance of children's literature and reading for students of all ages, so she tried to incorporate reading and other creative arts into her curriculum as much as possible. She was so successful that some of her students jumped two grade levels in their reading and writing capabilities. As often happens, however, she was saddled with an administration that had given up, had no imagination, and managed by following all the rules. Codell didn't stay long at that school, deciding instead to become a school librarian so that she could reach more children with books and by encouraging them to read. She now has a Web site, Planet Esmé (http://www.planetesme.com/), on which she promotes children's literature, and she has an actual bookroom, a resource center in Chicago, for parents to visit to learn more about encouraging reading in the home.

Subjects: Books and Reading; Chicago, IL; Diaries; Education; Elementary School Teachers; Teachers

Now Try: Codell has also written ***How to Get Your Child to Love Reading,*** with an afterword by Jim Trelease. Not just an annotated bibliography, it is also a resource for parents and teachers, with biographies of authors, recipes, creative activities, and stories, along with hints about helping children gain and sustain an interest in reading. Phillip Done has the same mix of humor and intelligence that Codell has, which he reveals as a third-grade teacher in ***32 Third Graders and One Class Bunny: Life Lessons from Teaching***. New teachers are often told that the way to establish control in the classroom is "not to smile until Christmas." Kevin Ryan uses this dictum as his title for a collection of reminiscences by a number of first-year teachers, ***Don't Smile Until Christmas; Accounts of the First Year of Teaching***. Another first-time teacher was Donna Moffett, who left her job as a legal secretary to take a position through the New York City Teaching Fellows Program. The reporter Abby Goodnough followed her through that year, wrote an award-winning series about it, and then published ***Ms. Moffett's First Year: Becoming a Teacher in America***.

Conway, Jill Ker (1934–)

A Woman's Education. Knopf, 2002, 2001. 143pp. 9780679421009. Also available in Braille and e-audiobook. 378.0092

This is the third title in Conway's autobiographical trilogy. The trajectory of her life has been education—of herself and of others, particularly women. The oeuvre is important as a whole, given her goal in writing it: to "try to write a lively picture of the way a woman's mind developed and how her intellectual vocation was formed" (*A Woman's Education*, p. 122). In this third volume Conway talks about both her own continuing education and the education of the women in her constituency in her new position as the first woman president of Smith College, striving to keep Smith a single-sex institution. All the while she is dealing with the increasingly severe illness (manic depression) of her husband and, finally, his death. The first volume of Conway's autobiography, ***The Road from Coorain***, is about her childhood in the outback in Australia, continuing through her adolescence and education in Sydney, until she finally leaves for the United States to get a more liberal education in university. Her second volume, ***True North: A Memoir***, describes her time at Harvard and her move to Toronto, where she becomes a professor of history and then vice president for two years at the University of Toronto.

Subjects: Australia; Australian-Americans; Classics; College Presidents; Harvard University, MA; Higher Education; Intellectual Life; Smith College, MA; University of Toronto, ON; Women's Education

Now Try: With so many stories available about women victimized by narrow attitudes, it is always refreshing to read about women who make a difference in surprising venues, such as the tale of the eighteenth-century American playwright Mercy Otis Warren, whose influence Nancy Rubin Stuart describes in ***The Muse of the Revolution: The Secret Pen of Mercy Otis Warren and the Founding of a Nation***. Gracefully written is one way to describe both Conway's writing and that of Geraldine Brooks, who tells the fictional story of an independent woman interested in furthering her own education in book conservation in ***People of the Book: A Novel***. If you'd like to understand more about why Conway strove to keep Smith College single-sex, you may want to read Karen Stabiner's ***All Girls: Single-Sex Education and Why It Matters***.

Esquith, Rafe (1954–)

Teach Like Your Hair's on Fire: The Methods and Madness Inside Room 56. Viking, 2007. 244pp. ill. 9780670038152. Also available in audiobook and e-audiobook. 370.1

The title of Rafe Esquith's memoir comes from an incident when he was so "in the zone" of teaching that he didn't even realize his hair had caught fire while doing a science experiment with his class. Esquith has been teaching the fifth-grade class at Hobart Elementary in inner-city Los Angeles for over twenty-five years. He has two guiding principles for his students: a) Be nice, work hard; and b) There are no shortcuts. He also believes in regarding failure as a learning tool rather than as a source of shame. Esquith takes his kids around the country to learn history and culture; he teaches them Shakespeare and helps them prepare for the class dramatic presentation of Shakespeare each year; and he gives his kids ownership of their education, teaching them how to assume responsibility for their learning.

Esquith is the only teacher to have won the National Medal of Arts.

Subjects: Education; Elementary School Teachers; Hobart Elementary School, CA; Los Angeles, CA; Moral Education

Now Try: There is a documentary video available in libraries, ***The Hobart Shakespeareans***, about Esquith and his students learning Shakespeare. In 1992 Esquith won the Walt Disney National Outstanding Teacher of the Year Award. Another teacher who also won that award is Ron Clark, now a former teacher who travels to explain to other teachers his philosophy, encompassed in ***The Essential 55:***

An Award-Winning Educator's Rules for Discovering the Successful Student in Every Child. Experiential teaching can be life-changing for both teacher and student. Tierney Cahill ran for Congress, prompted by and with the help of her campaign managers, her sixth-grade students, an experience that taught them all about the electoral process. With the help of Linden Gross, in her memoir ***Ms. Cahill for Congress: One Fearless Teacher, Her Sixth Grade Class, and the Election That Changed Their Lives Forever,*** Cahill also describes her students eight years later and the effect that this campaign had on them. For teachers who are becoming burned-out, Parker J. Palmer has written an inspiring, restorative book, ***The Courage to Teach: Exploring the Inner Landscape of a Teacher's Life***.

McCourt, Frank (1930–2009)

Teacher Man: A Memoir. Scribner, 2005. 258pp. 9780743243773. Also available in large print, audiobook, and e-audiobook. 371.10092

This is the third in a well-known trilogy by Irish-American Frank McCourt. (For ***Angela's Ashes: A Memoir,*** see p. 226.) This memoir covers McCourt's thirty years of teaching before he was known as a Pulitzer Prize–winning memoirist. A high school dropout himself, he managed to get a college education on the GI Bill and taught English in New York City until he was in his fifties. Like most teachers who write about teaching, he had frightful experiences in the classroom, but suffered more frustration at the hands of the bureaucracy. McCourt developed some very creative teaching tactics, including telling stories from his own life as a way to demonstrate colorful storytelling and to encourage the students to tell their own. He finally decided to end his teaching career, finding it somewhat shameful that he had spent so many years teaching English and composition and yet had never written anything himself.

McCourt was inducted into the Academy of Achievement and when asked what book he would recommend, cited Mark Twain's ***The Adventures of Huckleberry Finn***.

Subjects: Adolescents; Education; High School Teachers; Irish-Americans; New York, NY; Teachers

Now Try: Another teacher's story, from the other side of the country, is that of Jaime Escalante, a Bolivian immigrant who spent ten years trying to attain a teaching job in a barrio in East Los Angeles. When he finally succeeded, his dedication and skill in teaching math were such that his students excelled, and the school lost its image of being gang dominated. Jay Mathews tells his story in ***Escalante: The Best Teacher in America***. (Escalante was also the subject of the movie ***Stand and Deliver***.) One of the highlights in McCourt's memoir is his gift for dialogue; this same gift is an appealing element in Sam Shepard's collection, ***Great Dream of Heaven: Stories***. Anyone who has read Frank McCourt is well aware of his dark humor combined with his facility with language. This successful combination works well for Brock Clarke in his unusually titled ***An Arsonist's Guide to Writers' Homes in New England: A Novel***.

Swope, Sam

I Am a Pencil: A Teacher, His Kids, and Their World of Stories. H. Holt. 2005, 2004. 297pp. 9780805078510. 372.623

A children's writer, Sam Swope was invited to teach a third-grade writing class in Queens, New York, a highly diverse area with a lot of new immigrants. The course was meant to last for ten days, but Swope was so entranced by the children and the experience that he made arrangements with the principal to take over a storage closet as his office, and he stayed with the same children through the fifth grade. Apart from teaching them writing and the use of writing and language to empower themselves, he also became involved in their challenging lives as young immigrants. Swope tells stories of outings, of individual children and teachers (all of whose names have been changed to protect their privacy), and of the importance of developing the imagination as a vehicle for learning and for coping with life. In his epilogue he regretfully says how this experience, carried on in the 1990s, would not be possible now with the rigid test-driven standards schools face.

Subjects: Children of Immigrants; Children's Writers; Education; Elementary School Teachers; English Language; Immigrants; Queens (New York, NY); Writing

Now Try: Vivian Gussin Paley is an award-winning kindergarten teacher who also believed in nurturing the imagination of her students and encouraged them to tell their stories, an experience she describes in ***Wally's Stories***. Fifth grade is what Chris Zajac taught in Massachusetts, when Tracy Kidder followed her for a school year to write about the efforts of a good and dedicated teacher, caring about and teaching her class, in ***Among Schoolchildren***. Stephen O'Connor also used writing to help his inner-city students deal with the traumas of their daily lives; his story and his students' can be found in ***Will My Name Be Shouted Out? Reaching Inner City Students Through the Power of Writing***.

Media Personalities

This section profiles a variety of media people in both print and broadcasting. Some have come into your living room regularly for years, and others are better known in their local areas. Network newscasters mix with a gossip columnist, a television talk-show host, and newspaper reporters. Through the eyes of these media people, you will also learn the nature of the business of reporting and will discover how influential the media can be. A common thread running through the memoirs of the "old guard" is how journalism has changed from a serious profession to one of celebrity. You'll also see what a small world it is, in which everyone really does know everyone else. There is one major omission here: Walter Cronkite. His reporting was of such significance that you will find him in Chapter 10, "Changing Lives in History," p. 427.

The media personalities in this section reveal how the profession of journalism has changed through the decades, both in medium and in perspective. With changing technologies, the methods used to inform the public of current news and events have developed to reach an ever-growing audience, and as those reporting on these news items and events have come more and more in the public eye, so too has the focus changed, from the news itself to the reporter.

Bradlee, Benjamin C. (1921–)

A Good Life: Newspapering and Other Adventures. Simon & Schuster, 1996, 1995. 514pp. ill. 32 pp. of plates. 9780684825236. Also available in audiobook (read by the author) and e-book. 070.41092

Bradlee began his journalism career by buying a small newspaper in New Hampshire and, when that failed, he obtained a job as crime reporter for *The Washington Post*. He left the *Post* in 1951 for Paris, where he moved from a job as press attaché to one as a writer for *Newsweek*. Transferred back to Washington, he learned that the owner of *Newsweek* was interested in selling his magazine; Bradlee convinced Philip Graham of *The Washington Post* to buy it. Bradlee was the Washington Bureau Chief for *Newsweek* until after Graham's suicide, when Katharine Graham appointed him managing editor of the *Post*. Bradlee says in his autobiography that it is as much a history of America from 1945 onward as it is a history of his life. He also discusses the issue of truth in journalism and politics and admits that politicians are proficient in lying to the public. He also decries the way in which journalists have become celebrities, believing that muckraking journalism covering incidents such as Watergate has contributed to the celebrity cult.

Subjects: Graham, Katharine; Graham, Philip; Journalism; Journalists; Kennedy, John F.; Newspaper Publishing; *Newsweek* (Magazine); Nonagenarians; Social History, United States; *The Washington Post* (Newspaper)

Now Try: Edward Bennett Williams was a powerful Washington lawyer who encouraged the *Post* to publish the *Pentagon Papers*. His controversial life story is told by Evan Thomas, reporter for *Newsweek* and the *Post*, in ***The Man to See: Edward Bennett Williams; Ultimate Insider; Legendary Trial Lawyer***. At one point Bradlee was married to the sister of Mary Pinchot Meyer, a mistress of Bradlee's close friend President John F. Kennedy. Meyer was shot after Kennedy's assassination, a story told in Nina Burleigh's ***A Very Private Woman: The Life and Unsolved Murder of Presidential Mistress Mary Meyer***. Readers who enjoy stories of journalists and their profession may be entertained and informed by ***Infamous Scribblers: The Founding Fathers and the Rowdy Beginnings of American Journalism*** by Eric Burns.

King, Larry (1933–)
Fussman, Cal, coauthor

My Remarkable Journey. Penguin Canada, 2010, 2009. 294pp. 9780143173564. Also available in audiobook (read by the author), e-audiobook, and e-book. 791.44092

At the end of each anecdotal chapter of this memoir are comments by King's friends and family, which provide more analysis of the person Larry King than his own words do. What King has done in his autobiography is to provide the stories of who and what made him what he is today. He gives the reader a history of his life, from the death of his father, to his name change (from Zeiger) when he got a job in Miami radio, to his eight marriages and the children he has sired but not fathered, to his arrest for grand larceny. He was hired in 1985 by Ted Turner when CNN was just starting out and was host of *Larry King Live* until his retirement in 2010. As a man who has been interviewing people on the radio and on television for more than fifty years, he has his share of stories about people to relate, many of them now friends. Through his stories King provides a cultural history of the United States as well, as he has used current issues as the impetus for his selection of guests. Known for his heart ailments, Larry King has established the Larry King Cardiac Foundation (http://www.lkcf.org) to help fund cardiac procedures for those who wouldn't be able to afford them on their own.

Larry King has been inducted into the Academy of Achievement.

Subjects: CNN (Television Network); Divorce; *Larry King Live* (Television Program); Marriage; Radio Broadcasters; Social History, United States; Television Broadcasters; Television Personalities

Now Try: Diane Rehm is the well-respected radio host of NPR's *The Diane Rehm Show*. She has had to deal with a physical ailment throughout her career, a spasmodic dysphonia she describes in ***Finding My Voice***. Television hosting has many faces, including the late-night show. The late-night show has also had many faces, one of them being Jay Leno's. With the help of Bill Zehme, Leno has written a memoir, ***Leading with My Chin***. Another television personality who has appeared in a variety of guises is Regis Philbin. Also with the help of Bill Zehme, he has told a number of stories to amuse in ***Who Wants to Be Me?***

Kuralt, Charles (1934–1997)

A Life on the Road. Ivy Books, 1995, 1990. 338pp. ill. 16pp. of plates. 9780345484840. Also available in large print, Braille, and audiobook (read by the author). 917.30492

After apprenticing as a newspaper journalist in North Carolina, where he was born and went to university, Charles Kuralt went to New York, where he wrote copy for CBS television. By the time he was twenty-three, he had his dream job, as a CBS news correspondent. He traveled all over the world covering stories and people, and ten years after his first windfall came another one. He began to travel for *CBS Evening News*, creating the segment "On the Road with Charles Kuralt." He spent years traveling the country, reporting on Americana. While he was covering a story in Reno he met the woman who would become his mistress for thirty years, a relationship that came to light only after his death.

Kuralt won many awards for his journalism and was inducted into both the Broadcasting & Cable Hall of Fame and the Academy of Achievement. The book that he recommended to the Academy of Achievement as one of his favorites was ***My Name Is Aram*** by William Saroyan, a book illustrated by Don Freeman; he loved the stories for their humor and style.

Subjects: Americana; CBS (Television Network); *CBS Evening News* (Television Program); *CBS Sunday Morning* (Television Program); *On the Road with Charles Kuralt* (Television Program); Road Trips; Social History, United States; Television Journalists; Television News Anchors; Travel, United States

Now Try: Another television journalist who traveled around the United States did it literally, traveling the coastlines by boat; with drawings by David Canright, Walter Cronkite describes his view of America in ***Around America: A Tour of Our Magnificent Coastline***. The woman with whom Kuralt shared a secret life was Pat Shannon, who has told her story in ***Charles and Me: Notes in the Margin***. Kuralt's memoir is a happy one, full of funny anecdotes; another happy memoir, also full of funny stories, is that of Charles Strouse, a Broadway musical composer: ***Put on a Happy Face: A Broadway Memoir***. One of the lures to New York for Kuralt was the presence of Edward R. Murrow, his hero. Bob Edwards takes a look at Murrow and his world in ***Edward R. Murrow and the Birth of Broadcast Journalism***.

Mitchell, Andrea (1946–)

Talking Back—To Presidents, Dictators, and Assorted Scoundrels. Updated ed. with new Introduction. Penguin Books, 2007, 2005. 415pp. ill. 16pp. of plates. 9780143038733. 070.92

Andrea Mitchell presents an overview of American politics and world events over the past thirty years in this memoir of her journalistic career. She began as a cub reporter in Philadelphia and worked her way up to a spot as NBC-TV's chief foreign affairs correspondent. Along the way she encountered presidents—of the United States and elsewhere; traveled in war zones; and covered such disparate stories as the Three Mile Island nuclear meltdown, the Jonestown massacre, and the Clarence Thomas hearings for confirmation to the Supreme Court. Within her tales of reporting events, Mitchell also discusses her own development as a journalist, how she started out as a "gender pioneer," but how gender quickly slipped to the background. She even discusses the difficulties in maintaining her independence as a journalist through her marriage to Alan Greenspan. Readers of this memoir will get a picture of both current affairs over the past thirty years and the glitterati of Washington, as Mitchell accompanies her husband to a variety of black-tie affairs.

Subjects: Foreign Correspondents; Greenspan, Alan; Journalism; Journalists; NBC (Television Network); Newswomen; Politics; Television Journalists

Now Try: María Elena Salinas also had a gender barrier to overcome; hers was in the Latino news world. Her success is recounted in ***I Am My Father's Daughter: Living a Life Without Secrets***, written with the help of Liz Balmaseda. Traveling for her job just as Mitchell does, Annie Griffiths Belt talks about juggling family and career as a photographer for *National Geographic* in ***A Camera, Two Kids, and a Camel: My Journey in Photographs***. Another revealing memoir by a woman involved in politics is that of Jean Carnahan, the widow of Mel Carnahan, who was the former governor of Missouri and posthumous winner of a seat in the Senate, a seat his wife took over, as she tells in ***Don't Let the Fire Go Out!***.

Newman, Peter C. (1929–)

Here Be Dragons: Telling Tales of People, Passion, and Power. McClelland & Stewart, 2004. 733pp. ill. 24pp. of plates. 9780771067921. 070.92

Peter C. Newman, arguably Canada's most important journalist, tells a riches-to-rags-to-riches story, as he was born to a wealthy tradesman in Czechoslovakia, but fleeing from the Nazis in the early 1940s, they had to leave most of their belongings behind. As a "war child," Newman was given a scholarship to the prestigious Upper Canada College in Toronto. He held a number of increasingly important posts as a journalist, rising from assistant editor at the *Financial Post* to editor-in-chief at the *Toronto Star* and then editor-in-chief at *Maclean's* magazine, a periodical that he took from a foundering monthly to a vibrant weekly news magazine. As a trailblazer in investigative journalism, Newman has written several notable books.

Newman has been named a Companion of the Order of Canada. ***Here Be Dragons*** was awarded the Writers' Trust of Canada Drainie-Taylor Biography Prize.

Subjects: Businessmen; Czech-Canadians; Immigrants, Canada; Journalists; *Maclean's* (Magazine); Newspaper Journalists; Octogenarians; Politics, Canada; *Toronto Star* (Newspaper); Writers' Trust of Canada Drainie-Taylor Biography Prize

Now Try: Newman pulls no punches when he writes; a good example of that is his publication of years of interviews with one of Canada's former prime ministers, Brian Mulroney. Despite the title, Mulroney knew that whatever he said to Newman would eventually wind up in a book and so it did, in ***The Secret Mulroney Tapes: Unguarded Confessions of a Prime Minister***. Christina McCall, Newman's first wife, was an award-winning journalist herself, specializing in creative nonfiction; she died before she could complete her autobiography, but her husband, Stephen Clarkson, published ***My Life as a Dame: The Personal and Political Writings of Christina McCall***. In his memoir one of the people that Newman holds up for high praise is Jack McClelland, a major Canadian publisher and advocate of Canadian literature. Noted biographer James King has written McClelland's story, ***Jack: A Life with Writers: The Story of Jack McClelland***. Newman's book has been written with verve, a characteristic of Hugh Kenner's writing, particularly in ***The Elsewhere Community***, his look at the need to travel and to know, a need that Newman evinced as well.

O'Reilly, Bill (1949–)

A Bold Fresh Piece of Humanity. Broadway Books, 2010, 2008. 256pp. ill. 9780767928830. Also available in large print, audiobook (read by the author), e-audiobook, and e-book. 070.92

Bill O'Reilly's title dates back to his third-grade teacher, who described him thus one day when she was particularly frustrated with him. He invokes his parochial education a fair bit in this memoir of who he is and how he became who he is. He had affection for his father, but not much respect, as his father was not a scrapper and was too weak for O'Reilly to respect. He had to become everything his father wasn't, which is the reason he gives for his success: that he successfully fought against all resistance. Apart from the personal anecdotes, taking us through his schooling, his teaching, his reporting, and his broadcasting career, O'Reilly also weighs in on topics he deems important. Not surprisingly, one of those topics is religion in general and the scandal in the Catholic Church in particular; another is the presence of evil in the world; the third is politics, as one would expect. He also spends a chapter going back in U.S. cultural history to talk about specific singers, movies, television shows, and even Spiro Agnew, Richard Nixon's vice president.

Subjects: Catholics; Childhood and Youth; Conservatives; Family Relationships; Fathers and Sons; Journalists; *The O'Reilly Factor* (Television Program); Television Broadcasters; Writers

Now Try: Those who enjoy hearing Bill O'Reilly will find common ground in the late William F. Buckley Jr., a man about whom Lee Edwards has recently written ***William F. Buckley Jr.: The Maker of a Movement***. James (Jim) Lehrer is a radio and television newscast host, also with a large following; readers may enjoy his memoir, ***A Bus of My Own*** (reflecting his family business and the acquisition of his own 1946 personal bus). Norman Podhoretz is another conservative writer who offers his opinions on the current climate in the United States in ***My Love Affair with America: The Cautionary Tale of a Cheerful Conservative***.

Schieffer, Bob (1937–)

This Just In: What I Couldn't Tell You on TV. Berkley Books, 2004, 2003. 432pp. ill. 16pp. of plates. 9780425194331. Also available in large print, audiobook (read by the author), e-audiobook, and e-book. 070.92

So many journalists seem to succeed by being in the right place at the right time, and that has certainly been true of Bob Schieffer. A local newspaper reporter in Fort Worth when President John F. Kennedy was assassinated, Schieffer happened to get to the paper's office in time to field a phone call asking for a ride to Dallas; he refused until the caller identified herself as Lee Harvey Oswald's mother. It is stories like this that fill Schieffer's memoir, as he recounts some of his harrowing and his moving experiences, working his way to CBS, where he replaced Dan Rather as Washington bureau chief. He anchored the CBS *Saturday Evening News* for twenty years and has been the host of *Face the Nation* since 1991. Schieffer's memoir also has much in it for the budding journalist: advice and pointers, and he even talks about the risks to a marriage when one is often sent away on assignment.

Schieffer has been inducted into the Broadcasting & Cable Hall of Fame.

Subjects: CBS (Television Network); *Face the Nation* (Television Program); Journalism; Journalists; Politics; Television Journalists; Television News Anchors; Texas; Washington, DC

Now Try: The night of the 2000 election, Bob Schieffer was part of the CBS team, following the Senate races. Jeff Greenfield from CNN has written a book about that election and its flawed news coverage in ***"Oh Waiter! One Order of Crow!" Inside the Strangest Presidential Election Finish in American History***. Schieffer was in Washington during the "glory days" cited by journalist Roger Mudd in ***The Place to Be: Washington, CBS, and the Glory Days of Television News***. Dan Rather, whom Schieffer replaced in Washington, and who was still an important part of the CBS team, has written several memoirs, the most recent of which is ***Deadlines and Datelines***.

Smith, Liz (1923–)

Natural Blonde: A Memoir. Hyperion, 2000. 460pp. 32pp. of plates. 9780786863259. Available in large print and audiobook (read by the author). 070.92

Growing up in Texas, Liz Smith's greatest love was the movies. After getting a degree in journalism in Texas, she moved to New York City, where she has lived ever since. Although she has written for a variety of magazines as disparate as *Cosmopolitan* and *Sports Illustrated* and has done quite a bit of book reviewing, her real fame comes from her gossip column, which is syndicated across the country. Smith's form of gossip is benign and tasteful, a fact that she said encourages celebrities to come to her with their stories, as they know she'll treat them fairly. She does the same in her book; it's not a tell-all, even about her own life. She talks about her bisexual relationships, but not in personal detail. Her memoir is full of stories of the celebrities she has met over the years, many of whom became her friends, so that the reader will find anecdotes about a variety of people like Jackie Kennedy Onassis, Madonna, Frank Sinatra, Katharine Hepburn, and Donald Trump, to name but a few.

Subjects: Bisexuals; Celebrities; Gossip Columnists; Journalists; New York, NY; Octogenarians; Social History, United States

Now Try: In a prologue to her memoir, Smith talks about the history of gossip, dating it back to the time of Homer. Samantha Barbas takes a historical approach to her subject as well in ***The First Lady of Hollywood: A Biography of Louella Parsons***, the woman who created the role of gossip columnist. If you enjoy the humor in Smith's memoir, you may also enjoy reading about another columnist, Jancee Dunn, who still seems surprised at her success. Her title says it all: ***But Enough About Me: A Jersey Girl's Unlikely Adventures Among the Absurdly Famous***. From the other side of the gossip fence comes the wry memoir of someone whose personal experience allows her to give advice on how to live the celebrity life: ***Confessions of an Heiress: A Tongue-in-Chic Peek Behind the Pose*** by Paris Hilton, with help from Merle Ginsberg and photographs by Jeff Vespa and WireImage.

Stahl, Lesley (1941–)

Reporting Live. Simon & Schuster, 2000. 444pp. ill. 16pp. of plates. 9780684853710. Also available in large print, audiobook (read by the author), and e-book. 070.92

Stahl starts her memoir from the age of thirty: "I was born on my thirtieth birthday." She starts out as a cub reporter in Boston, but soon gets a gig with CBS in Washington. One of the "affirmative action babies," hired along with Connie Chung and Bernard Shaw, she was sent out to investigate a third-rate burglary while others were covering the Nixon and McGovern presidential campaigns. The locale of her burglary story was the hotel and office complex known as the Watergate, the burglary an event that toppled Richard Nixon from the presidency. This was the beginning of her rise through coverage of three presidents, to hosting *Face the Nation*, to reporting for *60 Minutes*, a position she still holds. In her memoir she also talks a bit about her personal life, her marriage to Aaron Latham and his clinical depression, and her being the one to work outside the home. She also talks about the changes in network news and the evolution of journalism to what it is today.

Subjects: CBS (Television Network); Depression; Journalism; Journalists; Latham, Aaron; Mothers and Daughters; Newswomen; Politics; Television Journalists

Now Try: After much experience as a television journalist herself, Linda Ellerbee wrote ***"And So It Goes": Adventures in Television***. Stahl's is a Horatio Alger story; surprisingly, so is Dawn Steel's story, as she describes her rise to the top of Columbia Pictures in ***They Can Kill You—But They Can't Eat You: Lessons from the Front***. Lindy Boggs also set out to do a job that's difficult for a mother, particularly a widowed mother. Written with the help of Katherine Hatch, Boggs's memoir, ***Washington Through a Purple Veil: Memoirs of a Southern Woman***, describes her life as a legislator.

Thomas, Helen (1920–)

Front Row at the White House: My Life and Times. Scribner, 2006, 1999. 415pp. ill. 16 pp. of plates. 9780684868097. Also available in audiobook and e-audiobook. 070.92

"Our priority is the people's right to know—without fear or favor. We are the peoples' servants." This is the philosophy that has inspired Helen Thomas for sixty-seven years and counting, as she stated in her first memoir, ***Dateline: White House***. Thomas worked her way up the ladder with UPI (United Press International) from copy-girl to reporter to White House correspondent, then senior White House correspondent and finally bureau chief. She left UPI, as she said she would, when it was bought out by News World Communications, Inc. in 2000, and at eighty years old she was then hired by the Hearst Corporation to write two columns a week. As a woman in the Washington press corps, Thomas has broken several glass ceilings;

perhaps the most significant was the National Press Club, which barred women, even women reporters, from entering. In 1971 she finally succeeded in opening their doors to women as the first female member of the club; she was eventually named its president. Thomas is perhaps best known for her signature, "Thank you, Mr. President," which she has said at the end of each press conference for ten presidents, beginning with President Kennedy. She was the first reporter to ask a question of President Obama at his first press conference. Embroiled in a controversy over a comment about Israel that she made publicly, Thomas retired in 2010, not long before her ninetieth birthday.

Subjects: Journalism; Journalists; Newspaper Journalists; Newswomen; Nonagenarians; Political Journalists; Politics; Trailblazers; United Press International; Washington, DC; White House, Washington, DC

Now Try: Concerned with the direction the media have been heading in, particularly since the Bush administration cracked down on investigative journalism, Thomas has recently written ***Watchdogs of Democracy? The Waning Washington Press Corps and How It Has Failed the Public***. Donald A. Ritchie provides a historical look at the Washington press corps in ***Reporting from Washington: The History of the Washington Press Corps***. Helen Thomas may be a pioneer and trailblazer, but she has some wonderful role models, as demonstrated in ***Mary Ann Shadd Cary: The Black Press and Protest in the Nineteenth Century*** by Jane Rhodes and ***Nellie Bly: Daredevil, Reporter, Feminist*** by Brooke Kroeger, a former UPI reporter.

Wallace, Mike (1918–)
Gates, Gary Paul (1935–), coauthor

Between You and Me: A Memoir. Hyperion, 2005. 292pp. Includes videodisc. 9781401300296. Also available in large print, audiobook (read by the author), e-audiobook, and e-book. 070.92

Gary Paul Gates collaborated with Mike Wallace on an earlier memoir as well, ***Close Encounters***. The earlier memoir was more personal; ***Between You and Me*** features many of Wallace's interviews with people from *60 Minutes*, the show he started with Harry Reasoner and producer Don Hewitt in 1968 and from which he retired in 2006. He is now "Correspondent Emeritus" and does occasional work for CBS. Wallace was known for his hard-hitting questions in his interviews and pulled no punches in his investigative journalism. He was at the heart of several controversies, some involving stories (e.g., one on General William C. Westmoreland) that CBS pulled because they didn't want to face lawsuits, even though Wallace's information was correct. He also evolved in his political thinking, not afraid to admit that views he had held earlier had changed as more information came forward (the war in Vietnam is a good example: he had originally favored it and finally came out swinging against it).

Winner of many Emmys, Wallace was inducted into both the Academy of Achievement and the Broadcasting & Cable Hall of Fame and even has a star on the Hollywood Walk of Fame.

Subjects: *60 Minutes* (Television Program); CBS (Television Network); Death of a Child; Depression; Journalism; Journalists; Social History, United States; Television Journalists

Now Try: Since his retirement, Wallace has published a collection of interviews with notables from around the world, ***The Way We Will Be 50 Years from Today: 60 of the World's Greatest Minds Share Their Visions of the Next Half Century***. Another of the controversies surrounding Wallace was CBS management pulling his story about a tobacco company—how it lied in its advertising and added more nicotine to addict smokers. A feature film, ***The Insider***, was made about that incident, with Christopher Plummer playing Mike Wallace. Through extensive research, the historian Allan M. Brandt backs up Wallace's claims in ***The Cigarette Century: The Rise, Fall, and Deadly Persistence of the Product That Defined America***. A former president of CBS, Bill Leonard, has written about his company in ***In the Storm of the Eye: A Lifetime at CBS***. And Don Hewitt, the longtime producer of *60 Minutes*, has written his story about that program, ***Tell Me a Story: Fifty Years and* 60 Minutes *in Television***.

Walters, Barbara (1929–)

Audition: A Memoir. Knopf, 2008. 612pp. ill. 9780307266460. Also available in large print, audiobook (read by the author), e-audiobook, and e-book. 070.92

In 1961 Walters began writing for NBC's *Today* show, and she joined Hugh Downs as cohost in the mid-1960s, although she wasn't actually given that title until 1974. She was not allowed, however, to ask any questions of the guest until Downs had asked three questions, so Walters started interviewing people outside the studio; this way she could ask all the questions. She was hired in 1976 by ABC to cohost *ABC Evening News* with Harry Reasoner, but he was very unhappy with that posting, and the show actually failed. She was under contract with ABC, however, for $1 million, so they gave her specials to do, in which she interviewed newsworthy people; she had finally found her niche. She hosted *20/20* for twenty years, conducting groundbreaking interviews and finally stepping down in 2004 after ABC managers insisted she interview a child molester rather than George W. Bush. Walters continues to air two annual shows, the pre–Academy Awards interview and *10 Most Fascinating People*, and she is also a regular participant in ABC's morning show, *The View*.

Walters has been awarded Emmys for her programs and has been inducted into the Broadcasting & Cable Hall of Fame.

Subjects: *20/20* (Television Program); ABC (Television Network); Adoption; NBC (Television Network); Newswomen; Television Journalists; Television News Anchors; Trailblazers

Now Try: Barbara Walters is one of several women recognized for her achievements by Kay Bailey Hutchison in ***American Heroines: The Spirited Women Who Shaped Our Century***. Her achievements also paved the way for women broadcast journalists; Liz Trotta talks about the difficulties for a woman in the business in ***Fighting for Air: In the Trenches with Television News***. For a perspective of ABC News from its president, you may enjoy Roone Arledge's ***Roone: A Memoir***. (Arledge was also responsible for creating *Monday Night Football*.) Walters's memoir has been very well-received, cited as "compulsively readable." Eleanor Coppola, wife of the director Francis Ford Coppola, has also written a compulsively readable memoir, ***Notes on a Life***, but her take on life is different from that of Barbara Walters.

Williams, Marjorie (1958–2005)
Noah, Timothy, ed.

The Woman at the Washington Zoo: Writings on Politics, Family, and Fate. Public Affairs, 2006, 2005. 365pp. 9781586484576. 975.3

Williams was a newspaper columnist and essayist, writing primarily for *The Washington Post*, *Vanity Fair*, and *Slate* magazine. Her beat was Washington, DC, particularly its movers and shakers, and her usual habit was to look at a specific person and peel away the façade. Quoting her oncologist, she was "hit by lightning" when she contracted liver cancer, diagnosed when she was forty-three, and given three months to live. She managed to live and continue to write until she was forty-seven. ***The Woman at the Washington Zoo*** is a collection of her essays compiled by her husband, Timothy Noah, a writer for *Slate* magazine. The first part comprises some of what Noah considers to be Marjorie's most interesting profiles, of people like Barbara and Jeb Bush and the relationship between Bill Clinton and Al Gore; the second section is personal essays and stories, looking back at her childhood in New Jersey and her marriage and motherhood. The final section is the previously unpublished "Hit by Lightning: A Cancer Memoir."

The Woman at the Washington Zoo won the PEN American Center Martha Albrand Award for First Nonfiction.

Subjects: Journalists; Liver Cancer; Newspaper Columnists; Newswomen; PEN American Center Martha Albrand Award for First Nonfiction; Personal Essays; Political Culture; *Vanity Fair* (Magazine); Washington, DC; *The Washington Post* (Newspaper)

Now Try: The one doctor whom Williams would mention by name, because of the high quality of his attitude toward her illness, was Jerome E. Groopman, a hematologist, oncologist, researcher, and writer; one of his books that cancer patients may find helpful is ***The Anatomy of Hope: How People Prevail in the Face of Illness***. Williams's writing about her plight is unsentimental, as is the writing of Amy Silverstein, a young woman needing a heart transplant, who tells her story in ***Sick Girl***. Political culture is Williams's milieu, and it is also the setting for Marge Piercy's novel, ***The Third Child***, about the youngest child of a former governor, running for the Senate.

Crime Fighters

This is quite a broad field, covering not just lawyers, judges, and the police, but also spies, criminal profilers (FBI), and forensic scientists, people in a relatively new field that seems to fascinate a broad spectrum of readers. Many of the criminal cases in these memoirs will likely be familiar to you. Some of these books will read at the narrative level and pace of a good thriller, and others are more introspective and ruminative.

Crime fighters include policemen and policewomen, judges, special agents, and forensic scientists. But they also include people who happened upon a crime and became involved in trying to solve it. Readers learn about more than the memoirist and the profession, however; gender discrimination is often present in these accounts, as women writers describe their experiences breaking into previously male-dominated professions.

Baer, Robert (1952–)

See No Evil: The True Story of a Ground Soldier in the CIA's War on Terrorism. Crown, 2002. 284pp. ill. 8 pp. of plates; maps. 9780609609873. Also available in large print, audiobook, e-audiobook, and e-book. 327.12730092

Robert Baer was a case officer for the Central Intelligence Agency (CIA) in the Middle East for twenty-one years and received the Career Intelligence Medal in 1997, the year he retired. His disillusionment with the CIA grew over the years as the agency changed, beginning to rely more on technical advances such as satellite photos than on ground operatives in the arena. The agency was no longer concerned to put people with appropriate language skills in the global offices and seemed to rebuff any intelligence that couldn't be proven technologically. Baer describes his career with the CIA, but gives much of his attention to the bombing of the American embassy in Beirut in 1983, an event whose repercussions he believes are still being felt. Despite his disillusionment, Baer is not bitter and laces his story with humor. The movie ***Syriana*** was suggested by Baer and this book.

Subjects: Central Intelligence Agency; Intelligence Officers; Islamic Fundamentalism; Lebanon; Middle East; Terrorism

Now Try: Following this book, Baer wrote another, ***Sleeping with the Devil: How Washington Sold Our Soul for Saudi Crude.*** Michael A. Sheehan has spent much of his career in counterterrorism and offers his own suggestions for winning the war against terrorism in ***Crush the Cell: How to Defeat Terrorism Without Terrorizing Ourselves.*** Another perspective on the substance of Baer's memoir comes from Bob Graham, a former member of the Senate Intelligence Committee, in ***Intelligence Matters: The CIA, the FBI, Saudi Arabia, and the Failure of America's War on Terror,*** written with the help of Jess Nussbaum. The technology that Baer is wary of relying on completely is described in a book by Robert Wallace, H. Keith Melton, and Henry R. Schlesinger, ***Spycraft: The Secret History of the CIA's Spytechs from Communism to Al-Qaeda.***

Bass, William M. (1928–)
Jefferson, Jon, coauthor

Death's Acre: Inside the Legendary Forensic Lab—the Body Farm—Where the Dead Do Tell Tales. Foreword by Patricia Cornwall. Berkley Books, 2004, 2003. 304pp. ill. 9780425198322. Also available in audiobook and e-book. 614.1

After several years teaching anthropology in Kansas, Bass was asked to head the Department of Anthropology at the University of Tennessee. It was while he was there, consulting on homicide cases with the police, that he realized very little was known about the body postmortem. With the blessing of the university, in 1972 he created the Forensic Anthropology Center, an outdoor research facility, known popularly as "The Body Farm," which would give scientists a controlled area to study postmortem decay in a variety of situations. Donated bodies are left out in the open, buried in water, buried in shallow or deep graves, locked in trunks, burned, etc., so that the scientists can explore the insect and floral growth as well as the surrounding environment to determine how one can be specific about time of death. Dr. Bass and his team have thus often been able to lead homicide detectives to perpetrators of crimes and provide the evidence to back up the arrests in court.

Subjects: Crime Laboratories; Crime Victims; Criminalists; Forensic Anthropologists; Homicide Investigations; Octogenarians; Scientists; University of Tennessee, TN

Now Try: Bass and Jefferson have followed up ***Death's Acre*** with a sequel, ***Beyond the Body Farm: A Legendary Bone Detective Explores Murders, Mysteries, and the Revolution in Forensic Science***. The two have also collaborated on a fiction series, under the pen name Jefferson Bass, **The Body Farm Mysteries**; the first in the series is ***Carved in Bone: A Body Farm Mystery***. Two nonfiction titles of particular interest in forensic anthropology, each dealing with different aspects of the subject, are Kenneth V. Iserson's ***Death to Dust: What Happens to Dead Bodies?***, a sociological look at the topic, and Jessica Snyder Sachs's ***Corpse: Nature, Forensics, and the Struggle to Pinpoint Time of Death***, with a botanical focus on the subject. Emily A. Craig had been a student at the Body Farm and went on to have a successful career as a forensic anthropologist for the state of Kentucky. She describes her work in ***Teasing Secrets from the Dead: My Investigations at America's Most Infamous Crime Scenes***.

Berger, Thomas R. (1933–)

One Man's Justice: A Life in the Law. Douglas & McIntyre, 2002. 346pp. 9781550549195. 340.092

As a lawyer working on his own, Berger soon began to make a name for himself in his constant fight for justice; he was often asked to take on important inquiries on behalf of the government and other agencies, within and outside Canada's borders. He became well-known as an advocate for Aboriginal rights, particularly in two renowned cases, one on the rights of Aboriginals to have a distinct place in Canadian law and one that stopped the proposed Mackenzie Valley Pipeline and recognized that Aboriginal peoples have a right to self-determination. Perhaps the most important step Berger took for Aboriginal peoples, however, was to speak out vociferously when their rights, originally included in the Canadian Charter of Rights and Freedoms, were then withdrawn shortly before ratification. Because of his advocacy, these rights were reinstated, but Berger was strongly chastised for his lack of objectivity as a sitting judge on the British Columbia Supreme Court. He then resigned his seat as judge and returned to the practice of law, fighting for justice one case at a time.

Berger's book was a finalist for the Hubert Evans Non-fiction Prize (BC Book Prizes), and he was awarded the Order of Canada.

Subjects: Aboriginal Peoples, Canada; Aboriginal Rights, Canada; Canada; Judges, Canada; Lawyers, Canada; Social Activists, Canada; Supreme Court of British Columbia, Canada

Now Try: Berger also took on the case of a conscientious objector who did not want her federal taxes to go toward military spending. Another interesting group of conscientious objectors volunteered to starve themselves to help doctors understand how to feed the starving victims of concentration camps; this heroic effort was recounted by Todd Tucker in ***The Great Starvation Experiment: The Heroic Men Who Starved So That Millions Could Live***. Another famous case that Berger took on was that of Linda Macdonald, brainwashed in a notorious study in Montreal; brainwashing is one of the tactics used in boot camps for troubled teens, as revealed by Maia Szalavitz in ***Help at Any Cost: How the Troubled-Teen Industry Cons Parents and Hurts Kids***. The Mackenzie Valley Pipeline is the backdrop for Elizabeth Hay's award-winning ***Late Nights on Air: A Novel***, set in Yellowknife, Northwest Territories.

Conlon, Edward (1965–)

Blue Blood. Riverhead Books, 2005, 2004. 562pp. 9781594480737. Also available in audiobook. 363.2092

Having majored in English at Harvard, Conlon appreciates his knowledge of writing for the reports he has to write and for the articles he wrote pseudonymously for *The New Yorker*, but day-to-day policing is what makes him excited to go to work each day. This is what he brings to ***Blue Blood***: the daily life of a regular NYPD policeman, with spurts of excitement, danger, tragedy, and grittiness along with extended lulls of waiting, watching, patrolling, and writing reports. His father, who left the NYPD to work with the FBI, wanted Conlon to find a different profession, although Conlon's uncle and great-grandfather had also been NYPD policemen. But Conlon found that he did not want only to write the story, he wanted also to be part of it. For him, being a policeman in New York is like participating in a play by Shakespeare, full of theater: " 'you knock on a door and someone has to tell you a story' " (Italiano, 2004).

Blue Blood was a finalist for the *Los Angeles Times* Current Interest Book Prize, the Anthony Award for Best Critical Work, and the National Book Critics Circle Award in Nonfiction.

Subjects: Crime; Family Portraits; Irish-Americans; New York, NY; New York Police Department; Police; Writers

Now Try: One of the stories that Conlon touches on is the infamous killing of Amadou Diallo, an innocent man who was shot by the police forty-one times in his doorway. Diallo's mother, Kadiatou, went to New York from her home in Guinea to protest not only the killing but the slanderous reports that were being spread about her son. With the help of Craig Wolff, she tells her story in ***My Heart Will Cross This Ocean: My Story, My Son, Amadou***. Across the country is another equally famous police force, the Los Angeles Police Department. Miles Corwin spent a year with the Homicide Unit and wrote about it in ***Homicide Special: A Year with the LAPD's Elite Detective Unit***. Although he writes in the literate manner one would expect from a Harvard graduate, Conlon's book comes across as streetwise, as indeed he needs to be able to communicate with the people he meets on the street. One of those street people, Lee Stringer, also took up writing, first for *Street News*, the paper sold by the homeless, and then in ***Grand Central Winter: Stories from the Street***.

DeLong, Candice (1952–)
Petrini, Elisa, coauthor

Special Agent: My Life on the Front Lines as a Woman in the FBI. Hyperion, 2002, 2001. 370pp. 9780786890330. Also available in audiobook, e-audiobook, and e-book. 363.2082092

Candice DeLong was no stranger to deviant behavior when she applied to join the FBI; she had been the head nurse in a maximum-security psychiatric ward in Chicago. She found that one of the obstacles in her rigorous training in the FBI was the blatant sexism she encountered, due in part to J. Edgar Hoover's aversion to women. DeLong started in 1980, eight years after the first women had been accepted. She found her way, however, and was involved in such notorious cases as the Tylenol tampering and the Unabomber. She was also in on the early stages of profiling, and by the time she left the FBI, she was serving as a head field profiler. In addition to discussions of sexism and stories of her cases, some with gruesome details, DeLong also talks about personal safety and what to do in the event of a personal attack.

Subjects: Criminal Investigation; Criminal Profilers; Federal Agents; Federal Bureau of Investigation; Hoover, J. Edgar; Sex Discrimination; Violent Crimes

Now Try: DeLong's style and tone are conversational. So too are the style and tone of the novelist and former policeman Hugh Holton in his nonfiction work, ***The Thin Black Line: True Stories by Black Law Enforcement Officers Policing America's Meanest Streets***. DeLong has been compared to Clarice Starling, the fictional federal agent created by Thomas Harris, first appearing in ***The Silence of the Lambs***. There are relatively few biographies or memoirs of policewomen at either the federal or local level. One that may prove of interest to readers is by Gina Gallo: ***Armed and Dangerous: Memoirs of a Chicago Policewoman***.

Dew, Rosemary
Pape, Pat, coauthor

No Backup: My Life as a Female FBI Special Agent. Carroll & Graf, 2004. 302pp. 9780786712786. 363.2082

Rosemary Dew is writing this exposé of the FBI from a distance in time, believing in its potential good but concerned about the intrinsic flaws that date back to its first head, J. Edgar Hoover. Although she received eight commendations from different directors and was promoted to Field Supervisor (only one of seven women in its history at that point), she felt the presence of gender bias and sexual harassment very strongly. Dew takes us from her training through her assignments to cases that the readers will be familiar with, to her posting as Field Supervisor. Her primary concern, however, is to make public the entrenched problems, in the hopes that attention will be paid. She describes the culture at the FBI that failure is not an option, so any failures that do occur need to be covered up, a culture that dates back to Hoover's concern that he be perceived as perfect. Very troubling to Dew is the inability of the FBI to share information, a factor that she believes contributed to the attacks on the World Trade Center in 2001. Because she worked as a consultant in law enforcement after her thirteen years with the FBI, Dew has been able to offer suggestions to the agency to help it become what it has the potential to be; rather than a disgruntled employee, she is a law-enforcement specialist with executable suggestions to make.

Subjects: Criminal Investigation; Federal Agents; Federal Bureau of Investigation; Hoover, J. Edgar; Sex Discrimination

Now Try: Anthony Summers offers a biography of J. Edgar Hoover, ***Official and Confidential: The Secret Life of J. Edgar Hoover,*** which reveals the man as he really was, terrorizing all the people in Washington who might otherwise have lobbied for his removal from his position. Although Dew wrote her book once she was no longer a federal agent, she could still be referred to as a whistleblower, one who shows much courage in bringing to light workplace offenses. Harry Markopolos tried to blow the whistle on Bernie Madoff, the felonious investment counselor who defrauded thousands of people, but as Markopolos explains with the help of Frank Casey et al., ***No One Would Listen: A True Financial Thriller***. Readers may enjoy the fictional FBI female agent in **The Maggie O'Dell Series** by Alex Kava; the first in the series is ***A Perfect Evil.***

Douglas, John E. (1945–)
Olshaker, Mark (1951–), coauthor

Mindhunter: Inside the FBI's Elite Serial Crime Unit. Pocket Star Books, 1996, 1995. 397pp. ill. 8pp. of plates. 9780671528904. Also available in large print, audiobook (read by the author), and e-book. 363.2092

When Douglas moved over to the Behavioral Science Unit in 1977 after seven years as an FBI agent, he finally found his niche and made his mark. He began the Criminal Profiling Program, initially by applying criminal psychology to cases. Realizing that they needed hard data to back up their ideas, he began to go into penitentiaries to interview serial killers and rapists, people like Ted Bundy and Charles Manson. By asking for very detailed information about the crimes they committed, he garnered enough information from these criminals to enable his department to draw up profiles of probable criminal behavior based on personality and past behavior. In practical terms, these profiles aided in finding probable cause for search warrants when police had a suspect in mind and provided insight when there was as yet no suspect. He was involved in such notorious cases as the Green River killings, the Tylenol tampering, and the Atlanta child murders. He retired from the FBI when he was fifty and continues to consult and to write books (with Mark Olshaker) about his various profiling cases.

Mindhunter was a finalist for the Edgar Award Best Fact Crime.

Subjects: Behavioral Science Unit, FBI; Behavioral Scientists; Criminal Investigation; Criminal Profilers; Federal Bureau of Investigation; Forensic Psychology; Homicide Investigations; Human Behavior; Serial Murder; Violent Crimes

Now Try: Apart from all his nonfiction on profiling, Douglas (with Olshaker) has begun a fiction series, **Broken Wings Thrillers**, the first of which is ***Broken Wings***. Another major FBI profiler was Robert K. Ressler, who was involved in setting up ViCAP, the Violent Criminal Apprehension Program; his story, told with the help of Tom Shachtman, is ***Whoever Fights Monsters***. David Reichert, the sheriff who was responsible for the investigation into the Green River killings, has written about that terrible time in ***Chasing the Devil: My Twenty-Year Quest to Capture the Green River Killer***. Among the various forensic sciences used in criminal investigation is one described by Jeanne Boylan, who combines her ability to interview victims and eyewitnesses sensitively with her artistic abilities. ***Portraits of Guilt: The Woman Who Profiles the Faces of America's Deadliest Criminals*** is her story of creating identikits for the police.

Preston, Douglas J. (1956–), and Mario Spezi

The Monster of Florence. With a new Afterword. Grand Central Publishing, 2009, 2008. 344pp. ill. 9780446581271. Also available in large print, audiobook, e-audiobook, and e-book. 363.1523

This story could be seen as a Keystone Kops kind of adventure if it weren't so serious. Mario Spezi, one of the two coauthors, was a reporter for the Italian newspaper *La Nazione* and had been covering a gruesome serial murder case for decades when Douglas Preston, the thriller writer, moved with his family to a villa outside Florence. Learning that one of the murders had taken place near his property, Preston contrived to meet Spezi to hear about the crimes and the investigations that had gone on for so long. Preston soon got caught up in Spezi's obsession and became involved with him in trying to sort it all out and determine who the real killer was. In their book they provide all the background detail from the years of investigations, accusations, trials, and lives ruined. They also tell the story of how they themselves became implicated, with Spezi arrested and Preston and his family deported, ostensibly for planting evidence and obstructing an ongoing criminal investigation. The new Afterword illustrates how the story continues.

Subjects: Corruption; Criminal Investigation; Florence, Italy; Freedom of the Press; Italy; Journalists; Serial Murders; Social History, Italy; True Crime; Writers

Now Try: Magdalen Nabb is the author of the **Marshal Guarnaccia Mysteries**, Marshal being a member of the Florence carabinieri. In the tenth novel in the series, ***The Monster of Florence,*** he becomes involved in this serial murder plaguing the city. (Nabb's novel was written more than ten years before Preston and Spezi's book.) Mismanagement of justice is one of the themes in Preston and Spezi's book, as it is in the story of four servicemen imprisoned for a crime they didn't commit, a story told by Tom Wells and Richard A. Leo, ***The Wrong Guys: Murder, False Confessions, and the Norfolk Four.*** The journalist Carlton Stowers tells the story of an investigator, John Little, given a cold case from Wichita Falls, Texas; assigned to investigate four unsolved murders, he links them to a fifth, with an outcome more successful than Preston's, as recounted in ***Scream at the Sky: Five Texas Murders and One Man's Crusade for Justice.*** Another novelist who sets her police procedurals in Italy (Venice) is Donna Leon, author of the **Commissario Brunetti Mysteries**, the first of which is ***Death at La Fenice.***

Queen, William

Under and Alone: The True Story of the Undercover Agent Who Infiltrated America's Most Violent Outlaw Motorcycle Gang. Fawcett, 2006, 2005. 260pp. ill. 16pp. of plates. 9780345487520. Also available in audiobook, e-audiobook, and e-book. 364.1066092

Queen begins his harrowing memoir with a review of his role as Special Response Team Agent with the Bureau of Alcohol, Tobacco, Firearms and Explosives (ATF). Then he dives right in with his account of hanging out in biker gear at the known haunts of one of America's most vicious motorcycle gangs, The Mongols, in southern California. He gradually insinuates himself into the organization, passing test after test, until the point where he receives a badge of membership and solidarity. Throughout his tenure undercover he works at keeping himself alive and not becoming completely immersed in the culture, trying to avoid the drugs and trying to avoid killing anyone. He also talks honestly about what effect his work had on his real family, who eventually had to move away under fictitious names while Queen was testifying.

Among the many awards he has won for his ATF work, Queen was awarded the Distinguished Service Medal from the ATF.

Subjects: Bureau of Alcohol, Tobacco, Firearms and Explosives; California; Crime; Criminal Investigation; Motorcycle Gangs; True Crime; Undercover Operations

Now Try: Bob Leuci is likely a familiar name to many for his undercover work, hiding in plain sight as a detective in the New York Police Department while acting as a confidential informant for the federal government in its investigation of corruption across the criminal justice system in New York. ***Prince of the City: The True Story of a Cop Who Knew Too Much,*** by Robert Daley, is Leuci's story. Hunter S. Thompson was perhaps the first writer to bring to light the biker lifestyle; after spending two years riding with the Hell's Angels and nearly getting kicked to death by some of them, he wrote ***Hell's Angels; A Strange and Terrible Saga***. Queen provides harrowing details in his narrative; so too does Jay Dobyns, relating with the help of Nils Johnson-Shelton his perilous undercover work in ***No Angel: My Harrowing Undercover Journey to the Inner Circle of the Hells Angels***.

Stoll, Clifford

The Cuckoo's Egg: Tracking a Spy Through the Maze of Computer Espionage. With a new Afterword. Pocket Books, 2005, 1989. 399pp. 9781416507789. Also available in audiobook. 364.168

Clifford Stoll had his doctorate in astrophysics, but was unemployed due to defunding. When he found a job at Berkeley as systems administrator for the Lawrence Laboratory computer system, his first assignment was to track down a discrepancy in billing of seventy-five cents, a task that took him a year to complete. What he discovered through this discrepancy was that someone was hacking into the system at Berkeley. But through Stoll's intelligence and plain doggedness, he also discovered that Berkeley was not the only target. Eventually the FBI, the CIA, the military, and the German police all got involved, breaking a spy ring of hackers who traded secrets with the Soviets for money and drugs. Stoll's story details all of this—how he discovered the hacker, how he tracked him, and what the federal agencies did, though they were initially reluctant to get on board. He also includes details of his personal life and the day-to-day workings of his work environment. Because of this job he became very popular on the lecture circuit and even appeared before the Senate.

Subjects: Computer Crime; Computer Espionage; Counterintelligence; Espionage, Soviet; Hackers: Hess, Markus; Military Secrets

Now Try: Stoll has gone on to write a number of other books, most recently ***High-Tech Heretic: Why Computers Don't Belong in the Classroom and Other Reflections by a Computer Contrarian***. Stoll's telling of his story reads like a thriller, something in the vein of a Tom Clancy work. Clancy's **Net Force** series, created with Steve Pieczenik, is all about cyberspace, and the first title is ***Tom Clancy's Net Force***. Another creative nonfiction narrative that reads like a thriller is also a true-crime story, set in a different century. Erik Larson's ***The Devil in the White City: Murder, Magic, and Madness at the Fair That Changed America*** is the story of Daniel Hudson Burnham, the architect of the 1893 Chicago World's Fair and H. H. Holmes, *né* Herman Webster Mudgett, a serial killer who built his killing grounds very near to the fairgrounds. If you'd like to read the story of a hacker from his point of view, you might want to try Ejovi Nuwere's book, written with David Chanoff. In ***Hacker Cracker: A Journey from the Mean Streets of***

Brooklyn to the Frontiers of Cyberspace, Nuwere recounts how he started out as a hacker and then used those skills to become a computer security specialist.

Tenet, George (1953–)
Harlow, Bill (1950–), coauthor

At the Center of the Storm: My Years at the CIA. HarperCollins, 2007. 549pp. ill. 16pp. of plates. 9780061147784. Also available in large print, audiobook, e-audiobook, and e-book. 327.12730092

Despite the title, this memoir really focuses on Tenet's time since he was made director of the Central Intelligence Agency in 1997, a time fraught with threats from terrorists. He discusses his work on the Israeli–Palestinian issue, his efforts to convince the Bush administration that a major terrorist attack was imminent before September 11, 2001, and the fallout from his comment about the question of weapons of mass destruction being a "slam dunk." He enlightens the reader about his take on the Bush administration, particularly the lower-level bureaucrats, and on how the CIA tried to make sense of Islamic militancy. One point that he clarifies is that policymakers did not so much tread on his turf of intelligence, as that he himself crossed over into the policy arena when he should have remained on the intelligence-gathering side.

Tenet was awarded the Presidential Medal of Freedom in 2004 by President George W. Bush.

Subjects: Bush, George W.; Central Intelligence Agency; Foreign Policy, United States; Greek-Americans; Intelligence Officers; Iraq; Terrorism

Now Try: There are two books in particular in Tenet's memoir that he discusses in order to contradict accusations in them. The first is veteran reporter Bob Woodward's ***Plan of Attack***, and the other is by former CIA intelligence officer Tyler Drumheller (with help from Elaine Monaghan): ***On the Brink: An Insider's Account of How the White House Compromised American Intelligence***. If you'd like to read about the CIA even before Tenet's time, you may enjoy Tim Weiner's ***Legacy of Ashes: The History of the CIA***. Tim Shorrock offers a disturbing twenty-first-century view of the American intelligence community in ***Spies for Hire: The Secret World of Intelligence Outsourcing***. A number of writers who describe the intelligence community lay blame at their feet for not preventing the September 11, 2001, attacks on the World Trade Center. Gerald L. Posner explains why in ***Why America Slept: The Failure to Prevent 9/11***.

Thomas, Clarence (1948–)

My Grandfather's Son: A Memoir. Harper Perennial, 2008, 2007. 289pp. ill. 16pp. of plates. 9780060565565. Also available in large print and audiobook (read by the author). 347.73263

Clarence Thomas offers here a candid view of his life, from the early days when his father had left his mother destitute, and his mother, in desperation, gave her children to her own father, Myers Anderson.

Clarence called his grandfather "Daddy," but there was little affection there. He describes a stern grandfather who ran a boot camp rather than a home, but the end result is that Thomas credits the tenacity and endurance his grandfather taught him for his getting to where he is today. His memoir is rather complex, however, as he also bears a great resentment for the kind of childrearing he was subjected to. He discusses his higher education, going as far as Yale Law School, but he also describes his unfortunate first marriage, his financial difficulties, and his trouble with alcohol. Thomas also recounts the nomination hearings for his position on the Supreme Court and the accusation of sexual harassment levied by *Anita Hill* (see p. 541). Initially a radical Black man growing up in the Jim Crow south, Thomas ultimately became a conservative, convinced that the only way African-Americans were going to get ahead was by pulling themselves up by their own bootstraps and not taking any handouts. And that is how he describes himself living his life.

Subjects: African-American Men; Anderson, Myers; Conservatives; Hill, Anita; Judges; Lawyers; Race Relations; United States Supreme Court

Now Try: The writer Stephen L. Carter looks at how federal appointments are made, particularly to the Supreme Court, and suggests how the process could be improved, in ***The Confirmation Mess: Cleaning Up the Federal Appointments Process***. Once they are appointed, the nine members of the Supreme Court have a great responsibility in the decisions they make; Jeffrey Toobin provides some insights into how those decisions are made and the people who make them in ***The Nine: Inside the Secret World of the Supreme Court***. Earl Warren was a very significant judge, becoming Chief Justice during a crucial period in U.S. history. In ***The Memoirs of Earl Warren***, he describes the decisions he is proud of as well as those he regrets.

Scientists

Some scientists work in the field—whether it's literally a field, a canopy in the trees, a jungle, or an ocean—while others work in a lab, and some do both. What they all have in common is the quest for an extension of knowledge. Some will use their empirical knowledge to further their own lab work, and others will provide the information for fellow scientists to build on. This is how science has developed over the centuries, with people adding bits of knowledge to what has come before, thus creating a new knowledge base. Some of the science written about here has been remarkable within its own community, while other discoveries and theories have shaken the thinking world to its core. The scientists represented here range in specialty from anthropology to physics to primatology, from biology to computer technology to neuroscience.

Science has a broad representation here of both men and women, in fields as diverse as computer technology and tree biology. The scientists describe their particular fields, how they first became interested, and how they pursued their scientific goals. They also share with the reader what they have learned from their scientific pursuits, making recommendations for future behavior among the scientists and the public alike.

Berners-Lee, Tim (1955–)
Fischetti, Mark, coauthor

Weaving the Web: The Original Design and Ultimate Destiny of the World Wide Web by Its Inventor. HarperSanFrancisco, 2000, 1999. 226pp. 9780062515872. Also available in audiobook (read by the author) and e-audiobook. 025.04

If you were to be asked who invented the World Wide Web or who Tim Berners-Lee was, would you be able to answer? Always modest about his invention, Tim Berners-Lee finally wrote the story of how acronyms like www, http, html, and url became a part of daily life, both at work and at home. Berners-Lee is a physicist who went to the CERN (European Organization for Nuclear Research) lab in Switzerland as a consultant and wanted to find a faster way of accessing the information he had already found for his research. The Internet, a system for networking among academics, had already been created, but its use was clumsy and time-consuming. Berners-Lee created a program for himself that he called Enquire, which enabled him to retrieve quickly documents he had already stored on his computer. A few years later he refined what he had done earlier, creating the software for hypertext transfer and markup protocols and for what was originally referred to as universal document identifiers (now universal resource locators). He put all of this information on the World Wide Web, as he called it, for free, universal use. He subsequently became the director of the World Wide Web Consortium at MIT, with a view to keeping the Web open and available to all.

Apart from a knighthood and many other awards, Berners-Lee is the recipient of a MacArthur Fellowship.

Subjects: Computer Technology; Electronic Industries; European Organization for Nuclear Research; Internet; Inventors; Technology; World Wide Web

Now Try: The first global browser that enabled nonacademics to use the World Wide Web was called Mosaic, developed at the University of Illinois by Marc Andreessen and Eric Bina. Marc and Jim Clark went on to create Netscape, the browser that really started the universal use of the World Wide Web. Jim Clark, with the help of Owen Edwards, recounts the excitement of those days in ***Netscape Time: The Making of the Billion-Dollar Start-Up That Took on Microsoft***. Michael M. Lewis captures early Silicon Valley days in ***The New New Thing: A Silicon Valley Story***. To remind ourselves that the Internet and the World Wide Web have not always been with us is Katie Hafner and Matthew Lyon's history, ***Where Wizards Stay Up Late: The Origins of the Internet***.

Campbell, David G.

The Crystal Desert: Summers in Antarctica. Houghton Mifflin, 2002, 1992. 308pp. maps. 9780395589694. Also available in e-book. 508.9892

David Campbell is a scientist who is also a writer. The books he has written—as much literary nonfiction as scientific—document his studies in the far-ranging places he's been, from the Bahamas to the Amazon. He also spent three summers—from October to May each time—in Antarctica, as a member of the Brazilian expedition to Antarctica, to study the parasitic life there. These summers he describes in ***The Crystal Desert***, recounting his scuba diving in a hailstorm, visiting penguin rookeries, and climbing a mountain to change the lightbulbs in a twenty-foot crucifix. He also describes how Antarctica was originally part of a much larger continent, Gondwanaland, which basically constituted the Southern Hemisphere until tectonic forces separated Antarctica from the larger land mass and caused it to move much farther south.

Campbell was awarded a Houghton Mifflin Literary Fellowship for ***The Crystal Desert*** (unusual for a nonfiction writer), the John Burroughs Medal, and the PEN American Center Martha Albrand Award for First Nonfiction.

Subjects: Antarctica; Biologists; Comandante Ferraz Antarctic Station, Antarctica; Marine Biologists; Natural History, Antarctica; Naturalists; PEN American Center Martha Albrand Award for First Nonfiction; Polar Regions; Writers

Now Try: The only negative comment made about ***The Crystal Desert*** was the lack of accompanying photographs. A good book to accompany Campbell's, then, would be Bruce McMillan's ***Summer Ice: Life Along the Antarctic Peninsula,*** a collection of photographs that illustrate the flora and fauna of Antarctica. Another very poetically written book about Antarctica (highly recommended by Campbell) is Leslie Carol Roberts's ***The Entire Earth and Sky: Views on Antarctica***, an account of her trip there. The eloquence of Campbell's writing can also be found in Robert Macfarlane's ***The Wild Places***, his description of the as-yet-untamed parts of Ireland and England; he seems to have the same sensitivity toward the teeming biological life there as Campbell does toward life elsewhere. If you'd like to read some literary scientific fiction, you may enjoy ***The Expeditions: A Novel*** by Karl Iagnemma, the story of a nineteenth-century boy who runs away from home wanting to be a naturalist and winds up in Michigan's Upper Peninsula on an expedition.

Crane, Kathleen

Sea Legs: Tales of a Woman Oceanographer. Westview Press, 2004, 2002. 318pp. ill. 9780813342856. Also available in e-book. 551.46009

Crane begins her memoir with a call from the FBI in 2000, a fact that illustrates that the Cold War is not over for her, the Cold War that had such an interfering and negative effect on research in oceanography for so many years. In addition to the political problems she faced, Crane also had to deal with the fact that she had entered this male-dominated field in the early days for women. It was the same old story, that because women were perceived as distracting to men they had to have restrictions placed on them, instead of talking to the men about dealing professionally with women. All of that having been said, Crane still made a name for herself in the field, being among the first to posit the existence of deep-sea hot springs (vents) in the Pacific Ocean and then discovering them. But it was the Arctic Ocean that she made her own, working successfully with Russians to map the ocean. She was one of the first women to graduate from the Scripps Institution of Oceanography in San Diego, California, and is now U.S. Mission

Coordinator of the Arctic Research Office of the National Oceanic and Atmospheric Administration.

Subjects: Arctic Ocean; Cold War; Oceanographers; Scripps Institution of Oceanography, CA; Sea Stories; Sex Discrimination; Trailblazers; Woods Hole Oceanographic Institution, MA

Now Try: Sylvia A. Earle is another oceanic pioneer, a marine biologist and diver and cofounder of a company that makes deep-sea submersibles. In a reprise of Rachel Carson's award-winning ***The Sea Around Us,*** illustrated by Katherine L. Howe, Earle also raises the alarm in ***Sea Change: A Message of the Oceans,*** about what humans are so quickly doing to the oceans that sustain us. ***She's Such a Geek! Women Write About Science, Technology & Other Nerdy Stuff,*** edited by Annalee Newitz and Charlie Anders, is a fun look at the various male-dominated fields that women have entered. Reflecting on the effects of the Cold War on academia are Noam Chomsky and other essayists who have contributed to ***The Cold War & the University: Toward an Intellectual History of the Postwar Years.***

Fouts, Roger (1943–)
Mills, Stephen Tukel, coauthor

Next of Kin: What Chimpanzees Have Taught Me About Who We Are. Introduction by Jane Goodall. William Morrow, 1997. 420pp. ill. 16pp. of plates. 9780688148621. Also available in audiobook (read by the author), e-audiobook, and e-book. 156

Given a research assistantship at the University of Nevada, Fouts's first assignment was to work with a chimp named Washoe, to see if she could learn sign language. Studies had been carried out unsuccessfully to teach spoken language to chimpanzees, and now researchers were studying the capability of chimpanzees to learn sign language. Washoe learned about 240 of the signs of American Sign Language (ASL) and used the vocabulary she knew to sign vocabulary she didn't know—for example, Alka Seltzer was signed "listen drink." The results of his studies led Fouts to conclusions about language acquisition that enabled him to develop theories about working with autistic children. As a result of studying how chimpanzees are treated in biomedical research, Fouts has also become very active in animal rights, and in ***Next of Kin*** tells some very damaging tales about the treatment of animals. He is currently director of the Chimpanzee and Human Communication Institute (http://www.cwu.edu/~cwuchci/index.html).

Next of Kin was selected as a Notable Book by the American Library Association.

Subjects: ALA Notable Books; American Sign Language; Animal Rights Activists; Chimpanzees; Experimental Psychology; Human–Animal Communication; Language Acquisition; Primates; Psychologists; Washoe (Chimpanzee)

Now Try: A similar study regarding sign language and chimpanzees was being conducted at Columbia University, with differences of opinions held by each group about the other's work. Elizabeth Hess has written a powerfully engaging story of the chimp at Columbia, ***Nim Chimpsky: The Chimp Who Would Be Human.*** If you're interested in learning more about the fight for animal rights, you might want to read ***Rattling the Cage: Toward Legal Rights for Animals*** by Steven M. Wise, with a foreword by Jane Goodall. Fouts's book is a fascinating story, reading like fiction; so too is the story told by Tony Juniper about the efforts to find a mate for the last Spix's macaw in the wild: ***Spix's Macaw: The Race to Find the World's Rarest Bird.***

Galdikas, Biruté Marija Filomena (1946–)

Reflections of Eden: My Years with the Orangutans of Borneo. Little, Brown, 1995. 408pp. ill. maps. 9780316301817. 599.8092

After a felicitous meeting with Louis Leakey in Los Angeles, Galdikas became one of his sponsored scientists, as he sent her to Borneo to study the orangutans there. This autobiography recounts her trip there with her then-husband and the harsh conditions in which they found themselves, isolated with no conveniences. There were also difficulties in finding their subjects, as orangutans are shy and solitary, not traveling in groups the way other primates do. Galdikas combines her personal life—divorce from her first husband, marriage to an Indonesian, trips back and forth between Borneo and North America with her children—with her tales of the orangutans. She worked to free the animals who had been captured for zoos, and she was especially interested in nurturing the orphaned orangutans she found. Like Louis Leakey's other two *protégés*, Jane Goodall and Dian Fossey, she has worked hard at conservation, fighting off loggers who would ruin the primates' habitat and poachers who would capture or kill them.

Subjects: Animal Conservation; Animal Rescue; Animal Rights Activists; Borneo; Leakey, Louis; Orangutans; Primates; Primatologists

Now Try: Scientists who work in the wild with animals are generally opposed to zoos. The opposite view is eloquently posited in ***Sailing with Noah: Stories from the World of Zoos*** by zoo master Jeffrey P. Bonner. Stephen J. O'Brien has studied endangered species, including the orangutan, and has written up his findings in a fascinating book, ***Tears of the Cheetah: And Other Tales from the Genetic Frontier.*** Shawn Thompson adds to the library of orangutans and their near-extinction through interviews he conducted with a variety of researchers in a book that was a life-changing experience for him to write, ***The Intimate Ape: Orangutans and the Secret Life of a Vanishing Species.***

Goodall, Jane (1934–)

Through a Window: My Thirty Years with the Chimpanzees of Gombe. New Preface and Afterword. Houghton Mifflin Harcourt, 2000, 1990. 337pp. ill. 40pp. of plates. 9780547336954. 599.884419

In this second memoir, Goodall takes the reader into her chimpanzee community, illustrating how close they are to humans in their behavior. She recounts the war that breaks out among them, the rise of one and the defeat of another. She demonstrates variations in childrearing: one mother urges her offspring to do well; another doesn't. As Goodall has witnessed their reactions to events and behavior, she is convinced that they can feel emotion just as humans do. Chimpanzees are genetically similar to humans to a high degree and can get the same illnesses as humans; at Gombe both chimps and humans suffered through a polio epidemic in the 1960s. Apart from allowing the reader to see the chimpanzees through a window, Goodall also talks about another subject very close to her heart, namely conservation—specifically of the chimpanzees and more generally of wildlife.

Through a Window was selected as a Notable Book by the American Library Association. Jane Goodall, among her many honors, has been made a Dame of the British Empire, and was awarded both a National Geographic Hubbard Medal and the highest honor of the French Foreign Legion, the *Légion d'honneur*.

Subjects: ALA Notable Books; Animal Behavior; Animal Rights Activists; Chimpanzees; Environmental Activists; Gombe Stream National Park, Tanzania; Leakey, Louis; Primates; Primatologists; Tanzania; Trailblazers

Now Try: Jane Goodall's first memoir, ***In the Shadow of Man***, with photographs by her husband, Hugo Van Lawick, is a classic, describing her first ten years at Gombe and how she got there. When Dale Peterson, a former colleague, wrote her biography, ***Jane Goodall: The Woman Who Redefined Man***, he aptly divided the book into three sections: the naturalist, the scientist, and the activist. Other wildlife activists have turned to "rewilding," a movement to restore natural habitats and migration corridors, a campaign described by Caroline Fraser in ***Rewilding the World: Dispatches from the Conservation Revolution***. Goodall has also inspired other women scientists: Alexandra Morton had been studying orcas in captivity, but realized from Jane Goodall's example that she should be out in the ocean studying them. Her story is ***Listening to Whales: What the Orcas Have Taught Us***. Jane Goodall, Biruté Marija Filomena Galdikas, and Dian Fossey are all included in Milbry Polk and Mary Tiegreen's collection, ***Women of Discovery: A Celebration of Intrepid Women Who Explored the World***.

Lowman, Margaret (1953–)

Life in the Treetops: Adventures of a Woman in Field Biology. Foreword by Robert D. Ballard. Yale University Press, 2000, 1999. 219pp. ill. maps. 9780300078183. Also available in e-book. 577.34092

Lowman's memoir is comically dry, as she candidly talks about her naïveté in her early days as a field biologist. She conducted her doctoral studies at the University of Aberdeen in Scotland, studying temperate forests and writing her dissertation on the highland birch. She decided she needed to branch out and chose to do field work in the tropical forest; to this end she accepted a botany scholarship from the University of Sydney in Australia, completely ignoring the fact that Sydney was a thousand kilometers from a tropical forest. When she then decided to study the rain-forest butterflies, she was discouraged from doing so because of their elusive nature. She finally settled on leaves and found herself hundreds of feet up in the canopies of trees, studying herbivores and leaf predations. Part of her research, aside from studying the ecology of life in tree canopies, was developing various methods of getting up there. When she was pregnant in Australia, she finally used a cherry picker to raise her to her "laboratory," but her more normal conveyances have been balloon exploration rafts, with aerial walkways also built among the trees. In ***Life in the Treetops***, each of her sons contributed an essay on "going to work" with their mother. Her second memoir, ***It's a Jungle up There: More Tales from the Treetops***, was cowritten with her sons Edward and James Burgess, both students at Princeton at the time.

Subjects: Australia; Ecologists; Field Biologists; Rain Forest Ecology; Single Mothers; Trailblazers; Trees

Now Try: Lowman regretted not having a mentor, another woman/field scientist/mother to help her figure out how she could juggle her obligations, but the reason for this was that she was the pioneer; now she could mentor other women, women such as Martha L. Crump, who describes similar problems in her book, ***In Search of the Golden Frog*** in Central and South America. Canopy research is more common now, since Lowman first started; the creative-nonfiction writer Richard Preston accompanied some "canopy voyagers" to their work among the redwoods in Northern California, writing about it in ***The Wild Trees: A Story of Passion and Daring***. Other women who have battled for the environment are described in Mary Joy Breton's ***Women Pioneers for the Environment***.

Sacks, Oliver W. (1933–)

Uncle Tungsten: Memories of a Chemical Boyhood. Vintage Books, 2002, 2001. 337pp. ill. 9780375704048. Also available in large print, Braille, and e-book. 616.8092

The title character in this childhood memoir is Oliver Sacks's Uncle Dave, a man who had a factory that manufactured lightbulbs using tungsten wires. He introduced Sacks to the wonders of tungsten specifically and to metals in general, an interest that was encouraged by Sacks's mother. The book alternates between stories of his life as a child, the son of two doctors and nephew of a variety of scientists and polymaths, and stories of his chemistry heroes. Sacks was given a room at home in which he was allowed to conduct scientific experiments (resulting at one point in a fire), and he was an avid reader of scientists throughout the ages, particularly interested in their biographies. One of the many lessons Sacks learned was how scientific discoveries were generally built upon earlier discoveries, so that to understand the present it was necessary to study the past. The book takes us through his childhood to his early adolescence, when he starts to lose interest in chemistry and gain more interest in biology.

Subjects: Boarding Schools; Chemistry; Childhood and Youth; England; Landau, Dave; Neurologists; Scientists; Uncles

Now Try: The writer Tahir Shah also had an interesting childhood, but his magic was not chemistry; it was real magic, as he was apprenticed to a conjuror, the story of which can be found in ***Sorcerer's Apprentice***. If the scientific aspects of Sacks's memoir interest you, you may also enjoy Neil Shubin's exploration into the history of fish, ***Your Inner Fish: A Journey into the 3.5-Billion-Year History of the Human Body***, particularly as this history sheds light on the evolution of the human body; Shubin tells his story with the same storytelling magic as Sacks tells his. C. Alan Bradley has created a charming new mystery series, the **Buckshaw Chronicles**, whose child protagonist, Flavia de Luce, is reminiscent of the young Sacks in her wit and in her keen interest in chemistry. The first in the series is ***The Sweetness at the Bottom of the Pie.***

Sapolsky, Robert M. (1957–)

A Primate's Memoir. Simon & Schuster, 2002, 2001. 304pp. 9780743202411. Also available in large print, audiobook, and e-book. 599.8092

When he was a young boy, Robert Sapolsky wanted to live in the African dioramas in the American Museum of Natural History in New York. While majoring in biological anthropology at Harvard, Sapolsky got his chance to go to Africa, stationing himself in the Serengeti in Kenya with a troop of baboons, which he would continue to visit every year for more than twenty years. In the field he's a primatologist; he initially looked at behavior and stress in baboons, not only observing the behavior of the baboons, but also conducting tests on their blood. More recently, however, he has been looking at the different cultures within the baboon troops and whether the cultural differences have any effect on their health. Back at Stanford in the lab he is a neuroscientist, where of late the lab has been focusing on gene therapy, to see how neurons can be saved from neurological diseases.

Sapolsky was the recipient of a MacArthur Fellowship when he was only thirty and has since won several awards, not only for his research, but also for his teaching and writing.

Subjects: Baboons; Brain; College Professors; Kenya; Nature Writers; Neuroscientists; Primates; Primatologists; Stress

Now Try: Another primatologist who has spent her life with baboons in Kenya is Shirley C. Strum, who recounts her first fifteen years there in ***Almost Human: A Journey into the World of Baboons,*** with drawings by Deborah Ross. In the vein of Sapolsky's writing, hilarious and poignant at the same time, Douglas Adams and Mark Carwardine have written a book about vanishing species, ***Last Chance to See.*** Robert Sapolsky has contributed to a collection by Lynn Margulis and Eduardo Punset, ***Mind, Life, and Universe: Conversations with Great Scientists of Our Time,*** which may sound dry, but is actually fascinating, covering a variety of sciences. There have been incredible advances in the broad field of science, a phenomenon that John Brockman attests to in his collection of essays from a number of scientists, ***The Next Fifty Years: Science in the First Half of the Twenty-First Century.***

Shirley, Donna (1941–)
Morton, Danelle, coauthor

Managing Martians. Bantam, 2000, 1998. 304pp. ill. 9780767902410. Also available in e-book. 629.1092

Donna Shirley broke most of the expected molds growing up in Oklahoma, the daughter of prominent parents in a small town. She did win a beauty contest, but she also acquired her pilot's license at age sixteen, switched from home economics to mechanics, and entered the University of Oklahoma as the only woman in the mechanical and aerospace engineering degree program (after being told by an advisor there that women could not be engineers). Gender discrimination was obvious at the beginning, but she battled it with wit and ingenuity, and as she moved up the ladder and proved her worth, it became less and less of an issue. Her dream as a child had always been to go to Mars, and she did so vicariously, managing the Mars Exploration Program for NASA and successfully landing the Pathfinder on the planet. She opens the book with the breathtaking story of its landing and then moves back in time to her childhood and her move up the organizational ladder.

The first woman to manage a NASA program, Shirley has been awarded the NASA Outstanding Leadership Medal and been inducted into the Academy of Achievement and the Women in Technology International Hall of Fame.

Subjects: Aerospace Engineers; Firsts; Mars Pathfinder Project; National Aeronautics and Space Administration; Oklahoma; Sex Discrimination; Small Towns; Trailblazers

Now Try: Shirley made a good choice in studying aerospace engineering rather than aviation; the accomplished women pilots who fought to become part of the original space program, despite excelling at the tests they took, were not given the opportunity to realize their dreams of becoming astronauts. Martha Ackmann tells their story in ***The Mercury 13: The Untold Story of Thirteen American Women and the Dream of Space Flight***. Some women did manage to become active astronauts, however, and their story, along with the story of those kept back, can be found in ***Almost Heaven: The Story of Women in Space*** by Bettyann Kevles. There is a fascinating story about a rock from Mars, discovered by a geologist in Antarctica and originally misidentified at the Johnson Space Center; the mystery of this rock unfolds in Kathy Sawyer's ***The Rock from Mars: A Detective Story on Two Planets***.

Teller, Edward (1908–2003)
Shoolery, Judith L., coauthor

Memoirs: A Twentieth-Century Journey in Science and Politics. Perseus, 2002, 2001. 628pp. ill. 9780738207780. 530.092

Known as the "Father of the Hydrogen Bomb," Edward Teller was also the purported model for Stanley Kubrick's movie ***Doctor Strangelove or: How I Learned to Stop Worrying and Love the Bomb***. As a young boy living in his birth country of Hungary, Teller had a strong affinity for mathematics, but eventually discovered physics to be his forte, developing an interest in that field when he started hearing about work in atomic theory. He moved to the United States in 1933 when he realized that Europe was no place to be for a Jew and in 1943 joined the secret lab in Los Alamos, working on an atomic bomb. Once that was accomplished, he then became very interested in creating a hydrogen bomb. While others were against pursuing it, Teller proved to be quite convincing in the political realm and managed to achieve permission not only to pursue his interest, but also to set up a separate lab for it, the Lawrence Radiation Laboratory at Livermore. Teller continued to exert an influence in the political world as a great supporter of Reagan's Strategic Defense Initiative. To read Teller's memoir is to get a close-up view of the members of the scientific community in the United States and the scientific work usually done behind the scenes. It also reveals the link between science and governing.

Just months before his death in 2003, Edward Teller was awarded the Presidential Medal of Freedom by President George W. Bush.

Subjects: Atomic Bomb; Hungarian-Americans; Hydrogen Bomb; Los Alamos Scientific Laboratory, NM; Nonagenarians; Oppenheimer, J. Robert ; Physicists; Technology

Now Try: In his memoir Teller discusses his role in the hearings questioning J. Robert Oppenheimer's security clearance and includes his testimony as an appendix; by testifying against his colleague, Teller lost many friends in the scientific community. Kai Bird and Martin J. Sherwin spent many years researching their book on Oppenheimer, ***American Prometheus: The Triumph and Tragedy of J. Robert Oppenheimer***. Andrei Sakharov was working on the atomic bomb in Russia, but unlike Teller, he grew disenchanted with the work they were doing and became a peace activist. He describes his own career in his ***Memoirs,*** translated from the Russian by Richard Lourie. If you'd like more information—on not too technical a level—about the bomb, you might find useful Gerard J. De Groot's ***The Bomb: A Life***.

Wilson, Edward O. (1929–)

Naturalist. Island Press/Shearwater Books, 2006, 1994. 394pp. ill. 16pp. of plates. maps. 9781597260886. Also available in audiobook and e-book. 508.092

Pulitzer Prize–winning author and scientist Edward O. Wilson divides his life story into two sections, "Daybreak in Alabama" and "Storyteller." Part One deals with his childhood, when he wandered swamps and beaches in search of natural life, primarily insects and snakes. A fishing accident blinded him in one eye, making it necessary to examine things closely; he thus chose to examine the minutiae of the natural world. Part Two relates the story of his life as an adult, revolutionary scientific thinker, often at the heart of controversy, including the "molecular wars" at Harvard, when the new molecular scientists ousted the traditional evolutionary biologists. Wilson is responsible for the advancement of a number of sciences, namely evolutionary biology, which he would extend further than *Charles Darwin* did; sociobiology; and biodiversity. An ardent conservationist, he believes that his life story reflects how one evolves as one's worldview changes with experience.

Wilson was inducted into the Academy of Achievement. ***Naturalist*** was a finalist for the National Book Critics Circle Award in Biography/

Autobiography and won the *Los Angeles Times* Book Prize for Science & Technology.

Subjects: Biological Diversity; Biology; College Professors; Evolution; Harvard University, MA; *Los Angeles Times* Book Prize for Science & Technology; Naturalists; Octogenarians

Now Try: One of the remarkable elements of Wilson's autobiography is his writing. A fellow entomologist (Berenbaum, 1995) suggested that Wilson's success as a writer enabled him to communicate and clarify not only his own ideas but those of his colleagues as well. With that in mind, the reader might enjoy other natural-science–related titles that feature literary writing. Stephen Jay Gould has always been lauded for his writing style in his science writing; one collection of essays from his articles for *Natural History* is ***The Lying Stones of Marrakech: Penultimate Reflections in Natural History***. Edwin Way Teale's ***Dune Boy; The Early Years of a Naturalist,*** illustrated by Edward Shenton, is another classic that fits in nicely with Wilson's memoir. Brad Leithauser wrote ***Darlington's Fall: A Novel in Verse,*** with drawings by Mark Leithauser, about an early twentieth-century naturalist, Russel Darlington, whose life seems to have many parallels with Wilson's.

Wozniak, Steve (1950–)
Smith, Gina, coauthor

iWoz: Computer Geek to Cult Icon; How I Invented the Personal Computer, Co-Founded Apple, and Had Fun Doing It. Norton, 2007, 2006. 313pp. ill. 9780393330434. Also available in audiobook and e-audiobook. 621.39092

Knowing that Steve Wozniak was the person who started the first Dial-a-Joke hotline in the Bay Area in California gives the reader an idea of what to expect in this memoir. In 1975 he had the idea of putting a typewriter together with a video screen and some computer circuitry; from that idea came what is regarded as the best personal computer ever made, the Apple II. Wozniak describes the initial meetings of the Homebrew Computer Club, which led to the kind of brainstorming that often contributes to revolutions. He tells how he met up with Steve Jobs and how they put the Apple company together. He goes beyond Apple, however, and talks about his personal life, becoming a new father, teaching fifth graders, and surviving a plane crash. He wrote this book because he was tired of all the misinformation published about him and wanted to set the record straight. (He offers a nine-page glossary for the nongeek.)

Steve Wozniak was inducted into the National Inventors Hall of Fame and the Consumer Electronics Hall of Fame.

Subjects: Apple Computer Inc.; Computer Engineers; Computer Industry; Electronic Industries; Inventors; Jobs, Steve; Technology

Now Try: Oliver W. Sacks shows in his childhood memoir how each new scientific development is built on an earlier one. There are some very important inventors in American history whose work enabled Wozniak to do his, Benjamin Franklin being one of them. Gordon S. Wood has written a very rounded biography of Franklin, ***The Americanization of Benjamin Franklin***. Samuel Morse, the American version of Leonardo da Vinci, is another of the important inventors. ***Lightning Man: The Accursed***

Life of Samuel F. B. Morse is a very well-received biography by Kenneth Silverman. For those who would like to know more about the computer revolution, there is a book by Jeffrey Zygmont, ***Microchip: An Idea, Its Genesis, and the Revolution It Created***.

Health Scientists

This relatively small section of health professionals represents a wide variety of disciplines, from a doctor conducting research in a brothel to a medical school professor to a veterinarian. There are also two stories of pediatric neurosurgeons. Their stories, while different, offer much inspiration and hope. What they all have in common is that by their work they have done much to help the living and the dying, the latter particularly served by Elisabeth Kübler-Ross.

Those involved in the health sciences are the focus here, whether they are doctors, nurses, social workers, or veterinarians. In some cases the memoirists share their experiences, wanting the readers to know about the patients they have treated. In other cases, the writers have their own theories to propound, hoping to make a difference in the mind of the reader.

Albert, Alexa (1968–)

Brothel: Mustang Ranch and Its Women. Ballantine Books,. 2002, 2001. 258pp. 9780449006580. 306.74097932

When Alexa Albert was a medical student, she asked for and received permission to interview the women working at Mustang Ranch, a legal brothel in Nevada. Her study was to investigate how the women there protected themselves from sexually transmitted infections, but her interest in the women grew, such that over a period of four years she spent several months with them, getting to know them, seeing what it was like to live in the community there (no different from any other community in its interpersonal relationships), and getting to know the customers as well. Her memoir of her time spent there is a mix of scientific study and her experiences and reactions to the women and their life. Albert has continued her studies in the sex industry.

Subjects: Brothels; Nevada; Physicians; Sex Workers

Now Try: Eva J. Salber is another physician who believes in community health, although her community is broader. In her memoir, ***The Mind Is Not the Heart: Recollections of a Woman Physician***, she talks about treating the poor, in South Africa where she was born, and in Boston and rural North Carolina after moving to the United States. Kate Holden describes the life of a sex worker from her own perspective as a working girl in Australia in ***In My Skin: A Memoir***. A different kind of brothel, supported by a corrupt civic government, is illuminated in Chris Wiltz's ***The Last Madam: A Life in the New Orleans Underworld.***

Carson, Ben (1951–)
Murphey, Cecil (1933–), coauthor

Gifted Hands. Zondervan Books, 1996. 224pp. ill. 9780310214694. Also available in audiobook, e-audiobook, e-book, and video. 617.48092

Ben Carson grew up in inner-city Detroit, with his mother working two or three jobs to make do for herself and her two sons. From a scholarship to Yale he went on to the University of Michigan Medical School and from there to Johns Hopkins as a neurosurgery resident. By the age of thirty-two he was the director of the Pediatric Neurosurgery Center at Johns Hopkins. In addition to his pioneering neurosurgery (separating twins conjoined at the head; removing one hemisphere from the brain to eliminate intractable seizures), Carson has also established a scholarship fund for children in elementary school, hoping to find tomorrow's leaders and help them achieve their potential (http://carsonscholars.org/). He is also very concerned about health-care costs, and with a view to helping those who cannot afford the kind of health care his hospital provides, has set up the Benevolent Endowment Network (BEN) Fund.

Carson was awarded membership in the Horatio Alger Association of Distinguished Americans, inducted into the Academy of Achievement, and awarded the Presidential Medal of Freedom in 2008 by President George W. Bush.

Subjects: African-American Men; Detroit, MI; Fatherless Children; Mothers and Sons; Neurosurgeons; Pediatric Surgeons; Poverty; Role Models; Spirituality; Technology, Medical

Now Try: While Carson's use of current technology is truly impressive, it is also amazing to think about the doctors who pioneered brain surgery, people such as Harvey Cushing, whose biography Michael Bliss has written: ***Harvey Cushing: A Life in Surgery.*** Allan J. Hamilton is also a neurosurgeon, one who has had his own beliefs shaken in the work that he does. He raises some very interesting questions in ***The Scalpel and the Soul: Encounters with Surgery, the Supernatural, and the Healing Power of Hope.*** Providing a perspective of childhood illness from the parent's point of view is Kelly Corrigan's book of letters to her two little daughters, ***Lift,*** particularly referring to the story of her four-month-old's struggle with viral meningitis.

Epstein, Fred (1937–2006)
Horwitz, Joshua (1955–), coauthor

If I Get to Five: What Children Can Teach Us About Courage and Character. H. Holt, 2003. 190pp. 9780805071443. Also available in audiobook. 617.48092

" 'I ask you, reader, whoever you may be, take my trembling hand and warm it with care and sympathy' " (Miller, 2006). Those words, in a letter written by a young patient who died, changed Dr. Fred Epstein's life. He was already pioneering techniques in brain-stem and spinal-tumor removals, but his focus was completely on the available technology that allowed such surgeries. What he realized with that child's words was the importance of the human touch—literally and figuratively. To that end, he created the Hyman-Newman Institute for Neurology and Neurosurgery (INN) at the Beth Israel Medical Center in New York City, a name that sounds highly technical, but it includes beds in patients' rooms so that parents can stay with the children, a resident clown, parties, and a humanistic approach to patient care. The title of this book comes from one of his four-year-old patients, who kept making plans for herself if she got to be five years old: she would learn to tie a double-knot, to ride a two-wheeler, and to jump rope backwards.

If I Get to Five was the winner of a Christopher Award.

Subjects: Children; Christopher Awards; Courage; Hope; Illness in Children; Learning Difficulties; Neurosurgeons; Pediatric Surgeons; Spirituality; Technology, Medical

Now Try: Prior to ***If I Get to Five,*** Epstein had written another book, ***Gifts of Time,*** with the help of Elaine Fantle Shimberg, in which he outlined some of his cases and the procedures he used to treat them. Stories involving sick children are always gripping, particularly where delicate surgery is involved. Readers may find fascinating Michael Ruhlman's look at one particular hospital, the Cleveland Clinic, in ***Walk on Water: Inside an Elite Pediatric Surgical Unit.*** At the other end of the economic scale is the Gesundheit Institute (http://www.patchadams.org/), founded by Doctor Patch Adams, offering free health care and humor to thousands; he told his story, with the help of Maureen Mylander, in ***Gesundheit! Bringing Good Health to You, the Medical System, and Society Through Physician Services, Complementary Services, Humor, and Joy.*** His story was also made into a movie, ***Patch Adams.*** Epstein's book is full of stories of children who inspire; Frank Deford's story of his daughter, a child with cystic fibrosis, ***Alex, the Life of a Child,*** is also heartwarming and inspiring.

Firlik, Katrina

Another Day in the Frontal Lobe: A Brain Surgeon Exposes Life on the Inside. Random House, 2007, 2006. 271pp. 9780812973402. Also available in e-book. 617.48092

Although she doesn't really call herself a brain surgeon, since the majority of her work focuses on the spine, Firlik felt that her stories of neurosurgery on the brain would be more interesting to the reader. This memoir lets the reader into the world of the neurosurgical intern and resident—a seven-year stint for Firlik, from her first year as an intern (and the first female neurosurgeon) at the University of Pittsburgh Medical Center, to her years as junior and senior resident, and finally as Chief Resident of Neurosurgery. She talks about the history of neurosurgery—what it is and what it isn't—and reflects on why she finds it so satisfying. Describing the kind of work involved, the tools used, and the technological future of this branch of medicine, she offers an inside look to anyone who might be considering such a career. For those who prefer to be armchair doctors, she offers specific stories and case histories—some quite detailed, though, and not for the squeamish.

Subjects: Brain; Medicine; Nervous System; Neurosurgeons; Spine; Technology, Medical; University of Pittsburgh Medical Center, PA

Now Try: Residency is the time of no sleep for most medical practitioners. Emily R. Transue describes her life as a resident in ***On Call: A Doctor's Days and Nights in Residency***. If the brain itself is of interest to you, you might really enjoy Diane Ackerman's humanistic and literary look at the brain in ***An Alchemy of Mind: The Marvel and Mystery of the Brain***. Whereas neurosurgery might be considered the elite of the medical branches, general medicine is what helps the majority of patients. Danielle Ofri got her education at Bellevue Hospital Center in New York, a locum that provided her with the greatest cross-section of people and disease that a medical student could hope to find; she tells her story in ***Singular Intimacies: Becoming a Doctor at Bellevue***.

Kübler-Ross, Elisabeth (1926–2004)

The Wheel of Life: A Memoir of Living and Dying. Touchstone, 1998, 1997. 286pp. ill. 9780684846316. Also available in audiobook. 150.92

Rather than "rage against the dying of the light" (Thomas, 2003), Kübler-Ross raged against the attitude toward that dying of the light and the treatment of those experiencing it. With a degree in psychiatry, Kübler-Ross became a research fellow at Manhattan State Hospital and was outraged when she saw how the dying were treated. She sought and eventually received permission to create a program whereby she could help these patients in their last stage in life. She furthered her studies by interviewing dying people, but still met resistance. The publication in 1969 of ***On Death and Dying*** established her reputation and enabled her to change the curriculum of medical teaching so that death and dying were part of it. Hospices and palliative care can be laid directly at her feet.

Kübler-Ross was posthumously inducted into the National Women's Hall of Fame.

Subjects: Children and Death; Death; Dying; Future Life; Palliative Care; Psychiatrists; Swiss-Americans

Now Try: The inevitable next step after the pioneering work that Kübler-Ross did would be to hear from people who work in palliative care, for them to detail what they have learned. Maggie Callanan and Patricia Kelley have done that, elaborating on theories they developed over many years of hospice care, particularly what they call "Nearing Death Awareness." ***Final Gifts: Understanding the Special Awareness, Needs, and Communications of the Dying*** is for both the dying and the caregiver. One of Kübler-Ross's theories is that those who have led a full, contributing life have less resistance to death than others. David Guterson seems to believe this, as he demonstrates in his protagonist in ***East of the Mountains***, a novel about a doctor with terminal cancer. Jerome E. Groopman is an oncologist who has listened to his dying patients and shares with others what he has learned from them in ***The Measure of Our Days: New Beginnings at Life's End***.

Thomas, Lewis (1913–1993)

The Youngest Science: Notes of a Medicine-Watcher. Penguin Books, 1995, 1983. 270pp. 9780140243277. Also available in large print, audiobook, and e-audiobook. 610.92

Lewis Thomas's subtitle is a reference to two collections of essays he wrote for *The New England Journal of Medicine,* which were then published as books, the subtitles of which were *Notes of a Biology Watcher* (***The Lives of a Cell***) and *More Notes of a Biology Watcher* (***The Medusa and the Snail***). The first part of his title refers to his take on modern medicine. Thomas grew up with a doctor father and a nurse mother who practiced medicine in their home. It was still the horse-and-buggy kind of doctoring, where there was little to be done for serious illness except to make the patient comfortable, understand what was happening, and apply humanistic touches. When Thomas arrived at medical school, the profession was on the cusp of major changes, moving from an art to a science, where technology would reign and the human touch would disappear (reminiscent of Fred Epstein's concern). The title, then, reflects Thomas's optimism that the recognition of the need for humanism in medicine is coming back and that the science is thus very young. An academic in medical universities, Thomas had a gift of being able to share his optimism and knowledge with laypeople, elucidating his notions of the connectedness of man and the universe in clear but lyrical language. He was a Renaissance man in his love of science, language, and music.

Subjects: Biology; College Professors; Essayists; Medical Sciences, History; Octogenarians; Personal Essays; Physicians; Writers

Now Try: Lewis Thomas was mentor to Gerald Weissmann, Thomas's first chief resident at Bellevue Hospital Center. With a nod to Thomas (and a chapter on him), Weissmann has written ***Galileo's Gout: Science in an Age of Endarkenment,*** in which he discusses his concern about today's lack of scientific understanding and the encroachment of religion into science. A scientific essayist who is often compared to Thomas for his ability to humanize science and make it comprehensible to the layperson is Stephen Jay Gould; readers may enjoy his ***Dinosaur in a Haystack: Reflections in Natural History***. Another writer who has been compared favorably to Lewis Thomas is Matt Ridley in ***Genome: The Autobiography of a Species in 23 Chapters***. The lyricism and gentle humor in Thomas's essays can also be found in Ann Zwinger's ***Downcanyon: A Naturalist Explores the Colorado River Through the Grand Canyon***.

Trout, Nick

Tell Me Where It Hurts: A Day of Humor, Healing, and Hope in My Life as an Animal Surgeon. Broadway Books, 2008. 286pp. 9780767926430. Also available in large print, audiobook, e-audiobook, and e-book. 636.8097

A staff surgeon at the Angell Animal Medical Center in Boston, Nick Trout has pulled various stories from his twenty-five years of experience to create a fictional twenty-four-hour day. By doing this, his idea is to give the reader a glimpse into the daily life of a small-animal veterinarian at work. As he describes various procedures, beginning with emergency surgery at 2:47 a.m., he also comments on the societal ramifications of what he is doing. Technology has moved along in veterinary science as well as in other medical sciences, and Trout raises the moral and ethical issues of what should be done in terms of continuing an animal's life. He also addresses the issues of cosmetic surgery (ear and tail clipping, for example), of the high cost of veterinary care, and of euthanasia. Trout believes that not only has technology changed, but also the place of the pet in the North American culture; he calls his pets' owners "pet parents." Because he had a high school student interested in veterinary medicine accompany him for a while, the reader also learns Trout's views on education .

Subjects: Angell Animal Medical Center, MA; Animal Care; Pets; Veterinarians

Now Try: Trout followed this first memoir with the story of two dogs in particular, ***Love Is the Best Medicine: What Two Dogs Taught One Veterinarian About Hope, Humility, and Everyday Miracles***. Jeff Wells has some very unusual stories to tell, illustrated by June Camerer, in ***All My Patients Have Tales: Favorite Stories from a Vet's Practice***. Moving from small-animal veterinary science to large animals is the story of a wildlife veterinarian, William B. Karesh's ***Appointment at the Ends of the World: Memoirs of a Wildlife Veterinarian***. With courage and honesty Loretta Gage (with help from her sister Nancy) describes what her life was like becoming a veterinarian, in ***If Wishes Were Horses: The Education of a Veterinarian***.

Consider Starting With . . .

Bass, William M. *Death's Acre: Inside the Legendary Forensic Lab—the Body Farm—Where the Dead Do Tell Tales*

Carson, Ben. *Gifted Hands*

Child, Julia. *My Life in France*

Conlon, Edward. *Blue Blood*

Darwin, Charles. *The Voyage of the Beagle*

Goodall, Jane. *Through a Window: My Thirty Years with the Chimpanzees of Gombe*

King, Larry. *My Remarkable Journey*

Kuralt, Charles. *A Life on the Road*

Newman, Paul, and A. E. Hotchner. *In Pursuit of the Common Good*

Teller, Edward. *Memoirs: A Twentieth-Century Journey in Science and Politics*

Fiction Read-Alikes

Archer, Jeffrey. *The Prodigal Daughter*. The daughter of a hotel baron gives up her inheritance and builds her own business empire.

Bohjalian, Christopher A. *Midwives: A Novel.* A successful midwife, Sybil Danforth finds herself on trial when a woman in her care dies in childbirth and Sybil performs surgery to release the infant.

Cheever, Benjamin. *The Plagiarist: A Novel.* Standing in the shadow of his famous father (a writer), Arthur Prentice finally gets a lucrative job on the copy desk with a well-established magazine in New York City.

Darnton, John. *The Darwin Conspiracy.* This historical novel combines a modern-day anthropologist along with his colleague, a Darwinian expert, and Charles Darwin himself as it goes back and forth in time.

Goodman, Allegra. *Intuition: A Novel.* Ambition reigns supreme in a research lab in Cambridge, Massachusetts, where several scientists are competing for a major grant.

Green, Tim. *American Outrage.* Jake Carlson is a reporter for a tabloid who turns his investigative skills to his own use when he tries to track down the birth mother of his adopted son.

Hunter, Evan. *The Blackboard Jungle; A Novel.* The classic bleak story of a first-year teacher in a tough high school in the Bronx remains current with contemporary problems in education.

Margolin, Phillip. *The Undertaker's Widow.* Following in his father's footstep as a judge with integrity, Richard Quinn finds his first case in homicide court a risky one.

Michelsen, G. F. *Hard Bottom: A Novel.* An independent fisherman off Cape Cod, Ollie Cahoon is faced with stiff competition from the commercial fleets.

Smiley, Jane. *Moo: A Novel.* This satire of an agricultural college (Moo U) sends up all the constituents of a university, from students to faculty to researchers.

Works Cited

Ambrose, Stephen. 1998. Interview. *Academy of Achievement,* May 22. Accessed March 23, 2009. http://www.achievement.org/autodoc/page/amb0int-1.

Berenbaum, May. 1995. Review of *Naturalist,* by Edward O. Wilson. *BioScience* 45: 792+. Reproduced in *Biography Resource Center.* Accessed June 30, 2009. http://galenet.galegroup.com/servlet/BioRC.

Grimes, William. 2006. "Julia Child's Memoir of When Cuisine Was French for Scary." Review of *My Life in France,* by Julia Child. *The New York Times,* April 8. Accessed July 18, 2009. http://www.nytimes.com/2006/04/08/books/review/08grim.html?pagewanted=all.

Italiano, Laura. 2004. Review of *Blue Blood*, by Edward Conlon. *People Weekly*, April 19. Reproduced in *Biography Resource Center*. Accessed April 16, 2009. http://galenet.galegroup.com/servlet/BioRC.

Miller, Stephen. 2006. "Fred Epstein, 68, Leading Pediatric Neurosurgeon." *The Sun*, July 12. Accessed April 19, 2009. http://www.nysun.com/obituaries/fred-epstein-68–leading-pediatric-neurosurgeon/35920/.

Seaman, Donna. 2005. Review of *No One Loved Gorillas More: Dian Fossey, Letters from the Mist*, by Camilla de la Bédoyère. *Booklist*, February 15.

Terkel, Studs. 1974. *Working; People Talk About What They Do All Day and How They Feel About What They Do*. New York: Pantheon Books.

Thomas, Dylan. 2003. *The Poems of Dylan Thomas*. Edited by Daniel Jones. New York: New Directions.

Chapter 5

Place and Time

Description

Place is a concept that at first seems very simple: a story is told, set in a specific place. Place is often referred to as setting—a country, a region, a city, a building. Setting could be defined as urban or rural, international or local, fantasy world or real world. But place often involves more than setting; it can be an interior place, the inner world of the writer's mind and heart. This type of "place" is more spiritual, though, and is dealt with in Chapter 8, "The Inner Life."

Time is also part of this concept. Often in memoirs the writer harks back to a specific time, when life might have seemed easier or less complicated. Very often when the writer is dealing with a specific time, the story relates to the age of the writer at that time, often the time of childhood. Thus many of these stories, particularly those taking place in small towns, are coming-of-age tales.

In this chapter, place has a very specific meaning, but within that meaning the stories can be quite varied. Place also plays an important role in the writing of the story: without the place, there would be no story. Writing from a sense of place, as the authors in this chapter do, involves not only setting, but time and environment. It makes use of all the senses, with the writer absorbing "the sights, sounds, smells, feel of what's there" (Gwyther, 2009), capturing the spirit of a place.

There is much discussion in the literature about regional writing and whether or not it has the same cachet or value as "universal" writing. As the author Eudora Welty explains, however, everyone is from a region, and if they are writing what they know about, all writing could be seen as regional, particularly if the writing comes from a sense of place (2002). Another author, Rudolfo A. Anaya, believes that writing from this perspective "means that the writers . . . have a special attachment to the people and the land of the region." Each locale has its own "historical, culture, and language traditions" (Anaya, 1995) that define it and that inform the author's writing.

As in the rest of this book, many of the authors here could have been placed in other chapters; their sense of place stands out, however, which is why they have been put here. On the other hand, because place is an integral part of anyone's story, it could perhaps be argued that most of the stories in this book could have been put into this single chapter; for obvious reasons, that hasn't been done. In this chapter the stories could only have been told by each writer in that place, that environment, that time, whether in a slum in Ireland or on a ranch in the West.

Memoirs of place and time focus on the environments memoirists found so special at one point in their lives. These memoirs often tell of the writers' childhoods, whether in a small town in the Midwest or in a city in Turkey. Other memoirs revolve around the place, whether a place in the woods or a harem in Iran.

Appeal

Readers love to immerse themselves in books, and for many the setting is of great import, a place not only to visit, but to get to know well, to feel its spirit, and to learn its landmarks. In some of the stories here, the reader learns the history of a place, at times a contemporary history amplifying stories previously heard only on the nightly news. Thus the learning experience can also be found here, more so in some stories than in others.

The chance to live vicariously in another time and place, to experience a lifestyle very different from one's own, appeals greatly. On the other hand, the sense of place may be very familiar to the reader, offering an opportunity to see that place from someone else's perspective, either to share in the familiar or to have one's eyes opened to a new way of seeing that environment.

Keep in mind that in the midst of whatever place is being written from, the writer is telling a story, often the story of childhood; along with that story, the reader is offered an interesting insight into that part of the writer's life. "Writing from a sense of place does not limit the exploration of universal human emotions" (Anaya, 1995); thus the reader's own experiences may resonate in the story told. Again, Rudolfo A. Anaya sums it up well: "To be moved into the realm of the characters of the story means to feel the place, the food, music, language, and history of the character's surroundings." While Anaya may be referring to fiction, the same obviously holds true for memoir.

Organization of This Chapter

This chapter is comprised of four main sections. It begins with five classic works related to the theme of this chapter, namely the environment in which one grows up or develops, whether that environment is nature itself or a contained space, either local or global.

The second section represents nature writing in its broadest sense, some stories involving sanctuaries, some occurring on ranches, but all concerned with the outdoors. This category includes the various environments where nature prevails—the wilderness, the farm or ranch, the forest, the water, the prairie.

Following that is a group of memoirists who grew up largely in small towns, recalling their lives as small people; time is a major theme here, as the writers focus on childhood and on the small world that was theirs. Because of this the reader is often treated to a view of life in another day and age.

We then move to the larger world, to various places around the world. With some exceptions, these are also tales of childhood, with an exotic flavor for the North American reader.

Classics

Some of the titles in this section have long been held up as exemplars of nature writing, particularly Dillard's and Thoreau's works. Isak Dinesen's story of life on a coffee plantation is known far and wide, and Ivan Doig's writings about the West have been long admired. Perhaps less of a household name is John Muir, unless you are an ardent conservationist; John Muir was one of the first.

> Classic memoirs of time and place often reflect how the environment formed the writer. These memoirs are more reflective than many, generally offering less story and more observation about the place or time itself, yet still providing a sense of the writer's life.

Dillard, Annie (1945–)

Pilgrim at Tinker Creek. Harper Perennial, 2007, 1974. 290pp. ill. 9780061233323. Also available in large print, Braille, audiobook, e-audiobook, and e-book. 508.9755

With a master's degree in English literature, focusing on Henry David Thoreau's ***Walden***, Annie Dillard decided to spend a year (four seasons) in the Blue Ridge Mountains of Virginia, at Tinker Creek. She spent her time there observing and meditating. After her year, she felt she needed to write, and extended her stay for this purpose, initially filling twenty journals, from which she then wrote this book. Her meditations are on the relationship between God and this world, on the nature of death and violence in the world, and on one's level of consciousness as we make our way through this world. One might expect a contemplative style, misty and quiet, but Dillard's style is as natural as the world she describes; in fact, it can be more like a trumpet blast. The book is full of the natural violence she sees on a daily basis, descriptions of a water bug sucking the life out of a frog or a praying mantis eating her mate.

Pilgrim at Tinker Creek won the Pulitzer Prize for General Nonfiction. It was also selected as a Notable Book by the American Library Association.

Subjects: ALA Notable Books; Classics; Landscape; Natural History; Nature Writers; Pulitzer Prize for General Nonfiction; Solitude; Spirituality; Thoreau, Henry David; Tinker Creek, VA; Virginia; Writers

Now Try: If you'd like to try some of Dillard's fiction, you may want to pick up ***The Maytrees***, a novel set on Cape Cod. With the unlikely title ***Stirring the Mud: On Swamps, Bogs, and Human Imagination***, Barbara Hurd also offers a meditative look at one aspect of nature, swamps, in this case. Hurd was a finalist for the Annie Dillard Award for Creative Nonfiction. There are many ways to observe and reflect on nature; Akiko Busch uses swimming as her path of exploration. In ***Nine Ways to Cross a River: Midstream Reflections on Swimming and Getting There from Here***, she talks about the various rivers across the United States that she has swum and what those rivers have taught her. Gretel Ehrlich's ***The Solace of Open Spaces*** focuses on a sheep farm in the West but, like Dillard's book, makes connections between the natural life there and the people who live in the environs.

Dinesen, Isak (1885–1962)

Out of Africa. Random House, 2002, 1952. 389pp. 9780375508455. Also available in large print, Braille, audiobook, e-book, and video. 916.762

Karen Blixen chose the pseudonym Isak Dinesen so that people would think she was a male writer. For her to create such a myth was completely in keeping with her character. Her memoir, ***Out of Africa***, is also considered by many to be mythical. More an evocation of place than a recounting of her years on the coffee plantation that she and her husband bought in Kenya, she opens the book with a sentence that has become famous: "I had a farm in Africa, at the foot of the Ngong Hills." Throughout the book she conjures up the spirit of Africa in general and that farm in particular, of the Masai and Kikuyu who worked with them, thereby creating almost an idyllic setting for herself, true to her affinity with the country, her spirit of place. Glossing over unpleasantries such as her marital difficulties, she instead tells stories, describing in fond terms her friends and the table she would set for them, maintaining the niceties of the colonial household. She followed this title with another, ***Shadows on the Grass***, full of anecdotes about individuals who worked on the plantation.

Subjects: Classics; Coffee Plantations; Colonial Life, Kenya; Danish in Kenya; East Africa; Farm Life, Kenya; Kenya; World War I (1914–1918); Writers, Denmark

Now Try: If you'd like to get a truer sense of Blixen's life in Kenya, you would do well to read Linda Donelson's ***Out of Isak Dinesen in Africa: The Untold Story***. And to accompany that, Sara Wheeler's ***Too Close to the Sun: The Audacious Life and Times of Denys Finch Hatton*** will shed a clearer light on Blixen's lover. Kuki Gallmann is another person who found the allure of Africa a strong pull, and moved there from Italy with her husband; she tells her tale in ***I Dreamed of Africa***. Ernest Hemingway presents a somewhat different view of East Africa, although he was there when Blixen was, but Hemingway was on a big-game safari, which he describes in ***Green Hills of Africa***. A classic novel by a Kenyan, set in a later time during the Emergency in Kenya (1952–1959), is ***A Grain of Wheat*** by Ngũgĩ wa Thiong'o.

Doig, Ivan (1939–)

This House of Sky: Landscapes of a Western Mind. Harcourt, Inc., 1999, 1978. 314pp. 9780156899826. Also available in audiobook (read by the author), e-audiobook, and e-book. 978.6092

Because Ivan Doig's mother died when he was six years old, Ivan's father asked his mother-in-law to live with them, to care for his son. Doig's memoir is a tribute to both his father, Charles (Charlie) Doig, and his grandmother, Elizabeth (Bessie) Ringer, living hard to make a life in various locales on the edge of the Rockies in Montana, finally winding up on a sheep ranch. As was normal for boys growing up at that time, in that place, Ivan helped with ranch work, picking stones, haying, herding sheep, and lambing. He writes that he did just enough of each task to know he did not want to spend his life at it. But the pull of the land and that life is strong, as is the pull, for him, of family. He brackets his story with the death from asthma of his mother and the death from emphysema of his father. In between he pays homage to the continually heroic struggle of his father to create a life for them all and to the steadfastness and courage of his grandmother. To write this memoir, Doig interviewed his father and others, but he also carried out significant research into Montana and its history.

This House of Sky was nominated for the National Book Award for Contemporary Thought and was chosen as a One Book Montana selection.

Subjects: American West; Classics; Coming of Age; Doig Family; Family Relationships; Fathers and Sons; Grandmothers; Landscape; Montana; Motherless Children; Ranch Life

Now Try: ***Heart Earth*** is a prequel to ***This House of Sky,*** in which Doig describes finding his mother's letters and the influence they had on him. ***Inside This House of Sky: Photographs of a Western Landscape,*** a photographic album of Doig's story, with photos by Duncan Kelso, provides a nice visual accompaniment to Doig's writing. Wallace Stegner's novel ***Angle of Repose*** could almost be written about Doig, as it features a historian researching his pioneer grandparents. Doig said that he wanted his language to dance in ***This House of Sky*** and felt that good writers should not be tagged as regional, that their language should appeal universally. Language is an important aspect, not only of the subject, but also in the writing of ***The Invention of Clouds: How an Amateur Meteorologist Forged the Language of the Skies,*** by Richard Hamblyn. The nature writer Rick Bass offers a very specific view of Doig's state in ***Winter: Notes from Montana,*** as he describes living in a remote valley that has no electricity.

Muir, John (1838–1914)

Nature Writings: The Story of My Boyhood and Youth, My First Summer in the Sierra, The Mountains of California, Stickeen, Selected Essays. Library of America, 1997. 888pp. ill. 9781883011246. 508.74092

The Library of America has collected John Muir's major writings in this one edition, an offering that provides the reader with the story of Muir's childhood in Scotland until the age of eleven, when his family emigrated to Wisconsin. It also includes the much-loved tales of life in the wild with his dog, Stickeen. Perhaps most important, it makes available Muir's writings about his favorite place: nature, particularly the Sierra Nevada Mountains. As a child, Muir could not resist the fields and woods, despite his father's embargo against playing in them. As an adult, he could not resist climbing the mountains, sleeping in the meadows, or clinging to the top of a tall tree during a windstorm. His stories are full of the flora and fauna he encounters, but also the sights and scents he experiences. One reviewer (*The New York Times*, 1894) said of Muir's writing that his descriptions of what he has seen are better for tourists than even going themselves, as they'd never be able to capture everything that John Muir captured, sometimes because they would never dare go where he dared go. Muir is largely responsible for the creation of the national parks in the United States and was cofounder and first president of the Sierra Club.

Subjects: 19th Century; Classics; Conservationists; Natural History; Nature Writers; Personal Essays; Sierra Club; Sierra Nevada Mountains, CA; Wilderness

Now Try: Aaron Sachs places John Muir and Clarence King in context with other nineteenth-century environmentalists, illustrating how radical the movement was at that time, in ***The Humboldt Current: Nineteenth-Century Exploration and the Roots of American Environmentalism***. Edward Hoagland is the twentieth-century Muir; you may want to look at ***Hoagland on Nature: Essays***. If you're interested in the history of the Sierra Club, you might enjoy Tom Turner's ***Sierra Club: 100 Years of Protecting Nature***. To read more about John Muir, Donald Worster's ***A Passion for Nature: The Life of John Muir*** is said to be the definitive biography.

Thoreau, Henry David (1817–1862)

Walden. Wood engravings by Michael McCurdy. Foreword by Terry Tempest Williams. Shambhala, 2004, 1854. 303pp. ill. 9781590300886. Also available in large print, Braille, audiobook, e-audiobook, and e-book. 818.3

Walden records a two-year, two-month, two-day stay by Thoreau in a cabin he built by himself on the land surrounding Walden Pond. Often referred to as "an experiment in simple living," the purpose of this venture for Thoreau was to live in solitude and to commune with nature, in part for himself and in part for others, to show how it could be done and to raise awareness of the importance of protecting and living in harmony with the environment. Ralph Waldo Emerson had purchased the land in Walden Woods expressly for his friend Thoreau, who then leased the land from Emerson. When Thoreau wrote ***Walden***, he compressed his two years into one, using the four seasons as his mileposts. This edition celebrates the 150th anniversary of the original publication of what quickly became an American classic.

Subjects: 19th Century; Classics; Massachusetts; Naturalists; Nature Writers; Seasons; Solitude; Walden Woods, MA; Wilderness

Now Try: As so often happens when one writes about a place, extolling its virgin nature and encouraging others to share in a similar experience, the area being extolled suffers environmental degradation from the hordes of people wanting to emulate the writer. Such was the case with Walden Pond, as outlined by W. Barksdale Maynard, a consultant for the Walden Woods Project (http://www.walden.org/), in ***Walden Pond: A History***. A lovely book of photographs of Walden Pond and its environs has been created by Bonnie McGrath: ***Walden Pond***, with reflections by Henry David Thoreau. Henry Beston is another writer who became enamored of the nature surrounding him and turned a two-week vacation on Cape Cod in 1928 into a year-long sojourn; he beautifully describes his year in ***The Outermost House; A Year of Life on the Great Beach of Cape Cod***, illustrated with photographs by William A. Bradford and others. Roger Deakin didn't stay in one place, but rather traveled throughout Europe, England, and even Australia, wherever he found trees and those animals and humans that interacted with them. His story can be found in ***Wildwood: A Journey Through Trees***. Another classic in the vein of ***Walden*** is Aldo Leopold's ***A Sand County Almanac, and Sketches Here and There***, written about a farm in south central Wisconsin and illustrated by Charles W. Schwartz.

Natural Environments

Nature writing, some of which is referred to as ecobiography (Dresdner, 2005), reflects the relationship of the writer to the land, often from a conservationist point of view. In certain cases the writer is drawn to the landscape, whether the woods, the water, the farm, or the mountains, and in learning the environment and seeing the ecology of the place becomes an ardent conservationist. In other cases, a desire to preserve the land is what takes the writer to that place.

Paul Lindholdt makes the distinction between the "affective domain" of nature writing, where one communicates the feelings engendered by being out in nature, and the "effective domain," where one actually does something about the engendered feelings (Lindholdt, 1999). In these stories, the reader sees a variety of reactions and reflections, some reminiscent and/or nostalgic and some expository. In nature writing the senses come into play in high definition, seeing tiny insects, hearing bird calls, smelling the plants that abound, feeling the smoothness of stones created by ages of running water. Some of the stories in this section are remembrances of childhoods spent in a specific landscape: the prairie, the boreal forest, the ranch. Other stories tell of proactive ventures: deliberately moving to a farm in order to eat locally, working in a bird sanctuary, escaping to the water and the wilderness. All reflect the respect of the writer for the landscape, a respect the writer hopes to communicate in order to encourage others to feel the same.

Nature writing often takes the form of memoir writing, as the great outdoors and the individual writer's relationship with that environment become the focus. In this "Natural Environments" section, however, the memoirists also tell a story about one part of their lives, sometimes their youth, sometimes not. For the nature writer, encouraging others to respect the natural environment is part of a self-imposed mandate.

Blunt, Judy (1954–)

Breaking Clean. Vintage, 2003, 2002. 303pp. map. 9780375701306. Also available in large print. 978.6092

The conventional role of a woman in the isolated and large ranches of the West was to support the men: do the domestic chores, raise the children, grow and can the fruits and vegetables, make the children's clothes, etc. If Blunt had been given a say in the running of the ranch, if she'd been allowed to do the calving, as she knew how to do, if she had been recognized as an individual in her own right, she would likely have stayed. However, finding a need to be more than Mrs. Matovich, she enrolled in a class at Great Falls College, via teleconference phone calls. One day, because she was late getting lunch on the table, her father-in-law pulled the plug on her electric typewriter, yelling and screaming at her. This incident firmed up her resolution to complete her education, and when she witnessed in class the reaction of other students to her writing, she realized the power of the written word and changed her major from journalism to creative writing.

Blunt was honored with several prizes for this book: a PEN/Jerard Fund Award for a Work in Progress, the Whiting Writers' Award for an emerging writer, the Mountains & Plains Independent Booksellers Association Regional Book Award, and the WILLA Literary Award; the book was also selected as a Notable Book by the American Library Association.

Subjects: ALA Notable Books; Homesteading; Montana; Personal Essays; Poets; Ranch Life; Single Mothers; Writers

Now Try: Blunt tells the story of how her mother loved horses and used a family horse to babysit the children. Her mother would set all the children on the back of a gentle horse and let the horse roam around the yard while she worked in the garden; the horse was a safe animal for the children and the children couldn't get down. Mary D. Midkiff's collection of essays, illustrated by Nancy Denison, is all about women and horses: ***She Flies Without Wings: How Horses Touch a Woman's Soul***. One of the thirteen essays in Blunt's memoir, entitled "Salvage," describes the horrible blizzard of 1964 when the cattle lost ears and hooves to frostbite. Weather is such an important element in the life of ranchers that Susan Allen Toth has written about it in ***Leaning into the Wind: A Memoir of Midwest Weather***. An intergenerational saga of women migrating to find their own places is Charlotte Bacon's novel ***Lost Geography***.

Cariou, Warren (1966–)

Lake of the Prairies: A Story of Belonging. Anchor Canada, 2003, 2002. 318pp. ill. map. 9780385259613. 819.32

Warren Cariou's place of belonging was Meadow Lake, a small town in northern Saskatchewan that rarely sees tourists—a town of fishing, hunting, bingo halls, berry picking, and racism. Part of the boreal forest, replete with muskeg, lakes and rivers, and forested hills, the land was originally cleared by a variety of Europeans, but Aboriginal peoples have always lived there too, creating a racial tension in the small town and a personal tension within Cariou himself. As the book unfolds, so too does Cariou's story, as we hear the tales told by his family interwoven with his own stories of his life on their farm outside Meadow Lake: his love for his father, a lawyer in town and a captivating storyteller; fear of Aboriginal people, which he knows he must keep hidden; and arrowhead hunting, to name but a few elements. Through gradual revelations, Cariou discovers his family is not what it seems. He eventually moves away from Meadow Lake, but his roots are planted firmly in his northern Saskatchewan hometown.

Lake of the Prairies was short-listed for the Charles Taylor Prize for Literary Non-Fiction and won the Writers' Trust of Canada Drainie-Taylor Biography Prize.

Subjects: Aboriginal Peoples, Canada; Canada; Family History; First Nations; Meadow Lake, SK; Métis; Saskatchewan; Small Towns, Canada; Social History, Canada; Writers, Canada; Writers' Trust of Canada Drainie-Taylor Biography Prize

Now Try: If you'd like a sense of Cariou's fiction writing, you may want to read ***The Exalted Company of Roadside Martyrs: Two Novellas.*** The comforting sense of being rooted in a place, as seen in Cariou's memoir, is an integral part of Mona Simpson's novel ***Off Keck Road,*** in which a young woman returns to her small town in Wisconsin, secure in her sense of belonging. Cariou's well-crafted prose is also reflected in Scott R. Sanders's ***The Country of Language,*** a collection of essays in which he connects his writing with his love for nature. For the quality of Cariou's writing and the sense of intimacy in his portrayal of childhood and family, his memoir has been favorably compared to Wallace Stegner's classic ***Wolf Willow; A History, a Story, and a Memory of the Last Plains Frontier.***

Carter, Jimmy (1924–)

An Hour Before Daylight: Memories of a Rural Boyhood. Simon & Schuster, 2001. 284pp. ill. 9780743211932. Also available in large print, Braille, and audiobook. 973.926092

Rather than a presidential memoir (see p. 374), Jimmy Carter offers here a classic depiction of the rural American South in the 1920s and 1930s. Despite living during the time of the Great Depression, the Carter family was better off than most, as James Earl Carter Sr. was a successful farmer who allowed sharecroppers to work on his land. Most of the sharecroppers were African-American, playing an important role in the development of Jimmy Carter. His mentor was a tenant farmer, Jack Clark, and his best friends were two African-American boys; it wasn't until they were teens that Jimmy noticed a new deference in his friends' attitude toward him. Carter's tale vividly reflects his sense of place, not just in Georgia, but in rural Georgia, and makes clear to the reader why he later returned to his roots. Bracketing his presidential years are this memoir of his childhood and a memoir detailing his life of service in his later years, ***Beyond the White House: Waging Peace, Fighting Disease, Building Hope***.

Carter was awarded the Presidential Medal of Freedom in 1999 by President Clinton and was recipient of the Nobel Peace Prize. When inducted into the Academy of Achievement, Carter was asked which book he would recommend; he cited James Agee and Walker Evans's ***Let Us Now Praise Famous Men*** because it shows how the problems faced by the people in the South during the Depression were shared across the country. ***An Hour Before Daylight*** was a finalist for the Pulitzer Prize for Biography or Autobiography and winner of a Christopher Award.

Subjects: 1920s; 1930s; American South; Carter, Earl, Sr.; Childhood and Youth; Christopher Awards; Fathers and Sons; Georgia; Mothers and Sons; Nobel Prize Laureates; Octogenarians; Presidents; Rural Life

Now Try: Another story that evokes the same sense of the simple but happy life in a rural environment (North Carolina), in roughly the same time period, is Tony Earley's highly acclaimed ***Jim the Boy: A Novel***. Sense of place and sense of family are also combined in Leila Philips's look back at her father's farm, which has been in the family for almost two centuries: ***A Family Place: A Hudson Valley Farm, Three Centuries, Five Wars, One Family***. The descriptive detail found in Carter's memoir is also prevalent in Adam Seth Cohen's description of the first hundred days in Franklin Roosevelt's administration, ***Nothing to Fear: FDR's Inner Circle and the Hundred Days That Created Modern America***. This book would also be of interest to those who would like to learn about the roots of Roosevelt's rural programs that benefited communities like Carter's.

Herriot, Trevor

River in a Dry Land: A Prairie Passage. M & S, 2004, 2000. 356pp. ill. maps by the author. 9781551991221. 971.24092

The Qu'Appelle Valley in southeastern Saskatchewan is the prairie's little secret. Not until you have driven into it do you realize you are there, and as you drive out of it and look back, all you see is flat prairie. But the Qu'Appelle Valley is rich with history—natural and human—and Herriot treats it all in this book, in a manner described by several reviewers as "luminous." He includes his own family heritage, as his mother's family had settled there, providing him with a memorable place to spend his summers as a child. His "prairie passage" is a combination of family history, a look at the history of the natural environment, a recognition without rancor of the harm done to the area and its original inhabitants, and an unstated plea for reconciliation and forward movement in concert to save and/or restore whatever was possible.

Herriot won a City of Regina Writing Award based on the early work he had done on the book. After the book was published, it was a finalist for the Governor General's Literary Award for Non-Fiction. It won two Saskatchewan Book Awards (the Regina Book Award and the Book of the Year Award) and the Writers' Trust of Canada Drainie-Taylor Biography Prize.

Subjects: Aboriginal Peoples, Canada; Farm Life, Canada; First Nations; Herriot Family; Nature Writers, Canada; Prairie Life, Canada; Qu'Appelle Valley, SK; Saskatchewan; Writers' Trust of Canada Drainie-Taylor Biography Prize

Now Try: Herriot's book sets out no polemic, but simply tells the tale as it really occurred and recognizes the gap in cultural narrative and communication between the settlers and those whom they unsettled. This is how Crown Attorney Rupert Ross describes the gaps in communication he encountered with the Aboriginal peoples he had come to serve in the far reaches of northwestern Ontario. In ***Dancing with a Ghost: Exploring Indian Reality*** he hopes to redress injustices and create a platform for better understanding. Herriot's sense of place as a circular connection to story is also reflected in Keith H. Basso's ***Wisdom Sits in Places: Landscape and Language Among the Western Apache***. Kazuo Ishiguro, also a luminous stylist, takes his characters back to their childhood in what was ostensibly an idyllic time at a private school and gradually reveals the truth of their past in ***Never Let Me Go***.

Kingsolver, Barbara (1955–), Steven L. Hopp (1954–), and Camille Kingsolver (1987–)

Animal, Vegetable, Miracle: A Year of Food Life. Illustrated by Richard A. Houser. Harper Perennial, 2008, 2007. 370pp. 9781554681884. Also available in large print, audiobook (read by the authors), e-audiobook, and e-book. 641.0973

Barbara Kingsolver had already made a statement about her social activism by creating the Bellwether Prize for Fiction to support writers of literature for social change, an award funded by the financial success of ***The Poisonwood Bible: A Novel***. Now she writes at great and eloquent length about the actions that she and her family took to live out their beliefs. Recognizing that most of the food eaten in Tucson has been transported there from other parts of the country, thus creating a large carbon footprint, Barbara, her husband Steven L. Hopp, and their two daughters, Camille and Lily, pulled up stakes and moved to Virginia, to a farm Steven owned in the Appalachian Mountains. They determined to become locavores, eating whatever they could grow themselves and supplementing that with food grown locally. The book presents a mine of information, some provided by Steven the scientist, who scatters essays throughout on topics that range from bread machines to mad cow disease to the use of fossil fuels in providing food; some provided by Camille, who adds anecdotal recipes along with meal plans; and the rest provided by Barbara, who creates a narrative worthy of her fiction. An index is available online (http://www.animalvegetablemiracle.com/Indices.html).

Animal, Vegetable, Miracle was awarded the James Beard Foundation Writing on Food Book Award; was named the Book Sense Book of the Year Adult Nonfiction Winner; and was selected as a Notable Book by the American Library Association.

Subjects: ALA Notable Books; Appalachian Region; Book Sense Book of the Year Adult Nonfiction Winner; Food Habits; Food Writing; James Beard Foundation Writing on Food Book Award; Local Foods; Writers

Now Try: Michael Pollan's ***In Defense of Food: An Eater's Manifesto*** is becoming a classic in the contemporary sustainable-food movement and is often named in conjunction with Kingsolver's book. A movement that caught on in Canada was called the "hundred-mile diet," based on a book by that name, ***The 100 Mile Diet: A Year of Local Eating*** by Alisa Dawn Smith and J. B. MacKinnon. This couple decided not to eat anything they could not acquire within a radius of 100 miles from their British Columbia home. (The American title is ***Plenty: One Man, One Woman, and a Raucous Year of Eating Locally***.) Verlyn Klinkenborg grew up on farms and went on to become a member of the editorial board of *The New York Times*, writing a column entitled "The Rural Life." He has collected those essays in ***The Rural Life***, describing his efforts at rural living again and encouraging all to be mindful of the details of nature surrounding them.

MacDonald, Jake (1949–)

Houseboat Chronicles: Notes from a Life in Shield Country. Lyons Press, 2004, 2002. 291pp. 9781592285532. 917.1

Shield Country is a vast (1.7 million square miles) stretch of wilderness that covers parts of Canada, Greenland, and the United States, but for Jake MacDonald, it was the "pine trees and granite, big skies, blue waters" of northwestern Ontario. He first felt the lure of nature in the wild as a young boy when his family spent summers in a cottage north of Winnipeg, Manitoba. In his reminiscences he talks at length about his family, as it was with his family that he shared his first experiences in nature. This coming-of-age story details not only his growing awareness of the beauty of the land as a child, but also his continuing growth and development as a man, learning to understand the real meaning of Charles Darwin's theory of adaptability to one's own environment. MacDonald tells the reader how he adapts, and he does it with humor and with a novelist's skill.

Highly praised in all its reviews, ***Houseboat Chronicles*** was awarded two Manitoba Writing and Publishing Awards: the Alexander Kennedy Isbister Award for Non-Fiction and the McNally Robinson Book of the Year Award. It was also awarded the Writers' Trust of Canada Non-Fiction Prize.

Subjects: Canadian Shield; Coming of Age; Family Relationships; Houseboats; Intellectual Life, Canada; Nature Writers, Canada; Ontario; Outdoor Life; Wilderness; Writers' Trust of Canada Non-Fiction Prize

Now Try: Apart from fiction and a field guide, MacDonald has also written a tongue-in-cheek look at a different part of the wilderness—bear country in northern British Columbia: ***Grizzlyville: Adventures in Bear Country***. Alongside MacDonald's book, readers may also enjoy a fellow Canadian's award-winning nature memoir, ***A Life in the Bush: Lessons from My Father*** by Roy MacGregor. It was named a Rutstrum Award winner, deemed to be the best book on the wilderness in North America published between 1995 and 2000. MacDonald's humor has been compared to Mark Twain's, particularly his "comic iconoclasm" (Wilkins, 2002). Readers may enjoy picking up Twain's own tale of the Western "wilderness," ***Roughing It***. Houseboats as a way of life can be fascinating to many; if you'd like to read someone else's experience, in quite a different environment, you may enjoy Gwen Roland's ***Atchafalaya Houseboat: My Years in the Louisiana Swamp***, including photographs by C. C. Lockwood.

O'Connor, Sandra Day (1930–), and H. Alan Day

Lazy B: Growing Up on a Cattle Ranch in the American Southwest. Modern Library, 2005, 2002. 318pp. ill. maps. 9780679643449. Also available in large print, Braille, audiobook, and e-book. 917.8092

Sandra and her brother, Alan, describe a vanishing way of life in this story set on a large ranch straddling the Arizona–New Mexico border, a ranch that had been in the Day family for three generations. The unforgiving land and climate with little annual rainfall necessitated digging wells and building windmills to pump water from them. But DA, Sandra's father, and her mother, MO, diligent, intelligent people, were willing to do what was necessary to make the ranch work. They hired eccentric, hard-working, loyal hands, who stayed on the ranch for life and who provide much color in the anecdotes found in this memoir. Although Sandra was sent to El Paso from the age of six to live with her maternal grandparents and attend a private girls' school, she glosses over that time, content to describe her special place, her life on the ranch during summer vacations. As they faced the growing bureaucratization of the lands, particularly by the Bureau of Land Management, her brother, manager of the ranch after their parents' deaths, divided and sold the ranch.

O'Connor was presented with the Presidential Medal of Freedom in 2009 by President Obama and has been inducted into the National Women's Hall of Fame. ***Lazy B*** was the book choice in ONEBOOKAZ in 2008.

Subjects: American Southwest; Arizona; Bureau of Land Management; Cowboys; Day Family; Firsts; Judges; Octogenarians; Ranch Life

Now Try: In a completely different vein, Sandra Day O'Connor has written reflections of her life as the first woman to be appointed to the United States Supreme Court after her tenure as a senator in the Arizona State Legislature; this more contemplative book, edited by Craig Joyce, is entitled ***The Majesty of the Law: Reflections of a Supreme Court Justice***. A classic about family and ranch life in Colorado that you may enjoy is Ralph Moody's ***Little Britches;***

Father and I Were Ranchers, with illustrations by Edward Shenton. If you'd like to read about a more modern cowboy lifestyle, you might find interesting David McCumber's ***The Cowboy Way: Seasons of a Montana Ranch***. Montana in its early days is reflected in Margaret Bell's story of her pioneer childhood, a story that has been revived by Mary Clearman Blew in ***When Montana and I Were Young: A Frontier Childhood***.

Spragg, Mark (1952–)

Where Rivers Change Direction. Riverhead Books, 2000, 1999. 283pp. 9780573228251. Also available in e-book. 978.7420330492

In a collection of essays, Spragg provides the reader with a view of a young boy/ man coming of age in the unadorned life of a cowboy. His father had a dude ranch in Wyoming, just miles east of the gate to Yellowstone National Park, and by the age of ten Spragg was expected to join the men in the bunkhouse, working for money and meals. He describes the land and the horses, animals that are very important to him as a person, as a ranch hand, and as a guide for the easterners that came to stay at the ranch. He shares the joy of having a day off work to go to an auction house with his father to get his first horse, and he recounts the pain of years later having to put down his longtime friend. In these essays Spragg takes us from his early childhood to his first marriage, his divorce, and a second marriage. He also writes lovingly of his mother, who was dying of emphysema at the time. In fact he wrote these essays for her, wanting her to see how important her life had been to him and his brother. He felt that seeing it on paper would be more convincing to her than just hearing him say it.

Where Rivers Change Direction was the winner of the Regional Book Award for Nonfiction for the Mountains & Plains Independent Booksellers Association.

Subjects: American West; Childhood and Youth; Coming of Age; Family Relationships; Mothers and Sons; Park County, WY; Personal Essays; Ranch Life; Wyoming

Now Try: Rick Bass fell in love with the West, specifically Yaak, Montana, when he headed north and west from his home in the south. In a collection of essays he expresses that love in ***Why I Came West***. The evocation of place found in Spragg's book can also be found in Ivan Doig's writing, for example, ***English Creek***, a coming-of-age novel set in Montana. Those who enjoyed Mark Spragg's essays may equally enjoy Annie Proulx's fictional collection, ***Close Range: Wyoming Stories***, with watercolors by William Matthews.

Watt, Alison (1957–)

The Last Island: A Naturalist's Sojourn on Triangle Island. Illustrated by the author. Harbour Publishing, 2002. 192pp. map. 9781550172966. 508.7112

Watt, a biology and botany student, went to the bird sanctuary of Triangle Island, off the northern coast of Vancouver Island, British Columbia, to study with Anne Vallée, a young biologist working there with tufted puffins. Alison found in Anne an inspiring mentor and, after finishing her term, continued to work as a seabird researcher and naturalist in British Columbia Provincial Parks. Two years later, Anne died accidentally, but sixteen years passed before Alison was finally able to get back to the island. Upon her arrival, she was flooded with memories, not only of the work she had done with the puffins, but also of Anne herself. Through her memories, Alison provides the reader with stories of Aboriginal legends, the science of the ecological reserve, and the importance of maintaining a delicate balance between humanity and wildlife. Alison, also a poet and an artist, has illustrated this book with forty of her own watercolors.

The Last Island was nominated for two BC Book Prizes and was awarded both the Western Regional Book Design & Production Award and the Edna Staebler Award for Creative Non-Fiction.

Subjects: Aboriginal Legends; Biologists; Bird Sanctuaries; Birds; British Columbia; Diaries; Edna Staebler Award for Creative Non-Fiction; Natural History, Canada; Puffins; Triangle Island, BC; Vallée, Anne

Now Try: Another artist/naturalist from Canada is Robert Bateman, whose illustrations grace Peter Matthiessen's ***The Birds of Heaven: Travels with Cranes***. For his twenty-first birthday, Adam Nicolson was given some islands in the Outer Hebrides by his father. These islands, as he recounts in ***Sea Room: An Island Life in the Hebrides***, are an important part of his well-being as he watches their only other inhabitants—birds such as puffins and razorbills. Phillip Manning traveled around America looking at wildlife refuges and in ***Islands of Hope*** describes ten of them, illustrating their worth for the health of the wildlife community.

Wiebe, Rudy Henry (1934–)

Of This Earth: A Mennonite Boyhood in the Boreal Forest. Good Books, 2007, 2006. 391pp. ill. maps. 9781561486021. Also available in e-book. 971.24

Rudy Wiebe, the son of Mennonite immigrants fleeing Stalinist Russia, tells the story of his first twelve years, growing up on a homestead in the boreal forest of northern Saskatchewan. In Speedwell, a largely Mennonite community, low German was spoken, and the inhabitants shared common religious and social beliefs. But for Wiebe, of prime importance were both his family and his physical surroundings. Lying on the floor of the forest, looking up at the trees, he felt the presence of a loving God, not the often wrathful God portrayed by those in his community. Wiebe also finds room for barnyard humor and revels in his happy memories of childhood. His grounding in this rural, forested community is such that when he became a prize-winning novelist as an adult, he recognized that he found himself aligned more with Aboriginal peoples from northern Saskatchewan, since they all shared a common birthplace, something Wiebe felt to be more significant than ancestry, and they also shared the marginalization of nonmainstream communities.

Of This Earth was nominated for the Writers' Trust of Canada Non-Fiction Prize and was awarded the Grant MacEwan Author's Award and the Charles Taylor Prize for Literary Non-fiction.

Subjects: 1930s; 1940s; Aboriginal Peoples, Canada; Boreal Forest; Charles Taylor Prize for Literary Non-fiction; Death of a Sibling; Farm Life, Canada; Immigrant Life, Canada; Mennonites, Canada; Novelists, Canada; Saskatchewan; Speedwell, SK

Now Try: For the quality of his writing, Wiebe's memoir has been favorably compared to Winfried Georg Sebald's writing; readers may want to pick up Sebald's highly acclaimed ***The Rings of Saturn,*** translated from the German by Michael Hulse. The unembellished style of his memoir is similar to the style found in the journal of Osborne Russell, another keen observer and writer who loved his environment: ***Journal of a Trapper; or, Nine Years in the Rocky Mountains: 1834–1843; Being a General Description of the Country, Climate, Rivers, Lakes, Mountains, etc., and a View of the Life Led by a Hunter in Those Regions***. Wiebe's structure in his memoir is circular, following the paths his memories take him. Kristen den Hartog uses a similar structure in her novel about life in a small Ontario town on the edge of the woods, ***Origin of Haloes: A Novel.***

Williams, Terry Tempest

Refuge: An Unnatural History of Family and Place. Tenth anniversary edition. With a new Afterword. Vintage Books, 2001, 1991. 314pp. map. 9780679740247. Also available in audiobook and e-book. 362.196994490092

The Table of Contents of Williams's memoir reflects the recurring themes that the author addresses in her book. Each chapter (except the last) is named after a bird, and under each bird's name is the phrase "lake level" followed by a number. Williams is a naturalist by nature and by vocation, particularly close to birds and intrinsically wrapped up in the Bear River Migratory Bird Refuge. During the writing of this book she details the unnatural rising of the Great Salt Lake, an event that, given the saline nature of the lake, has had a lasting effect on the surrounding flora, fauna, and aviculture in the area. Threaded in with these changes is another story, that of the breast cancers suffered by both her mother, Diane Dixon Tempest, and her grandmother, Lettie Romney Dixon. Her mother had had cancer once before, and it has now come back. This is the significance of the final chapter title, "The Clan of One-Breasted Women." Living in Utah for a good part of their lives, they had been exposed to radiation from the nuclear testing that the government had conducted in the 1950s. At the age of thirty-four Williams becomes the matriarch of the family. Despite all this, the memoir is uplifting for nature lovers, given Williams's Mormon faith, which ties her to the land and to nature as its steward.

Subjects: Bear River Migratory Bird Refuge, UT; Birds; Breast Cancer; Classics; Grandmothers; Great Salt Lake, UT; Mormons; Mothers and Daughters; Naturalists; Utah

Now Try: Another book from Williams's *oeuvre* that has proven very popular is her meditation on the relationship between the human and the natural, ***Finding Beauty in a Broken World***. Sharon Butala evokes the natural world of her new home in the Saskatchewan prairie in her memoir ***The Perfection of the Morning: An Apprenticeship in Nature***. Norman Maclean expresses his love of the land in his novella and stories in ***A River Runs Through It, and Other Stories***. In his nature journal, ***Following the Water: A Hydromancer's Notebook***, complete with his own beautiful illustrations, David M. Carroll takes his readers through one season in his New Hampshire wetlands.

Small Worlds

Many of the stories here are coming-of-age tales, the writers recounting their days growing up and growing into their worlds. Their worlds start small—their families, their neighborhoods, their communities of school and friendship. As they continue to grow, influenced by the people and events in their small worlds, they begin to develop their life interests, interests that for most of them turned into writing careers: journalists, historians, travel writers, novelists, poets. Gates, Gildiner, and Hickam are also writers, but each has a different primary occupation: academic, psychologist, and engineer. The ultimate career of the memoirist in this section is not always obvious from the story told here, although Hickam's career does not come as a surprise when you read his tale.

> The small worlds written of here represent the worlds of small children; they also happen to be primarily small towns. The childhoods of people familiar to us as adults are the focus here, most of them spent in small-town America; given the general age of the writers, these childhoods were also spent in a time not familiar to the youth of today.

Brokaw, Tom (1940–)

A Long Way from Home: Growing Up in the American Heartland. Random House, 2002. 233pp. ill. 9780375507632. Also available in large print, audiobook, e-audiobook, and e-book. 070.92

Tom Brokaw's place is not just the Heartland of the United States, but also the time period—of the 1940s and 1950s, when people were coming out of the Great Depression economy and entering the postwar boom economy. His parents were of strong stock, believers in hard work, honesty, thrift, self-reliance, and self-esteem without pride. He compares his life to Tom Sawyer's, recognizing that while he had to work hard—even doing the domestic chores that his mother taught him and his two brothers—he also had the opportunity to play: sports, youth government, even some radio broadcasting. In this memoir Brokaw takes the reader through the first twenty-two years of his life in South Dakota. In 1962 he and his wife,

Meredith, left South Dakota, initially for Nebraska and ultimately for parts a long way from home.

Brokaw is the recipient of a Horatio Alger Award.

Subjects: 1940s; 1950s; American Midwest; Childhood and Youth; Family Portraits; Journalists; Small Towns; Social History, United States; South Dakota; Television Journalists

Now Try: For the reader who enjoyed Brokaw's stories of his little league baseball games, Mark Kreidler has written the story of another small town—across the country, in New Jersey—where little league baseball is of prime importance: ***Six Good Innings: How One Small Town Became a Little League Giant***. The nostalgia felt in Brokaw's memoir would appeal to readers of Billie Letts's novels, particularly ***The Honk and Holler Opening Soon***. Idyllic childhoods seem to be few and far between, but Walter R. Brooks, creator of the **Freddy the Pig** series, seems to have had one as well. Michael Cart tells Brooks's story in ***Talking Animals and Others: The Life and Work of Walter R. Brooks, Creator of Freddy the Pig***.

Bryson, Bill (1951–)

The Life and Times of the Thunderbolt Kid: A Memoir. Broadway Books, 2007, 2006. 270pp. ill. 9780767919371. Also available in large print, Braille, audiobook, e-audiobook, and e-book. 910.4092

In keeping with the wistful humor of his memoir, Bryson prefaces each of his chapters with a quote from a newspaper or magazine, outlining some bizarre event. His memoir is a mix of nostalgia about growing up in Des Moines, Iowa, in the 1950s and wry reflections on the various cultural aspects of that time: practices in school in the event of an atomic bomb; the coming of the new appliances (television, for one) that made life easier; learning to read with Dick and Jane; playing outside all day long. The title comes from the superhero he created in himself after he found a moth-eaten shirt in the basement with a thunderbolt on it. When he donned the shirt and tied a cape (a towel) around his neck, he could then zap anything or anyone undesirable and even deflect unwanted kisses from old ladies.

Bryson's memoir was a Book Sense Book of the Year Honor Book.

Subjects: 1950s; Childhood and Youth; Des Moines, IA; Family Relationships; Humorists; Iowa; Popular Culture; Reflections; Social History, United States; Travel Writers

Now Try: David Benjamin grew up in an environment (Wisconsin) similar to Bryson's and humorously retells childhood anecdotes in ***The Life and Times of the Last Kid Picked***. The nostalgia that Bryson creates is an element in Howard Frank Mosher's novel, ***Waiting for Teddy Williams***, about an eight-year-old in a small town in Vermont who learns how to play baseball. Writer and engineer Henry Petroski's coming-of-age story takes place in the suburbs of New York City in the 1950s, as he describes how his life opened up when he was given a bike for his birthday, in ***Paperboy: Confessions of a Future Engineer***.

Gates, Henry Louis (1950–)

Colored People: A Memoir. Vintage Books, 1995, 1994. 216pp. 9780679739197. Also available in audiobook and e-book. 975.4092

Piedmont, West Virginia, was a segregated town when Henry Gates was born, but he grew up as millions of other young children grew up in North America, secure in the love of his family, encouraged in his talents by the adults around him, and full of memories of childhood antics. His father worked in the paper mill, doing the only job "coloreds" were permitted: working on the loading dock, loading paper into trucks. His mother cleaned houses, but her most important job was mothering her two boys. Although his childhood life had challenges, as most do, Gates paints an elegiac picture of his youth in Piedmont. He describes his early sex education among the male adults waiting for a haircut at the barbershop, the large family gatherings, the annual all-Black picnic held by the paper mill. But he also describes his mother's descent into severe depression; his own physical collapse in high school, which rendered him immobile in the hospital for six weeks; and the efforts he made to gain his father's respect. His memoir is an elegy to a time past, a small-town childhood in the 1950s, when racial tensions did exist, but were not an integral part of his childhood.

Gates was the recipient of a MacArthur Fellowship, and ***Colored People*** was selected as a Notable Book by the American Library Association and was awarded the *Chicago Tribune* Heartland Prize for Nonfiction as well as the Lillian Smith Book Award.

Subjects: 1950s; African-American Men; ALA Notable Books; Childhood and Youth, African-American; College Professors; Coming of Age; Intellectuals; Lillian Smith Book Award; Piedmont, WV; Small Towns; West Virginia

Now Try: Clifton L. Taulbert has written a memoir in the same vein as Gates, ***Once upon a Time When We Were Colored***, the story of a community in a pre-civil rights small town (in the South), where racial tensions existed, but family and community prevailed. Connie Rose Porter's novel, ***All-Bright Court***, set in Buffalo, New York, features an African-American community whose main source of employment is the local steel mill; it has the same wistful atmosphere as Gates's memoir. "Gracefully written" is a phrase applied to Gates's writing and to A. Manette Ansay's narrative, ***Limbo: A Memoir***, about her own sudden physical disability, which changed her career path from concert pianist to writer.

Gildiner, Catherine (1948–)

Too Close to the Falls. Viking, 2001, 1999. 354pp. 9780670894635. Available in audiobook and e-book. 974.7092

Gildiner's first memoir takes her from the age of four, when she was put to work in her father's pharmacy to channel her hyperactivity, to her adolescence, when she came very close to the symbolic vortex of the Falls in an illicit relationship with a priest. Catherine was very precocious, perhaps because her parents were unusual themselves. Her mother was an intellectual and a feminist, and the family always ate their lunches and dinners at a restaurant, as Catherine's mother refused to cook. During her childhood, Catherine encountered serious pollution (Love Canal), the power of politics (Robert Moses vs. the Tuscarora Nation), sexism (the essay contest that could really be won only by a boy), and discrimination (the cruelties toward the town's dump-keeper, a woman with "Elephant Man's disease"). As she recounts in a humorous fashion, she also became closely acquainted with the television, a new technology in her town. Gildiner, a psychologist, has recently followed up her childhood memoir with one entitled ***After the Falls: Coming of Age in the Sixties***.

Too Close to the Falls was short-listed for the Trillium Book Award.

Subjects: 1950s; Catholics; Drugstores; Eccentrics; Fathers and Daughters; Friendships; Lewiston, NY; Mothers and Daughters; New York (State); Parenting; Social History, United States; Television

Now Try: Joyce Carol Oates has written a family story using Niagara Falls as the background, simply titled ***The Falls: A Novel***. Jessica Weiss interviewed parents and their baby-boom children to determine what life really was like in the 1950s and found that perhaps Catherine's mother was not all that unusual; Weiss discusses her findings in ***To Have and to Hold: Marriage, the Baby Boom, and Social Change***. The humor in Gildiner's memoir has been compared to that of Jean Shepherd, as in one of his collections, ***Wanda Hickey's Night of Golden Memories, and Other Disasters***.

Goodwin, Doris Kearns (1943–)

Wait till Next Year: A Memoir. Simon & Schuster, 1998, 1997. 261pp. ill. 9780684847955. Also available in large print, audiobook, and e-book. 796.357092

Goodwin interweaves stories of her beloved Brooklyn Dodgers with stories of growing up on Long Island in the 1950s in an environment of events that included McCarthyism, Little Rock, Julius and Ethel Rosenberg, polio, and bomb shelters. Loving baseball and seeing it as a way to bond with her father, she kept scorebooks on each game every year, in order to recount to her father the games she had heard on the radio. She describes her community in terms of which of the three New York teams they supported, and even her close friendship with Elaine Friedle was in jeopardy the year the Dodgers and the Yankees played against each other in the World Series. As she grows older, her world changes—Elaine moves away, the Dodgers move to California, and her mother dies, introducing a much darker mood than existed earlier in the book.

Goodwin was inducted into the Academy of Achievement and, when asked to recommend a book, talked about the first book she read that excited her interest in history enough for her to become a historian: ***Roosevelt: The Lion and the Fox*** by James MacGregor Burns.

Subjects: 1950s; Baseball; Brooklyn Dodgers (Baseball Team); Cold War; Death of a Parent; Fathers and Daughters; Historians; Integration in Schools; Long Island, NY; McCarthy Era; New York (State)

Now Try: The food writer Molly O'Neill also grew up in a house dedicated to baseball, with her brother Paul eventually playing for the New York Yankees; her story of how baseball defined her family is a wonderful counterpart to Goodwin's story: ***Mostly True: A Memoir of Family, Food, and Baseball.*** Readers who would like to revisit that time when the Dodgers were still in Brooklyn may enjoy Michael Shapiro's ***The Last Good Season: Brooklyn, the Dodgers, and Their Final Pennant Race Together***. In writing about baseball and how she reported the games to her father and in detailing the historical events that were part of her life, Goodwin looks at how it all influenced her career as a historian. Susan Allen Toth does something similar in her childhood memoir, gauging how her young life molded her as a writer, in ***Blooming: A Small-Town Girlhood***.

Hickam, Homer H. (1943–)

Rocket Boys: A Memoir. Delacorte Press, 1998. 368pp. 9780385333207. Also available in large print, Braille, audiobook, e-audiobook, and video. 629.4092

Until he watched the space satellite *Sputnik* streak overhead in the October sky, along with the other townspeople of Coalwood, West Virginia, Homer Hickam had always assumed he would be going down the mines like his father when he finished high school. Seeing the space satellite changed his mind and, ultimately, his life. He and his buddies decided to try making their own rocket. After the first one succeeded only in burning his mother's fence, they began to get serious about learning how to do this properly. Their interest in school, first in science class and later in math class, picked up, thus challenging their teachers in ways they'd never been challenged before. The endeavors of this group who formed their own Big Creek Missile Agency became a focal point of interest for the whole town. Hickam's purpose in writing the memoir was not just to recount the efforts of a group of adolescents in successfully trying to achieve a dream, but also to depict a small town in the 1950s and the struggles within that town over its very existence. Hickam has said that he conflated some characters and played around a bit with chronology, but still remained true to the heart and authenticity of the story. The memoir was renamed ***October Sky*** for the movie and subsequent releases of the book.

Rocket Boys was nominated for the National Book Critics Circle Award in Biography.

Subjects: 1950s; Adolescents; Aerospace Engineers; Coalwood, WV; Coming of Age; Mining Towns; Rocketry; Small Towns; West Virginia; Writers

Now Try: Hickam wrote more about his town in **The Coalwood Series**, the second and third titles being ***The Coalwood Way*** and ***Sky of Stone***. Gregory Martin also grew up in a coal-mining town that went bust, which he details in ***Mountain City***. Hickam idolized Wernher von Braun for the work he was doing that so inspired Hickam and his friends; M. G. Lord presents another picture of von Braun and his lab in ***Astro Turf: The Private Life of Rocket Science***. Rinker Buck also had a dream, and he also had a father to impress. He writes of his cross-country flights with his brother, both teenagers, in ***Flight of Passage*** and follows that story with several others.

Kalish, Mildred Armstrong (1922–)

Little Heathens: Hard Times and High Spirits on an Iowa Farm During the Great Depression. Bantam, 2008, 2007. 292pp. ill. 9780553384246. Also available in large print, audiobook, e-audiobook, and e-book. 977.76103

The interest that Mildred Kalish's granddaughter showed in her grandmother's farm stories sparked Kalish's resolve to write down for posterity a time and a way of life that have all but disappeared—except perhaps among certain Amish or Mennonite sects. Kalish has a real memory for detail and uses that detail as the yarn with which she weaves her story. She says that her childhood ended when she was five and her paternal grandparents banished her father from the family and the town. Her mother, shamed by the ensuing divorce and left with four children to care for, was devastated. Her parents-in-law settled the family in a farm outside of town, but had the children live with them in town during the winter so they could walk to school. Work became the children's lives, but for Kalish it was "a romp." She is matter-of-fact in the telling, but her story resounds with the joy she felt even then, working hard at tasks like plucking feathers from a chicken, planting potatoes, or shucking corn. She also describes the unforgettable scents and views of the flowering crabapple tree or a lamb sleeping in the sun. She offers recipes from those days and basically presents a diorama of farm life in Iowa in the 1930s. She was eighty-five when this, her first book, was published and enthusiastically received.

Subjects: 1930s; Family Relationships; Farm Life; Fatherless Children; Garrison, IA; Grandparents; Iowa; Methodists; Octogenarians; Rural Life

Now Try: Jeanne Marie Laskas describes early days on a farm, but from an adult's perspective, as she fulfills a dream by buying a farm, although she knows nothing about farming. The first of her several memoirs is ***Fifty Acres and a Poodle: A Story of Love, Livestock, and Finding Myself on a Farm***. David Kline has a different take on farm life, a slow and contemplative one, as he closely observes the creatures that make up his environment. His book, ***Scratching the Woodchuck: Nature on an Amish Farm***, is a collection of short, observational essays, with drawings by Wendell Minor. Michael Perry has already written about life in a small village (***Population, 485: Meeting Your Neighbors One Siren at a Time***), but now he has moved to a farm, an adventure he tells in ***Coop: A Year of Poultry, Pigs, and Parenting***.

Kimmel, Haven (1965–)

A Girl Named Zippy: Growing Up Small in Mooreland, Indiana. Broadway Books, 2002, 2001. 282pp. ill. photos. 9780767915052. Also available in large print, audiobook, e-audiobook, and e-book. 977.264

One might wonder what one could possibly say about growing up in a town with a population of 300, but Haven Kimmel manages to say enough to create a humorous, beguiling memoir. In Mooreland, Indiana, everyone pretty well knows everyone else, and it is this familiarity that creates a universal story. Kimmel writes from the child's point of view, describing how she saw people and events, placing them in her own self-centered context, as all children just assume the world revolves around them. Her story is not linear, but based on memories about specific topics, enhanced by old photographs. Kimmel also quotes from her baby book, lending an even greater sense of authenticity to her story; her mother's prayer, once Haven began to talk, was that God would finally give her hair. In Kimmel's sequel, ***She Got Up off the Couch: And Other Heroic Acts from Mooreland, Indiana,*** she is now in her early teens and her mother, Delonda Hartmann, has decided to go to college.

Subjects: 1960s; 1970s; American Midwest; Childhood and Youth; Family Relationships; Friendships; Indiana; Mooreland, IN: Small Towns

Now Try: Another writer who has written of childhood in Indiana is Philip Gulley, whose ***I Love You, Miss Huddleston and Other Inappropriate Longings of My Indiana Childhood*** exhibits the same childlike innocence that Kimmel does. Her fresh and funny approach is also seen in another quirky girl in Randa Jarrar's ***A Map of Home: A Novel.*** For a bit of a different take on growing up in the American Midwest, you might enjoy the story of Linda Furiya, the only Japanese-American in her small Indiana town, described in ***Bento Box in the Heartland: My Japanese Girlhood in Whitebread America.***

Mason, Bobbie Ann (1940–)

Clear Springs: A Memoir. Random House, 1999. 298pp. ill. map. 9780679449256. Also available in e-book. 813.54

Bobbie Ann Mason couldn't wait to get away from her western Kentucky roots, first moving from the farm to the city for her undergraduate degree, finally moving north for her graduate degrees and staying there. Yet in her fiction she returns to her roots time and again. She started doing some genealogical research on her family and finally reached the point where she wanted to write about her family and her life in western Kentucky, life on a farm near the town of Mayfield. She focuses on three generations: her paternal grandmother, her mother, Christina, (who is really at the heart of the memoir), and herself. She describes her life on the farm, where her family lived with her grandparents, and looks particularly at the dislocation they felt as the twentieth century, brought to them by World War II, was finally putting its stamp on the old ways. She talks about her leaving and her writing and then returns home at one point when her book, ***In Country: A Novel,*** is being filmed in Mayfield by Warner Brothers. She finally comes full circle as she buys property in Kentucky near Lexington.

Clear Springs was a finalist for the Pulitzer Prize for Biography or Autobiography.

Subjects: Childhood and Youth; Family Relationships; Farm Life; Grandmothers; Kentucky; Mothers and Daughters; Rural Life

Now Try: One of the issues that Mason treats in her memoir is the isolation of the farming community, each family on its own farm. Lisa Wingate includes this theme in her novel, ***Tending Roses***, about a young woman who reads her grandmother's diary to understand the importance of her farm. Before the town of Martin, Kentucky, is razed by the government to be rebuilt on higher ground, Michelle Slatalla researches her family history in light of that town and its people in ***The Town on Beaver Creek: The Story of a Lost Kentucky Community***. In ***A Place on Earth***, one in the **Port William** series by Wendell Berry, a rural community in Kentucky is brought to life.

Moehringer, J. R. (1964–)

The Tender Bar: A Memoir. Hyperion, 2006, 2005. 416pp. 9780786888764. Also available in large print, audiobook (read by the author), e-audiobook, and e-book. 070.92

J.R. Moehringer knew his father as "The Voice," a late-night disc jockey who had abandoned Moehringer's mother years before. His mother had to hold down more than one job in order to make any kind of life for herself and her son. Initially they lived with her father in Manhasset, on Long Island in New York, but she took Moehringer with her to Arizona, where she hoped to do better economically and to be closer to other family members. One summer she sent her son back to Manhasset, where his Uncle Charlie took him under his wing and introduced him to the pub culture, particularly Publicans, the tavern where Uncle Charlie was both a bartender and a customer. It was here that Moehringer finally found his male role models, and he had a broad range to choose from: Wall Street men and blue collar workers, policemen and bookies, poets and lawyers. Though he was too young to drink, he was still able to spend his days there, getting to know the men the way the regulars got to know each other. The book ends with a poignant epilogue, listing the Manhasset people Moehringer knew who died in the attacks on the World Trade Center in 2011, people with whom he had made great connections through Publicans.

Subjects: Bars; Childhood and Youth; Coming of Age; Family Relationships; Fatherless Children; Friendships; Journalists; Long Island, NY; New York (State); Uncles

Now Try: Wendy Bounds also found fellowship in a pub; rendered homeless by the attacks on the World Trade Center, she was gradually introduced to Guinan's, an Irish pub in Garrison, New York, near the Hudson, where she eventually found a new home. She tells her story in ***Little Chapel on the River: A Pub, a Town, and an Unexpected Journey***. Those who enjoy Moehringer's story may also enjoy the novel by Michael Raleigh, ***In the Castle of the Flynns: A Novel***, in which a young orphaned boy goes to live with his Irish-American grandparents and uncles in Chicago. Readers may like to go along for the ride with Pete McCarthy, touring bars along the west coast of Ireland—or at least all those that are called McCarthy's—in ***McCarthy's Bar: A Journey of Discovery in the West of Ireland***.

Faraway Places

Central to the stories in this section is the locale. If the memoirist had been born elsewhere, the heart of the story would not have taken place. The titles span the globe, stopping off in five of the seven continents (missing from this section are Antarctica and Australia/Oceania). They range geographically from Afghanistan to Zimbabwe, from China to Colombia. The stories offer a glimpse into the "language, tradition, food, music, tempo" (Anaya, 1995) of a place, as well as the history, a history that is often painful to read about and that was often painful for the writer to have lived. Some stories do not reflect the childhood of the writer, as the memoirist did not grow up there, but the setting is of prime importance to the memoir, as the reader will discover.

> Memoirs of faraway places represent lives lived in countries other than the United States or Canada. While the experiences of these writers are very different from those of people in North America, the reminiscences reveal how setting had much to do with the formation of the writers, just as it may have done with writers growing up in the United States or Canada.

Akbar, Said Hyder (1984–), and Susan Burton (1973–)

Come Back to Afghanistan: A California Teenager's Story. Bloomsbury, 2005. 339pp. maps. 9781582345208. Also available in e-book. 958.1047

Said Akbar was a teenager in California when his father was called back to Afghanistan after 9/11 by his friend Hamid Karzai. Akbar's father was initially President Karzai's press officer and then was appointed governor of a strategic and outlying province, Kunar. Once his high school exams were over, Akbar joined his father for the summer, something he was to repeat for two more summers. He initially reported on his visits on *This American Life*, produced for Chicago Public Media by Akbar's coauthor, Susan Burton. Now they have created this memoir of his time there as he meets the political men of the day, gapes at famous Afghan writers, interviews warlords and regular citizens, and tours the house of Osama bin Laden as other tourists do. Because of his fluency in Pashto, Dari, and Urdu he is able to assimilate himself into his heritage country. Akbar had never been to Afghanistan before that first summer, as his parents had fled the country during the Soviet invasion, and he was born in Pakistan. He has since made his father's country his life's work.

Subjects: Adolescents; Afghanistan; Akbar, Said Fazel; Biculturalism; Karzai, Hamid; Social History, Afghanistan; *This American Life* (Radio Program); Travel

Now Try: In ***Afghanistan's Endless War: State Failure, Regional Politics, and the Rise of the Taliban***, Larry P. Goodson, a history professor, explains the political situation in Afghanistan prior to 9/11, prior to Akbar's father's return home. Nicholas Jubber provides a completely different view of Afghanistan and Iran, using an eleventh-century epic poem as his touchstone, revealing the cultural fabric of the area through it in ***Drinking Arak Off an Ayatollah's Beard: A Journey Through the Inside-Out Worlds of Iran and Afghanistan***. The life of bicultural children is often difficult; Maryam Qudrat Aseel describes her own experience as a second-generation Afghan-American in ***Torn Between Two Cultures: An Afghan-American Woman Speaks Out***.

Bernstein, Harry (1910–)

The Invisible Wall: A Love Story That Broke Barriers. With a new Afterword. Ballantine Books, 2008, 2007. 321pp. 9780345496102. Also available in large print, audiobook, e-audiobook, and e-book. 813.54

The small industrial town of Lancashire, England, just before World War I is the setting of this memoir of a small child growing up in a poor and conflicted environment. There is conflict in his home, with an alcoholic, abusive father and sibling rivalries, mitigated by his loving mother. There is conflict in the neighborhood as well, with the Jewish population on one side of the street and the Christian population on the other; "never the twain shall meet." When Harry's Jewish sister Lily falls in love with a Christian man, Arthur Forshaw, the neighborhood situation eventually changes. Before the street opens up, however, Harry is witness to difficult times for all, but especially for Lily. Bernstein wrote this memoir after Ruby, his wife of sixty-seven years, died in 2002; Harry was in his mid-nineties at the time. His friends were all gone and he felt he had no future, so he decided to look at his past. After this first memoir he wrote ***The Dream: A Memoir***, about his family's emigration to the United States in search of the American Dream, and then ***The Golden Willow: The Story of a Lifetime of Love***, about life with Ruby.

Subjects: 1910s; Centenarians; Childhood and Youth; Coming of Age; England; Family Relationships; Jews, England; Lancashire, England; Mothers and Sons; Religious Discrimination

Now Try: The classic novel ***Bread Givers; A Novel*** by Anzia Yezierska also deals with a strict Jewish father as his daughter rebels against the strictures placed upon her. The British writer John J. Gross grew up in a later generation from Bernstein, but offers his own view of growing up Jewish in England in ***A Double Thread; Growing Up English and Jewish in London***. Lancashire is also the town that William Woodruff grew up in; he brings to life his working-class childhood in ***The Road to Nab End: A Lancashire Childhood***.

Carr, Rosamond Halsey (1912–2006)
Halsey, Ann Howard, coauthor

Land of a Thousand Hills: My Life in Rwanda. Plume, 2000, 1999. 248pp. ill. 16pp. of plates. 9780452282025. Also available in large print, audiobook, e-audiobook, and e-book. 967.571

Rosamond Carr traded the life of a socialite and fashion illustrator for that of a flower plantation owner in Rwanda. She had married a man twenty-four years older than she and agreed to go to Africa with him seven years after their wedding, in the hopes of saving a marriage already floundering. The marriage didn't last, but her love of Africa did, and she eventually made her home in Mugongo, Rwanda. Carr describes her way of life: the running of the flower plantation she set up; the society in which she traveled; and good friends, including the primatologist Dian Fossey. She also clearly explains the political strife in the country, underlining the centuries-long conflict between the Hutus and the Tutsis. During the Rwandan genocide she was forced to leave Rwanda for a few months, but after watching the news reports back in the United States she went home again to set up an orphanage for the children abandoned by the civil war (http://imbabazi.org/). Due to continuing political strife, she had to move the orphanage four times, but they all eventually made their way back to Mugongo.

Subjects: Americans in Rwanda; Businesswomen; Divorce; Expatriates; Fossey, Dian; Nonagenarians; Orphans, Rwanda; Plantation Life, Rwanda; Rwanda; Rwanda Civil War (1994)

Now Try: Élisabeth Combres has written a novel about one Rwandan orphan, five-year-old Emma: ***Broken Memory: A Novel of Rwanda*** (translated from the French by Shelley Tanaka). Louise Mushikiwabo was living in the United States during the genocide; in ***Rwanda Means the Universe: A Native's Memoir of Blood and Bloodlines***, written with the help of Jack Kramer, she describes how she lost most of her family, and she provides a close-up view of Rwanda and the relationships among its people. If you're interested in Carr's flower business, you might enjoy Amy Stewart's ***Flower Confidential: The Good, the Bad, and the Beautiful in the Business of Flowers***.

Doyle, John (1957–)

A Great Feast of Light: Growing Up Irish in the Television Age. Carroll & Graf, 2007, 2005. 321pp. 9780786718146. 070.92

John Doyle offers a memoir of his boyhood in the very small town of Nenagh, County Tipperary, and his adolescence in Dublin, all through the prism of the coming of television to Ireland. Looking back as an adult and recognizing how hidebound the small towns of Ireland were, tied to the Catholic Church with all its rules and to the anti-British government, Doyle uses his own childhood and introduction to television as the means of illustrating just how strong an influence television was on Irish culture and life. By seeing American personalities such as Donna Reed or the characters of *Dallas*, none of whom was attached to the Catholic Church, as well as such historic events as civil rights marches, the Irish began to see other ways of living and protesting their current way of life. For John Doyle, however, the influence was great enough to create in him a desire to leave behind his birth country and emigrate to Canada, where he still lives, working as a columnist (and television reviewer) for *The Globe and Mail*.

Subjects: Coming of Age; Humor; Ireland; Irish-Canadians; Newspaper Columnists, Canada; Social History, Ireland; Television

Now Try: Doyle's writing style and voice are very similar to those of fellow Irishman Hugo Hamilton, whose first memoir is entitled ***The Speckled People***, about his own bicultural family. Ireland isn't the only country strongly influenced by television. A far-reaching history of television and its cultural effects has been written by Gary Richard Edgerton, ***The Columbia History of American Television***. Irish dramatist Peter Sheridan grew up in Ireland at the same time as Doyle, a childhood he describes in ***44, Dublin Made Me: A Memoir***.

Eire, Carlos M. N. (1950–)

Waiting for Snow in Havana: Confessions of a Cuban Boy. Free Press, 2003. 383pp. ill. 9780743219655. Also available in large print. 972.91092

Carlos Eire, part of the comfortable middle class in Batista's Cuba, was one of 14,000 children airlifted from Cuba to Florida between 1960 and 1962 in Operation Pedro Pan (http://www.pedropan.org/). When Eire heard about the number of Americans who wanted to have the young boat refugee Elián González flown back from Florida to Cuba in 2000, he was aghast and came to recognize that Americans had no idea what this child would be sent back to. As a historian (he is T. Lawrason Riggs Professor of History and Religious Studies at Yale), he felt an obligation to set the record straight and to inform those who would listen about life under the dictatorship of Fidel Castro. His story, then, details his life as an ordinary boy, living in a rather unusual household until the Revolution and his exile from Cuba at the age of eleven. When Eire's mother decided that they had to send Carlos and his brother Tony away, his father agreed, but never agreed to follow them, as their mother did. The boys lived in foster homes for several years until their mother was able to join them, and they never saw their father again. This is the backstory of the book, but the core of the story is Eire's actual childhood in Cuba, when he was full of vim and vinegar, going to the movies, shooting off fireworks, playing at friends' houses, just doing what little boys normally do. Instead of having snowball fights, they had breadfruit fights, but their curiosity about snow was always with them.

Waiting for Snow in Havana won the National Book Award for Nonfiction.

Subjects: 1960s; Childhood and Youth; Coming of Age; Cuba; Cuban-Americans; Family Relationships; Fathers and Sons; Havana, Cuba; National Book Award for Nonfiction; Operation Peter Pan; Refugees, Cuba

Now Try: In a recent memoir, ***Learning to Die in Miami: Confessions of a Refugee Boy***, Eire describes his immigrant experience. The other mass exodus from Cuba was the Mariel Boatlift in 1980; Mirta A. Ojito was part of that and talks about her experience in ***Finding Mañana: A Memoir of a Cuban Exodus***. The difference between Eire's father and Lucette Matalon Lagnado's father is that the expatriate journalist's father accompanied them in their flight from Egypt, as she describes in ***The Man in the White***

Sharkskin Suit: My Family's Exodus from Old Cairo to the New World. Carlos Eire has been highly praised for his writing style, including the way he moves back and forth in his storytelling: because each of his chapters focuses on an image, he has not written in a linear style. This same style is characteristic of Julia Alvarez's ***In the Name of Salomé: A Novel,*** in which a daughter looks back at her childhood with memories of her poet mother, who died young.

Farman-Farmaian, Sattareh (1920–)
Munker, Dona, coauthor

Daughter of Persia: A Woman's Journey from Her Father's Harem Through the Islamic Revolution. Three Rivers Press, 2006, 1992. 410pp. ill. 9780307339744. Also available in audiobook and e-book. 955.0509

Sattareh Farman-Farmaian was the third child born to her mother, the sixteen-year-old third wife of Sattareh's father, a man who eventually had eight wives. The compound she grew up in had at least 1,000 people living in it, including thirty-five siblings and half-siblings. Her father did not believe in all Muslim restrictions against women, so Sattareh was able to travel to California for her undergraduate degree and her master's in social work. She describes the various political regimes her country was ruled by, from the American-backed coup in 1953 that ousted the democratically elected Mohammad Mosaddeq to the installation and regime of the Ayatollah Khomeini, who died in 1989. She did return to Iran and set up a school of social work there, helping the women with issues of family planning, day care, help for the poor, and help for prisoners' families. After the Ayatollah took over, however, she and her work were seriously at risk; she was arrested by gun-toting teenagers and almost executed. She now lives in the United States, but she doesn't mince words about her feelings regarding U.S. intervention in Iranian politics throughout the decades. She also interweaves stories and information about Iran's cultural history throughout her tale.

Subjects: Exiles; Foreign Policy, United States; Harems; Iran; Iran Revolution (1979–1997); Nonagenarians; Social Workers, Iran; Women in Iran

Now Try: Farman-Farmaian was not a wife in the harem, which would have given her a different perspective on that culture. Providing a picture of the culture from the adult woman's point of view is ***Harem: The World Behind the Veil*** by Alev Lytle Croutier. Farman-Farmaian expresses her deep-felt anger against President Eisenhower and his role in Iranian politics, a role that Stephen Kinzer elaborates on in ***All the Shah's Men: An American Coup and the Roots of Middle East Terror.*** Persis M. Karim, disturbed by everything she was reading in the papers and particularly by President Bush's phrase, "axis of evil," asked a number of Iranian women writers to contribute to a collection that would illustrate the real culture and richness of Iran. The result is ***Let Me Tell You Where I've Been: New Writing by Women of the Iranian Diaspora.***

Fuller, Alexandra (1969–)

Don't Let's Go to the Dogs Tonight: An African Childhood. Random House Trade Paperbacks, 2003, 2001. 315pp. ill. map. 9780375758997. Also available in large print, Braille, audiobook, e-audiobook, and e-book. 968.91092

Alexandra Fuller offers a child's view of life in war-torn Rhodesia, where she was taken at the age of two by her parents. Fuller puts her writing skills to good use to describe the essence of the land, with its wildlife, its birds and insects, its plants, and its smells; this is the backdrop, however, for the tragedies within the home, with her father often away for long stretches fighting in the Rhodesian civil war; her mother driven to alcoholism by the death of several children; and their lives in danger from land mines, even while going to the grocery store. Fuller later said that she felt it necessary to give some historical background to her story and when she did, she slipped out of her reminiscing child's voice into a more reportorial voice. But the voice is largely that of a child who does not understand why danger is such a constant in their lives.

Fuller's debut work garnered a nomination for the *Guardian* First Book Award and won the Winifred Holtby Memorial Prize; it was also named the Book Sense Book of the Year Adult Nonfiction Winner.

Subjects: Book Sense Book of the Year Adult Nonfiction Winner; Childhood and Youth; Children and War; Children of Alcoholics; English in Rhodesia (Zimbabwe); Farm Life, Rhodesia; Racism, Southern Africa; Rhodesia Civil War (1971–1979); Southern Africa; Zimbabwe

Now Try: Fuller followed her childhood story with one about a tour as an adult of war-torn Southern Africa, ***Scribbling the Cat: Travels with an African Soldier***. Two other White women have written their own memoirs of life in Africa, one eerily similar to Fuller's and one completely dissimilar. Wendy Kann also grew up in war-torn Rhodesia, also with an alcoholic mother; she had occasion to return to Africa and come to grips with her childhood after the accidental death of her sister. She writes about her experience in ***Casting with a Fragile Thread: A Story of Sisters and Africa***. Robyn Scott, on the other hand, grew up happily in Botswana, albeit with an eccentric family, and tells her story in ***Twenty Chickens for a Saddle: The Story of an African Childhood***. Lauren St. John was another child who grew up in war-torn Rhodesia. Her reminiscences can be found in ***Rainbow's End: A Memoir of Childhood, War and an African Farm***.

Guillermoprieto, Alma (1949–)

Dancing with Cuba: A Memoir of the Revolution. Vintage Books, 2005. 290pp. 978037525814. Also available in e-book. 972.91064 [Trans. by Esther Allen]

This is a political coming-of-age story by the journalist who was a recipient of a MacArthur Fellowship for her reporting on the Latin American world. Born in Mexico, she had always hoped to be a professional dancer and headed off to New York to fulfill her dreams. She studied with Martha Graham and Twyla Tharp, but it wasn't until moving on to work with Merce Cunningham that she was finally told she didn't have what it takes to be a professional.

Cunningham did, however, offer her the opportunity to teach dance in a high school in Havana, a prospect that appealed to Guillermoprieto. Once the twenty-year-old arrived in Cuba, though, where the students had neither mirrors nor music, Guillermoprieto found herself in a world that changed her forever. At first indifferent to politics, interested only in teaching her students modern dance, she soon got swept up in the ideals of Cuba's communism and then came face-to-face with the reality. She finally recognized that there was more to the world than just dance; there was political interference by other countries; there were homophobia, racism, and police brutality in an ostensibly ideal political state; there were abject poverty and deprivation. She didn't immediately become a journalist—that decision came later in Nicaragua—but she did realize in Cuba that Latin America in all its upheaval was her world to discover.

Subjects: 1970s; Castro, Fidel; Cuba; Cunningham, Merce; Dance; Guevara, Che; Journalists; Mexicans; Newswomen; Social History, Cuba; Translations

Now Try: In ***Looking for History: Dispatches from Latin America,*** Guillermoprieto collected a number of the articles she has written about her chosen field. If you'd like to read about Merce Cunningham, the man who changed Guillermoprieto's life by being honest with her, you might find interesting the memoir by the dancer Carolyn Brown, ***Chance and Circumstance: Twenty Years with Cage and Cunningham***. Jonathan Kozol also went to Cuba, but in his case it was to teach illiterate adults; he too gets more of an education than he perhaps provides. He describes his time there in ***Children of the Revolution: A Yankee Teacher in the Cuban Schools***. Reinaldo Arenas experienced firsthand the institutional homophobia of Cuba, as he describes in his memoir, ***Before Night Falls,*** translated from the Spanish by Dolores M. Koch.

Jaffrey, Madhur (1933–)

Climbing the Mango Trees: A Memoir of a Childhood in India. Vintage Books, 2007, 2006. 297pp. ill. 9781400078202. Also available in audiobook and e-book. 641.5092

Madhur Jaffrey is known to Western readers as a cookbook writer more than as an actress. In fact, she was one of the cookbook authors that Judith Jones snagged for Knopf with ***An Invitation to Indian Cooking***. In this memoir she recalls her childhood through a scrim of food, beginning with the honey that her grandmother placed on her tongue at birth, writing out the word *om* with the honey. She lived in a comfortable home with loving parents and extended family and has many cherished memories of her childhood in India. The difficulties are not glossed over, however, particularly when politics intervened in her own life, politics in the form of the partition of India, creating a Muslim Pakistan and separating the Hindu Jaffrey from her Muslim friends. An interesting tidbit that Jaffrey provides regarding food is that with the influx of Hindus from what used to be northwestern India (now Pakistan), regional cooking like tandoori and paneer made its way into mainstream Indian fare. Jaffrey failed at home economics, but when she moved to England to study drama and realized how much she missed her mother's cooking, she asked for recipes, reams of which her mother sent her. Many of those recipes form the appendix of her memoir.

Subjects: Actors; Childhood and Youth; Cooking, Indic; Delhi, India; Family Relationships; Food, India; Food Writers; India; Indians in England

Now Try: Those of us who are not professional cooks just assume that the professionals always knew how to cook, but Jaffrey proves that was not the case for her. Kimberly Witherspoon and Peter Meehan asked a number of chefs to contribute essays to ***How I Learned to Cook: Culinary Educations from the World's Greatest Chefs***. The political troubles between India and Pakistan flare up periodically over different issues. In the 1980s it was the question of Kashmir and its desire to separate. The journalist Basharat Peer is a Kashmiri who wrote a memoir explaining the conflict and his presence in its midst in ***Curfewed Night: One Kashmiri Journalist's Frontline Account of Life, Love and War in His Homeland***. Shoba Narayan also grew up in India, surrounded by memorable food, as she narrates in ***Monsoon Diary: A Memoir with Recipes***.

Kwan, Michael David (1934–2001)

Things That Must Not Be Forgotten: A Childhood in Wartime China. Soho, 2001. 244pp. 9781569472484. Also available in e-book. 951.04092

Michael David Kwan, the biracial son of a Chinese man and a Swiss woman who had left the family, suffered from both his European and his Chinese schoolmates at school, finding that he belonged to neither group. This is one thread of Kwan's story of his life in China until the age of twelve. The other is the political situation he was living in at the time. He was in a walled community, which provided some protection from the vicissitudes of politics, but his family was not completely immune. The Japanese invaded China when Kwan was four, and while Kwan's father was ostensibly working for the Japanese, he was also part of the resistance against them. At the same time, the battle between Chiang Kai-Shek and Mao Zedong was heating up, providing more conflict and tension. Kwan was finally sent to Hong Kong when he was twelve and didn't go back to China until he was hired to teach there as an adult in the 1980s.

Things That Must Not Be Forgotten was nominated for the Charles Taylor Prize for Literary Non-fiction and was the winner of the Kiriyama Prize and posthumous cowinner of the Canada-Japan Literary Award.

Subjects: 1930s; 1940s; Biracial Children; Canada-Japan Literary Award; Childhood and Youth; China; Chinese-Canadians; Coming of Age; Kiriyama Prize; Sino-Japanese Conflict (1937–1939); Writers, Canada

Now Try: J. G. Ballard's ***Empire of the Sun: A Novel*** also tells the story of a young boy in China on the brink of World War II from the child's viewpoint. The issue of interracial marriages and the resultant prejudice is also dealt with in Aimee Liu's novel ***Cloud Mountain***. If you'd like another picture of life as a child in China, you may enjoy Charles N. Li's memoir, ***The Bitter Sea: Coming of Age in a China Before Mao***.

Manley, Rachel (1947–)

Drumblair: Memories of a Jamaican Childhood. Key Porter Books, 2008, 1996. 407pp. 16pp. of plates. 9781554700509. 972.920922

Drumblair was the home of Norman and Edna Manley, grandparents to Rachel Manley. At the age of two-and-a-half Rachel was sent to Jamaica from England by her divorced father to live with Pardi and Mardi, as her grandparents were called. She lived there until the age of twenty, and although her father, Michael, eventually moved to Jamaica himself, she remained with her grandparents. Her grandfather was the first chief minister (then premier) of a Jamaica newly independent of Britain and initially part of the West Indies Federation. Rachel's grandmother, Edna, was a preeminent sculptor and artist in Jamaica and had her studio on the Drumblair property. Rachel's story, told from a child's perspective, revolves around her life with her grandparents and with the domestics who worked there and who provided much care and instruction for her. As she grew older, however, and particularly once she reached college age, she was made to feel self-conscious because of her white skin (although her heritage was of mixed race) and because of her family name, as her father became prime minister of Jamaica for many years. Manley's memoir is not just a reflection of her own childhood, but also an evocation of a place and the family within that place.

Drumblair was awarded the Governor General's Literary Award for Non-Fiction.

Subjects: Childhood and Youth; Colonial Life, Jamaica; Governor General's Literary Award for Non-Fiction; Grandparents; Homes and Haunts; Jamaica; Manley, Edna; Manley, Norman; Poets, Canada

Now Try: Rachel Manley has followed ***Drumblair*** with two subsequent memoirs: ***Slipstream: A Daughter Remembers*** is more about her father, Michael, and ***Horses in Her Hair: A Granddaughter's Story*** focuses on her grandmother, Edna. Sara Suleri Goodyear also spent her early life in a colonial locale, in Pakistan; her childhood perceptions are revealed in ***Meatless Days***. Living with grandparents is not all that unusual, but Max Apple's situation might qualify for "unusual status," as he tells in ***Roommates: My Grandfather's Story***, made into a movie of the same name. Perhaps even more famous than Jamaica's first family is Bob Marley, Jamaica's best-known musician. Timothy White tells his story in ***Catch a Fire: The Life of Bob Marley***.

Márquez, Gabriel García (1928–)

Living to Tell the Tale. Vintage International, 2005, 2003. 533pp. maps. 9781400034543. Also available in e-book. 863.64 [Trans. by Edith Grossman]

This is the first of three proposed volumes of memoir, this one taking the author to the age of twenty-eight, just at the point where he has proposed to the woman who would be his wife. We see already his love of and talent for writing, a talent that resulted in his being sought out by the newspapers. We learn about coastal Colombia, very different from Andean Colombia, but most important, we meet Márquez's family: his grandparents with whom he lived for most of his childhood and youth, and his parents, especially his mother, Luisa Santiaga Márquez. Readers of Márquez will recognize the provenance of locales, events, and characters in his fiction by the stories he tells of his life. The book begins during his adolescence and then flashes back to his earlier days. It then jumps to young adulthood: school and then journalism and finally a trip to Switzerland, where he stays for three years.

Márquez was awarded the Nobel Prize in Literature in 1982.

Subjects: Childhood and Youth; Colombia; Family Relationships; Grandparents; Mothers and Sons; Nobel Prize Laureates; Novelists, Colombia; Octogenarians; Translations

Now Try: Although Gregory Rabassa didn't translate this work of Márquez, he did translate his earlier fiction, bringing Márquez to the attention of the English-reading world. Rabassa has written a memoir, too: ***If This Be Treason: Translation and Its Dyscontents; A Memoir***. For its portrayal of a young writer developing his craft, Márquez's memoir has been compared favorably to a similar albeit fictional portrayal in William Styron's novel ***Sophie's Choice***. Readers who delight in the magic realism of Márquez's writing may also enjoy Barbara Hodgson's illustrated novel, a tale as mesmerizing as Márquez's memoir: ***The Lives of Shadows***.

McCourt, Frank (1930–2009)

Angela's Ashes: A Memoir. Scribner, 1996. 364pp. ill. 9780684874357. Also available in large print, Braille, audiobook, e-audiobook, and video. 929.2

In this first memoir McCourt describes a life of abject poverty in Limerick, Ireland, in a family with an alcoholic father who drinks his wages and a depressed mother who can do little more than beg for food for her children. McCourt himself says it's a wonder he survived his childhood, suffering from vermin infestations, starvation, typhus, and severe conjunctivitis, to say nothing of the petty crimes he committed in order to help feed his family. Far from depressing, McCourt's use of the voice of the child, coupled with his dry, Irish sense of humor and lyrical writing style, make this memoir a wonder to behold.

McCourt was inducted into the Academy of Achievement and when asked what book he would recommend, he cited ***The Adventures of Huckleberry Finn***, because after reading it he craved the freedom that Finn had in the book. ***Angela's Ashes*** was the recipient of the American Booksellers Book of the Year (ABBY) Award, the *Los Angeles Times* Book Prize for Biography, the National Book Critics Circle Award in Biography/Autobiography, and the Pulitzer Prize for Biography or Autobiography; it was also selected as a Notable Book by the American Library Association.

Subjects: ALA Notable Books; American Booksellers Book of the Year (ABBY) Award; Childhood and Youth; Children of Alcoholics; Ireland; Irish-Americans; Limerick, Ireland; *Los Angeles Times* Book Prize for Biography; National Book Critics Circle

Award in Biography/Autobiography; New York, NY; Poverty, Ireland; Pulitzer Prize for Biography or Autobiography

Now Try: McCourt followed this memoir with ***'Tis: A Memoir,*** the story of his first years in New York as a young man. (For his third memoir, ***Teacher Man: A Memoir,*** see page 153.) Elaine Crowley is a popular novelist who has written the story of her Irish childhood in ***A Dublin Girl: Growing Up in the 1930's***. A fictional and often humorous account of living poor in Ireland was written by Brendan O'Carroll in his series, **Agnes Browne**. The second in the series of four is perhaps the best known: ***The Mammy***. Some of the funniest writing in McCourt's book comes from his descriptions of Catholic rituals and how they are interpreted by the young child. Marilyn Sewell collected a variety of stories from Catholic writers for ***Resurrecting Grace: Remembering Catholic Childhoods***.

Mezlekia, Nega (1958–)

Notes from the Hyena's Belly: An Ethiopian Boyhood. Picador USA, 2002, 2000. 355pp. map. 9780312289140. 963.2

The hyena's belly in the title comes from a folktale about a lion, a leopard, a hyena, and a donkey in which the donkey winds up in the hyena's belly. Mezlekia cautions Ethiopian citizens that they are likely to wind up in the hyena's belly, if they're not careful. Intertwined with his childhood stories are Ethiopian fables and history. Life changed drastically in 1974 after a serious drought caused a widespread famine. Since the government did not want to embarrass the emperor by calling attention to the famine, they did nothing about it. The end result of this was a military junta in which the emperor was ousted and replaced with a reign of terror (the Red Terror). During this strife Somalia invaded the country, while drought and famine continued. Throughout all of his tales Mezlekia interjects descriptions of various ethnic and religious groups in the country, the relationships among them, and the relationships between the governing bodies and the people they govern—often with threats of execution. Mezlekia himself went through a series of upheavals and traumas before he escaped the tyranny.

Notes from the Hyena's Belly was nominated for the Charles Taylor Prize for Literary Non-fiction and was awarded the Governor General's Literary Award for Non-Fiction.

Subjects: Childhood and Youth; Coming of Age; Ethiopia; Ethiopian-Canadians; Governor General's Literary Award for Non-Fiction; Imprisonment; War; Writers, Canada

Now Try: In ***The God Who Begat a Jackal: A Novel,*** Mezlekia again provides much lore and color from his native land. Dinaw Mengestu was taken from Ethiopia by his family when he was two years old and so had no memory of the Red Terror. He researched it as an adult, however, and wrote an award-winning novel about the life of an exiled Ethiopian in America, ***The Beautiful Things That Heaven Bears***. Ethiopia is seen through the eyes of an American boy as Tim Bascom describes his life in that country as the son of missionaries in ***Chameleon Days: An American Boyhood in Ethiopia***. As Mezlekia makes clear, the problems that developed in Ethiopia were not all of internal origin; Western nations had interfered for years, adding to the complexity of the situation. Howard W. French looks at this issue in his award-winning ***A Continent for the Taking: The Tragedy and Hope of Africa***.

Pamuk, Orhan (1952–)

Istanbul: Memories and the City. Vintage International, 2006, 2005. 384pp. ill. 9781400033881. Also available in e-book. 949.61092 [Trans. by Maureen Freely]

The city of Istanbul is the backdrop for this memoir of Orhan Pamuk's childhood and adolescence. He has never left the city and steeps himself in its *hüzün* or melancholy as a way of explaining both himself and his city. This particular melancholy actually brings peace and contentment, so that to be without it is to be incomplete. Pamuk explains this notion throughout as he describes a city and its inhabitants caught between the past and the present. He himself is also caught, between the lifestyle and ambitions of his eccentric family and his own desires for creative expression, beginning with drawing and concluding with his final sentence: "I'm going to be a writer." Throughout the book he also offers, with text and over 200 illustrations, a portrait of Istanbul's culture: its history, art, literature, religion, and politics. Maureen Freely, the translator, has received several accolades in the reviews of this translation.

Istanbul was short-listed for the National Book Critics Circle Award in Autobiography/Memoir, and Pamuk was awarded the Nobel Prize in Literature.

Subjects: Childhood and Youth; Istanbul, Turkey; Mothers and Sons; Nobel Prize Laureates; Novelists, Turkey; Social History, Turkey; Translations; Turkey

Now Try: In his novel, ***Yalo*** (translated from the Arabic by Peter Theroux), Ilyās Khūrī does for Beirut what Pamuk did for Istanbul. If you'd like to get a larger picture of how Turkey stands as a link between the Old World and the New, you might enjoy Stephen Kinzer's ***Crescent and Star: Turkey Between Two Worlds***. Pamuk's writing has been described as breathtaking; so too has Jared Cohen's, in his story of backpacking through the Middle East to talk to young people of his own age: ***Children of Jihad: A Young American's Travels Among the Youth of the Middle East***.

Shah, Saira (1964–)

The Storyteller's Daughter. Knopf, 2003. 253pp. 9780375415319. Also available in large print, audiobook, e-audiobook, and e-book. 958.1046092

Saira Shah, daughter of the Sufi writer Idries Shah, grew up in England in the fantasy world of her father's stories. Although she didn't actually go to her parents' home country, Afghanistan, until she was twenty-one, she felt strong ties to it through the stories she heard at home. The contrast was shocking, as her first view of her heritage country was as a journalist during the Soviet invasion. This memoir comprises two themes: the narration of her visits to Afghanistan, from which she made the award-winning documentary ***Beneath the Veil***, about the Taliban's treatment of women, and Shah's reflections on the contrast between the Islam of the inner person that she grew up with and the strict and literal interpretation of the Qur'an that fundamentalist Muslims use to rule their world.

Subjects: Afghanistan; Afghans in England; Cultural Identity; Expatriates; Islam; Islamic Fundamentalism; Journalists, England; Reflections; Social History, Afghanistan; Taliban; Women in Afghanistan

Now Try: Khaled Hosseini's novel, ***A Thousand Splendid Suns,*** illustrates very clearly how the Taliban treat women, especially the child who grows up on her own father's stories, which include the grandeur of the Buddhas of Bamiyan statues, later destroyed by the Taliban. ***Veiled Threat: The Hidden Power of the Women of Afghanistan*** by Sally Armstrong reinforces Shah's reflections on Islam and illustrates how some Afghan women are fighting back to help themselves and their children. Azadeh Moaveni, like Shah, returned to her heritage country as an adult, having been born of Iranian immigrants in the United States. In her memoir she describes her life-changing experiences there in ***Honeymoon in Tehran: Two Years of Love and Danger in Iran.***

Soyinka, Wole (1934–)

You Must Set Forth at Dawn: A Memoir. Random House Trade Paperbacks, 2007, 2006. 499pp. ill. maps. 9780375755149. 822.914

Soyinka begins this third memoir after the death of Sani Abacha, the notorious Nigerian dictator who had forced Soyinka into exile once again. He can now return to his native country, no longer exiled to what he referred to as the "Arctic wastes" of Boston (Harvard). Unlike his earlier memoir, ***Aké: The Years of Childhood,*** a tale that recalled his early days with his parents, this memoir has a very political focus, primarily the politics of Nigeria, as it has seen almost nothing but strife since gaining its independence from Britain in the 1960s. Soyinka includes in his political musings leaders of various countries and memories of his own imprisonment. He also describes his friendships, many of those friends having already died, but some (like Nelson Mandela) still alive. He discusses the responsibility and honor he feels at having won the Nobel Prize in Literature, but at the same time he feels the added burden of recognition.

A renowned novelist and playwright, Soyinka was the first African to receive the Nobel Prize in Literature.

Subjects: Exiles; Firsts; Human Rights Activists, Nigeria; Imprisonment; Nigeria; Nobel Prize Laureates; Political Activists, Nigeria; Political Prisoners, Nigeria; Tyranny; Writers, Nigeria

Now Try: Soyinka's first memoir was ***The Man Died: Prison Notes of Wole Soyinka***. Perhaps the best-known Nigerian novelist is Chinua Achebe, who has recently published a collection of essays, some of them autobiographical: ***The Education of a British-Protected Child: Essays***. The writer Chimamanda Ngozi Adichie has written a novel, ***Half of a Yellow Sun,*** about one of the serious outbreaks of violence in Nigeria, the civil war involving Biafra's quest for independence. Soyinka has lived largely in Nigeria, occasionally exiled because of his political differences with the reigning government. A Nigerian who was executed for his political differences with the government in his state was Ken Saro-Wiwa, whose son, Ken Wiwa, wrote a memoir about living under the shadow of his mythic father, ***In the Shadow of a Saint: A Son's Journey to Understand His Father's Legacy***.

Vitebsky, Piers

The Reindeer People: Living with Animals and Spirits in Siberia. Houghton Mifflin, 2006, 2005. 464pp. ill. 16pp. of plates. maps. 9780618773572. 305.89

In northeastern Siberia the temperature can drop to ninety-six below zero. The Eveny people are nomads who live there, and their story revolves around the reindeer culture that has sustained this tribe for centuries. Anthropologist Piers Vitebsky has traveled among these people periodically for over twenty years, meeting the peoples, learning their ways, and watching them cope with the modern world being imposed upon them. In this memoir of his time with them, he focuses on three different herding families, illustrating their ways and letting the reader in on the kinds of discussions that go on around the campfire, discussions that could focus on Bill Clinton, Sancho Panza, government policies, or shamanism. Vitebsky describes the changes wrought initially by the Soviet bureaucracies and now by privatization, and he recounts many of the Eveny spiritual beliefs, including the story of how the reindeer came to be such an integral part of their culture.

The Reindeer People was awarded the Kiriyama Prize.

Subjects: Anthropologists, England; Eveny (Asian People); Kiriyama Prize; Nature Writers, England; Reindeer Herding; Shamanism; Siberia

Now Try: There are two novels that bracket in time the culture of the reindeer people: ***Reindeer Moon*** by Elizabeth Marshall Thomas is set in prehistoric days in Siberia, about 20,000 years ago, and ***Let the Northern Lights Erase Your Name: A Novel*** by Vendela Vida tells the story of a contemporary young woman who seeks answers to her heritage among the Sami peoples. The richly detailed writing in Vitebsky's book can also be found in ***Minotaur: Sir Arthur Evans and the Archaeology of the Minoan Myth*** by J. A. MacGillivray, an account of the archaeologist who discovered a different civilization in Crete. The imposition of the Soviet way of life on the Eveny tribe is reminiscent of the residential school system imposed on North American indigenous peoples. J. R. Miller has dispassionately but vividly outlined the history of this institution in ***Shingwauk's Vision: A History of Native Residential Schools***.

Wong, Jan (1953–)

A Comrade Lost and Found: A Beijing Story. Houghton Mifflin, 2010, 2009. 322pp. maps. 9780547247892. Also available in e-book. 915.1156

Jan Wong lived for years with the guilty conscience of a woman who had betrayed another woman. Caught up in the rhetoric of Mao Zedong even while living in Canada, she found herself in receipt of an invitation to study abroad in Beijing in 1973. Seduced by the Cultural Revolution, she was appalled when one of her classmates asked her for help in getting to America; Wong reported on her and the classmate disappeared. Back in Canada, as the years passed and

Wong grew up, she couldn't forget this woman. Taking her husband and teenage sons with her, she traveled back to Beijing to look for her or to find out what had happened to her. What Wong found was a Beijing completely foreign to any Maoist principles. On the eve of the Summer Olympics, the city was full of construction projects, but it was obvious to Wong that it had already become a modern, capitalist city. She describes the party her former teachers held for her, her reunion with old friends and colleagues, and finally her meeting with the woman she had traveled so far to see.

Subjects: Beijing, China; Betrayal; Canadians in China; China; Cultural Revolution, China (1966–1976); Journalists, Canada; Travel, China

Now Try: Prior to this memoir, Wong had written one that described her tenure in China, ***Red China Blues: My Long March from Mao to Now***. James M. Fallows has been reporting on modern China for *The Atlantic* and collected his dispatches in ***Postcards from Tomorrow Square: Reports from China***. Also limning today's China is the novel ***Brothers***—a best seller in China—about two very different brothers who vow to remain close despite their differences and the influences of the new China, by Hua Yu and translated by Eileen Cheng-yin Chow and Carlos Rojas. One story of a betrayal and its consequences is that of Agnès Humbert (translated by Barbara Mellor), ***Résistance: A Woman's Journal of Struggle and Defiance in Occupied France***.

Consider Starting With . . .

Bryson, Bill. *The Life and Times of the Thunderbolt Kid: A Memoir*

Dillard, Annie. *Pilgrim at Tinker Creek*

Doig, Ivan. *This House of Sky: Landscapes of a Western Mind*

Eire, Carlos M. N. *Waiting for Snow in Havana: Confessions of a Cuban Boy*

Goodwin, Doris Kearns. *Wait till Next Year: A Memoir*

Herriot, Trevor. *River in a Dry Land: A Prairie Passage*

Hickam, Homer H. *Rocket Boys: A Memoir*

Kingsolver, Barbara. *Animal, Vegetable, Miracle: A Year of Food Life*

McCourt, Frank. *Angela's Ashes: A Memoir*

Thoreau, Henry David. *Walden*

Fiction Read-Alikes

Anaya, Rudolfo A. *Bless Me, Ultima.* A seven-year-old boy develops a relationship with a *curandera*, Ultima, in rural New Mexico.

Ashcom, Robert L. *Winter Run.* Rural Virginia in the 1940s is the setting for this gentle story of a young boy learning the ways of the animals he encounters.

Bass, Rick. *The Sky, the Stars, the Wilderness.* Three novellas by wilderness writer Bass; each focuses on some aspect of the land.

Hogan, Linda. *Solar Storms: A Novel.* A young woman explores her past in her birthplace, a small town in the Boundary Waters region between Minnesota and Canada.

Lennon, J. Robert. *On the Night Plain: A Novel.* The son of Montana ranch farmers abandons the ranch until he is drawn back by the death of his mother and the disappearance of his father.

McCullough, Colleen. *The Thorn Birds.* Highly evocative of place, this best-selling novel is a family saga set during the first two-thirds of the twentieth century in the Outback of Australia.

Mitchell, W. O. *Who Has Seen the Wind.* A young boy comes of age on the Saskatchewan prairie in this classic Canadian novel.

Petterson, Per. *Out Stealing Horses.* A Dublin Impac Literary Award winner, this book tells the story of a Norwegian recalling his past as he establishes himself in a remote cabin near the Norway–Sweden border.

Seth, Vikram. *A Suitable Boy: A Novel.* India in the first ten years after its independence is the backdrop for this novel of culture clash in families between traditional and modern ways.

Wroblewski, David. *The Story of Edgar Sawtelle: A Novel.* A young boy learns about life as he and his dogs grow up together on a farm in northern Wisconsin.

Works Cited

Anaya, Rudolfo. 1995. "Foreword." In *Writing the Southwest*, edited by David King Dunaway and Sara L. Spurgeon, viii–xiv. New York: Plume.

Dresdner, Lisa. 2005. "Space/Place." In *Encyclopedia of Women's Autobiography*, edited by Victoria Boynton and Jo Malin, 522–525. Westport, CT: Greenwood Press.

Gwyther, Sheryl. 2009. "The Lure of PLACE . . . More Than Just a Setting." *Sheryl Gwyther—Author,* March 11. Accessed July 9, 2009. http://sherylgwyther.wordpress.com/2009/03/11/the-lure-of-place-more-than-just-a-setting/.

Lindholdt, Paul. 1999. "Writing from a Sense of Place." *Journal of Environmental Education* 30 (4) (Summer): 4–10.

The New York Times. 1894. "Mr. Muir's Mountain Climbing." Review of *The Mountains of California*, by John Muir. *The New York Times Archives,* October 29. Accessed June 8, 2009. http://query.nytimes.com/mem/archive-free/pdf?_r=1&res=9B03EED71531E033A2575AC2A9669D94659ED7CF.

Welty, Eudora. 2002. *On Writing.* New York: Modern Library.

Wilkins, Charles. 2002. "Mother Nature's Heart of Stone." Review of *Houseboat Chronicles: Notes from a Life in Shield Country,* by Jake MacDonald. *The Globe and Mail,* October 5: D4.

Chapter 6

Life Away from Home

Description

The stories in this chapter feature people who have left their home countries to live in another. At times they choose to do this; at other times they are forced to do so. The irony is that whether they go willingly or reluctantly, they all have similar issues to deal with, some more difficult than others. This kind of writing is called expatriate and immigrant literature; although many immigrant writers today have a problem with the term "immigrant literature," for the interest of simplicity, it is used here.

There is a fine line between the definitions of *expatriation* and *immigration*. One could say that expatriates are those who willingly leave a good (or sometimes not so good) life in their own countries to seek a new lifestyle elsewhere. The literati, such as Ernest Hemingway, who converged on Paris in the 1920s, for example, did so in order to find a richer environment in which to cultivate their craft, knowing they would be among like-minded people. Others, like Peter Mayle, might move to a new country because they had originally traveled there and loved what they saw.

Immigrants are usually depicted as those who seek a better life, sometimes for economic reasons, at other times for political or religious reasons. In the nineteenth century in North America, people were hired to induce citizens of other countries to come settle in Canada and the United States, promising land and prosperity. Many who were unsure of their economic stability at home were happy to make the trip, believing that what they were heading for could be no worse than what they were leaving behind.

Those who emigrate for political or religious reasons do so because they can no longer bear to be in what they consider an untenable position, surrounded by citizens and/or governments whose basic beliefs, laws, and customs run very contrary to their own. Now we come to another fine line: the distinction between those who leave on their own in protest against the religious or political face of their countries and those who are forced into exile for the same reason. Many people would have willingly stayed in their birth countries if they had not been coerced by their government to leave, or forced by violence, war, or the threat of execution to find refuge elsewhere.

For whatever reason people leave their home countries, when they arrive at their destination, they are all faced with similar issues: culture shock, feelings of alienation and dislocation, and discrimination. They often face language barriers and may find themselves facing the diiemma of choosing between remaining within their own cultural group or assimilating into the new group. Simply understanding how things are done in a new country can be bewildering, adding to the feelings of disorientation. Depending on what enticed them to choose that country, if the reality does not match the promise, they have feelings of discouragement and self-doubt to contend with. Many people leave their birth countries as professionals, only to be forced into working-class jobs in their new country, required to start over again to build a professional life.

Once people settle in, and even years after making a new life in their adopted country, they may still have issues with cultural identity. They had a certain life where they came from; they have a new life where they are, but the cultural touchstones are not the same. Unless they continue to live in an expatriate community, the people around them have no knowledge of the social history of their childhood. Yet if *émigrés* try to go home again, even for a visit, they often feel out of place; those they left behind have no knowledge of their current social history. This is no longer their country. They are not perceived as citizens, nor do they feel at home. They are now looking at their home country with eyes that have been altered by the country they emigrated to. Dislocation sets in once again.

A further challenge for those who leave their country for a new one is the culture clash that arises when they have children. Often the parents remain steeped in their birth culture and want to immerse their children in that same culture. The children, however, want to be like their friends and peers; they want to have the nationality they were born into. Yet these children have similar issues of cultural identity: Who are they, really? Often it is not until they visit their heritage country as adults that they finally establish a sense of peace with who they are.

Immigrant and expatriate memoirs form the core of this section, as the memoirists describe their lives away from their birth homes. The stories are often joyous, as the writers delight in new worlds, but they can also be somber, as the writers describe the difficulties they encounter in the challenges of new worlds, coupled with the pain of missing the old world, especially if the writers were forced to leave their homelands.

Appeal

As with the titles in other chapters, character is always of great appeal in a memoir, and the immigrant/expatriate memoir is no exception. Often the people are of remarkable character, brave, resilient, and resourceful. We usually meet not only the immigrants themselves, but their extended families, too, people left behind or those accompanying the writer.

Setting, too, is appealing to readers. In most cases the immigrant writers describe in detail the countries they left behind, so that readers can gain insights into the physical landscape or the cultural makeup of countries they may never have encountered before. In the case of expatriate literature, the focus is more likely to be on the new country; in Frances Mayes's ***Under the Tuscan Sun: At Home in Italy***, for example, we are treated to wonderful descriptions of the land, the food, the people, the architecture, and the history of Tuscany.

Story is often of prime importance, particularly in the case of the exile/refugee literature, as writers recount the horrors of what they left behind. But it is also of interest in the other narrations as we learn what the writers and their families have had to face and how they have had to cope, what they have had to overcome and how they have managed.

For readers who have left their own birth countries, there is an appeal of familiarity and resonance. It is comforting to know that the shock and confusion felt on arriving in the new country are generally felt by many people. In fact, a significant impetus for writing immigrant memoirs is to try to establish some order in the confusion engendered by the move—even if the move occurred decades before. Thus, reading another's story of a similar confusion can be comforting to readers, by validating their own experiences or helping them to recognize that perhaps their own experiences were not so bad in comparison.

Readers who have always lived "at home," have much to gain from reading immigrant literature. There is the learning experience, derived from descriptions of the "Old World," explaining the impetus for leaving. Readers learn about that country and its culture. But the culture is not dropped the moment the immigrant arrives in the new land, so that readers continue that learning experience. There is another important facet of the learning experience: readers may have had no idea of the difficulties encountered by new immigrants and may thus become more empathic. Readers may also begin to understand behavior previously misunderstood. Others' experiences may also open the eyes of those considering such a change, alerting them to both the negative and the positive aspects of making such a move. Readers' eyes may be opened in a new way as well to their own country in understanding how it is viewed by new immigrants, offering new perspectives and a new way of looking at the country they have never left.

Organization of This Chapter

The chapter begins with classic stories of expatriates, immigrants, and exiles, all written by people whose work is very well-known. It then moves on to include four types of migration stories. The first, "Expatriates," consists of the people who have chosen to set up a second home abroad, or who have gone abroad temporarily, often because of work, but also because of an interest in living in a new culture. The chapter moves on to "Immigrants," the stories of those who have themselves emigrated to a new land, or of their children who were born in that new land. Following that is "Exiles and Refugees," the tales of those who have been forced to leave their homes due to political upheaval and/or war. The final section, "The Return Home," includes stories of the people who left and have returned to their birth country, often in an effort to resolve their questions of cultural identity.

The travel memoirs in Chapter 1, "Travel and Adventure," offer a different view of countries around the world: people who travel to a country as tourists look at it with very different eyes from people who are planning to live in a country for any extended length of time.

Classics

Expatriates, children of immigrants, and refugees make up this small section of classic tales. With the exception of Maria Trapp, these memoirists are all writers, the two expatriates leaving home to hone their craft abroad. The two refugees fled the German uprising against the Jews. And the child of immigrants tells not just her story but her family's story as well, particularly her mother's.

> These classic immigrant stories have largely become part of the canon of immigrant literature, well-known and well-loved for the story they tell or because of the fame of the writer, or both. They are not all happy stories, but they reflect the strength of the writers in making new lives for themselves in unfamiliar environments.

Hemingway, Ernest (1899–1961)
Hemingway, Seán, ed.

A Moveable Feast: The Restored Edition. Introduction by Seán Hemingway. Foreword by Patrick Hemingway. Scribner, 2009, 1964. 240pp. ill. 9781416591313. Also available in Braille, audiobook, e-audiobook, and e-book. 818.5203.

In 1958 Hemingway began his memoir documenting the time he, his then-wife Hadley, and their young son Jack spent in Paris. Before it was published, however, he committed suicide. His widowed wife, Mary, heavily edited it and had it published. Now his grandson Seán has restored it to something closer to the author's original intent. ***A Moveable Feast*** is Hemingway at his best as a writer, but it also reveals much of Hemingway the man: the egotist and the unkind friend. He seemed especially vicious toward those who had been most helpful, particularly Gertrude Stein and F. Scott Fitzgerald. (You may want to read Stein's ***The Autobiography of Alice B. Toklas*** to see why he might have been so harsh;

see p. 239.) Included in the revised version is a section on the breakup of his marriage to Hadley, in which he takes some of the responsibility for taking up with her best friend, Pauline Pfeiffer, something that had not been part of the original edition. Of particular interest to writers, however, are Hemingway's various discussions on the art of writing or at least on his own practices. He spent much time in Paris with other writers, tales of which may prove of interest to the reader.

Hemingway was awarded the Nobel Prize in Literature, and the original publication of ***The Moveable Feast*** was selected as a Notable Book by the American Library Association.

Subjects: 1920s; ALA Notable Books; Americans in France; Classics; Expatriates; France; Intellectual Life, France; Journalists; Lost Generation; Love Affairs; Nobel Prize Laureates; Novelists; Paris, France

Now Try: Morley Callaghan, a Canadian writer in Paris at the same time as Hemingway, moved in the same circles, as he describes in ***That Summer in Paris; Memories of Tangled Friendships with Hemingway, Fitzgerald, and Some Others***. Many people are familiar with the literati of the 1920s in Paris, but there were many more who went to Paris and then wrote about it; Adam Gopnik collected the writings of people from Benjamin Franklin to Diana Vreeland in ***Americans in Paris: A Literary Anthology***. One of the people for whom Hemingway maintained affection was Sylvia Beach, owner of the bookstore Shakespeare and Company. Beach wrote the story of her enterprise in ***Shakespeare and Company***.

Kingston, Maxine Hong (1940–)

The Woman Warrior; China Men. Introduction by Mary Gordon. Knopf, 2005, 1976. 541pp. 9781400043842. Also available in large print, audiobook, e-book, and video. 979.461092

Not the usual linear autobiography, this memoir contains fantasy, interweaving the essence of the author's life with myth and legend from her heritage country. The book is divided into five sections, each detailing an incident in either Kingston's own history or her family's history. The family histories were communicated to her by her mother, Brave Orchid, in the Chinese tradition of "talk-stories," but after being told the story, Kingston was then commanded not to tell the story to anyone else. Suppression of voice is a major theme in the book, and this work is a triumph of someone who found her voice, to critical acclaim. Throughout the book she avenges the women of her culture, suppressed in history, whether in China or in the diaspora. Because her mother gave talk-stories without explanation, Kingston provides her own explanations, weaves her own myths. The subtitle of this memoir is *Memoirs of a Girlhood Among Ghosts*. The ghosts are both the ghosts in family legends and the White people Kingston lives among in her birth town of Stockton, California. They all formed her childhood and her vivid imagination. After the success of ***The Woman***

Warrior, Kingston went on to write another autobiographical work, ***China Men*** (winner of the National Book Award for General Nonfiction and included in this edition), this time focusing on her father and the other men in her family, included in this edition.

The Woman Warrior won the Anisfield-Wolf Book Award and the National Book Critics Circle Award in General Nonfiction and was selected as a Notable Book by the American Library Association.

Subjects: ALA Notable Books; Anisfield-Wolf Book Award; California; Children of Immigrants; Chinese-Americans; Classics; Culture Clash; Family Portraits; Mothers and Daughters; National Book Critics Circle Award in General Nonfiction; Stockton, CA

Now Try: The only Chinese-American author whose work Kingston had read before writing her own story, and in whose book Kingston could see herself, was Jade Snow Wong, author of the memoir ***Fifth Chinese Daughter***, with illustrations by Kathryn Uhl. Kingston is often mentioned along with Leslie Silko, a Laguna Pueblo writer who incorporates the myths and legends of her people. You may want to read one of Silko's novels, perhaps ***Ceremony***, in which the protagonist makes use of myth to help himself recover from the Vietnam War. Amy Tan is an American writer of Chinese heritage whose writing is infused with the theme of assimilation, for example, ***The Hundred Secret Senses***.

Nabokov, Vladimir Vladimirovich (1899–1977)

Speak, Memory: An Autobiography Revisited. Introduction by Brian Boyd. Knopf, 1999, 1961. 268pp. ill. 9780375405532. Also available in Braille, audiobook, and e-book. 813.54

Nabokov was exiled more than once, initially from Russia during the Bolshevik Revolution, when he and his noble family were forced to flee, losing all their money and possessions; then from Germany; and again from France during the rise of Hitler (Nabokov's wife, Véra, was Jewish). Taught English as a boy by his governess, his first effort to publish in English was a translation of his own novel, ***Despair***, from Russian into English in 1937. Reassured by its reception, he went on to publish his most famous (and infamous) works in English, particularly ***Lolita*** and ***Pale Fire; A Novel***. The success of ***Lolita*** in the United States enabled him to leave teaching altogether. Nabokov died with an unfinished novel that, after years of deliberation, his son Dmitri edited and decided to have published, against his father's wishes. ***The Original of Laura (Dying Is Fun)*** was published in 2009.

Speak, Memory was selected as a Notable Book by the American Library Association.

Subjects: ALA Notable Books; Classics; Immigrants; Lepidopterists; Nabokov, Dmitri; Nabokov, Véra; Novelists; Political Exiles; Russian-Americans; Short-Story Writers

Now Try: Brian Boyd, who wrote the introduction to Nabokov's revised autobiography, also wrote the definitive biography, in two volumes: ***Vladimir Nabokov: The Russian Years*** and ***Vladimir Nabokov: The American Years***. But the picture would not be complete without reading Stacy Schiff's Pulitzer Prize–winning biography of Véra:

Véra (Mrs. Vladimir Nabokov): A Biography. One of the several techniques that Nabokov used in his writing is the intrusion of himself or the narrator into the narrative; Don DeLillo uses the same noticeable technique in ***White Noise***. One aspect of the Bolshevik Revolution that exiled the Nabokov family has been documented by Lesley Chamberlain in ***Lenin's Private War: The Voyage of the Philosophy Steamer and the Exile of the Intelligentsia***. If you'd like to read more about the scientific side of Nabokov, Stephen Jay Gould has included an essay on Nabokov's butterfly research in ***I Have Landed: The End of a Beginning in Natural History***.

Stein, Gertrude (1874–1946)

The Autobiography of Alice B. Toklas. Penguin Books Canada, 2001, 1933. 272pp. 9780141185361. Also available in e-book. 818.5209

When one thinks of expatriate Americans living in Paris, Gertrude Stein is generally one of the first to come to mind. She held a salon in Paris and was responsible for the nurturing of many careers in art and in literature. Constantly asked for her memoirs, she finally agreed to write something and in the space of six weeks completed the project. She treats the memoir as though it were written by her life partner, Alice B. Toklas, using Alice's voice rather than her own and only revealing her own identity at the end of the book. Because the focus shifts to Stein from Toklas at the very beginning of the book, it is almost as though Toklas were writing the biography of Stein. The memoir details Stein's education in the United States, her arrival in Paris to join her brother Leo, her meeting Toklas, her interest in modernist art and literature, and her life with those artists, but also her life with Toklas, a woman who had great admiration for Stein and was happy to be her wife, supporting her domestically and in her writing. Because Stein did not refrain from saying what she thought about specific people, she lost the friendship of such people as Pablo Picasso and Ernest Hemingway. The publication was immensely successful; the acclaim for this memoir was of great satisfaction to Stein, who had always chafed at her lack of recognition. She wrote a subsequent work, ***Everybody's Autobiography***, in which she discusses the effects of the success of the first one.

Subjects: Americans in France; Art, France; Classics; Expatriates; France; Intellectual Life, France; Lesbians; Lost Generation; Paris, France; Social Life and Customs, France; Toklas, Alice B.; Writers

Now Try: There have been several biographies of Gertrude Stein, but one that was particularly well-received is a dual biography of both Stein and Toklas: ***Gertrude and Alice*** by Diana Souhami. Elliot Paul was an American journalist living in Paris during the First World War and following, who wrote about his time there in ***The Last Time I Saw Paris***. Stein mentored an artist's model, Fernande Olivier, and was subsequently responsible for the American publication of Olivier's memoir detailing her affair with Picasso, which also includes letters to Stein: ***Loving Picasso: The Private Journal of Fernande Olivier***, translated from the French by Christine Baker and Michael Raeburn. For fun you may like to read Monique T. D. Truong's captivating novel about a Vietnamese man who cooks for Gertrude Stein and Alice B. Toklas, ***The Book of Salt***.

Trapp, Maria Augusta (1905–1987)

The Story of the Trapp Family Singers. Perennial, 2002, 1949. 312pp. ill. 9780060005771. Also available in Braille and video. 782.5092

Maria Trapp wrote this memoir not long after her husband died, in hopes of promoting her singing group, the Trapp Family Singers. Dividing her story into two parts, she details in the first section leaving the convent where she was a novice to be a governess for the widowed Count Georg von Trapp, a man with several children, one of whom was bedridden. Trapp recounts her life there for the next twelve years until they were forced to leave, penniless, to avoid Hitler's takeover. Maria had arranged a concert tour in America, so that was their first stop in what would initially be a series of voyages to various countries as their visas expired. The second half of the book covers their post-Austrian life, relating the trials of the immigrant who needs to learn the language in order to understand the currency and be able to buy food, who needs to understand the culture to be able to earn a living.

Subjects: Austria; Austrian-Americans; Catholics; Family Relationships; Octogenarians; Political Exiles; Singers; Trapp Family; Trapp, Georg

Now Try: Although the actual Trapp family garnered very little income from the broader success of their story as portrayed in ***The Sound of Music***, others made more. One person who benefited was Charmian Carr, the actress who played the character of Liesel in the movie. Carr and Jean A. S. Strauss have written Carr's story in ***Forever Liesel: A Memoir of "The Sound of Music"***. Another family that combined singing with their spiritual beliefs was the Ward family; one of the group, Willa Ward-Royster, has told their story to Toni Rose, captured in ***How I Got Over: Clara Ward and the World-Famous Ward Singers***. If you're interested in life in Austria just prior to the *Anschluss*, you might enjoy the story of a financially successful family by Alexander Waugh, ***The House of Wittgenstein: A Family at War***.

Expatriates

Expatriate stories could also be deemed immigrant stories, yet there is generally a different flavor to them. Because the characters in the stories in this section have moved elsewhere largely for the adventure rather than to escape a difficult life, you will find these stories lighter in tone, with more humor than angst over the necessary adjustments. In addition, these are mostly stories of Anglos (particularly North Americans, but also some British) moving to other countries, rather than the reverse. Another increasingly popular publishing phenomenon is the tale of the person who goes abroad to live, finding an old house to refurbish and becoming part of the community through the renovation process.

Expatriate literature here comprises memoirs by writers who have set out on their own to get a taste of a new culture by living in that culture. The tone is generally celebratory, with wry self-deprecation thrown in, as the writer admits to blunders and misunderstandings, most of which provide a vein of humor throughout the memoir.

Cohan, Tony (1939–)

On Mexican Time: A New Life in San Miguel. Broadway Books, 2001, 2000. 289pp. 9780767903196. Also available in audiobook and e-book. 972.41

Tony Cohan is a lyricist and a travel writer who went with his artist wife, Masako Takahashi, to San Miguel de Allende in Mexico for a vacation. Returning home to the crime-ridden, capitalistic atmosphere of life in Los Angeles, where everyone was always rushing and grocery stores bordered on "pathological," they decided they much preferred the slower lifestyle of open-air markets and a daily siesta. Selling their American home, they bought a 250-year-old home badly in need of some loving care and settled into the small central Mexican town. They soon got to know their neighbors and the surrounding folklore, both historic and current. They describe the ongoing renovations to their new house and little adventures and tragedies that occur in the neighborhood. Cohan was later asked to do some travel writing throughout Mexico, thus following up this memoir with tales of his Mexican travels: ***Mexican Days: Journeys into the Heart of Mexico***.

Subjects: Americans in Mexico; Homes and Haunts; Lyricists; Mexico; San Miguel de Allende, Mexico; Takahashi, Masako; Travel Writers

Now Try: Marlena De Blasi is known for her several books set in Italy, most of which involve food and recipes. She too moved into an old building—a sixteenth-century palazzo in Umbria—and writes about it in ***The Lady in the Palazzo: At Home in Umbria***. The well-known Mexican writer Carlos Fuentes offers a collection of personal essays that reflect his life and his thoughts in ***This I Believe: An A to Z of a Life***, translated by Kristina Cordero and providing local insights into Cohan's adopted country. The journalist Barry Golson and his wife did much the same as Cohan, leaving Manhattan for Mexico, building their own home, and narrating their experience in ***Gringos in Paradise: An American Couple Builds Their Retirement Dream House in a Seaside Village in Mexico***.

Gopnik, Adam (1956–)

Paris to the Moon. Random House Trade Paperbacks, 2008, 2000. 338pp. ill. 9780375758232. Also available in large print, audiobook, e-audiobook, and e-book. 944.3600413

When Gopnik was asked by *The New Yorker* to move to Paris to write from there, he was delighted. Living in Paris had always been a dream, and in 1995 he, his wife, Martha Parker, and their baby boy settled in Paris for five years, happy to learn its ways and live the Parisian life. A collection of personal essays and journal entries, this book details not only daily life in Paris, but also life with a baby, both challenges for the uninitiated. Gopnik said that in both cases it was necessary to learn a new language, new rules, and new routines. Gopnik's essays ostensibly deal with the minutiae of living in a new city—joining a gym, frequenting cafés, trying to get a Thanksgiving turkey during a strike; their overarching point, however, leads to a discussion of larger issues: the place French culture now holds in the world, the effects of globalization, the status of French cuisine. The title refers to an illustration the Gopniks saw shortly after arriving, a drawing of a train on its way from Paris to the moon, something they felt was quite apt, as Henry James had referred to Paris as a celestial city in ***A Little Tour in France***.

Subjects: Americans in France; France; Journalists; Parenting; Paris, France; Personal Essays; Social Life and Customs, France

Now Try: Thaddeus Carhart is an American expatriate living in Paris who was only able to gain entry through the doors of a special shop because he understood what was required in terms of social niceties and routines, as he describes in ***The Piano Shop on the Left Bank: Discovering a Forgotten Passion in a Paris Atelier***. Another journalist who was sent abroad with children in tow was Anthony Doerr, whose adventures are described in ***Four Seasons in Rome: On Twins, Insomnia, and the Biggest Funeral in the History of the World***. Mary Blume is a journalist who wrote for the *International Herald Tribune*, and, like Gopnik, collected her articles into a book: ***A French Affair: The Paris Beat, 1965–1998***, with drawings by Ronald Searle.

Mayes, Frances (1941–)

Under the Tuscan Sun: At Home in Italy. Broadway Books, 2003, 1996. 311pp. 9780767916066. Also available in large print, Braille, audiobook, e-book, and video. 945.5092

When Frances Mayes, a creative writing professor at San Francisco State University, suffered through a divorce, she decided to use the money from her divorce settlement to buy some property in Italy, a land she had come to love. The property she found, an old abandoned villa southeast of Florence, required a lot of work and dedication. But Mayes had fallen in love—with another creative-writing professor and with the villa in Italy. She and her partner Ed Kleinschmidt spent summers and Christmas vacation in Tuscany renovating the house, Bramasole ("yearning for the sun"). As they worked, she also fell in love with Tuscany, its people, its history, its landscape, and most of all, its food. She discovered a vineyard in her garden and grew food for her table. Mayes vividly describes excursions into villages and various food markets and details the meals she makes from all the fresh foodstuffs; she also relates many hilarious anecdotes about the renovations. She followed this memoir with a sequel, ***Bella Tuscany: The Sweet Life in Italy***.

Subjects: Americans in Italy; College Professors; Food, Italy; Gastronomy; Home Renovations; Homes and Haunts; Italy; Poets; Social Life and Customs, Italy; Tuscany, Italy

Now Try: Buying a house in a foreign country and renovating it is currently a popular endeavor, and others have not only done it, but written about it as well. Suzanna Clarke and her husband, Sandy McCutcheon, bought a *riad* in Fez, Morocco, one that was broken down and in much need of renovation, an experience she recounts in ***A House in Fez***. And Carol Drinkwater did the same in France, telling her story in ***The Olive Farm: A Memoir of Life, Love, and Olive Oil in the South of France***. Many have taken to Mayes's story because of her adventuresome spirit. Another woman who showed a similar spirit is Alice Steinbach, who gave up everything to travel the world, as she recounts in ***Without Reservations: The Travels of an Independent Woman***.

Mayle, Peter (1939–)

Encore Provence: New Adventures in the South of France. Knopf, 1999. 226pp. ill. 9780679441243. Also available in large print, audiobook (read by the author), and e-audiobook. 944.920838

Peter Mayle has made Provence his territory, beginning with the move there with his wife, Jennie, eleven years prior to this book; hence the diary-like memoir, illustrated by Judith Clancy, ***A Year in Provence***. Having had time now to assimilate himself, becoming more comfortable with and more respectful of his French neighbors, he regales the reader with more stories of food, people, cafés, and meals in a collection of essays reflecting his expatriate life in the south of France. He has one chapter specifically on lavender, one of the best-known exports of Provence, and another chapter on *foie gras*. His least typical chapter is an angry rebuttal of an article by food writer Ruth Reichl in which she writes disparagingly of Provence and its food. Throughout each of these essays on one particular aspect of his adopted area Mayle is present, letting the reader into his life in Provence; he is not just writing a guide. In ***Toujours Provence***, the sequel to Mayle's first memoir, also illustrated by Judith Clancy, he details how their house became a tourist attraction, an unwelcome result of the popularity of his first narration.

Subjects: English in France; Food, France; France; Personal Essays; Provence, France; Social Life and Customs, France; Travel, France; Writers, England

Now Try: If you'd like to read more about Provence, you may enjoy ***The Magic of Provence: Pleasures of Southern France*** by Yvone Lenard. Peter and Jennie Mayle are not the only expatriates to buy a house abroad; you can read about others who have done so in ***A House Somewhere: Tales of Life Abroad***, edited by Don George and Anthony Sattin. And if you'd like to enjoy a new cozy mystery series set in another part of southern France, the Dordogne, you might try the debut book in the series, ***Bruno, Chief of Police***, by Martin Walker.

Parks, Tim (1954–)

An Italian Education: The Further Adventures of an Expatriate in Verona. Perennial, 2001, 1995. 338pp. 9780380727605. Also available in audiobook. 945.34

This memoir is a sequel to Parks's first book on life in Italy, ***Italian Neighbors, or, A Lapsed Anglo-Saxon in Verona***. In this book he has been in Italy for several years, has two children with one on the way, and has become a successful writer of both fiction and nonfiction. He had never wanted to be a Peter Mayle or Frances Mayes, but he explains in his book why he is writing a second book on Italy when he had said he would never write even one. He realized that in his daily living he had done a lot of musing on the character of the Italian, on how Italian children become Italian in nature. With two young bilingual children of his own whose mother is Italian, he became much more observant of how children are raised in Italy, from pregnancy (considered a pathology) to the mother–son relationship. He is affectionate in his reflections, happy to receive an education in the Italian character from his friends and neighbors and happy to educate the reader in what he learns.

Subjects: Biculturalism; College Professors; English in Italy; Family Relationships; Italy; Parenting, Italy; Reflections; Social Life and Customs, Italy; Verona, Italy; Writers

Now Try: James Chatto is a food writer who moved to Greece, loving the people and its food, as he recounts in ***The Greek for Love: A Memoir of Corfu***. Mark Rotella didn't settle down in Italy, but he did visit long enough to share his experiences in ***Stolen Figs and Other Adventures in Calabria***. In a turnabout, Sarah Lyall focuses the microscope on the English in ***The Anglo Files: A Field Guide to the British***.

Shah, Tahir (1966–)

The Caliph's House. Bantam Books, 2007, 2006. 349pp. ill. 9780553383102. Also available in e-book. 964.38053

An Englishman of Afghan heritage, Shah had already spent time vacationing in Morocco, so that he knew he loved the country when he moved his little daughter and his pregnant wife, Rachana, there. Because his wife was from India, he used the lure of the sun after the grey skies of London to convince her to move. What they encountered there, however, was not at all what he had promised her. They bought a deserted house that had belonged to a caliph which, because it had been deserted, was now filled with *djinns*, according to local beliefs. Not sure they actually believed in such a thing, Shah and his wife went about trying to renovate the house, only to realize that in fact they would have to exorcise the house of its demons. They have many adventures in their year of renovation, some of them hair-raising, but throughout Shah relishes the new experiences and reveals his respect for this new community.

Subjects: Biculturalism; Casablanca, Morocco; English in Morocco; Haunted Houses; Historic Buildings; Home Renovations; Homes and Haunts; Morocco; Travel Writers

Now Try: Shah followed this book with one about travels he subsequently made in Morocco, ***In Arabian Nights: A Caravan of Moroccan Dreams***. William Dalyrmple encountered *djinns* in Delhi, India, spirits he knew all along existed there, which is why he went to discover and then write about them in ***City of Djinns: A Year of Delhi***, with illustrations by Olivia Fraser. The graphic artist Craig Thompson spent some time in Morocco, among other countries, and offers not only his narrative telling, but his illustrations as well in ***Carnet de Voyage***. During his year rebuilding his new house, Shah is introduced to an Islam he had not encountered in London. One Islamic custom that was centuries old there is the trek to the salt mines of Taoudenni from Timbuktu. An intrepid adventurer, Michael Benanav joined the caravan on what may have been one of the last before modern transportation supplants the camel; he describes his journey and its history in ***Men of Salt: Crossing the Sahara on the Caravan of White Gold***.

Stewart, Chris (1951–)

Driving over Lemons: An Optimist in Andalucía. Pantheon Books, 1999. 248pp. ill. maps. 9780375410284. Also available in large print, audiobook (read by the author), and e-book. 946.82

The former drummer for the musical group Genesis, Chris Stewart is the optimist and his wife Ana the pessimist. She has reason to be pessimistic when Chris convinces her to move from England to a small, rundown farm in the mountains south of Granada in Spain. They are on the wrong side of the river and have no amenities, including no real road to the farm. What they do have is an abundance of lemons (hence the title), olives, and peppers. They also have a neighbor who matches his capabilities with his generosity in helping out. Despite the difficulties in fixing up their house so that it will be livable and they will have potable water, they thrive there, harvesting their bounty, acquiring sheep, and having a baby. Stewart is very much aware of his status as an expatriate, a fact that makes him sensitive to cultural differences that he needs to accept, but that also makes him appreciate the welcome and the help that are available to him and his family. He followed this memoir with another, ***A Parrot in the Pepper Tree***.

Subjects: Andalucía, Spain; English in Spain; Friendships; Home Renovations; Homes and Haunts; Rural Life, Spain; Spain; Writers

Now Try: Something about Spain seems to bring out the intrepidness in people; Polly Evans left her job as an editor in Hong Kong to bike around Spain, including through the mountains, a tale she tells in ***It's Not About the Tapas***. Mario Batali, the restaurateur, traveled through Spain with actress Gwyneth Paltrow in search of food and culture, which they share in the PBS companion to the television series, ***Spain: A Culinary Road Trip***. A big production, this work was designed by Douglas Riccardi and Lisa Eaton, written with Julia Turshen, and photographed by Moises Saman and Quentin Bacon. The novelist Derek Lambert is another transplanted Anglo who set up his home in a village on the Mediterranean coast of Spain, a story told in ***Spanish Lessons: Beginning a New Life in Spain***.

Immigrants

These stories feature those who have been forced or enticed, often because of economic straits or political disagreements, to seek a better life elsewhere. They "come as a stranger to a strange land, hoping for welcome and going on trust" (Kennedy, 2009). The emigrants often have high expectations of their new homes, expectations that are rarely met; the resultant shock and disappointment lead the more literate among them to tell their stories.

The immigrant "brings with him a deep-rooted tradition, a system of culture and tastes and habits—a point of view which is as ancient as his national experience and which has been engendered in him by his race and environment" (Boelhower, 1982) and then finds himself or herself faced with "the pressures to abandon a language, a community, a religion, and a tradition" (Holte, 1982). Reflecting a more positive outlook, the Nigerian writer Ken Wiwa said, " 'I was moving to a place that encourages you to bring your past with you. You get a pretty hefty baggage allowance when you come to Canada' " (Egan and Helms, 2002). Many immigrants see their situation as a loss and a source of grief, while others see it as a source of opportunity.

Children born in the new country often feel a sense of displacement, sometimes even in their own homes, pulled between the heritage country of their parents and the country that they have always called home. They are often hybrids—not quite the nationality of their parents, not quite the nationality of their birth country.

The characters featured in this section's stories come from such disparate countries as Afghanistan, the Netherlands, and Peru. Some of the children, however, were born in the host country—either the United States or Canada—and their parents came from widely varied countries such as Jordan, China, or Greece.

Immigrant literature would suggest that it is solely the immigrants who have stories to tell, stories of moving from one country to another, along with the difficulties of doing so, of adjusting to new cultures, new languages, and new geographies. But the children of immigrants also have a story to tell, of being caught between two cultures, their heritage culture and their birth culture. This often creates even more unhappiness in the lives of the immigrants, as they find themselves losing control as parents.

Abu-Jaber, Diana (1960–)

The Language of Baklava. Anchor Books, 2006, 2005. 330pp. 9781400077762. Also available in e-book. 641.5956

A waiter said of Abu-Jaber while watching her enjoy her Chinese meal that she obviously comes from cooking. That is certainly a large part of her upbringing, her identity as the daughter of a Jordanian father called Bud, whose real name is Ghassan Saleh, and an American mother with Irish and German roots; it is also a large part of her memoir. As her father suffers from homesickness and cooks to link himself to his Bedouin heritage, she loves the culinary delights. But his homesickness also causes him to uproot the family several times, including one year-long stay in Jordan. For Abu-Jaber to negotiate the pitfalls of simply growing up, adding this tug-of-war between her birth country and her father's contributes to her struggle to find her own identity. She also discusses in her memoir her desire to be a writer and what that means for her. For readers who love Middle Eastern food, there are recipes at the end of each chapter.

The Language of Baklava won the Pacific Northwest Booksellers Association Award.

Subjects: Arab-Americans; Children of Immigrants; Coming of Age; Cooking, Middle Eastern; Food, Jordan; New York (State); Syracuse, NY

Now Try: Family and food are major components of Patricia Volk's life and her memoir, ***Stuffed: Adventures of a Restaurant Family***. Nora Janssen Seton recognizes that the kitchen is often the heart of the woman, the woman's realm for establishing and cementing relationships. In ***The Kitchen Congregation***, she recounts how it was so for her own mother, a writer, and how it will be so for her. Laila Halaby understands the conflicts of the immigrant child, an understanding reflected in her award-winning, ***West of the Jordan: A Novel***.

Ansary, Mir Tamim (1948–)

West of Kabul, East of New York: An Afghan American Story. Picador, 2003, 2002. 300pp. 9780312421519. Also available in audiobook (read by the author) and e-book. 973.04927

The day after the attacks on the World Trade Center in 2001, Mir Tamim Ansary sent an e-mail to several of his friends, detailing his fears of unjustified American reprisals against the Afghan people, comparing them to the victims of the Holocaust, Osama Bin Laden to Adolf Hitler, and the Taliban to the Nazis. This e-mail became viral, reaching into hundreds of thousands of homes, and suddenly the children's book writer and columnist for Microsoft *Encarta* became known for his informed and reasonable views on that fiery political situation. His memoir is a result of that situation. In it he describes his childhood in pre-Soviet Afghanistan, a member of the first Afghan-American family to live in Afghanistan, as his mother was a Finnish-American. He then narrates their move to the United States so that he could get an education and how he still belongs nowhere. Seeking to find his religious roots, he travels to Muslim countries in North Africa and the Middle East, disturbed to find an Islam different from the one in which he was raised. Then he is back in the United States, making his life as an Afghan-American, when suddenly his birth country becomes a household name.

West of Kabul has been chosen as a One Book selection in New Hampshire; Waco, Texas; Orland Park, Illinois; and San Francisco.

Subjects: Afghan-Americans; Afghanistan; Cultural Identity; Dislocation; Islam; Muslim Men; September 11 Terrorist Attacks, 2001; Writers

Now Try: The issue of militant Islam concerns the world; Fawaz A. Gerges has traveled to learn about the various factions among the militant Muslims and has rendered a very personal account of his research in ***Journey of the Jihadist: Inside Muslim Militancy***. Jon Lee Anderson was able to get into Afghanistan not long after the September 11 attacks and sent dispatches back recounting the reactions in Afghanistan to the attacks. He has collected those reports in ***The Lion's Grave: Dispatches from Afghanistan***, including photographs by Thomas Dworzak. Bicultural identity is a fact of life for millions of Americans, and Luis Alberto Urrea is no exception, as he describes in ***Nobody's Son: Notes from an American Life***.

Arana, Marie (1949–)

American Chica: Two Worlds, One Childhood. Dial Press, 2005, 2001. 309pp. 9780385319638. Also available in e-book. 070.92

Marie Arana's parents met in Massachusetts, where her Peruvian father, Jorge, was studying engineering at MIT and her American mother, Elverine, was a classical violinist. When they moved to Peru after their wedding, Marie's mother refused to accept the Peruvian way of life, nor was she accepted by her husband's family; she also tried to raise Marie as an American. However, in Peru Marie was surrounded by indigenous servants who taught her Peruvian legends and folklore, and whose children were her friends. Then, at age ten, she and her family moved to New Jersey, where she was the only Latina in her class. Throughout her childhood, she was caught between two worlds. On her first day as deputy book editor at *The Washington Post*, Marie Arana was asked if she was a "minority hire." She had never thought of herself in those terms before, and after being asked to improve diversity at the paper and add more Latina material, she began to look back at her childhood, a messy childhood she had packed away in order to tidy her life. Her memoir is a family portrait in a bicultural environment, made even more obvious when she moved from her birth country to the United States.

American Chica was nominated for a National Book Award and for the PEN American Center Martha Albrand Award for the Art of the Memoir, was winner of the Books for a Better Life Award, and was selected as a Notable Book by the American Library Association.

Subjects: ALA Notable Books; Biculturalism; Biracial Children; Cultural Identity; Culture Clash; Family Portraits; Journalists; Novelists; Peru; Peruvian-Americans; Wyoming

Now Try: Li-Young Lee also traces a family history lyrically and seems to have had the same emotional environment in his childhood as Marie Arana, although his country of origin was China and his problems were vastly different; his story is told in ***The Winged Seed: A Remembrance***. The young heroine in Laura Riesco's first novel (translated from the Spanish by Mary G. Berg), ***Ximena at the Crossroads***, seems to resemble the young Marie Arana in their love of story and in their fathers, both of whom worked for North American businesses in Peru. Family and the annual trip from Chicago to Mexico are at the heart of Sandra Cisnero's novel, ***Caramelo, or, Puro Cuento: A Novel***.

Choy, Wayson (1939–)

Paper Shadows: Memoir of a Past Lost and Found. Picador USA, 2000, 1999. 342pp. ill. 9780312262181. 819.54

Wayson Choy began his life in postwar Vancouver's Chinatown, but he begins his childhood memoir with a phone call he received as an adult in his late fifties, a call that alerted him to the fact that he had been adopted. He doesn't return to his adoption until toward the end of the book, so the fact of his adoption frames his reminiscences of life as the child of Chinese immigrants in a country that as yet would not allow them citizenship. Armed with the knowledge of his adoption, the specific details and impressions of his childhood take on a different significance—Did his love of Chinese opera come from the possibility that his father may have been one of the singers in the operas that he had attended as a child? The writing of this memoir was spurred by that illuminating phone call.

Paper Shadows was a finalist for the Charles Taylor Prize for Literary Non-Fiction, a nominee for the Governor General's Literary Award for Non-Fiction, a finalist for the City of Vancouver Book Award, and the winner of the Edna Staebler Award for Creative Non-Fiction.

Subjects: Adoptees, Canada; Childhood and Youth; Chinatown, Vancouver, BC; Chinese-Canadians; Edna Staebler Award for Creative Non-Fiction; Family Secrets; Immigrant Life, Canada; Novelists, Canada; Vancouver, BC; Writers, Canada

Now Try: Choy has recently written a new memoir, sparked by two close encounters with death, four years apart: ***Not Yet: A Memoir of Living and Almost Dying***. The nature of Choy's adoption was very different from the current adoption of Chinese children; journalist Jeff Gammage and his wife adopted a Chinese girl, which he writes about in ***China Ghosts: My Daughter's Journey to America, My Passage to Fatherhood***. Judy Fong Bates's novel, ***Midnight at the Dragon Café***, deals with the difficulties of owning a Chinese restaurant in Ontario while coping with family secrets. Growing up Chinese in North America has similarities for many, whether the country is Canada or the United States; Ben Fong-Torres relates his life growing up Chinese-American in Oakland, California, to become a successful journalist in ***The Rice Room: Growing Up Chinese-American; From Number Two Son to Rock 'n' Roll.***

Dumas, Firoozeh (1965–)

Funny in Farsi: A Memoir of Growing Up Iranian in America. Random House Trade Paperbacks, 2008, 2003. 227pp. 9780812968378. Also available in audiobook (read by the author) and e-book. 979.40092

Dumas's father had been in the United States as a graduate student and loved it, so when he was transferred by his Iranian company to Whittier, California, he happily took his entire family with him for what was to be a two-year stint. Firoozeh was seven when she arrived in California in 1972. With humor throughout, she describes their misadventures and their delight with and confusion over American culture. Firoozeh even changed her name to Julie, the pronunciation of her Iranian name got so garbled. They return to Iran but, disconcerted by the Iranian Revolution, return to the United States, a not-so-welcoming place this time, after the hostage crisis. However, they are there to stay, and the extended family joins them, also falling in love with the strange culture that they perceive as the United States. Dumas also recounts her higher education and marriage to a French man, adding even more to her melting pot.

Funny in Farsi was a finalist for both the PEN Center USA Literary Awards for Creative Nonfiction and the Thurber Prize for American Humor.

Subjects: California; Humor; Immigrants; Iran Hostage Crisis (1979–1981); Iran Revolution (1979–1997); Iranian-Americans; Social History, United States

Now Try: Dumas followed up this memoir with a collection of autobiographical essays, ***Laughing Without an Accent: Adventures of an Iranian American, at Home and Abroad***. Terence Ward's family, having been forced to flee Iran, returned in 1998 to look for a dear friend. While recounting their search, they also share much of Persian culture with the reader, in ***Searching for Hassan: An American Family's Journey Home to Iran***. On a more serious level, the question of identity for an Iranian immigrant to the United States is raised in Gelareh Asayesh's ***Saffron Sky: A Life Between Iran and America***. Davar Ardalan has been back and forth between Iran and the United States, and in her memoir, ***My Name Is Iran: A Memoir***, she includes not only her own story but those of her parents and of her American grandmother, who fell in love with a Persian.

Hart, Elva Treviño (1949–)

Barefoot Heart: Stories of a Migrant Child. Bilingual Press/Editorial Bilingüe, 2006, 1999. 236pp. 9780927534819. Also available in large print and e-book. 973.04687

More than the story of a migrant child, this is the story of a young girl living in several worlds: the Latino world, working largely for White people; the migrant world, which necessitates travel; and the world of a close-knit but tension-ridden family that stays together throughout the travels. Her father was a storyteller, and she fashioned her memoir from the stories he told. Her father also firmly believed in education and pushed the family to work hard so that all of the six children could finish high school and get away from the life of their parents. This meant a life of poverty, loneliness, and backbreaking work as they toiled in summer fields far from their winter home in Texas, but it also meant the fulfillment of a dream, as Hart was able to acquire a graduate degree in computer science. By offering anecdotes of her life as a migrant child, Hart brings into the reader's view a lifestyle that relatively few will be aware of, although we all benefit from the work of these people.

Subjects: Child Labor; Family Relationships; Mexican-Americans; Migrant Workers; Minnesota; Texas

Now Try: Perhaps the best-known depiction of migrant life in fiction is John Steinbeck's ***The Grapes of Wrath***, although the Joad family is not an immigrant family, simply one migrating from the dustbowl of Oklahoma to the fertile fields of California, looking for work. Rubén Martínez traces the lives of another Mexican-American migrant family in ***Crossing Over: A Mexican Family on the Migrant Trail***. Cesar Chavez's family, like the Joads, moved to California to try to earn a living. Chavez's shock at the working conditions was so great that he started the United Farm Workers' Union. Susan Ferriss, Ricardo Sandoval, and Diana Hembree cover this history, with photographs edited by Michele Mackenzie, in ***The Fight in the Fields: Cesar Chavez and the Farmworkers Movement***; a documentary movie of the same name was made around the same time that the book was published.

Horn, Michiel (1939–)

Becoming Canadian: Memoirs of an Invisible Immigrant. University of Toronto Press, 1997. 336pp. 16pp. of plates. 9780802008558. Also available in e-book. 971.004

Michiel (pronounced Michael in English) Horn emigrated to Canada with his parents in 1952. They moved to Canada for economic and political reasons, sailing from Europe to Victoria, British Columbia, where his father worked as a draughtsman while qualifying for his Canadian architect's papers. Although he came from a Western European country, with many similarities to Canada, Horn still had to get used to a different educational system, different food, even a different climate. And though he had learned English in the Netherlands, Canadian English was new to him. Of course none of these changes was harrowing, but they created in him a sense that he was neither here nor there. He felt like an immigrant, trying to assimilate (a conscious decision he made), trying to determine just what it means to be a Canadian, yet remembering his happy childhood in the Netherlands, wondering where he really belonged. His memoir, written in his mid-forties initially for his family, covers the years from his childhood to the mid-1970s.

Subjects: Assimilation; British Columbia; Dutch-Canadians; Historians, Canada; Immigrants, Canada; Intellectual Life, Canada; Netherlands; Victoria, BC

Now Try: A Dutch immigrant who is left to his own devices in post-9/11 New York is the main character in Joseph O'Neill's award-winning novel ***Netherland***. Because Horn's family did not emigrate until after the war, they suffered through the German occupation there. A fellow Dutch-Canadian writer, Kristen den Hartog, and her sister, Tracy Kasaboski, have written about their family's experiences during that time in ***The Occupied Garden: A Family Memoir of War-Torn Holland***. Edward William Bok was a Dutch immigrant who also believed in assimilation; so successful at it was he that he became the editor of *The Ladies' Home Journal*, creating a new direction in women's magazines. In his classic ***The Americanization of Edward Bok: The Autobiography of a Dutch Boy Fifty Years After***, he describes how he made his new country his home country.

Santiago, Esmeralda (1948–)

When I Was Puerto Rican. Da Capo Press, 2006, 1993. 278pp. 9780306814525. Also available in large print, Braille, and e-book. 974.71092

When Puerto Ricans arrive in the mainland United States they are already American citizens, but they are treated, and indeed regard themselves, as immigrants. Santiago describes her life in Puerto Rico before moving to the United States with her mother and some of her siblings at the age of thirteen. Life was hard in Puerto Rico, as the family was very poor. In addition, the parents fought and were never married, often separating and then reuniting. But in Puerto Rico, Santiago had the freedom to play safely, fresh air to run around in, and wonderful local produce to enjoy. When her mother finally decided she had had enough, she took some of her children with her to Brooklyn, where her own mother lived. Moving from a rural environment to an urban one, from the Spanish language to English, from a temperate climate to a cold northern one, and from a relatively safe environment to a dangerous one on the edge of the projects were all elements that Santiago had to deal with. She realized that education was her way out, and though her English was weak, she made valiant efforts that were recognized by her teachers, who encouraged and helped her. The book ends with her audition for the Performing Arts High School.

Subjects: Brooklyn (New York, NY); Childhood and Youth; Coming of Age; Cultural Identity; Immigrant Life; Poverty; Puerto Rico

Now Try: Santiago followed her debut memoir with ***Almost a Woman*** and then ***The Turkish Lover***. She also coedited with Joie Davidow a collection of stories, ***Las Mamis: Favorite Latino Authors Remember Their Mothers***. Julia Alvarez has written a coming-of-age novel, ***How the García Girls Lost Their Accents***, about four sisters who move from the Dominican Republic to New York. A male perspective, again Dominican, can be found in the novel ***The Brief Wondrous Life of Oscar Wao*** by Junot Díaz. Judith Ortiz Cofer also had difficulties with her cultural identity, as her father was in the navy and she and her mother spent half the year in Puerto Rico and half the year in the barrio in Paterson, New Jersey, as Cofer relates poetically in ***Silent Dancing: A Partial Remembrance of a Puerto Rican Childhood***.

Spanos, Alex (1923–)
Seal, Mark (1953–), and Natalia Kasparian, coauthors

Sharing the Wealth: My Story. Foreword by Rush Limbaugh. Regnery Publishing, 2002. 254pp. ill. 16pp. of plates. 9780895261588. Also available in e-book. 338.761796332092

Alex Spanos initially worked for his father, a Greek immigrant, in his bakery in Stockton, California, but decided to leave and branch out on his own. Borrowing $800 from the bank to start a business selling sandwiches to the migrant workers in the fields, he moved on from what became a very successful catering business to an even more successful construction and real estate business. He reached the culmination of his dreams in 1984, when he was able to buy a controlling interest in the San Diego Chargers. When not busy with his enterprises, making money, he was busy spending it in philanthropic ventures, earning him an Ellis Island Medal of Honor. Spanos did not visit Greece until he was an adult, but fostering Greek-American relations became very important to him, and he spent hundreds of thousands of dollars supporting Greece in various efforts, whether helping the Greeks in their bid for the Olympics, restoring classical ruins, or assisting with natural disasters. He was also executive producer for a documentary film, ***Greece: Secrets of the Past***. Apart from recounting his life in this memoir, he also outlines his philosophies of success, something he is keen to share with his readers.

In addition to other awards, Alex Spanos received a Horatio Alger Award.

Subjects: Businessmen; Children of Immigrants; Family Relationships; Football Team Owners; Greece; Greek-Americans; Octogenarians; Philanthropists; San Diego Chargers (Football Team)

Now Try: Peter G. Peterson is another son of Greek immigrants who made it big in America; he shares his story in ***The Education of an American Dreamer: How a Son of Greek Immigrants Learned His Way from a Nebraska Diner to Washington, Wall Street, and Beyond***. An important part of Greek culture is family, and Spanos names it number one in his list of secrets to success. Michael Cunningham traces the life of a family of Greek immigrants in his novel ***Flesh and Blood***. Another well-known Greek-American is the actress Olympia Dukakis, whose success is in a different realm from that of Spanos; readers may enjoy her memoir, written with Emily Heckman, ***Ask Me Again Tomorrow: A Life in Progress***.

Exiles and Refugees

A refugee is someone who isn't really welcome in any country—including their own . . . especially their own.—Riverbend (2007)

In this section the reader will find stories of people who have been displaced by political upheaval and war, their good fortune lying in their finding a new country. But they still suffer from what went before and face the necessity of coping with an entirely new life. The writers come from continents and countries as disparate as Liberia and Chile, but they all found refuge at some point in the United States.

Memoirists have become exiles and refugees through war, revolution, and political change in their own homes, forcing them to flee their lands, often to save their very lives. While the situation may not have been dire for all the writers here, there is still a sense of displacement, perhaps pain at what their countries have become, and a longing to return to how they had originally lived. Nostalgia can be a major characteristic of these memoirs, as the writers seek to share with their readers what their countries used to be like.

1 2 3 4 5 6 7 8

Allende, Isabel (1942–)

My Invented Country: A Nostalgic Journey Through Chile. Perennial, 2004, 2003. 199pp. map. 9780060545673. Also available in audiobook and e-audiobook. 863.64 [Trans. by Margaret Sayers Peden]

On September 11, 1973, when she was living in Chile, Allende witnessed the coup that toppled her father's cousin, Salvador Allende, from his position as president of Chile. On September 11, 2001, she was living in the United States, her adopted country, when the Twin Towers in New York were toppled. It was on that day that she finally realized how her adopted country had become her own country. This recognition sparked her interest in looking back at her heritage country (she was actually born in Peru, where her Chilean father was a diplomat), as a way of reviewing her life as an exile. She had been forced to move from Peru to Chile to Bolivia and back to Chile, which she finally fled in 1975 for safety in Venezuela. Once Allende had successfully published her first novel, ***The House of the Spirits*** (translated by Magda Bogin), she was then free to flee her marriage and move to the United States. All of this dislocation is part of this memoir of her country, interwoven with stories of its historical, political, cultural, and social makeup. Apart from offering her readers a view of Chile they may not have encountered before, Allende also provides background for much of her fiction.

Subjects: Allende, Salvador; Chile; Chilean-Americans; Dislocation; Exiles; September 11 Terrorist Attacks, 2001; Social History, Chile; South America; Translations; Writers

Now Try: Murīd Barghūthī was also an exile, whose memoir, ***I Saw Ramallah,*** translated from the Arabic by Ahdaf Soueif, is written in the same impressionistic style as Allende's. Mary Taylor Simeti is an expatriate who wrote a reflective memoir about her adopted country, Italy—specifically Sicily. She also provides the country's history along with her own in ***On Persephone's Island: A Sicilian Journal***. If you'd like to read more about the political situation in Chile, the book by President Allende's translator, Marc Cooper, might prove interesting: ***Pinochet and Me: A Chilean Anti-Memoir***.

Cooper, Helene (1966–)

The House at Sugar Beach: In Search of a Lost African Childhood. Simon & Schuster, 2009, 2008. 354pp. ill. map. 9780743266253. Also available in large print, audiobook, and e-book. 305.8966620753092

Helene Cooper and her family were part of the Liberian elite, happily living in their grand house at Sugar Beach, when their lives changed dramatically through political upheaval. In the first half of this book Cooper describes her life and the people who were part of that life in Liberia. When their house is raided by rebels and her mother is gang-raped, Helene's mother decides they will leave; because of their financial and social status they are able to do that quickly, moving to Tennessee, where they had relatives. Helene then recounts her life in the United States, often referring back to incidents and people in Liberia. Although she tries to put Liberia and its troubles out of her mind, she is not always able to do so. Finally, when she is injured as a journalist in Iraq, she decides that it is time to go back to Liberia and face up to her demons.

Subjects: Childhood and Youth; Dislocation; Exiles; Journalists; Liberia; Liberia Coup (1980); Liberian-Americans; Newswomen; Upper Class

Now Try: William Powers is an American who went to help out in Liberia and grew to love the people and the landscape, as he recounts in ***Blue Clay People: Seasons on Africa's Fragile Edge***. Liberia is the African country settled by freed American slaves in the nineteenth century. (Helene Cooper is a descendant of these former slaves.) If you'd like more information about this, you might find James T. Campbell's book very useful: ***Middle Passages: African-American Journeys to Africa, 1787–2005***. Exile and dislocation happen to people all over the world, and Agate Nesaule's Latvian story would resonate with many. She describes her own experience in ***A Woman in Amber: Healing the Trauma of War and Exile***.

Dorfman, Ariel (1942–)

Heading South, Looking North: A Bilingual Journey. Penguin, 1999, 1998. 282pp. 9780140282535. Also available in e-book. 863

"Dorfman's family history is driven by exile" (*Kirkus Reviews*, 1998). His grandparents fled pogroms and then Nazi persecution, settling in Argentina. When his father protested the purging at the university during the Perón regime, they fled to the United States. His father was again forced into exile, this time to Chile, during the McCarthy era. Dorfman had to flee Chile when Allende, for whom he worked, was overthrown. The effect of all this on Dorfman was a schizophrenia of language. During his first stay in the United States he refused to speak Spanish and embraced all things American. Back in South America, he came to recognize the beauty of Latin culture and the Spanish language and eventually embraced both languages. Even his name reflected the issues of identity he struggled with, created by so much drastic uprooting. His parents named him Vladimiro (after Vladimir Lenin), but he took on the name Edward when he was in the United States, for the prince in Mark Twain's ***The Prince and the Pauper: A Tale for Young People of All Ages***, "a story about duality and identity" (Weiner, 1998). He finally adopted the name Ariel, his given middle name, because it was also the title of a well-known book published in 1900 that spoke of opposition to the United States. Dorfman alternates his chapters among his own story, the story of language, and the situation in Chile with Allende, the story of death.

Subjects: Allende, Salvador; Bilingualism; Chileans in America; Exiles; Identity (Psychology); Jewish Men; McCarthy Era; Perón, Juan

Now Try: Pablo Neruda is a fellow Chilean who was also exiled; while the tone of his ***Memoirs***, translated from the Spanish by Hardie St. Martin, is quite different from Dorfman's, the perspective of another writer who was also a friend of Allende is interesting. As one may gather from her title, the main thread in Eva Hoffman's classic memoir, ***Lost in Translation: A Life in a New Language***, is language, particularly for the new immigrant. Wendy Lesser asked a number of uprooted writers to discuss the question of language and culture in a book she published as ***The Genius of Language: Fifteen Writers Reflect on Their Mother Tongues.***

Hakkākiyān, Ru'yā (1966–)

Journey from the Land of No: A Girlhood Caught in Revolutionary Iran. Crown, 2006, 2004. 245pp. 9781400046119. Also available in e-book. 955.053092

This is a coming-of-age memoir in more ways than one. The author was nine when her parents sent her brother to the United States for safety during the regime of the Shah. For this reason they were all excited to welcome the return of the exiled Ayatollah Khomeini, a man who would oust the Shah and end the repressive regime they had suffered under. What they didn't understand was how much more repressive the new regime would be. And for a Jewish family, as the Hakkākiyāns were, it was even worse. The toilets and drinking fountains were segregated, and all Jewish businesses had to be declared non-Muslim. Swastikas began to appear, and for many it was too much like Germany in the 1930s. Hakkākiyān's memoir covers the years from 1977 to 1984, when she and her mother fled, reflecting the progression from a happy preadolescent, secure in her family's love and acceptance among the larger, artistic community in which they traveled, to an anxious, angry adolescent, writing rebelliously in her school papers, frightened by the repressive changes, and finally forced to flee her homeland.

Subjects: Childhood and Youth; Coming of Age; Iran Revolution (1979–1997); Iranian-Americans; Jews, Iran; Khomeini, Ayatollah; Poets, Iran; Refugees, Iran; Women in Iran

Now Try: Farideh Goldin was also a Jewish girl growing up in Tehran. In her memoir, ***Wedding Song: Memoirs of an Iranian Jewish Woman,*** she describes the pre-revolution relationship between Muslims and Jews in Iran. Like Hakkākiyān, Afschineh Latifi had a privileged childhood during the Shah's regime, as her father was a colonel in his army. ***Even After All This Time: A Story of Love, Revolution, and Leaving Iran,*** written with the help of Pablo F. Fenjves, is her story of both the steps her mother had to take to keep the family safe after her father was killed and their subsequent flight from Iran. The protagonist in Gina Barkhordar Nahai's novel, ***Caspian Rain: A Novel,*** struggles with the class differences between her parents, both Jews living in Tehran, as well as the turmoil surrounding her in the larger arena of political Tehran, not long before the fall of the Shah.

Said, Edward W. (1935–2003)

Out of Place: A Memoir. Vintage Books, 2000, 1999. 295pp. ill. 9780679730675. Also available in e-book. 973.049274

Diagnosed with leukemia in his early sixties, the renowned scholar Edward Said decided he wanted to write about his childhood, about a place that no longer exists as it was, to describe a world he wanted to preserve in writing. The title is significant, as Edward Said has felt out of place for most of his life, both internally, from highly critical and demanding parents, and externally, through forced exile. A Christian Palestinian born in Jerusalem when it was part of Palestine, he and his family fled to Cairo in 1947 when he was twelve, in face of the unrest and changes about to take place in what had been their homeland. They spent their summers in the mountains in Lebanon, another country changed by turmoil. Said then moved to the United States, where he finished high school and went on to Harvard and earned three degrees. Everywhere he went he felt like an exile. Despite his being a pro-Palestinian political activist, the memoir doesn't actually focus much on politics, but more on his life with his parents and other relatives, yet the fact of political upheaval can't help but be present, given the forced changes in their lives.

For ***Out of Place*** Said was awarded both *The New Yorker* Book Award for Nonfiction and the Anisfield-Wolf Book Award.

Subjects: Anisfield-Wolf Book Award; Childhood and Youth; College Professors; Cultural Historians; Exiles; Intellectuals; Middle East; Palestine; Palestinian-Americans; Said Family; Writers

Now Try: Said was the only boy of five children; one of his sisters, Jean Said Makdisi, has also written a memoir, but from quite a different perspective. She has chosen to explore the women in the family in ***Teta, Mother, and Me: Three Generations of Arab Women***. In his seminal work, ***Orientalism***, Edward Said defined his concept of that philosophy, the effects of which Sherry B. Ortner experienced when she studied the sherpas who guide mountain climbers in the Himalayas. This she describes in ***Life and Death on Mt. Everest: Sherpas and Himalayan Mountaineering***. André Aciman also left his country of birth, a community of Jewish settlers in Alexandria, Egypt, that has all but vanished. He traces his family history in this community in ***Out of Egypt: A Memoir***. For a clearer understanding of the Palestinian question, readers may find Karl Sabbagh's ***Palestine: A Personal History*** of interest.

The Return Home

Why do people go back to the homes they left behind? For some, there is an emotional attachment, "a love of the landscape, and a knowledge of the place" (Stanford, 2007), as well as family to visit or to care for. For others, it is a "search for identity in one's familial, personal past" (Jay, 2003). The person going home is often conflicted and at times seeks to resolve that conflict by making the journey. But the journey can also result in further feelings of alienation, of belonging nowhere, accepted by neither the new home country nor the old, since the facility with language, the wardrobe, and the cultural outlook may all have changed. Somehow those returning home are often immediately recognized as not belonging. Although only five stories comprise this section, each is powerful—as much so for the writer as for the reader.

Those who return home do so for a number of reasons. Sometimes they simply travel back to their country with their parents. At other times they travel to their parents' country to get to know it or their parents better. Whatever the reason, there is usually a pull for the writer between the old country and the new, creating a tension in the divergence of cultures and in nostalgia for an older way of life, now disappeared.

Bahrampour, Tara

To See and See Again: A Life in Iran and America. University of California Press, 2000, 1999. 357pp. 9780520223547. 979.50049155

Tara Bahrampour's father was Iranian, her mother was American, and she always lived in a family that mixed the two cultures. She also lived a life between two countries, spending her young, formative years in Iran and returning to the United States as an adolescent during the Islamic Revolution. In both America and Iran she is bewildered by the differences in customs and culture and easily embarrassed by her relatives as they apply behavior appropriate to one culture in the other culture, where that behavior is inappropriate. Bahrampour decided to return to Iran in 1990 and discovered, as many do, that she was neither Iranian nor American but a mix of the two. The Iran she returned to was very different from the one she had left. She had grown up in a cosmopolitan environment, typical of the educated elite in Tehran at the time. When she returned, she discovered a "readjustment" school for Iranians who had been abroad, to teach the girls how to wear the chador, for example. She discovered the omnipresence of the morals police, but she also found little resistances among the people. Bahrampour now had the added adjustment to make of not just being Iranian and American, but of being from a different Iran, one that no longer exists.

Subjects: Biculturalism; Family Relationships; Identity (Psychology); Iran; Iran Revolution (1979–1997); Iranian-Americans; Journalists; Multiculturalism; Social History, Iran; Women in Iran

Now Try: Although Abbas Milani was born earlier than Bahrampour, as he relates in ***Tales of Two Cities: A Persian Memoir***, his experiences are not that dissimilar, as he learned to deal with the differences between Iran and the United States and between an earlier Iran and the one in which he was imprisoned. Alice Carey grew up quite differently from Tara Bahrampour; the daughter of an Irish immigrant to New York, she describes how she finally found home in ***A Daughter's Search for Home in Ireland***. Nahid Mozaffari and Ahmad Karimi Hakkak have collected various pieces to offer North Americans a good sampling of Persian and Iranian literature in ***Strange Times, My Dear: The PEN Anthology of Contemporary Iranian Literature***.

Godwin, Peter (1957–)

When a Crocodile Eats the Sun: A Memoir of Africa. Little, Brown, 2007, 2006. 344pp. ill. 8pp. of plates. map. 9780316158947. Also available in e-book. 968.91092

Born and raised in Rhodesia, Peter Godwin left shortly after finishing his military service to study in England, where he became a journalist for *The Sunday Times* and for the BBC. He was eventually sent back to his country to cover the changeover from the colonial Rhodesia to the independent Zimbabwe. Disillusioned by the political situation, he then emigrated to the United States, often returning to Zimbabwe, however, to visit his parents. These return visits to his parents, the secrets he learned about their history, and what he saw going on in his birth country led him to write ***When a Crocodile Eats the Sun***. Because the life of his father so closely paralleled the life of Zimbabwe, Godwin had no choice but to write a very personal book. As his father's physical condition deteriorated, so too did the health of Zimbabwe. Every time Godwin left Zimbabwe he felt tremendous guilt at leaving his parents and his country behind. He had to convince himself that he must not behave as an exile in New York, with his heart back home, but rather as an immigrant, with his heart full of hope.

When a Crocodile Eats the Sun was selected as a Notable Book by the American Library Association.

Subjects: ALA Notable Books; Family Relationships; Family Secrets; Fathers and Sons; Immigrants; Journalists; Race Relations, Zimbabwe; Southern Africa; Zimbabwe

Now Try: At one point, Godwin's parents are faced with their beloved retired servant forced at their door to accuse them of owing her back wages. Christina Lamb has written of a similar situation with another White family and their Black servant in ***House of Stone: The True Story of a Family Divided in War-Torn Zimbabwe***. A Zimbabwean novelist, Tsitsi Dangarembga, wrote the story of Rhodesia from the viewpoint of a Black adolescent young woman keen to get an education, ***Nervous Conditions: A Novel***. Carolyn Jourdan went home reluctantly—back to East Tennessee from her high-powered job in Washington, D.C.—planning to fill in as receptionist at her father's medical office until her mother was well enough again to take over, and she describes in ***Heart in the Right Place*** that one actually can go home again. Peter Godwin has been "home" several times, latterly in secret with his sister, Georgina, to research the political terror in Zimbabwe for his latest book, ***The Fear: Robert Mugabe and the Martyrdom of Zimbabwe***.

Moaveni, Azadeh (1976–)

Lipstick Jihad: A Memoir of Growing Up Iranian in America and American in Iran. PublicAffairs, 2005. 249pp. 9781586481933. 305.48092

Moaveni's parents were exiled from Iran even before the revolution in 1979, so she was born in the United States. But the political upheavals in Iran reached across borders and affected members of the Iranian diaspora, entering their homes and creating personal upheavals. So it was with Moaveni's family, and it was not until 2000 that Moaveni had an opportunity to visit her heritage country as a journalist for *Time* magazine, to see life there and to try to solve for herself her own issues of cultural identity. She traveled largely with the upper-middle-class crowd, people of her generation who grew up after the revolution, and found that Iran was not the country of her childhood fantasies. She was interested to see how people seemed to be fighting back, trying to acquire more freedom of movement and apparently succeeding for a while. Even during her brief stay of one year, however, she could see the hardliners taking over and the young who had tried to rebel growing tired of their battle and cynical about any possibility of success. Moaveni herself had to leave as she found her own journalistic freedoms being pulled back.

Subjects: Children of Immigrants; Iran; Iranian-Americans; Islam; Journalists; Mothers and Daughters; Muslim Women; Social History, Iran

Now Try: Casting light on the politics and culture of postrevolutionary Iran is Ray Takeyh's ***Hidden Iran: Paradox and Power in the Islamic Republic***. A number of Iranian writers have contributed to a collection of views of Iranian life in Lila Azam Zanganeh's ***My Sister, Guard Your Veil, My Brother, Guard Your Eyes: Uncensored Iranian Voices***. Moaveni's is a nuanced portrait of Iran, but Iran is not the only country suffering from fundamentalist hardliners. Azhar Abidi offers a nuanced portrait of Pakistan in the 1980s, a country under the joined fists of the mullahs and the generals, in ***The House of Bilqis***.

Ondaatje, Michael (1943–)

Running in the Family. Emblem Editions, 2001, 1982. 189pp. ill. photos. 9780771068966. Also available in audiobook (read by the author) and e-audiobook. 819.5409

Michael Ondaatje left his birth country of Ceylon to join his mother in England when he was eleven. He never came to know well the man who was his father, as his parents had separated when he was five. Once he finished high school, his brother Christopher urged Michael to join him in Canada, where he moved in 1962. After establishing a life as an academic and writer, he started taking trips back to what had become Sri Lanka. His father had been the superintendent of a large tea plantation on the island, and Ondaatje's parents had thus been part of the colonial society, with mixed heritages of Dutch, English, Sinhalese, and Tamil. By the time Ondaatje returned, his father had died, so he spent his time touring familiar parts of the island and asking family members to recount stories to him, especially about his father. This memoir, then, is an assemblage of stories from the past about Ondaatje's family in the 1920s and 1930s, told to him by such people as his eighty-year-old aunt, along with poetic renderings of his time in Sri Lanka in the late 1970s and early 1980s, as he wrote this book. It includes photographs that friends and family were able to find for him.

Running in the Family was selected as a Notable Book by the American Library Association.

Subjects: 1920s; 1930s; 1980s; ALA Notable Books; Fathers and Sons; Immigrants, Canada; Ondaatje Family; Sri Lanka; Sri Lankan-Canadians; Writers, Canada

Now Try: Ondaatje has set a novel in Sri Lanka, ***Anil's Ghost***, featuring a forensic anthropologist trying to determine the source of the organized murder campaigns occurring during the civil war. Another Sri Lankan writer, Romesh Gunesekera, has also written a novel about Sri Lanka, ***Reef***, with the same lyrical beauty in writing and description as Ondaatje. The high life of Ondaatje's parents brings to mind the serio-comic sociology book of Richard Conniff, ***The Natural History of the Rich: A Field Guide***. While Blake Morrison did live with his father, he still felt he did not really know him as a person; in learning who that person was as a man and not just as a father, he wrote a memoir, ***And When Did You Last See Your Father?***

Pham, Andrew X. (1967–)

Catfish and Mandala: A Two-Wheeled Voyage Through the Landscape and Memory of Vietnam. Farrar, Straus & Giroux, 2000, 1999. 344pp. 9780374119744. 915.9704092

Pham's odyssey back to Vietnam begins with a bicycle trip to Mexico. As a Vietnamese refugee, a "boat person," he had settled with his family in California when he was ten. Life in a new country was not easy, learning the language, learning the ways, and dealing with a family scarred by the war and by his father's experiences in a North Vietnamese concentration camp. In Mexico he met Thor, a blond American living hand-to-mouth by choice, a Vietnam vet, as it turned out, whose guilt on seeing Pham caused him to break down and confess what he had done in Vietnam and ask Pham's forgiveness. This chance meeting led Pham to Vietnam, where his first encounter was with an immigration official who sneered at him, calling him a "foreign Vietnamese." As he travels through the country, barely recognizing anything, suffering from the slurs against him, feeling a survivor's guilt when he perceives the poverty around him, Pham starts to realize that perhaps he is American after all. Despite the sadness around him, Pham recognizes the beauty of the country as well, providing a travelogue through Vietnam as well as through his family's history from Vietnam to California.

Catfish and Mandala won the Whiting Writers' Award, was a finalist for the *Guardian* First Book Award, and was a cowinner of the Kiriyama Prize.

Subjects: Cultural Identity; Cyclists; Kiriyama Prize; Refugees,Vietnam; Self-Discovery; Solo Travel; Travel, Vietnam; Vietnamese-Americans

Now Try: Pham has also written a book on behalf of his father, Thong Van Pham, focusing on the three wars his father endured in Vietnam: ***The Eaves of Heaven: A Life in Three Wars***. Bicycle trips are not an unusual form of road trip for Americans. Erika Warmbrunn also traveled through Asia, although for reasons different from Pham's. She recounts her journey in ***Where the Pavement Ends: One Woman's Bicycle Trip Through Mongolia, China & Vietnam***. Kate Gadbow is the author of the award-winning novel ***Pushed to Shore: A Novel***, about a teacher whose ESL class is made up of Vietnamese and Hmong refugee children. There are over a million Vietnamese-Americans living in the United States; Andrew Lam, a refugee himself at the age of eleven, has become an expert on the Vietnamese diaspora and has collected a number of essays, some autobiographical, in ***Perfume Dreams: Reflections on the Vietnamese Diaspora***.

Consider Starting With . . .

Allende, Isabel. *My Invented Country: A Nostalgic Journey Through Chile*

Choy, Wayson. *Paper Shadows: Memoir of a Past Lost and Found*

Godwin, Peter. *When a Crocodile Eats the Sun: A Memoir of Africa*

Gopnik, Adam. *Paris to the Moon*

Hakkākiyān, Ru'yā. *Journey from the Land of No: A Girlhood Caught in Revolutionary Iran*

Kingston, Maxine Hong. *The Woman Warrior; China Men*

Mayes, Frances. *Under the Tuscan Sun: At Home in Italy*

Ondaatje, Michael. *Running in the Family*

Santiago, Esmeralda. *When I Was Puerto Rican*

Trapp, Maria Augusta. *The Story of the Trapp Family Singers*

Fiction Read-Alikes

Dubus, Andre. *House of Sand and Fog*. Through a bureaucratic error, a young abandoned woman finds herself in a battle with an Iranian-American for her home, a home that had become his dream.

Hegi, Ursula. *The Vision of Emma Blau*. A family saga spanning almost a century, this story centers around a vision that Stefan Blau has, causing him to emigrate from Germany to America.

Lahiri, Jhumpa. *The Namesake*. The American-born child of immigrants from India is named after the Russian poet Gogol, adding one more stress to his difficulties in navigating the culture clashes in his life.

Levy, Andrea. *Small Island*. This award-winning novel tells the story of Hortense and Gilbert, moving from one island (Jamaica) to another (Britain), adjusting to life in a boarding house with Queenie, whose life is complicated when her husband comes home from the war—two years after it ends.

Mukherjee, Bharati. *Desirable Daughters: A Novel*. Daughter of a Bengali Brahmin family, Tara Chatterjee shocks her family by divorcing her millionaire husband and taking her son with her to California.

Ng, Fae Myenne. *Bone*. Chinatown, San Francisco, is the home of the Leong family, trying to cope with their new life at the same time that they are trying to understand the sadness of their middle child.

Roberts, Gregory David. *Shantaram: A Novel*. An escaped convict from Australia hopes to hide in the slums of Mumbai, and in doing so learns much about life, in this autobiographical novel.

See, Lisa. *Shanghai Girls: A Novel.* Victims of their father's hard luck, two sisters from 1930s Shanghai are sold in marriage to men from California, who take them back to America.

Shteyngart, Gary. *The Russian Debutante's Handbook.* In this award-winning debut novel, the son of immigrant Russian Jews has no expectations for his own success until he is noticed by a very rich young woman.

Tam, Amy. *The Joy Luck Club.* Mah jong is a source of comfort for a group of Chinese immigrant women in San Francisco in the late 1940s as they form the Joy Luck Club, a group that continues even when their children are grown women.

Works Cited

Boelhower, William Q. 1982. "The Brave New World of Immigrant Autobiography." *MELUS* 9 (2) (Summer): special issue, "Ethnic Biography and Autobiography." Accessed July 16, 2009. http://www.jstor.org.ezproxy.library.wisc.edu/stable/466962.

Egan, Susanna, and Gabriele Helms. 2002. "Auto/biography? Yes. But Canadian?" *Canadian Literature* 172: 5–16.

Holte, James Craig. 1982. "The Representative Voice: Autobiography and the Ethnic Experience." *MELUS* 9 (2) (Summer): special issue, "Ethnic Biography and Autobiography." Accessed July 16, 2009. http://www.jstor.org.ezproxy.library.wisc.edu/stable/466963.

Jay, Paul. 2003. "Memory, Identity and Empire in Michael Ondaatje's *Running in the Family*" (paper presented at the Midwest Modern Language Association, Chicago, IL). Accessed July 27, 2009. http://home.comcast.net/~jay.paul/ondaatje.htm.

Kennedy, Cecilia. 2009. "My Genes Are Dutch, but I Am Not." Facts & Arguments, *The Globe and Mail,* July 1.

Kirkus Reviews. 1998. Review of *Heading South, Looking North: A Bilingual Journey* by Ariel Dorfman. *Novelist,* March 1. EBSCO*host.* Accessed August 26, 2010.

Riverbend. 2007. Baghdad Burning blog, October 22. Accessed August 26, 2010. http://riverbendblog.blogspot.com/.

Stanford, Peter. 2007. "Peter Godwin: Truth in Black and White." *The Independent,* March 9. Accessed July 25, 2009. http://www.independent.co.uk/arts-entertainment/books/features/peter-godwin-truth-in-black-and-white-439376.html.

Weiner, Eileen. 1998. "Torn Between Two Languages." Review of *Heading South, Looking North,* by Ariel Dorfman. *Pittsburgh Post-Gazette,* June 21. Accessed August 26, 2010. http://www.postgazette.com/books/reviews/19980621review59.asp.

Chapter 7

Life with Others

Description

The relational memoir is one in which "the focus may be on another person to an equal or greater extent than on the autobiographer's own life" (Tridgell, 2005). Here the memoirist is usually less self-referential than in the memoirs found elsewhere. The word "relational" has another meaning as well, as the people who are central to the story are often relations of the memoirist. And if not relations, then they are close friends.

The stories in this chapter offer a broad mix. Heartfelt stories praise a parent, a lover, a friend. There are equally heartfelt stories about working through a difficult relationship—usually with a parent. Many of these stories, some heartrending, some celebratory, could have easily found their way into the chapter that focuses on loss, illness, difficult childhoods, and addiction; because the relationship is of prime importance in the story, though, they have been put here. And there are family histories as well, interesting for the knowledge they impart and important to the writer in developing a sense of cultural identity. This chapter also includes stories about friends in the larger sense, as there is also a section on animal friends, companions close to the hearts of the memoirists.

The relational memoir raises an ethical issue crucial to most memoirs, but particularly so here. What right does the memoirist have to bring into public view the lives of people other than himself or herself? In some few cases (Christopher Dickey, for example), the other central character has died, but in many cases there are still family members around who will obviously be affected by the public airing of the family story.

One of the reasons put forth to justify this kind of memoir writing is the notion that it is helpful to both the writer and the reader. If the writer has suffered through difficulties because of the family in general, or a parent in particular, it is therapeutic for the writer to work it all out through writing. Then, of course, one could say that's fine, but just don't publish the written product. However, the reader can also benefit by having someone else articulate his or her own experiences and feelings, offering comfort to the reader.

Another rationale given is that it is especially important to bring out into the open the shameful secrets, to shed light on them in order to defuse them. The shame diminishes, freeing the memoirist to move on. Memoirs usually have a counterpoint: the writer looks back as a witness to the participant that writer used to be. Writing through the difficulties presented by family, according to this theory, helps the writer integrate that past with the present in order to move on to a healthier, more productive future (Waxler, 2008).

There is no question, however, that memoir writing that includes family and friends (as most must do) involves the distinct possibility of betrayal (Bechdel, 2007). Writers like William Faulkner believe that such a drawback simply goes with the territory; a writer must write. "Everything goes by the board: honor, pride, decency, security, happiness, all, to get the book written. If a writer has to rob his mother, he will not hesitate" (Stein, 1958).

However, one writer suggested that reading a memoir is like having a conversation with friends in which one talks about the hardships of life, yet the ideas put forth are done so "more forcefully or poignantly from literature, if the writer is more skilled and articulate than my lunchtime friends might be, more able to distill the core of his or her experience" (Mills, 2004).

In the case of this chapter, two writers have added another dimension to their writing skills: their drawing skills; two of the memoirs here are written in graphic-narrative format.

Life-with-others memoirs focus as much on other people as on the memoirists themselves. Because the writers are describing their relationships with family and friends, it necessarily follows that readers will be introduced to and get to know the family and friends of the memoirists. Some of the stories are elegiac in nature and tone, and others are accusatory, reflecting the relationship the writers had with the people in question.

Appeal

Readers who enjoy character-driven stories have a wide array of choices in this chapter, from the upper classes to the homeless, from determined dads and moms to parents with too much baggage of their own. Even the animals in this chapter are worthy characters to add to the mix.

Though character-driven, these memoirs are also story-driven, particularly those in which the parent is writing about the child, although the story appeal is not limited to just those memoirs.

One of the major appeals of this type of memoir has already been touched upon: the expression by the writer of feelings experienced by the reader. In the words of one writer who is also a reader, "I am strengthened, enormously relieved, blessed by the sense that I am not so utterly alone" (Mills, 2004). There is also the possibility that the reader will gain new perspectives on a particular situation with a particular person, seeing the difficulties in a new light or perhaps stopping to think about what created the difficulties in the first place, what created the other person's personality that would cause such a situation to arise.

Not everyone who reads another's memoir about a relationship with a parent, a sibling, or a friend sees a reflection in the mirror—the opposite may be the case. There may be a feeling of great relief that that situation does not represent the reader's life. There may also be an innocent feeling of disbelief that such a family or relationship could even exist. As with much literature in which new situations appear for the reader, there is also the possibility of a new empathy arising in the reader for people who experience such lives.

In the case of the family histories, in addition to the story of the family, the author provides historical background so that the reader can learn more about Italy, China, Russia, or Newfoundland, particularly as the first three countries relate to immigration to the United States. But there is also much to be learned from other stories—about the *Kulturbund* during the war in Germany (Goldsmith), about disease politics (Kondracke), or about the plight of orphans in Zimbabwe (Tucker).

Organization of This Chapter

The chapter begins with a few representative classics, titles that have been added to the canon of memoir literature, touching on each of the various sections. The first section following "Classics" is the "Family" as a whole, where the story would not be complete without bringing in more than one individual. Following that is a focus on both parents, from the point of view of the child. The chapter then moves on to the individual parents, first the "Mothers," then the "Fathers." "Children" follow the parents, and then we have the "Siblings" section. There is a small section of bittersweet stories of "Lovers," bittersweet because they are written after the death of the loved one. These stories differ from those in Chapter 13 ("Surviving Life") in that they focus more on the loved person than on the fact of the loss. Finishing up the familial relationship is "Family History," in which the focus goes far beyond the immediate family. The next section is "Friends," first friendships found with humans, then "Animal Friends."

1 2 3 4 5 6 7 8

Classics

This section provides a small sampling of older titles that focus on relationships. The ties that bind here are between a father and his son, among the members of a large family, between a man and his village and their animals, between two brothers, and between a son and his mother.

> These classic relational stories represent a variety of relationships, some wonderful, some not so wonderful. They all serve to remind the reader of the pains and joys involved in loving others, particularly family. The stories here are largely narrative, although they also include reflections on the difficulties within the family and what might have caused them.

Dorris, Michael (1945–1997)

The Broken Cord. Foreword by Louise Erdrich. Harper Perennial, 1999, 1989. 300p. 9780833553348. Also available in large print, Braille, audiobook, and video. 362.1968

As much as this is a book about fetal alcohol syndrome, it is even more the story of a father's love for his adopted son, called Adam in this memoir. When he was young and single, Dorris successfully adopted a three-year-old boy from the Sioux Nation in South Dakota. It was not until several years later that Dorris discovered the real diagnosis of the problems he had encountered from the beginning with Adam: fetal alcohol syndrome (FAS). In his memoir, Dorris describes how he was initially in denial, blaming everyone but Adam for his son's inability to learn, his poor judgment, and his seizures. After adopting two more children, however, and seeing their developmental progress compared to Adam's, Dorris thought he had finally discovered the problem: that his oldest son was developmentally delayed. As time went on, though, Dorris really did learn the truth of Adam's disorder and was able to accept that his son was who he was because of his mother's drinking; he then set out to learn as much about FAS as he could and to tell the world about it.

The Broken Cord was the winner of a Christopher Award, the *Chicago Tribune* Heartland Prize for Nonfiction, and the National Book Critics Circle Award in General Nonfiction; it was also selected as a Notable Book by the American Library Association.

Subjects: Adoption; ALA Notable Books; American Indians; Christopher Awards; Classics; Family Relationships; Fathers and Sons; Fetal Alcohol Syndrome; National Book Critics Circle Award in General Nonfiction; Sioux Nation; Writers; Writers in the Family

Now Try: When Dorris wrote his memoir, not so much was known about FAS as in 2005, when Bonnie Buxton wrote her memoir about adopting an FAS child, ***Damaged Angels: An Adoptive Mother Discovers the Tragic Toll of Alcohol in Pregnancy.***

Another story of fathers and FAS in an American Indian community is the novel by Craig Lesley, ***Storm Riders***. Dorris's story is heart-wrenching from the parent's point of view. Jennings Michael Burch has written a heart-wrenching story from the child's point of view, ***They Cage the Animals at Night***, about a child who could never find an adoptive father like Dorris.

Gilbreth, Frank B. (1911–2001), and Ernestine Gilbreth Carey (1908–2006)

Cheaper by the Dozen. HarperCollins, 2005, 1948. 207pp. 9780060763138. Also available in large print, audio, and video. 658.540922

This title is more a family memoir than the story of any one individual. Frank and Ernestine, siblings, tell the story, in hilarious fashion, of growing up with their ten other siblings. Their parents were highly educated and had established careers as sought-after efficiency experts, bringing their ideas into the home both to test and to facilitate raising such a large brood. For example, the children were all encouraged to button their shirts from the bottom up, as it was more efficient and shaved seconds off getting dressed. While that sounds as though their life would be dreary and prescribed, it was not, as reading the story proves. The twelve grew up in a loving, adventurous family.

Subjects: Classics; Domestic Life; Efficiency Experts; Family Relationships; Gilbreth, Frank Bunker; Gilbreth, Lillian Moller; Industrial Engineers; Parenting

Now Try: Frank and Ernestine together wrote a sequel, ***Belles on Their Toes***, illustrated by Donald McKay, about the early death of their father and how their mother took over the family business and raised the children herself. In today's society, a family of twelve is an unusual occurrence. However, there are some very large families still around; Michelle and Jim Bob Duggar tell the funny, heartwarming story of their large group in ***The Duggars: 20 and Counting! Raising One of America's Largest Families—How They Do It***. Marion Winik published a collection of lighthearted essays on parenting and life with a large-ish family in ***Above Us Only Sky: Essays***. The author and humorist Calvin Trillin also wrote a collection of essays, offering his take on family in ***Family Man***.

Herriot, James (1916–1995)

All Creatures Great and Small. St. Martin's Griffin, 2004, 1972. 442pp. 9780312330859. Also available in large print, Braille, audiobook, e-audiobook, and video. 636.098092

When Alf Wight (see p. 302) decided to realize his ambition of converting his daily notes into a memoir (using the pseudonym of a Scottish soccer player), he unwittingly began what was to become practically a cottage industry. In this first volume of several, James Herriot describes his early days as an apprentice for a quirky but able Yorkshire veterinarian, also pseudonymously named, Siegfried Farnon. Knowing how much his British audience loved animals, Herriot made sure to include stories about the various animals he treated, including one story about a gypsy pony. He describes his various experiences in the barns and fields in the Yorkshire Dales around the fictitiously named town of Darrowby (Thirsk), where he also met and courted Joan Danbury, the woman who would become his wife. There are five titles in the memoir series, the second one being ***All Things Bright and Beautiful***, but Herriot didn't stop there: he wrote children's stories about animals and travel guides to Yorkshire, an area that became a tourist destination because of his books.

Subjects: Animal Care; Animals; Apprenticeships; Classics; England; Small Towns, England; Veterinarians, England; Yorkshire, England

Now Try: People who read James Herriot generally love reading other animal stories. One unlikely story is that of a group of animal-loving bikers. The subtitle of their story, told by Denise Flaim, tells it all: ***Rescue Ink: How Ten Guys Saved Countless Dogs and Cats, Twelve Horses, Five Pigs, One Duck, and a Few Turtles***. Another unusual hero—Wilbur in E. B. White's ***Charlotte's Web*** notwithstanding—is the pig Christopher Hogwood, an animal that changed the life of the naturalist Sy Montgomery, as she describes in ***The Good Good Pig: The Extraordinary Life of Christopher Hogwood***. Yorkshire is a locale that appeals to many readers, for its moors, its dales, and its atmosphere. Readers may enjoy steeping themselves in the environs by joining Inspector Alan Banks as he investigates crime in Yorkshire in the **Inspector Banks Mystery Series** by Peter Robinson; the first title in the series is ***Gallows View: An Inspector Banks Mystery***.

Wideman, John Edgar (1941–)

Brothers and Keepers. Houghton Mifflin, 2005, 1984. 242pp. 9780618509638. 364.3092

John Wideman is an award-winning novelist whose younger brother is still serving a sentence for a murder that occurred during the commission of a crime by a gang in 1976. In his memoir, Wideman looks at the issue of how two brothers raised by the same mother could turn out so differently. It also causes him to look at himself very closely in an effort to come to grips with who he really is as an African-American man succeeding in the world of academia as an English professor. Determined to listen to his brother Robby as he had never listened before, Wideman visits him in prison and encourages him to talk about his story—not just his story of prison life, nor the immediate story of how he got there, but also the story of his youth, his rebellion against all that the rest of his family stood for. The result of this listening is Wideman's recording of Robby's story in Robby's voice: the slang and the anger, a voice in sharp contrast to Wideman's own. At the same time, Wideman also paints a damning picture of the prison system and prison life as he witnesses it.

John Wideman was the second African-American to be a Rhodes scholar, and was the recipient of a MacArthur Fellowship. His book, ***Brothers and Keepers,*** was a finalist for the National Book Critics Circle Award in General Nonfiction and was selected as a Notable Book by the American Library Association.

Subjects: African-American Men; ALA Notable Books; Brothers; Classics; College Professors; Identity (Psychology); Imprisonment; Murder; Novelists; Pittsburgh, PA; Prisons, United States; Wideman, Robert Douglas

Now Try: John Wideman was living in Laramie, Wyoming, when Robert and his friends fled west from their crime in Pittsburgh to stay briefly with him. Laramie is also the location of the gay bashing and murder of Matthew Shepard some months later that same year. Moisés Kaufman and the members of the Tectonic Theater Project wrote a play, ***The Laramie Project***, using not two voices, as Wideman does, but several voices of the townspeople to depict that awful crime. The novelist Robert Ellis Gordon spent nine years teaching writing in Washington State prisons. He offers his views on prison life in ***The Funhouse Mirror: Reflections on Prison***. In the award-winning memoir ***Brother to a Dragonfly***, Will D. Campbell writes movingly of his brother, a man whose path also differed from his own.

Wolff, Tobias (1945–)

This Boy's Life: A Memoir. Grove Press, 2000, 1989. 288pp. 9780802136688. Also available in large print, Braille, audiobook, and video. 813.54

Tobias Wolff was five, and his brother, Geoffrey, was twelve when their parents divorced. Geoffrey went with his father, Arthur (Duke), to the East and Tobias went with his mother, Rosemary, to the West, and the brothers didn't meet up again until Geoffrey was at Princeton. Their young lives were very different, as one would see by reading both this memoir and Geoffrey's, ***The Duke of Deception: Memories of My Father***. Obviously Tobias Wolff's memoir focuses more on his mother, but his own behavior—strikingly like his father's—figures large as well. Tobias was well on his way to becoming at least an earl of deception, culminating in forging his way into acceptance at a prep school in the East. Much of his early delinquent behavior might have been a backlash against the petty and abusive meanness of his stepfather. Wolff's attitude toward both his mother, a woman conditioned by tyrannical men, and his stepfather are more sympathetic than bitter. His is a coming-of-age memoir as he recounts his youthful escapades, recognizing all the while that the miscreant he is describing was not his real self.

This Boy's Life was nominated for the National Book Critics Circle Award in Biography/Autobiography and won the *Los Angeles Times* Book Prize for Biography.

Subjects: Authoritarian Households; Childhood and Youth; Children of Divorce; Classics; Coming of Age; *Los Angeles Times* Book Prize for Biography; Mothers and Sons; Stepfathers; Wolff, Geoffrey; Wolff, Rosemary; Writers

Now Try: Thad Ziolkowski is also a writer, a poet; he escaped his stepfather by surfing, as he describes in ***On a Wave***. Craig Lesley had an abusive stepfather and a problematic father, as he describes in ***Burning Fence: A Western Memoir of Fatherhood***. Wolff's classic memoir is almost like a nonfiction version of J. D. Salinger's novel ***The Catcher in the Rye***.

Family

Tolstoy's famous first line in ***Anna Karenina*** is, "Happy families are all alike; every unhappy family is unhappy in its own way." Here the reader will find both happy and unhappy families, but contrary to Tolstoy's dictum, the happy families are not alike. There is a great variety here, from Chinese to Haitian to Mennonite families, and different family members being featured—aunts and uncles as well as grandparents. There is trauma and there is goodness, and for many of the writers, there is reconciliation.

Family memoirs may tell the story of how the writer relates to several members of the family, particularly while growing up. The family memoir could also demonstrate how the family dynamic, particularly involving the parents, formed the relationships among the various family members. In two cases here, the family memoir also stretches to the extended family, as the writer seeks to learn more about a special aunt or uncle.

Chang, Pang-Mei Natasha (1965–)

Bound Feet & Western Dress. Anchor Books, 1997, 1996. 215pp. ill. 8 pp. of plates. 9780385479646. Also available in audiobook. 305.420951

Studying Chinese history at Harvard, American-born Pang-Mei Natasha Chang came across the name of her grandaunt, Chang Yu-i, in a history book. She had met this grandaunt when she was a young girl, but had never realized that she might have done anything extraordinary. What she discovered when she sought her out to hear her story was that Chang Yu-i grew up without her feet being bound, was the first Chinese woman to have a Western-style divorce, and had directed the Shanghai Women's Savings Bank. Hearing her grandaunt's story helped Pang-Mei resolve her own issues of cultural identity and break out of traditional expectations by marrying outside her cultural heritage. At the same time that she tells her grandaunt's story, in Chang Yu-i's voice, Pang-Mei also paints a vivid portrait of China in its last days of Confucianism.

Subjects: China; Chinese-Americans; Culture Clash; Family Portraits; Feminists; Generation Gap; Grandaunts; Social History, China; Women in China; Yu-i, Chang

Now Try: Another Chinese-American has written a memoir in dual voices: William Poy Lee uses his own and his mother's voices to describe his mother's life as an immigrant to the United States in ***The Eighth Promise: An American Son's Tribute to His Toisanese Mother***. Foot binding, a long-standing tradition in China, is fascinating to many Westerners; readers may be quite interested in Beverley Jackson's illustrated history of the practice, ***Splendid Slippers: A Thousand Years of an Erotic Tradition***. Children of immigrants often look to the older people in their family lineage to derive a sense of their cultural heritage. In the case of Sasha Su-Ling Welland, she followed the story of her grandmother and her grandaunt, both independent women, and writes about them in ***A Thousand Miles of Dreams: The Journeys of Two Chinese Sisters***.

Danticat, Edwidge (1969–)

Brother, I'm Dying. Knopf, 2007. 272pp. 9781400041152. Also available in large print, audiobook, e-audiobook, and e-book. 813.54

Danticat begins this family memoir on the day that she receives the joint news of her pregnancy and the terminal illness of her father. She then goes back and forth in time to recall Uncle Joseph, her "second father," who raised her in Haiti for eight years while her parents were trying to make a better life for them all in the United States. She describes her uncle's efforts to help his fellow Haitians, initially through politics, and then through his Baptist ministry, and his gentle parenting of her in the absence of her own parents. She describes her life as an exile in New York City after she is brought there by her parents at the age of twelve. Danticat includes Haitian social conditions and history as part of her family history and ends with the ugly story of her uncle's death, at the age of eighty-one, while being detained in the Krome Detention Center in Miami.

Danticat was nominated for the National Book Award for Nonfiction and was the winner of a Christopher Award and the National Book Critics Circle Award in Autobiography for ***Brother, I'm Dying***; she was the recipient of a MacArthur Fellowship in 2009.

Subjects: Christopher Awards; Death of a Parent; Family Relationships; Fathers and Daughters; Haiti; Haitian-Americans; Homeland Security; National Book Critics Circle Award in Autobiography; Politics, Haiti; Social History, Haiti; Uncles; Writers

Now Try: Conditions in Haiti are difficult for most people, but one group not often heard about are the poor, illegitimate children who are taken to be unpaid "servants" of the rich. One such child, Jean-Robert Cadet, made his way to the United States, where he was able to get an education and then tell his story in ***Restavec: From Haitian Slave Child to Middle-Class American***. Keith Fleming, as he describes in ***The Boy with a Thorn in His Side: A Memoir***, lived with a very different kind of uncle, the writer Edmund White, but was equally loved and cared for by him, after suffering from an abusive father. Despite the sorrows in her memoir, Danticat's book is uplifting, a trait of Billie Letts's novel about two children in search of a family, ***Made in the U.S.A.***

Gilmore, Mikal (1951–)

Shot in the Heart. Anchor Books/Doubleday, 1995, 1994. 403pp. ill. 9780385478007. Also available in audiobook, e-audiobook, e-book, and video. 364.15230973

Fifteen years after his older brother Gary was executed by firing squad in Utah, Mikal Gilmore began the research into his family and its history that he hoped would shed some light on why his brother had become a killer. Mikal already knew that both parents were violent in word and deed, toward each other and their children, but he needed to explore further, to see where the truths lay in the stories they told and where the myths were. Because for much of Mikal's life the family's attention had been directed toward Gary and the trouble he got into, Mikal's purpose in writing this book was also to find his own place in the family, so that the book is not so much the story of his brother, but of the family as a whole, a family that for all its dysfunction still held together as a unit.

Shot in the Heart was nominated for the Hammett Prize and won the *Los Angeles Times* Book Prize for Biography and the National Book Critics Circle Award in Biography/Autobiography; it was also selected as a Notable Book by the American Library Association.

Subjects: ALA Notable Books; Brothers; Domestic Violence; Dysfunctional Families; Executions; Family Relationships; Fathers and Sons; Gilmore, Gary; *Los Angeles Times* Book Prize for Biography; Mormons; Murder; National Book Critics Circle Award in Biography/Autobiography

Now Try: Two years after Gary Gilmore's execution, Norman Mailer published an award-winning novel about the event, ***The Executioner's Song***. It's not often that the family member of a murderer will write about the murderous relative, but Jeffrey Dahmer's father, Lionel, also did so, also in an effort to understand how his son's sociopathic behavior could have happened, which he explores in ***A Father's Story***. Michael Patrick MacDonald also grew up with violence, but it was outside his house in South Boston; he too looks at his family history, as he lost four brothers to violence, in ***All Souls: A Family Story from Southie***. One of the more newsworthy items in Gilmore's case was that he fought legally to have himself executed; a different look at capital punishment is provided by John Grisham in ***The Chamber***.

Harrison, Kathryn (1961–)

The Kiss. Random House, 1997. 207pp. 9780679449997. Also available in audiobook (read by the author). 306.8742

While this memoir is ostensibly about the incestuous relationship Harrison had with her father for four years, it is also about her mother and Kathryn's emotionally impoverished childhood. The affair Harrison recounts in the present tense, but she provides flashbacks to her childhood, revealing how her maternal grandparents sent her teenage father away when she was six months old. Her mother left when she was six, leaving Kathryn with her grandparents. A childhood of self-cutting, eating disorders, and suicidal depression followed. When her father visited her family when Kathryn was twenty, they all spent a week together, at the end of which Kathryn took her father to the airport. He kissed her good-bye in a sexually provocative manner and thus began their affair. The writing style is emotionless and numb, meant to be a catharsis for her, as she said the fact of this affair was getting in the way of her writing. A later book, ***The Mother Knot***, detailing her depression and reversion to anorexia when she was in her forties, would suggest that her first memoir was not as successful as she'd hoped.

Subjects: Adult Children; Dysfunctional Families; Eating Disorders; Family Relationships; Fathers and Daughters; Grandparents; Incest; Mothers and Daughters; Writers

Now Try: Harrison's memoir has received much praise for its writing, described as "powerfully written." Ironically, that same phrase was used to describe Simone de Beauvoir's trailblazing book on feminism, ***The Second Sex,*** edited and translated from the French by H. M. Parshley. What goes on in Harrison's book is very disturbing to most readers—there is hardly any explicit sex, but the fact of it is understood. Robert M. Polhemus studies the relationships between older men and younger women throughout history in ***Lot's Daughters: Sex, Redemption, and Women's Quest for Authority***. The emotionally wrenching nature of Harrison's memoir can also be found in Richard Flanagan's award-winning novel, ***The Sound of One Hand Clapping,*** the story of a young Tasmanian girl abandoned by her mother and beaten by her father.

Hogan, Linda (1947–)

The Woman Who Watches Over the World: A Native Memoir. W. W. Norton, 2002, 2001. 207pp. 9780393323054. 818.5409

Linda Hogan has suffered much pain in her life, but though she had expected her memoir to be about pain, she was surprised to find that it was, after all, about love. It's not a linear, chronological tale, but rather snippets of anecdotes, remembrances, and reflections about herself and her family life and also about the larger family, the American Indian family, to which she belongs. She tells stories about those who have gone before as well as stories of those who were in her present. Her father was an alcoholic army sergeant, so she lived abroad as well as Stateside; her mother was withdrawn and silent. Hogan had what she calls a "love affair" with a much older man when she was a very young teen. As an adult, after overcoming alcoholism, she adopted two children who suffered from attachment disorders; she fell from a horse and suffered amnesia; she had fibromyalgia. She discusses the treatment of her people at the hands of the invaders and the treatment of the earth at the hands of all humans. Throughout it all, however, she offers a calmness and hope that life will be better—for her, for her people, and for the earth.

Subjects: Adoption; Alcoholics; American Indian Women; Chickasaw Nation; Family Relationships; Fathers and Daughters; Mothers and Daughters; Pain; Reflections; Self-Acceptance; Writers

Now Try: Barry Holstun Lopez is a great admirer of Hogan as a poet and writer; his collection of stories, ***Field Notes: The Grace Note of the Canyon Wren,*** is quite in keeping with Hogan's theme of stewardship of the land. Brenda Peterson, a naturalist who has worked with Linda Hogan, has written her own memoir, a love story about her relationship with animals, ***Build Me an Ark: A Life with Animals***. Readers who enjoy Linda Hogan's writing may also enjoy the writing of Lee Maracle, a member of the Stó:lō Nation in British Columbia; a novel that seems particularly apt here is Maracle's ***Daughters Are Forever***.

Homes, A. M. (1961–)

The Mistress's Daughter. Viking, 2007. 238pp. ill. 9780670038381. Also available in large print, audiobook, and e-audiobook. 362.734092

Novelist Amy Homes was thirty-one when her biological mother came looking for her. As Homes learned, her mother had arranged for adoption even before the birth, as the father was an older married man with whom Ellen Ballman had been having an affair. Having discovered her parents, Homes became preoccupied with learning about her biological heritage, although her father was less than cooperative. The first half of this memoir was originally conceived as an article for *The New Yorker*, narrating the story of her mother's appearance; included here with that story are Homes's subsequent efforts to learn more about her own biological background and a mock trial wherein she angrily interrogates her father. She concludes, however, with a return to the family who raised her, providing a loving tribute to her adoptive grandmother.

Subjects: Adoptees; Adoption; Birth Mothers; Family Relationships; Fathers and Daughters; Grandmothers; Identity (Psychology); Mothers and Daughters

Now Try: Homes discovered that through her biological father she was eligible to apply for membership in the Daughters of the American Revolution (although he refused to help her); Sarah Culberson, in tracing her own biological parents, discovered that her father was a Sierra Leone prince, a story she tells with the help of Tracy Trivas in ***A Princess Found: An American Family, an African Chiefdom, and the Daughter Who Connected Them All***. Although Homes's mother did not appear distressed at giving up her daughter, many women from that time period suffered greatly from societal pressure regarding pregnancies outside of marriage. Ann Fessler has created a collage of oral histories from women in mid-century America who gave their children up for adoption, ***The Girls Who Went Away: The Hidden History of Women Who Surrendered Children for Adoption in the Decades Before* Roe v. Wade**. Maureen O'Brien wrote a novel, ***B-Mother***, about a teenager who gives up her child for adoption and how she anticipates his various childhood stages while waiting for him to be old enough to search out his birth mother.

Janzen, Rhoda

Mennonite in a Little Black Dress: A Memoir of Going Home. Henry Holt and Co., 2009. 241pp. 9780805089257. Also available in large print, audiobook, and e-audiobook. 811.6

Rhoda Janzen, a poet and college professor, thought her life was in good shape until she suffered a number of setbacks in a relatively short time. Her first upset came from botched surgery that rendered her almost an invalid for several months, a time she got through with the help of her husband and her girlfriends. Once she was back on track, however, her husband told her he was leaving her for a man he'd met on the Internet; that same week she was hurt in a car accident. The only solution she could come up with to nurse her wounds was to go home to California, to her Mennonite parents, to a way of life she had exchanged for another. Her mother's love and ebullience, along with her own self-examination and recognition of the life that actually had not been in such good shape, help her find her way again.

Subjects: Accident Victims; College Professors; Family Relationships; Gay Husbands; Homecomings; Humor; Mennonites; Mothers and Daughters; Poets

Now Try: Going home again is a fairly common theme in literature, home meaning many things to many people. In Pamela Duncan's novel ***Plant Life,*** the protagonist goes back to her small town in North Carolina, determined not to work in the textile plant there. The wry humor in Janzen's memoir has been compared to Garrison Keillor, as he depicts a different religious culture, Minnesotan Lutherans, in ***Life Among the Lutherans***, edited by Holly Harden. Being married to a closeted gay man is not so uncommon as one might think; Dina Matos McGreevey, the wife of New Jersey's former governor, Jim McGreevey, tells her own story in ***Silent Partner: A Memoir of My Marriage***.

Sage, Lorna (1943–2001)

Bad Blood. Perennial, 2003, 2000. 281pp. 9780060938086. Also available in large print, audiobook, e-audiobook, and e-book. 942.939

While Lorna Sage's father was fighting in World War II, she and her mother lived with her grandparents in the small village of Hanmer, Wales, near the English border. Her grandfather was a vicar, but a lecherous, eccentric man, and her grandmother was an iconoclast in the realm of domesticity, refusing to take care of her home or anyone living in it. Sage's mother was not much better, with the result that Sage grew up a very neglected child. Life at school was not good either, Dickensian in nature and rough in the schoolyard. Somehow, though, Sage inherited her grandfather's love of books and reading and was able to attain a scholarship to Durham University. Iconoclastic in her own way, she kept the child she bore as a teenager and married the child's father, both of them determined to succeed at university. A noted literary critic, Sage obviously did succeed at university, and in writing this memoir, she also recognizes how she was part of the new generation establishing new mores, by keeping her child and forging ahead to make a life for herself and her family.

Bad Blood was the winner of the Whitbread Literary Award in Biography (now the Costa Book Award).

Subjects: 1950s; Childhood and Youth; Dysfunctional Families; England; Grandparents; Literary Critics, England; Small Towns, England; Teenage Mothers; Whitbread Literary Award in Biography; Working-Class Families

Now Try: Noted biographer Michael Holroyd also brought himself up from a dismal childhood in England, one aspect of which he describes in ***Basil Street Blues***. Susan Fletcher's novel, ***Eve Green,*** tells the story of a young girl also living with her grandparents in rural Wales. Those who enjoy the wry humor of Sage's memoir may also enjoy Kate Bingham's novel, ***Mummy's Legs: A Novel,*** the wryly told story of a young girl who feels obliged to take on the domestic responsibilities that her parents abnegate.

Seth, Vikram (1952–)

Two Lives. HarperCollins, 2005. 503pp. ill. 24pp. of plates. 9780060599669. Also available in Braille, audiobook (read by the author), and e-book. 828.91409

Vikram Seth's mother suggested he write something about his "Shanti Uncle," particularly as his uncle was not doing well following the death of his wife, Henny. In interviewing his uncle, Seth discovered much about Indian history in the twentieth century, as well as the story of how his uncle had lost his right forearm during World War II yet became a successful dentist. He also learned about Shanti's studies in Germany, which is how Shanti came to meet Henny, whose letters Vikram discovered in a trunk in the attic. He realized he had found a gold mine, and the story took on a life of its own. Apart from his uncle's story, he now had the story of his Jewish aunt's correspondence after the war, trying to discover what had actually happened in Germany during the war with family and friends, and how she discovered the tragic fate of her mother and her sister. This final product, then, is the story of two people from widely divergent cultures and histories, their lives separate and together, and the histories of their countries as well, with the author's presence interwoven.

Two Lives was a finalist for the National Book Critics Circle Award in Autobiography/Memoir.

Subjects: Aunts; Family Relationships; Germany; India; London, England; Seth, Henny; Seth, Shanti; Uncles; World War II (1939-1945); Writers, Indic

Now Try: Christopher Isherwood wrote a family memoir similar to Seth's, but his subjects were his own parents, ***Kathleen and Frank***. Vikram Seth's first book, ***The Golden Gate,*** was a novel in verse. Padma Hejmadi is an Indic writer whose prose is also poetic, as seen in ***Room to Fly: A Transcultural Memoir***. Another intercultural marriage affected by world affairs is the subject of a novel by Kurban Said, ***Ali and Nino,*** translated from the German by Jenia Graman.

Staples, Brent A. (1951–)

Parallel Time: Growing Up in Black and White. Perennial, 2000, 1994. 274pp. 9780380724758. 070.41092

When he was being interviewed for a job at *The Washington Post,* Brent Staples was asked the kinds of questions he had been asking himself all his life; he wrote this memoir to help find the answers. Why did he, the oldest of nine children in a poor African-American family living in a small industrial town, wind up with a doctorate in psychology when many others in his family were hooked on drugs and/or crime? He frames his book with the death of his younger brother, Blake, a drug dealer shot down by a rival when he was twenty-two. He begins with the autopsy report on his brother and ends with a trip to his grave, visiting the site for the first time. But it is not just his brother who haunts him; his father had been an alcoholic who drank most of his wages, forcing them all to move often because of eviction, but his mother would offer her hand to anyone who needed help. Even as Staples's path began to diverge seriously from that of other members of his family, he still was part of that family, and began to wonder "how do I as an achiever and educated person love and nurture my family?" (Peterson, 1994).

Parallel Time was a finalist for the *Los Angeles Times* Current Interest Book Prize and won the Anisfield-Wolf Book Award.

Subjects: African-American Men; Anisfield-Wolf Book Award; Chester, PA; Children of Alcoholics; Death of a Sibling; Family Relationships; Journalists; Murder; Newspaper Editors; Poverty; Small Towns

Now Try: Apart from family, one of the overriding themes in Staples's life is the stereotype of the Black male. Mark Anthony Neal has written a book, ***New Black Man***, on his idea of what the twenty-first-century Black male should be striving for. Staples's title has differing reference points; one is the word "White" and the White world of academe in which he found himself. Brian Copeland grew up literally in a White world, the White suburb of San Leandro, California; he describes what that life was like in ***Not a Genuine Black Man, or, How I Learned to be Black in the Lily-White Suburbs***. The racist overtones of *The Washington Post* interviewer's questions notwithstanding, there is a new publication by that newspaper that has collected essays from a variety of staff, ***Being a Black Man: At the Corner of Progress and Peril***, edited by Kevin Merida.

Thompson, Craig (1975–)

Blankets: An Illustrated Novel. Top Shelf, 2006, 2003. 582pp. ill. 9781891830433. 741.5973092

In this coming-of-age graphic narrative of growing up in rural Wisconsin in a religious fundamentalist family, Craig Thompson begins with his early childhood and his younger brother, Phil. Normal sibling rivalry was part of their growing up, particularly as they shared a bed and a thin blanket. He illustrates the kind of family life he experienced, with fundamentalist parents and their religious community. He was also a victim of abuse by a babysitter when he was young and suffered much bullying from his peers and many adults as he grew older, all of which he illustrates clearly. He moves on to his adolescence and his relationship with another outsider he met at a winter religious camp. Using his illustrations to complement his words, he depicts the beauty and angst of first love. He also reveals how his parents and their community decried his art, particularly the more imaginative depictions he created. By the end of the memoir he has lost Raina, his first love, and his religion, but he has realized that his art will be his medium, as he so deftly illustrates in this memoir.

Subjects: Alienation; Bullying; Coming of Age; Family Relationships; First Love; Graphic Narratives; Religious Fundamentalism; Wisconsin

Now Try: David B. also penned a graphic narrative, ***Epileptic***, about his family after they discovered that his brother had epilepsy. Alissa Torres and illustrator Choi combined their talents to create the illustrated memoir ***American Widow***, about Torres's loss of her husband on September 11, 2001. The lyricism in Thompson's memoir can also be found in another book about love, a collection of love stories edited by Jeffrey Eugenides, ***My Mistress's Sparrow Is Dead: Great Love Stories from Chekhov to Munro.***

Tucker, Neely (1963–)

Love in the Driest Season: A Family Memoir. Three Rivers Press, 2005, 2004. 276pp. ill. 9781400081608. Also available in audiobook and e-audiobook. 364.734092

The first family to be created in this memoir is that of the author and his wife, Vita, an African-American woman eleven years Tucker's senior; initially their common bond was that their families came from the South—hers from Alabama and his from Mississippi, although he grew up in a White, racist community. They met in Detroit as next-door neighbors and fell in love. As a journalist for the *Detroit Free Press* Neely was sent to Zimbabwe to cover the political situation there. Unable to get a work permit, Vita volunteered to work in an orphanage. It was not long before they discovered a baby who captured their hearts and whom they wanted to adopt to complete their family. Given the fact that through their intervention they saved the baby's life and kept her alive, they thought that adopting her in Robert Mugabe's nationalistic, anti-American country would be relatively easy. As Neely describes in this memoir, however, such was not the case. Apart from the wrenching story of this infant found abandoned in the high grass and the bureaucratic frustrations the Tuckers suffered time and again, this memoir also paints a picture of the tragedies visited upon Zimbabwe by both AIDS and the country's autocratic president.

Love in the Driest Season was the winner of a Christopher Award.

Subjects: Adoption; African-American Women; Christopher Awards; HIV/AIDS; International Adoption; Interracial Marriage; Journalists; Mugabe, Robert; Orphanages; Zimbabwe

Now Try: Interracial adoption is not that unusual, but for Sharon Rush, a White civil rights law professor, adopting an African-American child was an eye-opener for her as she discovered how much she had to learn about racism. She tells her tale in ***Loving Across the Color Line: A White Adoptive Mother Learns About Race.*** The Tuckers were overwhelmed by witnessing every day the ravages of HIV/AIDS. Greg Behrman has taken the United States to task for ignoring this global situation, offering portraits of those trying to help and those in need in ***The Invisible People: How the U.S. Has Slept Through the Global AIDS Pandemic, the Greatest Humanitarian Catastrophe of Our Time.*** On the uplifting side is Melissa Fay Greene's story of how an Ethiopian woman, Haregewoin Teferra, is doing what she can, one child at a time, in ***There Is No Me Without You: One Woman's Odyssey to Rescue Africa's Children.***

Parents Through the Child's Eye

Here the focus is on the parents from the point of view of the child. In most cases, the memoir is a remembrance of growing up with those parents, but in the case of Martin Goldsmith, it is the story of discovering his parents' history when he himself is an adult. Not surprisingly, there are both happy families and unhappy families here, along with a broad spectrum of experiences.

Memoirs of parents through a child's eye are a look back by an adult writer at the child and how that child was raised, often as a means of coming to understand the parents better. If the childhood was difficult, the story usually does not reflect well on the parents. In one case in this section, however, the adult child makes a discovery about his parents that he wants to share with readers.

Goldsmith, Martin (1952–)

The Inextinguishable Symphony: A True Story of Music and Love in Nazi Germany. Wiley, 2000. 346pp. ill. 9780471350972. Also available in audiobook and video. 940.53180922

Martin Goldsmith was forty when he learned about his parents' past as musicians in Nazi Germany, both members of the Jüdische Kulturbund, a Jewish cultural association. After visiting the Holocaust Museum in Washington, DC, radio announcer Goldsmith asked his father what it was like to have lived in Germany at that time. What his father finally told him, after years of silence, led Goldsmith on a mission to research his parents' story and perhaps at the same time to get a better sense of himself. He tells the story of his parents: their love, their participation in the Kulturbund, and their fortunate and timely escape from Nazi Germany. He also talks about the relatives (his grandfather and uncle among them) who didn't make it. At the same time he offers the history of the Kulturbund, with reflections on what it meant to both the Nazis and the Jewish community. Goldsmith initiated a project whose formal name is The Jüdischer Kulturbund Project, a multimedia project designed to inform people about the Kulturbund (http://www.judischekulturbund.com). He took his book title from a work of that name by the Danish composer Carl Nielsen.

Subjects: Germany; Goldsmith, George; Goldsmith, Rosemary; Holocaust, Jewish (1939–1945); Jewish Men; Jewish Musicians; Jüdischer Kulturbund; Musicians; Self-Discovery

Now Try: Alma Rosé, the niece of Gustav Mahler, was an orchestra conductor in Auschwitz, mitigating the harshness of life for many women in the camp. Although she herself died in the camp, her story has been researched and told by Richard Newman and Karen Kirtley: ***Alma Rosé: Vienna to Auschwitz.*** The power of music for both performer and listener is reflected in Nathan Shaham's ***The Rosendorf Quartet: A Novel,*** translated from the Hebrew by Dalya Bilu, featuring musicians who fled Germany for Palestine. A more modern setting of war is Sarajevo; Steven Galloway's novel, ***The Cellist of Sarajevo,*** focuses on that war, as the title character honors the dead by playing solo in the street every afternoon.

Gray, Francine du Plessix (1930–)

Them: A Memoir of Parents. Penguin, 2005. 529pp. ill. 9781594200496. Also available in e-book. 974.70922

Gray, a biographer and novelist, has turned her research and writing talents to her mother and stepfather, tracing their story from their early days in Czarist Russia to their deaths in New York City. Gray's mother, Tatiana, was initially married to a French count, Francine's father. After the count was killed in the Second World War, Tatiana married Alexander Liberman, a wealthy playboy. Once they moved to New York they quickly made their way to the top of the haut monde, she as a hat designer for Saks and he, first as artistic editor of *Vogue* and then as second-in-command to the director of Condé Nast. Francine was sorely neglected as a child, but she made her own life, finding friends and relatives to act as surrogate parents and immersing herself in school. The world she depicts, the world of her parents, drips with names from the fashion and design world, as well as the world of culture—music, literature, and dance. Despite the detached parenting she received, by the time she has finished her memoir she has come to understand her parents better and, apparently, has come to forgive them as well.

Them was the winner of a National Book Critics Circle Award in Autobiography/Memoir.

Subjects: Condé Nast Publications; Fashion Designers; Iakovleva, Tatiana; Immigrants; Liberman, Alexander; Narcissism; National Book Critics Circle Award in Autobiography/Memoir; New York, NY; Stepfathers; Upper Class; Writers

Now Try: Alexander Liberman, Francine's stepfather, was an artist in his own right and a man of great influence in the publishing world. Readers may be interested in reading more about him, perhaps the biography by Barbara Rose, ***Alexander Liberman***. Sean Wilsey grew up in high society as well, but on the other side of the country, a world he describes in ***Oh the Glory of It All***. Gray was inspired to write her own memoir of her parents because of writers who had gone before her, notably Mary Gordon, whose ***Circling My Mother*** discusses Gordon's relationship with her mother, who suffered from alcoholism and dementia. (Gray's mother was addicted to prescription drugs.) Gray's portrait of her parents was referred to as an unforgettable memoir, as was Fergus M. Bordewich's memoir of his mother, LaVerne Madigan, a woman he was very close to and whose tragic death he witnessed. He found a hidden woman though, as he researched his memoir, ***My Mother's Ghost***.

Lindbergh, Reeve (1945–)

Under a Wing: A Memoir. Isis Publishing, 2009, 1998. 223pp. ill. 9780684807706. Also available in large print, audiobook, and e-book. 629.13092

Reeve Lindbergh is the youngest of the five children that Charles A. Lindbergh and Anne Morrow Lindbergh had after the kidnapping of their first-born son. Her parents were deeply affected by that tragedy, particularly her father, who insisted on absolute privacy and moving several times when the children were small, in an effort to maintain the isolation he craved. The children, however, were largely unaware of the tragedy that had befallen their parents. While their father was rigorous in his expectations of his children, their mother was a gentler sort, and the children grew up quite happily in their New England home. Lindbergh, a novelist, describes both difficult and tender moments, not just of their childhood, but also of their adulthood, such as the time her mother sat with her at the deathbed of her own child, sharing a similar grief.

Subjects: Death of a Child; Family Relationships; Fathers and Daughters; Lindbergh, Anne Morrow; Lindbergh, Charles; Mothers and Daughters; Pilots; Writers; Writers in the Family

Now Try: Lindbergh has just recently published a memoir more about herself, ***Forward from Here: Leaving Middle Age—and Other Unexpected Adventures***. The eloquence of Lindbergh's recollections is also found in those of another writer, Chris Offutt, who describes going back to his old home in Kentucky in ***No Heroes: A Memoir of Coming Home***. Readers who appreciate the gentleness of Lindbergh's memoir are likely to appreciate as well the memoir of Lewis Buzbee, ***The Yellow-Lighted Bookshop: A Memoir, a History***. Another daughter who grew up as a happy child of famous parents is Cheryl Rogers-Barnett, who tells the story of her childhood with help from Frank Thompson, in ***Cowboy Princess: Life with My Parents, Roy Rogers and Dale Evans***.

Uhlberg, Myron (1933–)

Hands of My Father: A Hearing Boy, His Deaf Parents, and the Language of Love. Bantam Books, 2009, 2008. 232pp. ill. 9780553806885. Also available in large print and e-book. 306.87409

Growing up as the hearing child of deaf parents, Uhlberg's first language was American Sign Language. Once he learned his oral language, he became his parents' interpreter. But his father especially wanted to know more than just what hearing people (such as Myron's teachers) were saying. He was fascinated by the concept of sound and was forever asking Myron to describe such sounds as those made by waves, a challenge difficult to consider. Myron grew up near Coney Island in Brooklyn, in a world of love and reading and Jackie Robinson. He also grew up bearing the responsibility of listening for his epileptic brother's seizures and facing prejudices because of his parents' disability. But his love and respect for his parents, engendered by their own resilience and love of life, shine through in this memoir.

Subjects: 1940s; American Sign Language; Books and Reading; Brooklyn (New York, NY); Children of Deaf Adults; Children's Writers; Deaf Culture; Epilepsy; Family Relationships

Now Try: Lennard J. Davis had a similar childhood to Uhlberg's, which he describes in ***My Sense of Silence: Memoirs of a Childhood with Deafness***. If you're interested in reading more about deaf culture, you might find interesting

Deaf in America: Voices from a Culture, by Carol Padden and Tom Humphries. The novelist Joseph Heller also grew up in 1940s Brooklyn, an environment he describes in ***Now and Then: From Coney Island to Here***.

Walker, Rebecca (1970–)

Black, White, and Jewish: Autobiography of a Shifting Self. Riverhead Books, 2001. 320pp. 9781573221696. 973.04092

Rebecca Walker might have thought she was simply born at the wrong time. Her mother, the writer Alice Walker, married a Jewish civil rights lawyer at the beginning of the Civil Rights Movement. Their marriage was illegal in Mississippi, but it was, among other things, an attempt to prove that one could easily integrate Black and White. Their marriage collapsed, however, with Alice Walker and Mel Leventhal deciding to divide their daughter's time between them in two-year segments. This meant that she lived in her mother's Afric-centered Bohemian community in California for two years and then in her father's White, Jewish community on the East Coast for two years. Back and forth she went, wondering who she was, where she belonged. She was dealing not only with culture, but also with religion, and, obviously, with a broken home, with parents who allowed her too much freedom in lieu of attention. In her memoir, Rebecca openly talks about the fallout, but she finally encountered some wise teachers who, recognizing her situation, told her to concentrate on her own skills and talents, allowing her to put her cultural-identity issues in the background.

Subjects: African-American Women; Biracial Children; Children of Divorce; Fathers and Daughters; Identity (Psychology); Interracial Marriage; Jewish Women; Mothers and Daughters; Walker, Alice

Now Try: When parents of mixed cultures marry, they often don't realize that their children will have issues that they themselves cannot understand: Where do they belong? A number of biracial "children" are now writing about this in their own memoirs, as they have struggled through or perhaps continue to struggle through their confused emotions. Danzy Senna is one of these, a writer who has penned her own journey of self-discovery, ***Where Did You Sleep Last Night? A Personal History***. William S. Cohen and Janet Langhart Cohen cowrote the memoir of their marriage, ***Love in Black and White: A Memoir of Race, Religion, and Romance***; he is half-Jewish and White, she African-American, a story not unlike the story of Walker's parents. The situation that Walker and others like her find themselves in is not always so different from the situation that children of immigrant parents find themselves in. The stories collected by Angela Jane Fountas reveal the similarities: ***Waking Up American: Coming of Age Biculturally; First-Generation Women Reflect on Identity***.

Mothers

Here the reader will find books of praise for the writer's mother from three men and a woman. Two other daughters, however, had very difficult times with their mothers, finding themselves with much to work through. Adding something different to the mix is the story of a mother and her adult daughter traveling together and coming closer together as a result.

These memoirs about mothers are largely elegiac in tone, describing the hardships the writers' mothers endured and the strong efforts they made to raise their children well. As the children become adults they learn a new appreciation for the sacrifices their mothers made. But illness also plays a part for two daughters, as they look back at what life was like with mothers who suffered from mental illness.

Bragg, Rick (1959–)

All Over but the Shoutin'. Vintage Books, 1998, 1997. 329pp. ill. 9780679774020. Also available in large print, audiobook, and e-book. 070.92

Bragg was often told by others as he was growing up that he was nothing but "poor, White trash." He might have stayed that way, but for his mother. Married to an abusive alcoholic who had a habit of abandoning her and returning, only to leave again, she worked hard all her life to raise her children honorably and to help them make something of their lives that she could never make of her own. While a depiction of the harshness of Bragg's childhood, this is also a book in homage to his mother. Part of Bragg's story is his journey toward becoming a journalist; he wins a Pulitzer Prize for his feature writing for *The New York Times*. He recounts in great detail his mother's first flight ever, going to New York for the award ceremony, and her introduction to such things as an escalator. He ends the story with his delight at being able finally to buy her a house of her own.

All Over but the Shoutin' was an American Booksellers Book of the Year (ABBY) Honor book and was selected as a Notable Book by the American Library Association.

Subjects: ALA Notable Books; Alabama; American South; Bragg, Margaret; Childhood and Youth; Children of Alcoholics; Journalists; Mothers and Sons; Poverty; Rural Life; Working-Class Families; Working Poor

Now Try: Bragg followed this memoir with one about his mother's family and her childhood, ***Ava's Man***. Novelist Harry Crews also had a hardscrabble life, in Georgia; he doesn't skimp on the details in his memoir, ***A Childhood, the Biography of a Place***. Lorna Goodison, a Jamaican poet, pays homage to her mother, a woman who raised nine children in difficult circumstances in Kingston, in ***From Harvey River: A Memoir of My Mother and Her Island***. The evocative writing style of Bragg is echoed in Tony Earley's fiction, for example, ***The Blue Star: A Novel***, the sequel to ***Jim the Boy: A Novel***, set in North Carolina.

Faderman, Lillian (1940–)

Naked in the Promised Land. Houghton Mifflin, 2003. 350pp. ill. 9780618128754. Also available in e-book. 305.48092

Much of Lillian Faderman's early life was devoted to the idea of helping and/or rescuing her mother, Mary. Her mother was a Jewish immigrant who had come to the United States with her younger sister with high hopes of success. Instead she could find work only in a sweatshop, and she became pregnant by a man who would not acknowledge his paternity. Compounding her guilt and adding to her psychoses was the fact that her family did not survive the Holocaust. Because of her mother's fragility, Faderman set herself the goal of becoming an actress in order to free her mother from her life of drudgery. As her memoir details, her plans too took a different route, as she found herself posing for "girlie" magazines in high school and working in burlesque and at a strip club to support herself through university. She also describes coming to recognize her sexual orientation and details the various relationships she had until she finally met the right woman. Currently an expert in the field of gay studies and particularly lesbian history, Faderman provides a clear picture of life for lesbians in the 1960s and 1970s.

Naked in the Promised Land was selected as a Notable Book by the American Library Association and won the Lambda Literary Award for Autobiography/Memoir.

Subjects: ALA Notable Books; College Professors; Exotic Dancers; Fatherless Children; Feminists; Lambda Literary Award for Autobiography/Memoir; Lesbians; Los Angeles, CA; Mothers and Daughters; Trailblazers

Now Try: Betty Berzon suffered mentally because of her sexual orientation. She underwent serious psychiatric treatment that ended in her becoming a gay activist, all of which she recounts in ***Surviving Madness: A Therapist's Own Story***. Women of all sorts work in strip clubs; Diablo Cody tried it on a whim and liked it, as she tells in her memoir, ***Candy Girl: A Year in the Life of an Unlikely Stripper***. Elizabeth Berg has written a collection of short stories that may resonate with readers who appreciate Faderman's breaking of the mold: ***The Day I Ate Whatever I Wanted: And Other Small Acts of Liberation***.

Holman, Virginia

Rescuing Patty Hearst: Memories from a Decade Gone Mad. Simon & Schuster, 2003. 244pp. 9780743222853. Also available in large print and audiobook. 616.89092

Although Patty Hearst was Holman's idol as a child, she doesn't actually figure much in this memoir of growing up with a mother whose schizophrenia develops into a severe and untreatable psychosis. In addition to narrating the years spent in a cabin with her mother and younger sister, prepared and waiting for a war that didn't come and that didn't bring the expected wounded children, Holman also raises questions about how her mother's illness was allowed to proceed to the point of no return and how her children were allowed to participate in the fantasies of that illness. Holman's father did what he believed best, but his best proved not to be enough against the strong will of his wife, who refused treatment until it was too late to repair her broken mind.

Holman originally submitted part of this manuscript for *DoubleTake Magazine*, an essay for which she won a Pushcart Prize.

Subjects: Illness in the Family; Mental Health; Mothers and Daughters; Schizophrenia; Virginia

Now Try: Jacki Lyden's mother also refused to accept treatment for her mania, which created in her such delusions as the notion that she was the Queen of Sheba—thus the title for Lyden's memoir, ***Daughter of the Queen of Sheba***. Leslie Garis is the granddaughter of Howard R. Garis, the creator of Uncle Wiggily Longears, and of Tom Swift, under the pseudonym Victor Appleton; her grandmother, Lilian, wrote some of the early *Bobbsey Twins* stories. Growing up with these storytellers was not so wonderful as one might think, however. Garis reveals the mental and physical illness that seemed to be a part of her childhood in her memoir, ***House of Happy Endings***. Patrick Austin Tracey took an almost clinical interest in the schizophrenia that was part of his family life, his two sisters having fallen victim to it. In ***Stalking Irish Madness: Searching for the Roots of My Family's Schizophrenia***, he returns to Ireland, wondering if there is something in the Irish makeup itself that would contribute to such an illness.

Kidd, Sue Monk (1948–), and Ann Kidd Taylor

Traveling with Pomegranates: A Mother-Daughter Story. Viking, 2009. 282pp. 9780670021208. Also available in large print, audiobook, e-audiobook, and e-book. 818.6

Both mother and daughter were on the brink of new phases in their lives when they decided to travel together, first to Greece and Turkey, and then to France. Kidd was about to turn fifty and was trying to make sense of having visualized a swarm of bees, wondering if she could create something from that. (***The Secret Life of Bees*** was published two years after they ended their travels.) Taylor (Kidd at the time) had graduated from college and was unsure of where she should head, having been turned down at graduate school. In alternating chapters each woman offers riffs on their travels, on the significance of the sights they see, and on the relationship that is strengthening between them. Theirs is a collaboration in a meditative, spiritually oriented dual memoir of time that helps them see their way more clearly.

Subjects: France; Greece; Mothers and Daughters; Novelists; Self-Discovery; Spirituality; Travel; Turkey; Writers

Now Try: Kate Walbert wrote a collection, ***Where She Went: Stories***, featuring a mother and daughter, wherein the mother urges her daughter to be more adventuresome. Patricia Stephens Due and Tananarive Due are another mother–daughter duo who wrote their story in alternating chapters; theirs too was a story of change, but change of a different sort, as reflected in their book's title: ***Freedom in the Family: A Mother-Daughter Memoir of the Fight for Civil Rights***. Readers who enjoy the travel part of the Kidds' story may also enjoy the story of Patricia Storace's year in Greece, ***Dinner with Persephone***, a reflection that looks at Greece in its modern incarnation, but also as the source of the mythical stories that provide spiritual touchstones in ***Traveling with Pomegranates***.

McBride, James (1957–)

The Color of Water: A Black Man's Tribute to His White Mother. 10th anniversary ed. Riverhead Books, 2006, 1996. 328pp. ill. 9781594481925. Also available in large print, Braille, audiobook, and e-audiobook. 974.70092

James McBride was thirty when he began to appreciate his mother and to recognize in her more than the confusing, embarrassing woman he had seen in his adolescence and early adulthood. Already a journalist, he wrote an article about her that garnered both a large response and the idea that he should write a book about her. But it took him some time after that to convince her to tell her story, which she only did when she realized it was time she let it out. Her story was as much a revelation to her children as it is to the reader. All she would say about her ethnicity as her twelve children were growing up in the projects in Harlem was that she was "light-skinned" and that God was the color of water, meaning no color. As she tells in this dual-voiced memoir, she is the daughter of an Orthodox Jew who fled the pogroms in Europe, only to encounter anti-Semitism in the American South. Her father was a violent and racist man himself, browbeating his polio-stricken wife and sexually abusing his daughter. James also tells his own story, growing up economically poor in Harlem, but given an education in a Jewish neighborhood and loved by both his mother and his stepfather, his own father having died of cancer before he was born.

The Color of Water received the Anisfield-Wolf Book Award and was selected as a Notable Book by the American Library Association.

Subjects: African-American Men; ALA Notable Books; American South; Anisfield-Wolf Book Award; Biracial Children; Education; Family Relationships; Harlem (New York, NY); Incest; Jewish Women; McBride-Jordan, Ruth; Stepfathers

Now Try: At the same time that McBride's book was published, another memoir of a biracial child was also being published; although the details of Scott Minerbrook's story differ, the search for the mother's family in the South was the end result for both of them in their search for identity. Minerbrook's title is ***Divided to the Vein: A Journey into Race and Family***. Tim McLaurin grew up poor but loved in the South, with a resourceful mother and a family and way of life he pays tribute to in ***Keeper of the Moon***. An interesting counterpoint to Ruth's story of her father's store in the South is Stella Suberman's story, ***The Jew Store***, about her family's move by horse and wagon from the Bronx to Tennessee before she was born.

Ryan, Terry (1946–2007)

The Prize Winner of Defiance, Ohio: How My Mother Raised 10 Kids on 25 Words or Less. Simon & Schuster, 2001. 321pp. ill. 9780743211222. Also available in large print, e-audiobook, and video. 977.1092

Terry Ryan was the writing side of T. O. Sylvester, creator of a syndicated cartoon out of San Francisco, and the sixth of Evelyn and Kelly Ryan's ten children. Her father was an abusive alcoholic who drank much of his income, and her mother was a cheerful optimist who gave up an opportunity to be a writer in order to be a housewife and mother. Evelyn put her writing talents to work, however, to create successful jingles and slogans for a wide variety of products whose ad agencies offered prizes for the best. Ryan describes their financially poor life in a household with so many children, where her mother initially had no time for friends because she was so busy doing housework and researching contests to enter. Because of her mother's skill, however, they always managed to skirt disaster, such as when they were about to be evicted from their rented home and Evelyn won a prize large enough to put a down payment on a house. Apart from telling the reader about their home life, Ryan also illuminates an interesting part of 1950s American culture, particularly the advent of television commercials.

Subjects: 1950s; Advertising; Children of Alcoholics; Defiance, OH; Mothers; Ohio; Poverty; Prize Contests; Ryan, Evelyn; Working-Class Families

Now Try: The irrepressible nature of Evelyn Ryan can also be seen in Venetia Summers, a single mom who tries to make a new life for her children in rural England after moving there from the city, in Raffaella Barker's novel ***Hens Dancing***. Just as Ryan presents the 1950s in a quick-witted style, Jane Smiley does the same for the 1980s in her novel ***Good Faith***. The baby-boomer reader will recognize many of the slogans that Evelyn Ryan created; for a fascinating review of advertising lines that have become household phrases, readers may be interested in Thomas Andrew Bailey's ***Voices of America: The Nation's Story in Slogans, Sayings, and Songs***, written with the assistance of Stephen M. Dobbs.

Smith, Dennis (1940–)

A Song for Mary: An Irish-American Memory. Warner Books, 2000, 1999. 369pp. 9780446524476. Also available in Braille, audiobook (read by the author), and e-book. 813.54

Even when he was about to do something illegal, Dennis Smith had his mother's voice in his head. He, his older brother, and his mother lived in a rundown tenement in the Lower East Side of New York City. Using the present tense, Smith creates an immediacy of time, place, and event. He brings the reader into the ghetto and ghetto life with him; he relives his wild childhood, loved and scolded by the global village of his environs, but in trouble all the time anyway. He runs with the wildest kids, he can't settle down at school, and he gets into alcohol and drugs. All the while he wonders about his absent father: Why has he been in the hospital all this time, leaving his mother to receive welfare while occasionally moonlighting to bring in a bit of extra money to help feed her children? Dennis was on the verge of imprisonment when he was given the option of joining the armed forces. By the time he was discharged and became a firefighter, his life had come full circle. Once rescued from a tenement fire by a firefighter, he was able to do the same for others in the Bronx.

Subjects: 1950s; Catholics; Childhood and Youth; Coming of Age; Fatherless Children; Firefighters; Irish-Americans; Mothers and Sons; New York, NY; Poverty; Smith, Mary; Urban Youth; Working-Class Families

Now Try: Thomas J. Fleming explores Hoboken, New Jersey, to discover the story behind his Irish-American father, a search that starts with the discovery of a ring belonging to Fleming lost thirty years ago. He recaptures his father in ***Mysteries of My Father***. The Irish-American mother often proves to be very strong in the face of hardship, as Madeleine Blais describes in the story of her own mother, left a widow with five children to raise in poverty in Massachusetts. As she relates in ***Uphill Walkers: Memoir of a Family***, her mother was determined that they all be educated. One of New York City's most elite groups of firefighters is depicted in Tom Downey's ***The Last Men Out: Life on the Edge at Rescue 2 Firehouse***.

Fathers

For some reason, contemporary writers seem to focus more on telling the stories of their fathers than those of their mothers, so that there are almost three times as many titles in this section as there are in the mothers section. In many cases, the father was an absent figure—either literally or figuratively—and the adult child is trying to discover who that man was. Other memoirs, by both sons and daughters, are celebrations of the father, coupled with a desire to tell others about him. And Michael Chabon and Michael M. Lewis both share their thoughts on what it is like to be a father. In this section the reader is treated to another graphic narrative, this one by Alison Bechdel.

These memoirs about fathers are a mix of praise and blame. The fathers of many of the writers were absent, either physically or emotionally, so that the memoirists are trying as adults to discover them. This type of memoir will be more reflective than the narratives that describe how wonderful the fathers have been.

Bechdel, Alison (1960–)

Fun Home: A Family Tragicomic. Houghton Mifflin, 2006. 232pp. ill. 9780618477944. 741.5973

Alison Bechdel grew up in a hamlet in Pennsylvania, living in a large Victorian house that served as the town funeral home (the "Fun Home" of the title), with an emotionally repressed father. Her graphic memoir took her seven years to write, as she worked on coming to terms with secrets she learned about her father and her parents' marriage shortly before her father's death—whether by accident or suicide was never legally determined. When she announced in a letter home from college that she was a lesbian, her mother replied with the admission that her father was also gay. Four months later he was dead. Much of the book, however, is about Bechdel's apprenticeship as a creative artist under her father's watchful eye; she chose the comic strip as her medium because it was something he would never touch; it was too lowbrow for him. But the literature they shared gave her the gift of words to accompany her drawing, so that this graphic narrative is a complete work, offering the best of both words and illustrations.

Fun Home was a finalist for the National Book Critics Circle Award in Autobiography/Memoir, won the Lambda Literary Award for Lesbian Memoir/Biography and the Stonewall Book Award-Israel Fishman Non-Fiction Award, and was selected as a Notable Book by the American Library Association.

Subjects: ALA Notable Books; Artists; Death of a Parent; Fathers and Daughters; Funeral Homes; Graphic Narratives; Lambda Literary Award for Lesbian Memoir/Biography; Lesbians; Queer Parents; Stonewall Book Award-Israel Fishman Non-Fiction Award

Now Try: Bechdel has been a successful syndicated comic strip artist for decades; her comic strip has been collected in an omnibus, ***The Essential Dykes to Watch Out For***. Another daughter who learned about her father's relationships with men is Honor Moore, who tells the story of her family life in ***The Bishop's Daughter: A Memoir***. Noelle Howey and Ellen Samuels have collected essays by a number of people who have grown up with queer parents in ***Out of the Ordinary: Essays on Growing Up with Gay, Lesbian, and Transgender Parents***. Bechdel's memoir is haunting; so too is a novel that is the reverse of ***Fun Home***. In ***The Every Boy*** by Dana Adam Shapiro, the child dies, and the father tries to learn about the boy he was emotionally distant from.

Carroll, James (1943–)

An American Requiem: God, My Father, and the War That Came Between Us. Houghton Mifflin, 1996. 279pp. ill 8pp. of plates. 9780395779262. Also available in large print and Braille. 813.54

James Carroll grew up feeling a close bond with his father, a former seminarian and an FBI agent turned brigadier general and founder of the Defense Intelligence Agency at the Pentagon. As he grew up, Carroll changed his ambition from the Air Force to the seminary and became a priest. He recounts the story of a filial relationship irreparably sundered and his life trajectory from priest to pacifist, rebel, writer, husband, and father. In telling his story he re-creates the American world of the 1960s and 1970s, with the generationally divisive Vietnam War and the Civil Rights Movement. He reveals the power of the Catholic Church, the FBI, and the Pentagon. And he discloses what he discovered about his father when it was too late for any reconciliation.

An American Requiem was awarded the National Book Award for Nonfiction.

Subjects: 1960s; 1970s; Catholic Ex-Priests; Catholics; Coming of Age; Fathers and Sons; National Book Award for Nonfiction; Pacifists; Pentagon; Social History, United States; Vietnam War (1961–1975)

Now Try: Originally a poet and novelist, Carroll has turned his hand to writing a number of nonfiction works on varying topics. One of particular interest here is ***House of War: The Pentagon and the Disastrous Rise of American Power***. The Vietnam War created many familial casualties, one of which Tom Bissell tried to heal on a trip to Vietnam with his father, a former Marine who became an alcoholic after his return from duty; Bissell describes that trip and his relationship with his father in ***The Father of All Things: A Marine, His Son, and the Legacy of Vietnam***. Frank Schaeffer and his son John have a slightly different take on the father/son conflict about the military. It is Frank's son who joins up, and together they tell their stories of adjustment; unlike Carroll, they do have the opportunity to reconcile their differences. The Schaeffers' story is told in ***Keeping Faith: A Father-Son Story About Love and the United States Marine Corps***. If you are interested in the religious aspect of Carroll's story, you may want to try John Cornwell's memoir, ***Seminary Boy***, as he reveals a life full of challenges and difficulties.

Chabon, Michael (1963–)

Manhood for Amateurs: The Pleasures and Regrets of a Husband, Father, and Son. Harper, 2009. 306pp. 9780061490187. Also available in large print, audiobook, and e-audiobook. 913.54

Not just a novelist, Chabon has also written essays, particularly for the magazine *Details*. For this latest publication, he collected a number of those essays about such topics as fatherhood, gender roles, child's play today as compared to his own childhood days, and even why men should carry purses. Through these essays he also sheds light on himself—his childhood, his family relationships, and his views on parenting. He believes he has a much greater emotional connection to his children than his own father did, and lays that at the doorstep of gender roles.

Subjects: Fatherhood; Gender Roles; Manhood; Marriage; Parenting; Personal Essays; Writers

Now Try: Chabon's wife, Ayelet Waldman, has just written her own perspective on parenting, particularly for mothers: ***Bad Mother: A Chronicle of Maternal Crimes, Minor Calamities, and Occasional Moments of Grace***. Despite the humor in his essays, Chabon is also thoughtful, reflecting on gender roles. William S. Pollack has interviewed boys himself to learn what they are thinking and what their concerns are and has collected his interviews, with help from Todd Shuster, in ***Real Boys' Voices***. Chabon also looks closely at the role of the father in today's family. Robert Rummel-Hudson does the same, looking specifically at himself and whether or not he is the right man to be father to his daughter, afflicted with a brain disorder that has rendered her mute. He brings his thoughts to light in ***Schuyler's Monster: A Father's Journey with His Wordless Daughter***. If you enjoy Chabon's humor in these essays, you may also want to read Al Roker's collection of humorous essays on parenting, ***Don't Make Me Stop This Car! Adventures in Fatherhood***.

Coates, Ta-Nehisi (1975–)

The Beautiful Struggle: A Father, Two Sons, and an Unlikely Road to Manhood. Spiegel & Grau, 2009, 2008. 227pp. map. 9780385527460. Also available in audiobook, e-audiobook, and e-book. 975.26092

Paul Coates, a former Black Panther and founding owner of the publishing company Black Classic Books, is the father of seven children with four different mothers. He set out to raise his children to become race-conscious Black adults who could think for themselves, while avoiding the minefield of the crack-addicted neighborhood in which they were living in Baltimore. A librarian at Howard University, Coates was determined that each of his children would obtain college degrees there. Ta-Nehisi is one of those children, now a freelance writer for several magazines, who describes life with his father, a strong, loving man who would use whatever means at his disposal to ferry his children safely to adulthood.

Subjects: 1980s; African-American Men; Baltimore, MD; Black Classic Books; Books and Reading; City Life; Coates, Paul; Family Relationships; Fatherhood; Fathers and Sons; Librarians; Street Life

Now Try: Michael Datcher would like to have had a father like Paul Coates; instead he determined that he would be the father he never had, as he narrates in ***Raising Fences: A Black Man's Love Story***. David Matthews also grew up with an activist Black father, although David was White and Jewish through his mother; his complex story of developing his own identity is told in ***Ace of Spades: A Memoir***. Ta-Nehisi Coates is warmly praised for the quality of his writing, particularly its rhythmic nature. Louis Armstrong, rhythmic musically, proved to have the same gift in writing, as demonstrated in ***Louis Armstrong, in His Own Words: Selected Writings***, edited and with an introduction by Thomas Brothers.

Dickey, Christopher (1951–)

Summer of Deliverance: A Memoir of Father and Son. Simon & Schuster, 1999, 1998. 287pp. 9780684855370. Also available in audiobook, e-audiobook, and e-book. 811.54

Christopher Dickey's story is a painful one of watching his famous father, a well-respected poet and novelist, slide down an alcoholic slope to the point of near-death from liver damage. Before they reached the point of his hospitalization, however, Dickey père had already been responsible for the alcoholic death of Christopher's mother, was engaged in a volatile and abusive relationship with a second wife, and was father to a young girl greatly neglected by both parents. Christopher points to the summer when his father's best-selling novel, ***Deliverance,*** was made into a movie as the lever that pushed his father into increasingly self-destructive behavior. Estranged from his father for many years, it was only when James was hospitalized that Christopher joined forces with his brother and his half-sister to try to rescue their father, an effort that succeeded in two years of sobriety and reconciliation before James Dickey actually died.

Subjects: Children of Alcoholics; Dickey, James; Family Relationships; Fathers and Sons; Poets; Reconciliation; South Carolina; Writers; Writers in the Family

Now Try: Readers of Dickey's memoir will find many similarities in the story of a man trying to cope with his emotionally absent father in Andrew Sheehan's ***Chasing the Hawk: Looking for My Father, Finding Myself.*** Reconciliation is a major theme in Dickey's memoir, as it is in Mark Spragg's ***An Unfinished Life: A Novel,*** the story of a broken family in Wyoming. The gut-wrenching nature of Dickey's story is also present in Laurie R. King's novel about a Vietnam vet who rescues a young boy from his abusive father, ***Keeping Watch.***

Fiorito, Joe (1948–)

The Closer We Are to Dying: A Memoir of Father and Family. Picador USA, 2000, 1999. 321pp. 9780312261368. 070.92

Joe Fiorito grew up in Fort William, Ontario, before it was amalgamated with Port Arthur and renamed Thunder Bay. His father, known as Dusty, was a mailman and a womanizer, and money was not easily come by in the family. His father was also an Italian immigrant, and Italians did not seem to be well-liked in northern Ontario. This was Joe Fiorito's childhood: poor, Italian, and, to make matters worse, bookish. His father was also abusive, which only added to Fiorito's difficulties. But his father was a storyteller, too, and the stories he would recount about his family, including five other brothers, were legion. When his mother called him to say his father was dying, Fiorito flew to Thunder Bay to sit vigil with his dying father and to hear all these stories once again. It gave him a chance to reflect on the man and to reconcile his confused feelings for him.

Subjects: Domestic Violence; Dying; Family Relationships; Fathers and Sons; Fiorito, Dusty; Italian-Canadians; Journalists, Canada; Storytelling; Thunder Bay, ON; Working-Class Families

Now Try: Dan McGraw's connection to his dying father was football, as he returned to Cleveland to be with his father; he tells his story in ***First and Last Seasons: A Father, a Son, and Sunday Afternoon Football.*** Rick Bragg, who had sat at his dying father's bedside, also takes another look at his father from the vantage point of the adult in ***The Prince of Frogtown.*** The stories that Fiorito's father told were larger than life. Paul Paolicelli heard similar stories about his grandfather; in ***Dances with Luigi: A Grandson's Determined Quest to Comprehend Italy and the Italians*** he describes how he decided to visit Italy to understand the source.

Flynn, Nick (1960–)

Another Bullshit Night in Suck City: A Memoir. W. W. Norton, 2005, 2004. 357pp. ill. 9780393329407. 811.6

Suck City is Scituate, Massachusetts, where Nick Flynn was born, and where his father abandoned the family, leaving his mother to cope with two children. The title comes from something Flynn's father, Jonathan, said to him in a harangue one day. Flynn draws his own life beside his father's in a somewhat parallel structure, portraying his father's descent into alcoholism, crime, prison, and eventual homelessness as well as his own descent into drugs and alcohol, barely keeping himself from winding up completely like his father, particularly after his mother's suicide. Nick Flynn began working at the Pine Street Inn homeless shelter in Boston, where he finally encountered his father, after erratic phone calls and letters throughout their twenty years of separation. Jonathan had always wanted to be a writer, and his son had the talent to do so, becoming an award-winning poet and now memoirist.

Another Bullshit Night in Suck City received the PEN American Center Martha Albrand Award for the Art of the Memoir.

Subjects: Alcoholics; Boston, MA; Children of Alcoholics; Death of a Parent; Fathers and Sons; Homeless Shelters; Homelessness; Massachusetts; PEN American Center Martha Albrand Award for the Art of the Memoir; Poets; Scituate, MA

Now Try: Not long before the birth of his first child, Nick Flynn wrote another memoir, ***The Ticking Is the Bomb: A Memoir***. In the many accolades this memoir has received, several reviewers have compared it to Frank Conroy's classic, ***Stop-Time***, for being both unforgettable and wonderfully written. At the same time that Flynn's book was being published, another memoir of a homeless parent was also on the market: ***West of Then: A Mother, a Daughter, and a Journey Past Paradise*** by Tara Bray Smith. Shaughnessy Bishop-Stall is a journalist who spent some time living with homeless people in Toronto, in an area that he describes in his highly acclaimed investigation, ***Down to This: Squalor and Splendour in a Big-City Shantytown***.

Greene, Bob (1947–)

Duty: A Father, His Son, and the Man Who Won the War. Perennial, 2001, 2000. 295pp. 9780380814114. Also available in large print, audiobook, and e-book. 940.544092

In one final effort to make a connection with his father, Robert, Bob Greene returned to his hometown of Columbus, Ohio, where his father was dying. His father had been a well-decorated infantry soldier in the Second World War, but had spoken little about his experiences. He also knew by sight Paul Tibbets, a fellow Ohioan who had been the pilot of the *Enola Gay*, the bomber that dropped the atomic bomb on Hiroshima. Although Tibbets was his hero, and Robert knew him by sight, he would never approach him to engage in conversation. Greene, a journalist, decided to seek out Paul Tibbets, to learn his story and by extension to learn his own father's story better. This memoir is a combination of what Greene found by going through his father's papers, by listening to a tape his father had made of his war experiences, and by having several conversations with Paul Tibbets, finally coming to understand something of the cultural and societal differences between his father's generation and his own.

Subjects: Fathers and Sons; Generation Gap; Greene, Robert; Hiroshima, Japan; Journalists; Tibbets, Paul; World War II (1939–1945)

Now Try: Bob Greene has written a number of memoirs, the most recent dealing with his career as a journalist, ***Late Edition: A Love Story***. Tom Brokaw held Greene's father's generation in great esteem and published a book about them to reflect that esteem: ***The Greatest Generation***. But that generation also lived through the war and the horrific bombing of Hiroshima. John Hersey wrote a classic investigative work on that day, simply titled ***Hiroshima***. Louise Steinman is another offspring, like so many, of a father who kept his war stories to himself. She delves into his story as an infantryman in the Pacific War and describes what she found in ***The Souvenir: A Daughter Discovers Her Father's War***.

Lewis, Michael M. (1960–)

Home Game: An Accidental Guide to Fatherhood. Photographs by Tabitha Soren. W. W. Norton, 2009. 190pp. ill. 9780393069013. 306.8742092

Michael Lewis was bewildered to find that his reactions to his first-born were not what he had expected. He wasn't the adoring, emotional father he had expected to be, but was instead rather detached and observant. He kept a journal of his children's first years and in doing so made a discovery that he shares with the reader: if you want to have appropriate emotional reactions to your children, you need to engage with them on a regular basis, in a very domestic way. Although that sounds serious, his look at his parenting style is actually quite light and humorous. The book is divided into three sections, one for each of his children—two girls and a boy—and includes photographs taken by his wife, ending with a discussion of the surgery that will preclude their having any more children.

Subjects: Family Relationships; Fatherhood; Humor; Parenting; Vasectomies

Now Try: One of the books Lewis made use of in learning about fatherhood was Bill Cosby's classic, ***Fatherhood***. Another humorous story of fatherhood is by Steve Doocy, ***Tales from the Dad Side: Misadventures in Fatherhood***. Before Lewis became a dad, he was first the husband of a pregnant woman. In his wry reflections, ***Yes, You're Pregnant, but What About Me?***, the comic Kevin Nealon comments on the role of the expectant father.

MacIntyre, Linden (1943–)

Causeway: A Passage from Innocence. HarperCollins, 2006. 361pp. ill. 9780002007245. 971.6904

An investigative journalist, Linden MacIntyre was born in Newfoundland, but grew up on Cape Breton Island in Nova Scotia. He begins his childhood memoir with the first day of construction of the Canso Causeway linking the island to the mainland, hoping that it will mean his father will be home more often, that he will be able to get a job building the causeway. Poverty was such in Cape Breton that men often had to leave in order to find employment, and many of these men, like Dan Rory MacIntyre, wound up in mines, sometimes as far away as Quebec. Much of MacIntyre's childhood, then, as well as his memoir, is full of the longing of a boy for his father; compounding the problem is that even when his father was there, Linden still felt as though he weren't, such were his inattention and detachment. MacIntyre also creates a picture of a vanishing way of life in Port Hastings, the town where he grew up with his fey grandmother, Peigeag.

Causeway was awarded the Evelyn Richardson Memorial Literary Prize for Non-Fiction and the Edna Staebler Award for Creative Non-Fiction.

Subjects: 1950s; 1960s; Canso Causeway, NS; Cape Breton Island, NS; Childhood and Youth; Coming of Age; Edna Staebler Award for Creative Non-Fiction; Fathers and Sons; Grandmothers; Journalists, Canada; Nova Scotia

Now Try: If you'd like to read some of Linden MacIntyre's fiction, you could start with his award-winning ***The Bishop's Man: A Novel***. Alistair MacLeod paints a vivid portrait of the life of the men who work "away" in his novel, ***No Great Mischief***. Island life has its own particular rhythms and culture, but is often subject to change. MacIntyre's style of island life would vanish with the construction of the causeway; Tom Horton describes another island with its own way of life in ***An Island out of Time: A Memoir of Smith Island in the Chesapeake***. Anita Diamant replicates MacIntyre's melancholic tone as she describes the historical community of Dogtown in ***The Last Days of Dogtown: A Novel***.

Miller, Sue (1943–)

The Story of My Father: A Memoir. Knopf, 2003. 173pp. ill. 9780375414794. Also available in large print, audiobook (read by the author), e-audiobook, and e-book. 813.54

James Nichols, the father of the novelist Sue Miller, was a minister and a church historian, his final teaching position at Princeton. When his behavior became noticeably odd, Miller took him to the doctor, where he was diagnosed with Alzheimer's disease. Her memoir is a combination of recounting the progress of this disease, whereby a man who had occupied his life with history would soon have no memory of his own history, with remembrances of the man he had been, the attentive parent he had been when her mother had not been so. She also incorporates her life as a writer and what it meant to her to be able to write this memoir, a nonfiction work about her father, whereas she had written a novel, ***The Distinguished Guest***, about her mother.

Subjects: Adult Children; Aging Parents; Alzheimer's Disease; Cambridge, MA; Family Relationships; Fathers and Daughters; Novelists

Now Try: Sandra Sabatini, whose father also suffered from Alzheimer's disease, wrote a collection of short stories, each one from the point of view of a different person in the life of a man with Alzheimer's disease. The collection, ***The One with the News***, is more compassionate and empathic than desolate. At the end of her life Anne Morrow Lindbergh, her mind failing, went to live with her daughter Reeve Lindbergh and her family, a poignant time that Reeve describes in ***No More Words: A Journal of My Mother, Anne Morrow Lindbergh***. Carmen

Renee Berry and Lynn Barrington interviewed a number of fathers and daughters to put together a collection, ranging chronologically from the birth of a daughter to the death of a father, entitled ***Daddies and Daughters***.

Roth, Philip (1933–)

Patrimony: A True Story. Vintage Books, 1999, 1991. 238pp. 9780099914303. Also available in large print, Braille, audiobook, and e-book. 813.54

" 'I must remember accurately,' I told myself, 'remember everything accurately so that when he is gone I can re-create the father who created me.' " This poignant sentence from Roth's memoir about the living and dying of his father encapsulates the goal he set for himself: to capture his father for all time, now that Roth has come to recognize his father's mortality in the diagnosis of a growing brain tumor. Between descriptions of the care and conversations involved in his father's illness are reminiscences of the father and husband who was such a strong influence on the writer. Roth also describes the issue of role reversal usually present in the care-giving of a dying parent: for the first time in his life, Roth said to his father, "Do as I say."

Patrimony won the National Book Critics Circle Award in Biography/Autobiography and was selected as a Notable Book by the American Library Association. Roth was also awarded the Gold Medal in Fiction by the American Academy of Arts and Letters as well as the National Medal of Arts.

Subjects: ALA Notable Books; Anti-Semitism; Family Relationships; Fathers and Sons; Jewish Men; National Book Critics Circle Award in Biography/Autobiography; Novelists; Roth, Herman

Now Try: Roth's subtitle, "A True Story," reflects the reality of his father's death, the fact of which he found shocking, even after caring for his father throughout the two years of his illness. David Shields, faced with a father whose vitality at ninety-seven seemed more than Shields could manage, looks at the issue of death with humor and through the lens of his own degenerating body in ***The Thing About Life Is That One Day You'll Be Dead***. The writer Walter Dumaux Edmonds lovingly invokes his father in his autobiography, ***Tales My Father Never Told,*** as he goes back in time to portray their life in the Adirondacks. The graceful prose found in Roth's memoir can also be found in Ann Beattie's collection of stories, ***Perfect Recall: New Stories***.

Russert, Tim (1950–2008)

Big Russ and Me: Father and Son, Lessons of Life. Miramax, 2005, 2004. 336pp. ill. 16pp. of plates. 9781401359652. Also available in large print, Braille, audiobook, and e-book. 070.92

In this memoir journalist Tim Russert wrote a paean to his father, Tim Sr., whom he called "Big Russ," a man he called his hero. Russert grew up in South Buffalo in the 1950s and 1960s, in a Catholic, Irish-American environment. He describes the routines of his life, with his father working two jobs in order to feed his family of four children well and in order to be able to send them to Catholic school.

With Tim Sr. being a war veteran, the American legion was also a big part of their lives, so that home, church, and the legion were the touchstones of a childhood overseen by his father. This memoir is not just a homage to his father, however; it is also a guidebook for Russert to pass on to his son, Luke, the various lessons that Tim had learned from his father, lessons revealed in some of the chapter headings: "Respect," "Work," "Faith." He also talks about his own career, from his work for Senator Daniel Moynihan to his role as interviewer on *Meet the Press*, so that it is really a dual biography.

Subjects: 1950s; 1960s; Buffalo, NY; Catholics; Fathers and Sons; Irish-Americans; Journalists; Russert, Tim, Sr.; Television Journalists; Working-Class Families

Now Try: Jim Nantz, a sports journalist, has a relationship with his dad similar to Tim Russert's, a loving relationship he describes with help from Eli Spielman in ***Always by My Side: A Father's Grace and a Sports Journey Unlike Any Other***. Growing up Catholic and Irish in the United States can be the same regardless of the city. Michael Pearson shares his stories, some quite similar to Russert's, in ***Dreaming of Columbus: A Boyhood in the Bronx***. Daniel Moynihan was referred to as Russert's intellectual father. If you'd like to read more about him, Godfrey Hodgson has written an acclaimed biography, ***The Gentleman from New York: Daniel Patrick Moynihan; A Biography***.

Salinger, Margaret Ann (1955–)

Dream Catcher: A Memoir. With a new Afterword by the author. Pocket Books, 2001, 2000. 450pp. ill. 24pp. of plates. 9780671042820. 813.54

Margaret Salinger has written a memoir of her life with her famous father, J. D. Salinger, almost in self-defense, or at the very least, as a way of making sense of her childhood and upbringing and as a means of ensuring that she won't do to her son what was done to her. In her memoir, apart from describing life in the Salinger home with a father who very likely loathed women, she also sheds light on her father's early years and his stint in the war. He was involved in some of the major battles of World War II and was one of the first to liberate a concentration camp, all of which had a lifelong effect on him. One of the unusual aspects of her memoir is her analysis of his work in light of his life. While J. D. Salinger did not publish anything after 1965, his daughter says that he had boxes of material to be published after his death.

Subjects: Family Relationships; Fathers and Daughters; Hermits; Privacy; Salinger, J. D.; World War II (1939–1945); Writers

Now Try: Joyce Maynard made some waves when she published her gossipy memoir, ***At Home in the World: A Memoir***, about her affair with J. D. Salinger, which occurred when she was eighteen (two years older than his daughter) and he was fifty-three. The father of journalist Lucinda Franks shared experiences similar to Salinger's in World War II; Franks also tries to understand her father by understanding what he suffered then. She tells her story in ***My Father's***

Secret War: A Memoir. When Margaret Salinger was growing up, she suffered from both anorexia and alcoholism; Jane Velez-Mitchell had similar problems and overcame her trials to become a journalist and activist. She describes her journey in ***iWant: My Journey from Addiction and Overconsumption to a Simpler, Honest Life***. Louisa May Alcott did not always have a smooth relationship with her father, particularly as she rebelled against his views on parenting. John Matteson wrote a Pulitzer Prize–winning biography of Alcott and her father, Bronson: ***Eden's Outcasts: The Story of Louisa May Alcott and Her Father***.

Sinatra, Tina (1948–)
Coplon, Jeff (1951–), coauthor

My Father's Daughter: A Memoir. Berkley Books, 2001, 2000. 388pp. ill. 32pp. of plates. 9780425181980. Also available in large print. 791.43028092

Tina Sinatra's mother, Nancy, was the first Mrs. Sinatra. Tina suffered through divorce and almost abandonment as a child. In her memoir she talks about what it is like to have a father she hears more on the radio and sees more on the television than in real life. Much of her memoir, however, deals with his marriages, to Ava Gardner and Mia Farrow, whom she liked, but more so his final marriage, to Barbara Marx, whom she disliked and mistrusted. Her father was bipolar for a good part of his life, although it wasn't diagnosed as such at the time, and this obviously played a role in his behavior and his relationships. One aspect of this book that fans of Sinatra will enjoy are all the photographs his daughter has included.

Subjects: Bipolar Disorder; California; Children of Divorce; Fathers and Daughters; Sinatra, Barbara Marx; Sinatra, Frank; Singers

Now Try: Other Sinatra daughters have also written about their father: Nancy Sinatra wrote a memoir, ***Frank Sinatra, My Father***, and then more recently, ***Frank Sinatra: An American Legend***. Julie Sinatra, who claims to be his daughter from an affair he had with her mother, Dorothy Bonucelli, has written ***Under My Skin: My Father, Frank Sinatra: The Man Behind the Mystique***. Sammy Davis Jr. was a member of the Rat Pack, the Hollywood group that featured Sinatra and others. Davis's daughter, Tracey, with help from Dolores A. Barclay, wrote a memoir of life with her father, ***Sammy Davis Jr., My Father***. Bebe Moore Campbell is another daughter whose father was in and out of her life, recounted in ***Sweet Summer: Growing Up with & Without My Dad***. The heartfelt tone of Sinatra's memoir can also be found in K. L. Cook's novel about a young girl missing her mother, ***The Girl from Charnelle: A Novel***.

Trussoni, Danielle (1973–)

Falling Through the Earth: A Memoir. Picador, 2007, 2006. 240pp. 9780312426569. 306.8742092

Trussoni weaves three major threads to create both a coming-of-age memoir and a portrait of her father, Daniel Trussoni, a man she often fought with, but whom she loved all the same. The element that binds these threads together is Vietnam. Her father had been a tunnel rat and suffered from post-traumatic stress disorder

(PTSD) as a result. The consequences of his PTSD were serious: he often became violent, to the point where his wife left him, taking all their children but Danielle, who chose to stay with her father. She researched the time of her youth that she wanted to write about, listening again to the music of the 1980s and reviewing the culture of the day as an *aide-mémoire* to recall her own memories and feelings of the time she spent with her father. To learn about her father's war experiences, Trussoni used tapes that he had made before being stricken with throat cancer—presumed to be a result of exposure to Agent Orange. Finally, she went to Vietnam to visit the tunnels in order to see what her father had seen.

Subjects: 1980s; Coming of Age; Fathers and Daughters; La Crosse, WI; Post-Traumatic Stress Disorder; Tunnel Rats, Vietnam; Veterans; Vietnam War (1961–1975); Working-Class Families

Now Try: Germaine Greer also lived with a father who suffered from his war experiences, suffering that obviously affected his family. She traveled far and wide to discover who her father really was and describes her efforts in ***Daddy, We Hardly Knew You***. The Vietnam War, like most wars, had a life-changing effect on thousands of people, many of whom were consulted for a book by Christian G. Appy, ***Patriots: The Vietnam War Remembered from All Sides***. Shirley Abbott came of age in an earlier time and in a different locale, but she too felt the need to come to terms with her father, which she does in ***The Bookmaker's Daughter: A Memory Unbound***.

Washington-Williams, Essie Mae (1925–)
Stadiem, William (1947–), coauthor

Dear Senator: A Memoir by the Daughter of Strom Thurmond. Regan Books, 2005. 223pp. ill. 9780060760953. Also available in e-book. 973.9092

When Essie Mae Washington was thirteen, she discovered that the woman she had always thought of as her mother was actually her mother's sister. Three years later she visited her mother in South Carolina and was taken to meet her father, Strom Thurmond, a politician and an outspoken racist. Essie Mae's memoir, written after her father's death, talks about his reaction to meeting her, his secret visits with her, and her concomitant silence. He funded her education—in a segregated college—but never acknowledged her publicly. Perhaps because of her age at the time of writing, there is no bitterness in this memoir. It is more a narration of her life, with and without her father, and how she felt about that and about his racism. She does, however, seem to have adopted her mother's attitude, that his racist behavior and comments were just politics.

Subjects: American South; Biracial Children; Fatherless Children; Fathers and Daughters; Octogenarians; Racism; Thurmond, Strom

Now Try: The story of White men impregnating Black women, usually slaves or servants, is an old one. Carrie Allen McCray tells the story of one such liaison and the daughter that the mixed-race couple had in ***Freedom's Child: The Life of***

a Confederate General's Black Daughter. One of the many adjustments that Essie Mae had to make was in moving from racially mixed Pennsylvania to segregated South Carolina. Lise Funderburg encounters a similar culture shock as she takes her Black father home to Georgia after they had lived with her White mother in the northern states. She describes this in ***Pig Candy: Taking My Father South, Taking My Father Home; A Memoir***. Holly Chamberlin has written a novel, ***One Week in December***, in which the daughter being raised in a Maine household is, like Essie Mae, really the daughter of her mother's sister.

Wight, Jim (1943–)

The Real James Herriot: A Memoir of My Father. Ballantine Books, 2001, 2000. 371pp. ill. 9780345434906. Also available in large print and audiobook. 636.089092

Jim Wight went to the same veterinary school as his father and then joined his father's practice in the small town of Thirsk in Yorkshire. He and his father were very good friends, and it was only natural that the younger Jim should write his father's biography, a story that automatically includes his own story. When James Herriot (a pseudonymous name) wrote his very popular tales of the life of a Yorkshire vet (see page 269), he changed the names of people and towns. Wight now brings the real people to light, describing them and their place in his father's life. He talks about his father's writing life and the fame it brought to him, and he describes how that fame was not a part of his father's storytelling. He also reveals his father's health problems, the fact that he kept his emotions close to his chest, resulting in a severe depression that required electroshock therapy. And finally, he describes his father's death from cancer. By writing this biography/memoir, Jim Wight wanted to show his father's readers that the real James Herriot, known to his family and friends as Alf Wight, was as much a gentleman as they might have deduced from reading his books.

Subjects: England; Fathers and Sons; Herriot, James; Small Towns, England; Veterinarians, England; Wight, Alf; Yorkshire, England

Now Try: One of the many avenues Wight took to research his father's life was to re-read all his books. His memoir, then, resonates with his father's style, a style that is also to be found in ***Tales from a Dog Catcher*** by Lisa Duffy-Korpics. By dint of his subject and his writing style, James Herriot created almost a genre of writing, so that if a reviewer says that Benet Tvedten is the James Herriot of the monastic world, because of his memoir, ***The View from a Monastery***, the reader will know to expect a heartwarming, entertaining story. Jim Wight, in describing his father's professional life, has depicted a world that no longer exists, with modern technology now coming into play. The same is true of the life depicted by Patrick Taylor in his novel, ***An Irish Country Doctor***.

Children

Parents bare their hearts and their pain in these stories of their children, stories in which the child is in great difficulty, perhaps from drug addiction, or perhaps from physical or mental illness. The one exception is Louise Erdrich's celebration of the birth of her third biological child.

> The memoirs of children that parents have written here illustrate the potential heartache in raising a child. Fears of illness or addiction strike every parent's heart, and when they actually strike the family, the parents are right at the core of the misery. Writers who take solace in the written word offer their experiences of such disasters with their children. But sometimes parenting is sheer joy, and that too can be found in this section.

Allende, Isabel (1942–)

Paula. Harper Perennial, 2008, 1995. 330pp. 9780061564901. Also available in large print and Braille. 863 [Trans. by Margaret Sayers Peden]

When Isabel Allende was in Spain promoting a novel, her daughter, Paula, living in Spain, was stricken by a hereditary disease, porphyria, and lapsed into a coma. Allende sat vigil by her bedside, devastated, but expecting at any moment that her daughter would awaken. When Allende's usual courage appeared to be failing her, her agent showed up with a stack of yellow note pads, and Allende started to write. She intended to write a long letter to her daughter, detailing her family history. Part of this memoir, then, is about the generations of family who went before and the events that surrounded their lives, with a particular focus on the overthrow in Chile of Salvador Allende, a member of Isabel's extended family. As Paula's condition deteriorated and grew increasingly hopeless, as she was transported to Allende's home in San Francisco, details of the vigil, of Paula's life and her dying and death, become more prominent in the memoir. Allende's daughter never awoke to read her mother's letter, but her mother managed to keep despair at bay through the power of her writing. She also established The Isabel Allende Foundation (http://www.isabelallendefoundation.org/) with the funds garnered from the sale of this memoir, a foundation meant to carry on the spirit of her daughter, helping nonprofit organizations that support women.

Paula was selected as a Notable Book by the American Library Association.

Subjects: ALA Notable Books; Allende Family; Chilean-Americans; Death of a Child; Family Relationships; Frias, Paula Allende; The Isabel Allende Foundation; Mothers and Daughters; Porphyria; Translations; Writers

Now Try: Allende followed ***Paula*** with the story of how she was coping after her loss, ***The Sum of Our Days***, also translated from the Spanish by Margaret Sayers Peden. A number of women contributed to an unusual collection of anecdotes about how they have coped with difficult events, each essay concluding with a "post-it" note message, ***Note to Self: 30 Women on Hardship, Humiliation,***

Heartbreak and Overcoming It All, edited by Andrea Buchanan. Geneviève Jurgensen suffered the loss of two daughters in a car accident; she also puts her writing to work, to help her come to grips with her tragedy, in ***The Disappearance***, translated from the French by Adriana Hunter. One can't separate the novelist from the grieving mother in Allende's memoir. Rosario Ferré has written a novel similar in style to Allende's fiction, going back in time to reveal the history of the family and the land, in this case Puerto Rico, in ***The House on the Lagoon***.

Erdrich, Louise (1954–)

The Blue Jay's Dance: A Birth Year. Perennial, 2002, 1995. 223pp. 9780060927011. Also available in e-book. 813.54

Erdrich has created a series of linked essays resembling diary or journal entries, written over the space of a year, from her pregnancy with her third biological child to the child's birth and early growth. She looks at the creative forces of a mother and a writer, sometimes the conflict, sometimes the joining together of the two. Because this covers a year, there is much more in the book than just "baby talk." She talks about her husband, Michael Dorris, and shares some of his recipes; they have three teenagers—all adopted—who still need nurturing, plus two other little girls. She still needs to write, which she does in a little house across the road from their New Hampshire home. A nature lover, Erdrich entwines the natural life around her into her writing as well, using the emotions engendered in nature to reflect the varying emotions of a pregnant and new mother.

Subjects: Childbirth; Dorris, Michael; Infants; Journals; Motherhood; Mothers and Daughters; Nature Writers; New Hampshire; Novelists; Personal Essays; Seasons; Writers in the Family

Now Try: Louise Erdrich is primarily a novelist, but she has written one other memoir that reflects her strong ties to nature: ***Books and Islands in Ojibwe Country***. Other writers also make connections between their writing and having children; Christina Baker Kline has collected a number of essays from writers, ***Child of Mine: Writers Talk About the First Year of Motherhood***. Erdrich may have found a kindred spirit in novelist Rachel Cusk, who also wrote about motherhood in ***A Life's Work: On Becoming a Mother***, expressing many of the same sentiments as Erdrich. Those who enjoy the love and observation of nature in Erdrich's memoir may also enjoy the unusual story of another kind of nurturing in nature, ***The Daily Coyote: A Story of Love, Survival, and Trust in the Wilds of Wyoming*** by Shreve Stockton.

Greenberg, Michael (1951–)

Hurry Down Sunshine. Vintage Books, 2009, 2008. 234pp. 9780307473547. Also available in audiobook and e-audiobook. 362.19689

When Greenberg's daughter Sally was fifteen, she suffered a psychotic breakdown in New York City, later diagnosed—much to Greenberg's relief—as bipolar disorder. Greenberg's brother has a serious mental disorder, leaving Greenberg to fear a diagnosis of schizophrenia in his daughter. The diagnosis did not minimize her illness, however, and Greenberg takes us through her illness along with its effects on her family: her mother, her stepmother, her brother, her father. He also takes us on a guided tour of the psychiatric ward to which she is committed for several weeks. By the end of the memoir, Sally has been stabilized and is out of the hospital, but everyone recognizes that life will never be the same, for Sally or her family.

Subjects: Adolescents; Bipolar Disorder; Fathers and Daughters; Health Care; Illness in the Family; Mental Health; New York, NY

Now Try: A columnist for the *Times Literary Supplement,* Greenberg has obviously been earning his living as a writer. Following this memoir of his daughter, he wrote another memoir, ***Beg, Borrow, Steal: A Writer's Life,*** in which he describes the various jobs he has worked at when writing was not enough to pay the bills. Pete Earley is another writer whose teenager had a breakdown, resulting in Earley's investigation into how mental illness is treated. He discusses both issues in ***Crazy: A Father's Search Through America's Mental Health Madness.*** Bebe Moore Campbell takes on the subject of a child's mental illness in ***72 Hour Hold: A Novel.*** The elegiac tone in Greenberg's story is matched by another novelist, William Wharton, as he writes of the tragic loss of his daughter, her husband, and their two children in ***Ever After: A Father's True Story.***

Sheff, David (1955–)

Beautiful Boy: A Father's Journey Through His Son's Addiction. Mariner Books, 2009, 2008. 340pp. 9780547203881. Also available in large print, audiobook, and e-audiobook. 362.299

Nic Sheff was a loving, talented young man before he became a meth addict. His father has struggled painfully with his son's addiction and, as a writer, needed to share his story. In this memoir of father and son, he details many of the heartbreaking scenes with his son, the depths his son would sink to, the repeated rehabs and relapses, the costs to David's new family, Nic's stepmother and half-brothers. He also discusses all the research he has done into meth addiction and being the parent of an addicted child, a parent who blames himself for his son's problem. In the midst of his trials with his son, Sheff himself had a brain hemorrhage, but no one could say if it was caused by the stress in his life. Sheff ends the book on a realistic note, hoping that his son is permanently sober, but knowing that his situation is a slippery slope.

Subjects: Adolescents; California; Children of Divorce; Drug Abuse; Fathers and Sons; Illness in the Family; Methamphetamine Abuse; Sheff, Nic

Now Try: Nic Sheff published his own memoir for younger people at the same time that his father's book came out: ***Tweak: Growing up on Methamphetamines.*** Julie Myerson, a mother in England, suffered many of the same heartaches as David Sheff, a story she has told in ***The Lost Child: A Mother's Story.*** The writer David Gilmour was having difficulties with his teenage son and tried something new to engage his son; readers may enjoy reading what he did in ***The Film Club.*** In Martha Tod Dudman's novel, ***Augusta, Gone: A True Story,*** the author describes life with a teenage daughter who seems to be heading down the same path Nic Sheff did.

Steel, Danielle (1947–)

His Bright Light: The Story of Nick Traina. Delta, 2000, 1998. 303pp. ill. 9780385334679. Also available in large print and audiobook. 616.8950092

Nick Traina was Danielle Steel's second-oldest child, adopted by her third husband. From the time he was a toddler she knew he was different—very precocious and often out of control. In this memoir she details his behavior, which was often shocking and resulted in several school expulsions. Convinced that his problems were mental, she went from doctor to doctor, hospital to hospital, until her son finally received a diagnosis of early-onset manic depression and a prescription for lithium. That seemed to make a difference, and for two years Nick led a life of fulfilling his potential as a musician and being the person his mother believed him to be. He fell into the trap, however, of many people suffering from a bipolar disorder: believing themselves cured, they take themselves off their medication. What follows then is the description of his spiral downward. Apart from narrating her son's story, interspersed with excerpts from his journals, Steel also raises the issue of mental health problems in teenagers—How well are they diagnosed? How much influence can a parent have in their care? What do people do who don't have the resources that someone like Danielle Steel has?

Subjects: Adolescents; Bipolar Disorder; Children of Divorce; Family Relationships; Health Care; Illness in the Family; Mental Health; Mothers and Sons; Suicide; Traina, Nick

Now Try: Judy Collins also suffered the loss of a child through suicide; she offers her own thoughts about coping in her memoir, ***Sanity and Grace: A Journey of Suicide, Survival, and Strength***. Danielle Steel is unsparing in her portrayal of her son's difficulties, and so is Marc Parent. His children, though, are not his own, but they are very much at risk, as he discusses in ***Turning Stones: My Days and Nights with Children at Risk***. Gail Griffith shares Steel's views on the issue of teen depression and suicide, made more pointed through her own son's experience, recounted in ***Will's Choice: A Suicidal Teen, a Desperate Mother, and a Chronicle of Recovery***.

Siblings

Surprisingly, this section is not about sibling rivalry. It is comprised of stories told by adult children, of relationships with siblings, some painful and some restorative. In all cases the writer comes to know the brother or sister better through the circumstances that have brought them together.

The memoirs of siblings here tell about the relationships that have developed between siblings at the adult level, rather than when the writers were very young. They are largely narrative, describing a set period of time with that sibling, but they also reflect how the relationship changed because of that time spent.

Eggers, Dave (1970–)

A Heartbreaking Work of Staggering Genius. Vintage Books, 2001, 2000. 437pp. ill. 9780375725784. Also available in large print and e-book. 973.92092

This memoir began as an effort by the author to deal with the very real emotions spawned by his parents' deaths, one within five weeks of the other, both caused by cancer. As a result of circumstances Eggers, at twenty-two, becomes the de facto primary caregiver of his eight-year-old brother Christopher (Toph). He describes how he and Toph move to Berkeley from the Chicago area to be near their sister, a law student. The first part of the book deals largely with his "parenting"; as one might expect, this is not necessarily conventional parenting, although he does attend Toph's Little League games as well as parent–teacher interviews. The second half of the book focuses on his efforts with the Gen-X magazine, *Might*. The memoir begins with a preface, a list of "Rules and Suggestions for Enjoyment of This Book" (such as skip the middle part of the book), and twenty pages of acknowledgments, all of which offer a hint to the reader not to expect a standard memoir.

Eggers's book was nominated for the *Guardian* First Book Award and the Pulitzer Prize for General Nonfiction and was selected as a Notable Book by the American Library Association.

Subjects: ALA Notable Books; Berkeley, CA; Brothers; Death of a Parent; Humor; Media; *Might* (Magazine); Orphans; Parenting; Siblings

Now Try: The humor in Eggers's book is often compared to that of David Foster Wallace, whose ***Infinite Jest: A Novel,*** might be enjoyed by those who liked this memoir. Despite his edgy humor, Eggers doesn't hide the depth of pain of such a tragic loss; Kiara Brinkman communicates that same sense of loss in her novel about a nine-year-old boy who loses his mother, ***Up High in the Trees: A Novel.*** The death or near-death of parents when one is still young is obviously life-changing. Allison Gilbert faced that crisis and, finding nothing to help her, she and Christina Baker Kline wrote a book to help others. ***Always Too Soon: Voices of Support for Those Who Have Lost Both Parents*** is a collection of essays by people who have suffered this tragedy, whether famous people like Yogi Berra, or people who have lost their parents in disasters like the Oklahoma City bombing.

Kincaid, Jamaica (1949–)

My Brother. Farrar, Straus & Giroux, 1998, 1997. 197pp. 9780374525620. Also available in audiobook (read by the author) and e-book. 813

Jamaica Kincaid's half-brother Devon Drew was born when she was thirteen. Since she moved to the United States as an *au pair* when she was sixteen, Jamaica barely knew her brother, yet on hearing of his diagnosis of full-blown AIDS, she made the trip home to her birth country of Antigua to spend time with him and to help her mother nurse him. Kincaid (a legal name change) has always written autobiographical fiction, and much of her writing is based on her contentious relationship with her mother. This habit—Kincaid writing to save herself and to try to come to grips with her family—continues in this memoir, as she recounts what is happening with her brother and her efforts to help him, along with memories of her years in Antigua. She is very honest in her portrayal of her brother: his squandered life, his Rastafarianism, and his messy death. Her greatest disappointment is learning only after his death that he was gay, wishing his circumstances had been such that he could have been open about it. The scorn he would have met on the island if he had come out was not unlike the scorn she would have encountered if she had stayed on the island to write.

My Brother was a finalist for the National Book Award for Nonfiction.

Subjects: Antigua; Brothers; Death; Drew, Devon; Dying; Family Relationships; HIV/AIDS; Mothers and Daughters; Rastafarians; Sexual Orientation

Now Try: For an even clearer picture of her mother, readers may want to pick up Kincaid's novel, ***The Autobiography of My Mother***. Kincaid is widely respected for her prose, "incantatory" being one of the many adjectives used to describe her writing. Alice McDermott too shares such accolades, so readers of Kincaid may enjoy McDermott's novel, ***That Night***. While this memoir is really not an AIDS memoir, Kincaid did contribute to a collection edited by Sarah Brophy, ***Witnessing AIDS: Writing, Testimony, and the Work of Mourning***. Kincaid's return home refreshes painful memories. Lois Gould also had a difficult relationship with her mother and recalls her own painful memories in ***Mommy Dressing: A Love Story, After a Fashion***.

Latus, Janine (1959–)

If I Am Missing or Dead. Simon & Schuster Paperbacks, 2008, 2006. 309pp. ill. 9780743296540. Also available in large print, audiobook, and e-audiobook. 362.82092

Janine Latus has written a double memoir—one of herself and one of her sister—as her sister can't speak for herself, and Latus wanted to provide a cautionary tale for other women in similar circumstances. Involved in a relationship whose abusiveness she denied for several years, Latus nonetheless saw very clearly the abusive situation her sister, Amy, was in. Each refused to see her own life clearly, while the other's circumstances seemed blatantly clear. Finally, Janine realized that her own life had become untenable and, just after she left her husband, she learned that her sister was missing. Two weeks later, Amy's murdered body was found. Janine fought long and hard to have Amy's boyfriend brought to justice, based in part on a note found in Amy's desk, pointing the finger at him if something befell her. Part of this memoir is an exploration by Latus into why both she and her sister had weight issues (Latus aimed for the perfect body, while her sister allowed herself to gain a lot of weight) and why they both were in abusive relationships. As she remembers and recounts their childhood and youth, she finally realizes that their behavior was a direct result of the abuse they had suffered from their father.

Subjects: Abuse (Parental); Abuse (Spousal); Death of a Sibling; Domestic Violence; Eating Disorders; Fathers and Daughters; Latus, Amy; Murder; Sisters

Now Try: Connie May Fowler has done something similar to Janine Latus in baring her own abusive relationships, illuminating for others what denial can do to a person's sense of self-worth. Her story is told in ***When Katie Wakes: A Memoir***. Judith Strasser shares the disbelief of so many women after they have left an abusive marriage: How could she have stayed so long? To help herself and others understand, she wrote ***Black Eye: Escaping a Marriage, Writing a Life***. Haunting and heartbreaking is ***Skinner's Drift: A Novel***, by Lisa Fugard, about a woman who returns to her birth country of South Africa, to a home where violence was part of the norm.

Simon, Rachel (1959–)

Riding the Bus with My Sister: A True Life Journey. Plume, 2003, 2002. 296pp. 9780452284555. Also available in video. 305.9092

Rachel Simon's sister, Beth, is referred to as "mentally retarded"; one of the journeys Rachel takes in this year with her sister is to determine just what that constitutes and what one could do about it. Finding her sister to be more of a burden and nuisance than anything, Rachel had become a writer and a professor and immersed herself in her work. Her sister finally challenged her to make contact, asking her to ride the bus with her over the course of a year. This is something Beth did every day but Sunday for several hours a day, so Rachel did too; she would take a few days every two weeks for a year and get to know her sister and her sister's world. She was amazed at what she discovered and found by the end that not only did she come to understand and appreciate her sister, but she also came to understand her own self-imposed barriers.

Subjects: Children of Divorce; College Professors; Family Relationships; Mental Disabilities; Pennsylvania; Sisters

Now Try: Terrell Dougan enjoyed a heartwarming relationship with her sister, Irene, whom her parents had been advised to institutionalize when she was young, a relationship and a sister she shares with readers in ***That Went Well: Adventures in Caring for My Sister***. Sister relationships can be very close or very problematic. Debra Ginsberg enjoyed the friendship of her three sisters and reminisces about their lives together in ***About My Sisters***. Riding the bus with her sister was a touching journey for Rachel and for the reader who is able to share that journey later. Marlee Matlin's story is also a touching journey, as she recounts her life as a deaf child and actress in her memoir, ***I'll Scream Later***, written with the help of Betsy Sharkey.

Sparks, Nicholas (1965–), and Micah Sparks

Three Weeks with My Brother. Warner Books, 2006, 2004. 356pp. ill. 9780446694858. Also available in large print, Braille, audiobook, e-audiobook, and e-book. 813.54

Just as he was struggling with a bit of writer's block, Nicholas Sparks received a brochure in the mail from his alma mater, promoting a trip around the world. As his wife was not able to accompany him, Sparks convinced his brother Micah to join him, and together they traveled to such varied spots as the Incan temples in Peru and the Killing Fields in Cambodia. As they traveled they reminisced, about their childhood of poverty and their family tragedies, losing both parents in separate accidents and losing their sister to a brain tumor. They recognized their differences—evident even on this trip, as they reacted differently to the sites and the travel—but they also recognized the elements that held them close together. The memoir is part travelogue, part reminiscence, with photographs illuminating both aspects of the book.

Subjects: Brothers; Death of a Parent; Death of a Sibling; Grief; Novelists; Poverty; Self-Discovery; Travel

Now Try: Franz Wisner also took a trip with his brother, but one that was prompted by something quite different. As his book title suggests, ***Honeymoon with My Brother: A Memoir***, Wisner was jilted at the altar by his fiancée and decided to travel instead with his brother. But rather than the usual two-week honeymoon, they traveled together for two years. Reading Sparks's memoir offers some insight into the private life of a best-selling author. Michael Korda provides a wealth of information about writers from his position as editor-in-chief at Simon & Schuster in ***Another Life: A Memoir of Other People***, and he does so with the same perceptiveness seen in Sparks's book. Travel is often a source of self-discovery, or even recovery; William Fiennes embarks on a long journey after recuperating from an illness, a journey involving the snow geese with whom he had become obsessed. He tells his story in ***The Snow Geese: A Story of Home***.

Lovers

The stories in this section involve friendship of a very deep nature: that between two people who love each other enough to create a life together and who continue to love each other during that life together. In these particular stories there is much drama, perhaps in the relationship or perhaps in the fate that befalls the nonwriting partner. The two women represented here, by mere fluke, were both married to adventurers who each died at the age of forty-four. The men remember their wives in the face of the illness that each of them suffered, from which each of them died.

Memoirs about lovers are elegies by a spouse for the spouse who has become ill or who has died. Rather than focusing on their loss, these writers tell of the relationships they shared with their spouses, recounting their lives together in a better time. These are love stories, celebrations of deep friendships, even in the face of death.

Bayley, John (1925–)

Elegy for Iris. Picador, 2000, 1999. 275pp. 9780312253820. Also available in large print, audiobook, and video. 823.914

As he is caring for his wife of forty-seven years, Bayley remembers what she was like before Alzheimer's disease took away the woman he loved. He recalls when he fell in love with her, the moments of shared humor and private jokes, the intellectual pairing of the two, he a noted literary critic and she the noted novelist and writer, Iris Murdoch. But he doesn't shy away from revealing the feelings engendered in him by this disease as he tries to make life easier for her—his frustrations and even his rage.

Subjects: Alzheimer's Disease; College Professors; Coping in Men; Death of a Spouse; Literary Critics, England; Love; Married Couples; Murdoch, Iris; Novelists, England; Octogenarians

Now Try: Bayley followed up this elegy with a memoir that, despite the title, delves more into his own childhood, ***Iris and Her Friends: A Memoir of Memory and Desire***. Perhaps one of the most famed literary couples with a loving marriage is the Brownings. Readers might enjoy ***Dared and Done: The Marriage of Elizabeth Barrett and Robert Browning*** by Julia Markus, a biography that illuminates the love and intellectual partnership of the two. C. S. Lewis is another writer who was taken by surprise in his love for an American woman, a love that was cut short by her premature death. Brian Sibley tells their story in ***C. S. Lewis: Through the Shadowlands***. The jazz icon Charles Mingus married a woman very unlike himself, but theirs was a love that sustained them through life with his volatile personality as well as his defeat by ALS. Sue Mingus tells their story in ***Tonight at Noon: A Love Story***.

Irwin, Terri (1964–)

Steve & Me. Simon Spotlight Entertainment, 2008, 2007. 273pp. ill. 16pp. of plates. 9781416954743. Also available in large print and e-book. 597.9092

Terri Baines is an American zoologist who went to Australia for vacation. One of her stops was the Australian Zoo, where she watched a man giving an impassioned talk about crocodiles. He saw her in the audience, and they both say it was love at first sight. For Terri the idea of being able to chase a man with a snake and not have him run away was refreshing. Steve Irwin was referred to as a "wildlife warrior," hunting various species of dangerous animals to implant transmitters so they could study their habits to improve their protection and conservation. Terri describes their life together, their dating (in a canoe in a swamp in the night), their honeymoon—filmed and becoming the first episode of *The Crocodile Hunter*—their children, their life together, and his untimely death.

Subjects: Australia; Australia Zoo; Conservationists; *The Crocodile Hunter* (Television Program); Environmental Activists; Irwin, Steve; Married Couples; Nature Writers, Australia; Widows; Zoologists; Zoos

Now Try: Steve and Terri Irwin had written a joint memoir before his death at the age of forty-four, ***The Crocodile Hunter: The Incredible Life and Adventures of Steve and Terri Irwin***. Before he went missing, another adventurer named Steve had written tales of his exploits, although his adventures took place more in the sky than in the mud; his story, told with the help of Will Hasley, is ***Chasing the Wind: The Autobiography of Steve Fossett***. One doesn't always expect people passionate in their careers to be close to their families, but Steve Irwin was a real family man; so too was Charles Darwin, as his great-great-grandson Randal Keynes discovered and relates in ***Darwin, His Daughter, and Human Evolution***. Mary D. Leakey also worked with her husband, Louis, in their world-altering studies; she describes their life together and their work in ***Disclosing the Past***.

Kondracke, Morton (1939–)

Saving Milly: Love, Politics, and Parkinson's Disease. Ballantine, 2002. 229pp. ill. 8pp. of plates. 9780345451972. Also available in large print and e-book. 362.10092

This is a love story. Kondracke writes about how he initially resisted marrying Milly and describes their loving marriage once he realized the error of his ways. He talks about life with their children and how Milly was always a fighter, even after she was diagnosed with Parkinson's disease while she was still in her forties. It took them a while to come to grips with this life sentence, but once they did, Kondracke became an activist for the disease, joining forces with Michael J. Fox. He writes of his own personal transformation into not just an activist, but also a caregiver, and he details for the reader just what it is like to have Parkinson's disease, an illness for which there is still no cure. Milly lived for another two years after the publication of this book.

Subjects: Coping in Men; Disease Politics; Health Care; Illness in the Family; Journalists; Kondracke, Milly; Love; Married Couples; Parkinson's Disease

Now Try: Cokie and Steve Roberts have written a joint biography of their marriage, ***From This Day Forward***, discussing at the same time the institution of marriage in the United States. Nancy Reagan found herself in the role of caregiver as well; Anne Edwards has written the story of Nancy and Ronald Reagan's marriage through health and sickness, ***The Reagans: Portrait of a Marriage***. A young couple face the devastating news of the woman's life-threatening illness in the novel ***Where the River Ends*** by Charles Martin.

Saint-Exupéry, Consuelo de (1901–1979)

The Tale of the Rose: The Passion That Inspired "The Little Prince". Random House Trade Paperbacks, 2003, 2001. 308pp. ill. 16pp. of plates. 9780812967173. Also available in large print and e-book. 848.9 [Trans. by Esther Allen]

Consuelo de Saint-Exupéry wrote this memoir in French as a letter to her husband, who had gone missing during a flight over France during the Second World War. It lay undiscovered until the 1990s and has now been translated into English. The night that Antoine met Consuelo in Buenos Aires, he proposed to her. She was not yet thirty and had already been widowed twice; she fled to France but he chased her there, taking as a gift a caged puma. Thus was their marriage and their relationship. Theirs was a marriage in which they couldn't live with each other or without. He was unfaithful but always went back to her, and she always took him back; she was his muse and he could not write without her. She is the rare rose, loved by The Little Prince portrayed in Saint-Exupéry's story ***The Little Prince*** (***Le Petit prince***). And she loved him back. Despite their stormy relationship, this letter she wrote to him is a love letter.

Subjects: Argentina; Death of a Spouse; France; *The Little Prince;* Married Couples; Pilots; Saint-Exupéry, Antoine de; Translations; Widows; Writers

Now Try: The Fitzgeralds were well-known as a couple, very much in love and very much at war; their love letters to each other in ***Dear Scott, Dearest Zelda: The Love Letters of F. Scott and Zelda Fitzgerald*** (edited by Jackson R. Bryer and Cathy W. Barks) illustrate the more loving aspect of their relationship. Simone de Beauvoir and Jean-Paul Sartre were another couple whose passionate relationship was well-known. Hazel Rowley sheds light on this pair in ***Tête-à-Tête: Simone de Beauvoir and Jean-Paul Sartre.*** Norris Church Mailer was twenty-six when she met Norman Mailer, a man twice her age who had been married five times already. She describes their thirty-three-year marriage in ***A Ticket to the Circus: A Memoir.***

Trillin, Calvin (1935–)

About Alice. Random House, 2007, 2006. 78pp. 9781400066155. Also available in large print, audiobook, and e-audiobook. 814.54

This little book is short on pages, but long on love and respect for Calvin Trillin's wife, Alice. She died in 2001 at the age of sixty-three; Trillin originally wrote an essay about her for *The New Yorker,* where he has been a staff writer since 1963. He then developed that article into this eulogy. In his books (***Travels with Alice*** or ***Alice, Let's Eat: Further Adventures of a Happy Eater***) and in his articles, he often invoked Alice, so that when she died, Trillin received many letters from his readers saying they felt they had known her and had also lost a friend. He admits that he often treated her as though she were a character in a sitcom, but now he describes the real woman, the woman of definite ideas, great generosity, and warm intelligence.

Subjects: Congestive Heart Failure; Family Relationships; Illness in the Family; Love; Lung Cancer; Married Couples; Teachers; Trillin, Alice Stewart; Writers

Now Try: George Burns is another humorist whose wife was an integral part of his profession. He pays tribute to her and their forty-year marriage in ***Gracie: A Love Story.*** The writer Fenton Johnson has written a poignant memoir, ***Geography of the Heart: A Memoir,*** describing his relationship with his life partner, Larry Rose, a man he loved and then took care of until Larry's death from AIDS. Just three years before her death at ninety, author and columnist Nardi Reeder Campion wrote a memoir, ***Everyday Matters: A Love Story,*** about her happy marriage to Thomas Campion, a writer for *The New York Times.*

Family History

This section features history, of both the family and the country where the families have come from. The memoirs often demonstrate great courage, as ancestors made significant moves for a better life for themselves and their families. The memoirists come to better understand both themselves and their more immediate families as they explore their families and where they came from. Here the reader is treated to investigations of family histories in Russia, Newfoundland, Iraq, China, and Italy.

Memoirs of family history go back in time, sometimes as far back as a century, to reveal the histories of the writers' families. By discovering their family histories, the memoirists find that they can thus discover more about themselves. These memoirs necessarily add a history of the family's culture, the country where they originated, or the country to which they may have emigrated.

Ball, Edward (1959–)

Slaves in the Family. Ballantine Books, 2001, 1998. 505pp. ill. 48pp. of plates. 9780345431059. Also available in large print and audiobook (read by the author). 975.79150099

Edward Ball has been able to trace his family history back to 1698, when an ancestor arrived in Charleston, South Carolina, and began what became a slave dynasty. A journalist, Ball read countless pages of family history and records—the Ball slave owners were meticulous record-keepers—to uncover the history of his family, owners of several plantations and roughly 4,000 slaves. Through master–slave relations the Ball genealogy grew until Edward Ball was able to count over 75,000 members in the family, both White and biracial. He tried to meet as many of his living relatives as he could, partly in expiation for what he saw as his ancestors' sins, as the records indicate they were not benevolent masters. One gift he was able to offer those who were interested was their own genealogy records, something that would be difficult for the ancestors of slaves to acquire.

Slaves in the Family won the National Book Award for Nonfiction.

Subjects: American South; Charleston, SC; Family History; Family Portraits; National Book Award for Nonfiction; Plantation Life, South Carolina; Slaveholders; Slavery; South Carolina

Now Try: Perhaps the currently best-known genealogical story of African-Americans is Alex Haley's ***Roots***, although its veracity has been called into question and it is often referred to as fiction. Readers might do better with Thulani Davis's story of her diverse family in ***My Confederate Kinfolk: A Twenty-First Century Freedwoman Confronts Her Roots***. Lawrence Hill, in his award-winning novel ***Someone Knows My Name***, paints a clear picture of life in Charleston during the same time period that Ball's ancestors were trading and owning slaves. By tracing the Hemings family in ***The Hemingses of Monticello: An American Family***, Annette Gordon-Reed has brought into the open the family that was started by Thomas Jefferson.

Ignatieff, Michael (1947–)

The Russian Album. Penguin, 2009, 1987. 224pp. 9780143141652. 947.65

A Canadian himself, Michael Ignatieff comes from a line of Russian nobility, a family whose nobility came to an end with the Russian Revolution. Making use of diaries, photographs, family stories, and a trip to the Soviet Union, Ignatieff has pieced together the story of his family, going back four generations, but focusing primarily on his grandfather, Count Paul Ignatieff, the man who resigned his post as minister of education for the Czar when his liberal views received no hearing, and on his grandmother, Princess Natasha Mestchersky, the woman who was ultimately responsible for getting the Ignatieff family to Canada (the Eastern Townships, to be specific) after the revolution. Ignatieff doesn't pull punches, revealing the skeletons in his family history as well: his great-grandfather persecuted Jews, and one of his ancestors sent Fyodor Dostoyevsky to jail.

The Russian Album was awarded both the British Royal Society of Literature's Heinemann Prize and the Governor General's Literary Award for Nonfiction.

Subjects: Belarus; Czar Nicholas II; Exiles; Family History; Governor General's Literary Award for Non-fiction; Ignatieff Family; Multigenerational Stories; Nobility, Russia; Russian Revolution (1917–1921); Writers

Now Try: Ignatieff followed this memoir of his father's lineage with one of his mother's lineage, the Grant family, a heritage that has a strong role in Canadian history: ***True Patriot Love: Four Generations in Search of Canada***. Readers who become immersed in Ignatieff's story may want to revisit (or visit for the first time) Robert K. Massie's classic ***Nicholas and Alexandra***. There are some amazing stories to come out of prerevolutionary Russia. One is the story of the poet Alexander Pushkin's great-grandfather, a Black man adopted by Peter the Great, whose story is told by Hugh Barnes in ***The Stolen Prince: Gannibal, Adopted Son of Peter the Great, Great-Grandfather of Alexander Pushkin, and Europe's First Black Intellectual***. Another Black man features in a little-known part of Russian-exile history: Jimmy Winkfield, an African-American jockey who fled the Jim Crow laws to live in Russia. His amazing story is told by Joe Drape in ***Black Maestro: The Epic Life of an American Legend***.

Johnston, Wayne (1958–)

Baltimore's Mansion: A Memoir. Anchor, 2001, 1999. 272pp. maps. 9780385720304. 819.354

Wayne Johnston could not tell the history of his family without including the history of his province, Newfoundland. In fact the title takes the reader back to the seventeenth century, when the colonizing Lord Baltimore

(George Calvert) came over from England, had a mansion built for himself, and then left the following year, unable to tolerate the climate. His mansion was left to rot. Johnston has woven three themes throughout his book. He looks back at his own childhood in Newfoundland and also tells episodic stories of his father, Arthur (Art) and grandfather, Charlie. Intertwined with their stories is the story of Newfoundland, particularly its confederation with Canada in 1949, a move that was very controversial for many Newfoundlanders, Johnston's family included.

Baltimore's Mansion was a finalist for the Governor General's Literary Award for Non-Fiction and winner of the first Charles Taylor Prize for Literary Non-fiction.

Subjects: Charles Taylor Prize for Literary Non-fiction; Childhood and Youth; Family History; Fathers and Sons; Homes and Haunts; Island Life; Multigenerational Stories; Newfoundland; Novelists

Now Try: Johnston's skill as a writer shines in this memoir, and readers may want to try his fiction as well, particularly his award-winning novel, ***The Colony of Unrequited Dreams***, a fictional look at Joey Smallwood, the man who brought Newfoundland together with Canada. British writer John Gimlette also has family ties to Newfoundland, using them to interweave in his travel tale, ***Theatre of Fish: Travels Through Newfoundland and Labrador***. If you'd like more historical fiction related to Newfoundland, you would do well to read Michael Crummey's ***River Thieves***, a novel that includes the Beothuk, an Aboriginal nation now extinct. Both the beauty of Johnston's writing and the droll tone are reflected in the biography by Maggie Fergusson of a much-loved British poet, ***George Mackay Brown: The Life***.

Sabar, Ariel

My Father's Paradise: A Son's Search for His Jewish Past in Kurdish Iraq. Algonquin Books of Chapel Hill, 2009, 2008. 344pp. ill. map. 9781565129337. Also available in e-book. 305.8924

Growing up in Los Angeles, Ariel Sabar considered himself too cool to have any time for his father, a quiet man who spent his life cataloguing a language (Aramaic) that was practically dead. Finally a father himself, Ariel started to look again at the man who had been mainly a source of embarrassment to him and regretted not having understood him earlier. Here was a man born in a small village of illiterate people in Kurdish Iraq who still spoke Aramaic, the language of Jesus and his neighbors, who studied at Yale and then became a professor of Hebrew at UCLA. Yona Sabar also published the only extant dictionary of Aramaic. In order to learn who his father really was, Ariel and his father took a trip back to Zakho, Iraq, a place Yona hadn't been to since all the Jews had been airlifted out of there to Israel after the establishment of that country. Yona's was the last bar mitzvah, the fact of which laid a large responsibility on him to preserve the Jewish history from that place. Ariel traces back his family history and even tries unsuccessfully to look for his aunt, who had been kidnapped as a baby.

My Father's Paradise was the winner of the National Book Critics Circle Award in Autobiography.

Subjects: Aramaic (Language); California; Fathers and Sons; Iraq; Israel; Jews, Iraq; Kurdish Jews; National Book Critics Circle Award in Autobiography; Sabar, Yona

Now Try: Aaron Lansky tried to save the Yiddish language by collecting all the books written in Yiddish that he could find. His title indicates what a task that turned out to be: ***Outwitting History: The Amazing Adventures of a Man Who Rescued a Million Yiddish Books.*** Helen Epstein went in search of her mother's history and discovered a world among the Jews in Czechoslovakia, as she relates in ***Where She Came From: A Daughter's Search for Her Mother's History.*** In his memoir ***Messages from My Father,*** *Calvin Trillin* touches on many of the same themes as Sabar, particularly the importance of generational connections.

See, Lisa (1955–)

On Gold Mountain: The One-Hundred-Year Odyssey of My Chinese-American Family. Vintage, 1996, 1995. 394pp. ill. 30pp. of plates. 9780679768524. Also available in audiobook. 929.2

Lisa See, with her red hair and freckles, does not look Chinese, but most of her relatives in California are indeed fully Chinese. She became fascinated with her family history and began serious research, interviewing countless people in both California and China and harking back to family legends. She begins with her great-grandfather, Fong See, a man who came to the United States in 1871, a teenager following his father and older brothers. See tells how he became an entrepreneur and married a White woman. Interspersed with her family history is the history of the Chinese in America, as one cannot be separated from the other. Fong See went back to China several times and started a family there as well, so that we are treated to a picture of his Chinese life as well as his American life on Gold Mountain, the Chinese name for America.

Subjects: 19th Century; 20th Century; Businessmen; California; China; Chinese-Americans; Family History; History, United States; Multigenerational Stories; See Family

Now Try: Denise Chong has also written a family history, one with a different focus, however. Her story about her Chinese grandfather and his offspring is the award-winning ***The Concubine's Children: Portrait of a Family Divided.*** Some Chinese obviously crossed the country to settle in New York City, as evidenced by the size of its Chinatown. Bruce Edward Hall (a transliteration of his ancestors' name Hor) provides a history of his family in ***Tea That Burns: A Family Memoir of Chinatown.*** See's memoir reads like a novel with page-turning anticipation, much like Joan Silber's ***The Size of the World: A Novel,*** the story of Americans in foreign countries.

Talese, Gay (1932–)

Unto the Sons. Random House, 2006, 1992. 577pp. 9780812976069. Also available in audiobook. 973.0451

In 1966 Gay Talese wrote an article for *Esquire* that resulted in his being hailed as the master of the "New Journalism," nonfiction writing that employed the writing techniques of fiction. And so it is with this history of his family, going back to the southern tip of Italy even before the unification of the country. As other family historians have successfully done, he interweaves Italian history with his family's history, at the same time braiding in American immigration history and his own history as a child up to the age of twelve. His grandmother was left in Italy with their children while his grandfather went to America to find prosperity, a not uncommon practice. Instead he found an early death in an asbestos mine. Talese's father eventually made his way to America via Paris, employing the tailoring skills he had learned in Italy. Talese (named after his grandfather Gaetano) grew up in a bit of an odd situation: he was an Italian Catholic surrounded by Irish Catholics, yet they all lived in Ocean City, New Jersey, a Protestant enclave, so he had more than the usual issues to deal with as the son of an immigrant.

Subjects: Family History; History, Italy; Italian-Americans; Italy; Journalists; Multigenerational Stories; New Jersey; Ocean City, NJ; Talese Family

Now Try: If you'd like to go further back into Italian history, you might enjoy Christopher Hibbert's gripping story of a famous Italian family, ***The Borgias and Their Enemies: 1431–1519***. Juliet Nicholson exhibits her own storytelling gifts in her microcosm of history, immediately before the world started to change drastically: ***The Perfect Summer: England 1911, Just Before the Storm***. Roland Merullo has written several stories about the Italian-American community in Revere, Massachusetts. Readers may want to pick up his story of days gone by, ***In Revere, in Those Days: A Novel***.

Friends

The importance of friendship comes through in this section as friends celebrate friendships or mourn friends lost through death. As the reader will see, some of these friendships have been forged out of highly unusual circumstances, as in the case of the accused man and the woman who erroneously accused him, or the two men who became friends despite the apparent walls between them of jailer versus jailed, Jew versus Palestinian.

In these memoirs about friends the writers celebrate their friends and the importance of friendship. The memoirs are largely narrative as the writers describe how the friendships began and what happened to make them noteworthy. What they all have in common is the recognition of how important and formative their friendships were to them.

Albom, Mitch (1958–)

Tuesdays with Morrie: An Old Man, a Young Man, and Life's Greatest Lesson. 10th anniversary ed. Afterword by the author. Broadway Books, 2007, 1997. 192pp. 9780767905923. Also available in large print, Braille, audiobook, e-audiobook, e-book, and video. 378.12092

Morrie Schwartz was a sociology professor at Brandeis University when he contracted ALS (Lou Gehrig's disease). Continuing to teach beyond his seventy-six years, he incorporated thoughts on living with death and dying into his lectures and caught the attention of the broadcast journalist Ted Koppel. Mitch Albom saw one of the excerpts featuring his former professor on Ted Koppel's *Nightline* and contacted Schwartz. Recapturing the relationship they'd had years before as professor and student, Albom visited Morrie every Tuesday until finally Morrie was too weak to have visitors. Albom has recaptured in this memoir many of the lessons he learned from Morrie about the important things in life. He also details the progress of Morrie's dreadful disease, so that the reader is almost there in the study with both men.

Tuesdays with Morrie was the winner of a Christopher Award and was an American Booksellers Book of the Year (ABBY) Honor Book.

Subjects: Amyotrophic Lateral Sclerosis; Christopher Awards; College Professors; Death; Dying; Intergenerational Relationships; Journalists; Schwartz, Morrie; Spirituality

Now Try: Intergenerational relationships usually provide great benefit to both parties. Sonny Kleinfield writes of one particular friendship between an elderly woman in a wheelchair and a teenage boy volunteering in the home where she lives: ***His Oldest Friend: The Story of an Unlikely Bond Across Generations***. Tim Madigan was also much younger than the man who became his mentor, Mr. Rogers; they developed a friendship largely through letters and e-mails, and Madigan shares what he learned through that correspondence in ***I'm Proud of You: My Friendship with Fred Rogers***. A lovely novel depicting the mutually beneficial friendship between a young boy and an old man in his neighborhood in Mobile, Alabama, is Ben Erickson's ***A Parting Gift***.

Edwards, Elizabeth (1949–2010)

Saving Graces: Finding Solace and Strength from Friends and Strangers. With a new chapter by the author. Broadway Books, 2007, 2006. 368pp. ill. 9780767925389. Also available in large print, audiobook, e-audiobook, and e-book. 973.931092

Elizabeth Edwards had her fair share of hard knocks, including the death of her teenage son in a car accident and a diagnosis of breast cancer, an illness she was not able to overcome. But this is not her focus in this book. Instead she talks about the various communities and friendships throughout her life that supported her, from the military families who surrounded her as a child, to the mothers' groups who provided support to a young mother, to the various friends she met as her husband became a politician and began campaigning in presidential elections. She describes how she could not have gotten through her various trials without the strong support of her friends, and to them she pays homage in this memoir.

Subjects: Breast Cancer; Coping in Women; Courage; Death of a Child; Edwards, John; Hope; Legislators' Spouses; Military Life

Now Try: Elizabeth Edwards wrote a second book, ***Resilience: Reflections on the Burdens and Gifts of Facing Life's Adversities.*** Women know all too well the joy and value of friendships, a fact that Carmen Renee Berry and Tamara Traeder highlight in ***Girlfriends: Invisible Bonds, Enduring Ties.*** Men also need to bond with friends, which Bob Greene has illustrated in his own story of his group of best friends: ***And You Know You Should Be Glad: A True Story of Lifelong Friendship.*** Nicholas Sparks describes the strength and importance of community in his novel, *Safe Haven.*

Goldberg, Jeffrey (1965–)

Prisoners: A Story of Friendship and Terror. With a new Afterword by the author. Vintage, 2008, 2006. 324pp. 9780375726705. Also available in e-book. 070.9222

Jeffrey Goldberg was an American Zionist when he traveled to Israel to live and work. He joined the military and was assigned to the Ketziot Prison, where many Palestinians were held. One of the prisoners was a young man, Rafiq Hijazi, a rising star in the Palestine Liberation Organization (PLO). Gradually over time, by engaging in conversations, the two formed a friendship in which each shared his own beliefs, developing a respect for each other as well as a feeling of amity. This memoir details their differences of opinion and their coming to an understanding and acceptance of each other. After his time in prison, Hijazi eventually made his way to Washington, DC, as a graduate student, a fact that facilitated the continuation of their friendship.

Prisoners was a finalist for the *Los Angeles Times* Book Prize for Biography.

Subjects: Arab–Israeli Conflict; Cultural Identity; Hijazi, Rafiq; Israel; Jewish Men; Ketziot Prison, Israel; Palestinian-Arabs; Prison Guards, Israel; Prisons, Israel; Zionists

Now Try: The conflict in the Middle East is a very complicated one, which Gregory Harms and Todd M. Ferry try to explain in their objective history, ***The Palestine-Israel Conflict: A Basic Introduction.*** Jimmy Carter, too, has tried to make some sense of it, in the hopes of brokering a lasting peace. He has written about this in ***Palestine Peace Not Apartheid.*** Another strong friendship was forged between an Arab and a Jew, as Sandy Tolan describes in ***The Lemon Tree: An Arab, a Jew, and the Heart of the Middle East.***

Hall, Ron (1945–), and Denver Moore (1937–)
Vincent, Lynn, coauthor

Same Kind of Different as Me. Thomas Nelson, 2008, 2006. 245pp. ill. 9780849919107. Also available in large print, audiobook, and e-book. 976.40922

This story of an unlikely friendship between two apparently very different men is told in two voices, the voices of each of the authors. Ron Hall is an international art dealer who reluctantly agreed to accompany his wife to a local homeless shelter to volunteer serving meals one day a week. Denver Moore is currently an artist, but when he met Deborah and Ron Hall, he was an illiterate and homeless man. He had grown up as a sharecropper's son; instead of paying them money, the farm owner gave them credit, so they were more like indentured servants. Moore finally left the farm and drifted, at one point winding up in Angola Prison for ten years. Continuing to drift after his release, he made his way to Fort Worth, where Deborah met him at the shelter. She felt there was something special about this man and urged her husband to come meet him. It took time, but eventually a strong friendship grew between the two men, particularly in light of Deborah's unsuccessful fight against cancer. The double memoir now has a reader's guide, and the screenplay for a movie has been written.

Subjects: African-American Men; Art Dealers; Artists; Death of a Spouse; Fort Worth, TX; Homeless Shelters; Homelessness; Illiteracy; Sharecropping; Volunteers

Now Try: An unexpected friendship sprang up between James Newman, a mathematician in Washington, DC, and the family maid, an illiterate but numerically savvy African-American woman. Newman's daughter Brooke writes about this friendship in ***Jenniemae & James: A Memoir in Black & White***. In his New York City legal thrillers, the **Butch Karp and Marlene Ciampi Series**, Robert Tanenbaum uses as characters homeless people who live under the city. Jennifer Toth has visited this underground city several times and writes about these people in ***The Mole People: Life in the Tunnels Beneath New York City***. Christian faith is very strong in ***Same Kind of Different as Me***; Michael Yankoski tests his faith by living on the streets for a period of time, as he describes in ***Under the Overpass***.

Patchett, Ann (1963–)

Truth & Beauty: A Friendship. Harper Perennial, 2005, 2004. 257pp. 9780060572150. Also available in large print, audiobook, and e-book. 362.196092

When Ann Patchett and Lucy Grealy became roommates at the Iowa Writers' Workshop, they recognized that theirs would be a special friendship. Patchett realized that she and Grealy were quite different, that Grealy was a risk-taker Patchett would never be, and she made an important decision. She decided that she would not worry about her disfigured friend, but she would be there to support her and pick up the pieces as and when necessary. For twenty years they remained friends, a friendship that Patchett describes in this moving memoir, using in part excerpts from letters she received from Grealy. They supported each other as writers, and Patchett supported Grealy in particular as her condition worsened (see p. 549).

Truth & Beauty was a finalist for the *Los Angeles Times* Current Interest Book Prize, a Book Sense Book of the Year Honor Book, and winner of the *Chicago Tribune* Heartland Prize for Nonfiction.

Subjects: Bone Cancer; Disfigurement; Female Friendships; Grealy, Lucy; Poets; Suicide

Now Try: Women rely on each other for a number of things in their friendships. Ellen Goodman and Patricia O'Brien have taken a look at the importance of women's friendships in ***I Know Just What You Mean: The Power of Friendship in Women's Lives***. And Madeleine L'Engle, revered children's writer, shared the pen with a longtime friend, Luci Shaw, as together they wrote ***Friends for the Journey: Two Extraordinary Women Celebrate Friendships Made and Sustained Through the Seasons of Life***. The sign of a true friendship is the gift that Martha McNeil Hamilton (a White woman) gave her good friend and colleague Warren Brown (an African-American man) in the form of a kidney donation. Together they share their story of friendship in ***Black and White and Red All over: The Story of a Friendship***.

Radziwill, Carole (1963–)

What Remains: A Memoir of Fate, Friendship, and Love. Scribner, 2007, 2005. 264pp. 9780743277181. Also available in large print, audiobook (read by the author), and e-book. 070.92

Carole DiFalco left her working-class town to marry a real prince, the nephew of Jackie Onassis and cousin of John F. Kennedy Jr. An ABC producer, Carole met Anthony Radziwill on the job (he too worked for ABC). Radziwill was very close to his cousin John, and Carole became best friends with the woman who was to become John's wife, Carolyn Bessette. For most of Carole's married life, she and her husband dealt with his rare cancer, a disease that took his life three weeks after a plane crash took the lives of his cousin John and Carole's best friend Carolyn, and her sister Lauren. In order not to lose them all once again, Carole began to write down stories about their lives together and finally decided to turn them into this memoir.

Subjects: Cancer; Death of a Friend; Death of a Spouse; Friendships; Kennedy, Carolyn Bessette; Kennedy, John F., Jr.; Nobility, Poland; Radziwill, Anthony; Television Journalists; Upper Class

Now Try: Radziwill's style in this book is impressionistic, as is Ellen Burstyn's in her own memoir, ***Lessons in Becoming Myself***. Given the circles she traveled in, readers will take vicarious pleasure in reading Radziwill's story of the new society in which she found herself. Such readers may equally enjoy the story of Belle Greene, who disguised the fact that her father was an African-American (the first to graduate from Harvard) and took a position at the Princeton Library, then became head of the Pierpont Morgan Library and confidante of J. P. Morgan himself. Heidi Ardizzone tells Greene's fascinating story in ***An Illuminated Life: Belle da Costa Greene's Journey from Prejudice to Privilege***. Radziwill's is an emotional tale, as is Maureen McCormick's ***Here's the Story: Surviving Marcia Brady and Finding My True Voice***.

Thompson-Cannino, Jennifer, Ronald Cotton, and Erin Torneo

Picking Cotton: Our Memoir of Injustice and Redemption. St. Martin's Griffin, 2010, 2009. 298pp. ill. 8pp. of plates. 9780312599539. Also available in audiobook, e-audiobook, and e-book. 362.8830922756

Jennifer Thompson was raped in her apartment when she was a college student, and she felt she got a good look at her rapist. She was White and he was Black. Because of her eyewitness testimony, Ronald Cotton was sentenced to fifty years in prison, despite his protestations of innocence. Eleven years later he was exonerated through DNA evidence, a fact that left Jennifer horrified and guilt-stricken. When she saw him on television and heard him wonder why he'd never been contacted by the woman who had accused him, she did contact him. Over the years they have forged not only a strong friendship, but a team advocating for improvements to the criminal justice system, particularly as it involves eyewitness testimony. Journalist Erin Torneo has taken their stories in their own words and juxtaposed them. For example, as Jennifer talks about the demeaning processes of having evidence gathered for a rape kit, Ronald talks about the demeaning processes of being prepared for a prison cell.

The three authors received a Soros Justice Media Fellowship for their book.

Subjects: Evidence Law; Eyewitness Testimony; Forgiveness; Friendships; Law Reform; North Carolina; Rape; Reconciliation; Trials (Rape); Violent Crimes

Now Try: There are various aspects of the criminal justice system that activists try to address, one of which is the prevalence of injudiciously placing people on death row. Dominique Green was one such young man, a man who came to the attention of such people as Desmond Tutu and Thomas Cahill. Cahill wrote Green's story, ***A Saint on Death Row: The Story of Dominique Green,*** published five years after Dominique's execution. Abbe Smith is a lawyer who recognizes that people are often wrongfully convicted, a fact that encouraged her to become a criminal defense attorney, as she relates in ***Case of a Lifetime: A Criminal Defense Lawyer's Story***. Forgiveness may be one of the most difficult attributes to attain, but its benefits can often prove worthy of the difficulty. Katy Hutchison's forgiveness of her husband's murderer has led to the same kind of collaboration as Jennifer and Ronald's. Katy and the young man, who is now out of prison, often speak together about the dangers of teenage drinking and drug use, as she relates in ***Walking After Midnight: One Woman's Journey Through Murder, Justice & Forgiveness***.

Verghese, A. (1955–)

The Tennis Partner: A Doctor's Story of Friendship and Loss. HarperCollins, 1998. 345pp. 9780060174057. Also available in audiobook. 610.92

Abraham Verghese was teaching in the medical school at Texas Tech when he became friends with one of his students. David Smith had been on the pro tennis circuit for a while, which gave Verghese an opportunity to rekindle his own interest in the game. Gradually over time and many tennis games they became close friends, each confiding in the other. Verghese opened up about the pain of the divorce he was going through, and David confessed to being a recovering cocaine addict. As their friendship progressed, though, David's original problems that had led to his addiction overtook him and, despite Verghese's best efforts, David relapsed and ultimately committed suicide. In his memoir Verghese offers the reader a glimpse of life in a teaching hospital, life on the tennis court, and life as a drug addict, all done with compassion and understanding.

Subjects: Death of a Friend; Divorce; Drug Abuse; Family Relationships; Friendships; Physicians; Smith, David; Suicide; Tennis; Texas Tech University, TX

Now Try: Verghese had written an award-winning memoir prior to this, about his sojourn in a town in Tennessee as an infectious-disease specialist, ***My Own Country: A Doctor's Story of a Town and Its People in the Age of AIDS***. Friendships are not always easy to sustain, but their importance cannot be denied. Beth Kephart has written about this very topic in ***Into the Tangle of Friendship: A Memoir of the Things That Matter***. The drug addiction that broke the friendship between Abraham and David is vividly described by one who suffered from it, William Cope Moyers (son of the broadcaster Bill Moyers). With the help of Katherine Ketcham, he wrote ***Broken: My Story of Addiction and Redemption***. Throughout Verghese's memoir his dedication to his profession shines through. This same dedication is seen in three young doctors who grew up in a very rough district of Newark, New Jersey. They made a pact as teenagers to support each other in their dreams to become medical professionals and, having succeeded, have written about it, with the help of Lisa Frazier Page, in ***The Pact: Three Young Men Make a Promise and Fulfill a Dream***. The three young men are Sampson Davis (an emergency medicine specialist), George Jenkins (a dentist and professor), and Rameck Hunt (an internist). Today they also work to encourage at-risk youth (http://www.threedoctors.com/index.php).

Animal Friends

Certain people will contend that the best friend is an animal friend, and some will be more specific and say that the best friend is a dog. There are several stories here about dogs—they do seem to prevail in the stories told about great friendships with animals—but the reader will also find a lion, horses, an owl, and a very special cat. Here also is the story of a man who caught the attention of England's Queen Mother with his unusual method of gentling horses.

Stories of life with animal friends are usually feel-good stories, as the writers recount how special their pets are to them and how the pets have actually helped the writers develop as people. While there is often much humor in these stories, there is also some poignancy as the readers witness the sensitivity of the animals toward their owners' needs.

Bourke, Anthony, and John Rendall

A Lion Called Christian. Broadway Books, 2009, 1971. Rev. and updated. 226pp. ill. 9780767932301. Also available in large print, audiobook, e-audiobook, e-book, and video. 599.757

Once again proving how influential the Internet can be, this book, originally published in the early 1970s, gained a new life after a YouTube video was circulated about the reunion, after a year, between the lion, Christian, and his two owners. Information about Christian and his human friends, two furniture shop owners who had bought Christian from the exotic animal department at Harrods, has been updated from the original story, but readers today are still entranced by the story of how this young cub moved from being born in a zoo to being integrated into the wild by George Adamson. John Rendall is currently a trustee for the George Adamson Wildlife Preservation Trust (http://www.georgeadamson.org/).

Subjects: 1970s; Adamson, George; Human–Animal Relationships; Kenya; Kora National Park, Kenya; Lions; London, England; Wild Animals as Pets; Wildlife Rehabilitation

Now Try: Christian was introduced to George Adamson through the agency of two actors who had played in the movie ***Born Free*** (originally a book by George's wife, the naturalist Joy Adamson) and who subsequently visited the furniture shop where they encountered the lion. Lions are not generally considered suitable for pets, but animal trainer Ralph Helfer bought a lion cub to prove how humane treatment could render animals gentle with humans. He describes his life with his lion in ***Zamba: The True Story of the Greatest Lion That Ever Lived***. Wildlife rehabilitation takes many forms, like Sheila and David Siddle's cattle ranch in Zambia, where they established the Chimfunshi Wildlife Orphanage. Sheila Siddle and coauthor Doug Cress describe this orphanage in ***In My Family Tree: A Life with Chimpanzees***. Linda Johns is a writer in Nova Scotia who established an unusual relationship too, in her case with a robin. She describes in ***Sharing a Robin's Life*** how her robin maintained its instinct for the wild even while living in her house.

Doty, Mark (1953–)

Dog Years: A Memoir. Harper Perennial, 2008, 2007. 215pp. ill. 9780061171017. Also available in large print, audiobook, e-audiobook, and e-book. 811.54

Mark Doty went to the local animal shelter to find a dog to keep their older dog, Arden, company and to provide a new distraction for his partner, dying of AIDS (see p. 583). He describes life with the four of them in the house, and then the three of them, and reveals how his dogs gave him the will to live and to go on. He finally finds a new partner, and when the dogs eventually adjust to Mark's new partner, they do so willingly and lovingly. Sadness enters the house once again, though, as Beau, the younger dog, develops a neurological illness, one that he cannot survive.

Dog Years won the Stonewall Book Award-Israel Fishman Non-Fiction Award.

Subjects: Death; Dogs; Golden Retrievers; Grief; Human–Animal Relationships; Loss; Love; Poets; Stonewall Book Award-Israel Fishman Non-Fiction Award

Now Try: It is not unusual to hear of animals who help grieving owners. Cindy Heller Adams was given a dog after her husband died, and though she initially resisted, she found that Jazzy was just what she needed, as she tells in ***The Gift of Jazzy***. Susan Richards describes how an abused horse she took in helped her get over her own past difficulties in ***Chosen by a Horse: A Memoir***. Because of the proven power of animals to help humans, animals have also been trained in pet therapy. Marty Becker is a veterinarian who, with the help of Danelle Morton, has written about this subject in ***The Healing Power of Pets: Harnessing the Amazing Ability of Pets to Make and Keep People Happy and Healthy.***

Grogan, John (1957–)

Marley & Me: Life and Love with the World's Worst Dog. Morrow, 2008, 2005. 308pp. ill. 9780061687204. Also available in large print, Braille, audiobook, e-audiobook, e-book, and video. 636.752092

When John Grogan was a columnist for *The Philadelphia Inquirer*, he often included stories about his dog, Marley, "the worst dog in the world." He received letters and e-mails from readers regaling him with stories about their own dogs, who were even worse. But when John started to write about Marley's failing health and then his death, more letters and e-mails poured in than ever before in the history of the paper. This response encouraged Grogan to write a book about Marley, a story that parallels his new married life with Jenny: their first house, their first pregnancy. As they grow up along with their children, so does Marley, until finally he just gets too old.

Marley & Me was a Book Sense Book of the Year Honor Book and winner of the Quill Award for Biography/Memoir.

Subjects: Dogs; Family Relationships; Human–Animal Relationships; Humor; Labrador Retrievers; Married Couples; Miscarriages; Newspaper Columnists

Now Try: Grogan has subsequently written another memoir, ***The Longest Trip Home: A Memoir***, about his childhood and coming of age, and then that trip back home to say good-bye to his dying father. As most pet owners will attest to, it's not just dogs that can get up to mischief. Nancy Ellis-Bell describes life with a parrot in ***The Parrot Who Thought She Was a Dog***. One of the most poignant scenes in Grogan's book occurs when Marley is still a puppy but displays a great sensitivity in the face of grief. Readers who appreciated that particular story may find it interesting to read ***Creature Comfort: Animals That Heal*** by Bernie Graham. Dean R. Koontz took a break from writing his suspense-filled stories to tell the loving story of his dog, Trixie, ***A Big Little Life: A Memoir of a Joyful Dog***.

Katz, Jon (1947–)

Dog Days: Dispatches from Bedlam Farm. Villard, 2007. 273pp. ill. 9781400064045. Also available in large print, audiobook, and e-audiobook. 636.0092

Jon Katz had picked up sticks and moved to the country, to a property in New York he named Bedlam Farm, and from that location has written a number of stories. In this particular memoir it is obvious that Katz is becoming familiar with being a farmer and that he has begun to recognize what is important with animals. He has a number of them on his farm, from dogs to donkeys, sheep to a steer. He also has come to know his neighbors and the people in his community.

In fact, he shares one of his dogs with a friend, a physical therapist, a decision that proves beneficial for everyone concerned. If you'd like to read his stories in order, the first title is ***A Dog Year: Twelve Months, Four Dogs, and Me***. He also has a Web site where he keeps a journal (http://www.bedlamfarm.com/).

Subjects: Bedlam Farm, NY; Dogs; Domestic Animals; Farm Life; Human–Animal Relationships; New York (State); Writers

Now Try: Bob Tarte is another writer who left the city for country life and has written to tell about it. His second foray into memoir writing is ***Enslaved by Ducks***. William Alexander decided he wanted to try his hand at growing vegetables, rather than animals. Once all was said and done, when he considered how much it actually cost him to grow his tomatoes, the figure came to $64.00 per tomato. If you read ***The $64 Tomato***, you'll find out why. Catherine Friend went reluctantly with her partner to a farm in Minnesota, but as she tells in ***Hit by a Farm: How I Learned to Stop Worrying and Love the Barn***, she was eventually converted.

Kerasote, Ted (1950–)

Merle's Door: Lessons from a Freethinking Dog. Harcourt, Inc., 2008, 2007. 398pp. ill. 8pp. of plates. 9780156034500. Also available in large print, audiobook, and e-audiobook. 636.7092

Kerasote is an award-winning nature writer who was on a camping trip in Utah with some friends when they were approached by a stray Labrador retriever. As though he had no choice, the dog looked back at the shore, sighed, and got on the raft the campers were about to sail on. Merle, as Kerasote named him, went back to Wyoming with his new owner, where both dog and man learned new ways of living. Kerasote cut a door for Merle, to give him the independence to go walking as the mood hit him, and he would do so every day, making his way to the village (where he was known as The Mayor) and completing his round of visits with the village people. Between anecdotes about his relationship with Merle, Kerasote sprinkles information that he has found by reading about domestic animals and discusses his own changing views about pet ownership. As in many other books about dogs, Merle does not live forever, and Kerasote does not hide his grief.

Subjects: Dogs; Human–Animal Relationships; Labrador Retrievers; Nature Writers; Wyoming

Now Try: Pam Houston has written the heartwarming ***Sight Hound: A Novel***, about an Irish wolfhound who changed lives around him. ***Amazing Gracie: A Dog's Tale***, illustrated by Meg Cundiff, is the story of a half-blind, albino Great Dane who gets herself adopted by two men, Dan Dye and Mark Beckloff. They recognize that she is developing anorexia and, as a result of cooking for her, start what becomes a national enterprise, Three Dog Bakery. Karin Winegar, using photographs by Judy Olausen, gathered stories of a number of rescued dogs who have in turn rescued those who saved them, ***Saved: Rescued Animals and the Lives They Transform***.

Myron, Vicki
Witter, Bret, coauthor

Dewey: A Small-Town Library Cat Who Touched the World. Grand Central Publishing, 2009, 2008. 269pp. ill. 9780446555418. Also available in large print, audiobook, and e-book. 636.80929

For nineteen years Dewey Readmore Books was the mascot of the public library in Spencer, Iowa. Left in the overnight drop-box when he was just a kitten, he was found the next day by the director, Vicki Myron. Vicki took him in, asked for approval from the board to keep him in the library—although she took him home on weekends and holidays—and watched him grow into an intelligent, sensitive cat who seemed to know who among the library patrons was in particular need of affection and support on any given day and who preferred to be left alone. Interspersed with Dewey stories is Myron's own story. She lost her farm, divorced her alcoholic husband, and was left to raise her daughter alone during economic hard times. But she persevered and eventually got her master's degree and became director of the Spencer Public Library. Dewey became known, not just all over Spencer, or just Iowa, but all over the world.

Subjects: Cats; Human–Animal Relationships; Iowa; Mascots; Public Libraries; Spencer, IA

Now Try: Peter Gethers made his cat, Norton, famous with a trilogy of books about him, the final one being ***The Cat Who'll Live Forever: The Final Adventures of Norton, the Perfect Cat, and His Imperfect Human.*** Willie Morris, like Peter Gethers, had not been a cat person until he actually got one. In fact, Willie Morris had always been a dog person (***My Dog Skip***), but once he found Spit McGee, he was a changed man (***My Cat Spit McGee***). Gwen Cooper became a changed woman after adopting a blind kitten, a story she tells in ***Homer's Odyssey: A Fearless Feline Tale, or How I Learned About Love and Life with a Blind Wonder Cat.***

O'Brien, Stacey

Wesley the Owl: The Remarkable Love Story of an Owl and His Girl. Free Press, 2009, 2008. 235pp. ill. 9781416551775. Also available in large print, audiobook, and e-audiobook. 598.97

Stacey O'Brien was a young assistant working on the Owl Project at Caltech when she came across a baby barn owl with nerve damage in one wing. Knowing the owl could never survive on his own, she adopted him, naming him Wesley. Taking her cue from Jane Goodall, she decided early on not just to treat him as another specimen to observe, but as an animal to engage with on all levels, learning much in the process, particularly how intelligent animals can be. She relates various anecdotes about life with a barn owl, such as having to order mice in bulk in order to feed him, watching how Wesley would interact (or not) with O'Brien's prospective suitors, and how Wesley gave her the courage to move on when she was diagnosed with a benign, inoperable brain tumor.

Subjects: Animal Behavior; Biologists; Birds; Human–Animal Relationships; Owls; Wild Animals as Pets

Now Try: Irene M. Pepperberg, a scientist specializing in animal communication, also discovered the unexpected intelligence of animals, in this case, an African grey parrot named Alex. After having published a scientific book on her findings with Alex, she has since written a memoir about her time with him, ***Alex & Me: How a Scientist and a Parrot Discovered a Hidden World of Animal Intelligence—and Formed a Deep Bond in the Process.*** Parrots have also been an important part of Mark Bittner's life, as he describes in ***The Wild Parrots of Telegraph Hill: A Love Story . . . with Wings.*** It seems that any group of animals, if studied carefully, has much to teach humans. Elizabeth Marshall Thomas is a naturalist who studied the deer on her farm in New Hampshire for a year. Her tale of that year and what she discovered can be found in ***The Hidden Life of Deer: Lessons from the Natural World.***

Roberts, Monty (1935–)

The Man Who Listens to Horses. Updated ed. Introduction by Lawrence Scanlan. Afterword by the author. Ballantine, 2009, 1997. 255pp. ill. 9780345510457. Also available in large print, Braille, and audiobook. 636.10835092

Monty Roberts's father would beat him whenever he found him training horses in the gentle manner he had developed as a teenager by watching mustangs' behavior in the wild. His father usually took three weeks, with great cruelty, to train, or break, a wild horse, whereas Monty Roberts developed a technique that could be accomplished in twenty minutes by gentling the horse and engendering trust in the animal. This memoir recounts Roberts's harsh upbringing and his discovery of horse interaction, leading to his development of this very special technique in training horses. In addition to the training, however, he also learned how to diagnose and help with problems in already-trained horses. What he doesn't tell the reader, but Scanlan does in the introduction, is how he applied those same techniques with at-risk youth, young people he has taken in on his ranch.

Subjects: Abuse (Parental); Animal Care; California; Cruelty to Animals; Family Relationships; Fathers and Sons; Horse Trainers; Human–Animal Communication

Now Try: Nicci Mackay is another horse gentler, who has written about her experiences in ***Spoken in Whispers: The Autobiography of a Horse Whisperer.*** Rupert Isaacson recounts the story of his autistic son's healing relationship with horses in ***The Horse Boy: A Father's Quest to Heal His Son.*** In her novel ***The Hearts of Horses,*** Molly Gloss tells the story of a young woman who gentles horses in Oregon during World War I.

Consider Starting With . . .

Bragg, Rick. *All Over but the Shoutin'*

Carroll, James. *An American Requiem: God, My Father, and the War That Came Between Us*

Eggers, Dave. *A Heartbreaking Work of Staggering Genius*

Erdrich, Louise. *The Blue Jay's Dance: A Birth Year*

Gilbreth, Frank B., Jr., and Ernestine Gilbreth Carey. *Cheaper by the Dozen*

Kincaid, Jamaica. *My Brother*

Patchett, Ann. *Truth & Beauty: A Friendship*

Roberts, Monty. *The Man Who Listens to Horses*

Talese, Gay. *Unto the Sons*

Walker, Rebecca. *Black, White, and Jewish: Autobiography of a Shifting Self*

Fiction Read-Alikes

Bausch, Richard. *Mr. Field's Daughter: A Novel.* A man raising his daughter on his own is devastated when she elopes, but is happy to take her back in when she arrives with her daughter in tow.

Duncan, David James. *The Brothers K.* Four brothers grow up with identical twin sisters, a father who was thwarted in his major-league baseball dreams, and a mother who gradually becomes obsessed as a Seventh-Day Adventist.

Evans, Diana. *26A.* Four biracial sisters, two of whom are identical twins, try to learn how to deal with the realities of life.

Findley, Timothy. *The Piano Man's Daughter.* After his mother's death, Charlie decides to write about her life, in an effort to come to terms with her own increasingly serious mental illness.

Gibbons, Kaye. *Charms for the Easy Life.* The youngest of three generations of feisty women in North Carolina relates the story of all three women.

Kelly, Mary Pat. *Galway Bay.* A multigenerational story narrates the exodus from the famine in Ireland of a young married couple to the streets of Chicago.

Lennon, J. Robert. *The Funnies.* A dysfunctional family's life was idealized by their father in his syndicated cartoon, and now his son has decisions to make about whether or not to continue the cartoon, and if so, how.

Parkhurst, Carolyn. *The Dogs of Babel.* A linguistics professor, Paul Iverson tries to teach his Rhodesian ridgeback to speak in order to be able to tell Paul how his wife actually died.

Robinson, Marilynne. *Home.* Gloria returns home to care for her dying father, where she is joined by her charismatic but alcoholic brother.

Wells, Rebecca. *Ya-Yas in Bloom: A Novel.* The friendships established in *Divine Secrets of the Ya-Ya Sisterhood: A Novel* continue to flourish as the women are now in their late sixties.

Works Cited

Bechdel, Alison. 2007. "What the Little Old Ladies Feel." *Slate,* March 27. Accessed January 31, 2010. http://www.slate.com/id/2162410/.

Mills, Claudia. 2004. "Friendship, Fiction, and Memoir: Trust and Betrayal in Writing from One's Own Life." In *The Ethics of Life Writing,* edited by Paul John Eakin, 101–20. Ithaca, NY: Cornell University Press.

Peterson, V. R. 1994. Review of *Parallel Time: Growing Up in Black and White,* by Brent Staples. *Essence* 25 (2) (June): 56. Reproduced in *Biography Resource Center.* Accessed September 5, 2010. http://galenet.galegroup.com/servlet/BioRC.

Stein, Jean. 1958. "The Art of Fiction No. 12." In *Writers at Work, the Paris Review Interviews,* edited by Malcolm Cowley, 119–26. New York: Viking Press

Tridgell, Susan. 2005. "Relational Autobiography." In *Encyclopedia of Women's Autobiography,* edited by Victoria Boynton and Jo Malin, 481–82. Westport, CT: Greenwood Press.

Waxler, Jerry. 2008. "Mothers and Daughters Don't Always Mix." *Memory Writers Network,* October 7. Accessed January 30, 2010. http://memorywritersnetwork.com/blog/mothers-daughter-abandonment/.

Chapter 8

The Inner Life

Description

This chapter of spiritual memoirs may be the most intimate of all the chapters, for here readers will find writers exposing their innermost secrets and flaws. Intimacy is often thought of as something physical, when in fact true intimacy is the sharing of one's inner core. In other chapters where secrets are told, particularly in the case of people who have been abused, the flaw is in the perpetrator, not the writer. In this chapter the flaw is in the writer, and for the writer to lay bare that flaw is an act of intimacy. There are differing reasons why a writer would do such a thing. One primary reason is at the core of most memoirs: to come to a greater understanding of oneself and to resolve the very issues written about. Another reason is to provide a cautionary tale for the reader to be wary lest the same trials befall him or her. But it can also be that the writer simply wants to share a remarkable experience with the reader. Or perhaps writers may "want to persuade their reader to accept the same truths that they themselves have come to believe. . . . Spiritual autobiography is written in order to influence the lives of readers" (cocopreme, n.d.).

The word "spiritual" often connotes formal religion, but not all of the memoirs in this chapter are about God or specific religious denominations. Spiritual can be defined "as relating to our values and to our psychological capacity for deep, perhaps even mystical, experiences in art and contemplation" (Wallraff, 2000–2007). The "spiritual memoir places one's life in relationship to something greater, whether that something be God or oneness or the earth or death" (Andrew, 2008). Where religion is involved, the memoir can be a retelling of the writer's journey of spiritual growth toward God and salvation (Logan, 2005).

The spiritual memoir dates from St. Augustine and ***The Confessions***, not very long after the initial spread of Christianity, when writers, men and women alike, began to look inward. With works by such men as Benvenuto Cellini, Michel de Montaigne (both of the sixteenth century), and Jean-Jacques Rousseau (eighteenth century), the autobiography, while confessional, was more of what used to be called an "apology," the revelation of one's thoughts and actions, but as a "personal self-defense or justification" (Kappel, 2001). Jumping to the latter half of the twentieth century, we find writers who are trying to find their place in the universe or who have made the journey from absolute wretchedness to contentment with their lives. These memoirs often "follow an account of the author's wayward past . . . his or her discovery of some sort of secular or sacred light, and then, finally, sweet redemption" (Yagoda, 2009).

The confessional autobiography or memoir is a classic example of a spiritual autobiography. It stems from the Roman Catholic practice of confession, wherein a penitent kneels before another in humility and repentance and confesses past transgressions with the hope of receiving forgiveness and absolution, along with the grace to work toward becoming a better person. In the confessional memoir the writer has gone through the stages of transgression, recognition of unworthiness, and reconciliation with God or some higher essence, and now endeavors to be a better person. The confessional aspect is completed in the writing of that story and in the sharing of it with others.

Conversion is closely aligned with confession. Often confession follows conversion, as in the case of Augustine. Conversion often suggests a momentous event (the image of Saul of Tarsus comes to mind), but can also be a gradual awakening that leads to an epiphany. With that "aha moment" the memoirist attempts to put aside earlier behaviors and beliefs and becomes better able to cope with life's vicissitudes (Sim, 2001).

The concept of journey is often present in the spiritual memoir. At times it is a metaphorical journey from transgression to redemption. Other times it is a physical journey, wherein the journeyer embarks on a pilgrimage or journey in humility "to seek wisdom and guidance" (Abood, 2006). In this chapter actual pilgrimages are undertaken by a Catholic (William F. Buckley) and two Muslims (Malcolm X and Qanta Ahmed), both religions known for their pilgrimages.

Memoirs about the inner life are often referred to as spiritual memoirs or autobiographies, but they are not necessarily related to religion. They reflect the inner lives of the writers, whether through confession, introspection, or narration of their life stories. These memoirs are naturally more contemplative in tone, less narrative, although there may be important stories that move the writers along in their spiritual development. The theme of a journey is often present in these memoirs, whether a literal passage or a spiritual one.

Appeal

The characters in this chapter are typical of those in most chapters in this book in that they include the very well-known and the completely unknown, but they are all strong individuals who have faced their demons and generally come out ahead. For people who enjoy character-driven stories, there is much here to find appealing.

The person's story can also be riveting, however, so that the reader might be fascinated by snake handling (Covington) or by searching out a father's assailant (Blumenfeld). The stories in this chapter take readers all over the map, throughout the United States, to Ireland, England, Saudi Arabia, Tanzania, India, Indonesia, and Tibet, so that the personal journey becomes literal as well as figurative.

The chapter also offers a number of opportunities for the learning experience as the reader encounters writers from a variety of religious denominations and sects, gaining some insight into and perspective on those religions. The reader can also gain a range of different and thoughtful outlooks on life in general and on one's own spirituality in particular by sharing in the thoughts of the writers.

Perhaps the most important appeal of these books, however, is the chance for the reader to commune with someone else on issues that he or she may not be willing to discuss in person. People who may be having spiritual doubts might find comfort in reading about Karen Armstrong's doubts. Those who feel an affinity for nature as the larger mystery may find that Jane Goodall's spiritual journey resonates with them. Those who feel they never have time to sort out their own inner feelings or beliefs may find that reading Tony Dungy is enough.

The other opportunity for a resonant experience is in the section on confession. The stories of John Cheever, Eric Clapton, and Mary Karr are not pretty, and readers may recognize themselves in those stories, relieved to know that change is possible. On the flip side of that coin could be the relief a reader feels at not having had to suffer through those experiences.

Organization of This Chapter

After the five classic works, which encompass the three categories within the chapter as a whole, the chapter then moves on to "Confession," stories of people whose lives were overtaken by their own weaknesses, but who found the strength to turn in another direction. Following that section is "Introspection," wherein the writer tells a life story, but with a notable depth of personal revelation. These are thoughtful memoirs, looking at how philosophies and beliefs of others may have changed the writers' philosophies and beliefs. The final section is "Spirituality," in which many of the stories revolve around a religious faith. Even if a religious denomination is not in the story, however, there is still a sense of spiritual growth, of recognition of a connection to a higher essence.

Classics

These classics cover a broad and strange spectrum of writers from St. Augustine to Malcolm X. Readers may be surprised to find Malcolm X here,

1 2 3 4 5 6 7 8

but his is really a conversion story. The three main topics of the chapter are covered here: confession (Augustine), introspection (Lindbergh), and spirituality (Black Elk). The classics vary in age and style, and even include a twentieth-century motorcyclist (Pirsig).

These classic stories of the inner life cover a wide range of spirituality, from an early Christian saint to a man who was a proponent of violence before he recognized a better way to accomplish his goals. These stories cover a wide range in the writers' lives as well, not focusing on the single epiphany that changed them, but reflecting on the overall development of their inner beliefs.

Augustine, Saint, Bishop of Hippo (354–430)
Rotelle, John E., ed.

The Confessions. Introduction by Maria Boulding. New City Press, 2000, 397 CE. 304pp. 9781565481541. 270.2092 [Trans. by Maria Boulding]

Augustine's ***The Confessions*** is acknowledged to be "the first major autobiographical work" (Kappel, 2001) in the Western world, written as a penance, but also as a way for him both to demonstrate and to work through his spiritual growth. He looks back at his youth and his young adulthood from an adult perspective, lamenting his bad behavior, addressing himself all the while to God. He admits his wrongdoings, so the autobiography is very frank about what he calls his sins. He talks about his mother, Monica, and he also talks about his concubine, who bore him a son. He wasn't baptized until he was thirty-two, but his mother—who had prayed for years for his conversion—lived to see his baptism. This particular edition was chosen among many possibilities because it is the first English translation to use inclusive language.

Subjects: 1st Century; Bishops; Catholic Church, Early; Classics; Conversion; Hippo (Extinct City); Monica, Saint; Religious Men; Saints, Roman Catholic; Spirituality; Theology; Translations

Now Try: The story of Margery Kempe, a thirteenth-century woman, is considered to be the first "as-told-to" autobiography, and it followed in the tradition of Augustine's. Because she was illiterate she dictated her story, ***The Book of Margery Kempe,*** to a man. Another early autobiography (but later than Margery Kempe's) that may be of interest is ***Teresa of Ávila: The Book of My Life,*** translated from the Spanish by Mirabai Starr. Almost as important as Augustine's ***The Confessions*** in the historical canon of Western literary autobiography is Jean-Jacques Rousseau's work of the same name, ***Confessions.*** It is far more secular than Augustine's, as Rousseau sought forgiveness and approval from society rather than from God.

Black Elk (1863–1950)
Neihardt, John G. (Flaming Rainbow) (1881–1973), coauthor

Black Elk Speaks: Being the Life Story of a Holy Man of the Oglala Sioux. Annotated by Raymond J. DeMallie. Illustrated by Standing Bear. SUNY Press, 2008, 1932. 334pp. 9781438425405. Also available in Braille, audiobook, and e-book. 978.0049752440092

Black Elk had been hearing voices and having visions as a very young child, but his great vision came when he was nine. When he was nearing sixty, he met the poet John Neihardt, who had come to Black Elk's reservation looking for a medicine man who would have participated in the Ghost Dance movement in the 1880s. Black Elk felt there was something special about Neihardt and adopted him (naming him Flaming Rainbow) so that he could tell Neihardt his story about his people and their traditional culture, about his visions, and about his mission to lead his people against the invader. This book, then, is part spiritual autobiography and part history of the Sioux Nation, with its great triumphs and its horrible defeats. We learn about pre-reservation life, but we see Black Elk living on a reservation, feeling that he had failed the Six Grandfathers in the mission they had given him in his visions. The Sioux Nation believes, however, that by telling his story, resulting in their newfound pride, Black Elk did accomplish his mission.

Subjects: American Indians; Classics; Crazy Horse; History, United States; Octogenarians; Oglala Sioux Nation; Religious Men; Spirituality

Now Try: If you would like to share in the spiritual nature of the Lakota Nation, you could read ***Meditations with the Lakota: Prayers, Songs, and Stories of Healing and Harmony,*** collected by Paul B. Steinmetz. Black Elk refers often to Crazy Horse in his autobiography. Although there is little published of Crazy Horse's own words, Larry McMurtry conducted much research to write a biography, ***Crazy Horse.*** Leonard Crow Dog was also a Siouan medicine man, one of a long line in his family, a history he narrates with Richard Erdoes in ***Crow Dog: Four Generations of Sioux Medicine Men.***

Lindbergh, Anne Morrow (1906–2001)

Gift from the Sea. 50th anniversary ed. Introduction by Reeve Lindbergh. Pantheon Books, 2005, 1955. 130pp. 9780679406839. Also available in large print, Braille, audiobook, e-audiobook, and e-book. 170.8222

Anne Lindbergh went to the Florida coast to take some time to regroup and, in her own words, she wrote this book "in order to think out my own particular pattern of living, my own individual balance of life, work and human relationships." She uses the natural rhythms of the sea as a means of understanding the rhythms of life, the ebb and flow. Although she set out to determine her own life patterns and how to deal with the elements in her life that she found challenging, what she discovered, and the manner in which she was able to convey it, have made these reflections universal; they speak to readers on various levels, depending on each reader's own particular needs.

Lindbergh was inducted into the National Women's Hall of Fame and awarded the National Geographic Hubbard Medal. ***Gift from the Sea*** was selected as a Notable Book by the American Library Association.

Subjects: ALA Notable Books; Classics; Conduct of Life; Nature Writers; Nonagenarians; Ocean; Personal Essays; Reflections; Solitude; Spirituality

Now Try: Lindbergh wrote several volumes of diaries and letters. If you are interested in exploring those, the first one is ***Bring Me a Unicorn; Diaries and Letters of Anne Morrow Lindbergh, 1922–1928***. Joan Anderson did something similar, but a little more extremely. She and her husband took a year's sabbatical from each other, and Joan went to Cape Cod, where she too worked to sort out her role as a woman at that point in her life. Her reflections in ***A Year by the Sea: Thoughts of an Unfinished Woman*** would blend well with Lindbergh's. Virginia Woolf too, considered woman's place in ***A Room of One's Own***. What the sea did for Lindbergh the garden did for Diane Ackerman, who offers her own reflections in ***Cultivating Delight: A Natural History of My Garden***.

Pirsig, Robert M. (1928–)

Zen and the Art of Motorcycle Maintenance: An Inquiry into Values. Harper Perennial, 2008, 1974. 418pp. 9780061673733. Also available in Braille, audiobook, e-audiobook, and e-book. 917.3042092

This memoir is ostensibly about a motorcycle journey that Pirsig took in 1968 with his young son, Chris, riding from Minnesota to the West Coast. He intertwines this journey with stories of his earlier self, whom he calls Phaedrus, who had suffered seriously from mental illness. Using the technology of motorcycle maintenance as a metaphor, coupled with his current journey and his past journey as Phaedrus, Pirsig offers his philosophy of life in a quest to reconcile the rational and the subjective in life.

Zen and the Art of Motorcycle Maintenance was selected as a Notable Book by the American Library Association.

Subjects: ALA Notable Books; Classics; Fathers and Sons; Motorcycle Travel; Octogenarians; Philosophy; Quests; Travel, United States

Now Try: Mark Richardson became a "Pirsig Pilgrim" and followed Pirsig's route, describing in ***Zen and Now: On the Trail of Robert Pirsig and "Zen and the Art of Motorcycle Maintenance"*** how he met many of the same people—or their offspring—whom Pirsig and his son had originally met. Scott R. Sanders did something similar to Pirsig, but used nature rather than technology as his source for developing a philosophy with his son, as they went on a nature hike. His thoughts are revealed in ***Hunting for Hope: A Father's Journeys***. Another philosophical cult classic, which came out shortly before Pirsig's book, is Richard Bach's ***Jonathan Livingston Seagull***, with photographs by Russell Munson. Rossie Benasco, the protagonist in William Kittredge's lauded novel ***The Willow Field***, embarks on a thousand-mile journey on horseback to learn what direction his life will take.

X, Malcolm (1925–1965)
Haley, Alex (1921–1995), coauthor

The Autobiography of Malcolm X. Penguin, 2007, 1965. 512pp. 9780141032726. Also available in Braille, audiobook, and video. 320.54092

Not long before his assassination, Malcolm X was interviewed over a period of time by Alex Haley, and the result is this autobiography, this conversion story. Malcolm X traces his history from a young boy enduring violent racism, to a young gang member imprisoned for armed robbery, to his entry into the Nation of Islam. The conversion was sparked by his initial discomfort with the racism and hatred he was seeing in the Nation of Islam and his eventual expulsion from that sect. But his conversion was complete after he made a Hajj to Mecca, discovering there Muslims of every color. Malcolm X created a new organization, Muslim Mosque, Inc., whose twofold purpose was to raise the level of morality among the Black community while at the same time developing a Black nationalism. His goal was to help create a larger community wherein Blacks and Whites could work harmoniously together.

The Autobiography of Malcolm X won the Anisfield-Wolf Book Award.

Subjects: African-American Men; Anisfield-Wolf Book Award; Black Muslims; Black Nationalism; Civil Rights; Classics; Conversion; Hajj; Islam; Muslim Men; Nation of Islam

Now Try: One of the daughters of Malcolm X, Ilyasah Shabazz, along with Kim McLarin, has written about Malcolm's family's life following his assassination in ***Growing Up X***. Muhammad Ali, the noted boxer originally known as Cassius Clay, had a very different career path from Malcolm X, but they were both initially formed spiritually by the same group, the Nation of Islam. Ali's autobiography, written with his daughter Hana Yasmeen Ali and including photographs by Howard Bingham, is also spiritually oriented, and readers of Malcolm X may enjoy ***The Soul of a Butterfly: Reflections on Life's Journey***. For something in quite a different tone, but rising out of Black Nationalism, readers may want to acquaint themselves with another classic, ***Soul on Ice***, the memoir of a follower of Malcolm X, Eldridge Cleaver. Vibert L. White Jr. offers a more current history of the Nation of Islam in ***Inside the Nation of Islam: A Historical and Personal Testimony by a Black Muslim***.

Confession

Some writers have taken on the task of baring their souls and showing the world their inner frailties. They do this in part to satisfy an "emotional need to unburden the self" (Egan, 1984). They may also do it, however, to warn the reader not to head down that slippery slope. Other writers (like Mary Karr and Anne Rice) also want to share their conversion experience and the satisfaction they now derive from their new way of life. While some of these stories might have found their place elsewhere in the book, they have been placed here

1 2 3 4 5 6 7 8

because of the personal nature of the story, the role of the inner life. Readers will be quite surprised to find Mother Teresa in this section; her story may prove comforting for some, but unsettling for others.

Confessional memoirs reveal the innermost secrets of the writers' hearts and often reflect their painful journeys from desolation to contentment. They are very often conversion memoirs as well, as the writers confess how low they have fallen and what happened to make them realize they needed to take their lives in hand and make some serious changes. For some these changes mean espousing a specific religion; for others they involve a radical change in behavior and outlook.

Blumenfeld, Laura (1964–)

Revenge: A Story of Hope. Washington Square Press, 2003, 2002. 367pp. ill. 8pp. of plates. 9780743463393. Also available in large print and audiobook (read by the author). 364.152095694

When Laura Blumenfeld's father, David, was shot and injured in Jerusalem by a member of the Palestine Liberation Organization (PLO), Laura vowed to avenge him. Ten years later, after she was married, she and her husband moved to Israel, and Blumenfeld's quest then became serious. She was in touch with the shooter and his family, but she also traveled extensively to talk to various groups and individuals about vengeance, how to actually go about achieving it, and the role it plays in their culture. In writing about her search she is open about herself and the effect this mission had on her family and her marriage. She also comes to a startling conclusion by the end of her quest.

Subjects: Arab–Israeli Conflict; Family Relationships; Fathers and Daughters; Israel; Jerusalem, Israel; Marriage; Middle East; Revenge; Self-Discovery; Travel, Israel; Violence

Now Try: David K. Shipler provides an overview of the rhetoric and emotional context in the Arab–Israeli conflict in ***Arab and Jew: Wounded Spirits in a Promised Land.*** Simon Wiesenthal was confronted with a moral dilemma about forgiveness when he was in a concentration camp and was always troubled by his response, whether it was right or wrong. Years later, he asked a number of noted people to answer the question: "Can one forgive evil?" Their thoughts can be found in ***The Sunflower: On the Possibilities and Limits of Forgiveness.*** Patricia Raybon has an interesting take on the racial divide and forgiveness in her memoir, ***My First White Friend: Confessions on Race, Love, and Forgiveness.***

Cheever, John (1912–1982)
Gottlieb, Robert (1931–), ed.

The Journals of John Cheever. Vintage Books, 2008, 1991. 399pp. 9780307387257. Also available in e-book. 818.5203

This one volume is a posthumous publication and the result of extrapolations of journals kept by the novelist for forty years. He kept the journals as an ongoing memoir and also as a writer's notebook, so that we hear Cheever's comments on other writers such as *Saul Bellow* or Norman Mailer, but we also hear his comments on his life as he perceives it. He confesses to a deep dissatisfaction and evinces many contradictions in his life. Cheever's two greatest troubles, however, were his alcoholism and his bisexuality. There was a time in his writing career when his alcoholism overtook his writing life, but he was finally able to stay sober after a sojourn at a treatment center and then continue writing. His bisexuality was something it took him a while to acknowledge and accept, but it was still a torment to him.

The Journals of John Cheever was a finalist for the National Book Critics Circle Award in Biography/Autobiography.

Subjects: Alcoholics; Alcoholism in the Family; Bisexuals; Family Relationships; Introspection; Journals; Marriage; Novelists; Short-Story Writers; Sobriety; Writers in the Family

Now Try: John Cheever's daughter, Susan Cheever, wrote her own memoir about her father, ***Home Before Dark***. The atmosphere of the household in Elizabeth Strout's psychologically harrowing ***Abide with Me: A Novel***, is similar to what Susan Cheever often experienced in her father's household. The writer Donald Barthelme also suffered from depression and alcoholism, the nature of which is revealed in ***Hiding Man: A Biography of Donald Barthelme*** by Tracy Daugherty. Rather than using journals to reveal the writer, F. Scott Fitzgerald used letters, many of which have been collected in ***Correspondence of F. Scott Fitzgerald*** by Matthew J. Bruccoli, Margaret M. Duggan, and Susan Walker. A new biography of Cheever that has received wide acclaim is Blake Bailey's award-winning ***Cheever: A Life***.

Clapton, Eric (1945–)

Clapton: The Autobiography. Broadway Books, 2008, 2007. 345pp. ill. 9780767925365. Also available in large print, Braille, audiobook, e-audiobook, and e-book. 787.87166092

Eric Clapton's story is what Stephen King refers to as a "drunkalogue [that] consists of three parts: what it was like, what happened and what it's like now" (King, 2007). Clapton begins with his childhood, when he learned after six years or so that the people he thought of as his parents were really his grandparents. He continues through his music successes, his heroin addiction, his marriage to Pattie Boyd, his alcoholism, his new relationship with the mother of the son Conor who died in a tragic accident, his rehabilitation through Alcoholics Anonymous, and his subsequent career. After his rehabilitation he also founded the Crossroads Centre in Antigua in the early 1990s (http://crossroadsantigua.org/index.aspx).

Subjects: Alcoholics; Alcoholism; Blues Music; Crossroads Centre (Antigua); Death of a Child; Drug Abuse; Guitarists; Rock Musicians, England; Sobriety

Now Try: Kyle Keegan, with the help of Howard B. Moss, describes what it is like to reach rock bottom through an addiction to both heroin and alcohol in ***Chasing the High: A Firsthand Account of One Young Person's Experience with Substance Abuse***. Eric Clapton always loved the blues, and when he reached sobriety and finally felt comfortable in his own skin, he went back to playing the blues. Robert Gordon has written the biography of Clapton's blues idol: ***Can't Be Satisfied: The Life and Times of Muddy Waters***. Neil Young also had his inner demons but great success nonetheless. Jimmy McDonough was given unprecedented access to Neil Young so that he could write ***Shakey: Neil Young's Biography***.

Derricotte, Toi (1941–)

The Black Notebooks: An Interior Journey. W. W. Norton, 1999, 1997. 205pp. 9780393319019. 811.5403

Toi Derricotte consciously led a double life, much of which she reveals in her journals. A light-skinned Black woman, she often passed for White, deliberately so, and both her reflections and her anguish at doing this form the bulk of this memoir. She recognizes the innate privilege in being accepted as a White woman in day-to-day encounters with others, but the downside is that it emphasizes for her even more the level of racism in American society. In acknowledging that when passing for White she can speak first to a stranger, can tease a salesperson, and can easily ask a pharmacist for help, she admits that if she were darker-skinned she would not have that ease: the barrier would be there, invisible but almost impenetrable. This places her in no-man's land, always worrying about being found out when she passes, facing racist boundaries when she doesn't.

The Black Notebooks was winner of both the Anisfield-Wolf Book Award and the BCALA Literary Award for Nonfiction.

Subjects: African-American Women; Anisfield-Wolf Book Award; BCALA Literary Award for Nonfiction; Journals; Passing (Identity); Poets; Race Awareness; Racial Identity; Racism; Reflections

Now Try: Shirlee Taylor Haizlip's memoir, ***The Sweeter the Juice***, deals with the issue of passing as well, since her mother and her mother's siblings could all pass for White. As Brooke Kroeger points out in ***Passing: When People Can't Be Who They Are***, it is not just African-Americans who may find themselves passing. Danzy Senna's first novel, ***Caucasia***, reveals the differences in outlook and consequence of two sisters whose skin colors are noticeably different.

Karr, Mary (1955–)

Lit: A Memoir. Harper Perennial, 2010, 2009. 386pp. 9780060596996. Also available in large print, audiobook, e-audiobook, and e-book. 811.54

This memoir could easily go into the chapter with others recovering from alcoholism, but it is the spiritual nature of Mary Karr's recovery that is the focus here. She writes this for her son, the child whose birth seemed to catapult her onto the road to severe alcoholism, and she acknowledges in her introduction, addressed to him, that her memories of his youth may be completely different from his. She describes with great honesty how she followed in her alcoholic parents' footsteps until finally she stumbled into a recovery group, unnamed, but likely Alcoholics Anonymous. Reaching sobriety wasn't the end, however. She then became severely depressed and suicidal, and it wasn't until she was in a mental hospital that she finally reached out for something bigger than herself. To her amazement, she found her agnostic self not only accepting God, but also accepting membership in a church—the Catholic Church. This is a combined confessional/conversion story, told with Karr's typical edgy humor and somewhat profane language.

Subjects: Alcoholics; Alcoholism; Catholics; Conversion; Fathers and Daughters; Marriage; Mothers and Daughters; Mothers and Sons; Poets; Sobriety

Now Try: This is the third of Karr's memoirs (see p. 528), but she also published a collection of poetry about her trajectory toward conversion, ***Sinners Welcome: Poems***. Brian "Head" Welch was a guitarist with the group Korn whose recovery and conversion happened in a different order from Karr's but for the same reason: to save his relationship with his child. He tells the story in ***Save Me from Myself: How I Found God, Quit Korn, Kicked Drugs, and Lived to Tell My Story***. A number of women offer their stories of spiritual awakening in ***Face to Face: Women Writers on Faith, Mysticism, and Awakening***, edited by Linda Hogan and Brenda Peterson. The Christian comedienne Chonda Pierce suffered from a debilitating depression for more than a year and describes, with her trademark humor, what may have caused it, what it was like, and how she recovered, in ***Laughing in the Dark: A Comedian's Journey Through Depression***.

Rice, Anne (1941–)

Called out of Darkness: A Spiritual Confession. Anchor Books, 2010, 2008. 245pp. 9780307388483. Also available in audiobook, e-audiobook, and e-book. 813.54

Growing up in New Orleans in the 1940s and 1950s, Anne Rice was secure in her faith, surrounded as she was by Catholicism. In her memoir she describes how that comfortable bubble gradually shrank and then disappeared, first with the death of her mother due to alcoholism, then her father's quick remarriage to a Baptist, and finally their move to a Protestant enclave in Texas. Bewildered by the life she witnessed outside the Catholic Church, Rice became increasingly disillusioned with her faith, until she finally broke with the church and her faith and became an atheist. She focuses largely on her early life and then concentrates on her conversion back to religion and specifically back to Catholicism. This memoir will explain to the multitude of fans of her earlier writing why she is now writing faith-based fiction rather than vampire fiction.

Subjects: 1940s; 1950s; Atheism; Catholics; Children of Alcoholics; Conversion; Faith; New Orleans, LA; Novelists; Spirituality; Texas

Now Try: One of the elements that caused Rice to leave the church and then to rejoin it was the changes in the Catholic Church that have taken place over the past fifty years. Kerry Kennedy Cuomo interviewed a number of Catholics to ask them their views on their religion and collected the responses in ***Being***

Catholic Now: Prominent Americans Talk About Change in the Church and the Quest for Meaning. Colette Livermore describes how she gave up her life in England to join Mother Teresa's Missionaries of Charity and ultimately lost her faith in ***Hope Endures: Leaving Mother Teresa, Losing Faith, and Searching for Meaning***. If the picture that Rice paints of New Orleans is of interest, you might like to pick up Dan Baum's ***Nine Lives: Death and Life in New Orleans***, in which his look at nine different people illuminates the subcultures of New Orleans over the past forty years.

Teresa, Mother (1910–1997)
Kolodiejchuk, Brian, ed.

Mother Teresa: Come Be My Light; The Private Writings of the "Saint of Calcutta." Commentary by Father Brian Kolodiejchuk. Doubleday, 2007. 404pp. 9780385520379. Also available in large print, audiobook, and e-book. 271.97

Many who felt they knew what Mother Teresa must have been like, or who may have envied her her relationship with God, will be very surprised to read this collection of writings by a tormented person. She had been sent to India for a period of retreat and recuperation, and while there felt that she had been given a mission by God to remain and to care for the most abject of India's people. Almost as soon as she accepted what she perceived to be God's will, she began what St. John of the Cross has described as "the dark night of the soul," in his poem of the same name. Only one of her series of confessors, Father Joseph Neuner, a theologian, seemed to be able to help her accept her ongoing crisis of faith. She had a brief hiatus for several weeks, but then once again became steeped in her feelings that she had been completely abandoned by God. Those pursuing her canonization believe that her continuous work in the face of such crises is proof of her sainthood.

Mother Teresa was awarded the Presidential Medal of Freedom by President Reagan in 1985 and was named one of *Time*'s People of the Century in the Heroes & Icons category. She was also awarded the Nobel Peace Prize.

Subjects: Catholics; Christian Life; Despair; Faith; Missionaries of Charity; Nobel Prize Laureates; Nuns; Octogenarians; Religious Women; Spiritual Leaders; Spirituality

Now Try: Although she could find little spiritual comfort for herself, Mother Teresa knew how to offer counsel and comfort to others, such as through her thoughts on how to find one's way spiritually in ***A Simple Path***, compiled by Lucinda Vardey. One might wonder at how much Mother Teresa was able to accomplish while still trying to have a prayerful life. Joanna Weaver addresses this question in ***Having a Mary Heart in a Martha World: Finding Intimacy with God in the Busyness of Life***. Mother Teresa chose her name because of Saint Thérèse de Lisieux, a nun who died very young but who still left a journal behind, published as ***The Story of a Soul; The Autobiography of Saint Thérèse of Lisieux***. James Martin is a Jesuit priest who has long been interested in saints; in his memoir he uses saints—and includes twentieth-century people like Mother Teresa and Pope John XXIII—to put forth his own spiritual views in ***My Life with the Saints***.

Introspection

These stories may not always be of a religious nature, but they all include reflections by the authors on what they have learned from their life experiences. The events are varied, whether involving basketball, reading, snake handling, or searching for one's personal identity based on race or gender. The writers have gone through spiritual changes because of the lessons learned from their life experiences, and they reveal these changes with great honesty about their thoughts and feelings.

> Introspective stories take us into the minds and hearts of writers as they wrestle with their philosophies of life, developed through specific experiences. There is some narrative content here, but the focus is primarily on reflection.

Ahmed, Leila

A Border Passage: From Cairo to America—a Woman's Journey. Penguin Books, 2000, 1999. 307pp. 9780140291834. 305.4209

Because she believes that politics is intrinsically entwined with identity, Ahmed offers a close look at the history and politics of the Middle East region in general and Egypt in particular over the last several decades, through the lens of one who has studied in England and taught in America. The author of ***Women and Gender in Islam: Historical Roots of a Modern Debate***, Ahmed has spent much of her life examining the question of her identity, especially through the prism of feminism. Originally disdainful of her mother and her female relatives and friends, through an honest study of herself and what she refers to as the Islam of women, Ahmed has come to understand and appreciate how the women in her life have made sense of their lives. Despite the history in these essays, Ahmed offers a layperson's guide to her thoughts as she makes sense of her own life, through recollection of her younger years and reflections on her studies. Her contemplations include the fact of Girton College at Cambridge being a single-sex institution, which she compares to a harem.

Subjects: Arab Women; Childhood and Youth; College Professors; Egypt; Egyptian-Americans; Feminists; Islam; Muslim Women; Personal Essays; Reflections; Social History, Egypt; University of Cambridge, England; Women in Egypt

Now Try: Geraldine Brooks, a non-Muslim feminist, looks at the issue of how the male Muslim has changed his interpretation of Islam's view of women and what the Muslim women's feminist response to that is in ***Nine Parts of Desire: The Hidden World of Islamic Women***. Fatima Mernissi takes on many of the same issues as Ahmed in her cultural study, ***Scheherazade Goes West: Different***

Cultures, Different Harems. In G. Willow Wilson's memoir, ***The Butterfly Mosque***, the author makes a reverse border passage, going from her life in America as an atheist to her life in Egypt as a Muslim.

Conroy, Pat (1945–)

My Losing Season. Dial Press, 2006, 2002. 402pp. 9780553381900. Also available in large print, audiobook, e-audiobook, and e-book. 796.323092

Pat Conroy looks back at a formative and affirming year in college when he and his basketball buddies were on a losing team. He considers how the effort to do better than the last time and to prove to their coach that he should have faith in them coalesced the group and made them stronger for each other. He realizes that not winning a lot of games was good preparation for life, a life that would not always be a winning game. It was also good for them to recognize the bonding that can come with disappointment, that the faith each had in the others only served to boost the others to do better. Although his military-school environment and his coach too closely resembled his childhood environment and his abusive father, Conroy's team members and his supportive teachers all served to help him establish confidence in the gifts he really did have.

My Losing Season was a Book Sense Book of the Year Honor Book.

Subjects: Abuse (Parental); Athletes; Basketball; Charleston, SC; Citadel Academy, SC; College Sports; Failure; Fathers and Sons; Friendships

Now Try: If you'd like to see the emotional reality of Conroy's childhood, you might want to read his novel, ***The Great Santini***, the title character modeled on his father whose actual nickname was the Great Santini. John Edgar Wideman also measured himself against his performance on a basketball court; he combines a look back along with a look at his current self in ***Hoop Roots***. W. Hodding Carter came to learn Conroy's lessons at a much later age after he decided to return to competitive swimming when he was forty-two, and then wrote about it in ***Off the Deep End: The Probably Insane Idea That I Could Swim My Way Through a Midlife Crisis—and Qualify for the Olympics***. One of the pleasures of reading Conroy's memoir is his combination of research and richness of description. Nicholas Dawidoff uses the same successful combination in ***The Fly Swatter: How My Grandfather Made His Way in the World***.

Covington, Dennis (1948–)

Salvation on Sand Mountain: Snake Handling and Redemption in Southern Appalachia. 15th anniversary ed. New Foreword by the author. Da Capo, 2009, 1995. 249pp. ill. 9780306818363. 289.92

When Dennis Covington went to Scottsboro, Alabama, to cover the trial of a preacher accused of trying to kill his wife with rattlesnakes, he did not expect to get caught up in a spiritual renewal of his own. Fascinated by the stories he heard at the trial, he started to investigate the practices of the Church of Jesus with Signs Following, practices that included snake handling. He had already been on a spiritual quest of his own to find a faith that would sustain him, and for a while he thought that the ecstasy he reached in snake handling was it. By the end of the book, however, while he believes in what the snake handlers are doing, he cannot reconcile that practice with the fact that people actually die from being bitten, since the practitioners don't seek medical help afterward. He realized that he was more interested in the fruit of the spirit—giving of oneself to others—than the gift of the spirit—the ecstasy one finds in certain religious practices.

Salvation on Sand Mountain was a finalist for the National Book Award for Nonfiction and winner of the *Boston Book Review* Rea Non-fiction Prize. It was also selected as a Notable Book by the American Library Association.

Subjects: ALA Notable Books; Appalachian Region; Christian Life; Church of Jesus with Signs Following; Ecstasy (Christianity); Journalists; Snake Cults

Now Try: If you'd like to know more about snake handling, you might enjoy Thomas G. Burton's ***Serpent-Handling Believers***. Jeff Biggers presents a new view of Appalachia in ***The United States of Appalachia: How Southern Mountaineers Brought Independence, Culture, and Enlightenment to America***. Covington has written his book in the rhythmic cadence of the language he heard spoken, combining it with the rhythms of the language in the King James version of the Bible; William Hoffman re-creates the rhythmic language of rural Virginia in his novel, ***Lies***.

Denby, David (1943–)

Great Books: My Adventures with Homer, Rousseau, Woolf, and Other Indestructible Writers of the Western World. Simon & Schuster, 1996. 492pp. 9780684809755. Also available in e-book. 909.09812

As a middle-aged man, David Denby decided to return to Columbia University, to take again the courses on the Great Books that he had once taken as an undergraduate. This memoir is a combination of his story as a mature student in the midst of young students and his reflections on the books themselves, particularly in the context of the current debate over them, namely that they are largely authored by "dead White males" and are therefore irrelevant to many. He sees these works with new eyes and in relating them to various events in his life recognizes even more clearly their importance for making readers take note and ponder the truths they find within. His own take on the debate is that neither the left nor the right has looked at these great works for what they really are and for the ongoing discussions they could still engender.

Great Books was selected as a Notable Book by the American Library Association.

Subjects: ALA Notable Books; Books and Reading; Education; Film Critics; Humanities; Literature; Reflections; Western Civilization

Now Try: Michael Dirda also offers a contemplative look at the books that have been important in his own life in ***Book by Book: Notes on Reading and Life***. In ***How Beautiful It Is and How Easily It Can Be Broken: Essays***, Daniel Adam Mendelsohn studies modern films in much the same way that Denby looked at older classics, relating them to today's culture and ethos. Suggesting the importance of books and reading is ***The Book That Changed My Life: Interviews with National Book Award Winners and Finalists,*** edited by Diane Osen.

Obama, Barack (1961–)

Dreams from My Father: A Story of Race and Inheritance. Three Rivers Press, 2009, 1995. 457pp. 9781400082773. Also available in large print, Braille, audiobook (read by the author), e-audiobook, and e-book. 973.0405092

In this contemplation on his cultural identity, Barack Obama begins with his childhood: born in Hawai'i to a White woman from Kansas and a Black man from Kenya. First living in Hawai'i and then in Indonesia with his mother, S. Ann Dunham Soetero, and stepfather, he had a variety of racial-identity issues to deal with. His father had left his mother when Barack was just a toddler, with the result that Obama had only one subsequent major encounter with him—a month's stay in Kenya. Confused about who he was and where he stood as a person and as an American, he read many of the classics in the Black canon. He also initially turned to drugs and alcohol, realizing soon, however, that whatever he was to become would have to be of his own doing. Going back to Kenya to visit with his father's large family and particularly with his half-siblings, Obama started finally to get a sense of who he was. Feeling more comfortable with his own identity, he then wrote ***Of Thee I Sing: A Letter to My Daughters,*** to give his daughters a sense of who they are in the context of their strengths and of those international figures who came before them evincing the same strengths.

Barack Obama was awarded the Nobel Peace Prize.

Subjects: African-American Men; Biracial Children; Chicago, IL; Fathers and Sons; Hawai'i; Kenya; Lawyers; Nobel Prize Laureates; Obama, Barack Hussein, Sr.; Presidents; Racial Identity; Racism

Now Try: Obama's father received a master's degree from Harvard in the 1960s. The story of how he got there was told by Tom Shachtman in ***Airlift to America: How Barack Obama, Sr., John F. Kennedy, Tom Mboya, and 800 East African Students Changed Their World and Ours***. Obama's mother is the subject of a new biography by Janny Scott: ***A Singular Woman: The Untold Story of Barack Obama's Mother***. One of the many books that Obama read to help define himself was ***The Autobiography of W. E. B. Du Bois; A Soliloquy on Viewing My Life from the Last Decade of Its First Century,*** the story of the man who did much to advance the cause of African-Americans. In ***Race Matters*** Cornel West takes a long and differing look at race issues in America in the hopes of effecting significant change. Rosemary Bray McNatt's story proves inspiring in the way that Obama's does, as she overcame the disadvantages that were part of her life growing up poor in Chicago and became one of the first Black women at Yale. She shares her story in ***Unafraid of the Dark: A Memoir***. (For Obama's other memoir, please see p. 384.)

O'Faolain, Nuala (1942–2008)

Are You Somebody: The Accidental Memoir of a Dublin Woman. H. Holt, 1998, 1996. 215pp. 9780805056631. Also available in large print and audiobook. 070.92

A journalist in Ireland, O'Faolain offered to write an introductory blurb about herself for a collection of her articles that was being published. Once she started writing, however, she couldn't stop, and thus her first memoir was born. She was one of nine children in a typical poor Irish family and watched her mother, given full responsibility for all the children, sink into a reclusive alcoholism. Holding a mirror to her mother, she saw reflected there not only the potential for her own life, but also the faces of countless Irish women who had little significance except their ability to bear and perhaps raise children. O'Faolain deliberately chose a different life for herself, eschewing traditional marriage and childbirth, but she still felt a lack of connectedness and love with a special companion. Her memoir, then, is both an honest declaration of her loneliness as a woman—a loneliness shared by hundreds, if not thousands, of other Irish women—and a reflection of the social culture in Ireland in the last half of the twentieth century.

Subjects: Children of Alcoholics; Ireland; Irish; Journalists, Ireland; Loneliness; Women in Ireland

Now Try: Edna O'Brien's ***Mother Ireland,*** published with photographs by Fergus Bourke, is another autobiographical piece that portrays both a life and the country that gave birth to that life. Rosemary Mahoney returned to Ireland to witness what she perceived as a change among women and how they were considered. Interweaving her own experiences there with the stories of women she met, she wrote ***Whoredom in Kimmage: Irish Women Coming of Age***. Julia Scully's life differed significantly from O'Faolain's except for one major detail: born poor and neglected, she too made something of herself, telling her story in ***Outside Passage: A Memoir of an Alaskan Childhood.***

Spirituality

Formal religion is more evident in this section than in the other sections. The people represented here might be spiritual leaders, or they might be laypeople learning more about their own religion or seeking out other religions. Not all of the stories deal with actual religions, however. Jane Goodall finds spirituality in the work she has spent her life doing with chimpanzees in Tanzania, and Tony Dungy finds his on the football field. Both Kathleen Norris and Elizabeth Gilbert find spiritual renewal in a religious environment different from their own, while Don Piper died to find his. The true tenets of Islam are illuminated by the faith journeys of two Muslim women (Ahmed and Hasan).

Memoirs focusing on spirituality often speak of specific religions and how the writers came to embrace those religions. But they can also tell the stories of writers who, outside of religion, have learned that it is the life of the spirit that holds much importance, perhaps more so than the material life. These memoirs involve more narrative than other introspective memoirs, as the writers describe how they have come to recognize the importance of good spiritual health.

Ahmed, Qanta

In the Land of Invisible Women: A Female Doctor's Journey in the Saudi Kingdom. Sourcebooks, 2008. 454pp. 9781402210877. Also available in e-book. 610.82092

A British-born Muslim doctor working temporarily in the United States, Ahmed moved on to accept a position in a hospital in Saudi Arabia. Initially excited at the prospect, she was not prepared for what she actually found there. Although she had always been a believing Muslim, she had never lived in a Muslim country before, in this case a country that included both fundamentalist, militant security guards and traditional, peace-loving Muslim doctors. She railed against the former and learned much about practicing her faith from the latter. A major spiritual benefit to her of living in Saudi Arabia was the ease with which she could make Hajj to Mecca, a journey she embarked on for the first time in her life, a journey that greatly enhanced her spirituality, drawing her closer to her faith and her religion.

Subjects: English in Saudi Arabia; Hajj; Muslim Women; Pakistani-English; Physicians; Saudi Arabia; Wahhabis (Islam); Women in Saudi Arabia

Now Try: Rosemary Mahoney embarked on several pilgrimages, primarily to Christian shrines, but also to a Hindu shrine in Varanasi, India. As she explains in ***The Singular Pilgrim: Travels on Sacred Ground***, she did it to discover what believers see in these pilgrimages; she came away still skeptical, but also recognizing that she too was a woman of faith. Another woman who made the Hajj to Mecca is Asra Q. Nomani, a Muslim single mother whose faith was renewed by her pilgrimage; her story can be found in her memoir, ***Standing Alone in Mecca: An American Woman's Struggle for the Soul of Islam***. The Moroccan scholar Abdellah Hammoudi offers his own view of the Hajj in ***A Season in Mecca: Narrative of a Pilgrimage***, translated from the French by Pascale Ghazaleh.

Armstrong, Karen (1944–)

The Spiral Staircase: My Climb out of Darkness. Anchor Books, 2005, 2004. 305pp. 9780385721271. Also available in large print, audiobook (read by the author), e-audiobook, e-book, and video. 200.92

This is Armstrong's third memoir (after ***Through the Narrow Gate*** and ***Beginning the World***), but she is writing this one to correct the first two, which she felt were untrue both in their perspective and in their emotional rendering. Using the image provided by T. S. Eliot's ***Ash-Wednesday*** of the spiral staircase, an artifact that takes one in a circular fashion but ultimately reaches the light, she describes her difficult journey. Providing highlights (or lowlights) from her life in a cloistered convent, she moves on to her unsuccessful academic career, all the while suffering from a misdiagnosed illness. Once she learns she has epilepsy and is given medication for it, she is so relieved that she is able to see better the light at the top of the staircase. Though still confused spiritually in her search for God and therefore for herself, she is sent to Jerusalem by her employer to make a documentary on St. Paul; there she finds her life's work as a writer who will try to create unity in diversity by illuminating the teachings of and similarities among the three Abrahamic religions: Judaism, Christianity, and Islam.

The Spiral Staircase was a finalist for the *Los Angeles Times* Current Interest Book Prize.

Subjects: Catholics; Christian Life; Convent Life; Epilepsy; Ex-Nuns; Religion; Writers, England

Now Try: Joan Chittister is a woman who stayed in the convent, but also writes about the commonalities among the three great Western religions. After writing several books on that topic, she has written a more personal story, ***Called to Question: A Spiritual Memoir***. Sue Monk Kidd describes her own search for God in ***The Dance of the Dissident Daughter: A Woman's Journey from Christian Tradition to the Sacred Feminine***. One of Armstrong's discoveries on her path was how important art could be in one's spiritual development; Madeleine L'Engle made the same discovery, as she describes in ***Walking on Water: Reflections on Faith & Art***.

Braestrup, Kate

Here If You Need Me: A True Story. Back Bay Books, 2008, 2007. 211pp. 9780316066310. Also available in large print, audiobook, and e-book. 813.54

Kate Braestrup's life took some unexpected turns, which makes for some unexpected reading in a section on spirituality. She was married to Drew, a member of the Maine State Police, a man who had planned to become a minister when he retired from the State Police. Killed in a car accident, Drew was never able to fulfill that dream, but his wife, Kate, did. She wanted to be of service to others and eventually became the chaplain for the Maine Warden Service. Accompanying the wardens when they were called to help, she gave comfort to the families whose child or spouse had gone missing, to those hurt in the park, and to the wardens as well, when they had to deal with particularly troubling tragedies. Given her own tragedy, she was well-equipped to offer empathy to others. In a collection of essays Braestrup discusses her husband's death and what followed, her education at the seminary, her four children, and her work, full of detail about search-and-rescue operations, for example. She also offers her take on religion, on God, on heaven and hell. Because she felt that Maine was such a small state and she had the issue of confidentiality to deal with, Braestrup changed names and identifying features, both personal and geographic, when telling her stories.

Subjects: Chaplains; Death of a Spouse; Maine; Personal Essays; Religious Women; Rescue Work; Unitarian Universalists; Widows; Writers

Now Try: Kim Chernin grew up in a radical household but eventually made her way to a spiritual life, engendered by the realization of the spiritual importance of caring for others; her journey is recounted in ***In My Father's Garden: A Daughter's Search for a Spiritual Life***. Joni Eareckson Tada became quite spiritual after the diving accident that paralyzed her. She describes her spiritual journey in ***The God I Love: A Lifetime of Walking with Jesus***. Chaplains can be found in a variety of interesting, and often dangerous, places. Michael Daly tells the story of a chaplain for the New York City Fire Department, ***The Book of Mychal: The Surprising Life and Heroic Death of Father Mychal Judge***.

Bstan-'dzin-rgya-mtsho, Dalai Lama XIV (1935–)

Freedom in Exile: The Autobiography of the Dalai Lama. HarperCollins, 2008, 1990. 320pp. ill. 9780060987015. Also available in large print and audiobook. 294.3923092

The freedom to which the Dalai Lama refers in his title is a spiritual freedom that he has found. Living in exile from Tibet allows him to practice his religion and to preach it to others. It allows him to continue to be a self-described "simple Buddhist monk." But his spiritual freedom is only one of many topics in this memoir. He describes his lonely childhood, taken from his parents and a familiar environment to an austere monastery when he was just a toddler. The responsibilities he faced as a teenager—head statesman of the country and head religious figure for all the Tibetan Buddhists—particularly in the face of the increasing hostilities from China, were more than any teenager should ever have to bear. He also describes his life in exile, the political meetings, the statesmen he has met, and what he has perceived in human behavior around the world. He has written this book in English—obviously not his first language—so that sometimes there is a quaintness in his expressions.

The Dalai Lama was awarded the Nobel Peace Prize.

Subjects: Buddhism; China; Dalai Lamas; Exiles; Government-in-Exile; Nobel Prize Laureates; Refugees, Tibet; Religious Men; Spiritual Leaders; Spirituality; Tibet

Now Try: In conversations with Thomas Laird, the Dalai Lama has also offered a picture of Tibet, its geography, history, and culture, in ***The Story of Tibet: Conversations with the Dalai Lama***. A highly acclaimed introduction to Buddhism has been cowritten by Huston Smith and Philip Novak: ***Buddhism: A Concise Introduction***. Barbara Brown Taylor is an Episcopal minister who left formal preaching to teach at university. She has written a book, ***An Altar in the World: A Geography of Faith***, which illustrates the kind of spirituality that the Dalai Lama would recommend, the recognition of how one can practice a religious faith in even the smallest details of day-to-day life. Readers who are interested in the Eastern aspects of the Dalai Lama's story and religion may also be interested in pursuing another Eastern religion in the classic ***Autobiography of a Yogi*** by Paramahansa Yogananda.

Buckley, William F. (1925–2008)

Nearer, My God: An Autobiography of Faith. Harcourt Brace, 1998, 1997. 313pp. ill. 9780156006187. Also available in e-book. 282.092

William Buckley's Catholic childhood was not a typical American childhood, spent as it was in English boarding schools, travels in Europe, and life in homes with servants. But it was still a childhood of strong Catholic faith that carried on throughout Buckley's adulthood. In this autobiography, reflecting on his faith in God and the Catholic Church, he also voices his opinions on the changes that have taken place in the Church over the last several decades and discusses some of the major issues challenging the church, such as contraception and women priests. In addition, he calls upon some prominent Catholic converts to weigh in with their thoughts. He is very personal in this autobiography, sharing very deep, very real reactions to such events as his pilgrimage to Lourdes.

Buckley was awarded the Presidential Medal of Freedom in 1991 by President George H. W. Bush.

Subjects: Catholics; Christian Life; Faith; Journalists; Muggeridge, Malcolm; Political Commentators

Now Try: Buckley subsequently wrote a more secular autobiography, ***Miles Gone By: A Literary Autobiography***. In his spiritual autobiography he devotes an entire chapter to meeting Malcolm Muggeridge, the renowned British journalist and writer. Muggeridge, a convert to Roman Catholicism, has written his own autobiography, ***Confessions of a Twentieth-Century Pilgrim***. Paul Wilkes is another author who has written a book to describe what his Catholic faith means to him: ***In Due Season: A Catholic Life***. The United States has some important Catholic writers, whose stories Paul Elie has gathered together. ***The Life You Save May Be Your Own: An American Pilgrimage*** includes the stories of Flannery O'Connor, Dorothy Day, Walker Percy, and Thomas Merton.

Dungy, Tony (1955–)
Whitaker, Nathan, coauthor

Quiet Strength: A Memoir. Foreword by Denzel Washington. Tyndale House, 2007. 301pp. ill. 16pp. of plates. 9781414318011. Also available in audiobook, e-audiobook, and e-book. 277.3083092

Dungy presents his life from his childhood and the strong influence of his parents to his Super Bowl win as head coach of the Indianapolis Colts, the first African-American to do so. He talks about specific games and about coaching, but he also talks about the suicide in 2005 of his eldest son, James. The main thrust of Dungy's memoir, however, is the inclusion of his life principles, reflecting a strong belief in God and in the importance of doing significant things with your life. By significant he doesn't mean winning games or making a lot of money; he means making a difference in other people's lives by the example one sets and by the good one can do for others. He believes that his faith has helped him get through the tragedy of his son's death. Following this memoir, he wrote an even more spiritual book, with Nathan Whitaker, ***Uncommon: Finding Your Path to Significance***.

Subjects: African-American Men; Christian Life; Conduct of Life; Death of a Child; Firsts; Football; Football Coaches; Indianapolis Colts (Football Team); Spirituality; Super Bowl

Now Try: Denzel Washington, who wrote the foreword for Dungy's book, has compiled a book with Daniel Paisner on the importance of role models, including several disparate stories of significant mentoring: ***A Hand to Guide Me***. There is often much adversity to overcome in professional sports, some of it self-imposed. Such is the story of Josh Hamilton, a baseball player who had it all and almost threw it away. He describes how his faith helped him overcome his own weaknesses that nearly ruined his career in ***Beyond Belief: Finding the Strength to Come Back***, written with Tim Keown. The coach of a sports team has an opportunity to be a constructive influence on many young people. Andrew Blauner interviewed a number of high school and college players who went on to be writers, asking them to talk about the coaches who had the most positive influence on them; he collected the responses in ***Coach: 25 Writers Reflect on People Who Made a Difference***.

Gilbert, Elizabeth (1969–)

Eat, Pray, Love: One Woman's Search for Everything Across Italy, India and Indonesia. Penguin, 2007, 2006. 334pp. 9780143038412. Also available in large print, audiobook, e-audiobook, e-book, and video. 910.4

While her professional life was in full swing, Elizabeth Gilbert was experiencing a serious personal crisis. After much upheaval and much angst, she finally decided to embark on a year's travel in search of her real self. Choosing three countries to help her in her quest, she assigned a specific purpose for each country. Italy was to give her comfort—in its food, its people, and its language. Here she indulged herself. India was to provide her with spiritual sustenance, so she stayed in an ashram for several months, learning to meditate, practicing yoga, and discovering new things about herself. Indonesia proved to be the source of her emotional healing, where she made new friends, learned even more about herself, and fell in love. Her writing is honest and open; we see her warts and all, as she struggles in her spiritual quest, but it is also quite humorous so that we can laugh with her as she bumbles about.

Subjects: Ashrams; Humor; India; Indonesia; Italy; Quests; Self-Discovery; Solo Travel; Spirituality; Travel

Now Try: Gilbert has continued her story with a new book, ***Committed: A Skeptic Makes Peace with Marriage***. Dani Shapiro, too, decided she needed to take a serious look at herself and what her life was all about. The result is her new book, ***Devotion: A Memoir***. Natalie Goldberg didn't feel she had to leave the United States for her quest of self-realization. In her memoir, ***Long Quiet Highway: Waking Up in America***, she describes the various people she met who helped her "wake up" to the world and to who she was. Jessie Sullivan, the protagonist in Sue Monk Kidd's novel, ***The Mermaid Chair***, has a problem similar to Elizabeth Gilbert's: she is professionally successful and personally suffering. She returns to her childhood home, ostensibly to help her mother, but in doing so she also helps herself.

Goodall, Jane (1934–)
Berman, Phillip (1956–), coauthor

Reason for Hope: A Spiritual Journey. Warner, 2005. 304pp. ill. 9780446676137. Also available in large print, audiobook (read by the author), e-audiobook, e-book, and video. 590.92

Although she has written other autobiographies (see p. 178), in this memoir Jane Goodall uses the trajectory of her life to illustrate her spiritual views as they have developed through the years. She traces her life from her childhood through her career, the birth of her son, Hugo ("Grub"), the death of her second husband, Derek Bryceson, and her ensuing grief. She uses the knowledge she has gained from her work with chimpanzees to understand human nature better, so she is filled with hope that humankind will assume the responsibility that is ours alone to take care of the planet and its inhabitants. She recognizes that the possibility exists that greed might prevail, but she has great hope in the younger generation. She also discusses such serious matters as evolution and her belief in the existence of a God or a higher being.

Among her many awards, Jane Goodall was made a Dame of the British Empire and awarded both a National Geographic Hubbard Medal and the highest honor of the French Foreign Legion, the *Légion d'honneur*.

Subjects: Animal Rights Activists; Chimpanzees; Environmental Activists; Evolution; Gombe Stream National Park, Tanzania; Jane Goodall Institute; Primatologists; Spirituality; Tanzania

Now Try: After writing this autobiography Goodall published a work in conjunction with Marc Bekoff, an animal behaviorist, as a guideline for human interaction with animals: ***The Ten Trusts: What We Must Do to Care for the Animals We Love***. In conducting her important studies on elephant communication, Katharine Payne has also developed a spiritual philosophy about the importance of nonhuman forms of life and our interaction with them. She explains this, along with her work with elephants, in ***Silent Thunder: In the Presence of Elephants***. It was because of Louis Leakey that Goodall became involved in the study of chimpanzees and subsequently in environmentalism in the first place. Along with Virginia Morell, Leakey's son, Richard E. Leakey, a paleontologist and conservationist, has written about his fight for conservation of the wildlife in Africa in ***Wildlife Wars: My Fight to Save Africa's Natural Treasures***. Goodall's ideas about the hope to be found in youth are exemplified in Robin Kadison Berson's ***Young Heroes in World History***.

Graham, Billy (1918–)

Just as I Am: The Autobiography of Billy Graham. 10th anniversary ed., rev. and updated. HarperOne, 2007, 1997. 801pp. ill. 9780061171062. Also available in large print, Braille, and audiobook. 269.2092

Billy Graham offers a look at his early life growing up in North Carolina and his interest in God and in preaching, something that came fairly early to him. He also describes his belief that he was given the gift of faith by God and that there was no point in questioning it. He always tried to communicate this belief in God and God's caring for everyone in the hundreds of crusades he conducted, crusades that are recounted in his book. Another aspect of his book deals with the difficulties of being a good family man when he traveled so much through his ministry. He admits that he felt it was his calling to travel in order to evangelize, and his wife's calling, then, would be to follow and to take responsibility for their family. And finally, we learn much in his story about his friendships and relationships with powerful politicians, particularly U.S. presidents, from Dwight Eisenhower onward.

Billy Graham was named one of *Time*'s People of the Century in the Heroes & Icons category and received a Horatio Alger Award. In 1983 he was awarded a Presidential Medal of Freedom by President Reagan, and in 1996 he received the Congressional Gold Medal.

Subjects: Absentee Fathers; Billy Graham Evangelistic Association, NC; Christian Life; Evangelists; Faith; Family Relationships; Graham, Ruth Bell; *Hour of Decision* (Radio Program); Nonagenarians; Religious Men; Spiritual Leaders

Now Try: Graham's wife, Ruth Bell Graham, wrote her own story, ***Footprints of a Pilgrim: The Life and Loves of Ruth Bell Graham***. Robert Harold Schuller is another renowned preacher who also grew up on a farm. His autobiography is ***My Journey: From an Iowa Farm to a Cathedral of Dreams***. For quite a different view of the evangelical life, you might be interested in Jay Bakker's book, written with Linden Gross, ***Son of a Preacher Man: My Search for Grace in the Shadows***, about his own faith, given the upsets he had in his family life with a preacher father, Jim Bakker, who went astray. Faith is an integral part of Graham's ministry, but it shows itself in various ways. Mitch Albom also discusses the importance of faith and reveals its presence in two very different men ministering to their people, in ***Have a Little Faith: A True Story***.

Hasan, Asma Gull (1974–)

Why I Am a Muslim: An American Odyssey. With a new Preface by the author. Element, 2005, 2004. 172pp. 9780007175345. 297.4

A self-proclaimed "Muslim feminist cowgirl" raised in Colorado, Hasan sets out to explain why she chose to remain Muslim. She distances true Islam from fundamentalist Islam, seeing the religion founded by Mohammed as one that fosters religious tolerance and equality for women. She also believes that the basic principles of Islam are closely aligned with the basic principles of the American Founding Fathers. She offers seven chapters, each providing a reason for her choice, using incidents from her own life to back up her choices.

Subjects: Colorado; Islam; Muslim Women; Pakistani-Americans; Sufis (Islam)

Now Try: Hasan has written a subsequent memoir as well, ***Red, White, and Muslim: My Story of Belief***. Hassan Qazwini is an imam in a different sect of Islam, the Shi'a sect, but he agrees with Hasan on the importance of illuminating true Islam, which he does with the help of Brad Crawford in ***American Crescent: A Muslim Cleric on the Power of His Faith, the Struggle Against Prejudice, and the Future of Islam and America***. Eboo Patel used to be a radical Muslim, but after changing his ways and embracing a more inclusive Islam, he created the Interfaith Youth Core to promote religious tolerance. His story is ***Acts of Faith: The Story of an American Muslim, the Struggle for the Soul of a Generation***. Sadia Shepard is a half-Muslim, half-Christian woman with a Jewish grandmother who travels to India to discover her family's past in a small Jewish community in India in ***The Girl from Foreign: A Search for Shipwrecked Ancestors, Forgotten Histories, and a Sense of Home***.

Lamott, Anne (1954–)

Traveling Mercies: Some Thoughts on Faith. Anchor, 2000, 1999. 275pp. 9780385496094. Also available in large print, audiobook (read by the author), e-audiobook, and e-book. 813.54

In her first two memoirs, ***Bird by Bird: Some Instructions on Writing and Life*** and ***Operating Instructions: A Journal of My Son's First Year,*** Lamott had already introduced her readers to recurring characters in this third memoir, particularly her son, Sam. This memoir focuses on her "lurch" of faith as an undergraduate when she started to believe there really could be a God and continues from there. She is brutally honest about herself, about her struggles with alcohol and drugs, all the while aware of a Jesus and a God out there somewhere. This memoir also deals with the serious illness of two good friends introduced in her earlier books, and the death of her father, but her increasing faith, discussed irreverently, is the thread that winds through the book.

Subjects: Alcoholics; Drug Abuse; Faith; Fathers and Daughters; Friendships; Humor; Mothers and Sons; Single Mothers; Spirituality

Now Try: Lamott has continued her spiritual writing with ***Plan B: Further Thoughts on Faith*** and ***Grace (Eventually): Thoughts on Faith.*** Lamott has been compared to Flannery O'Connor in the subjects she treats and in the sharp humor she uses to get her point across. The reader might enjoy browsing through ***The Complete Stories*** of Flannery O'Connor. The writer who started Lamott on her journey toward faith was, oddly enough, Søren Kierkegaard, whose work, ***Journals and Papers,*** tells his life story as well as his faith history. Readers of Lamott might enjoy the irreverent (and sincere) lessons offered by Liz Curtis Higgs in her series beginning with ***Bad Girls of the Bible: And What We Can Learn from Them,*** in which she puts forth the idea that today's women are more like the flawed women in the Bible than the good women.

Norris, Kathleen (1947–)

The Cloister Walk. Riverhead Books, 1997, 1996. 385pp. 9781573225847. Also available in large print, audiobook, and e-book. 255

Norris paved the way for this illumination of the monastic life in her first spiritual autobiography, ***Dakota: A Spiritual Geography.*** In this memoir she presents a diary-like offering revealing what the monastic life means to her, as she had been given the opportunity to spend two separate nine-month periods studying and teaching at a Benedictine academic institute. She has been able to share in their life, with the readings of Scripture, the prayer, and the song, and she has been able to talk to both the Benedictine brothers and the visiting sisters about such topics as celibacy and virgin martyrs. As a poet she found the monastic life to be a haven from the stresses of her life, but more than that, it provided her with greater insight in her own spiritual journey toward faith. Although she is an oblate of the

Benedictine monastery, she is still a practicing Presbyterian, so her ecumenism adds another dimension to her spiritual story.

Subjects: Benedictines; Celibacy; Christian Life; Diaries; Faith; Liturgy; Monastic Life; Poets; Presbyterians; Spirituality

Now Try: Norris has since written another memoir, another very personal one: ***Acedia & Me: A Marriage, Monks, and a Writer's Life***. A convert from atheism to Catholicism, Thomas Merton has also written an autobiography extolling the monastic life, ***The Seven Storey Mountain***. A Franciscan sister, Mother Mary Angelica, who began an international faith-based television network from the garage of her monastery, offers reflections garnered from her monastic life in ***Mother Angelica's Little Book of Life Lessons and Everyday Spirituality***, edited by Raymond Arroyo. In ***When the Heart Waits: Spiritual Direction for Life's Sacred Questions***, Sue Monk Kidd offers her own thoughts on how a contemplative life—even among secular people living busy lives—can help those grappling with a search for more spirituality in their lives.

Piper, Don (1950–)
Murphey, Cecil (1933–), coauthor

90 Minutes in Heaven: A True Story of Death & Life. Revell, 2007, 2004. 205pp. 9780800719050. Also available in large print, Braille, audiobook (read by the author), e-audiobook, and e-book. 231.73092

Although Piper's title would suggest that much of his memoir focuses on his near-death (or death) experience, in fact that is only a small part of the book. Most of the book is taken up with the follow-up to the horrific car accident he was in, his recovery, the struggles he went through afterward, and the miracles he witnessed. He compares his post-accident life, not with his earlier life, but with what he saw and heard in heaven between the time he was declared dead at the scene of the accident and the time someone recognized that he was actually alive. He believes that even his injuries—or lack thereof—were miraculous. Although the steering wheel crushed his sternum, no internal organs were damaged, he had no brain injury, nor did he bleed copiously as would have been expected. He has followed this first story with ***Heaven Is Real: Lessons on Earthly Joy—From the Man Who Spent 90 Minutes in Heaven***.

Subjects: Christian Life; Christianity; Death; Future Life; Heaven; Life-Changing Events; Mortality; Near-Death Experiences

Now Try: Michael B. Sabom is a doctor who wrote ***Recollections of Death: A Medical Investigation*** and then set up The Atlanta Study to investigate the experiences of people who recounted their near-death experiences. In ***Saved by the Light: The True Story of a Man Who Died Twice and the Profound Revelations He Received***, Dannion Brinkley, with the help of Paul Perry, discusses his own near-death experience. Life-altering events are not just restricted to near-death experience. Cartoonist Judd Winick describes how his life changed by virtue of his being the roommate of Pedro Zamora, a young AIDS activist, in ***Pedro and Me: Friendship, Loss, and What I Learned***.

Spong, John Shelby (1931–)

Here I Stand: My Struggle for a Christianity of Integrity, Love, and Equality. HarperSanFrancisco, 2001, 2000. 464pp. ill. 9780060675394. Also available in e-book. 283.092

After writing several books on his ministry, including ***Why Christianity Must Change or Die: A Bishop Speaks to Believers in Exile; A New Reformation of the Church's Faith and Practice,*** this retired Episcopalian bishop has turned to his life story. Growing up in North Carolina, he lived with parents, who were very pious and also very racist and whose ethos he rejected at an early age. He talks about his dysfunctional family, his university days at the University of North Carolina, and his marriage to Christine, a woman whose compassion and love helped him to heal from his childhood days and to stand strong in his inclusive beliefs. He has pitted himself against fundamentalists from all over and even against his peers, particularly in his battle to open the door for noncelibate homosexuals into the church's ministry. He recognizes that many of today's people have become disenchanted with religion, and much of his writing has gone toward addressing that issue.

Subjects: Bishops; Christian Life; Christianity; Episcopal Church; Faith; Homosexuality; Inclusiveness; Racism; Religious Men; Spiritual Leaders

Now Try: Another clergyman who rejected his father's social beliefs and grew up fighting racism is Martin Luther King Sr., who tells his story with Clayton Riley in ***Daddy King: An Autobiography***. Shane Claiborne shares John Spong's desire to reach out despite detractors and does so in North Philadelphia, living with and supporting the homeless. In his memoir, ***The Irresistible Revolution: Living as an Ordinary Radical,*** he also tells stories about his various ministries around the world. John C. Danforth is both an Episcopal clergyman and a politician, who demonstrates courage by speaking forthrightly in ***Faith and Politics: How the "Moral Values" Debate Divides America and How to Move Forward Together***.

Consider Starting With . . .

Armstrong, Karen. *The Spiral Staircase: My Climb out of Darkness*

Conroy, Pat. *My Losing Season*

Graham, Billy. *Just as I Am: The Autobiography of Billy Graham*

Karr, Mary. *Lit: A Memoir*

Lindbergh, Anne Morrow. *Gift from the Sea*

Norris, Kathleen. *The Cloister Walk*

O'Faolain, Nuala. *Are You Somebody: The Accidental Memoir of a Dublin Woman*

Rice, Anne. *Called out of Darkness: A Spiritual Confession*

Teresa, Mother. *Mother Teresa: Come Be My Light; The Private Writings of the "Saint of Calcutta"*

X, Malcolm. *The Autobiography of Malcolm X*

Fiction Read-Alikes

Baldwin, James. *Go Tell It on the Mountain*. A young boy in Harlem, feeling an outsider in his community and in his home, undergoes a religious conversion in his stepfather's church.

Callanan, Liam. *The Cloud Atlas*. Sent to Alaska to disarm Japanese balloon bombs, Louis Belk embarks on a spiritual quest, one he describes in confessional flashbacks to a dying shaman.

Coelho, Paulo. *The Alchemist*. A young Spaniard learns about following his dreams and gaining wisdom as he travels from Spain to Egypt in search of a treasure.

Dostoyevsky, Fyodor. *Crime and Punishment*. After committing murder, Raskolnikov realizes he has to decide between committing suicide or confessing his crime.

Godwin, Gail. *Evensong*. As tensions between the local woman pastor and an evangelist grow in the small town of High Balsam, the reader is treated to a view of real-life spirituality.

Hosseini, Khaled. *The Kite Runner*. Amir emigrated from Afghanistan to the United States in his adolescence, after cravenly betraying his best friend; he is called home to help that friend, given one chance for atonement.

McEwan, Ian. *Atonement: A Novel*. Young Briony seeks atonement as an adult when she realizes that she may have unwittingly ruined the lives of her sister and her sister's boyfriend.

Percy, Walker. *The Moviegoer*. Binx Bolling, realizing his life has little direction or importance, seeks meaning in his life, often by watching movies in the local theater.

Richler, Mordecai. *Barney's Version: A Novel*. In Rousseau-like fashion, Barney tells his life story, justifying his actions so that he will be looked upon favorably by the people in his world.

Salzman, Mark. *Lying Awake*. Sister John of the Cross, a nun in contemporary Los Angeles, faces the decision of medically correcting her blinding headaches, knowing that she may lose her spiritual visions and insights at the same time.

Works Cited

Abood, Maureen. 2006. "In Memory of Me: An Interview with Patricia Hampl." *U.S. Catholic* 71 (9) (September): 24–25. Reproduced in *Biography Resource Center*. Accessed February 25, 2009. http://galenet.galegroup.com/servlet/BioRC.

Andrew, Elizabeth Jarrett. 2008. An excerpt from *Writing the Sacred Journey: The Art and Practice of Spiritual Memoir. Writing Resources*. Accessed January 29, 2009. http://www.spiritualmemoir.com.

cocopreme. n.d. "Spiritual Aautobiographies." *HubPages*. Accessed March 20, 2010. http://hubpages.com/hub/SpiritualAutobiographies.

Egan, Susanna. 2001. "The Literary Confession and Its Religious Model" [1984]. In *Autobiography*, edited by Lawrence Kappel, 40–59. San Diego, CA: Greenhaven Press.

Kappel, Lawrence. 2001. "A Historical Overview of the Autobiography." In *Autobiography*, edited by Lawrence Kappel, 14–31. San Diego, CA: Greenhaven Press.

King, Stephen. 2007. "Slowhand." *The New York Times*, October 28. Accessed February 12, 2010. http://www.nytimes.com/2007/10/28/books/review/King-t.html.

Logan, Lisa M. 2005. "American Women's Autobiography: Early Women Diarists and Memoirists (to 1800)." In *Encyclopedia of Women's Autobiography*, edited by Victoria Boynton and Jo Malin, 32–42. Westport, CT: Greenwood Press.

Sim, Stuart. 2001. "Spiritual Autobiography." *The Literary Encyclopedia*, January 1. Accessed June 18, 2007. http://www.litencyc.com/php/stopics.php?rec=true&UID=1377.

Wallraff, Dean. 2000–2007. "An Atheist on a Spiritual Quest." In *Millennium: Essays by Dean Wallraff*. Accessed June 18, 2007. http://www.arsnova.org/millennium/asq.html.

Yagoda, Ben. 2009. *Memoir: A History*. New York: Riverhead Books.

Chapter 9

The Political Life

Description

Readers should approach political memoirs with a slightly different perspective and attitude than toward other memoirs. Because of their potential importance in forming a historical record, political memoirs should be read with a questioning mind and should not necessarily be read in isolation from other books of the period. Politicos who write their memoirs do so for a variety of reasons. For some, the initial impetus is financial. Ulysses S. Grant's story is well-known: he was in dire financial straits and wanted to make sure that his soon-to-be widow would be cared for, so he agreed to write his memoirs. Sarah Palin, too, was able to benefit from writing her memoir to pay off debts she had incurred as governor of Alaska (Gwinn, 2009). Often presidents wrote their memoirs to help fund a presidential library in their name, or simply to fund their retirement.

Sometimes leaders write their memoirs to set the record straight, to explain why they made the decisions they did, what kinds of influences they were under at the time. These memoirs are often written with a self-serving purpose. If the leader had proven to be unpopular, he might want to redesign his legacy, put it into a new light for future generations. On the other hand, he might genuinely, as did Harry Truman, "like to record, before it is too late, as much of the story of my occupancy of the White House as I am able to tell" (Whitney, 2004). People who worked for and around the country's leader often tell their stories too, sometimes contradicting what the leader might say, sometimes confirming it.

A new phenomenon has crept into the world of political memoirs, the memoir as campaign fodder. Especially notable in the 2008 presidential campaign, major contenders (Hillary Rodham Clinton, John McCain, and Barack Obama) had written memoirs prior to running. But John McCain and Bill Bradley had already done so in the late 1990s as well (Denvir, 2010) and Jimmy Carter even earlier, in 1975 (Raban, 2009). Thus this form of political memoir will differ greatly from the reflective, retrospective autobiography one might expect from a figure who makes history during his or her tenure in the government house.

The question of authorship is another interesting element of the political memoir. Very few political leaders have an interest in isolating themselves in order to write their story, and very few actually have the talent, either (Raban, 2009). Ulysses S. Grant was noted for his literary skill, as is Barack Obama, but for the most part, being a president or prime minister does not a writer make. Just as their speeches are often ghostwritten, so too are their memoirs. Ronald Reagan is known for saying that he understood his memoir was a great read, and at some point he would get around to reading it (Whitney, 2004), leading one to question the accuracy of these ghostwritten memoirs and to wonder whose words are actually represented. Most subjects will acknowledge their cowriters, but occasionally (as in the case of Bill Clinton or Sarah Palin), the coauthor's name is nowhere to be found (Denvir, 2010). Pierre Elliott Trudeau's memoir was fashioned from hours of interviews he participated in for a documentary on his life, but he acknowledges all who were involved in both the documentary and his subsequent memoir.

It is generally recognized that serious historians of a period should read several of the memoirs from that administration—from both the major players and the behind-the-scenes people—in order to get an accurate picture of what actually went on. It is not uncommon that once a particular administration is over, several memoirs will then be published as everyone races to tell his or her own story, so that there is usually much to choose from to get an overview. And if the stories start to sound familiar, chances are good that those stories are what actually happened (Gwinn, 2009). Even so, readers must recognize that usually the writers have personal biases, an interest in putting themselves in the best light.

Political memoirs are often written by people who have reached the pinnacle of their political careers, but those at lower levels of the political hierarchy also add their voices to the mix, as do some family members of those involved in politics. These memoirs tend to focus on the time spent in politics, setting the record straight, explaining why and how decisions were made, and what life was really like behind the scenes. They may also be written for the purpose of providing fodder for the history books, which means that the writers might be more circumspect in their writing than they may otherwise have been.

Appeal

Character is a major appeal of political memoirs. In many cases the reader has seen the subject on television and in the newspapers, so that celebrity is part of the cachet. One assumes that in order to have succeeded in politics, leaders of a country and even those who work with them must be special, larger than life, so that the reader wants to get closer and find out what this person is really like.

Learning is another appeal: What really happened during that crisis, that scandal, that upset? There is often so much debate in the media about events, and currently there is so much polarizing of views, that readers may want to go to the primary source in the hopes of figuring things out themselves. But recognizing that one source alone may not yield the truth, the reader is grateful to have a number of memoirs to read. Often presidents or prime ministers like to depict their daily lives as well, giving the reader an inside view of the routines of governing and, in some cases, the details of the physical environment as well.

Organization of This Chapter

Beginning with classics from the nineteenth and twentieth centuries, the chapter moves on to the politicians of the United States. The scope then broadens to encompass international memoirs, many of which are from Canada, although other countries—China, Cuba, England, Kenya, Liberia, and Pakistan—are represented. Availability and currency of titles were limiting factors in the selection of titles for this final section.

Classics

In this section we have exceptions to the rule that heads of state are unable to write their own memoirs: Ulysses S. Grant, Theodore Roosevelt, and Winston Churchill are all known for their writing abilities, and Grant's memoir is reputed to be the finest of presidential memoirs (Whitney, 2004). With the exception of Albert Speer, this section features memoirs of specific heads of countries, although they don't all recount their lives after their political careers have ended. Winston Churchill's accomplishments have been so well-documented that it seemed fitting to represent the beginning of his career rather than the end. And Adolf Hitler had no opportunity to write about his exploits after his autobiographical manifesto. Two of the five classic memoirs are from the Third Reich, indicating the historical importance of that dreadful time.

These classic political memoirs represent men who have played a major role in the political life of the Western world over more than a century, some for the betterment of society, some not. The memoirs here, however, do not all reflect their time in office; instead, they portray the writers themselves at some point in their lives, providing insights to readers on how these men came to wield such influence.

Churchill, Winston (1874–1965)

My Early Life, 1874–1904. Introduction by William Manchester. Simon & Schuster, 1996, 1930. 372pp. ill. maps. 9780684823454. Also available in large print, audiobook, and e-audiobook. 941.084092

Knowing that Churchill won a Nobel Prize in Literature may add to the reader's anticipation of this witty and charming overview of his young life. An earlier subtitle is "My Roving Commission," and in this memoir Churchill roves from an unhappy childhood, both at home and at boarding school where he battled with math and with bullies, to his stint as a journalist in South Africa during the Boer War, and then his beginning life in politics back home in England. Apart from his early life, Churchill also offers an intelligent picture of the late Victorian era. The fact that Churchill wrote this from the perspective of an older man only enhances the work.

Churchill was named one of *Time*'s People of the Century in the Leaders & Revolutionaries category.

Subjects: Boer War (1899–1902); Childhood and Youth; Classics; Foreign Correspondents, England; Journalists, England; Leaders; Nobel Prize Laureates; Nonagenarians; Politicians, England; Prime Ministers, England; South Africa

Now Try: Much of Churchill's prolific writing is autobiographical, but readers may want to see the man through another's eyes. Paul Johnson offers a highly acclaimed biography, ***Churchill***. Benjamin Disraeli was comparable to Churchill in his colorful personality, his political acumen, and his great orating skills. Christopher Hibbert, in writing Disraeli's biography, ***Disraeli: The Victorian Dandy Who Became Prime Minister***, also depicts Victorian England. Peter Gay extends the view of the Victorian era to Europe and adds his own perspective on it, based on the plays of the Austrian playwright Arthur Schnitzler: ***Schnitzler's Century: The Making of Middle-Class Culture, 1815–1914***. For a lengthier explanation of the Boer War, readers may find informative Martin Meredith's ***Diamonds, Gold, and War: The British, the Boers, and the Making of South Africa***.

Grant, Ulysses S. (1822–1885)

Personal Memoirs of U. S. Grant. Cosimo Classics, 2006, 1885–1886. 514pp. 9781596059993. Also available in audiobook, e-audiobook, and e-book. 973.82092

Mark Twain, by promising to publish them himself, convinced Ulysses S. Grant to write his memoirs, a task that Grant undertook because of his dismal financial condition. Although he was suffering from throat cancer at the time, Grant managed to tell his life story, including a large and vivid section on his role in the Civil War, with great intelligence and even excitement. The memoirs were a great success at the time, a boon to Grant's widow, Julia, as Grant died a week after revising the proofs. Edmund Wilson has said of Grant's memoirs that reading them puts the reader right there at the table with Grant, planning and executing his war strategies, wondering how it will all turn out (Wilson, 1994).

Subjects: Civil War, United States (1861–1865); Classics; Generals; History, United States; Politicians; Presidents; Republicans; Sherman, William; Twain, Mark; United States Army

Now Try: Grant's wife, Julia, also wrote her memoirs, providing a different perspective on Grant's life: ***The Personal Memoirs of Julia Dent Grant (Mrs. Ulysses S. Grant)***, edited by John Y. Simon. While Grant was writing his memoirs, Mark Twain, also impoverished, was trying to write ***The Adventures of Huckleberry Finn***. Readers may be interested in reading the story of the friendship and simultaneous writing challenges of these two men in a biography by Mark Perry, ***Grant and Twain: The Story of a Friendship That Changed America***. Jim Fergus has written a novel, ***One Thousand White Women: The Journals of May Dodd***, whose basic plot conflict centers around a treaty between Grant and Little Wolf, chief of the Cheyenne Nation. When Grant ran for the presidency in 1872, he was challenged by the feminist suffragette Victoria Woodhull. Barbara Goldsmith depicts this controversial woman in ***Other Powers: The Age of Suffrage, Spiritualism, and the Scandalous Victoria Woodhull***.

Hitler, Adolf (1889–1945)

Mein Kampf. Introduction by Abraham H. Foxman. Houghton Mifflin, 2002, 1925. 694pp. 9780395951057. Also available in Braille, audiobook, e-book, and video. 943.086092 [Trans. by Ralph Manheim]

Hitler wrote this story of his life, his beliefs, and his plans when he was in prison for a failed revolutionary attempt in what was known as the Beer Hall Putsch. In his memoir he describes his early life with his parents and his political coming of age. He rants against the outcomes of World War I as they related to Germany and lays out his blueprint for what he will do when he gets into power. Apart from seeking revenge against the French, another major objective outlined in this book is to provide more room for the Aryan peoples of Germany. To accomplish this, Hitler plans to conquer other lands, putting all the undesirables, particularly Jews, to work for them. His book is a treatise on bigotry, hatred, and terrorism, one that was considered so outrageous when it was published that people reading it or hearing about it laughed and dismissed it as preposterous. Now, however, those who are concerned about the ease with which demagoguery can take hold urge all thinking people to read it as a cautionary tale.

Hitler was named one of *Time*'s People of the Century in the Leaders & Revolutionaries category.

Subjects: Bigotry; Classics; Germany; Hate Literature; History, Germany; National Socialism; Nazis; Revolutionaries; Terrorism; Translations

Now Try: William L. Shirer, a journalist who was at the Nuremberg trials, presents an award-winning perspective on the downfall of the Nazi war machine in ***The Rise and Fall of the Third Reich; A History of Nazi Germany***. Simon Berthon and Joanna Potts have looked at World War II with a somewhat different lens, focusing on the real personalities of four major combatant leaders, in ***Warlords: An Extraordinary Re-Creation of World War II Through the Eyes and Minds***

of Hitler, Churchill, Roosevelt, and Stalin. Timothy W. Ryback offers an interesting perspective on Hitler the man in ***Hitler's Private Library: The Books That Shaped His Life***, as he analyzes the titles of the books Hitler read and the marginal notes he made. Another proclamation in book form that was of global significance is Karl Marx's ***The Communist Manifesto***.

Roosevelt, Theodore (1858–1919)

The Rough Riders; An Autobiography. Library of America, 2004, 1899. 895pp. ill. 9781931082655. Also available in audiobook and e-audiobook. 973.8942

This particular volume includes two publications by Roosevelt. The first, ***The Rough Riders***, describes the exploits and losses of the "League of Extraordinary Gentlemen," the cavalry of cowboys who accompanied Roosevelt to Cuba during the Spanish–American War. The second, although entitled ***Autobiography*** and written after his tenure as president, is more a representation of Roosevelt's ideas about life using his own experiences to illustrate his points. Between the two volumes, however, the reader is able to see the outdoorsman, the conservationist, the politician, and the statesman that Roosevelt was.

Roosevelt was awarded the Nobel Peace Prize and was named one of *Time*'s People of the Century in the Leaders & Revolutionaries category.

Subjects: Classics; Conservationists; Cuba; Leaders; New York, NY; New York Police Department; Nobel Prize Laureates; Politicians; Presidents; Republicans; Spanish–American War (1898); Writers

Now Try: David G. McCullough has written an award-winning biography of the young Roosevelt, which might be interesting to read, to see what created the larger-than-life man: ***Mornings on Horseback: The Story of an Extraordinary Family, a Vanished Way of Life, and the Unique Child Who Became Theodore Roosevelt***. John Paul Jones became an American hero because Theodore Roosevelt felt that America needed a naval hero and raised Jones's reputation to achieve that. Evan Thomas has written Jones's story for today's reader: ***John Paul Jones: Sailor, Hero, Father of the American Navy***. With conservation so much in the forefront these days, it is interesting to see what was being done in earlier days. In his award-winning book, ***The Adirondacks: A History of America's First Wilderness***, Paul Schneider sheds light on centuries of conserving one particular wilderness area in America. Readers who like to learn their history through fiction might enjoy Elmore Leonard's historical novel, ***Cuba Libre***, a story of Cuba prior to the Spanish–American War.

Speer, Albert (1905–1981)

Inside the Third Reich: Memoirs. Introduction by Eugene Davidson. Foreword by Sam Sloan. Ishi Press International, 2009, 1970. 596pp. ill. 48pp. of plates. 9780923891732. 943.08609 [Trans. by Richard Winston and Clara Winston]

Albert Speer was the number two man in the Nazi war machine. He was first attracted to Hitler in the early days of Hitler's rise, particularly after Hitler described to Speer, an architect, his dreams for colossal architecture in Berlin that would be worthy of a thousand-year Reich. Speer's memoir is in three parts: the first part covers his childhood and youth leading to his meeting with Hitler and his appointment as Hitler's architect-in-chief; the second begins with his installation as Minister of Armaments and War Production; and the third deals with the long road to the trials at Nuremberg and Speer's subsequent sentencing to Spandau Prison for twenty years.

Inside the Third Reich was selected as a Notable Book by the American Library Association.

Subjects: ALA Notable Books; Architects, Germany; Classics; Germany; Hitler, Adolf; History, Germany; Labor Camps; Military History; National Socialism; Nazis; Nuremberg Trials; Spandau Prison, Germany; Translations; World War II (1939–1945)

Now Try: Using the known facts of the trials at Nuremberg, William F. Buckley created a fictional family to write a novel about the famous war trials, ***Nuremberg: The Reckoning***. Ironically, one of the colossal buildings that Speer managed to build was the stadium in Nuremberg. An architecture critic, Deyan Sudjic, offers an interesting view on the political ramifications of such grandiose architecture in his book, ***The Edifice Complex: How the Rich and Powerful Shape the World***. Of course Albert Speer was not the only person in Hitler's regime to be guilty of criminal behavior; several of the others are included in Anthony Read's study, ***The Devil's Disciples: Hitler's Inner Circle***.

The United States

Represented in this section is a broad spectrum of the women and men who have contributed to the political life of the United States. They are diplomats, political campaigners, fund-raisers, political consultants, speechwriters, mayors, legislators, and presidents. Several of them have had more than one role, working as legislators, becoming secretaries, and then perhaps moving on to diplomacy. Others have had very specific roles, such as Richard A. Clarke, in charge of counterterrorism, or Wilma Pearl Mankiller and Russell Means, fighting politically for their people.

The political memoirs from the United States illustrate the range of political roles that can influence much of what happens in the lives of all Americans. Some of the memoirs cover the lives of the politicians, while others focus on specific administrations in which they participated. Not all of these memoirs take place in Washington, DC, however, as they reflect the political life of the country as a whole, with a variety of possible roles.

Albright, Madeleine Korbel (1937–)
Woodward, Bill (1951–), coauthor

Madam Secretary. Miramax Books, 2003. 562pp. ill. 9780786868438. Also available in large print, audiobook (read by the author), and e-book. 327.73009

Madeleine Albright was the first female secretary of state in the United States, a position she reached through working hard and moving gradually up the political ladder. In her memoir she describes coming to the United States as a young immigrant, fleeing the Communist invasion into Czechoslovakia. Her father had been a diplomat back home so that it seemed natural for her to study political science at college. As she makes her way through the various political arenas to which she is assigned, she introduces the reader to the international heads of state who figured importantly during Bill Clinton's presidency. She also opens a small window into her personal life, her marriage, her children, her divorce, and the biggest surprise of all: the discovery that her family was originally Jewish, not Catholic, as she had been raised to believe.

Madeleine Albright was inducted into the National Women's Hall of Fame.

Subjects: Ambassadors; Cabinet Officers; Democrats; Diplomats; Firsts; Foreign Service, United States; Politicians; Trailblazers; United Nations; Women in Politics

Now Try: Madeleine Albright has since published another memoir, based on the jewelry she acquired while acting as a diplomat: ***Read My Pins: Stories from a Diplomat's Jewel Box***. She had several people helping her with that publication: Elaine Shocas, Vivienne Becker, and Bill Woodward helped with the writing; the photography was done by John Bigelow Taylor; and the photography composition was done by Dianne Dubler. Helen Fremont also grew up thinking she was Catholic, but her parents, like Albright's, had fled their Jewish life in Nazi Germany. She offers her family memoir in ***After Long Silence: A Memoir***. Another strong political woman who has also served in the cabinet is Elizabeth Dole, about whom several books have been written. Readers may want to pick up ***Elizabeth Hanford Dole: Speaking from the Heart*** by Molly Meijer Wertheimer and Nichola D. Gutgold. Strong women influencing political governance have a long history in the United States, as Woody Holton illustrates in his award-winning biography, ***Abigail Adams***.

Bradley, Bill (1943–)

Time Present, Time Past: A Memoir. Vintage Books, 1997, 1996. 450pp. 9780679768159. Also available in large print. 328.73092

Before this memoir Bradley had already written ***Life on the Run***, about his career as first a collegiate and then a professional basketball player. He went from basketball to politics, a career change he discusses in this memoir. He goes back in time to his childhood, a formative time that helped develop the values he held as a legislator, and he also discusses how his life on the basketball court continued to form his philosophies and beliefs. In addition to discussing how the Senate works and how legislation gets passed, Bradley also offers his own thoughts on and raises very deep and important questions about the future look of the United States.

Subjects: Basketball; Democrats; Legislators; Olympic Gold Medalists; Politicians; Politics; Senators

Now Try: William H. Frist was a Senate majority leader who also based his political service on his long-held values. A heart surgeon before he became a politician, he entitled his memoir ***A Heart to Serve: The Passion to Bring Health, Hope, and Healing***. Another athlete turned politician is J. C. Watts, a professional football player who became the highest-ranking African-American Republican in the House before he retired. Like Bradley, he does not shy away from discussing controversial topics in his memoir, ***What Color Is a Conservative? My Life and My Politics***, written with the help of Chriss Anne Winston. It is difficult for the common American to grasp clearly how the legislative process works; another politician who offers a look at this process is Robert B. Reich, former secretary of labor, who describes his working life in ***Locked in the Cabinet***.

Brazile, Donna (1959–)

Cooking with Grease: Stirring the Pots in American Politics. Simon & Schuster, 2005. 352pp. ill. 9780743253987. 324.7093092

Brazile began campaigning politically when she was nine years old, supporting a candidate for city council who promised to install a playground in her neighborhood in New Orleans. One of nine children, she spent a lot of time in the kitchen with her mother, Jean, from whom she learned to cook; from her grandmother Frances she developed a love of both reading and politics. After the assassination of Martin Luther King Jr., Brazile determined to become a social activist, and she has put that determination into her political campaigning for various members of the Democratic National Party. When Al Gore hired her in 2000 to run his presidential campaign, she was the first African-American woman to run a presidential campaign.

Subjects: African-American Women; Democrats; Firsts; Gore, Al; Grandmothers; New Orleans, LA; Political Campaigners; Political Consultants; Politics; Presidential Campaigns; Women in Politics

Now Try: Brazile's experience has taught her about the real intersection of race and politics; her ideas seem to be bolstered by Thomas Byrne Edsall and Mary D. Edsall in ***Chain Reaction: The Impact of Race, Rights, and Taxes on American Politics***. An earlier Black political activist was Shirley Graham Du Bois, wife of W. E. B. Du Bois; Gerald Horne has brought her into the spotlight in his biography, ***Race Woman: The Lives of Shirley Graham Du Bois***. Ida B. Wells was a noted journalist and social activist born into slavery whose biography Paula Giddings has written: ***Ida, a Sword Among Lions: Ida B. Wells and the Campaign Against Lynching***.

Bush, Barbara Pierce (1925–)

Barbara Bush: A Memoir. Scribner's Sons, 2003, 1994. 575pp. ill. 9780025196353. Also available in large print, audiobook (read by the author), e-audiobook, and e-book. 973.928092

Barbara Bush's is a straightforward memoir of a happy life begun in Rye, New York, and continuing in unexpected ways due to her marriage to *George Bush*. She recounts her life as the mother of six children, with all the activity that entails, particularly when her husband was so busy building up his business in the oil industry. She also describes their sadness at the death from leukemia of their young daughter Robin. Her husband's entry into politics added a new twist to her life, with political campaigns, moving and setting up house, and hosting dinner parties. She discusses her views on literacy and why that became such an important cause for her, eventually leading to the creation of the Barbara Bush Foundation for Family Literacy (http://www.barbarabushfoundation.com). Bush has followed up her memoir with another, detailing her life after she and her husband left the White House: ***Reflections: Life After the White House***.

Subjects: Barbara Bush Foundation for Family Literacy; Bush, George; Death of a Child; Family Relationships; First Ladies; Literacy; Octogenarians; Republicans; Upper Class; White House, Washington, DC

Now Try: People are often curious to know what goes on behind the scenes in political lives. Kati Marton has studied a number of presidential couples in ***Hidden Power: Presidential Marriages That Shaped Our Recent History***. Readers fascinated by political wives may enjoy reading Patricia Brady's biography of the first First Lady, ***Martha Washington: An American Life***. Byron Pitts is a living example of the importance of literacy. A journalist now, he tells his story of being functionally illiterate in his memoir, ***Step Out on Nothing: How Faith and Family Helped Me Conquer Life's Challenges***.

Bush, George (1924–)

All the Best, George Bush: My Life in Letters and Other Writings. Touchstone, 2000, 1999. 640pp. ill. 16pp. of plates. 9780743200417. Also available in audiobook. 973.928092

George Bush Sr. apparently has no interest in writing his autobiography and has therefore offered this collection of letters to stand in for his memoirs. His letters begin when he was eighteen and the youngest pilot in the U.S. Navy and continue through his courtship to Barbara Pierce and his various career choices: business, diplomacy, intelligence, and politics, all culminating in the presidency. His letters go beyond that, however, to his postpresidency years, and include letters to his family as well as to friends and colleagues. Normally a private man, his letters reveal his joys and sorrows, particularly over the death of his daughter Robin, as well as his candid thoughts on various political situations.

George Bush has been inducted into the Academy of Achievement.

Subjects: Bush, Barbara Pierce; Diplomats; Foreign Service, United States; Intelligence Officers; Letters; Octogenarians; Politicians; Politics; Presidents; Republicans; Texas

Now Try: In her biography of her father, ***My Father, My President: A Personal Account of the Life of George H. W. Bush***, George Bush's other daughter, Doro Bush Koch, fills in some of the blanks left by his letters. Letter writing is a disappearing art, but was practiced by several presidents; readers may find of particular interest the letters exchanged by Harry Truman and Eleanor Roosevelt and edited by Steve Neal, ***Eleanor***

and Harry: The Correspondence of Eleanor Roosevelt and Harry S. Truman. At the same time that George Bush was in power, so was John Roy Major in Britain; he tells his story, which obviously includes encounters with Bush, in ***John Major: The Autobiography.*** Given that George Bush had been the director of the Central Intelligence Agency (CIA) prior to being president of the United States, Stansfield Turner's book, ***Burn Before Reading: Presidents, CIA Directors, and Secret Intelligence,*** offers an intriguing perspective on the relationship between the two agencies.

Bush, George W. (1946–)

Decision Points. Crown, 2010. 497pp. ill. 32pp. of plates. 9780307590619. Also available in large print, audiobook (read by the author), e-audiobook, and e-book. 973.931092

Having read Ulysses S. Grant's presidential memoir, George Bush decided to follow the same format: rather than provide a chronological portrait of his life, particularly his presidential life, he centered each chapter on a weighty decision he had to make, either personally or professionally. He describes his childhood and his family relationships, particularly discussing his going sober in middle age and embracing Christianity. Some of the issues he covers are stem-cell research, Afghanistan, waterboarding, Iraq, Hurricane Katrina, and the financial crisis. He also talks about how he perceives himself making decisions, offering his memoir as a guide for those in management. His tone is folksy and casual, much as the man is, and he credits a lot of the work in writing the book to Peter Rough, his researcher, and Christopher Michel, his former speechwriter. Accusations of plagiarism and misinformation have been lobbied against the book, with reviewers citing specific passages taken from Bob Woodward's four books on George Bush, particularly ***Bush at War,*** as well as Robert Draper's ***Dead Certain: The Presidency of George W. Bush,*** along with other articles and interviews.

Subjects: Bush Family; Bush, George; Bush, Laura Welch; Decision Making; Governors; Politicians; Presidents; Republicans; Texas; War on Terrorism (2001–)

Now Try: Another book that Bush's researchers were said to have plagiarized from is ***American Soldier,*** the memoir of General Tommy Franks, who led American and Coalition Forces in Afghanistan and Iraq in the early part of the twenty-first century; he was helped in the writing of it by Malcolm McConnell. The similarities between George Bush and Rutherford Hayes are quite astounding, given their chronological distance of a century, but both were folksy in their manner, both were governors before becoming presidents, and both won the presidency despite having lost the popular vote. It is similarities like these that are recounted by the historian Roy Morris in ***Fraud of the Century: Rutherford B. Hayes, Samuel Tilden, and the Stolen Election of 1876.*** Karen Hughes was legal counsel to George W. Bush in Texas and moved her family to Washington, DC, upon his election. In her memoir, ***Ten Minutes from Normal,*** she describes how disruptive such a political life can be for a family and explains why she decided to move her family back to Texas. There are several biographies that have been written about George Bush, but a recent one offers a different perspective. Written by a personality scientist, Dan P. McAdams, the book is entitled ***George W. Bush and the Redemptive Dream: A Psychological Portrait.***

Bush, Laura Welch (1946–)

Spoken from the Heart. Scribner, 2010. 456pp. ill. 24pp. of plates. 9781439155202. Also available in large print, audiobook (read by the author), e-audiobook, and e-book. 973.931092

The first half of Laura Bush's memoir is a coming-of-age story, growing up in Midland, Texas, as an only child. She creates a clear picture of life in small-town Texas in the 1950s and 1960s, describing not only the social mores but the physical geography as well. She moves on to the car accident that formed her psyche, an accident wherein she ran into a friend's car, killing him. From there she details her education and her brief courtship with George W. Bush. The tone changes, then, as the former First Lady seems to recognize that her story is now someone else's story as well, so that she can provide details about the public life only. She does describe her life as a mother and as an activist for improving women's lives in developing countries, but she ultimately remains private about her life as the wife of the president.

Subjects: 1950s; 1960s; Bush, George W.; Car Accidents; Family Relationships; First Ladies; Librarians; Republicans; Texas; Washington, DC; White House, Washington, DC

Now Try: The letters of John and Abigail Adams, edited by Margaret A. Hogan and C. James Taylor, reveal the loving relationship between an earlier president and his wife, collected in ***My Dearest Friend: Letters of Abigail and John Adams***. Lady Bird Johnson began keeping a diary when she and her husband moved into the White House. Her diary was written as a memory-keeper, but she also knew it would be read by the public. It might be interesting to compare Johnson's ***A White House Diary*** with Bush's memoir to see how different or similar their public lives were. Chiang Kai-Shek's wife was quite different from Laura Bush, as Laura Tyson Li demonstrates in ***Madame Chiang Kai-Shek: China's Eternal First Lady***.

Carter, Jimmy (1924–)

White House Diary. Farrar, Straus & Giroux, 2010. 570pp. ill. 24pp. of plates. 9780374280994. Also available in audiobook and e-book. 973.926

When Jimmy Carter was in the White House (1977–1981), he dictated diary-like snippets throughout the day. These entries included the day-to-day trappings of a president's life as well as his observations and thoughts about them and about the people surrounding him. He offers his opinion on people in the global arena and on the events that overtook his presidency. The total output was around 5,000 pages, which Carter has whittled down to this manageable book. He has added clarifying comments as well as insights into his views now on certain topics, views created from a distance of thirty years. What readers will learn from this book is what the presidency looks like from within, how so many world issues can distract from domestic issues, and how difficult the job of president really is.

Subjects: 1970s; 1980s; Democrats; Diaries; History, United States; Iran Hostage Crisis (1979–1981); Octogenarians; Politicians; Politics; Presidents

Now Try: Not long after his presidency, Carter wrote his first presidential memoir, ***Keeping Faith: Memoirs of a President***. For those who may forget what the 1970s were really like, or for those who never knew, Edward D. Berkowitz offers an overview in ***Something Happened: A Political and Cultural Overview of the Seventies***. Perhaps one of the most memorable political events at the time was the Iran Hostage Crisis, an ordeal laid out by David Harris as he provides input from those who were closely involved, in ***The Crisis: The President, the Prophet, and the Shah—1979 and the Coming of Militant Islam***. Carter as a president is often compared to Herbert Hoover. Readers may find it interesting to read ***The Memoirs of Herbert Hoover*** to decide for themselves what the similarities are.

Cheney, Mary (1969–)

Now It's My Turn: A Daughter's Chronicle of Political Life. Threshold Editions, 2006. 239pp. ill. 8pp. of plates. 9781416520498. Also available in audiobook, e-audiobook, and e-book. 973.931092

Mary Cheney was very involved as a senior advisor in both presidential campaigns involving her father, Dick Cheney. While working full-time in the campaigns, she kept a very low personal profile, even though she is gay and was working for the administration that signed an amendment to a bill banning gay marriage. She chose to keep quiet because she did not want to be part of the political scrum and because she believed the country could not afford single-issue voters. She mentions this issue, along with some personal details such as her parents' reactions when she came out to them, but her focus in this memoir is the presidential campaigns of 2000 and 2004, providing an insider's view of the grueling life on the campaign trail.

Subjects: Bush, George W.; Cheney, Dick; Cheney Family; Children of Vice Presidents; Fathers and Daughters; Lesbians; Political Consultants; Politics; Presidential Campaigns; Republicans

Now Try: Mary's mother, Lynne V. Cheney, has written a family memoir, tracing her family and her husband's back a few centuries. She also discusses their family as a unit in ***Blue Skies, No Fences: A Memoir of Childhood and Family***. Readers may be curious to read more about Mary Cheney's father, the vice president for two terms. Barton Gellman has written an award-winning book, ***Angler: The Cheney Vice Presidency***. Unlike Mary Cheney, Candace Gingrich reached the point where she felt it important to challenge the views on homosexuality held by her half-brother, Newt Gingrich, as she explains in ***The Accidental Activist: A Personal and Political Memoir***, written with Chris Bull. One of the major elements that comes through in her memoir is Cheney's love for her father; Christine Brennan is a sports journalist who credits her success to her father's love and support for her career, as she recounts in ***Best Seat in the House: A Father, a Daughter, a Journey Through Sports***.

Clarke, Richard A.

Against All Enemies: Inside America's War on Terror. Free Press, 2004. 304pp. 9780743260244. Also available in large print, audiobook (read by the author), and e-book. 973.931

Apart from being an indictment of the American government's continuing resistance to recognizing its most serious enemy (Osama bin Laden and al-Qaeda), this is Clarke's memoir of his twenty-year career in counterterrorism in the U.S. government. Although he had worked under seven different administrations, he focuses on his years with Presidents George H. Bush, Bill Clinton, and George W. Bush. His book begins with the September 11 attack on the World Trade Center in 2001, when he was appointed crisis manager of the White House Situation Room by Condoleezza Rice, giving him a firsthand view of how the crisis was handled. His title comes from the phrase in the Constitutional Oath with which he ends his book, a pledge to protect the Constitution "against all enemies."

Subjects: al-Qaeda (Terrorist Group); Antiterrorist Policy; Counterterrorism; Politics; September 11 Terrorist Attacks, 2001; War on Terrorism (2001–); Writers

Now Try: Just at the point when he was asked to manage the Situation Room, Clarke had been about to take on a less prominent role in cybersecurity. He has turned his knowledge from that position into a thriller, ***Breakpoint***. The terrorist situation facing the United States is not new; if readers are interested in some historical background to this, they would do well to read Steve Coll's ***Ghost Wars: The Secret History of the CIA, Afghanistan, and bin Laden, from the Soviet Invasion to September 10, 2001***. Dexter Filkins takes the need for counterterrorism beyond 9/11 in his look at the Taliban and U.S. involvement in Afghanistan and Iran in ***The Forever War***. Politics and diplomacy are one way to combat terrorism. Another way is through actual combat, as practiced by a counterterrorism unit. Eric L. Haney describes the selection process, the training, and some of the secret missions of one such unit in ***Inside Delta Force: The Story of America's Elite Counterterrorist Unit***.

Clinton, Bill (1946–)

My Life. Knopf, 2004. 957pp. ill. 32pp. of plates. 9780375414572. Also available in large print, Braille, audiobook (read by the author), e-audiobook, and e-book. 973.929092

The short title of this memoir succinctly sums up the lengthy content. Clinton treats the reader to his life story from his childhood in Arkansas to the end of his presidency. We learn of his close relationship with his mother and the abuse he suffered at the hands of his stepfather (his father had died before he was born). While describing his childhood, he also depicts life in the segregated South. He takes us through his education, his political career in Arkansas, and his presidency. In discussing his presidency he doesn't ignore the scandals, but he does candidly express his views about both Ken Starr and his own perception of a conservative conspiracy to discredit him. He also illuminates the daily life of a president, both in Washington and in international affairs. (In a later edition, the publisher divided the memoir into two volumes: ***My Life: The Early Years*** and ***My Life: The Presidential Years***.)

My Life won the British Book Award for Best Biography and the Audie Award for Audiobook of the Year.

Subjects: Abuse (Parental); American South; Arkansas; Childhood and Youth; Clinton, Hillary Rodham; Democrats; Governors; Mothers and Sons; Politicians; Politics; Presidents; Rural Life; Stepfathers

Now Try: Clinton has spent much of his postpresidency life in humanitarian work and has written a book to that end, ***Giving: How Each of Us Can Change the World***. In his memoir Clinton gives his mother much credit for forming him. As Bonnie Angelo reveals in ***First Mothers: The Women Who Shaped the Presidents***, he is not the only president to have had a positive and formative relationship with his mother. Giving credence to the notion of a conservative conspiracy against Clinton is David Brock, a former reporter who pilloried Clinton in the press and who has since changed his views, as he reveals in ***Blinded by the Right: The Conscience of an Ex-Conservative***. Before he moved to Washington, Clinton spent many years in politics in Arkansas. Readers may enjoy learning more about the American South by reading James C. Cobb's book, ***Away Down South: A History of Southern Identity***.

Clinton, Hillary Rodham (1947–)

Living History. Scribner, 2004, 2003. With a new Afterword. 567pp. ill. 9780743222259. Also available in large print, Braille, audiobook (read by the author), e-audiobook, and e-book. 973.929092

Hillary Rodham grew up in a middle-class Republican suburb in Chicago and remained a Republican until the Vietnam War, when she began to rethink her political views. Her childhood and youth form the background for her memoir of life in the White House with her husband, *Bill Clinton*, and her subsequent election to the New York Senate. In her memoir, apart from describing her life and the people in it, she also discusses the causes that proved to be important to her and that she worked to improve as First Lady, causes such as early childhood development, health care for uninsured children, and microloans for women in developing nations. She credits the writing of the book to three women: Lissa Muscatine, Ruby Shamir, and Maryanne Vollers.

Hillary Clinton was inducted into the National Women's Hall of Fame.

Subjects: Arkansas; Children's Rights Activists; Democrats; First Ladies; Lawyers; Politicians; Politics; Senators; Trailblazers; White House, Washington, DC; Women in Politics; Women's Rights Activists

Now Try: Elaine Showalter has included Hillary Clinton in her wide-ranging look at strong women, ***Inventing Herself: Claiming a Feminist Intellectual Heritage***. There were several strong First Ladies who preceded Hillary Clinton, but one who may surprise today's readers is the politically ambitious Nellie Taft, whose biography is written by Carl Sferrazza Anthony, ***Nellie Taft: The Unconventional First Lady of the Ragtime Era***. Hillary's memoir is rich in detail, as is an award-winning biography, ***Lincoln***, by David Herbert Donald.

DeLay, Tom D. (1947–)
Mansfield, Stephen (1958–), coauthor

No Retreat, No Surrender: One American's Fight. Foreword by Rush Limbaugh. Preface by Sean Hannity. Sentinel, 2007. 189pp. ill. 8pp. of plates. 9781595230348. Also available in audiobook (read by the author), e-audiobook, and e-book. 328.73092

Tom Delay was Majority Whip for the Republican Party in the House of Representatives and then Majority Leader for a number of years before being indicted on a felony conspiracy charge and forced to step down. In his memoir he describes the events, particularly one in Havana when he was twelve, that influenced him, formed his conservative views, and led him into the political realm. His memoir is as much a statement of his political and religious credos as it is a life story. Before describing his childhood, he sets out in point form his political manifesto, a creed that includes a belief in God and a higher moral order, but he also later admits to revelry and womanizing. He provides a view for the reader into the workings of the Republican Party as well as his and his party's successes in political campaigning and fund-raising.

Subjects: Campaign Finances; Conspiracies; Corruption; Cuba; Fund-Raisers; Legislators; Politicians; Politics; Republicans; Texas

Now Try: Those who would like to understand better the influence that DeLay had on American politics might enjoy the dispassionate study by Steve Bickerstaff, ***Lines in the Sand: Congressional Redistricting in Texas and the Downfall of Tom DeLay***. Mitt Romney, a Republican politician, has recently written a book outlining his own manifesto of Republican beliefs and ideas, ***No Apology: The Case for American Greatness***. If readers found interesting Sean Hannity's preface to DeLay's book, they may also like his ***Deliver Us from Evil: Defeating Terrorism, Despotism, and Liberalism***. Mark R. Levin is a radio host who has also written a statement of beliefs in ***Liberty and Tyranny: A Conservative Manifesto***.

Ferraro, Geraldine (1935–2011)
Francke, Linda Bird, coauthor

Ferraro, My Story. Foreword by Marie C. Wilson. Northwestern University Press, 2004, 1985. 348pp. ill. 24pp. of plates. 9780810122116. Also available in large print. 973.927092

Geraldine Ferraro made history when she was invited by Walter Mondale to run as his vice presidential candidate in 1984. In her memoir she describes what led up to that selection and the election campaign itself, depicting the inner workings of American political campaigns. She also discusses the importance of women in politics, mentioning specific women who have had legislative positions in both the House and the Senate. This new edition has been updated to include her bout with cancer in the late 1990s, when she had been given a prognosis of three to five years to live.

Ferraro was inducted into the National Women's Hall of Fame.

Subjects: Democrats; Equal Rights Amendment; Firsts; Legislators; Politicians; Politics; Vice-Presidential Candidates; Women in Politics; Women's Rights Activists

Now Try: Bella Abzug was one of the influential women responsible for Ferraro's presence on the presidential ticket. Suzanne Levine and Mary Thom have sorted through Abzug's writing and created an "oral biography" of her, ***Bella Abzug: How One Tough Broad from the Bronx Fought Jim Crow and Joe McCarthy, Pissed Off Jimmy Carter, Battled for the Rights of Women and Workers, Rallied Against War and for the Planet, and Shook Up Politics Along the Way; An Oral History***. Pat Schroeder is another woman legislator who has put her stamp on congressional politics and helped blaze a trail for women. Her memoir is dryly entitled ***24 Years of House Work—and the Place Is Still a Mess: My Life in Politics***. Another first for women in politics was the appointment of Nancy Pelosi as Speaker of the House; Pelosi wrote a book to encourage young women to strive in their leadership capabilities, ***Know Your Power: A Message to America's Daughters***, written with Amy Hill Hearth.

Giuliani, Rudolph W. (1944–)
Kurson, Ken (1968–), coauthor

Leadership. With a new Introduction by the author. Hyperion, 2007, 2002. 407pp. 9781401360344. Also available in large print, Braille, audiobook, and e-book. 303.34

Giuliani begins his memoir with the event that catapulted him into international renown, the September 11 terrorist attack on New York City in 2001, where he was mayor at the time. Each of the chapter titles in his book is a phrase denoting an aspect of leadership, the ostensible subject of his book. He uses his personal experiences, however, to illustrate how he came to learn those leadership attributes and to illuminate his points. He invokes the lessons he learned from boxing with his father, Harold, gaining a love of reading from his mother, Helen, and having high standards set for him by Judge Lloyd MacMahon for whom he clerked as a young lawyer. He briefly refers to his postmayoral days, particularly in the decisions he made regarding his prostate cancer, decisions he felt were facilitated by lessons learned throughout his career.

Subjects: Lawyers; Leadership; Mayors; New York, NY; Politicians; Prostate Cancer; Republicans; September 11 Terrorist Attacks, 2001

Now Try: Being mayor of New York City is one of the more challenging mayoral positions in the United States. Joyce Purnick looks at Giuliani's successor in her biography, ***Mike Bloomberg***. Many readers would like to cultivate greater leadership skills and may therefore be interested in Marcus Buckingham's ***The One Thing You Need to Know: About Great Managing, Great Leading, and Sustained Individual Success***. For something a little lighter, readers may enjoy the mystery series by former New York mayor Ed Koch, in which he himself is the protagonist solving the mysteries. ***Murder at City Hall*** is the first in the Ed Koch Mystery Series, written with Herbert Resnicow.

Kennedy, Edward M. (1932–2009)

True Compass: A Memoir. Twelve, 2009. 532pp. ill. 40pp. of plates. 9780446539258. Also available in large print, audiobook, e-audiobook, and e-book. 978.92092

Ted Kennedy spent the last five years of his life writing this memoir, battling brain cancer at the end; this long-awaited book was published a month after he died. In it he describes what it was like to grow up as the youngest of the close-knit Kennedy clan; he reveals the heartache of his brothers' deaths, his sister's mental illness, and the later tragedies that befell the family. He also discusses the tragedy of Chappaquiddick and his divorce. His political life is naturally an important part of his memoir, as it was through his politics that he tried to effect the social and political changes—particularly in health reform—that were his goals.

Subjects: Brain Cancer; Democrats; Kennedy Family; Leadership; Massachusetts; Politicians; Politics; Senators; Social Activists

Now Try: Vincent Bzdek looks at Ted Kennedy as Act Three of the triumvirate of brothers in ***The Kennedy Legacy: Jack, Bobby and Ted and a Family Dream Fulfilled.*** Stories of the family dynasty fascinate readers who enjoy celebrity, but not all dynastic families are celebrities. Tad Friend, a writer for *The New Yorker*, tells his family story in ***Cheerful Money: Me, My Family, and the Last Days of WASP Splendor***. Speaker of the House Tip O'Neill was another lion in the Senate; his popular memoir, written with William Novak, is entitled ***Man of the House: The Life and Political Memoirs of Speaker Tip O'Neill.*** One of Ted Kennedy's friends was Orrin Hatch, a Republican senator from Utah, who describes his long career in the Senate in ***Square Peg: Confessions of a Citizen Senator.***

Mankiller, Wilma Pearl (1945–2010)
Wallis, Michael (1945–), coauthor

Mankiller: A Chief and Her People. With a new Afterword by the author. St. Martin's Griffin, 2000, 1993. 310pp. ill. 9780312206628. Also available in audiobook. 973.049750092

Wilma Mankiller's political coming of age did not arrive until after she had married a well-to-do Ecuadorean in San Francisco. Provoked by a combination of the women's movement and the occupation by American Indians of the island of Alcatraz, she started to develop a political awareness. This memoir was written after Mankiller had divorced her husband, taken her two children back to her home, Mankiller Flats, Oklahoma, and begun to get involved with her Cherokee Nation community. That involvement led eventually to her being elected the first woman leader of the Cherokee Nation, a position that she retained in a second election four years after the first. Her memoir includes not only her own history, but that of her nation as well, and doesn't mince words about the Europeans and other White people who did so much damage to American Indian cultures and peoples. She also includes Cherokee folklore, so that the reader gets a sense of her community as well as of this woman who led her people and fought for them for decades.

Mankiller was awarded the Presidential Medal of Freedom in 1998 by President Clinton and inducted into the National Women's Hall of Fame.

Subjects: American Indian Women; Cherokee Nation; Childhood and Youth; Democrats; Feminists; Firsts; History, United States; Oklahoma; Political Activists; Politicians

Now Try: Rigoberta Menchú is a strong indigenous female figure who has written a controversial memoir about her place in Guatemala's struggles, ***I, Rigoberta Menchú: An Indian Woman in Guatemala***, edited by Elisabeth Burgos-Debray and translated from the Spanish by Ann Wright. The controversy lies in the veracity of her stories, although the emotional truth is real. Theda Perdue, a historian, edited a collection of essays detailing lives of various American Indian women, ***Sifters: Native American Women's Lives***. Because her father participated in a government initiative to move from the reservation to the city, Mankiller did not spend her whole childhood on the reservation. Joseph Iron Eye Dudley did, living with his grandparents, a happy time that he describes in ***Choteau Creek: A Sioux Reminiscence***.

McAuliffe, Terry (1957–)
Kettmann, Steve, coauthor

What a Party! My Life Among Democrats: Presidents, Candidates, Donors, Activists, Alligators, and Other Wild Animals. Thomas Dunne Books, 2007. 406pp. ill. 16pp. of plates. 9780312357870. Also available in audiobook and e-audiobook. 324.2736092

The alligator in McAuliffe's title is one that he wrestled while fund-raising for Jimmy Carter and Walter Mondale in the 1980 presidential election. That was his beginning as a fund-raiser for the Democratic Party, and he has since made a name for himself in both fund-raising and political consulting. In his memoir he recounts stories of time spent with the major Democratic players in the final decades of the twentieth century, so that the reader gets cameo portraits of names in the news. He also details his work for the Democratic Party, culminating in his chairmanship of the Democratic National Committee, a successful tenure that saw him bring the committee out of debt. Although he rails against the Republican Party in his memoir, he also lashes out at the Democrats as well, citing them for a lack of courage and strength.

Subjects: Clinton, Bill; Democrats; Fund-Raisers; Political Consultants; Presidential Campaigns

Now Try: The general populace doesn't always get to see those behind the scenes in politics. Washington journalist Marjorie Williams offers a look at some of these people in ***Reputation: Portraits in Power***, edited by Timothy Noah. McAuliffe's energy earned him the name "Mad Dog"; he is not unlike Stephen Fry, who has also written a boisterous memoir, ***Moab Is My Washpot***. Because McAuliffe's memoir may seem larger than life, readers might like to hear what Robert Shrum, another political campaigner, has to say in ***No Excuses: Concessions of a Serial Campaigner*** about many of the same people in McAuliffe's story.

9 10 11 12 13

McCain, John (1936–)
Salter, Mark (1955–), coauthor

Worth the Fighting For: A Memoir. Random House, 2002. 396pp. ill. 9780375505423. Also available in large print, audiobook, e-audiobook, and e-book. 328.73092

This memoir, beginning after his return from Vietnam where he was a POW for five years, is a sequel to McCain's ***Faith of My Fathers***, also written with Mark Salter (see p. 491). After his rehabilitation he was able to fly again for the U.S. Navy and became the navy liaison with the Senate. In that position McCain met men who became mentors to him in his political career as he made his way to the House and then to the Senate. He gives a lot of time and high praise to John Tower and Henry Jackson, as well as to Morris Udall, who taught him much in the Senate. McCain openly discusses his role in the Keating Five scandal and finishes his memoir with the 2000 presidential election.

Subjects: Arizona; Jackson, Henry; Keating Five Scandal; Legislators; Politicians; Politics; Republicans; Senators; Tower, John G.; Udall, Morris; United States Navy

Now Try: McCain decries his role in the Keating Five scandal, although he was found to be one of the least culpable. Dennis F. Thompson looks at the issue of corruption and ethics in government in ***Ethics in Congress: From Individual to Institutional Corruption***. John G. Tower was quite influential in McCain's political development. This Republican from Texas has written his own story, ***Consequences: A Personal and Political Memoir***. A fellow U.S. Navy veteran turned politician is Jesse Ventura, another maverick, but one who presents a startling contrast to John McCain. Ventura has written several books, one of which is ***I Ain't Got Time to Bleed: Reworking the Body Politic from the Bottom Up***.

Means, Russell (1939–)
Wolf, Marvin J., coauthor

Where White Men Fear to Tread: The Autobiography of Russell Means. St. Martin's Press, 1996, 1995. 573pp. ill. 32pp. of plates. maps. 9780312147617. 305.89707

Russell Means, an Oglala Sioux, has been an actor, an accountant, an alcoholic, a data processor, a vice presidential candidate, and a leader in the American Indian Movement (AIM), and he relates it all in this autobiography. He initially found himself going the way of many American Indian people, spending much of his time in bars, but as he tells it, his tenure with AIM led him to realize the importance of his heritage and provided him with a spiritual environment in which to grow and transform. His autobiography is often angry as he recognizes and describes the treatment of his people at the hands of the White people. It is also full of action as he vividly narrates his encounters with the law, the fights he has been in, and the prison terms he has served. Throughout his story the reader can see why he has always remained a controversial figure among both his own people and those he has spent much of his life fighting against.

Subjects: Alcoholics; American Indian Movement; American Indian Rights; American Indians; History, United States; Libertarians; Oglala Sioux Nation; Politicians; Politics; Social Activists

Now Try: Wounded Knee was the site of a bloody massacre in the nineteenth century, where the American army killed about 300 Sioux, including their chief, Big Foot. Wounded Knee was thus chosen as the locale for a stand in 1973 against government treatment of American Indians in the twentieth century, an event that Means was heavily involved in. Dee Alexander Brown wrote a highly popular history of the American West, published not long before that confrontation in 1973 and just recently revised: ***Bury My Heart at Wounded Knee: An Indian History of the American West***, an illustrated edition that includes excerpts from writers such as Russell Means, Mary Brave Bird, and Elliott West. After the confrontation at Wounded Knee in 1973, Peter Matthiessen added to that history in a publication decrying the actions of the American government and its agent against American Indians and specifically against Leonard Peltier. Because of suits filed by the Federal Bureau of Intelligence, the publication of Matthiessen's ***In the Spirit of Crazy Horse*** was suppressed for eight years. Hyemeyohsts Storm is a self-described Breed (his North Cheyenne mother married a German) who has introduced by way of his well-received novel, ***Seven Arrows***, both the Medicine Wheels and the "Indian Wars" from the perspective of the American Indian peoples.

Myers, Dee Dee (1961–)

Why Women Should Rule the World. Harper, 2008. 280pp. 9780061140402. Also available in large print and e-book. 973.929092

When Dee Dee Myers was given the job of press secretary for President Clinton, she was both the youngest person and the first woman to hold that position. But she was also denied the normal press secretary's office, given a much smaller room, and paid significantly less than men in less important jobs. In her memoir she describes her life, including her personal experiences as press secretary, but she also recounts the history of women breaking into male-dominated worlds. With the research she has done into women's roles, Myers offers a manifesto for empowering women. Her thesis is not so much that women should hold all the positions of power as that there should be more women in governance, adding their own particular brand of thinking and perspectives on solving problems.

Subjects: Clinton, Bill; Democrats; Empowerment of Women; Firsts; Politics; Press Secretaries; Sex Discrimination; Women in Politics

Now Try: George W. Bush also hired a woman, Dana Perino, as press secretary; if you'd like to read about that role in Washington politics, you might find interesting Woody Klein's ***All the Presidents' Spokesmen: Spinning the News, White House Press Secretaries from Franklin D. Roosevelt to George W. Bush***, the foreword of which was written by Myers. Gender discrimination in employment is nothing new; one example can be seen in Liza Featherstone's ***Selling Women Short: The Landmark Battle for Workers' Rights at Wal-Mart.*** The differences between men and women are real, with scientists offering various opinions. Deborah Blum looks at the situation from one perspective in ***Sex on the Brain: The Biological Differences Between Men and Women.***

Obama, Barack (1961–)

The Audacity of Hope: Thoughts on Reclaiming the American Dream. Vintage, 2008, 2006. 448pp. 9780307455871. Also available in large print, audiobook (read by the author), e-audiobook, and e-book. 328.73092

Using his own experiences as a lawyer, a junior senator, a husband and father, and a Christian, Barack Obama presents his thoughts on how the United States can restore itself to the vision set out by the Founding Fathers. He discusses the current partisanship in the two major parties and refers back to the Constitution. He includes thoughts on values, on race, and on religion, offering a chapter on each. And he goes beyond the U.S. borders to look at the world around us. His title comes from a phrase spoken by his preacher in Chicago, but it was also a part of his speech at the 2004 Democratic National Convention, referring to an entrenched American optimism regarding the future.

Barack Obama was awarded the Nobel Peace Prize.

Subjects: African-American Men; Democrats; Ideals (Philosophy); Nobel Prize Laureates; Politicians; Politics; Presidents; Senators

Now Try: David Remnick has interviewed a broad swath of people, including Obama himself, to write a biography of the man in the context of the racial history of the United States, ***The Bridge: The Life and Rise of Barack Obama***. Richard G. Wilkinson and Kate Pickett have spent thirty years working on a study to prove why everyone has a vested interest in working toward the type of ideals outlined in Obama's memoir. In ***The Spirit Level: Why Greater Equality Makes Societies Stronger***, they illustrate how everyone benefits when the gap between the rich and the poor is significantly reduced. In his eclectic collection of essays, ***A Power Governments Cannot Suppress***, the historian Howard Zinn reveals America at its finest and at its worst, with a view to inspiring readers to work toward reclaiming the ideals of the Founding Fathers. Abraham Lincoln's philosophies have always been formative for Barack Obama. Frank J. Williams and William D. Pederson invited a number of Lincoln scholars to talk about their first encounters with the man's writing and what his ideas have meant to them. The result is ***Lincoln Lessons: Reflections on America's Greatest Leader***.

Palin, Sarah (1964–)

Going Rogue: An American Life. HarperCollins, 2010, 2009. 431pp. ill. 24pp. plates. 9780061939907. Also available in large print, audiobook (read by the author), e-audiobook, and e-book. 973.93109

Sarah Palin's memoir is basically in two parts. The first tells her story about growing up in Alaska, marrying, having children, and becoming governor. She reminisces about her early life and is quite open about her feelings when she discovered she was going to have a baby with Down syndrome. She then describes the phone call that changed her life, a call from Senator John McCain, asking her to stand as the first Republican woman to run for vice president. The remainder of the book becomes an *apologia*, wherein she reveals her views about politics, political issues, and the presidential campaign, but as a "personal self-defense or justification" (Kappel, 2001). Readers might expect that if she levies criticism in the latter half it would be against the Democrats and her opposing candidates. In fact she is quite bitter about the people who ran Senator McCain's campaign and in criticizing them offers her own perspective on her various actions that had been decried by the media. Palin has since written a second book, ***America by Heart: Reflections on Family, Faith, and Flag.***

Subjects: Alaska; Firsts; Governors; Politicians; Politics; Presidential Campaigns; Republicans; Vice Presidential Candidates; Women in Politics

Now Try: Much has been written about the 2008 presidential campaign, but for an objective overview, readers may want to pick up ***The Battle for America, 2008: The Story of an Extraordinary Election*** by Daniel J. Balz and Haynes Johnson. It became clear during Palin's campaign that Alaska is relatively unknown to many south of the 49th parallel. For a wide-ranging look, Larry Kaniut collected a variety of essays that he has included in ***Tales from the Edge: True Adventures in Alaska***. Another woman who made a name for herself in government is Condoleezza Rice, who has written a memoir of her childhood in Alabama, paying particular tribute to her family, ***Extraordinary, Ordinary People: A Memoir of Family***.

Powell, Colin L. (1937–)
Persico, Joseph E. (1930–), coauthor

My American Journey. Ballantine Books, 2003, 1995. 675pp. ill. 42pp. of plates. 9780345466419. Also available in large print, audiobook (read by the author), e-audiobook, and e-book. 355.0092

Colin Powell's parents were immigrants from Jamaica living in the South Bronx. He was an average student in college but found his way in the U.S. Army, an institution that provided him with a sense of order that he could work with. In his autobiography he details his rise in the army, his two tours in Vietnam (where he was wounded each time), and his stint in South Korea as a lieutenant colonel. He continued his education as he moved up the ranks and finally made his way to Washington. When he was appointed the twelfth Chairman of the Joint Chiefs of Staff, he was the youngest to hold that position and the first African-American. Powell has excelled as an administrator, one of the reasons for his several positions in Washington, and he has even included in his book a list of the rules he has worked by. His memoir, then, apart from detailing his own life, offers a broad view of the workings of American life and a general view of how one can succeed in administration, regardless of the venue.

Colin Powell was given the Horatio Alger Award, inducted into the Academy of Achievement, and awarded the Presidential Medal of Freedom twice: once in 1991 by George Bush, and then in 1993 by President Clinton.

Subjects: African-American Men; African-Americans in the Military; Cabinet Officers; Firsts; Generals; Politics; United States Army; Vietnam War (1961–1975); Washington, DC

Now Try: Henry Louis Gates interviewed a number of prominent African-Americans in order to write ***America Behind the Color Line: Dialogues with African-Americans.*** Henry H. Shelton was also the Chairman of the Joint Chiefs of Staff at one point and, with Ronald Levinson and Malcolm McConnell, has recently written a memoir, ***Without Hesitation: The Odyssey of an American Warrior.*** McGeorge Bundy, very instrumental in shaping the Vietnam War, has since stated that he was wrong in his decisions. This admission is revealed in the book by Gordon M. Goldstein, ***Lessons in Disaster: McGeorge Bundy and the Path to War in Vietnam.***

Reagan, Ronald (1911–2004)
Brinkley, Douglas (1960–), ed.

The Reagan Diaries. HarperCollins, 2009. 2v. 1173pp. ill. 32pp. of plates. 9780061346255. Also available in large print, audiobook, e-audiobook, and e-book. 973.927092

Unlike many other American presidents in the twentieth century, Ronald Reagan kept a daily diary of events and impressions during his tenure as president, begun as a "memory book" for himself and Nancy. His entries were each about a page long, jottings of what happened and his reactions to events. They also include the favorable reactions he received from others. Douglas Brinkley took five volumes of diaries and condensed them into one volume initially, publishing an abridged version in 2007. They present a clear picture of Reagan's presidency, the acuity of his first term, and the increasing diminution of his focus in the second term. For historians the diaries are of great interest because of the landmark events in the 1980s, such disparate events as the Iran-Contra affair or Perestroika and the fall of the Berlin Wall.

Reagan was awarded the Presidential Medal of Freedom in 1993 by President George Bush and was named one of *Time*'s People of the Century in the Leaders & Revolutionaries category. For his work as an actor he was inducted into the Broadcasting & Cable Hall of Fame.

Subjects: 1980s; Actors; Diaries; History, United States; Nonagenarians; Politicians; Politics; Presidents; Republicans

Now Try: Not long after the end of his tenure as president, Reagan had his autobiography ghostwritten: ***An American Life.*** Shortly before that, his wife Nancy had written hers with the help of William Novak, ***My Turn: The Memoirs of Nancy Reagan.*** The historian Sean Wilentz looks back at the American political scene, reflecting on the long-standing influence of Ronald Reagan as president in ***The Age of Reagan: A History, 1974–2008.*** While Reagan was in power in the United States, Margaret Thatcher was his counterpart in England. Hugo Young offers an objective biography of her in ***The Iron Lady: A Biography of Margaret Thatcher.*** Gerald Ford didn't keep a diary, but he did engage in many off-the-record conversations with the reporter Thomas M. DeFrank. The result of these interviews is DeFrank's ***Write It When I'm Gone: Remarkable Off-the-Record Conversations with Gerald R. Ford.***

Rove, Karl (1950–)

Courage and Consequence: My Life as a Conservative in the Fight. Threshold Editions, 2010. 596pp. ill. 16pp. of plates. 9781439191057. Also available in audiobook (read by the author) and e-book. 973.931092

In his memoir Karl Rove provides his political history, beginning with an incident when he was a young boy in Colorado. In college he became so immersed in politics that he actually didn't get his degree. He went on from there to Texas, where his fortunes and those of George W. Bush became entwined to the point that Rove was responsible for Bush's political success and accompanied him to Washington. In the course of his memoir Rove discusses many of the controversial issues of Bush's administration, such as torture, the war in Iraq, the government response to Hurricane Katrina, and the situation with Joseph C. Wilson's wife, Valerie Plame Wilson, offering his perspective on these topics and more.

Subjects: Bush, George W.; Hurricane Katrina (2005); Iraq War (2003–); Plame, Valerie; Political Consultants; Politics; Presidential Campaigns; Republicans

Now Try: Recognizing Rove's influence in molding George Bush's career are reporters James Moore and Wayne Slater, whose political biography of Rove, ***Bush's Brain: How Karl Rove Made George W. Bush Presidential,*** supplements Rove's own autobiography. Jordan Wright, who has a vast collection of presidential memorabilia, offers a history of presidential campaigns, ***Campaigning for President,*** dating back to George Washington and using that memorabilia to outline the history. Dana Milbank offers his view of current-day politics in Washington, skewering both parties in ***Homo Politicus: The Strange and Barbaric Tribes of the Beltway.*** Dick Morris is another political consultant who has had a tremendous influence on American politics. In his memoir, ***Behind the Oval Office: Winning the Presidency in the Nineties,*** he provides a close-up view of the political machine.

Sorensen, Theodore C. (1928–)

Counselor: A Life at the Edge of History. Harper Perennial, 2009, 2008. 556pp. ill. 16pp. of plates. 9780060798727. Also available in large print, audiobook (read by the author), e-audiobook, and e-book. 973.92209

When Ted Sorensen got off the train in Washington, DC, from Nebraska in the early 1950s, he was a real greenhorn. He describes his youth in Nebraska in this memoir and recounts how naïve he was when he started out after law school. But he made the acquaintance of John F. Kennedy, and each hitched his star to the other. In his memoir Sorensen discusses his writing for Kennedy the book ***Profiles in Courage,*** for which Kennedy won a Pulitzer Prize. He also reveals life in the White House with Kennedy, writing and advising on many often-quoted speeches. Sorensen's response to Kennedy's assassination was to write his biography, ***Kennedy.*** He also fills in the years after Kennedy, including a failed attempt at a Senate seat, an unpleasant nomination to be director of the Central Intelligence Agency (CIA), and his work in international law.

Subjects: Democrats; Kennedy, John F.; Lawyers; New York, NY; Octogenarians; Political Consultants; Politics; Speechwriters; Writers

Now Try: Citizens who listen to their presidents' speeches often assume the words spoken are the presidents' own. Robert Schlesinger, son of a Kennedy speechwriter and aide, Arthur M. Schlesinger, illustrates how some of the most famous lines in history were not penned by their speakers in ***White House Ghosts: Presidents and Their Speechwriters***. The general electorate is also not always aware of who is counseling their president or how much power that person might have. J. M. Fenster offers an investigation of Franklin Roosevelt's advisor in ***FDR's Shadow: Louis Howe, the Force That Shaped Franklin and Eleanor Roosevelt***. Sorensen always claimed he did not want to be Kennedy's friend, but rather his advisor. His memoir, however, is quite touching in its honesty and discretion. This same touching quality is reflected in a story of friendship among Boston Red Sox teammates, as described by David Halberstam in ***The Teammates: A Portrait of a Friendship***.

Wilson, Joseph C. (1949–)

The Politics of Truth: Inside the Lies That Led to War and Betrayed My Wife's CIA Identity; A Diplomat's Memoir. Carroll & Graf, 2005, 2004. 528pp. ill. maps. 9780786715510. Also available in e-book. 327.730092

The title of this memoir would suggest that it is almost entirely about what became known as "Plamegate," the public disclosure of Valerie Plame (Wilson's wife) as a CIA covert operative. It certainly is about that and about what spurred Wilson to go public about the lies that he knew George W. Bush was telling the American people to justify invading Iraq. More than that, however, it is Wilson's memoir about his more than twenty years serving in the U.S. Foreign Service under five presidents, from Jimmy Carter to Bill Clinton. He was recognized by George Bush as an American hero for his role in sequestering 800 potential American hostages in Iraq. He was also the last American official to speak to Saddam Hussein before Operation Desert Storm, and he was appointed by Clinton to be the Senior Director of African Affairs in the National Security Council.

Subjects: Africa; Bush, George W.; Central Intelligence Agency; Diplomats; Ethics; Foreign Service, United States; History, United States; Hussein, Saddam; Iraq War (2003–); Plame, Valerie; Politics

Now Try: Valerie Plame Wilson finally told her own story as well: ***Fair Game***. Robert D. Novak is the journalist who leaked Plame's name; called "The Prince of Darkness" by his colleagues, he used that nickname for the title of his memoir, ***The Prince of Darkness: 50 Years Reporting in Washington***. Norman Pearlstine was involved in "Plamegate" to a certain extent and now discourses on the issue of freedom of the press in ***Off the Record: The Press, the Government, and the War over Anonymous Sources***. Another man who was implicated in this entire story is Karl Rove, an analysis of whom is provided by James Moore and Wayne Slater in ***The Architect: Karl Rove and the Master Plan for Absolute Power***.

International

While we may or may not be aware of what goes on in our own government corridors, it is likely that we are even less aware of the political activity in other countries. Reading the memoirs of people who made a political difference in their own countries, countries as close as Canada and Cuba or as far away as Pakistan

9 10 11 12 13

or England, is one way to broaden our knowledge and discover at the same time that politics is pretty much the same the world over. The story of Wangari Maathai in Kenya, however, demonstrates how much one is able to accomplish for good by combining a strong spirit and a good political instinct.

These international political memoirs, with some exceptions, reflect the stories of leaders of countries in various parts of the world, describing what was involved in their arriving at such illustrious political positions and what went on while they were in power. They all deal with issues of governance, but in certain cases their situations are far more threatening than in others.

Bartleman, James (1939–)

On Six Continents: A Life in Canada's Foreign Service, 1966–2002. McClelland & Stewart, 2005, 2004. 253pp. ill. 16pp. of plates. 9780771010910. Also available in audiobook. 971.064092

James Bartleman is a Métis man (part Chippewa, part White) from the Muskoka area in Ontario who made a career in the Canadian foreign service. In this memoir he covers his twenty-six years of foreign service work on six continents, the only Canadian diplomat ever to do so. Part of his tenure also included working in Canada during the crisis with the *Front de libération du Québec* (FLQ) in Québec, when he was regarded as the expert in security involving terrorism. While describing the international leaders he met, Bartleman introduces the reader to the life of a diplomat and the diplomat's family. He also includes such personal details as his descent into depression, worsened by post-traumatic stress disorder (PTSD) after suffering a brutal attack in South Africa. Bartleman's story ends just before his appointment as lieutenant governor of Ontario in 2002.

Subjects: Aboriginal Peoples, Canada; Ambassadors, Canada; Biracial Persons; Canada; Chippewa Nation; Diplomats, Canada; Foreign Relations, Canada; Foreign Service, Canada; Lieutenant Governors, Ontario; Métis; Politics, Canada; Writers, Canada

Now Try: After he was attacked in South Africa, Bartleman began writing a series of memoirs, the first being ***Out of Muskoka***, the writing of which seemed to help him deal with his depression. In this memoir, ***On Six Continents***, he glosses over four years spent working with Jean Chrétien, as he knew he would be writing a book about that part of his career, a book entitled ***Rollercoaster: My Hectic Years as Jean Chrétien's Diplomatic Advisor, 1994–1998***. Charles Ritchie is another Canadian diplomat who has written several well-received memoirs, preceding the time period of Bartleman's writing; the first of these is ***The Siren Years: A Canadian Diplomat Abroad, 1937–1945***. The achievements of Ken Taylor, ambassador to Iran during the hostage crisis, have recently been in the news, and now a book by Robert A. Wright has been published to cover that event: ***Our Man in Tehran: The True Story Behind the Secret Mission to Save Six Americans During the Iran Hostage Crisis and the Foreign Ambassador Who Worked with the CIA to Bring Them Home.*** Another biracial diplomat is the former governor of New Mexico, Bill Richardson, who has written a memoir with Michael Ruby entitled ***Between Worlds: The Making of an American Life.***

Blair, Cherie (1954–)

Speaking for Myself: My Life from Liverpool to Downing Street. Little, Brown, 2009. 354pp. ill. 16pp. of plates. 9780316031455. Also available in audiobook (read by the author) and e-book. 941.0859092

Only one other British prime minister's wife besides Cherie Booth Blair had her own career, and that was Audrey Callaghan, wife of James Callaghan, successor to Harold Wilson. Cherie came to 10 Downing Street as a barrister, part-time judge, and human rights activist. In this memoir she describes her early childhood growing up in Liverpool, daughter of the actor Tony Booth, who abandoned the family. She met Tony Blair while they were both training in Chambers; by the time he was elected prime minister, they had three children, the fourth born while Tony was in office (the first child born to a prime minister in office since the nineteenth century). Blair describes her life as a prime minister's wife along with the people she meets, such as the royals, the Clintons, and the Bushes. She also relates stories about the run-ins she had with the British media, who were forever parked right outside 10 Downing Street.

Subjects: Barristers, England; Blair, Tony; Human Rights Activists, England; Judges, England; Marriage; Prime Ministers' Spouses, England

Now Try: Cherie Blair's husband, Tony, has recently released his own memoir, ***A Journey: My Political Life.*** Clementine Churchill apparently was one of the few prime ministers' wives who did not always stand by her man, not always supporting him in his political decisions. Their daughter, Mary Soames, edited a collection of letters between Clementine and her husband that reveal their disagreements as well as their love for each other: ***Winston and Clementine: The Personal Letters of the Churchills.*** Denis Thatcher is the only man thus far to have been a prime minister's spouse; their daughter Carol decided to write a biography of him to show that he was not the man pilloried in the media. Her book is ***Below the Parapet: The Biography of Denis Thatcher.*** Because the legal system in Britain is quite different from that of North America, readers may enjoy learning more about it through the fictional series featuring a female barrister, **Trish McGuire**. The first in the series by Natasha Cooper is ***Creeping Ivy.***

Campbell, Kim (1947–)

Time and Chance: The Political Memoirs of Canada's First Woman Prime Minister. Seal Canada, 1997, 1996. 434pp. ill. 16pp. of plates. 9780770427382. 971.0648092

Kim Campbell's political career is memorable for the number of "firsts" she accomplished, beginning in high school, when she was the first female president of student council. She worked her way from municipal to provincial to federal politics and, in Ottawa, worked her way from cabinet ministries to leader of the Conservative Party and then prime minister, the first woman to achieve that position. She did not stay in that position for long, however, and her party suffered an ignominious defeat, all of which is described in her book. She is direct and candid in her writing, putting forth her views on the people and events that had so much to do with her rise and fall.

Subjects: Firsts; Mulroney, Brian; Politicians, Canada; Politics, Canada; Prime Ministers, Canada; Progressive Conservative Party of Canada; Tory, John; Women in Politics

Now Try: Margaret Thatcher shares a "first" with Kim Campbell, in that she was the first woman prime minister in England. She provides an overview of how she arrived at that position in ***The Path to Power***. Another feisty Canadian who fights for what she believes in is Maude Barlow, the author of a number of books on water conservation and ownership as well as a memoir entitled ***The Fight of My Life: Confessions of an Unrepentant Canadian***. There are a number of women who have held the highest position in their country's government, as Gunhild Hoogensen and Bruce O. Solheim demonstrate in their book, ***Women in Power: World Leaders Since 1960*** (with a foreword by Kim Campbell).

Castro, Fidel (1926–)
Ramonet, Ignacio (1943–), coauthor

Fidel Castro: My Life; A Spoken Autobiography. Scribner, 2008, 2006. 723pp. ill. 9781416553281. Also available in audiobook and e-audiobook. 972.91064092 [Trans. by Andrew Hurley]

Ignacio Ramonet is the editor of the leftist magazine *Le Monde Diplomatique* and professor of communication theory in Paris. He spent 100 hours with Castro, interviewing the Cuban leader about his life and his political views; this translation by Andrew Hurley allows English-speaking readers to see the man up close. The book is in interview format and will be the only autobiographical work available by Castro. Castro discusses his childhood as the son of a prominent landowner, taught by Spanish Jesuits. He moves on to his revolutionary stances and the people with whom he shared similar beliefs, particularly Che Guevara. He also discusses the United States—the Bay of Pigs invasion and the embargo against Cuba. He expresses his views on the world as he sees it, particularly focusing on globalization. Castro also reveals a deep faith in the Cuban people, that they will continue the revolution after he is gone. Ramonet is a sympathetic interviewer and allows Castro free rein without challenging him, where others may have.

Subjects: Childhood and Youth; Cuba; Cubans; Guevara, Che; History, Cuba; International Relations, Cuba; Octogenarians; Politics, Cuba; Presidents, Cuba; Revolutionaries; Translations

Now Try: Ann Louise Bardach is a journalist who has steeped herself in Cuban history. By interviewing scores of people in Miami, Washington, DC, and

Havana, she has opened even more windows on Castro, particularly on his medical ailments, and on projections of Cuban life after Castro, in ***Without Fidel: A Death Foretold in Miami, Havana, and Washington***. Ernesto Che Guevara is a folk hero in the eyes of many and wrote several diaries of his adventures; perhaps the best-known is ***The Motorcycle Diaries: Notes on a Latin American Journey***. This particular edition (2003) includes a preface by Guevara's daughter, Aleida Guevara March, and was translated by Alexandra Keeble. The man Castro revolted against was Fulgencio Batista, a leader who was a revolutionary in his own right. The historian Frank Argote-Freyre has published ***Fulgencio Batista***, the first of a two-volume biography of Batista, this one going up to his election in 1940. One of Castro's favorite writers is Ernest Hemingway; readers may want to reacquaint themselves with the Cuban fisherman, Santiago, in ***The Old Man and the Sea***.

Chrétien, Jean (1934–)

My Years as Prime Minister. With a new Introduction by the author. Vintage Canada, 2008, 2007. 435pp. ill. 32pp. of plates. 9780676979015. 971.0648092

In his earlier memoir, ***Straight from the Heart***, Jean Chrétien wrote about his personal life and his childhood, as well as his years as cabinet minister in the federal government. Now he focuses on his three terms as prime minister of Canada from 1993 to 2003. He describes life as a prime minister—what is involved and how politics works in Ottawa—but he also discusses specific issues. Primary among those issues are the reduction of the deficit, his refusal to send Canadian troops to participate in the Iraq War, and the Québec referendum. He also discusses his rivalry with his former finance minister, Paul Martin. Dictated to Ron Graham, the book still has Chrétien's trademark sense of humor and folksy way of speaking. He spoke no English until he was thirty and, having learned English "on the street" as it were, he has his own signature style.

Subjects: Bush, George W.; French-Canadians; Liberal Party of Canada; Martin, Paul; Politicians, Canada; Politics, Canada; Prime Ministers, Canada; Québec

Now Try: Paul Martin has written his side of the story in ***Hell or High Water: My Life in and out of Politics***. Johnnie L. Cochran is another lawyer whose oratorical style has been characterized as folksy, the evidence of which is in his memoir, ***A Lawyer's Life***, written with David Fisher. The issue of Québec separation loomed large during Chrétien's tenure, but it didn't start there. Keith Spicer was an outspoken advocate of national unity while also championing the Québécois. His memoir, ***Life Sentences: Memoirs of an Incorrigible Canadian***, may provide interesting background to Chrétien's.

Johnson-Sirleaf, Ellen (1938–)

This Child Will Be Great: Memoir of a Remarkable Life by Africa's First Woman President. Perennial, 2010, 2009. 353pp. ill. 8pp. of plates. 9780061353482. Also available in large print, audiobook, and e-book. 966.62033

Recurring throughout Johnson-Sirleaf's life is a remembrance of the prophecy of an old man on seeing her as a baby: he told her mother that this child would be great, a prediction they all laughed at when she had to flee an abusive marriage, when she was imprisoned for her political views, or when she was sent into exile for the same. She had the determination and the smarts to be great, and she finally succeeded, after running three times, in winning the presidency of Liberia, the first woman in Africa to be elected as head of state. Liberia is the other thread that runs through her memoir: her love of the country and her willingness to fight for it, even if she had to do it from the United States, where she acquired her graduate degrees, or Kenya, where she worked in finance while in exile. She does not shy away from stating her views and speaking honestly about the age-old problems in Liberia that stem from the settlers, former American slaves, who never quite fit in properly with the indigenous peoples. She has also challenged her people to solve their problems on their own without waiting for handouts from superpowers.

Johnson-Sirleaf was awarded a Presidential Medal of Freedom by President George W. Bush in 2007.

Subjects: Africa; Doe, Samuel; Exiles; Firsts; Liberia; Political Prisoners, Liberia; Politicians, Liberia; Politics, Liberia; Presidents, Liberia; Taylor, Charles; Women in Politics

Now Try: Gerry Adams has been very instrumental in trying to create peace in his country, Ireland. One of the several books he has written deals specifically with the peace process that led to the Good Friday Agreement, ***A Farther Shore: Ireland's Long Road to Peace***. Benazir Bhutto also suffered exile before she was elected to be Pakistan's first woman prime minister. She told her story in ***Daughter of Destiny: An Autobiography***. If you're interested in how freed American slaves arrived in Liberia, you might enjoy Alan Huffman's ***Mississippi in Africa***.

Maathai, Wangari (1940–)

Unbowed: A Memoir. Anchor Books, 2007, 2006. 326pp. ill. 16pp. of plates. 9780307275202. Also available in audiobook, e-audiobook, and e-book. 333.72092

Maathai was awarded the Nobel Peace Prize (the first African woman to be so honored) for her work in founding the Green Belt Movement (http://www.greenbeltmovement.org/), an effort to both reforest Kenya and provide rural Kenyan women with a livelihood. To date the movement has been responsible for the planting of millions of trees, not just in Kenya, but throughout Africa. Maathai recounts her life story, from her beginnings in a mud hut, where women were not expected to get an education, through that unexpected education, to her completion of a doctorate in veterinary anatomy (the first woman in East and Central Africa to earn a doctorate). She has followed her work as a feminist and an environmental activist with political work, acting as Assistant Minister for Environment and Natural Resources in the Kenyan government.

Unbowed was the recipient of the Hurston/Wright Legacy Award, an award for books of high quality by writers of African descent.

Subjects: Environmental Activists; Feminists, Kenya; Firsts; Green Belt Movement; Hurston/Wright Legacy Award; Kenya; Nobel Prize Laureates; Politicians, Kenya; Trees; Women in Politics

Now Try: Maathai's indomitable spirit is matched by William Kamkwamba, a young boy in Malawi who was determined to provide a windmill for his village so they could have electricity. In ***The Boy Who Harnessed the Wind: Creating Currents of Electricity and Hope*** by Kamkwamba and Bryan Mealer, we learn how he did that with old car parts and an old bicycle wheel. The issue of women's rights in developing countries is an urgent one, as Maathai recognized. Nicholas D. Kristof and Sheryl WuDunn address this in their inspirational book of stories, ***Half the Sky: Turning Oppression into Opportunity for Women Worldwide***, a book that is not only about the plight of women but also about what they're doing for themselves. Women of any age have inspired others, and that includes Doris Haddock, the ninety-year-old "Granny D," who walked from Los Angeles to Washington, DC, to lobby for campaign finance reform. She kept a diary, which she and Dennis Burke later published as ***Granny D: Walking Across America in My Ninetieth Year***.

Mandela, Nelson (1918–)

Long Walk to Freedom: The Autobiography of Nelson Mandela. Back Bay Press, 1995, 1994. 638pp. ill. 24pp. of plates. 9780316548182. Also available in large print, audiobook, e-audiobook, and e-book. 968.064092

The adopted son of a tribal chief, Nelson Mandela grew up in a traditional culture, but was still aware of the brutal fact of apartheid. It was in law school that he started to become politicized, moving from there to revitalizing the African National Congress, working underground in the hopes of achieving change for his people in White-dominated South Africa. He describes all this as well as his many years at Robben Island, the prison in which he wrote his story, hiding his pages under the floor of his cell. He relates how he finally managed to negotiate not only his freedom, but also the end of apartheid, with then President F. W. de Klerk, the man who shared the Nobel Peace Prize with Mandela.

Mandela was awarded the Presidential Medal of Freedom in 2002 by President George W. Bush and was named one of *Time*'s People of the Century in the Leaders & Revolutionaries category. ***Long Walk to Freedom*** was also the winner of a Christopher Award.

Subjects: Apartheid; Christopher Awards; Civil Rights Activists; Firsts; Leaders; Nobel Prize Laureates; Nonagenarians; Political Activists; Politics, South Africa; Presidents, South Africa; Racism, Southern Africa; Robben Island, South Africa; South Africa

Now Try: Bishop Desmond Tutu is perhaps the only other man in South Africa held in as much esteem as Nelson Mandela. As head of the Truth and Reconciliation Commission following the end of apartheid, Tutu witnessed the victims' challenges to the oppressors and the oppressors' confessions and apologies to the victims. He then wrote a spiritual overview of that experience in ***No Future Without Forgiveness***. The South African poet and journalist Antjie Krog won an award for her coverage of that commission's work, which she details in her book, ***Country of My Skull: Guilt, Sorrow, and the Limits of Forgiveness in the New South Africa***. The courage to speak out is strong in Mandela and in many people trying to wrest their countries from corruption and despotism. Ingrid Betancourt is another example of this courage to speak out; she too was captured and held prisoner, but not by her Colombian government. She tells her story of capture by leftist guerrillas in ***Even Silence Has an End: My Six Years of Captivity in the Colombian Jungle***.

Mulroney, Brian (1939–)

Memoirs: 1939–1993. McClelland & Stewart, 2007. 1121pp. ill. 9780771065361. 971.0647092

This voluminous memoir begins with Mulroney's childhood and takes him up to the point where he left office after serving as Canada's prime minister from 1984 to 1993, succeeded by Jean Chrétien. He describes his life as the son of a mill worker in rural Québec, growing up bilingual and with an interest in politics. He reveals what life is like for a political leader, not only in terms of pressures of the job, but also in terms of the lack of privacy for one's family. Readers get an inside view of the controversial decisions he made regarding free trade and the goods and services tax, and see Mulroney's own reactions to the Meech Lake Accord discussions and results. He is not shy about discussing his views about his Canadian political rivals, and he shares his encounters with global leaders like Margaret Thatcher, Ronald Reagan, and Boris Yeltsin.

Subjects: Free Trade Agreement; Politicians, Canada; Politics, Canada; Prime Ministers, Canada; Progressive Conservative Party of Canada; Québec

Now Try: Pat Carney is a politician who was also very involved in the creation of the Free Trade Agreement, playing on that part of her political life in the title of her memoir, ***Trade Secrets: A Memoir***. The Progressive Conservative Party has changed its political face considerably in the last two decades, a fact that Hugh Segal cogently analyzes in ***The Long Road Back: The Conservative Journey in Canada, 1993–2006***. Leaders in power constantly receive correspondence from their constituents. Stephen Harper, a Conservative successor to Brian Mulroney, has been in receipt of a unique type of communication from the writer Yann Martel: a biweekly delivery of a book with accompanying note. This practice of Martel's has gone on since 2007, and he has now published a book listing those titles and providing his accompanying letters annotating the books: ***What Is Stephen Harper Reading? Yann Martel's Recommended Reading for a Prime Minister (and Book Lovers of All Stripes)***.

Musharraf, Pervez (1943–)

In the Line of Fire: A Memoir. Free Press, 2006. 354pp. ill. 16pp. of plates. 9780743283441. Also available in e-book. 954.91053

Musharraf's memoir is unusual for two reasons: it is rare for a political leader to write a memoir while still in power, as Musharraf has done, and it is unlikely that many other leaders would have such perilous tales to tell. Musharraf describes the violence that precipitated his coming into power in Pakistan (although the *coup d'état* itself was nonviolent); the various assassination attempts on him; his efforts to hunt out the Taliban; and the abduction and beheading of the journalist, Danny Pearl. He also discusses the international issues he has had to deal with, primarily from George W. Bush and in particular, Richard Armitage, Bush's then Deputy Secretary of State, particularly after the September 11, 2001, attacks. His required role and his actual role as leader of such a large Islamic country in the midst of the war on terror are complex, a fact he does not hide.

Subjects: Armitage, Richard; Bush, George W.; Muslims, Pakistan; Pakistan; Pearl, Daniel; Politicians, Pakistan; Politics, Pakistan; Presidents, Pakistan; September 11 Terrorist Attacks, 2001; Taliban; Terrorism; War on Terrorism (2001–)

Now Try: Nicholas Schmidle, a journalist who lived in Pakistan, offers his view of the political and military life of the country in ***To Live or to Perish Forever: Two Tumultuous Years in Pakistan***. In his memoir Musharraf discusses the efforts made to find the assassins of journalist Danny Pearl. After his death, Pearl's pregnant wife, Mariane, also a journalist, wrote her story, with Sarah Crichton, about the difficulties of organizing the search for him and then dealing with his murder: ***A Mighty Heart: The Brave Life and Death of My Husband, Danny Pearl***. In ***The Duel: Pakistan on the Flight Path of American Power***, Tariq Ali, a well-known commentator on Pakistan, has delved into the situation Pakistan finds itself faced with vis-à-vis the United States.

Trudeau, Pierre Elliott (1919–2000)

Memoirs. McClelland & Stewart, 1995, 1993. 379pp. ill. 9780771085871. Also available in video. 971.0644092

When a little boy makes his way to the principal's office on his second day of school to register a complaint, it's to be expected that that child will grow up to make a name for himself, as Pierre Trudeau did. He recounts this and many other adventures in his life before he headed to Ottawa as a federal politician in his forties. He was a controversial prime minister, but respected enough by the electorate to lead the country from 1968 to 1984 with a brief hiatus. His memoir is also full of the people he met, from John Lennon and Yoko Ono to Zhou Enlai and *Fidel Castro*. Readers will also gain insights into firm stands Trudeau took in situations such as the crisis with the *Front de libération du Québec* (FLQ) in Québec or the repatriation of the Constitution. In his memoir he makes it apparent that his decisions stemmed from his love of the country and its people.

Subjects: Canada; Castro, Fidel; French-Canadians; International Relations, Canada; Liberal Party of Canada; Octogenarians; Politicians, Canada; Politics, Canada; Prime Ministers, Canada

Now Try: John English has written an award-winning, two-volume biography of Trudeau, ***Citizen of the World: The Life of Pierre Elliott Trudeau*** and ***Just Watch Me: The Life of Pierre Elliott Trudeau, 1968–2000***. Perhaps a little-known fact about Trudeau was his friendship with Fidel Castro, a friendship that led Castro to travel to Canada for Trudeau's funeral. In ***Three Nights in Havana: Pierre Trudeau, Fidel Castro and the***

Cold War World, Robert A. Wright traces this friendly relationship that began with Trudeau's visit to Castro in 1976. One of Trudeau's drives was to warm up the Cold War by engaging with political leaders of Communist countries. John Lewis Gaddis provides a layman's history of that political time in ***The Cold War: A New History***. Charismatic leaders can be found in political arenas around the world, and one of them is Hugo Chávez, the Venezuelan leader whose story, ***Hugo Chávez,*** is told by Cristina Marcano and Alberto Barrera Tyszka, and translated from the Spanish by Kristina Cordero.

Zhao, Ziyang (1919–2005)
Ignatius, Adi, ed.

Prisoner of the State: The Secret Journal of Zhao Ziyang. Foreword by Roderick MacFarquhar. Simon & Schuster, 2009. 306pp. ill. 8pp. of plates. 9781439149386. Also available in e-audiobook and e-book. 951.05809 [Trans. by Bao Pu and Renee Chiang]

Although he was ostensibly China's highest-ranking official in 1989, premier of the country, and chief of the Chinese Communist Party, Ziyang Zhao was put under house arrest for life when he suggested negotiating with the uprising students instead of using military force against them. On May 19 he was divested of his power, and on June 3 the massacre in Tiananmen Square began. Despite the close watch kept on him, Zhao managed to record about thirty hours' worth of tapes, describing his political life, even pointing out that he was the real architect of economic reform and criticizing the political regime in China, both in its processes and in the specific individuals, an elite group, that continue to wield power. The tapes were smuggled out to Bao Pu and Renee Chiang, a married couple who run New Century Press in Hong Kong and who translated and coedited the work with Adi Ignatius.

Subjects: China; House Arrest, China; Octogenarians; Political Atrocities; Political Prisoners, China; Politicians, China; Politics, China; Premiers, China; Tiananmen Square Massacre (June 3–4, 1989); Translations

Now Try: Ma Jian wrote a novel, ***Beijing Coma,*** translated from the Chinese by Flora Drew, about one victim of Tiananmen Square who lies in a coma for ten years and wakes up to a different China. Maurice J. Meisner is an eminent history professor who has studied the China of Deng Xiaoping and written ***The Deng Xiaoping Era: An Inquiry into the Fate of Chinese Socialism, 1978–1994.*** Following chronologically on Zhao's book is a new study by Andrew J. Nathan and Bruce Gilley, ***China's New Rulers: The Secret Files.***

Consider Starting With . . .

Albright, Madeleine Korbel. *Madam Secretary*

Castro, Fidel. *Fidel Castro: My Life: A Spoken Autobiography*

Clinton, Bill. *My Life*

Grant, Ulysses S. *Personal Memoirs of U.S. Grant*

Kennedy, Edward M. *True Compass: A Memoir*

Maathai, Wangari. *Unbowed: A Memoir*

Mandela, Nelson. *Long Walk to Freedom: The Autobiography of Nelson Mandela*

Reagan, Ronald. *The Reagan Diaries*

Trudeau, Pierre Elliott. *Memoirs*

Zhao, Ziyang. *Prisoner of the State: The Secret Journal of Zhao Ziyang*

Fiction Read-Alikes

Anonymous. *Primary Colors: A Novel of Politics.* This *roman à clef* centers on the governor of a Southern state who has ambitions for the White House.

Beinhart, Larry. *American Hero.* A political satire, this novel posits Operation Desert Storm as nothing more than a Hollywood movie filmed to enhance George Bush's chances to be reelected.

Boxer, Barbara. *A Time to Run: A Novel.* In this debut of her series set in Washington, DC, the senator from California features a young woman whose political career begins when she takes over for her husband, who dies while campaigning for a seat in the Senate.

Isegawa, Moses. *Snakepit.* Bat Katanga returns home to Uganda after studying in England to get a job with the government of Idi Amin, a government he discovers to be corrupt and brutal.

Kadare, Ismail. *The Successor: A Novel.* The man expected to succeed the Albanian dictator, Enver Hoxha, is found shot dead in his bed, in this political *roman à clef* by the Albanian winner of the first Man Booker International Prize.

Mantel, Hilary. *Wolf Hall: A Novel.* Thomas Cromwell takes over from Cardinal Wolsey in advising King Henry VIII, particularly in Henry's wish to divorce his current wife and marry Anne Boleyn.

McCarry, Charles. *Shelley's Heart: A Novel.* The reelection of the president is challenged by his rival, who cites computer rigging as the cause for the incumbent's victory.

Moore, Brian. *The Revolution Script.* The kidnapping of a British diplomat and a Québec minister force the prime minister to invoke the War Measures Act in this journalistic re-creation of a serious challenge facing Pierre Trudeau and Canada.

Vidal, Gore. *Burr: A Novel.* Vidal begins his fictional **American Chronicle** series with a "biography" of Jefferson's vice president, Aaron Burr.

Warren, Robert Penn. *All the King's Men.* A classic tale of politics in the South, told by the idealistic yet cynical aide to the governor.

Works Cited

Denvir, Daniel. 2010. "Authors for President: The Curious History of Political Memoirs." *The Huffington Post,* February 9. Accessed April 5, 2010. http://www.huffingtonpost.com/daniel-denvir/authors-for-president-the_b_455195.html.

Gwinn, Mary Ann. 2009. "Best Tell-all Political Memoirs." *The Seattle Times,* November 16. Accessed March 31, 2010. http://seattletimes.nwsource.com/html/books/2010271356_litlife16.html.

Kappel, Lawrence. 2001. "A Historical Overview of the Autobiography." In *Autobiography,* edited by Lawrence Kappel, 14–31. San Diego, CA: Greenhaven Press.

Raban, Jonathan. 2009. "All the Presidents' Literature." *The Wall Street Journal,* January 10. Accessed March 31, 2010. http://online.wsj.com/article/SB123154076720569453.html.

Whitney, Gleaves. 2004. "Presidential Memoirs: An Oversold Genre?" Ask Gleaves, *The Hauenstein Center for Presidential Studies.* Accessed March 31, 2010. http://www.gvsu.edu/hauenstein/index.cfm?id=6098314B-F326–7A68–25EF7857C976EA6A.

Wilson, Edmund. 1994. *Patriotic Gore: Studies in the Literature of the American Civil War*. New York: W. W. Norton.

Chapter 10

Changing Lives in History

Description

The title of this chapter has a deliberately double meaning. The word "changing" has both an active and a passive connotation here, in that some of the people in this chapter have changed the lives of others through their actions, and some have had their lives changed by the events they describe. Some of the memoirists are known worldwide, and some are likely not well-known beyond their neighborhood, if even there. Some of the people in this chapter have had a tremendous influence on history, and others have simply lived a long time, observing the changes that have taken place over the decades or over a century, witness to change and development. "Witness" is a word that occurs with some frequency throughout the annotations, as many of these people have been witness to history in the making, in some cases while participating in making that history.

There are a number of reasons why people will write their stories. The case of Vernon E. Jordan is not unusual: his daughter had no understanding of what the lives people of Vernon's generation and those preceding him had been like. He wrote his memoir to help her understand not only the Jim Crow laws but also the efforts people had made to fight those laws for themselves and their children and what positive outcomes had grown from that. Others, like James Orbinski, tell their stories to inform readers of dire situations and to raise difficult questions that should be part of the global conversation. Elie Wiesel writes his story in an effort to prevent anyone else from having to live it. And George Dawson may have written his story simply because of the sheer joy in his life, a joy whose message he wanted to share with others.

In this chapter are books by feminists, by Black authors, and by a Sioux woman. The diversity among the memoirists reflects the changing attitudes toward their liberation, toward hearing their stories. It also brings home again the question of truth in memoir. For years, one major demographic group had written the history books. Now the narratives are being written by the participants, but participants whose perspective might be quite different from that of the major demographic group. " 'Whose story was true?' historians wondered. The answer depended on the perspective. . . . Some historians concluded . . . that truth was subjective. It wasn't that there wasn't truth but that truth—the past—looked different depending on where one stood" (Gutkind and Fletcher, 2008).

Some of the people in this chapter could easily have gone elsewhere—Hank Aaron into the sports section of the chapter on celebrities (Chapter 2), Walter Cronkite into the media section of "The Working Life" (Chapter 4), for example. What they represent, however, goes beyond their profession: Aaron for what he did to extend desegregation, particularly in sports, and Cronkite for how he witnessed major events through the century. Leaders of the country are very often change-makers, so that Nelson Mandela, for example, could easily have been put here instead of in the preceding chapter on political lives. The purpose of this chapter, though, is to highlight those who did not run for a political position but chose to make their changes using other vehicles.

Memoirs of changing lives in history include those people who actually played a role in making history and those who lived in historical times and have borne witness to what they have seen. The differences the writers have made are in a variety of fields, from social sciences (particularly in fighting discrimination) to politics to science. These memoirs are largely narrative as the writers recount what they and those surrounding them did to effect change.

Appeal

The stories in this chapter contain a variety of appeal factors. One of the major appeals is character, as the reader sees extraordinary but familiar people like Benjamin Franklin up close, or extraordinary but unknown people like the Delany sisters, hearing their stories, marveling at their accomplishments. Depending on the generation reading these stories, for some, reading about Joan Baez, for example, may be getting to know better a person one had long admired and enjoyed listening to; for others, reading about Joan Baez may be getting to know a person for the first time. Reading stories of people like Craig Kielburger or Erin Gruwell, ordinary people at first glance, may inspire a reader to try to emulate their behavior. Readers might marvel at the courage of a Melba Beals or Khassan Baiev, or they might simply be grateful to read about how others went before them to prepare a better way.

Again, depending on the generation enjoying some of these stories, the appeal can be of reading about an experience shared, either through news reports or actual participation. Seeing someone like John Lewis on television as an active member of Congress and then reading about his courage during the Civil Rights Movement can be an enlightening experience, bringing history to life, helping the reader understand that what was studied in perhaps dry history classes actually was current events at one time. "Seeing the arc of history through the eyes of those who lived it, even created it, is as close to being there as we can get" if we didn't actually participate ourselves (Wyatt, 2007). Learning, then, is also part of the appeal of this chapter: learning for the younger reader, who did not hear the news reports, and learning for the older reader, who was never that close to the action. Given the current political climate and debates in the United States, these stories need to be read, so that readers can learn for themselves what the issues were and continue to be, not just what happened, but why.

The actual subject matter or story line has great appeal in history-oriented books, too. People who want to understand more about economics in today's world will want to read both Muhammad Yunus's and Alan Greenspan's stories. Daniel Ellsberg's ***Secrets: A Memoir of Vietnam and the Pentagon Papers*** reads like a thriller. What must it have been like to marry a royal? Reading Queen Noor's or Empress Farah Pahlavi's stories will give one perspective. What actually went on during the Civil Rights Movement? Several sides of that story are told here.

Organization of This Chapter

The chapter begins with classics—from the seventeenth, eighteenth, nineteenth, and twentieth centuries—and moves from there to the current time. The second section is about people who are actively changing lives, primarily in other parts of the world, but at the same time changing their own lives. Following that section are those who have had an influence in a broader sphere—activists in civil rights, women's rights, indigenous rights, and the environment. The chapter ends with people who have witnessed much in their lives, whether through a very long life or through the nature of their profession or personality.

Classics

These classics cover a span of centuries, with a glimpse of London in the seventeenth century providing much detail about the social mores of the time as well as the cultural and newsworthy events of the day, moving forward to equivalent detail about life in the United States and abroad in the eighteenth century. The nineteenth century and its politicians are limned here, and the twentieth century is represented by two women blazing trails for others, women in particular.

> Classic stories of writers changing lives in history represent men and women from two continents and several centuries who have portrayed for their readers not only life as it was lived in their time, but also changes that they themselves may have contributed.

Adams, Henry (1838–1918)
Chalfant, Edward, and Conrad Edick Wright, eds.

The Education of Henry Adams: A Centennial Version. Massachusetts Historical Society, 2007, 1907. 500pp. 9781401603250. Also available in e-audiobook and e-book. 973.07202

Written in the third person, this work by Henry Adams offers glimpses into both his life and the political life of the United States. His great-grandfather was John Adams, his grandfather, John Quincy Adams, and his father, Charles Adams, a senator and ambassador. Henry chose not to follow in his ancestors' political footsteps but rather to be the observer and the writer. As a journalist in Washington, DC, and a history professor at Harvard, he did just that, and readers who know Washington find Adams's autobiography an interesting lens through which to view the current city. Because of his family, Adams rubbed elbows with noted people of the nineteenth century, offering to his readers snapshots of such people as presidents and literati.

Adams's book was originally published in a limited edition in 1907 and after his death was edited and republished by the Massachusetts Historical Society, an edition that won the Pulitzer Prize for Biography or Autobiography.

Subjects: 19th Century; Classics; Education; Historians; Journalists; Octogenarians; Pulitzer Prize for Biography or Autobiography; Reflections; Self-Education

Now Try: If you're interested in seeing Henry Adams as a part of his larger familial legacy, you might enjoy Richard Brookhiser's ***America's First Dynasty: The Adamses, 1735–1918.*** Part of the time period covered in Adams's book is the so-called Gilded Age, a time that Christopher E. G. Benfey brings to life in ***The Great Wave: Gilded Age Misfits, Japanese Eccentrics, and the Opening of Old Japan,*** particularly in America's looking eastward to Japan. Following in time on the heels of Henry Adams was H. L. Mencken, another journalist and one of great influence. Marion Elizabeth Rodgers has written his definitive biography, ***Mencken: The American Iconoclast,*** a biography that is as exhaustive as Adams's autobiography. Howard Zinn was a historian of today's time, a man not as detached as Adams. For a historian's view of today's world, seen through the lens of his own life, you may want to read Zinn's ***You Can't Be Neutral on a Moving Train: A Personal History of Our Times.***

Franklin, Benjamin (1706–1790)

The Autobiography of Benjamin Franklin. Cosimo Classics, 2007, 1793. 136pp. 9781602069602. Also available in large print, audiobook, e-audiobook, and e-book. 973.3092

A Renaissance man skilled in business, science, and letters, Benjamin Franklin was also a political man, yet capable of changing his perceptions, converting from Loyalist attitudes to revolutionary precepts and behavior. Although this autobiography is short for a man who lived so long and so illustriously, it still covers much ground. He begins with a letter to his son, including for him details of their family heritage. But he soon backtracks to his own childhood and adolescence, making the man who is an icon for twentieth-century readers into a flesh-and-blood person. It took him several years to complete this work, beginning in 1791 and not resuming for another thirteen years. Finishing not long before he died, he takes his account up to his mid-life when he was fifty-one. Interestingly, his book was first published in France in 1791 and then translated into English two years later.

Subjects: 18th century; Classics; Founding Fathers; Inventors; Octogenarians; Philadelphia, PA; Publishers; Scientists; Social History, United States

Now Try: For a broader look at one area in which Franklin had a great influence, readers may want to pick up the award-winning book by Joseph J. Ellis, ***Founding Brothers: The Revolutionary Generation***. To accompany that book is another that current readers may find particularly topical: Carol Berkin's ***A Brilliant Solution: Inventing the American Constitution***. Many readers like to learn their history through fiction. Jeff Shaara, known for his Civil War novels, has also written a **Revolutionary War Series**, the first of which is ***Rise to Rebellion***.

Goldman, Emma (1869–1940)

Living My Life. Cosimo Classics, 2008, 1931. 2v. 993pp. 9781605204208; 9781605204185. Also available in e-book. 335.83092

Known as Red Emma and "the most dangerous woman in America" (Vanderford, 2005), Emma Goldman spoke out all her life about her beliefs in the importance of liberty for all. She came from a comfortable background in Lithuania, but suffered when she saw the treatment of her family's servants—a typical situation in her world. All her life she fought for improvement in the lives of the disenfranchised, whether it meant fighting for birth control, abolition of conscription, or freedom of speech. Her personal creed is made obvious in her autobiography, but she writes a personal story, rather than one of doctrine. She talks about her life in New York and elsewhere (she was deported in 1919), her jail sentences, and her many love affairs. She also talks about the people who joined her in her fight, women such as Margaret Sanger, who shared Goldman's belief in women's rights.

Subjects: Anarchists; Birth Control; Classics; Freedom of Speech; New York, NY; Pacifists; Women's Rights Activists

Now Try: Although at first glance it may not seem likely, Emma Goldman and Eleanor Roosevelt had beliefs in common, both interested in social change and women's rights. Roosevelt's autobiographical volumes were published together as ***The Autobiography of Eleanor Roosevelt***. When President McKinley was assassinated, Emma Goldman was reviled as being partly responsible for it, as it was rumored that her speeches stirred up McKinley's assassin. Eric Rauchway has investigated that killing and the killer, along with the country at the time of the event, in ***Murdering McKinley: The Making of Theodore Roosevelt's America***. Goldman begins her autobiography with her arrival in New York City, the place that was to feed her passions. In his study of Greenwich Village, ***Republic of Dreams: Greenwich Village, the American Bohemia, 1910–1960***, Ross Wetzsteon explains how influential a place it really was, given the people who lived there.

Pepys, Samuel (1633–1703)
Le Gallienne, Richard, ed.

The Diary of Samuel Pepys. Abridged and edited by Richard Le Gallienne. Preface by Richard Le Gallienne. Introduction by Robert Louis Stevenson. Modern Library, 2003, 1825. 310pp. 9780812970715. Also available in audiobook, e-audiobook, and e-book. 914.2036

This edition, abridged from eleven volumes of text, will give the reader a taste of Pepys's diary, to determine if further reading would be interesting. Although Pepys died in 1703, the first published edition of his diary didn't come out until 1825. The diary, written over a period of roughly ten years, from 1660 to 1669, is a superb view of life in seventeenth-century London, a view that illustrates the universality of humankind even over centuries. Although the time period is only ten years, Pepys covers the plague, the Restoration, the Dutch War, and the Great Fire of London. As the naval administrator for King Charles II, Pepys treats his readers to commentary on all manner of subjects, from coffeehouses to taverns, education to science, government to holidays. For Pepys and history aficionados there is a wonderful Web site that offers a daily entry from his diary along with much more information about the author and his writing: *The Diary of Samuel Pepys* (http://www.pepysdiary.com/about/).

Subjects: 17th Century; Charles II, King of England; Classics; Diaries; England; London, England; Social History, England

Now Try: Because Pepys's diary covers only ten years, readers may want to learn more about his long life, which they can do by reading Claire Tomalin's award-winning biography, ***Samuel Pepys: The Unequalled Self***. The time period that Pepys lived in was full of drama, intrigue, and tragedy; one example of that is the Great Fire of London, about which Adrian Tinniswood has written, ***By Permission of Heaven: The Story of the Great Fire of London***. The architect Christopher Wren was a major London figure at the time, a man whose story has been told by Lisa Jardine in ***On a Grander Scale: The Outstanding Life of Sir Christopher Wren***. Pepys's eye for detail is one of the characteristics that adds such appeal to his writing. This same attention to detail has been used by Diana Preston in ***Cleopatra and Antony: Power, Love, and Politics in the Ancient World***.

Steinem, Gloria (1934–)

Outrageous Acts and Everyday Rebellions. 2d ed. New Preface and Notes by the author. H. Holt, 1995, 1983. 406pp. 9780805042023. Also available in audiobook (read by the author) and e-audiobook. 304.420973

This collection of essays by Gloria Steinem reveals the progress she personally has made as a feminist, as she describes her journey from a girl reporter to a woman becoming aware of the political differences between women and men in the field of journalism: for women the lower salaries and the exclusion from the better assignments, and the role assigned most women in political campaigns. As is clear from her essays on the political campaigns, the penny finally dropped for her in the 1968 campaign when she wasn't allowed into a "council" meeting because of her gender. Her growing consciousness led her to start writing and pushing for women to stand up for themselves, creating *Ms. Magazine* in 1971 for that very purpose. In this collection Steinem also includes an unpublished memoir essay, "Ruth's Song (Because She Could Not Sing It)," about her mother, a woman who suffered from mental illness.

Gloria Steinem was inducted into the National Women's Hall of Fame.

Subjects: Classics; Feminists; Journalists; Mothers and Daughters; *Ms. Magazine*; Personal Essays; Presidential Campaigns; Sex Discrimination; Women's Rights Activists

Now Try: Gloria Steinem was one of the initiators of the second wave of feminism, with other strong women preceding her in the first wave. Two of those women had a long friendship, the story of which is told by Geoffrey C. Ward in ***Not for Ourselves Alone: The Story of Elizabeth Cady Stanton and Susan B. Anthony; An Illustrated History***, with contributions by Martha Saxton, Ann D. Gordon, and Ellen Carol DuBois. Betty Friedan's name is often associated with Gloria Steinem's, although her classic feminist manifesto, ***The Feminine Mystique***, came before Steinem's own awakening. Friedan also wrote a memoir, ***Life So Far***. To illustrate just how far women have come in terms of their legal rights (or how far behind they had been), Fred Strebeigh has written ***Equal: Women Reshape American Law***.

Making a Difference Now

The stories here help us "understand the interconnected problems of real human experiences . . . [wherein the] writer provides a human experience, a narrative surrogate whose reach extends beyond ours" (Carr, 2004). The titles here focus on certain individuals in today's world, rather than in earlier times. The writers have heard about or encountered firsthand situations that need remedying and offer their creative thinking, their skills, and their courage to address the problem. By doing so and by writing about it, they inform others of the need for further work and remind us that even we everyday readers could find something similar to do that might strike a chord within us. They also give a sense of hope to readers that indeed something can be done, that by helping in one little corner of the world, one is helping to make positive change. Readers also gain insight into the person telling the story, recognizing that these heroes have doubts and fears and resentments about the work they are doing, just as we expect we would.

Memoirists who are making a difference now are those who have stepped outside themselves to help others on both an individual and a global scale. They have seen specific groups in dire straits and have set out to make changes for that group, often enlisting help from others and often making changes in themselves because of performing their humanitarian work. These memoirs tell not only the story of actions taken but also the plight of the people involved, with a hope on the part of the writer that permanent change can be effected if enough people become concerned.

Baiev, Khassan (1963–)
Daniloff, Ruth, and Nicholas Daniloff (1934–), coauthors

The Oath: A Surgeon Under Fire. Walker & Co., 2003. 376pp. ill. maps. 9780802714046. Also available in large print and audiobook. 947.52

The conditions in which Baiev worked in his native Chechnia during the mid-1990s often closely resembled those of the American Civil War, conducting surgeries without electricity or running water, performing amputations with local anesthetics and saws, and trying to save lives while being bombarded all around by bombs and shelling. In this memoir he describes his childhood in Chechnia, his lucrative work as a cosmetic surgeon in Russia, and his decision to return home at the outbreak of war. At one point he was the only surgeon for 80,000 residents and 5,000 refugees. He also describes the effect the war had on him personally, his desire to commit suicide, and his restorative Hajj to Mecca. He wrote his book for two reasons: to depict the horrors of war and to bring to life for outsiders his homeland of Chechnia. (Baiev's book was reprinted in 2005 under the title ***Grief of My Heart: Memoirs of a Chechen Surgeon.***)

Subjects: 1990s; Chechnia (Russia); Chechnia (Russia) Civil War (1994–); Courage; Medical Assistance; Muslim Men; Refugees; Spirituality; Surgeons; War

Now Try: We often hear major news reports from Chechnia, without really understanding what is going on there. Carlotta Gall and Thomas de Waal were Moscow correspondents during the brunt of the war in Chechnia and have provided their own account, ***Chechnya: Calamity in the Caucasus,*** with background information helping the North American reader understand the situation. The war in the former Yugoslavia provided similar working conditions for the medical people there, as Sheri Fink describes in ***War Hospital: A True Story of Surgery and Survival.*** Baiev gave up a comfortable job and almost sacrificed his life to help his fellow Chechens. Tracy Kidder investigated the life of another doctor who has spent his life offering help to the neediest, regardless of their geographic location, in ***Mountains Beyond Mountains: The Quest of Dr. Paul Farmer, a Man Who Would Cure the World.***

Gruwell, Erin (1969–), and the Freedom Writers

The Freedom Writers Diary: How a Teacher and 150 Teens Used Writing to Change Themselves and the World Around Them. 10th anniversary ed. Foreword by Zlata Filipović. Broadway Books, 2009. 314pp. ill. 8pp of plates. 9780385494229. Also available in Braille, audiobook (read by the authors), e-audiobook, e-book, and video. 305.235

When Erin Gruwell began teaching in an underserved community in California, she found herself in a classroom of intolerant children who had already suffered more in their lives than others ever do in their lifetimes and who were completely ignorant of the world beyond their own. Gruwell brought in reading materials by people their own age who had also suffered, books such as ***The Diary of a Young Girl*** by Anne Frank and ***Zlata's Diary: A Child's Life in Sarajevo*** by Zlata Filipović. Gruwell encouraged them to start keeping diaries themselves, and the Freedom Writers (the name taken from the Freedom Riders in the 1960s

Civil Rights Movement) were born. She was also able to raise funds to have people like Filipović and Miep Gies, the woman who helped hide the Franks, visit her classroom. The book includes a narrative by Gruwell and anonymous diary entries by the Freedom Writers, all of whom graduated from high school and went on to college. Gruwell has set up a foundation to share and promote her ideas on teaching (http://www.freedomwritersfoundation.org).

Subjects: California; Courage; Diaries; Education; Freedom Writers Foundation; Holocaust, Jewish (1939–1945); Race Relations; Racial Segregation; Teachers

Now Try: Gruwell has continued writing about the Freedom Writers, with a teacher's guide, a follow-up story, ***Teaching Hope: Stories from the Freedom Writer Teachers and Erin Gruwell,*** and a memoir, ***Teach with Your Heart: Lessons I Learned from the Freedom Writers; A Memoir.*** Other individuals are also trying to help fix the broken education system in the United States, people such as Mike Feinberg and Dave Levin, who began the Knowledge Is Power Program (KIPP), providing another opportunity for underserved children. Jay Mathews wrote about their work in ***Work Hard. Be Nice. How Two Inspired Teachers Created the Most Promising Schools in America.*** The notion of a hard-to-reach classroom audience has been around for a long time, as evidenced by the classic fictional memoir written in the 1950s by E. R. Braithwaite, ***To Sir, with Love.*** More recently LouAnne Johnson wrote ***My Posse Don't Do Homework,*** which was subsequently made into ***Dangerous Minds,*** a movie with Michelle Pfeiffer, and reprinted under the same title.

Kielburger, Craig (1982–)
Major, Kevin (1949–), coauthor

Free the Children: A Young Man Fights Against Child Labor and Proves that Children Can Change the World. Harper Perennial, 2000, 1998. 321pp. ill. 9780060930653. Also available in video. 331.31092

Craig Kielburger was twelve years old, living in a comfortable community in the Toronto area, when he read in the newspaper about another twelve-year-old, Iqbal Masih, who was assassinated for his work in trying to end child labor in Pakistan. Kielburger rushed to his local library (that he had earlier advocated to save from being closed) to get more information and thus began what has become his life's work. This story is told from the perspective of the fifteen-year-old Craig, after he had made several trips to South Asia to witness firsthand the plight of child workers and to speak to various heads of countries and heads of state to advocate for the freedom of children. He begins the book with the story of Iqbal coming to America just a few months before his death to receive the Reebok Human Rights Award. Even before writing this book, Kielburger had founded Free the Children, an organization of youth helping youth (http://www.freethechildren.com/). With his older brother Marc, Kielburger subsequently wrote ***Me to We: Finding Meaning in a Material World*** and then founded a social enterprise, Me to We (http://www.metowe.com/).

9 10 11 12 13

Subjects: Adolescents, Canada; Child Advocates, Canada; Child Labor; Children's Rights Activists; Free the Children (Organization); Me to We (Organization); Social Activists, Canada

Now Try: David L. Parker took his camera into shops that had child workers and published ***Before Their Time: The World of Child Labor***. Adults don't have to travel abroad to find children living unacceptable lives. Jonathan Kozol spent time in one section of the Bronx, and in ***Amazing Grace: The Lives of Children and the Conscience of a Nation***, presents his readers with a view of children's lives almost as horrible as what Kielburger saw on the other side of the world, but the view also includes the resilience and courage of some of these kids. For parents who would like to encourage their own children to develop a social conscience, Barbara A. Lewis, with editorial help from Pamela Espeland, has told the stories of several such children: ***Kids with Courage: True Stories About Young People Making a Difference***. Parents could also visit the Web site, Kids Are Heroes (http://www.kidsareheroes.org).

Mortenson, Greg (1957–)
Relin, David Oliver (1957–), coauthor

Three Cups of Tea: One Man's Mission to Fight Terrorism and Build Nations—One School at a Time. Penguin Books, 2007, 2006. 349pp. ill. 16pp. of plates. 9781439504895. Also available in large print, Braille, audiobook, e-audiobook, and e-book. 371.82209

Recently called into question for its veracity, this book remains a popular read, so the annotation stands as originally written. With time, we may know the truth behind the story and the accusations.

Mortenson is honest about discussing his own frailties in his efforts to fulfill a promise made to a tiny hamlet in Pakistan. A nurse who worked only until he had enough funds to climb mountains, Mortenson failed in his attempt to reach the top of K2, and by the time he found any people to help him on his return, he was in dire need of assistance. After his impoverished hosts spent seven weeks nursing him back to health, he promised he would return to build them a school. This was a promise not made lightly, but it was also a promise that he wondered how he would possibly be able to honor. Honor it he did, however, and the story of that commitment and its completion is what makes up the bulk of the book. He also founded the Central Asia Institute. Mortenson has written a sequel, ***Stones into Schools: Promoting Peace with Books, Not Bombs, in Afghanistan and Pakistan***, narrating how it has become his life's mission to provide schools in Pakistan and Afghanistan, insisting that the student population be comprised of at least 50 percent girls.

Subjects: Afghanistan; Americans in Asia; Central Asia Institute (Organization); Education; Humanitarians; Muslims, Pakistan; Pakistan; Taliban

Now Try: If readers would like a better understanding of the political situation in Central Asia, they might find Ahmed Rashid's book useful: ***Taliban: Militant Islam, Oil, and Fundamentalism in Central Asia***. Sarah Chayes, a journalist working out of Afghanistan for NPR, decided she needed to do more for the people she encountered there every day; she reveals in her memoir, ***The Punishment of Virtue: Inside Afghanistan After the Taliban***, just how difficult such an effort can be. In California

Oral Lee Brown made a promise to a classroom of children, and with the help of Caille Millner tells how she honored that pledge, in ***The Promise: How One Woman Made Good on Her Extraordinary Pact to Send a Classroom of First Graders to College.***

Orbinski, James (1960–)

An Imperfect Offering: Humanitarian Action in the Twenty-First Century. Walker, 2009, 2008. 431pp. ill. maps. 9780802717627. 610.9222

The "imperfect offering" in the title is Orbinski's own—his imperfect attempt to answer the bigger questions surrounding the issue of humanitarianism in the face of the political atrocities that often lead to the need for humanitarian aid. Orbinski was the director of Doctors Without Borders (*Médecins sans Frontières*) and under its aegis traveled to such disparate countries as Peru (cholera epidemic), Afghanistan (refugee camps), Kosovo (war victims), and Rwanda (genocide). It seemed that everywhere he went he encountered humankind's inhumanity to humankind and eventually developed an understanding that simply putting Band-Aids on the walking wounded was not enough: one could not be bipartisan in the fight to eliminate political atrocity. Readers should know that Orbinski's memoir is very graphic in portraying the horrors suffered by the people he and his fellow doctors helped. As he made his way through various countries, Orbinski also came to recognize the great need that developing countries had for lifesaving drugs, particularly to combat AIDS. He has started an organization, Dignitas International, to help with that need (http://www.dignitasinternational.org/).

James Orbinski accepted the Nobel Peace Prize on behalf of *Médecins sans Frontières*.

Subjects: Dignitas International (Organization); Doctors Without Borders (Organization); Humanitarians, Canada; Medical Assistance; Nobel Prize Laureates; Physicians; Political Atrocities; Rwanda; Suffering; War Relief

Now Try: Michael J. Sandel is a professor at Harvard who deals with issues of ethics. He has recently written a book based on his lectures, ***Justice: What's the Right Thing to Do?***, a thoughtful investigation that would go well with Orbinski's questions. Bill Gates's father, William H. Gates, offers similar thoughts in his reflective memoir, cowritten by Mary Ann Mackin, ***Showing Up for Life: Thoughts on the Gifts of a Lifetime.*** The man who started the Canadian chapter of Doctors Without Borders is Richard Heinzl, a doctor who writes about the time he spent in Asia in ***Cambodia Calling: A Memoir from the Frontlines of Humanitarian Aid.***

Wood, John (1964–)

Leaving Microsoft to Change the World: An Entrepreneur's Odyssey to Educate the World's Children. Updated ed. Collins, 2007, 2006. 278pp. ill. 16pp. of plates. 9780061121081. Also available in e-book and video. 370.917340954

John Wood was in senior management with Microsoft in Asia, dissatisfied with the direction his life was taking. Trekking through the mountains of Nepal became a life-changing vacation for him as he encountered a remote school there, one with very few books in its library. A promise to return with some books led him to leave Microsoft, create the nonprofit organization Room to Read (http://www.roomtoread.org/Page.aspx?pid=183), and return to Nepal and countries beyond with not only books but also schools. To date the organization has built over 1,000 schools and distributed over seven million books. In his memoir he discusses how one can apply corporate-management theories and skills to nonprofit management, using the lessons he learned at Microsoft.

Subjects: Americans in Asia; Education; Humanitarians; Microsoft Corporation; Nepal; Room to Read (Organization)

Now Try: David Bornstein also offers advice on how to become a successful social entrepreneur in ***How to Change the World: Social Entrepreneurs and the Power of New Ideas***. Social awareness is becoming a much greater force in the world, one that Paul Hawken has recognized and written about in ***Blessed Unrest: How the Largest Movement in the World Came into Being, and Why No One Saw It Coming***. Wendy Kopp practiced her own social entrepreneurship at home, creating the organization Teach for America, an endeavor that has been providing educators for underserved children for over twenty years. She tells her story in ***One Day, All Children—: The Unlikely Triumph of Teach for America and What I Learned Along the Way***.

Yunus, Muhammad (1940–)
Jolis, Alan (1953–2000), coauthor

Banker to the Poor: Micro-Lending and the Battle Against World Poverty. Rev. and updated ed. PublicAffairs, 2007, 1999. 273pp. ill. 9781586481988. Also available in audiobook and e-audiobook. 332.1095492

After getting his doctorate in economics in the United States, Muhammad Yunus returned to his home in Bangladesh but felt unable to settle down in either the corporate or the academic worlds. Surrounded by poverty, he tried to determine how he could apply his knowledge to helping his fellow citizens. His solution seemed simplistic, but with it he started the Grameen Bank to give small loans to small-business entrepreneurs. Called microcredit, this practice involves loaning a very small amount of money to a person endeavoring to start a business—it could be something as simple as helping a woman buy a wheelbarrow so she can make deliveries. In his book Yunus explains how it works, but he also explains the philosophies behind it, beginning with his beliefs that it is possible to eradicate worldwide poverty and that access to credit is a right, not a privilege. The site for the Grameen Foundation also explains how banking to the poor works (http://www.grameenfoundation.org/).

Yunus was given the Presidential Medal of Freedom in 2009 by President Obama and was awarded the Nobel Peace Prize.

Subjects: Bangladesh; Banking; Economists, Bangladesh; Global Economy; Grameen Foundation; Microcredit; Nobel Prize Laureates; Poverty, Bangladesh; Working Poor

Now Try: The economic advisor Jeffrey Sachs also believes that the world can rid itself of poverty, as he explains in ***The End of Poverty: Economic Possibilities for Our Time***. Jacqueline Novogratz has been trying to find a way to end global poverty and describes her efforts in ***The Blue Sweater: Bridging the Gap Between Rich and Poor in an Interconnected World*** (the blue sweater refers to one she donated to Goodwill and later discovered on a child in Rwanda). Mark Winne brings his interest in bridging the gap closer to home, looking at the differences in diet between the rich and the poor in the United States. In ***Closing the Food Gap: Resetting the Table in the Land of Plenty*** he puts forth his ideas about achieving that.

History Makers

The history books come alive in this section as we read about the people who largely felt they had had enough with their personal situations, which were not germane solely to them, but to their demographic group, and decided to do something about it. The bulk of the section deals with the Civil Rights Movement, but the stories are not necessarily the same. Stokely Carmichael was tired of passive resistance and started preaching Black Power; John Hope Franklin felt he could use his academic and research training to effect change. Some, like David T. Suzuki or Susan Brownmiller, almost backed into their activism, their eyes gradually opening to what was happening right before them. The stories all have at least one element in common: they were part of the history of the world in the twentieth century.

Memoirists who are also history makers have often risked their lives to effect change, thereby creating history. The writers in this section have dared to speak up and to stand tall in the face of often brutal opposition, and by writing their stories they illuminate the crucial history of their time. While many of these memoirs deal with major participants in the Civil Rights Movement, they also cover other important issues that the writers have contributed to, primarily in the field of the social sciences.

Aaron, Hank (1934–)
Wheeler, Lonnie (1952–), coauthor

I Had a Hammer: The Hank Aaron Story. Harper Perennial, 2007, 1999. 457pp. ill. 9780061373602. Also available in Braille, audiobook, and e-book. 796.357092

Although he was a record-setting baseball player, more important, Hank Aaron was a significant player in the move to desegregate baseball. In each of the chapters in this autobiography, sports columnist Lonnie Wheeler sets the stage. Then Aaron takes over, remembering people, events, and

9 10 11 12 13

plays throughout his career. He believed that he was Jackie Robinson's successor, fighting to keep what Robinson had won and to extend it. Aaron offers a social history of race relations in the United States, beginning with his childhood in Alabama and continuing through his playing in the Negro American League; integrating the South Atlantic League; and joining the Milwaukee Braves, who were then moved to Atlanta. He describes the racist mail he received after breaking Babe Ruth's home-run record in 1974 (a record he held until 2007). But he also received high accolades and respect and was hired as a senior executive with the Atlanta Braves after his playing career was over, making him the highest-ranking African-American in baseball management for a long time.

Hank Aaron was inducted into the Baseball Hall of Fame and was awarded the Presidential Medal of Freedom in 2002 by President George W. Bush. He was also given the Horatio Alger Award.

Subjects: African-American Men; Alabama; Baseball; Civil Rights; Depression (Economic); Integration in Sports; Negro American League; Race Relations; Social History, United States; South Atlantic Baseball League

Now Try: Proving that Aaron's setting a new home-run record was more than a sports accomplishment is Tom Stanton's ***Hank Aaron and the Home Run That Changed America***. Jackie Robinson's integration into baseball was a landmark event, a situation with many unknowns at the beginning, as Jonathan Eig describes in ***Opening Day: The Story of Jackie Robinson's First Season***. Illustrating the example set by Robinson for Hank Aaron in terms of working toward racial equality is a collection of letters by Robinson, ***First Class Citizenship: The Civil Rights Letters of Jackie Robinson***, edited by Michael G. Long. Basketball was another sport that contributed to the lowering of barriers, particularly in one game, the 1966 NCAA championship game, described by Frank Fitzpatrick in ***And the Walls Came Tumbling Down: Kentucky, Texas Western, and the Game That Changed American Sports***. Sports can be a very exclusive club, initially barring people of color, often barring women, and making life difficult for gay athletes. Mark Tewksbury tells his story of coming out as a gay athlete in ***Inside Out: Straight Talk from a Gay Jock***.

Baez, Joan (1941–)

And a Voice to Sing With: A Memoir. Introduction by Anthony DeCurtis. Simon & Schuster, 2009, 1987. 381pp. 30pp. of plates. 9781439169643. Also available in Braille. 784.492

Suffering from prejudice in high school because of her dark skin and Mexican name and raised in a Quaker household with an activist mother, it seems only natural that Joan Baez would combine her vocal talent with her social conscience to fashion her career. Her memoir is a social history of the protest movements of the 1960s and 1970s, with concerts and events associated with such names as Woodstock, Greenwich Village, Cambodia, Vietnam, and Live Aid. She sang for people like Martin Luther King Jr. and Lech Wałęsa. But she also reveals something of her personal life, which did not run completely smoothly. She had earlier written a reflective memoir, ***Daybreak***, which included an essay on her brother-in-law, Richard Fariña, who died very young. In 1969 Baez sang "We

Shall Overcome" for the Civil Rights Movement, and she sang it forty years later, in 2009, for the people of Iran.

Apart from musical awards, including a Grammy Lifetime Achievement Award, Baez has also been honored with several peace and humanitarian awards.

Subjects: 1960s; 1970s; Family Relationships; Folk Singers; Human Rights Activists; Mothers and Daughters; Pacifists; Peace Activists; Singers; Woodstock Festival, NY (1969)

Now Try: Baez's mother, Joan (or Big Joan, as she was known), was arrested twice with Joan and Mimi, Joan's sister. A writer herself, she wrote about this time in her life in ***Inside Santa Rita: The Prison Memoir of a War Protester***. Woody Guthrie was another singer who put his talents—compositional and vocal—to use to protest injustices, often for the working man. He wrote an autobiography, now a classic, ***Bound for Glory***. 2009 was the fortieth anniversary of Woodstock, an event celebrated by its co-creator, Michael Lang, with the publication of ***The Road to Woodstock***. Joan Baez went to northern California to lend support to an environmentalist who spent 738 days in a tree to prevent the clear-cutting of age-old redwoods. Julia Butterfly Hill has since written about her experience, ***The Legacy of Luna: The Story of a Tree, a Woman, and the Struggle to Save the Redwoods***.

Beals, Melba (1941–)

Warriors Don't Cry: A Searing Memoir of the Battle to Integrate Little Rock's Central High. Pocket Books, 1995, 1994. 312pp. ill. 9780671866396. Also available in large print, Braille, and e-book. 370.19342

Melba Beals knew that the only school that would give her the education she required to go on to college was Central High School in Little Rock, Arkansas, where she lived. Her desire for higher education gave her the courage to fight for her rights and join eight other students in a landmark battle to desegregate the all-White high school. They did this in the face of physical and violent opposition from the students and teachers; from other uninvolved citizens of Little Rock; from the governor of Arkansas; and even from their own families, who feared the ensuing violence. Using her own diaries and a diary kept by her mother, Lois, an English teacher with a PhD, Beals is able to re-create the events, the fear, the hatred, and the success of their venture.

Warriors Don't Cry was selected as a Notable Book by the American Library Association.

Subjects: African-American Women; ALA Notable Books; American South; Arkansas; Central High School, Little Rock, AR; Civil Rights; Courage; Hatred; Integration in Schools; Little Rock Nine; Race Relations

Now Try: Beals later wrote a second memoir, ***White Is a State of Mind: A Memoir***, beginning with her senior year in high school. Elizabeth Jacoway had researched the Little Rock Nine and published an overview for the fiftieth anniversary of the event, ***Turn Away Thy Son: Little Rock, the Crisis That Shocked the Nation***.

Filled as it is with violence and hatred, Beals's first memoir is nonetheless uplifting for the courage exhibited by the Little Rock Nine and those who supported them. Such is the story of Marian Anderson's concert in front of the Lincoln Memorial, an event described by Raymond Arsenault in ***The Sound of Freedom: Marian Anderson, the Lincoln Memorial, and the Concert That Awakened America***. The courage and determination exemplified by Beals can also be found in Barbara Robinette Moss, who succeeded despite all odds in achieving her own career goal of becoming an artist. Her ultimately uplifting story is told in her second memoir, ***Fierce: A Memoir***. Another member of the Little Rock Nine was Daisy Bates; she also wrote a memoir of the time, ***The Long Shadow of Little Rock, a Memoir***.

Brave Bird, Mary (1953–)
Erdoes, Richard (1912–2008), coauthor

Lakota Woman. Harper Perennial, 1997, 1990. 263pp. ill. 16pp. of plates. 9780060973896. Also available in large print and video. 978.362

Although a biracial woman, Mary Brave Bird (also known as Mary Crow Dog because of her marriage to Leonard Crow Dog) aligns herself with her Sioux heritage. Abandoned by her White father, she left her overburdened mother and her oppressive Catholic school to wander, mixed up in a delinquent life. Meeting up with people from the American Indian Movement (AIM), marching on Washington in the Trail of Broken Treaties march, and then participating in the sit-in at Wounded Knee, where she gave birth to a son, all contributed to her coming of age as a concerned member of the American Indian peoples. This memoir, dictated to Richard Erdoes, takes her up to 1977, and she follows it with ***Ohitika Woman*** (also dictated to Erdoes), which adds details to the first and continues with her life to 1992.

Lakota Woman was given an American Book Award from the Before Columbus Foundation.

Subjects: American Book Award; American Indian Movement; American Indian Rights; American Indian Women; Crow Dog, Leonard; Feminists; Racism; Rosebud Indian Reservation, SD; Sioux Nation; Spirituality

Now Try: One of the aspects of Brave Bird's change in direction was the spirituality she discovered through the American Indian Movement. Vine Deloria elaborates on religion from the perspective of American Indians in ***God Is Red: A Native View of Religion***. Eden Robinson is a Haisla woman from British Columbia who created a memorable First Nations heroine in her debut novel, ***Monkey Beach***. If you'd like to read more about American Indian women and their efforts to maintain tribal customs, you might enjoy ***Messengers of the Wind: Native American Women Tell Their Life Stories***, edited by Jane Katz.

Brownmiller, Susan (1935–)

In Our Time: Memoir of a Revolution. Dell, 2000. 360pp. ill. 9780385318310. 305.420973

Susan Brownmiller was a freelance journalist when she attended her first women's liberation movement meeting in 1968, a meeting that changed her thinking and

9 10 11 12 13

her life's work. In her memoir, using her own experiences, Brownmiller offers a history of the second wave of feminism, bringing to the fore the well-known names of women like Gloria Steinem and Kate Millett. She also discusses the role of the women who have not been so much in the public eye. In her honest rendering of this movement, Brownmiller also talks about the divisiveness within the movement, particularly the debate sparked by the "Pornography Wars." One of Brownmiller's personal outcomes of her involvement in working for women's rights was the publication of her pioneering book on rape, ***Against Our Will: Men, Women, and Rape***, a book that changed perspectives everywhere on that violent crime.

Subjects: Feminists; Journalists; Social Reform; Women's Liberation Movement; Women's Rights Activists; Writers

Now Try: If you'd like to delve into one of the earliest writings on women's rights, you may enjoy reading ***A Vindication of the Rights of Woman, with Strictures on Political and Moral Subjects*** (1792) by Mary Wollstonecraft, the mother of ***Frankenstein***'s author, Mary Shelley. A contemporary liberation activist is Eleanor Holmes Norton, a congresswoman from Washington, DC, who has made a career of fighting for many rights, among them civil, women's, and gay rights. She authorized Joan Steinau Lester, a friend, to write ***Fire in My Soul***. Phyllis Chesler has been an outspoken writer for people's rights and has recently taken a look at feminism today, ***The Death of Feminism: What's Next in the Struggle for Women's Freedom***.

Carmichael, Stokely (1941–1998)
Thelwell, Ekwueme Michael (1939–), coauthor

Ready for Revolution: The Life and Struggles of Stokely Carmichael (Kwame Ture). Scribner, 2005, 2003. 848pp. 9780684850047. Also available in e-book. 973.0196073092

The Student Nonviolent Coordinating Committee (SNCC) changed its tenor in 1966 when Stokely Carmichael replaced its leader, John Lewis. Carmichael had been a Freedom Rider but eventually grew dissatisfied with the slow progress in legal changes affecting Black people at the time. He coined the phrase "Black Power" and became a member of the Black Panther Party. His autobiography is a firsthand view of the changing Civil Rights Movement, but he also provides details of his life both in Trinidad before moving to New York in his youth and in Africa, where he moved in the late 1960s, taking the name Kwame Ture in honor of two African revolutionaries. Knowing he was dying of cancer, he dictated his autobiography to his friend Ekwueme Michael Thelwell, who then published it posthumously.

Subjects: African-American Men; Black Muslims; Black Panther Party; Civil Rights Activists; Civil Rights Movement; Freedom Riders; Immigrants; Muslim Men; Revolutionaries; Social History, United States; Student Nonviolent Coordinating Committee; Trinidadian-Americans

Now Try: Peniel E. Joseph's book, ***Waiting 'til the Midnight Hour: A Narrative History of Black Power in America,*** provides an overview of the movement in which Carmichael so largely figured. David Hilliard, who cofounded the Black Panther Party, offers a history of the movement in the context of his own life in his autobiography, written with Lewis Cole: ***This Side of Glory: The Autobiography of David Hilliard and the Story of the Black Panther Party***. The man who initiated the Freedom Rides was James Farmer, also the founder of CORE, the Committee (later, Congress) of Racial Equality. Farmer also gives an overview of the Civil Rights Movement and beyond in his autobiography, ***Lay Bare the Heart: An Autobiography of the Civil Rights Movement***.

Chestnut, J. L., Jr. (1930–2008)
Cass, Julia, coauthor

Black in Selma: The Uncommon Life of J. L. Chestnut, Jr. With a new Foreword and Afterword by Julia Cass. University of Alabama Press, 2007, 1990. 444pp. ill. 9780817354619. 340.092

J. L. Chestnut was part of the Selma Black middle class. When he returned from law school at Howard, however, he was the first Black lawyer in Selma. He admits that he drunkenly slept through the initial stages of the Civil Rights Movement in Selma, but once he became sober, he became very involved in helping effect changes, particularly with relation to the Voting Rights Act. In his autobiography he focuses on the grassroots people rather than on the names in the news, and he continues his story beyond the Civil Rights Movement, with discussions of the difficulties of Black people having political power without economic power.

Black in Selma won a Lillian Smith Book Award and was selected as a Notable Book by the American Library Association.

Subjects: African-American Men; ALA Notable Books; Alabama; Civil Rights Activists; Civil Rights Movement; Lawyers; Lillian Smith Book Award; Selma, AL; Voting Rights Act

Now Try: Frank M. Johnson Jr. was a judge in Alabama at the same time that Chestnut was a lawyer; an award-winning biography by Jack Bass, ***Taming the Storm: The Life and Times of Judge Frank M. Johnson and the South's Fight over Civil Rights*** illustrates how he was highly instrumental in upholding the laws put in place to establish civil rights. Selma witnessed notorious incidents during the Civil Rights Movement, but so did Birmingham, a city whose role in the movement is documented by Diane McWhorter in ***Carry Me Home: Birmingham, Alabama, the Climactic Battle of the Civil Rights Revolution***. In showing how civil rights legislation, including the Voting Rights Act, managed to be enacted, Nick Kotz provides an in-depth look at the working relationship between Martin Luther King Jr. and Lyndon Johnson in ***Judgment Days: Lyndon Baines Johnson, Martin Luther King, Jr., and the Laws That Changed America***.

Ellsberg, Daniel (1931–)

Secrets: A Memoir of Vietnam and the Pentagon Papers. Penguin, 2003, 2002. 500pp. ill. 9780142003428. Also available in Braille, audiobook, e-audiobook, and e-book. 959.7043373

" 'A time comes when silence is betrayal' " (King, 1967). This quote from Martin Luther King Jr. is one of the elements that persuaded Daniel Ellsberg to settle the battle within his conscience and make public thousands of pages of reports on government lies about the war in Vietnam, lies that had been perpetrated since the Truman administration. In his memoir he talks about his conversion from an anticommunist supporter of the war and his government to his recognition that he and his fellow citizens had been deceived by their government. He describes copying the papers for Congress and *The New York Times*, his subsequent trial, and life following the trial. He also discusses the ramifications of making the Pentagon Papers public: Nixon's resignation from office and the ending of the war in Vietnam.

Secrets was a finalist for the *Los Angeles Times* Book Prize for Biography and winner of the American Book Award from the Before Columbus Foundation and the PEN Center USA Literary Award for Creative Nonfiction.

Subjects: American Book Award; Courage; Deception; Foreign Policy, United States; McNamara, Robert; Military Secrets; Octogenarians; Patriotism; Peace Activists; PEN Center USA Literary Award for Creative Nonfiction; *Pentagon Papers, The*; Vietnam War (1961–1975)

Now Try: An award-winning documentary has recently been made by Judith Ehrlich and Rick Goldsmith, entitled ***The Most Dangerous Man in America: Daniel Ellsberg and the Pentagon Papers***. David Maraniss took a snapshot of America at a very specific time, covering the war, the protests, and the Johnson administration in ***They Marched into Sunlight: War and Peace, Vietnam and America, October 1967***. On the other hand, Rick Perlstein, while ostensibly writing about one president, offers an overview of the protest movement over a period of years in ***Nixonland: The Rise of a President and the Fracturing of America***. It took Ellsberg some time to find his moral compass regarding the war, but I. F. Stone seems to have seen the writing on the wall much sooner, as Myra MacPherson illustrates in her biography of Stone, ***All Governments Lie: The Life and Times of Rebel Journalist I. F. Stone***.

Evers, Charles (1922–)
Szanton, Andrew (1963–), coauthor

Have No Fear: The Charles Evers Story. Wiley & Sons, 1997. 333pp. ill. 9780471122517. Also available in e-book. 323.092

Charles Evers and his younger brother Medgar Wiley Evers made a pact that if anything happened to one of them, the other would carry on. Charles was in Chicago, making a lot of money through illicit means (the mob, brothels, etc.) and sending some of that money to Mississippi to help support his brother as a civil rights worker. When Medgar was assassinated, Charles moved back to Mississippi, where he carried on his brother's work, heading up the Mississippi chapter of the National Association for the Advancement of Colored People (NAACP). Outspoken and controversial, he was nevertheless successful in becoming the first Black mayor in

Mississippi in a century, running the city of Fayette for twenty-five years. Apart from recounting all his activities, Evers also introduces the reader to many of the active figures he worked with, people as disparate as Robert Kennedy and George Wallace.

Subjects: African-American Men; Civil Rights Activists; Civil Rights Movement; Evers, Medgar Wiley; Mayors; Mississippi; National Association for the Advancement of Colored People; Octogenarians; Race Relations; Social History, United States

Now Try: Another major player in the Civil Rights Movement in Mississippi was Fannie Lou Hamer, a woman who was badly beaten while trying to register to vote and who later brought her determination to bear in acquiring biracial representation in the Mississippi delegation to the Democratic National Convention. Kay Mills has told Hamer's story in ***This Little Light of Mine: The Life of Fannie Lou Hamer***. Thurgood Marshall, the first African-American to be appointed to the Supreme Court, figures largely in Evers's memoir and is the subject of an award-winning biography by Juan Williams, ***Thurgood Marshall: American Revolutionary***. Unita Blackwell also grew up in Mississippi, and her memoir, written with JoAnne Pritchard Morris, ***Barefootin': Life Lessons from the Road to Freedom***, offers another slice of history.

Evers, Medgar Wiley (1925–1963)
Evers-Williams, Myrlie (1933–), and Manning Marable (1950–), coeditors

The Autobiography of Medgar Evers: A Hero's Life and Legacy Revealed Through His Writings, Letters, and Speeches. Basic Civitas Books, 2005. 352pp. ill. 16pp. of plates. 9780465021772. Also available in e-book. 323.1196073092

Because of his early death, Evers was not able to write a memoir, but his widow, with the help of a historian, collected his monthly reports, speeches, articles, and other writings, and combined them with her own recollections to form this autobiography for him. He was the field secretary of the National Association for the Advancement of Colored People (NAACP) in Mississippi and put his life in danger by recruiting people to the NAACP, working on voter registrations, fighting to have James Meredith enrolled in the University of Mississippi, and calling attention to the murders of such victims as the young Emmett Till. Evers was assassinated in his driveway at the age of thirty-seven. Myrlie Evers-Williams followed her work on her husband's life with one on her own, with the help of Melinda Blau: ***Watch Me Fly: What I Learned on the Way to Becoming the Woman I Was Meant to Be.***

Subjects: African-American Men; Assassinations; Civil Rights Activists; Civil Rights Movement; Mississippi; National Association for the Advancement of Colored People; Race Relations

Now Try: Several films have been made about Medgar Evers, but perhaps the best-known is ***Ghosts of Mississippi***. Although it was known for a long time who had shot Evers, it was thirty years before the murderer was finally convicted. Bobby DeLaughter tells the story of the trial of Byron De La Beckwith in ***Never Too Late: A Prosecutor's Story of Justice in the Medgar Evers Case***. The NAACP has been an essential part of the Civil Rights Movement, which Patricia Sullivan illustrates in her history, ***Lift Every Voice: The NAACP and the Making of the Civil Rights Movement.*** Bringing to life the story of James Meredith's fight to become a student at the University of Mississippi is William Doyle's award-winning ***An American Insurrection: The Battle of Oxford, Mississippi, 1962.***

Franklin, John Hope (1915–2009)

Mirror to America: The Autobiography of John Hope Franklin. Farrar, Straus & Giroux, 2006, 2005. 401pp. ill. 9780374530471. Also available in audiobook (read by the author). 973.04960730092

John Hope Franklin participated academically in the Civil Rights Movement, particularly in carrying out important research for Thurgood Marshall and the National Association for the Advancement of Colored People (NAACP) for the historically important case *Brown v. Board of Education.* He also spent his life working to change the depiction of African-Americans in American history. Beginning with his doctoral work on the free Blacks in antebellum North Carolina, he continued to research and write about the true history of Black people in America and as a professor of history taught it to his students. He made that knowledge available to the world in his seminal work, ***From Slavery to Freedom; A History of American Negroes*** (1947), a book that has seen several changes in the ensuing editions, one being a title change to ***From Slavery to Freedom: A History of African-Americans*** in the 1994 edition. While he was working on his memoir, he asked Evelyn Higginbotham to update the book, which she has done for the ninth edition (2011). In his memoir Franklin is proving to be a witness to a wider history, depicting most of twentieth-century America from the viewpoint of a Black man.

Mirror to America received the Robert F. Kennedy Book Award and the Hurston/Wright Legacy Award. Franklin himself was given the Presidential Medal of Freedom in 1996 by President Bill Clinton.

Subjects: African-American Men; Civil Rights; College Professors; Historians; Hurston/Wright Legacy Award; Integration in Schools; Marshall, Thurgood; Nonagenarians; Race Relations; Racial Segregation; Trailblazers

Now Try: One of the many issues Franklin deals with in his autobiography is racism in the military, citing his own example when he was told that he qualified completely except for his color. Gail Lumet Buckley has written an award-winning history of Black people in the U.S. military, ***American Patriots: The Story of Blacks in the Military from the Revolution to Desert Storm.*** Franklin's was a remarkable life, as was Dorothy I. Height's, although she may have been more unsung than Franklin. Readers can enjoy getting to know her and her accomplishments in her memoir, ***Open Wide the Freedom Gates: A Memoir.*** The debate continues to rage about the efficacy of the decision in *Brown v. Board of Education*, a debate that James T. Patterson clarifies in ***Brown v. Board of Education: A Civil Rights Milestone and Its Troubled Legacy.***

Greenspan, Alan (1926–)

The Age of Turbulence: Adventures in a New World. Penguin Books, 2008, 2007. 563pp. ill. 32pp. of plates. 9780143114161. Also available in large print, audiobook, e-audiobook, and e-book. 332.11092

Greenspan begins his memoir with the September 11 attacks on the World Trade Center in 2001, illustrating the various events that can alter the economic health of the world. He then moves back to his childhood, youth, education, and entry into the world that made him famous. He includes his time as the long-standing Chairman of the Board of Governors of the Federal Reserve System, a position of much importance and worldwide influence. He also talks about his love of music and studying the clarinet at the Juilliard School along with his early career as a jazz musician. By taking his readers through his life in this manner, he helps them come to an understanding of economics and world markets similar to his own. Once he has finished telling his life story, he offers his views on the global economy and his thoughts about what the future holds economically.

Alan Greenspan was awarded the Presidential Medal of Freedom in 2005 by President George W. Bush.

Subjects: Clarinetists; Economics; Economists; Federal Reserve Board; Global Economy; Octogenarians; Politics

Now Try: Elucidating another aspect of economic reality is John Perkins, whose ***Confessions of an Economic Hit Man*** reveals how economic threats can be wielded against government leaders. Warren Buffett is a name well-known to most readers as a man who has made a success out of his understanding of economics. Alice Schroeder conducted interviews with him that led to ***The Snowball: Warren Buffett and the Business of Life***. Sara Bongiorni looks at one very specific aspect of the global economy when she writes about her family's experiment and what it led her to understand about world economics: ***A Year Without "Made in China": One Family's True Life Adventure in the Global Economy***.

Jordan, Vernon E. (1935–)
Gordon-Reed, Annette (1958–), coauthor

Vernon Can Read! A Memoir. Basic Civitas Press, 2003, 2001. 343pp. ill. 16pp. of plates. 9780465036974. Also available in large print, audiobook (read by the author), and e-book. 323.092

Vernon Jordan's daughter Vickee had no understanding of the Jim Crow culture in which her father had grown up, leading him to write this memoir, the story of his life until the 1980s, in order to bridge the knowledge gap between his generation and his daughter's. After gaining a law degree from Howard University, Jordan became prominent in Georgia in the Civil Rights Movement, helping to desegregate the University of Georgia (he had gone to DePauw in Indiana, the only Black person to graduate in his undergraduate class), acting as field secretary of the Georgia National Association for the Advancement of Colored People (NAACP), and leading the drive for voter registrations. He left his position as Executive Director of the United Negro College Fund to head up the National

Urban League, an organization that works for the economic empowerment of the Black community. Jordan's title comes from a statement made when he had a summer job driving for a known racist while in college; his employer was shocked to find him reading and announced in amazement in front of both his friends and Jordan that Vernon could read.

Vernon Can Read! won the Anisfield-Wolf Book Award as well as the BCALA Literary Award for Nonfiction.

Subjects: African-American Men; Anisfield-Wolf Book Award; BCALA Literary Award for Nonfiction; Civil Rights Activists; Civil Rights Movement; Georgia; Lawyers; National Urban League; Political Activists; Racial Segregation

Now Try: Jordan has recently published a book of his speeches, first laying out the context in which they were given: ***Make It Plain: Standing Up and Speaking Out***. Vernon Jordan replaced Whitney Young as head of the National Urban League when Young drowned in an accident in Nigeria. To learn more about this unsung civil rights worker, you could read Dennis C. Dickerson's biography, ***Militant Mediator: Whitney M. Young, Jr.*** Also providing an understanding of the generations that preceded Jordan's daughter is Richard Wormser's history of the legal status of African-Americans, ***The Rise & Fall of Jim Crow: The African-American Struggle Against Discrimination, 1865–1954***. Many of the civil rights workers were lawyers, including William L. Taylor, who helped write the brief relating to desegregation of schools in Little Rock, Arkansas. Taylor's story is entitled ***The Passion of My Times: An Advocate's Fifty-Year Journey in the Civil Rights Movement***.

Lewis, John (1940–)
D'Orso, Michael (1953–), coauthor

Walking with the Wind: A Memoir of the Movement. Harcourt Brace, 1999, 1998. 526pp. ill. 16pp. of plates. 9780156007085 Also available in e-book. 328.73092

John Lewis was a teenager in 1955 when he first heard Martin Luther King Jr. on the radio preaching nonviolence in the goal for social justice. This became Lewis's guiding principle, which saw him through Freedom Rides, protest marches, vicious beatings, and imprisonment. It also led him to work for voter registration, leading the march from Selma to Montgomery to advocate for voters' rights. It was while crossing the Edmund Pettus Bridge in Selma that the marchers were attacked by Alabama State Troopers; this violence against the peaceful demonstrators, later referred to as "Bloody Sunday," fanned the flames of outrage across the country and contributed to the success of the Civil Rights Movement. Because of his belief in nonviolence, Lewis left the Student Nonviolent Coordinating Committee (SNCC) because it was becoming more militant (see Stokely Carmichael, p. 417) and moved on to the Voter Education Project. Lewis's memoir, while describing his youth as the son of a sharecropper, focuses most of its attention on the Civil Rights Movement.

Walking with the Wind was the winner of a Christopher Award, the Anisfield-Wolf Book Award, the Lillian Smith Book Award, and the

Robert F. Kennedy Book Award. John Lewis was inducted into the Academy of Achievement.

Subjects: 1950s; 1960s; African-American Men; Anisfield-Wolf Book Award; Christopher Awards; Civil Rights Activists; Civil Rights Movement; Courage; King, Martin Luther Jr.; Legislators; Lillian Smith Book Award; Student Nonviolent Coordinating Committee; Voters' Rights

Now Try: Illustrating the driving and influential force for both Mahatma Gandhi and Martin Luther King Jr. is Michael J. Nojeim's book, ***Gandhi and King: The Power of Nonviolent Resistance***. John Lewis believes he received his life's calling from Martin Luther King Jr., a call that he has spent his life answering. King was assassinated before he could write his own story, but at the request of King's family, Clayborne Carson collected memories and King's speeches and writings and created ***The Autobiography of Martin Luther King, Jr.*** John Lewis has been an important part of many of the events of the Civil Rights Movement. Readers can revisit those events with Charles E. Cobb Jr.'s ***On the Road to Freedom: A Guided Tour of the Civil Rights Trail***.

Suzuki, David T. (1936–)

David Suzuki: The Autobiography. Greystone Books, 2007, 2006. 405pp. ill. 9781553652816. 333.72092

In this second autobiography, Suzuki expands on his first, ***Metamorphosis: Stages in a Life***, describing his childhood, wherein it was natural for him to spend his days outdoors with his father, camping, fishing, and hunting. His life changed dramatically when he was interned with other Japanese-Canadians, facing blatant racism during World War II. But even in the internment camp he was able to be among the forests and rivers with the wildlife that roamed there. He describes how he gradually became an environmentalist, at first just reporting the bad news he was learning from scientists and from his own work, but eventually offering suggestions to inquiring citizens as to how one can Think Globally and Act Locally. He and his wife, Tara Cullis, set up the David Suzuki Foundation (http://www.davidsuzuki.org/) for this very purpose, and he continues to educate the public with his television documentary series *The Nature of Things*.

David Suzuki won the Canadian Booksellers Association Libris Award for Non-Fiction Book of the Year as well as the BC Booksellers' Choice Award in Honour of Bill Duthie.

Subjects: Canadian Booksellers Association Libris Award for Non-Fiction Book of the Year; David Suzuki Foundation; Environmental Activists; Geneticists, Canada; Japanese-Canadians; Japanese Internment; *The Nature of Things* (Television Program); Nature Writers, Canada; Racism, Canada; Scientists, Canada; Television Journalists, Canada

Now Try: Before David Suzuki became a preeminent environmentalist, Rachel Carson made her name as a vocal proponent of saving the planet with her trailblazing work, ***Silent Spring***, with drawings by Lois and Louis Darling. Linda J. Lear has written an award-winning biography of her, ***Rachel Carson: Witness for Nature***. Of late, former vice president Albert Gore has been making a name for himself as an ardent environmentalist, making a film and publishing a book, ***An Inconvenient Truth: The***

Planetary Emergency of Global Warming and What We Can Do About It. Internment as a Japanese-Canadian was puzzling for adults, but even more so for children. Julie Otsuka writes of the internment of two children and their mother in her novel, ***When the Emperor Was Divine: A Novel.***

Witness to History

The writers in this section have seen a lot in their lives. In the case of Timothy B. Tyson, it was largely one incident, but that was enough to change his life. In the case of George Dawson, it was a century's worth of incidents. Some have made history while observing it; others are simply reporting on it. Studs Terkel chose to recount the histories of others, and in doing so educated his readers about specific groups of people often overlooked. But they all want to share with the reader their perspectives on what they have seen and what they have done. They "evince empathy and compassion, touching something deeper and more resonant than history courses care to tell us" (Carr, 2004).

> Writers who shared what they have witnessed in history have been able to do so through their professions, their life choices, or simply their long lives. By being on the scene at the time, they can offer their perspective of what was going on, why people reacted as they did, and more important, what actually happened. Some of the memoirists reflect back on decades of changes, so the narratives are combined with a contemplative tone as the writers consider how the world has changed.

Clarkson, Adrienne (1939–)

Heart Matters: A Memoir. Penguin Canada, 2009, 2006. 274pp. ill. 16pp. of plates. 9780143171515. 971.07209

The closest position Canada has to head of state is the governor-general, the queen's representative in Canada. Adrienne Clarkson held that position for six years, from 1999 to 2005. In her memoir she narrates the life that led up to that prestigious posting: her flight with her family from Japanese-invaded Hong Kong to Canada; her home life with a father, William Poy, she was very close to and a mother, Ethel Poy, who suffered from mental illness; and her life as a wife and mother, journalist, writer, film producer, and host of several talk shows, *Adrienne Clarkson Presents* among them. As both journalist and governor-general she has traveled the world, seeking to inform herself and her fellow Canadians about the plight of others. She has also met with leaders from other countries, such people as Vladimir Putin and Nelson Mandela.

Among her many awards, Clarkson was named a Companion of the Order of Canada and was also recently named the Colonel-in-Chief of the Princess Patricia's Canadian Light Infantry.

Subjects: Chinese-Canadians; Family Relationships; Governors-General, Canada; Journalists, Canada; Refugees, China; Social Activists, Canada; Television Journalists, Canada; Writers, Canada

Now Try: Since writing her memoir, Clarkson has written a biography, ***Norman Bethune,*** in the **Extraordinary Canadians** series. Another well-known governor-general is actually better known for the sports cup named after him. Kevin Shea and John Jason Wilson have written a well-received biography, ***Lord Stanley: The Man Behind the Cup,*** a book for which Clarkson wrote the introduction. Readers interested in learning more about the Japanese invasion of Hong Kong that led to Clarkson's refugee status could read Philip Snow's ***The Fall of Hong Kong: Britain, China, and the Japanese Occupation.*** Dorothy Schiff was another remarkable woman, a social activist and owner of the *New York Post*. Marilyn Nissenson has written Schiff's biography, ***The Lady Upstairs: Dorothy Schiff and the "New York Post".***

Cooper, Anderson (1967–)

Dispatches from the Edge: A Memoir of War, Disasters, and Survival. Harper, 2007, 2006. 222pp. ill. 8pp. of plates. 9780061136689. Also available in large print, audiobook (read by the author), e-audiobook, and e-book. 070.92

Anderson Cooper, the son of Gloria Vanderbilt, found himself drawn to a life that would keep him moving and distracted, a life reporting the news from around the world. In his life and in his memoir he travels to the trouble spots of the world, witnessing natural disasters like the Asian tsunami and Hurricane Katrina, war-torn areas such as Bosnia and Iraq, genocide in Rwanda, and famine in Somalia. In writing about the tragedies of others, Anderson also looks at himself to try to understand why he seems determined to visit and report on the worst that life seems to offer citizens of the world. In seeing others' tragedies, however, he puts his own (the deaths of his father and brother, for example) into perspective, recognizing a common humanity across the globe.

Subjects: Childhood and Youth; Death of a Parent; Death of a Sibling; Disasters, Natural; Fathers and Sons; Foreign Correspondents; Hurricane Katrina (2005); Mothers and Sons; Television Journalists; Vanderbilt, Gloria; War

Now Try: Chris Rose is a journalist—a newspaper reporter—who lives in New Orleans and who collected his columns about Katrina into a book, ***1 Dead in Attic: After Katrina.*** Jackie Spinner offers a slightly different view from Cooper's of reporting from Iraq in her memoir, ***Tell Them I Didn't Cry: A Young Journalist's Story of Joy, Loss, and Survival in Iraq.*** Jackie's twin sister, Jenny, added her own stories to the book, describing how she watched her sister from afar by reading her articles in *The Washington Post*. Apart from telling stories of his global adventures, Cooper also discusses the changes television journalism has seen. Lynn Sherr, a journalist for *20/20*, does the same in her memoir, ***Outside the Box: A Memoir.***

Cronkite, Walter (1916–2009)

A Reporter's Life. Random House, 1997, 1996. 609pp. ill. 16pp. of plates. 9780679774143. Also available in large print, audiobook (read by the author), and e-book. 070.92

To recount the events that Walter Cronkite covered as a journalist—in newspaper, radio, and television—is to recount twentieth-century history: the Great Depression, World War II, the Nuremburg trials, the Korean War, the Civil Rights Movement, the Vietnam War, the assassination of President Kennedy, and the struggles in South Africa, to name but a few. He was able to track down and interview people in hiding: Takeo Yoshikawa, a Japanese spy, and Daniel Ellsberg, the man who blew the whistle on the Nixon administration. In addition to revealing his personal and professional lives, Cronkite also discourses on the history of news reporting, decrying the "infotainment" that it has become. His own reputation as a television journalist for CBS News was such that the term "anchorman" was coined with reference to him.

Among his numerous awards and honorary doctoral degrees, Cronkite was awarded the Presidential Medal of Freedom in 1981 by President Carter and inducted into the Broadcasting & Cable Hall of Fame.

Subjects: 20th Century; CBS (Television Network); Foreign Correspondents; Journalism; Nonagenarians; Television Journalists

Now Try: What Cronkite was to television, Lowell Thomas was to radio. A prolific author as well, he wrote two memoirs: ***Good Evening Everybody: From Cripple Creek to Samarkand*** and ***So Long Until Tomorrow: From Quaker Hill to Kathmandu.*** David Brinkley was another major broadcaster who coanchored *The Huntley-Brinkley Report* from the NBC news desk with Chet Huntley. Brinkley shares his own experiences in ***Brinkley's Beat: People, Places, and Events That Shaped My Time.*** And at the ABC desk was the Canadian Peter Jennings, whose life was captured by Kate Darnton, Kayce Freed Jennings, and Lynn Sherr in ***Peter Jennings: A Reporter's Life.***

Dawson, George (1898–2001)
Glaubman, Richard, coauthor

Life Is So Good. Penguin, 2001, 2000. 260pp. 9780141001685. Also available in large print, audiobook, and e-book. 976.4192

The oldest child in his family and the grandson of slaves, George Dawson was not able to go to school, as he had to work to help support his family. He managed to hide his illiteracy from his seven children, whom he "helped" with homework. One literacy volunteer in his neighborhood knew that George could not read, though, so he knocked on George's door one day to say that lessons were being taught down the street. George asked him to wait while he got his coat, and he never stopped going to school after that. George was ninety-eight at the time. His memoir offers the reader an inside view of the tremendous changes that occurred over a century—changes in technology and in culture. George witnessed the coming of the automobile and the first flight to the moon. He also witnessed the lynching of a friend and the end of Jim Crow laws. Readers see what life was really like for the common Black man living in the South. George's attitude throughout life, ingrained in him by his father, was that life was good and everyone should just accept that.

Life Is So Good was the winner of a Christopher Award.

Subjects: 20th century; African-American Men; Aging; American South; Centenarians; Christopher Awards; Literacy; Racism

Now Try: Jane Pittman is also a centenarian, a fictional one who recalls her experiences in the Civil War as she is emancipated, in ***The Autobiography of Miss Jane Pittman*** by Ernest J. Gaines. Bernard Edelman offers a look at the twentieth century through the eyes of a number of centenarians in ***Centenarians: The Story of the Twentieth Century by the Americans Who Lived It.*** Ella Mae Cheeks Johnson was also the child of former slaves; born in 1904, she lived long enough to attend the inauguration of President Obama in 2009. With the help of Patricia Mulcahy, she told the story of her long, eventful life in ***It Is Well with My Soul: The Extraordinary Life of a 106-Year-Old Woman.***

Delany, Sarah Louise (1889–1999), and A. Elizabeth Delany (1891–1995) Hearth, Amy Hill (1958–), coauthor

Having Our Say: The Delany Sisters' First 100 Years. Dell, 1999, 1993. 299pp. ill. 16pp. of plates. 9780785769699. Also available in large print, Braille, audiobook (read by the sisters), and video. 973.04960730092

The Delany sisters grew up in North Carolina with a father (Henry Beard Delany) who was a freed slave and the first Black man to be elected an Episcopal bishop. Their strength and determination were such that no one man could hold their interest, so they lived together all their lives and quietly broke race barriers as they went about their business. Sadie (Sarah) was the only Black female student in her Columbia University Dental School class, and her sister, Bessie, integrated the school system in Mount Vernon, New York, where she taught high school. They introduce the reader to the illustrious people they knew, people such as Booker T. Washington, W. E. B. Du Bois, and Paul Robeson. They involved themselves in the Harlem Renaissance and mixed with Black activists. Bessie, the younger sister, did not live as long as her sister, and Sadie pays tribute to Bessie by writing a book of her life without her sister by her side: ***On My Own at 107: Reflections on Life Without Bessie,*** also written with the help of Amy Hill Hearth, and accompanied by illustrations by Brian M. Kotzky.

Having Our Say was selected as a Notable Book by the American Library Association, was named an Honor Book by the American Booksellers Association, and was the winner of a Christopher Award. The play, adapted by Emily Mann, was nominated for a Tony Award.

Subjects: 20th Century; African-American Women; ALA Notable Books; Centenarians; Christopher Awards; Delany Family; Fathers and Daughters; Firsts; Race Relations; Racial Segregation; Sisters; Trailblazers

Now Try: Jessie Lee Brown Foveaux was another feisty centenarian, a woman who divorced her alcoholic husband, although she then had to raise eight children on her own. Her memoir, published when she was ninety-eight, tells a remarkable story: ***Any Given Day: The Life and Times of Jessie Lee Brown Foveaux.*** Amy Hill Hearth, coauthor of the Delany sisters' story, discovered in her own family a Lenni-Lenape ancestor, Marion "Strong Medicine" Gould, living in New Jersey; Hearth wrote her ancestor's story in ***"Strong Medicine Speaks": A Native American Elder Has Her Say: An Oral History.*** Pauli Murray was a spirited woman like the Delany sisters and came from an interesting family who made her thus, a family whose history she provides in ***Proud Shoes; The Story of an American Family.***

Farah, Empress, Consort of Mohammad Reza Pahlavi, Shah of Iran (1938–)

An Enduring Love: My Life with the Shah; A Memoir. Miramax, 2004. 447pp. ill. 32pp. of plates. 9781401359614. Also available in large print and e-book. 955.53092 [Trans. by Patricia Clancy]

Farah Diba was an Iranian architecture student in Paris when she met the man who would become her husband, Mohammad Pahlavi, Shah of Iran. In her memoir she describes her childhood with her father, Sohrab, whose early death was tragic for her; her studies in Paris; and her new life as a royal in Iran. She also discusses the politics of the time, the efforts her husband made to modernize and liberalize his country, and the increasing opposition by people such as the Ayatollah Khomeini. She continues her story up to the point of the death of their daughter and the death of her husband, in exile.

Subjects: Death of a Child; Death of a Spouse; Iran; Khomeini, Ayatollah; Married Couples; Mohammad Reza Pahlavi, Shah of Iran; Politics, Iran; Royalty; Translations; Women in Iran

Now Try: The award-winning British novelist James Buchan offers a different perspective on life in the Shah's Iran in his novel, ***The Persian Bride.*** American readers are quite familiar with British royals but less so with royalty from other parts of the world. Ben Hills describes the life of the woman who married the son of Emperor Akihito in Japan, ***Princess Masako: Prisoner of the Chrysanthemum Throne.*** To gain a better understanding of Iran, readers would do well to read Elaine Sciolino's ***Persian Mirrors: The Elusive Face of Iran.***

Klemperer, Victor (1881–1960)

I Will Bear Witness: A Diary of the Nazi Years 1933–1941. Modern Library, 1999, 1998. 519pp. ill. photos. 9780375753787. Also available in e-book. 943.086092 [Trans. by Martin Chalmers]

This is the first of a three-volume work by Klemperer, bearing witness to what happens when a society loses its moral compass and runs completely amok. The second volume gives witness to life for Jews in Nazi Germany, entitled ***To the Bitter End: The Diaries of Victor Klemperer 1942–1945***, and the final volume is ***The Lesser Evil: The Diaries of Victor Klemperer 1945–1959***. This first volume is of particular interest for painting the life of a Jew as Nazism was starting to take hold and of the society that was created during that time. Born a Jew, Klemperer converted to Protestantism when he married his Gentile wife, Eva, but that did not preclude his being persecuted by the Nazis. According to their highly legalistic system, Klemperer was still a Jew. But because he was married to an Aryan, he was initially saved from being deported. Klemperer was a professor of Romance languages when Hitler came to power, and when he was deprived of his position (and his house, his typewriter, his cat, his driver's license), he began to keep a diary of his life. His wife couriered the papers to a friend, who then hid them.

This volume was selected as a Notable Book by the American Library Association, and the second volume was nominated for the National Book Critics Circle Award in Biography/Autobiography.

Subjects: 1930s; 1940s; ALA Notable Books; College Professors; Courage; Diaries; Dresden, Germany; Germany; Hitler, Adolf; Holocaust, Jewish (1939–1945); Holocaust Survivors; Jews, Germany; National Socialism; Translations

Now Try: The historian Sebastian Haffner, in his book (translated from the German by Oliver Pretzel), ***Defying Hitler: A Memoir***, gives a clear picture of the social conditions in Germany that led to the successful power grab by Hitler. Germany, of course, is not the only country to hold its citizens in a state of permanent fear. Nadezhda Mandel'shtam recounts the nightmare life that she and her poet husband (Osip) endured in Communist Russia in ***Hope Against Hope; A Memoir***, translated from the Russian by Max Hayward. ***The Pieces from Berlin*** is a well-received novel by Michael Pye that looks into the long-term results of one specific degradation suffered by Jews during Hitler's regime—the theft and reselling of their personal belongings and treasures.

Noor, Queen, Consort of Hussein, King of Jordan (1951–)

Leap of Faith: Memoirs of an Unexpected Life. Miramax Books, 2003. 467pp. ill. 16pp. of plates. 9780786867172. Also available in large print, audiobook, e-audiobook, and e-book. 956.95044092

Queen Noor is an Arab-American, born of Jordanian and Swedish parents and raised and educated in the United States. She became the fourth wife of King Hussein and describes in her memoir the difficulties in adjusting to royal life, parenting their four children along with Hussein's eight other children, and being the wife of a politically important man. Her memoir will interest a wide group of people because it portrays not only the life of a royal, but also the life of a country's leader in a volatile part of the world. Noor discusses the many issues her husband dealt with, particularly the Arab–Israeli conflict and Jordanian–

American relations, providing a perspective not often seen by Americans. Noor offers a look at politics in the Middle East over a twenty-two-year span, from 1978 to 1999, when her husband died.

Subjects: Arab–Israeli Conflict; Hussein, King of Jordan; Jordan; Married Couples; Middle East; Politics, Jordan; Royalty; Women in Jordan

Now Try: Noor's memoir has been compared to the musical by Rodgers and Hammerstein, ***The King and I***, but the real and even more fascinating story of the governess (Anna Harriette Leonowens) who so impressed the king of Siam has been told by Susan Morgan in ***Bombay Anna: The Real Story and Remarkable Adventures of the "King and I" Governess***. Readers are often enthralled by the lives of royalty, vicariously living a life they could never capture. Grace Kelly's story appears to be one of those fairy tales come true, a story that J. Randy Taraborrelli tells in ***Once upon a Time: Behind the Fairy Tale of Princess Grace and Prince Rainier***. On a more serious note, for those interested in the political dealings in the Middle East, Patrick Tyler presents one perspective in ***A World of Trouble: The White House and the Middle East—from the Cold War to the War on Terror***.

Schlesinger, Arthur M. (1917–2007)

A Life in the Twentieth Century: Innocent Beginnings, 1917–1950. Houghton Mifflin, 2002, 2000. 592pp. 9780618219254. 973.91092

Arthur Schlesinger was the son of a historian, also Arthur Schlesinger, and his childhood was steeped in books (read to him by his mother, Elizabeth), history, and an intellectual life. He followed in his father's footsteps, showing a particular interest in the politicians in U.S. history, particularly the men who were prominent in his own day. He also put social history on the map, writing for the general populace as well as fellow historians. This first volume of his memoirs reveals his childhood and youth; his education; his work for the Office of Strategic Services (OSS) during the war; and his subsequent development of a liberal philosophy, particularly in the face of both McCarthyism and the Cold War. Schlesinger's sons, Andrew and Stephen, worked to gather his journals for publication, hoping to finish in time for his ninetieth birthday, but Schlesinger died months before. They did prevail in publishing the results of their efforts, however, as ***Journals, 1952–2000***, completing the picture of Schlesinger's full and productive life.

Arthur Schlesinger was awarded the National Humanities Medal in 1998 by President and Mrs. Clinton.

Subjects: Childhood and Youth; Fathers and Sons; Historians; History, United States; Octogenarians; Social History, United States

Now Try: Daniel Aaron is a historian who embraced American studies, shedding light on the world in which he traveled and on many of the same people who so engaged Schlesinger. Aaron's memoir is entitled ***The Americanist***. The historian John Lukacs offers a biography, ***George Kennan: A Study of Character***, about one of the men who played an important role at the beginning of the Cold War in Truman's day, the diplomat and writer George Kennan. Offering an overview of the major political changes in ideology during the period covered in Schlesinger's first volume is David Plotke's ***Building a Democratic Political Order: Reshaping American Liberalism in the 1930s and 1940s.***

Terkel, Studs (1912–2008)
Lewis, Sydney, coauthor

Touch and Go: A Memoir. New Press, 2007. 269pp. ill. 8pp. of plates. 9781595580436. Also available in audiobook, e-audiobook, and e-book. 384.54092

Terkel claims that it was his childhood in Chicago, living in the boarding houses run by his parents, that engendered his interest in ordinary people, in what he referred to as the "etceteras of history." Initially involved in acting and in broadcasting, he cast his net further afield and made his name by studying people in various situations: those who lived through the Great Depression; those who lived through World War II; working people; Blacks and Whites; people facing death—either through their professions or their circumstances; and movie and theater people. He didn't just study people, however; he also lived a varied and full life himself. As just one example, he had his own television show in the 1950s, *Studs' Place*, which was canceled when he was blacklisted by Joe McCarthy. Reading Terkel's memoir is reading a social and political history of the United States from the point of view of a not-so-common common man. A nice companion volume to this is another by Terkel published shortly before his death, ***P.S.: Further Thoughts from a Lifetime of Listening.***

Subjects: Chicago, IL; McCarthy Era; Nonagenarians; Oral Historians; Radio Broadcasters; Social History, United States; *Studs' Place* (Television Program); Writers

Now Try: John McPhee is another writer who enjoys depicting the lives of interesting but unknown people. His collection of essays, ***The John McPhee Reader,*** edited by William L. Howarth and taken from McPhee's first twelve books, offers a wide-ranging example of his personal profiles. Another book reminiscent of those written by Studs Terkel is the study done by Dale Maharidge and Michael Williamson (photographer) fifty years after ***Let Us Now Praise Famous Men,*** the book that resulted from Walker Evans photographing and James Agee writing about Southern sharecroppers. ***And Their Children After Them: The Legacy of Let Us Now Praise Famous Men, James Agee, Walker Evans, and the Rise and Fall of Cotton in the South*** looks at the children of the families studied by Agee and Evans. The StoryCorps Project (http://storycorps.org/), originally inspired by Studs Terkel, was developed to gather oral histories of everyday people in the United States. David Isay collected some of the more outstanding interviews in ***Listening Is an Act of Love: A Celebration of American Life from the StoryCorps Project.***

Tyson, Timothy B. (1959–)

Blood Done Sign My Name: A True Story. Three Rivers Press, 2005, 2004. 355pp. 9781400083114. Also available in audiobook (read by the author), e-audiobook, e-book, and video. 975.6092

Just ten years old in Oxford, North Carolina, when a young Black man, Henry Marrow, was murdered by three White men, Timothy Tyson's life trajectory was set, although he didn't know it for several years. His father was a White pastor in a local Methodist church, preaching racial tolerance long before it was common to do so. After running away from home at the age of seventeen, Tyson finally decided to go to college, but not before he went back to Oxford to ask Robert Teel, one of the murderers (acquitted by an all-White jury) why he had killed Henry Marrow. Tyson's memoir is a recounting of that time in Oxford, along with stories of the lives of the major participants in the tragedy and its subsequent fallout: racial violence and unrest. His book is not just a reminder of a violent time in American history, but also a study of what racial intolerance can beget. Tyson eventually became a professor of African-American studies.

Blood Done Sign My Name was nominated for the National Book Critics Circle Award in General Nonfiction and was the winner of a Christopher Award.

Subjects: Childhood and Youth; Christopher Awards; Civil Rights; College Professors; Marrow, Henry; Murder; North Carolina; Oxford, NC; Racism; Reel, Robert; Trials; Whites, United States

Now Try: Offering a perspective on White people in the South during the Civil Rights Movement is Jason Sokol's ***There Goes My Everything: White Southerners in the Age of Civil Rights, 1945–1975***. Willie Morris also grew up in the South and during his college years lived in Texas during desegregation. He wrote a classic memoir of that time, ***North Toward Home***. Bringing the racial divide forward to the 1990s is Alex Kotlowitz's investigation into the death of a Black teenager found in the river between two communities in Michigan—one White (St. Joseph) and one Black (Benton Harbor): ***The Other Side of the River: A Story of Two Towns, a Death, and America's Dilemma***.

Wiesel, Elie (1928–)

All Rivers Run to the Sea: Memoirs. Schocken Books, 1996, 1994. 432pp. ill. 16pp. of plates. 9780805210286. Also available in large print, audiobook (read by the author), and e-book. 843.092 [Trans. by Jon Rothschild]

In this first of two volumes, bringing the author up to 1969, Wiesel describes his life as a young boy in Romania, the son of Shlomo, a rabbi, and a child very interested in mystical Judaism. His life is tragically interrupted by deportation with his father to Auschwitz. Witnessing his father's death there, but surviving the ordeal himself, was a deciding moment for Wiesel. He recounts his life and education in France and subsequent move to the United States as a journalist for an Israeli newspaper; here he met the woman who would become his wife, Marion Erster Rose. The second volume, ***And the Sea Is Never Full: Memoirs, 1969–*** , translated from the French by his wife, Marion Wiesel, was published in 1999, covering the next thirty years of his life, including the creation of The Elie Wiesel Foundation for Humanity (http://www.eliewieselfoundation.org/).

Elie Wiesel was awarded the Congressional Gold Medal by President Reagan in 1982 and was given the Presidential Medal of Freedom in 1992 by George Bush. He was also awarded the Nobel Peace Prize. Inducted into the Academy of Achievement, Wiesel recommended Franz Kafka's ***The Metamorphosis, In the Penal Colony, and Other Stories***, translated from the German by Willa and Edwin Muir, because, while he was so caught up in it that he read it through the night, it made him grateful that he had a normal life.

Subjects: Childhood and Youth; Death of a Parent; Elie Wiesel Foundation for Humanity; Fathers and Sons; Holocaust, Jewish (1939–1945); Holocaust Survivors; Jewish Men; Nobel Prize Laureates; Octogenarians; Translations; Wiesel, Marion Erster Rose; Writers

Now Try: The Israeli novelist Aron Appelfeld was also a victim of the Holocaust and describes in his memoir, ***The Story of a Life***, translated from the Hebrew by Aloma Halter, how he escaped the camps as a young boy and what he had to do to survive. Viktor E. Frankl is another man who decided to turn his experiences in the concentration camp to something for good, developing a form of psychotherapy to help people reach out toward the future instead of focusing on the past. His autobiography is ***Viktor Frankl—Recollections: An Autobiography***, translated from the German by Joseph and Judith Fabry. Isaac Bashevis Singer, a fellow Nobel Laureate, also grew up immersed in Judaism. His biographer, Dvorah Telushkin, became first Singer's assistant and finally his *protégée*, which she describes in ***Master of Dreams: A Memoir of Isaac Bashevis Singer***.

Consider Starting With . . .

Aaron, Hank. *I Had a Hammer: The Hank Aaron Story*

Adams, Henry. *The Education of Henry Adams: A Centennial Version*

Cooper, Anderson. *Dispatches from the Edge: A Memoir of War, Disasters, and Survival*

Cronkite, Walter. *A Reporter's Life*

Delany, Sarah Louise, and A. Elizabeth Delany. *Having Our Say: The Delany Sisters' First 100 Years*

Ellsberg, Daniel. *Secrets: A Memoir of Vietnam and the Pentagon Papers*

Franklin, Benjamin. *The Autobiography of Benjamin Franklin*

Gruwell, Erin, and the Freedom Writers. *The Freedom Writers Diary: How a Teacher and 150 Teens Used Writing to Change Themselves and the World Around Them*

Lewis, John. *Walking with the Wind: A Memoir of the Movement*

Suzuki, David T. *David Suzuki: The Autobiography*

Fiction Read-Alikes

Barnes, Julian. *Arthur & George*. Barnes tells the story, based on a real event, of Sir Arthur Conan Doyle coming to the aid of the Anglo-Indian George Edalji, the result of which was the establishment of the Court of Criminal Appeal in England.

Dangor, Achmat. *Bitter Fruit*. Twenty years after being victimized by an Afrikaans policeman, Silas Ali is not convinced that bringing the policeman before the Truth and Reconciliation Commission will satisfy his need for vengeance.

Earling, Debra Magpie. *Perma Red*. Louise White Elk is torn between staying on her reservation to be near the traditional man she loves and leaving for the wider world.

Harris, Robert. *Imperium: A Novel of Ancient Rome*. Cicero's life is revealed through the reminiscences of his confidential secretary, also depicting the political life of the time.

Huyler, Frank. *Right of Thirst: A Novel*. A doctor's offer to help in a refugee camp following an earthquake becomes a personal journey for himself as he probes his reactions to his wife's premature death.

Kim, Eugenia. *The Calligrapher's Daughter: A Novel*. Najin, the independent daughter of a traditional man in early nineteenth-century Korea, witnesses firsthand the political changes that befall her country.

Marciano, Francesca. *The End of Manners*. Maria is assigned to Afghanistan to photograph young girls as they participate in interviews with her partner about their attempts at suicide to avoid marriage to much older men.

Pārsī'pūr, Shahrnūsh. *Touba and the Meaning of Night*. The reader is treated to seeing eight decades of Iranian life through the life story of Touba, just a young girl when her progressive father died.

Ragen, Naomi. *The Covenant*. Elise is desperate for help when her husband and daughter are abducted by terrorists in Judea, where Elise and her husband had set up their home.

Stockett, Kathryn. *The Help*. A recent White college graduate seeks out the stories of the Black women who work as maids for middle-class White women of Jackson, Mississippi, in the early 1960s.

Works Cited

Carr, David. 2004. "Many Kinds of Crafted Truths: An Introduction to Nonfiction." In *Nonfiction Readers' Advisory*, edited by Robert Burgin, 47–65. Westport, CT: Libraries Unlimited.

Gutkind, Lee, and Hattie Fletcher, eds. 2008. *Keep It Real: Everything You Need to Know about Researching and Writing Creative Nonfiction*. New York: W. W. Norton & Company.

King, Martin Luther, Jr. 1967. "Beyond Vietnam—A Time to Break Silence." Speech delivered at Riverside Church, New York City, April 4.

Vanderford, Audrey. 2005. "Goldman, Emma (1869–1940)." In *Encyclopedia of Women's Autobiography*, edited by Victoria Boynton and Jo Malin, 250–52. Westport, CT: Greenwood Press.

Wyatt, Neal. 2007. *The Readers' Advisory Guide to Nonfiction*. Chicago: American Library Association.

Chapter 11

Life on the Dark Side of History

Description

This chapter could easily be entitled "Humanity's Inhumanity to Humanity." It represents some of the darkest days and darkest events in recent world history. But it also represents the ability of the individual to recover, to fight back, even to rejoice. Most of these memoirs could also go into Chapter 13, "Surviving Life," which includes books that feature triumph over adversity. These particular stories, however, reveal not just the individual but the society as a whole. We see a nation's history, or a good part of it. We see how the world in general responds to what goes on in different countries. And we see the confluence of politics, government, history, and the individual citizen as each has its effect on the other.

One of the more remarkable aspects of this particular chapter is the blossoming of the female voice from countries that had so long suppressed them. Many of the stories in this chapter come from countries where women have been deemed secondary to men. For them to tell their stories in writing had been unthinkable for centuries. Their traditional role was in storytelling among themselves, or perhaps in literally weaving their narratives into tapestries (Milani, 1990). To tell their stories in public, to the public, would be considered a shameful act.

With the opening of these countries to the West, however, change was inevitable. People left their oppressive countries, and women found themselves encouraged by others to tell their stories. Or women (and men) found the urge to share their stories too great to suppress. For many exiles, caught between the loss of their birth countries and the relief of being in a greater freedom, writing their stories was a way to keep their countries close to the heart. It was also a way to counteract Western media views of their countries. Marjane Satrapi, for example, said that she wrote ***Persepolis*** because she wanted to show Iran as she saw it, not as it was reflected in European television: " 'pictures of women in chadors and guys with guns' " (Goldin, 2004). Readers will find, then, that the writers often describe a childhood within the context of the country—its culture, folklore, food, family relationships—as a way of bringing close that country, that time. The contrast for the writer and the reader between that familiar home environment and the change and violence that ensue is even more shocking and difficult to bear.

Genocide is a recurring theme in this chapter, not just the Jewish Holocaust, but also the genocides that have occurred in countries as varied as Rwanda, the former Yugoslavia, Sudan, Cambodia, and Armenia. The stories are what David Carr refers to as "the regard of extreme politics by challenged mortals" (Carr, 2004). Woven throughout these stories of genocide, however, are the portraits of people who offered help and rescue. Captivity is another theme, whether mental (life in a cult) or physical (life in prisons, as slaves, as hostages, or as prostitutes). Again there is a ribbon of light shining in the stories of those who came to the aid of the captives. Through it all runs the theme of oppression: how one group elects to oppress another. Often the writers chose to write their stories in the hopes of preventing future oppression. Whether or not they have succeeded is a decision for future history books.

"Devastating works demonstrate the myth of 'closure' and resolution. Perhaps this is why we also have enduring bodies of nonfiction devoted to wars, crimes, disasters, and losses: they will always be open" (Carr, 2004).

Memoirs reflecting the dark side of history include stories of genocide, slavery, and oppression. They are written primarily by the victims but also, in certain cases, by witnesses to the crimes. Their tone is often bleak, particularly from those who are witnesses; the survivors often inject a tone of positive optimism as they face a new life away from the horror.

Appeal

A dominant appeal of the memoir genre is reflected here as the reader looks upon the life of the writer through the lens of the reader's life: in most cases the reader's life is likely to be better on some level, providing a new perspective to that life, making one grateful to have been born or to be living in a country where life seems better than it was for the writer. But in reading another's story, despite the difference in location and culture, we also recognize that we are all basically the same: human beings with hearts, minds, feelings, troubled and/or close relationships, likes and dislikes. All of which is to say that character is a large appeal here: getting to know the person's background, seeing the difficulties, watching how that person behaves during the worst or the best, and rejoicing in a rescue, if there is one.

The appeal of character is closely entwined here with story. The stories may be similar (imprisoned for speaking out) or they may be quite different (escape from a suicidal cult), but each story is different because of the character living and telling it. The stories in this chapter are hair-raising, very grim to read, very tragic in parts, and often quite unbelievable to readers born and raised in countries that have not yet experienced a totalitarian government. But they are gripping stories, tales of lives largely lived in countries few of us have traveled to. They often read like a novel, beginning with fairly calm scenes, introducing the conflict, and living through the conflict, with a resolution—of some sort or other—at the end.

Because the stories are so different from the North American reader's own experience, the opportunity for learning is great. To read about the genocide in Rwanda is to learn how deep and how strong are intertribal rivalries. Reading about the Red Guard in China opens the reader's eyes not only to the realities of Mao's Cultural Revolution but also to the dangers of brainwashing and demagoguery, how easy it seems for one powerful man to sway millions of people—and of course the same thing can be said of Hitler. These stories are the sort that may lead us to read further, wanting to know more about the event, more about the country in which the event took place, and more about peripheral aspects.

Organization of This Chapter

The chapter begins with five classics, some known to all (***The Diary of Anne Frank*** is available in over 5,000 libraries in North America) and others perhaps less familiar, but no less important or telling. The ensuing sections could be perceived as moving from larger affected groups to smaller, beginning with stories of the Holocaust and other twentieth-century genocides, involving at times the victims, their family members, or those who experience the aftermath. Still affecting large groups, but seen through the porthole of individual stories, are the books on oppression—largely by oppressive governments. We move then to stories that are no less traumatic, of individuals caught up in someone else's drama that has become their own.

Classics

These five classics date from the early nineteenth century to the late twentieth century and cover four continents. They include a slave narrative (an important genre in American literature and history), and stories of the Holocaust, of apartheid, of citizen internment, and of political imprisonment. They all speak of oppression.

If you would like to read more about the slave narrative, only lightly covered here, you might want to pick up ***African American Slave Narratives: An Anthology,*** a collection of nineteenth-century narratives edited by Sterling Lecater Bland Jr. There are also three Web sites of particular interest: *Born in Slavery: Slave Narratives from the Federal Writers' Project, 1936–1938* (http://lcweb2.loc.gov/ammem/snhtml/); *American Slave Narratives: An Online Anthology* (http://xroads.virginia.edu/~hyper/wpa/wpahome.html); and *"Been Here So Long,"*

Selections from the WPA American Slave Narratives (http://newdeal.feri.org/asn/index.htm).

Classic stories illustrating the dark side of history are representations of a long history of oppression and brutality.They are narrative stories of captivity, slavery, and sheer basic hatred. By the same token, they also reflect hope for a better tomorrow.

Douglass, Frederick (1818–1895)

Narrative of the Life of Frederick Douglass, an American Slave, Written by Himself. Essays by Angela Y. Davis. City Lights, 2010, 1845. 254pp. ill. 9780872865273. Also available in large print, Braille, audiobook, e-audiobook, and e-book. 973.8092

This first of three autobiographies by the preeminent nineteenth-century orator and abolitionist is unusual in that Douglass was able to convert his oratorical skills to the written page, something not commonly found in his day and age. The original work had prefaces by each of two White abolitionists in order to give Douglass credibility, to verify that he had indeed written the narrative and that he was who he said he was. Full of details of the cruelties he encountered as a slave, both personally and to others, the book skimps on the facts surrounding his successful escape in an effort to protect those who had helped him. Of particular interest in this volume is his recognition of the importance of language and reading, along with his tales of how he actually learned to read in secret. Spurring him on was the comment by one of his owners that if slaves knew how to read the Bible, they would no longer be fit to be slaves. Throughout his narrative he also stresses the importance for all people to be masters of their own fate, not to be subject to the dictates and cruelties of other people. Following this autobiography are ***My Bondage and My Freedom*** (1855) and ***Life and Times of Frederick Douglass*** (1881).

Subjects: 19th Century; Abolitionists; African-American Men; Classics; Human Rights Activists; Maryland; Orators; Racism; Slave Narratives; Slavery

Now Try: Harriet A. Jacobs's classic slave narrative is almost as well-known as Douglass's: ***Incidents in the Life of a Slave Girl: Written by Herself.*** Another well-known slave narrative is ***The Interesting Narrative of the Life of Olaudah Equiano or Gustavus Vassa, the African/Written by Himself,*** a man who bought his freedom and used his narrative as a means of publicizing the horrors of slavery. It is common knowledge that Thomas Jefferson had slaves; not so well-known is that another Founding Father did too, but Robert Carter freed his, thus breaking ties with his colleagues. Andrew Levy is the author who has brought all this to light, in ***The First Emancipator: The Forgotten Story of Robert Carter, the Founding Father Who Freed His Slaves.***

Frank, Anne (1929–1945)
Frank, Otto H., and Mirjam Pressler, eds.

The Diary of a Young Girl: The Definitive Edition. Doubleday, 1995, 1947. 340pp. ill. 9780385473781. Also available in large print, Braille, audiobook, e-audiobook, e-book, and video. 940.53092 [Trans. by Susan Massotty]

Because she died of typhus at Bergen-Belsen, Anne Frank was not able to see her book published, a diary she wrote while in captivity, which she had planned to publish after the war to fulfill her dream of becoming a writer. After Frank and her family were captured, Miep Gies, a woman who had helped them in hiding, found the diary and gave it to Anne's father, Otto, after the war. He published an expurgated edition of her book in an effort both to gloss over some of the more personal entries and to reveal the universality of Anne's story. This definitive edition includes the sections initially excluded. Anne's diary, written in part to keep her still when silence was so important for their safety, is taken up largely with life hidden from the Nazis, life with her family and another family, also living with them, who also had a child, Peter. It is a coming-of-age work as much as a story of a life lived in fear, as Anne was an adolescent at the time of the writing. Her development over the two years of their life hiding in Amsterdam is evident as she reveals her own thoughts and feelings as well as the daily ups and downs of such a life.

Anne Frank was named one of *Time*'s People of the Century in the Heroes & Icons category.

Subjects: Adolescents; Classics; Coming of Age; Diaries; Family Relationships; Holocaust, Jewish (1939–1945); Jews, Netherlands; Netherlands; Translations; World War II (1939–1945)

Now Try: Miep Gies (who recently died at the age of 100 from a fall) told her own story, with the help of Alison Leslie Gold, about her connection to the Frank family: ***Anne Frank Remembered: The Story of the Woman Who Helped to Hide the Frank Family.*** Edith Velmans-Van Hessen was another Dutch adolescent who suffered during the Holocaust. Managing to survive, she wrote her memoir from diaries kept during that time: ***Edith's Story.*** Hélène Berr's journal was made public sixty-three years after she also died of typhus at Bergen-Belsen. She also brings a literary skill and liveliness to her writing, translated from the French by David Bellos as ***The Journal of Hélène Berr.*** For a different perspective on a childhood in Nazi Germany—that of a young German Gentile—readers may want to try Irmgard A. Hunt's memoir, ***On Hitler's Mountain: Overcoming the Legacy of a Nazi Childhood.***

Houston, Jeanne Wakatsuki (1934–)
Houston, James D. (1939–2009), coauthor

Farewell to Manzanar; A True Story of Japanese American Experience During and After the World War II Internment. Laurel-Leaf Books, 2007, 1973. 9780553272581. Also available in large print, Braille, and video. 940.54727

Jeanne Wakatsuki was married to her husband for fifteen years before he learned about her time in the American concentration camp, Manzanar, during the Second World War. No one spoke of their time in the camps, but when she was asked by her nephew how she had felt while living there, Jeanne burst into tears and finally decided to write her story for her family. Once she started, however, she found it almost too difficult to continue, as her life in the camp was so intertwined with the negative changes in her father after the treatment he received from the American government. Her husband then helped her, insisting that the story be written for a larger audience; they were then asked to write the screenplay for a film, and both the film and the book entered the school curriculum for American children. Jeanne was seven years old when she and her family were sent to Manzanar, where they remained for four years. One of the details she mentions is how the family units disintegrated because they were forced to eat in mess halls with large groups of people, rather than being allowed to eat as individual families.

Subjects: Childhood and Youth; Classics; Concentration Camps, United States; Fathers and Daughters; Japanese-Americans; Japanese Internment; Manzanar War Relocation Center, CA; World War II (1939–1945)

Now Try: Lawson Fusao Inada pored over legal and government documents, diaries, and interviews to fashion a history of Japanese-Americans in World War II: ***Only What We Could Carry: The Japanese American Internment Experience***. Canada also interned its Japanese citizens, which Ken Adachi addressed in his seminal work, ***The Enemy That Never Was: A History of the Japanese Canadians***. Joy Kogawa offers a fictional illustration of life for Japanese internees, both during the Second World War and following, in her award-winning novel ***Obasan***.

Mathabane, Mark (1960–)

Kaffir Boy: The True Story of a Black Youth's Coming of Age in Apartheid South Africa. Simon & Schuster, 1998, 1986. 354pp. ill. 9780684848280. Also available in Braille and e-book. 968.0040092

Although apartheid as an official South African government policy is over now, Mathabane's story of a young boy's life under the weight of such a system still speaks to the reader. In his memoir he recalls that at the age of ten he was suicidal because his life was so bleak. But his mother believed in him and in the power of education and pushed him forward. He also had a special talent for tennis and was inspired by seeing Arthur Ashe playing tennis in South Africa. Due to his determination and courage, along with the help of some White people, he was able to obtain a tennis scholarship in the United States, thus taking him away from the cruelties, the fears, and the privations of life under apartheid. Reading his book is not for the fainthearted, as most readers will be unfamiliar with the depths of poverty in which he and his family lived, poverty exacerbated by fear of stepping out of bounds or of reprisals even while staying in bounds.

Kaffir Boy was the winner of a Christopher Award.

Subjects: Apartheid; Ashe, Arthur; Childhood and Youth; Christopher Awards; Classics; Coming of Age; Poverty, South Africa; South Africa; Tennis

Now Try: Mathabane has followed this memoir with others, the most recent being the story of his sister, told in her voice, ***Miriam's Song: A Memoir***. Explaining how apartheid came to exist in South Africa is Dominique Lapierre's history of the country, ***A Rainbow in the Night: The Tumultuous Birth of South Africa***, translated from the French by Kathryn Spink. Not only Black people were subject to government oppression, however; André P. Brink's novel, ***A Dry White Season*** was banned, and Nadine Gordimer's ***July's People*** was also banned. Aelred Stubbs collected many activist essays by Steve Biko after his murder, published as ***I Write What I Like: A Selection of His Writings Edited with a Personal Memoir***.

Wiesel, Elie (1928–)

Night. Foreword by François Mauriac. Preface by the author. Hill and Wang, 2006, 1958. 120pp. 9780374399979. Also available in Braille, large print, audiobook, and e-audiobook. 940.5318 [Trans. by Marion Wiesel]

This edition of Wiesel's classic is a new translation by his wife, making the text more contemporary and rendering his language more as he had intended. It also includes a new preface by the author wherein he exhorts the reader to be vigilant about humankind's inhumanity to humankind and to stand up against it. In the memoir Wiesel recounts how he and his family were sent off first to Auschwitz in 1944, where his mother and one sister died, and then to Buchenwald, he a boy of fifteen. He was able to stay with his father, Shlomo, and then had to watch him die a slow death. Throughout the physical and emotional sufferings they endured, Wiesel also had a crisis of faith: How could a merciful God allow such behavior? He initially vowed never to speak of the death camps, but the author François Mauriac persuaded him to write about his experiences. Once he had done that, he vowed to dedicate his life to telling others about the Holocaust and the potential for evil throughout the world.

Wiesel was inducted into the Academy of Achievement and awarded the Congressional Gold Medal by President Reagan in 1982, the Nobel Peace Prize in 1986, and the Presidential Medal of Freedom from President George Bush in 1992.

Subjects: Auschwitz (Concentration Camp); Buchenwald (Concentration Camp); Classics; Death of a Parent; Despair; Germany; Holocaust, Jewish (1939–1945); Holocaust Survivors; Jewish Men; Nobel Prize Laureates; Octogenarians; Poland; Translations; World War II (1939–1945)

Now Try: Imre Kertész is a Hungarian Jew, a winner of the Nobel Prize in Literature, who had also been sent to Auschwitz with his father. He wrote a novel about that experience, newly translated from the Hungarian by Tim Wilkinson as ***Fatelessness: A Novel***. Seventy years later a question remains, which Theodore S. Hamerow sets out to answer in his highly acclaimed work: ***Why We Watched: Europe, America, and the Holocaust***. Primo Levi's name is often coupled with Wiesel's, perhaps for his noted skill as a writer. His ***Survival***

in Auschwitz, translated by Stuart Woolf, is considered as much a classic as Wiesel's *Night*.

Holocaust/Genocide

In this section it "is difficult to separate politics and government from contemporary issues" (Carr, 2004). For genocide to occur, the government has to be implicated, and politics is at the core—whether it's a political belief of superiority or a political will to grab land. The phrase "ethnic cleansing" seems to go hand-in-hand with the word "genocide"—in most cases one group has decided to wipe out another ethnic or religious group. That it happened over several years in Armenia was bad; that it happened again in both Germany and Russia two decades later was worse. The question remains: How could it have happened again in the 1970s and on into the twenty-first century in four completely separate locales? This is the type of question with which readers find themselves faced when reading the books in this section. Readers will see how families are still affected by these genocides years later. They will see what the aftermath looks like, the investigations that must be conducted. And they will be right there in the middle of it all, seeing the horror. The genocide that occurred during Pol Pot's regime in Cambodia is not specifically addressed here, but the horrific effects of it are seen in the next chapter, "Life at War," in the section "Victims of War."

Memoirs portraying a holocaust or genocide are stories told by survivors, by the children of survivors, and by those trying to help during the slaughter or sent in afterward to help. The telling is often matter of fact and dispassionate, as the writers describe unimaginable horrors.

Balakian, Peter (1951–)

Black Dog of Fate: A Memoir. Basic Books, 2009, 1997. 357pp. geneal. map. 9780465010196. Also available in e-book. 811.54

Applying a poet's language to his life story, Balakian intertwines his own narrative, growing up in New Jersey surrounded by family, with the story of that family—particularly the older ones—victimized and horrified by the genocide in Armenia by the Ottoman Turks. While he was growing up, spending time with his grandmother, sitting around the table eating typical Armenian food, Balakian often heard subtle references to something of which he had no concept. It was after he had graduated from college that he read a memoir by Henry Morgenthau, American ambassador to Turkey during the First World War. From ***Ambassador Morgenthau's Story*** Balakian learned for the first time of the Armenian genocide. At the next family celebration he presented a poem he had written, which asked questions and finally sparked his family to speak to him about what they had experienced. This knowledge changed the direction of Balakian's life, as he set out to learn as much as he could about the massacre and then to tell others about it.

Black Dog of Fate was awarded the PEN American Center Martha Albrand Award for the Art of the Memoir.

Subjects: Armenian-Americans; Armenian Massacres (1915–1929); Coming of Age; Family Relationships; Genocide, Armenia; Grandmothers; History, Turkey; New Jersey; PEN American Center Martha Albrand Award for the Art of the Memoir; Poets

Now Try: Whereas the main connection to Armenia for Balakian was his grandmother, for Michael J. Arlen it was his father, Michael. His personal investigation, ***Passage to Ararat,*** is as much a homage to Arlen's father as it is an exploration of Armenian history, which his father tried to obliterate from his own history. Vartan Gregorian, the president of the Carnegie Corporation of New York, has written his own story, ***The Road to Home: My Life and Times,*** but rather than focus on the genocide, he nostalgically describes life in the small Armenian enclave in Tabriz, Iran. The Armenian genocide is seen somewhat from the Turkish perspective in Turkish author Elif Shafak's novel, ***The Bastard of Istanbul.***

Dallaire, Roméo (1946–)
Beardsley, Brent, coauthor

Shake Hands with the Devil: The Failure of Humanity in Rwanda. Carroll & Graf, 2005, 2003. 562pp. maps. 9780786715107. Also available in video. 967.5710431

When General Roméo Dallaire was first appointed as Force Commander of the UN Assistance Mission for Rwanda, he wasn't even sure where Rwanda was. Once he arrived, however, he learned not only where it was, but that it was at the beginning of a civil war, a war whose goal was for the Hutu tribe to wipe out the Tutsi tribe. Within the space of 100 days they almost succeeded, with 800,000 dead. Dallaire was witness to this, increasingly frustrated in his attempts to generate action and response from the United Nations and from any other political body that might help. Because his was a peacekeeping force, he was forbidden to engage in anything resembling warfare; he regularly sought permission to change this status. His story is one of bureaucracy allowing genocide, but also one of individual efforts to stem the violence or at least to help save some of the potential victims. And it is also the story of a high-ranking officer's post-traumatic stress disorder (PTSD), an illness that almost led to both the breakdown of his family and his own suicide. Following the publication of this memoir, Dallaire has worked on raising awareness about PTSD to engender much-needed research into its cause, prevention, and treatment. He has also lectured about PTSD to various military units. Recently the former governor-general of Canada, Michaëlle Jean, admitted in Rwanda that both Canada and the United Nations had let Rwanda down, thus vindicating Dallaire and his men.

Shake Hands with the Devil won the Canadian Booksellers Association Libris Award for Non-Fiction Book of the Year, the Governor General's Literary Award for Non-Fiction, and the Writers' Trust of Canada Shaughnessy Cohen Prize for Political Writing.

Subjects: Canadian Booksellers Association Libris Award for Non-Fiction Book of the Year; Generals, Canada; Genocide, Rwanda; Governor General's Literary Award for Non-Fiction; Peacekeeping Forces; Rwanda Civil War (1994); United Nations Peacekeeping Forces; War Atrocities, Rwanda; Writers' Trust of Canada Shaughnessy Cohen Prize for Political Writing

Now Try: The Canadian journalist Gil Courtemanche wrote a dispassionate and powerful novel about a Canadian journalist's sojourn in Kigali during the Rwandan genocide, ***A Sunday at the Pool in Kigali,*** translated by Patricia Claxton. Michael N. Barnett worked in New York with the U.S. Mission to the UN during the time of the genocide and offers the UN perspective on the action (or inaction) witnessed by Dallaire; Barnett raises disturbing ethical questions in ***Eyewitness to a Genocide: The United Nations and Rwanda***. Peacekeeping forces were deployed in the latter half of the twentieth century more than ever before. In ***The Mission: Waging War and Keeping Peace with America's Military,*** Dana Priest explores the conflicts these forces encounter as they head into the countries where they are assigned to keep peace.

Eisenstein, Bernice (1949–)

I Was a Child of Holocaust Survivors. Riverhead Books, 2006. 187pp. ill. 9781594489181. 971.3092

Eisenstein's parents, who met in Auschwitz toward the end of the war, were married not long after the Liberation. Originally from Poland, they and their remaining family members moved to Toronto, Ontario, where they lived with their tattooed forearms and their memories. Eisenstein's parents rarely talked about their experiences, however, which created in their daughter a fascination with the Holocaust, a desire to understand what her parents had been through, how it had formed them into the people they now were and how they might have been otherwise. Using poetic language and a graphic-narrative format in places, she tells stories about her parents and her aunts and uncles, along with stories about her own youth, growing up with her sister.

I Was a Child of Holocaust Survivors was a finalist for the Trillium Book Award.

Subjects: 1950s; Children of Holocaust Survivors; Family Relationships; Holocaust, Jewish (1939–1945); Holocaust Survivors; Illustrated Narratives; Jews, Canada; Polish-Canadians

Now Try: Joseph Berger had a somewhat similar experience to Eisenstein's, as he describes life with his family in ***Displaced Persons: Growing Up American After the Holocaust***. An interesting companion volume for Eisenstein's memoir is a collection of essays written by women who forge a living through art of one genre or another: ***Daughters of Absence: Transforming a Legacy of Loss,*** edited by Mindy Weisel, herself an artist. Through her own graphic narrative, ***We Are on Our Own: A Memoir,*** Miriam Katin tries to come to terms with her childhood in a world where she and her mother,

Hungarian Jews, were forced to flee German soldiers and hide in the countryside disguised as a Russian woman and illegitimate child.

Hari, Daoud
Burke, Dennis Michael, and Megan M. McKenna, coauthors

The Translator: A Tribesman's Memoir of Darfur. Random House, 2009, 2008. 207pp. 9780812979176. Also available in large print, audiobook, e-audiobook, and e-book. 962.4040392

Daoud Hari is a Sudanese of the Zaghawa tribe, proud of his heritage and of his country as it was before the civil war and the genocide that put it on the global map. In this memoir he describes the country as it was, explaining its history, its hierarchy, and its culture. He then goes on to explain what happened to put him in a refugee camp in Chad and how he made himself indispensable by translating for the visiting journalists and putting them in touch with people he knew they would want to speak to. Wanting the world to know about the dire situation in his country, he moved back there with the journalists, risking his safety and his life by being in a country that forbade journalists. In fact he was captured, imprisoned, and tortured, but even that couldn't daunt his positive spirit or his continuing goal of informing the world about what was happening to his country. That was one of the driving forces behind his narrating this account to Burke and McKenna: further distribution of his story.

Subjects: Darfur Conflict (2003–); East Africa; Genocide, Sudan; Sudan; Torture; Translators; Victims of Violence; War Atrocities, Sudan

Now Try: Once again the world looks on while a genocide takes place, which is roundly criticized by Brian Steidle and Gretchen Steidle Wallace in their book, ***The Devil Came on Horseback: Bearing Witness to the Genocide in Darfur***. Don Cheadle, the actor who starred in ***Hotel Rwanda***, has written a book about Darfur, not only outlining what has happened, but also offering suggestions for making a difference. The title of his book, written with John Prendergast, ***Not on Our Watch: The Mission to End Genocide in Darfur and Beyond***, is also the name of a foundation (http://notonourwatchproject.org/) he and some other actors founded to bring a focus to large-scale global atrocities, for the purpose of stopping and/or preventing them. Offering an analysis of the problems in Darfur by highlighting global responses to them and by explaining the larger history of the region is Mahmood Mamdani's ***Saviors and Survivors: Darfur, Politics, and the War on Terror***.

Ilibagiza, Immaculée (1972–)
Erwin, Steve, coauthor

Left to Tell: Discovering God Amidst the Rwandan Holocaust. Foreword by Wayne Dyer. Hay House, 2006. 215pp. ill. 16pp. of plates. map. 9781401908966. Also available in audiobook, e-audiobook, and e-book. 282.092

For ninety-one of the one hundred days of the Rwandan genocide, Immaculée Ilibagiza huddled in the house of a Hutu pastor in a tiny bathroom with seven other Tutsi women. She could hear the cries of the Interahamwe (the name given to those seeking to obliterate the "cockroaches," the Tutsis) outside the window and she occasionally heard stories from others about the massacres of her parents and her two brothers. While sequestered in the bathroom, Immaculée, already a devout Catholic, began to pray and to forge a strong relationship with God, whom she credits with saving her and many others through the power of prayer. When she left the bathroom, eventually making her way to Mother Teresa's Orphanage in Kigali, she was determined to forgive the murderers, as she did not want them to continue their soul-destroying work by harboring hatred and thoughts of revenge inside herself. In her memoir, she leads up to the horrors of the genocide by describing her life in what she referred to as "Paradise," a life in which she was able to get an education, ending up at university studying mechanical engineering. She now spends her time as a motivational speaker and fund-raiser for her foundation, Left to Tell (http://www.lefttotell.com/fund/index.php), which supports Rwandan orphans and promotes forgiveness and reconciliation.

Left to Tell was the winner of a Christopher Award.

Subjects: Catholics; Christopher Awards; Courage; Forgiveness; Genocide, Rwanda; Left to Tell Charitable Fund; Reconciliation; Rwanda Civil War (1994); Spirituality; War Atrocities, Rwanda

Now Try: The fact that Ilibagiza was able to stay in the home of a Hutu pastor was not a given, as many pastors throughout Rwanda were implicated for contributing to the massacres. Bishop John Rucyahana, an Anglican leader who lost several members of his family, has spent his postgenocide time in Rwanda trying to help the survivors heal, acknowledging to them how the clergy failed them, and trying to help them reach a state of forgiveness and reconciliation; he has told his story in ***The Bishop of Rwanda***, written with James Riordan. South Africa is no stranger to the concept of reconciliation, particularly as seen in the story of Pumla Gobodo-Madikizela. She was a psychologist on the Truth and Reconciliation Commission who confronted one of South Africa's worst perpetrators of mass murder, Eugene de Kock, sentenced to 212 years' imprisonment. How she brought herself to a state of forgiveness and understanding is told in ***A Human Being Died That Night: A South African Story of Forgiveness***. For a look at the rebuilding of Rwanda and the positive effects of Rwandans' efforts at reconciliation, readers may want to pick up Stephen Kinzer's story of Paul Kagamé, ***A Thousand Hills: Rwanda's Rebirth and the Man Who Dreamed It***.

Klein, Gerda Weissmann (1924–)

All but My Life. Hill and Wang, 1996, 1957. 261pp. 9780809015801. Also available in large print, audiobook, and e-audiobook. 940.5318092

By the time Gerda Weissmann was liberated from the German labor camps (by the man who would become her husband), she had been stripped of all but her life—her family, friends, community, and possessions. One other element that remained intact, however, was her optimistic belief in the genuine capability of humankind for goodness. She divides this classic memoir into three parts, beginning with life in Poland with her close family. She then moves on to the rise of Nazism and its impact on her family, resulting in the deaths of her parents. She recounts the various death marches she was forced on (including one that was 350 miles long), the labor camps she suffered in, and the friendships she developed that were then taken away through the deaths of those friends. She also describes the inner strength that allowed her to continue and to give strength to others. The book's final section is her liberation and life afterward with Kurt Klein, the American Army lieutenant who found her standing in front of a booby-trapped warehouse the day before she turned twenty-one, weighing sixty-eight pounds.

Subjects: Classics; Courage; Holocaust, Jewish (1939–1945); Holocaust Survivors; Hope; Jewish Women; Labor Camps; Poland; World War II (1939–1945)

Now Try: Much less is written about the labor camps than the concentration camps; Sala Kirschner is another woman sentenced to the Nazi labor camps, who kept her life there a secret until she finally told her daughter her story. Her daughter Ann has since written ***Sala's Gift: My Mother's Holocaust Story***. Forced labor was also a part of the Soviet punishment system, the history of which is told by Anne Applebaum in her award-winning ***Gulag: A History***. Strength of spirit enabled many people to survive the Holocaust. Renee Rockford and Linda J. Raper collected and edited the stories of many of these survivors, and photographs were taken by Nick Del Calzo, who also created the book: ***The Triumphant Spirit: Portraits & Stories of Holocaust Survivors, Their Messages of Hope & Compassion***.

Koff, Clea (1972–)

The Bone Woman: A Forensic Anthropologist's Search for Truth in the Mass Graves of Rwanda, Bosnia, Croatia, and Kosovo. Random House, 2005, 2004. 276pp. ill. 16pp. of plates. 9780812968859. 364.151092

While working as a graduate student in forensic anthropology, Clea Koff was asked to accompany a team of scientists with the United Nations International Criminal Tribunal for Rwanda, to apply her forensic skills to the bodies unearthed from mass graves there. The purpose of this work was to help identify the bodies and to determine cause of death, in order to provide some semblance of closure for the families and some idea of the magnitude of the crimes committed against humanity. It was to help set history straight. After Rwanda she went elsewhere, to other sites of genocides and mass graves. One irony she encountered in Croatia was the strong resistance by the mothers (one in particular) of disappeared young men. They did not want to learn that their boys' bodies were in those graves; they wanted to keep alive the hope of their boys coming home. In her memoir Koff describes her feelings about the work she does, including her reaction to the mothers in Croatia. Initially she wondered about the value of her work, but ultimately decided it needed to be done, if only to lay bare what is actually going on in this world.

Subjects: Bosnia and Hercegovina; Croatia; Forensic Anthropologists; Genocide, Rwanda; Genocide, Yugoslavia; Kosovo; Rwanda Civil War (1994); War Atrocities; Yugoslav War (1991–1995)

Now Try: The book that sparked Koff's interest in forensics was the story of forensic anthropologist Clyde Snow, told by Christopher Joyce and Eric Stover, ***Witnesses from the Grave: The Stories Bones Tell***. In Srebrenica, the situation was made more difficult because of the secondary graves that were found—the Bosnian Serbs had unearthed the original graves and thrown the bodies into secondary mass graves. Sarah E. Wagner was an anthropologist working in these graves, where DNA was the only means of identifying the now-mixed-up bodies. She describes the situation and their efforts in ***To Know Where He Lies: DNA Technology and the Search for Srebrenica's Missing***. Telling the difficult story of those left to search for their loved ones in the former Yugoslavia is Wojciech Tochman, whose ***Like Eating a Stone: Surviving the Past in Bosnia*** has been translated from the Polish by Antonia Lloyd-Jones.

Rusesabagina, Paul (1955–)
Zoellner, Tom, coauthor

An Ordinary Man: An Autobiography. Penguin, 2007, 2006. 207pp. ill. photo inserts. 9780143038603. 967.57104092

Paul Rusesabagina, the son of a Hutu father and a Tutsi mother, was managing two hotels during the Rwandan genocide. As the manager of the hotel Mille Collines, he housed and saved over 1,200 fellow Rwandans during the 100-day siege. His memoir narrates his childhood and education, along with some history of Rwanda and an explanation of the ethnic rivalries that led to the horrific genocide. Once the genocide itself was over, he determined to tell the world about it, his frustration at the inactivity of the global community evident throughout his book. To this end, he agreed to the making of ***Hotel Rwanda*** and then founded the Hotel Rwanda Rusesabagina Foundation (http://hrrfoundation.org/) to aid the orphans of the Rwandan genocide and to foster tolerance and a prevention of future such atrocities.

Rusesabagina was awarded the Presidential Medal of Freedom by President George W. Bush in 2005.

Subjects: Courage; Genocide, Rwanda; Heroism; Hotel Rwanda Rusesabagina Foundation; Human Rights Activists; Rwanda Civil War (1994); War Atrocities, Rwanda

Now Try: The journalist Philip Gourevitch wrote a harrowing account of personal stories in ***We Wish to Inform You That Tomorrow We Will Be Killed with Our Families: Stories from Rwanda,*** the main title coming from a note sent by a group of Tutsi pastors to their church leader. Another journalist, Jean Hatzfeld, went into the prisons after the war to talk to many of the perpetrators of the butchery and found them ready to speak openly about their crimes. The resulting book is ***Machete Season: The Killers in Rwanda Speak; A Report,*** translated from the French by Linda Coverdale. Rusesabagina has often been compared to Oskar Schindler, the Nazi who saved so many Jews in Nazi Germany. Thomas Keneally wrote the original novel, ***Schindler's List*** (made into an award-winning movie) and then wrote a memoir, ***Searching for Schindler: A Memoir***, explaining why and how he had written that novel.

Spiegelman, Art (1948–)

Maus: A Survivor's Tale. Pantheon Books, 2008, 1986. 2v. ill. 9781435262355. Also available in e-book. 741.5973

The first volume of Spiegelman's classic graphic narrative was followed by a second, ***Maus II: A Survivor's Tale; And Here My Troubles Began***. The first volume ends when his father, Vladek, and his mother Anja, entering Auschwitz, are separated for the duration of the war, and Anja gives birth to a son who dies. Throughout this volume is the story of Spiegelman's parents before they were finally captured: their efforts to escape from Poland, their betrayal at the Hungarian border, and their separation at Auschwitz. Volume II is a commingling of his parents' story with his own.

A breakthrough in the format of graphic narrative, ***Maus*** was a finalist for the National Book Critics Circle Award in Biography/Autobiography and was a winner of the Pulitzer Prize Special Awards and Citations—Letters.

Subjects: Auschwitz (Concentration Camp); Children of Holocaust Survivors; Death of a Parent; Fathers and Sons; Graphic Narratives; Holocaust, Jewish (1939–1945); Holocaust Survivors; Illustrators; Poland; Spiegelman, Vladek

Now Try: Spiegelman was so affected by the September 11 attacks on New York in 2001 that he felt compelled to create another graphic narrative, ***In the Shadow of No Towers***. Leslie Gilbert-Lurie had problems as the child of a Holocaust survivor. She finally realized that her mother, Rita Lurie, had passed on her own fears to her daughter, almost like an "unwanted gene." She discusses this in her memoir, written with her mother, ***Bending Toward the Sun: A Mother and Daughter Memoir***. Remarkable as it may seem, there are several stories of Jewish couples reuniting after the war. In the case of Jack and Rochelle Sutin, however, they both met again during the war after each had separately escaped. In ***Jack and Rochelle: A Holocaust Story of Love and Resistance***, their son Lawrence tells their story of fighting back from their place in the woods after they escaped. Spiegelman's life as the child of Holocaust survivors was difficult for him, not knowing what it could have been like for his parents and not feeling justified in complaining about anything in his own life. This is not unusual among the children of Holocaust survivors. Eva Hoffman has studied this phenomenon and written her findings in ***After Such Knowledge: Memory, History, and the Legacy of the Holocaust***.

Szpilman, Władysław (1911–2000)

The Pianist: The Extraordinary Story of One Man's Survival in Warsaw, 1939–45. Foreword by Andrzej Szpilman. Epilogue by Wolf Biermann. With Diary Extracts of Wilm Hosenfeld. Picador, 2003, 1999. 222pp. ill. 9780312311353. Also available in Braille, large print, audiobook, and video. 940.5318092 [Trans. by Anthea Bell]

When Szpilman and his family were rounded up by the Nazis in Warsaw, a German soldier who recognized Władysław as the well-known pianist and composer that he was pushed him off the transport, saving his life while taking his family to their deaths. Szpilman left the Ghetto and managed to survive the remainder of the war in the Aryan sector of Warsaw through his wits and by hiding, growing increasingly hungry and thin. A German officer, Wilm Hosenfeld, discovered him in hiding and saved his life by bringing him food and a quilt. Some of Hosenfeld's diary entries are excerpted in this volume; they speak to his horror about what his fellow Germans had done. Hosenfeld himself died in a Soviet labor camp several years later. After the war ended, Szpilman wrote his book, but it was immediately squelched by Stalin. When Szpilman's son found the publication in his father's bookcase, he had it published in Germany.

Subjects: Holocaust, Jewish (1939–1945); Hosenfeld, Wilm; Jewish Men; Jewish Musicians; Octogenarians; Pianists, Poland; Translations; Warsaw Ghetto; World War II (1939–1945)

Now Try: Shirli Gilbert offers an overview of the role of music during the war for the Jewish communities in ***Music in the Holocaust: Confronting Life in the Nazi Ghettos and Camps***. A Ukrainian Jewish pianist, Zhanna (Arshansky) Dawson and her sister Frina (Arshansky) Boldt, saved themselves by changing their identity and performing for the Nazis. They eventually moved to the United States where Zhanna married the violist David Dawson; their son, Greg, has told his mother's story, ***Hiding in the Spotlight: A Musical Prodigy's Story of Survival, 1941–1946***. As honorable as Wilm Hosenfeld was, he fortunately was not the only Nazi who helped Jews. Michael Good's mother claims that the only reason she survived the Vilna work camp in Lithuania was because of the commander of the camp. Good recounts his research on this man in ***The Search for Major Plagge: The Nazi Who Saved Jews***. Both Karl Plagge and Wilm Hosenfeld are counted among Israel's "Righteous Among the Nations."

Oppression

Through no deliberate design, all the authors in this section are women. With some exceptions they come from China and from the Middle East and surrounding countries (Egypt and Afghanistan). The two exceptions are an American situated in Guatemala and an American situated in the United States, who relates her experiences with those (largely men) oppressed by her government. The women from Afghanistan, Egypt, Iran, and Yemen all have different stories to tell, some more torturous than others. Most tell of life in a country that has veiled its women, literally and figuratively, virtually placing them under house arrest. Some tell of speaking out and being imprisoned for it. For all of them, writing their stories is a declaration of independence, a public unveiling of their lives and those around them. It must not be forgotten that in telling their own stories, these women are also telling the stories of family and friends.

Writing their stories is also a testament to the education and the literacy of these women. They had been given an education, growing up initially in lands that fostered such a culture. But rulers change, and in reading these stories, readers should recognize that the oppression generally comes from the governing body, and that the citizens of the country should not be vilified for what their rulers have done. The fact of writing their stories attests to the writers' own regret that the countries they knew, rich in tradition and culture, were being destroyed at the hands of a rabid and influential few.

The Iranian and Afghan women come from a long line of oppression and disappointment. The Iranians first suffered under the regime of the Shah, and many of them supported, actively or philosophically, the revolution that overthrew the Shah. Much to their horror, however, what ensued proved to be even worse than what had gone before. The Afghans suffered from the invasion of the Soviets, fighting for the victory of the mujahideen over the Soviet invaders. When the mujahideen did succeed in pushing out the Soviets, life was chaotic for the Afghans and still violent, but nonetheless better, and women were able to make progress in their social evolution and education. Then came the Taliban, and life was worse than ever, with the Afghan women in much the same situation as the Iranian women, all victims of Islamic fundamentalism. Both Nujood Ali from Yemen and Nawāl Sa'dāwī from Egypt, separated in age by over sixty years, had to deal with child marriage, although Sa'dāwī's family was sufficiently well-off and sufficiently progressive to allow her to fight it. Ali fought it after the fact.

The Chinese women also had a long line of political regimes and policies to deal with, from the battle to create the People's Republic of China under Communist rule, to the political instability and massive famine in the 1950s, to the Cultural Revolution, to the one-child policy. The women in this section all participated in the Cultural Revolution, both confirming each other's stories and adding new elements.

The salient point of these stories is that all of these women have succeeded in "affirming their own sense of identity and political and religious beliefs against notions of authority that are overwhelmingly male dominated" (Hamouda, 2005).

> Stories of oppression are also stories of rebellion and revolution as the memoirists reveal their lives in repressive cultures and describe what they did to extricate themselves from the situation. These are narrative stories, but they often include historical accounts of what the writers' countries were like before oppression became the norm.

Ali, Nujood (1998–)
Minoui, Delphine (1974–), coauthor

I Am Nujood, Age 10 and Divorced. Three Rivers Press, 2010. 188pp. 9780307589675. Also available in e-audiobook and e-book. 306.8723 [Trans. by Linda Coverdale]

Unwilling to accept her situation as a child bride, separated from her family who had sold her, abused by her mother-in-law during the day and by her much-older husband during the night, Nujood hoarded bread money and, when she was in the city visiting her family, took the bus to the courthouse, where she knocked on the door and asked for a divorce. Her husband had promised not to consummate the marriage until Nujood had reached puberty, but he broke that promise on their wedding night. Her father had also broken the law by marrying her off before she was fifteen, but Nujood still faced cultural battles in achieving her goal. She was directed to good and helpful people, with one lawyer in particular taking up her case, so that finally she was granted a divorce.

Subjects: Abuse (Spousal); Arab Women; Child Marriage; Courage; Divorce; Forced Marriage; Poverty, Yemen; Social Conditions, Yemen; Translations; Yemen

Now Try: Readers may think that forced child marriages occur only elsewhere, but in fact Warren Jeffs of the Fundamentalist Church of Jesus Christ of Latter Day Saints has been convicted in Utah of being an accomplice to rape for insisting on the marriage of fourteen-year-old Elissa Wall (see p. 538). Stephen Singular recounts the story of Jeffs in ***When Men Become Gods: Mormon Polygamist Warren Jeffs, His Cult of Fear, and the Women Who Fought Back***. Nujood's story is remarkable for her courage and conviction, at such a young age, compelling her to do something to improve her own situation. Eve Ensler encourages girls and women around the world to recognize their own self-worth and realize their dreams in her book, ***I Am an Emotional Creature: The Secret Life of Girls Around the World***. Mukhtar Mai also took responsibility for her own future when, instead of committing suicide as was expected of her, she defied custom by instead pressing charges against men who had gang-raped her because her twelve-year-old brother had purportedly seduced an older woman. She told her story, ***In the Name of Honor: A Memoir***, with the help of Marie-Thérèse Cuny (translated from the French by Linda Coverdale).

Bin Ladin, Carmen (1954–)
Marshall, Ruth (1961–), coauthor

Inside the Kingdom: My Life in Saudi Arabia. Warner Books, 2005, 2004. 214pp. ill. 16pp. of plates. 9780446694889. Also available in large print, audiobook, and e-audiobook. 305.42092

Carmen Dufour met her future husband, Yeslam bin Ladin, in Switzerland, where she lived; she enjoyed her life with him when they lived in the Western world, but after they moved to Saudi Arabia, into the Bin Laden compound, Carmen's life changed drastically, as she lost her independence and her voice. Initially she made great efforts to understand her husband's culture and to abide by all the rules, particularly since he was sympathetic and still loved her. Gradually, however, as Islamic fundamentalism grew throughout the Middle East, so too did it start to take hold in the Bin Laden household, and Yeslam became increasingly reactionary. When she was visiting her family in Switzerland, he separated from Carmen, accusing her of adultery, thus signing her death warrant: if she were to step onto Muslim soil anywhere, she could be extradited to Saudi Arabia for execution. Living in Switzerland with her three daughters, she continued to fight for her freedom and was finally granted a divorce in 2006.

Subjects: Bin Laden Family; Bin Ladin, Yeslam; Interracial Marriage; Islam; Saudi Arabia; Wahhabis (Islam); Women in Saudi Arabia

Now Try: If you'd like to read more about the family that Carmen married into, you might find of interest Steve Coll's ***The Bin Ladens: An Arabian Family in the American Century***. Jean P. Sasson has written several books about the life of women—particularly royal women—in Saudi Arabia. Her first, at the behest of an Arabian princess, was ***Princess: A True Story of Life Behind the Veil in Saudi Arabia***. Coincidentally sharing the same book title as Carmen bin Ladin, Robert Lacey offers insights into today's Saudi Arabia in ***Inside the Kingdom: Kings, Clerics, Modernists, Terrorists, and the Struggle for Saudi Arabia***. Readers will have heard of Betty Mahmoody's ordeal in Iran, when her Iranian husband would not allow her to leave with her daughter; she tells her story with the help of William Hoffer in ***Not Without My Daughter***, a book that was made into a movie with the same name.

Chang, Jung (1952–)

Wild Swans: Three Daughters of China. Touchstone, 2003, 1991. 524pp. ill. 16pp. of plates. 9780743246969. Also available in Braille, audiobook, e-book, and video. 951.05092

This story of three women—grandmother, mother, and author—encapsulates Chinese history over the twentieth century. Jung Chang traces her grandmother Yu-fang's history, from her bound feet at the age of two to her being given away as a concubine to a local warlord. She became pregnant with Jung Chang's mother, Bao Qin, but after escaping from her husband, told him that their daughter had died. Bao Qin became a revolutionary and married a Communist official. When she gave birth to Jung Chang, she was initially accorded privileges because of her parents' standing. With the onset of the Cultural Revolution, however, their status changed, and Jung Chang was sent out to the countryside, untrained, commanded to work first as a doctor and then as an electrician. Things eventually started to shift, and the book ends in 1978 when Jung Chang is sent to England to study.

Wild Swans was awarded the British Book Awards Book of the Year.

Subjects: China; Communism; Cultural Revolution, China (1966–1976); Family Portraits; Grandmothers; Intergenerational Relationships; Mao Zedong; Mothers and Daughters; Social History, China; Women in China

Now Try: Yang Erche Namu had a very different upbringing from Chang's, largely because of where she grew up, in a matrilineal society among the Mosuo in southwestern China, almost in Tibet. Now a pop singer, she has written a memoir of her childhood, with the help of Christine Mathieu, ***Leaving Mother Lake: A Girlhood at the Edge of the World***. Helen Tse also tells the story of three generations of women, depicting their travails over a number of decades and political regimes, ending in Manchester, England, and all revolving around

Chinese cooking. ***Sweet Mandarin: The Courageous True Story of Three Generations of Chinese Women and Their Journey from East to West*** relates the story of the restaurant, Sweet Mandarin, by telling the story of the three women. The famine that Chang and her family suffered through was responsible for more deaths than those caused by Stalin and the Holocaust combined, due in large part to Mao's grandiose scheme to become a world leader in the production of steel. Jasper Becker studied this travesty in governance and published the results in ***Hungry Ghosts: Mao's Secret Famine***.

'Ibādī, Shīrīn (1947–)
Moaveni, Azadeh (1976–), coauthor

Iran Awakening: A Memoir of Revolution and Hope. Random House, 2006. 232pp. ill. map. 9781400064700. Also available in e-book. 323.34092

Shīrīn 'Ibādī happily answered the call of the Ayatollah Khomeini when from exile he exhorted his followers to eject the sitting ministers in Iran from their government offices. She believed in the revolution against the Shah, but within a year of the revolution she was forced to change her mind. A judge before the revolution, afterward she was demoted first to clerk and then to secretary in the court where she used to rule; women were suddenly reduced to the level of chattel with no rights. She decided to stay in Iran and fight for her own rights as well as those of other women and children in Iran, was occasionally imprisoned for her efforts, and was eventually awarded the Nobel Peace Prize. Once Iran realized that in fact the country did need women lawyers, 'Ibādī began to take on the most challenging cases, usually trying to find solutions within Koranic law, as she recognized that as the most realistic way to accomplish her goals. One of the ironies in her story is that she had to sue the U.S. Department of the Treasury to have her book published in the United States, because of a prohibition against writers from embargoed countries.

Subjects: Courage; Iran; Iran Revolution (1979–1997); Khomeini, Ayatollah; Lawyers; Nobel Prize Laureates; Social Conditions, Iran; Women in Iran; Women's Rights Activists

Now Try: Depending on the family situation and individual personalities, women's reactions to their plight in Iran can differ widely. 'Ibādī takes umbrage at the people who fled Iran rather than stay and fight, but novelist Nahid Rachlin explains why she left in ***Persian Girls: A Memoir***. Hālāh Isfandiyārī also left and became a professor at Princeton, but she often traveled back to Iran; she has published an accessible study, ***Reconstructed Lives: Women and Iran's Islamic Revolution***. For a look at a different Iran in the first half of the twentieth century, readers may enjoy ***A Mirror Garden: A Memoir*** by Monir Shahroudy Farmanfarmaian, written with the help of Zara Houshmand.

Khan, Mahvish Rukhsana

My Guantánamo Diary: The Detainees and the Stories They Told Me. Public Affairs, 2008. 302pp. ill. 9781586484989. Also available in audiobook and e-book. 973.931

Born in the United States of Afghan parents, Mahvish Khan grew up speaking Pashto, her parents' language. She was able to use that knowledge to offer her services as a translator for lawyers working for detainees in Guantánamo. She was shocked beyond her wildest imaginings at what she saw as flagrant contraventions of the American Constitution, a Constitution she knew as a law student and respected as an American citizen. Her memoir goes back and forth between her own experiences as a translator (and later, supervised legal counsel) at Guantánamo and the experiences of the inmates there, many of whom were there simply at the whim of those back home who were looking to share in the U.S. bounty offered for terrorists. Not denying that there are real terrorists at Guantánamo, Khan nonetheless insists on their right to a fair trial and works tirelessly to that end.

Subjects: Afghan War (2001–); Guantánamo Bay Detention Camp, Cuba; Human Rights Activists; Prisoners of War, United States; Prisons, United States; Translators; War on Terrorism (2001–)

Now Try: Murat Kurnaz, a Turkish citizen and legal resident of Germany, was one of the men detained at Guantánamo; after much public outcry at his arrest and detention (including by Amnesty International), he was finally released. He tells his story with the help of Helmut Kuhn, translated from the German by Jefferson Chase in ***Five Years of My Life: An Innocent Man in Guantanamo***. Jane Mayer looks at the erosion of civil rights and how it was enabled in the Bush administration by the war on terrorism in ***Dark Side: The Inside Story of How the War on Terror Turned into a War on American Ideals***. Omar Khadr was fifteen when he was shot and captured in Afghanistan in 2002; his father had known contact with al-Qaeda, but the fact of Khadr's youth and his Canadian citizenship have made him a *cause célèbre*. *Toronto Star* reporter Michelle Shephard has looked closely at his case and after extensively interviewing people involved in his story, has published ***Guantanamo's Child: The Untold Story of Omar Khadr***.

Latifa (1980–)
Hachemi, Shékéba, coauthor

My Forbidden Face: Growing Up Under the Taliban; A Young Woman's Story. Preface by Karenna Gore Schiff. Talk Miramax Books, 2003, 2001. 210pp. map. 9781401359256. Also available in large print, audiobook, and e-book. 305.4209581 [Trans. by Linda Coverdale]

Pseudonymous Latifa was sixteen, planning to attend a wedding the next day and looking forward to her university studies in journalism, when her brother ran home to announce that the Taliban's white flag was flying over his school. Overnight their world changed; her mother, a doctor, was no longer allowed to practice medicine. Since females were forbidden health care by male doctors, this effectively meant no health care for women. Women were forbidden to go outside without a male relative and without wearing at least a *chador*, a veil to cover hair, face, and arms. Secular schools were closed and boys allowed to attend religious schools only; girls were banned from attending these schools. Taking to her bed for weeks at this disastrous news, Latifa finally got up, helped her mother tend patients secretly at home as long as she could and as long as her meager supplies lasted, and then started a clandestine school (with no supplies) at home for those who wanted to continue to learn. For five years Latifa stayed in seclusion, writing in a diary, much like Anne Frank, until she and her family were rescued by an Afghan resistance group and sent to Paris.

Subjects: Afghanistan; Afghanistan Civil War (1979–); Courage; Islamic Fundamentalism; Social Conditions, Afghanistan; Taliban; Translations; Women in Afghanistan; Women's Rights Activists

Now Try: Deborah Ellis had originally written children's novels to introduce Canadian children to the plight of girls in Afghanistan. She finally turned her attention to an adult audience with the publication of her interviews with women sequestered in their homes or in refugee camps, ***Women of the Afghan War***. Harriet Logan did much the same but also took her camera along, creating an affecting collage of women's stories and photographs in ***Unveiled: Voices of Women of Afghanistan***. Lest readers think that the women of Afghanistan are passively accepting their plight, Cheryl Benard and Edit Schlaffer have written ***Veiled Courage: Inside the Afghan Women's Resistance***, a look at RAWA, the Revolutionary Association of the Women of Afghan (http://www.rawa.org/rawa.html).

Min, Anchee (1957–)

Red Azalea. Anchor Books, 2006. 306pp. 9781400096985. Also available in audiobook and e-book. 951.05092

A proper member and leader of the Little Red Guards, Anchee Min was urged to denounce her teacher as a reactionary; her reward was to be sent to a peasant farm, as peasants were regarded to be the most favored among society during the Cultural Revolution. The workload and working conditions belied that, however, as Min found the work grueling and most of her freedoms curtailed, including communication with the opposite sex. She was chosen, finally, to participate in a political film based on Madame Mao's opera, *Red Azalea*, wherein the director put her into the starring role and began an affair with her. When Chairman Mao died, Min's fortunes changed again; the director went into hiding and Min became a lowly peon at the theater. She eventually escaped China with the help of an actress who had already moved to the United States. After adjusting to immigrant life, working in several different jobs, Min was able to complete a master's of fine arts degree in Chicago. She then turned to writing, penning this memoir first and subsequently several novels.

Red Azalea won the Carl Sandburg Literary Award.

Subjects: China; Communism; Cultural Revolution, China (1966–1976); Mao Zedong; Red Guard; Social History, China; Women in China; Writers

Now Try: Depicting very clearly how youth can become caught up in the rhetoric of the day is Yuan Gao's story of his time as a Red Guard, ***Born Red: A Chronicle of the Cultural Revolution***. Even more damning is Bo Ma's pseudonymous work, a story (translated from the Chinese by Howard Goldblatt) that forced the Chinese to face up to what the Cultural Revolution really was, ***Blood Red Sunset: A Memoir of the Chinese Cultural Revolution***. Emily Yimao Wu begins her story at a younger age than Anchee Min. She was three when she first met her father in a concentration camp in China; in ***Feather in the Storm: A Childhood Lost in Chaos***, written with the help of Larry Engelmann, Wu describes how punishing life was for the family members of an enemy of the state, as her father was labeled.

Nafisi, Azar (1955–)

Reading Lolita in Tehran: A Memoir in Books. Random House, 2008, 2003. 380pp. 9780812979305. Also available in large print, Braille, audiobook, and e-audiobook. 820.9

Finally tired of all the battles she was fighting as a professor of literature at the University of Tehran, Nafisi resigned and then invited seven young women (former students) to form a book club of sorts at her home on Thursday mornings. They would enter in their black burqas, which, once shed, revealed their colorful outfits. Her memoir of these two years is divided by the major books and authors they discussed, weaving the stories of the books into their own lives against the backdrop of a repressive regime. As the women got to know each other and became more comfortable within the group, they began to share their own personal stories. Readers should be aware that there is much discussion of the actual books in this memoir, but Nafisi also does something unusual: she puts F. Scott Fitzgerald's ***The Great Gatsby*** on trial, as one of her students had labeled it immoral. Nafisi moved to the United States two years after beginning her book club in Tehran; after her success with her first memoir, she has written a more personal memoir of her childhood and family in Iran, ***Things I've Been Silent About: Memories***.

Reading Lolita in Tehran was a finalist for the PEN American Center Martha Albrand Award for the Art of the Memoir and was the Book Sense Book of the Year Adult Nonfiction winner.

Subjects: Book Sense Book of the Year Adult Nonfiction Winner; Books and Reading; College Professors, Iran; English Literature; Iran; Iran Revolution (1979–1997); Muslims, Iran; Self-Discovery; Social Conditions, Iran; Women in Iran

Now Try: Fatemeh Keshavarz, a professor of Persian and comparative literatures in Missouri, has chosen to refute the picture Nafisi has painted of Iran, suggesting that it smacks of New Orientalism. To counteract Nafisi's book she has written her own, highlighting Iranian and Persian writers and including some of her own story: ***Jasmine and Stars: Reading More Than "Lolita" in Tehran***. Christopher de Bellaigue has lived for several years in Tehran, filing stories from there. In a collection of his journalistic articles, ***The Struggle for Iran***, he offers a dispassionate view of postrevolutionary Iran. The link between reading and life is drawn in an entirely different way by Elizabeth D. Samet, an English professor at West Point, as she describes in ***Soldier's Heart: Reading Literature Through Peace and War at West Point***.

Ortiz, Dianna
Davis, Patricia, coauthor

The Blindfold's Eyes: My Journey from Torture to Truth. Orbis Books, 2004, 2002. 484pp. ill. 8pp. of plates. 9781570755637. 272.9092

In 1989, when she was a young nun teaching poor Guatemalan children in the local convent garden, Dianna Ortiz was grabbed by an army captain, a police intelligence officer, and a team of torturers, taken to a secret basement in the police training institute, and tortured for twenty-four hours. She had often received threats, but that was not unusual for religious workers in Guatemala: threats were regularly made against groups the Guatemalan government feared for their activism, and random people were regularly grabbed for torture as a way of instilling fear in others. The fact that she was tortured (burned with cigarettes; gang raped; and forced to use a machete on a dying woman, thereby killing her) for twenty-four hours only was due to the arrival of an American who had heard about her abduction on the news and berated her torturers for grabbing the wrong person. Most of her story deals with her efforts to heal (she lost all memory of her life up to the abduction) and to seek retribution against both the Guatemalan government for its sanctioning of torture and the American government for its cover-up of and complicity in her torture.

Subjects: Catholics; Guatemala; Guatemala Civil War (1960–1996); Human Rights Activists; Nuns; Rape; Social Conditions, Guatemala; Spirituality; Survivors of Rape; Torture; Victims of Violence; Violence

Now Try: The human rights worker Daniel Wilkinson, in investigating arson on a coffee plantation in Guatemala, found he needed to dig deeper to carry on his investigation; managing to get the normally silent Guatemalans to talk to him, he discovered a tradition of terror instilled in the Guatemalans by their American-backed government. The result is his book ***Silence on the Mountain: Stories of Terror, Betrayal, and Forgetting in Guatemala***. Backing up Ortiz's claim of U.S. involvement in Guatemalan torture is Jennifer Harbury's study, ***Truth, Torture, and the American Way: The History and Consequences of U.S. Involvement in Torture***. Dorothy Stang was also a Catholic nun, who made her way to Brazil and found herself working to better the way of life for the peasants she found there. The story of her life and murder, ***The Greatest Gift: The Courageous Life and Death of Sister Dorothy Stang***, has been told by the journalist Binka Le Breton.

Sa'dāwī, Nawāl (1931–)

A Daughter of Isis: The Autobiography of Nawal El Saadawi. Zed Books, 1999. 294pp. 9781856496797. Also available in e-book. 892.736 [Trans. by Sherif Hetata]

Written from the perspective of her sixty-plus years and her locale of North Carolina in exile (her name was on a death list published by Islamic fundamentalists in Egypt), Sa'dāwī offers a look at the rural world she was born into in Egypt, along with her lifelong fight for women's rights. Though she was given an education, her accomplishments were never acknowledged. In her autobiography she focuses largely on the females in her life. She recognizes and regrets the set roles they have, yet her emotional comforts came from them and the food and warmth they provided. They were also responsible, however, for her brutal circumcision at the age of six, which is graphically described. Throughout her narrative Sa'dāwī sets the stage for what may be a second volume to her life story. She points out the gender inequities as well as the class differences and the urban/rural differences in Egypt. She takes the reader up to her medical training and first position as a doctor in a rural Egyptian village but only alludes to her imprisonment, her writings, her activist work, and her exile.

Subjects: Arab Women; Classics; Egypt; Exiles; Female Circumcision; Feminists; Mothers and Daughters; Physicians, Egypt; Social History, Egypt; Translations; Women in Egypt; Women's Rights Activists; Writers, Egypt

Now Try: An earlier Egyptian feminist was Hudá Sha'rāwī, born into a harem, married at thirteen, and then divorced, which enabled her to get an education and write about the liberation of women. A leader in ending the harem system, she wrote her autobiography, ***Harem Years: The Memoirs of an Egyptian Feminist (1879–1924)***, translated from the Arabic and edited by Margot Badran. A well-thought-of autobiographical novel is Ahdaf Soueif's, ***In the Eye of the Sun***, which highlights Gamal Abdel Nasser's regime in Egypt and all the political troubles that occurred during his time, viewed from the distance of England. Bringing the state of Muslim women to today's world is Fawzia Afzal-Khan's collection of writings by a number of Muslim women, ***Shattering the Stereotypes: Muslim Women Speak Out***.

Satrapi, Marjane (1969–)

The Complete Persepolis. Pantheon Books, 2007. 341pp. ill. 9780375714832. Also available in e-book and video. 955.0542092 [Trans. by Mattias Ripa, Blake Ferris, and Anjali Singh]

This volume combines Satrapi's two award-winning graphic-narrative memoirs. The first, ***Persepolis***, describes her life as an only child in Iran with loving, Marxist parents; the fall of the Shah; the beginning of the Islamic Revolution; and the war with Iraq. The changes in their lives are clear to see. The first volume takes her to the age of fourteen, when her parents send her to Vienna to live: Marjane cannot keep her political views to herself and is in danger. The second volume, ***Persepolis 2: The Story of a Return***, depicts her unhappy life in Vienna and her eventual return home to Iran. Things are no better there, and Marjane falls into a depression. She sees that the revolutionary spirit has died and people just go on with their repressed lives—except for the partying, which her friends and family continue to do behind curtains. Throughout both volumes we see Marjane's coming of age, her relationships with others, and her growth as a woman and as a person. The second volume ends with her leaving Iran once again, this time for Strasbourg, France, to study illustration.

Subjects: Adolescence; Childhood and Youth; Coming of Age; Family Relationships; Graphic Narratives; Illustrators; Iran; Iran Revolution (1979–1997); Muslims, Iran; Social Conditions, Iran; Translations; Vienna, Austria

Now Try: Iran has changed greatly since Ayatollah Khomeini's death, a change that Robin B. Wright investigates in ***The Last Great Revolution: Turmoil and Transformation in Iran***. The graphic narrative has been used to great effect to tell serious stories. Joe Sacco looks at the Israeli–Palestinian conflict through the eyes of many of the participants in his graphic narrative, ***Palestine: The Special Edition***. In her novel ***The Septembers of Shiraz***, Dalia Sofer describes the life of a Jewish family in Tehran after the father is imprisoned during the Islamic Revolution.

Yang, Rae (1950–)

Spider Eaters: A Memoir. University of California Press, 1998, 1997. 285pp. ill. 9780520215986. Also available in e-book. 951.05092

Blame for the Cultural Revolution is usually directed at Chairman Mao. While he was responsible for inspiring it, he had millions to carry out his wishes/commands. This is made quite clear in Yang's memoir of her life as a Red Guard, one of the thousands of youth caught up in the propaganda. Yang's early years were spent in Switzerland, as her father was a diplomat, but she was raised as a member of the Communist Party and a Maoist revolutionary. Back in Beijing she attended an elite school and then became a Red Guard. She is unflinchingly honest in her description of her behavior as a victimizer, as she and her colleagues enthusiastically set out to do Mao's bidding, destroying lives on what at times appeared to be a mere whim. Caught up in Mao's rhetoric, she happily volunteered to work on a pig farm, where she soon became the victim. Disillusioned with the Cultural Revolution, she eventually made her way back home to her parents and on to the United States for higher education. Throughout her narrative, Yang also reveals her relationship with her family—particularly her grandmother and her nanny—and intertwines folklore learned at her nanny's knee into her story.

Subjects: Beijing, China; China; Communism; Cultural Revolution, China (1966–1976); Family Relationships; Grandmothers; Mao Zedong; Red Guard; Social History, China; Upper Class, China; Women in China

Now Try: As illustrated in Chen Chen's memoir, ***Come Watch the Sun Go Home***, the Chinese have suffered through more than Mao's Cultural Revolution; Chen Chen's trials began when she was a baby and her family fled the Second Sino-Japanese War, returning in the 1950s, only to suffer again under Mao. Weili Ye and Xiaodong Ma engage in a dialogue about their experiences in the Cultural Revolution in ***Growing Up in the People's Republic: Conversations Between Two Daughters of China's***

Revolution. For a change of pace readers may enjoy a collection of short stories by Yiyun Li, ***A Thousand Years of Good Prayers: Stories***, which encompasses a wide range of people, situations, and emotions in both China and the United States.

Zoya (c. 1978–)
Follain, John, and Rita Cristofari, coauthors

Zoya's Story: An Afghan Woman's Struggle for Freedom. Perennial, 2003, 2001. 239pp. 9780060097837. Also available in large print and audiobook. 958.1046.

Zoya learned when she was about eight that her mother was a member of the Revolutionary Association of the Women of Afghanistan (http://www.rawa.org/rawa.html). This explained why Zoya was raised more by Nabila, a woman she called Grandmother, than by her mother, but rather than feel neglected, Zoya wanted to work with her mother. Women in Afghanistan had suffered through the reigns of the mullahs, the Soviets, the mujahideens, and then the Taliban, but they were always fighting for each other, to improve the plight of women in Afghanistan. After her parents were killed by the mujahideen, Zoya and Grandmother were spirited out of Afghanistan by the RAWA to Pakistan, where Zoya was able to attend school. By the time the Taliban had taken over, Zoya was working for RAWA in refugee camps in Pakistan and speaking abroad to raise awareness about the lack of women's rights in Afghanistan.

Subjects: Afghanistan; Afghanistan Civil War (1979–); Courage; Death of a Parent; Exiles; Mothers and Daughters; Revolutionary Association of the Women of Afghanistan; Taliban; Women in Afghanistan; Women's Rights Activists

Now Try: Åsne Seierstad received permission to stay at the home of Sultan Khan, a bookseller in Kabul, as he appeared to her to be quite liberated and she wanted to write his story. Reading her subsequent tale, ***The Bookseller of Kabul***, translated from the Norwegian by Ingrid Christophersen, reveals, however, that while Khan may have been liberated, the women in his home were anything but. Several women who have been fighting for women's rights for over thirty years in Afghanistan have shared their stories with Sunita Mehta in the collection ***Women for Afghan Women: Shattering Myths and Claiming the Future***. Another positive note is provided by Awista Ayub, whose ***However Tall the Mountain: A Dream, Eight Girls, and a Journey Home*** tells about the Afghan girls she brought to the United States to learn soccer, and describes the courage and self-confidence they also learned through the experience.

Captivity

This section is not so far removed from the one preceding it in that many of the people here also suffered under oppressive regimes. In addition to governmental oppression, however, there is oppression by the criminal element, and we have that here as well. It is the criminal element that is responsible for the stories of slavery found in this section. Whether to do the work that a slave master doesn't want to pay for or to fill brothels, slavery has been with us for centuries and shows no signs of diminishing. This section features three stories of modern-day slavery, which may provide a learning experience for some readers. Other writers have been captured by their governments and imprisoned or by special-interest groups and taken hostage. One distressing story involves a woman imprisoned when seeking asylum; another woman seeks asylum when she realizes the dangers of the cult she has joined. The stories of how they escaped or were released are as gripping as the stories of their capture.

The stories of captivity here do not include traditional slave narratives, but they do include stories of modern-day slavery and escape. These stories are all told by writers who have endured one sort of captivity or another, at the hands of an oppressive government or at the hands of the criminal element.

Bok, Francis (1979–)
Tivnan, Edward, coauthor

Escape from Slavery: The True Story of My Ten Years in Captivity—and My Journey to Freedom in America. St. Martin's Griffin, 2004, 2003. 284pp. ill. map. 9780312306243. 305.567092

It has been a centuries-long habit of Arabs in northern Sudan to take Black slaves from southern Sudan, which is what happened to seven-year-old Francis Bok when he went to the local market for the first time to sell his mother's eggs and peanuts. Sold to a well-to-do Muslim, he was treated as an animal to tend the "other" animals, a life he lived for ten years. His third attempt at escape proved to be successful, although not without setbacks, including a stint in prison for saying in a refugee camp that he had been a slave—his crime here was for speaking against his government. He was finally granted refugee status and allowed to travel to the United States, where he currently works for the abolition of slavery and for the resolution of conflict between northern and southern Sudan.

Escape from Slavery won the Books for a Better Life/Suze Orman First Book Award.

Subjects: Antislavery Movements; Captivity; Refugees, Sudan; Slavery, Sudan; Social History, Sudan; Sudan; Sudan Civil War (1983–2005); Sudanese-Americans

Now Try: Most North Americans would be shocked to hear the statistics about modern-day slavery. E. Benjamin Skinner has spent four years of his journalistic career investigating this crime and states in ***A Crime So Monstrous: Face-to-Face with Modern-Day Slavery*** that there are more slaves today than there have ever been in history. Kevin Bales has also made it his mission to study modern-day slavery and offers his views on how it can be brought to an end in ***Ending Slavery: How We Free Today's Slaves.*** Bok's story is a harrowing one; Uwem Akpan is a Nigerian who has written a collection of harrowing stories about the plight of children in his country, ***Say You're One of Them***.

Burnham, Gracia (1959–)
Merrill, Dean (1943–), coauthor

In the Presence of My Enemies. Tyndale House, 2010, 2003. 334pp. ill. 9780842381390. Also available in large print, audiobook, and e-audiobook. 959.9048092273

Martin and Gracia Burnham had spent seventeen years in the Philippines, he as a missionary pilot and she as his assistant. Taking time off to celebrate their eighteenth wedding anniversary at a resort, they happened to be in the wrong place at the wrong time, as they and several others from the resort were kidnapped by the terrorist group Abu Sayyaf, known to have ties with al-Qaeda. Taken to the jungle and often moved about, many of the hostages either escaped, were let go, or were killed. Finally the terrorists were located, and a firefight ensued. Both Martin and a nurse were killed in the crossfire, and Gracia was wounded. In her memoir she talks about Stockholm syndrome and also describes with real honesty her weakening faith at times, her un-Christian reactions to and thoughts about their captors. She gives her husband credit for bolstering her faith.

In the Presence of My Enemies won the ECPA/Christian Book Award for Biography/Autobiography.

Subjects: Abu Sayyaf (Terrorist Group); Burnham, Martin; Captivity; Christians; Hostages, Philippines; Martin & Gracia Burnham Foundation; Missionaries; Philippines; Terrorism; Victims of Violence; Violence

Now Try: Greg Williams has the dubious distinction of being the first American missionary to have been captured by Abu Sayyaf, a nightmare he recounts in ***13 Days of Terror: Held Hostage by al Qaeda Linked Extremists—a True Story***. A classic story of kidnapping and hostage taking is that of Terry Waite, who had successfully negotiated for the release of hostages in the Middle East and was then himself captured and held hostage for almost five years, a story told in ***Taken on Trust***. He credits his faith with getting him through the ordeal. Sometimes people are aware that given their jobs or their locale, they are in danger of political abduction. But sometimes the abduction comes unexpectedly, as it did for Abdulrahman Zeitoun, a Syrian-American who was helping victims of Hurricane Katrina in New Orleans when he found himself captured without redress by military personnel and held for a month before he could contact his family. Dave Eggers has captured his story in the award-winning ***Zeitoun***.

Curry, Dayna (1971–), and Heather Mercer (c. 1977–)
Mattingly, Stacy, coauthor

Prisoners of Hope: The Story of Our Captivity and Freedom in Afghanistan. Waterbrook Press, 2003, 2002. 309pp. ill. 8pp. of plates. 9781578566464. Also available in large print, audiobook, and e-book. 266.0092273

Two women left their home in America to work in Afghanistan with Shelter Now International (since renamed Shelter for Life International), a relief organization that seeks to help the poorest of Afghanistan's people. Both women are devout Christians and were prepared to talk about Christ but not to proselytize. They knew that the Taliban had outlawed any religion other than Islam to be discussed, and they also knew that any Afghan who chose to convert to Christianity would be severely punished. One day they were heard discussing their religion with Afghans and were arrested and imprisoned for their crime. They state in their memoir that the Taliban never mistreated them, and they credit that, ironically, to their religion. They did live in fear for their lives, however, which created a personal spiritual crisis for Heather. During their trial the events of September 11, 2001 took place, complicating their situation and diminishing hope for them. Eventually, though, they were rescued by U.S. Special Forces.

Subjects: Afghanistan; Captivity; Christians; Missionaries; Political Prisoners, Afghanistan; Prisons, Afghanistan; Spirituality; Taliban

Now Try: Ana Tortajada, a Spanish journalist, has also seen what Dayna and Heather have seen in the very difficult lives of the Afghan people, particularly the women. Inspired by a lecture given by a member of the Revolutionary Association of the Women of Afghanistan (RAWA), she journeyed to Afghanistan, writing her story afterward: ***The Silenced Cry: One Woman's Diary of a Journey to Afghanistan***, translated from the Spanish by Ezra E. Fitz. Micah Garen was a journalist working on a documentary with his fiancée, Marie-Hélène Carleton, and their Iraqi translator, Amir Doshi, about the looting of Iraq's archaeological sites. Marie-Hélène went home to New York early, only to learn that Micah and Amir had been taken hostage. Micah and Marie-Hélène have told the story of how she worked for the men's release in ***American Hostage: A Memoir of a Journalist Kidnapped in Iraq and the Remarkable Battle to Win His Release***. One of the projects that Shelter for Life International has taken on in Afghanistan is helping farmers move from opium growing to saffron growing. Joel Hafvenstein has worked as an aid worker on a similar project, though not with Shelter for Life. He describes the situation and the difficulties in ***Opium Season: A Year on the Afghan Frontier***.

Kassindja, Fauziya (1977–)
Bashir, Layli Miller, coauthor

Do They Hear You When You Cry. Delta, 1999, 1998. 528pp. map. 9780385319942. Also available in audiobook. 305.48691

Kassindja's life drastically changed when she was fifteen, when her liberal father suddenly died. A man who had defied many Muslim and Togolese customs in the way he treated his daughters, he had also married outside his tribe and created much rancor among his own family. This rancor came to bear on Fauziya after her father's death, as she was soon faced with the prospect of marrying a man in his mid-forties, becoming his fourth wife, and undergoing female genital mutilation (FGM). Her sister and mother helped her escape on her wedding night, and she made her way to the United States, where another sort of nightmare began. Naïve about the workings of immigration, she had the misfortune of being questioned by a callous Immigration and Naturalization

Service (INS) worker who eventually had her put in chains and taken to prison, where she was strip-searched. For sixteen months Fauziya was in the prison system, abused, denied basic decency and medical attention. It was only after a reporter, Celia Dugger from *The New York Times*, who had heard of her story interviewed her and wrote a front-page article that Fauziya finally got a fair hearing, was released, and was granted asylum.

Subjects: Asylum, Right of; Captivity; Courage; Fathers and Daughters; Female Circumcision; Muslim Women; Prisons, United States; Refugees; Togo

Now Try: Along with Philip G. Schrag, the lawyer who tried to help him, David Ngaruri Kenney also faced the immigration system in the United States, after escaping from Kenya, where he was almost executed for having led a peaceful protest. They describe David's experience in ***Asylum Denied: A Refugee's Struggle for Safety in America***. Mark Dow has studied the American immigration system, publishing his findings in ***American Gulag: Inside U.S. Immigration Prisons***. Kassindja's case led to the legal recognition by the courts that women could seek asylum based on their sex, as female genital mutilation has been deemed a crime in the United States. Fadumo Korn, who had suffered through FGM as a seven-year-old, teamed up with Sabine Eichhorst to write ***Born in the Big Rains: A Memoir of Somalia and Survival***, translated from the German by Tobe Levin.

Layton, Deborah (1953–)

Seductive Poison: A Jonestown Survivor's Story of Life and Death in the Peoples Temple. Anchor Books, 1999, 1998. 309pp. ill. map. 9780385489843. 289.9

Disturbed by other public accounts of cults and the harm they do, Deborah Layton, once in the inner circle of Jim Jones's Peoples Temple, decided to tell her story. She pulls no punches in baring herself and her motivation to join his group (once deemed a worthy organization in San Francisco working for social justice) and to stay with him, despite the life she found herself living. Her mother, Lisa, a Holocaust survivor, and her brother, Larry, also eventually joined. The group of 900 or so people in Jones's cult made their way to Guyana, to what was meant to be a paradise on earth. What Layton found when she arrived, however, shocked her to the point of opening her eyes to the realities of Jones's paranoia and manipulations. Using the opportunity of a public-relations trip to Georgetown, she fled to the American Embassy there, where she sought asylum. When she arrived back in the United States she tried to warn people about what Jones was planning (they had already undergone several suicide drills), spurring Congressman Leo Ryan and some journalists to head to Guyana to investigate. Unfortunately, Ryan and several journalists were assassinated by Jonestown members, including Layton's brother. Layton wrote her book as much to warn about the dangers of cults and to inform about why people join them as she did to tell her story.

Subjects: Brainwashing; Cults; Guyana; Jones, Jim; Jonestown Mass Suicide, Guyana; Mass Suicide; Peoples Temple; San Francisco, CA

Now Try: Philip Jenkins offers an overview of cults in America in ***Mystics and Messiahs: Cults and New Religions in American History***. Also wanting to explain what leads young women in particular to join cults is Miriam Williams, a former cult member and author of ***Heaven's Harlots: My Fifteen Years as a Sacred Prostitute in the Children of God Cult***. Apparently the arrival of Ryan and the journalists sparked Jones into executing the real "suicide." This seems to be an unfortunately common consequence of official interference. Danny O. Coulson and Elaine Shannon look at the work of the FBI's hostage rescue unit in ***No Heroes: Inside the FBI's Secret Counter-Terror Force***.

Mam, Somaly (ca. 1971–)
Marshall, Ruth (1961–), coauthor

The Road of Lost Innocence. Foreword by Nicholas Kristof. Introduction by Ayaan Hirsi Ali. Spiegel & Grau, 2009, 2008. 205pp. 9780385526227. Also available in audiobook, e-audiobook, and e-book. 362.76092

Already a victim of the Khmer Rouge, having been separated from her family and living on her own in the forest around the age of nine, Mam was approached by a man who said he would take her to her family. That was the beginning of years of enslavement, of rape and torture, and of a brutal life in Cambodian brothels. She was not alone in this world, as one out of forty Cambodian girls was abducted or sold into the sex slave trade. She realized her only way out would be to marry a foreigner, so she did. She married a French aid worker, Pierre Legros, with whom she started an organization, AFESIP, to help girls in distress. She currently works through the Somaly Mam Foundation (http://www.somaly.org), which offers shelter, counseling, and hope for girls rescued from these brothels. Her youngest client is four years old.

Subjects: Abuse (Sexual); Cambodia; Child Prostitution, Cambodia; Child Slaves; Children, Crimes Against; Courage; Human Rights Activists, Cambodia; Legros, Pierre; Rape; Slavery, Cambodia; Somaly Mam Foundation; Survivors of Rape; Victims of Violence

Now Try: David B. Batstone has traveled the world to determine the extent of present-day human trafficking; his book, ***Not for Sale: The Return of the Global Slave Trade—and How We Can Fight It***, is a call for action. Currently young women are promised work in Western Europe or North America, only to have their money and identification taken when they arrive; they are then enslaved as prostitutes. Victor Malarek investigates this in ***The Natashas: Inside the New Global Sex Trade***. Very often prostitution is the only way a child can survive on the streets. Jaume Sanllorente discovered this on a trip to India, a trip he says changed his life, as he now devotes that life to keeping children off the streets in Mumbai. He recounts his story in ***Bombay Smiles***, translated from the Spanish by Gwendollyn Gout and Robert Dreesen.

Nazer, Mende (1980–)
Lewis, Damien, coauthor

Slave. Public Affairs, 2004, 2003. 350pp. 9781586482121. Also available in large print and audiobook. 306.362092

Mende Nazer is from the Nuba Mountains area of northern Sudan. Growing up she lived in a compound with thatched huts, unaware of the modern conveniences of the cities in Sudan and elsewhere. That changed when she was twelve; she was abducted by marauding mujahideen, raped, and sold off to an Arab family in Khartoum, where she became the property of the woman of the house. As she tells her story in her memoir, the reader sees the young adolescent separated from her family (likely killed by the raiding Arabs), treated worse than a family pet would be, more like the pigs the family owned, yet still marveling at the world around her—running water, cars, even mirrors. She lived with this family for seven years—beaten on a daily basis, fed the scraps from their table, sleeping on the floor of the garden shed—until she was sent to England to be the slave of her mistress's sister. Much older now, she was finally able to contact other Nubians, who helped her escape; one of the people instrumental in helping her was Damien Lewis, the coauthor of her book. Initially the British government refused to grant her asylum, until the public outcry changed their minds. Nazer now spends her time raising awareness of the very real problem of modern-day slavery.

Subjects: Asylum, Right of; Captivity; Child Slaves; Khartoum, Sudan; London, England; Nuba, Sudan; Slavery, Sudan; Social History, Sudan; Sudan; Upper Class, Sudan

Now Try: Kevin Bales, who has devoted his life to writing against modern slavery, has written (among other books) ***Disposable People: New Slavery in the Global Economy***. Jesse Sage and Liora Kasten collected stories of people who have been sold as slaves in ***Enslaved: True Stories of Modern Day Slavery***. It is difficult for those enslaved and for those reading about it not to become completely disheartened. Mariane Pearl, in the face of her own tragedy—the violent loss of her husband, the journalist Daniel Pearl—felt she needed to look for signs of hope, something she could share with her son. The fortunate result is ***In Search of Hope: The Global Diaries of Mariane Pearl***.

Nemat, Marina (1965–)

Prisoner of Tehran: One Woman's Story of Survival Inside an Iranian Prison. Free Press, 2008, 2007. 321pp. 9781416537434. Also available in large print and e-book. 365.45092

Reminiscent of Marjane Satrapi, Marina Nemat was vocal in her opposition to the fundamentalist Islamic regime set in place by the Ayatollah Khomeini, even in the classroom. Her behavior landed the sixteen-year-old in the infamous Iranian Evin Prison, where she was set to be executed by a firing squad. Saved at literally the last minute by a guard who had fallen in love with her, she was forced to convert to Islam and marry him. This was a secret marriage, so she was still in prison, serving a life sentence, often in solitary confinement. Her parents-in-law had embraced her as a daughter, and after their son was murdered by a rival faction, used their influence to have her released from prison. It wasn't until after her life began to settle down in Canada, where she had emigrated with her second husband, Andre, that she began to have nightmares and to feel the need to tell her story, hoping at the same time to encourage more tolerance. She has since written a follow-up, ***After Tehran: A Life Reclaimed***.

Subjects: Adolescence; Captivity; Christians; Courage; Evin Prison, Iran; Iran; Iran Revolution (1979–1997); Iranian-Canadians; Political Prisoners, Iran; Prisons, Iran; Social Conditions, Iran; Victims of Violence; Women in Iran

Now Try: A reporter protesting in print the strictures of the Islamic Revolution, Camelia Entekhabifard found herself in prison and also in a relationship with a guard, a man who secured her release. Fleeing Iran, she was able to tell her story in ***Camelia, Save Yourself by Telling the Truth: A Memoir of Iran*** (translated from the Persian by George Mürer). Perhaps the best-known (and longest-held) political prisoner is Aung San Suu Kyi, a Burmese national who has been fighting for democracy in her country for decades and has been under house arrest for much of that time. Justin Wintle has written a biography of her, ***Perfect Hostage: The Life of Aung San Suu Kyi, Burma's Prisoner of Conscience***. Zarah Ghahramani, with help from Robert Hillman, interweaves stories of her happy childhood and adolescence with stories of her imprisonment and beatings at Evin Prison for speaking out against the government in ***My Life as a Traitor***.

Oufkir, Malika (1953–)
Fitoussi, Michèle, coauthor

Stolen Lives: Twenty Years in a Desert Jail. Talk Miramax Books/Hyperion, 2001. 293pp. ill. map. 9780786867325. Also available in large print, audiobook, e-audiobook, and e-book. 365.45092 [Trans. by Ros Schwartz]

Oufkir begins her story by recounting the first part of her life, spent in great comfort in Morocco. As the daughter of a general and military aide to King Muhammad V, she became the adopted daughter of the king, living in the palace with his daughter. This first section, lushly described, is in sharp contrast to the second part, wherein she and her family try to survive in a desert prison. When Muhammad's son, King Hassan II, came to power, Malika's father led a coup against him, resulting in the death of Malika's father and the imprisonment of her and her family. They initially thought they were simply being exiled to the desert, able to take their books and clothes with them, but as the years went on and they suffered greater and greater privations, they realized they had been left to die there. They managed to create a tunnel through which to escape, but were recaptured. They endured five more years in their desert prison before being released.

Subjects: Arab Women; Captivity; Deserts; Fathers and Daughters; Morocco; Political Prisoners, Morocco; Prisons, Morocco; Survival; Translations; Upper Class, Morocco

Now Try: Oufkir follows her book of hardships with one of hope and peace, ***Freedom: The Story of My Second Life,*** translated from the French by Linda Coverdale. Although quite a different kind of imprisonment, Fatima Mernissi's life in a Moroccan harem was also circumscribed, as she describes in ***Dreams of Trespass: Tales of a Harem Girlhood,*** with photographs by Ruth V. Ward. Aline (Griffith), Countess of Romanones, often worked for the Office of Strategic Services (OSS). In her book, ***The Spy Wore Silk***, she describes how she and William Casey tried to offset the rumored coup against King Hassan, the very coup that resulted in the Oufkirs' imprisonment. The journalist Terry A. Anderson also became caught up in the web of politics when he was captured by Hezbollah, an ordeal he recounts in ***Den of Lions: Memoirs of Seven Years***.

Consider Starting With . . .

Ali, Nujood. *I Am Nujood, Age 10 and Divorced*

Bok, Francis. *Escape from Slavery: The True Story of My Ten Years in Captivity—and My Journey to Freedom in America*

Dallaire, Roméo. *Shake Hands with the Devil: The Failure of Humanity in Rwanda*

Douglass, Frederick. *Narrative of the Life of Frederick Douglass, an American Slave, Written by Himself*

Ilibagiza, Immaculée. *Left to Tell: Discovering God Amidst the Rwandan Holocaust*

Koff, Clea. *The Bone Woman: A Forensic Anthropologist's Search for Truth in the Mass Graves of Rwanda, Bosnia, Croatia, and Kosovo*

Mam, Somaly. *The Road of Lost Innocence*

Min, Anchee. *Red Azalea*

Satrapi, Marjane. *The Complete Persepolis*

Wiesel, Elie. *Night*

Fiction Read-Alikes

Arslan, Antonia. *Skylark Farm*. The author bases this story of one family's attempt to survive the Armenian genocide on her own family's history.

Cheng, Terrence. *Sons of Heaven: A Novel*. Two brothers live in political opposition as one marches in Tiananmen Square and the other is sent to pull him away from the protest.

Danticat, Edwidge. *The Dew Breaker*. Linked stories tell of Haitians in exile, some of whom suffered from the brutalities of Haiti's dictatorships and some of whom, like the "Dew Breaker," inflicted the brutalities.

Farah, Nuruddin. *Knots*. Returning to her home in Somalia, Cambara tries to retrieve her land from warlords and finds herself aided by a network of women.

9 10 11 12 13

Larsson, Stieg. *The Girl Who Played with Fire*. The trafficking of women from Eastern Europe to Sweden is at the heart of this novel featuring the journalist Mikael Blomkvist and the enterprising hacker Lisbeth Salander.

Littell, Jonathan. *The Kindly Ones: A Novel*. Although he hides his past as a Nazi officer from his neighbors in northern France, Max Aue cannot hide the atrocities he committed from himself.

Livaneli, Zülfü. *Bliss*. Raped by her uncle, Meryem is now expected to hang herself in the barn; when she refuses, her brother is ordered to take her to Istanbul and kill her there.

Mda, Zakes. *The Madonna of Excelsior*. A mixed-race family tries to work out how they are supposed to conduct themselves, first in apartheid South Africa and then in the ever-changing postapartheid society.

Némirovsky, Irène. *Suite Française*. Written by a woman who died in Auschwitz, and published sixty years after her death, this novel describes what life was like in France as the Germans invaded and the Parisians fled the city with hopes of safety in the country.

Stowe, Harriet Beecher. *Uncle Tom's Cabin*. A classic novel depicting the life of slaves in the American South, this work has come under criticism in the twentieth century but still remains seminal in the history of African-Americans.

Works Cited

Carr, David. 2004. "Many Kinds of Crafted Truths: An Introduction to Nonfiction." In *Nonfiction Readers' Advisory*, edited by Robert Burgin, 47–65. Westport, CT: Libraries Unlimited.

Goldin, Farideh. 2004. "Iranian Women and Contemporary Memoirs." *Iran Chamber Society*. Accessed June 28, 2010. http://www.iranchamber.com/culture/articles/iranian_women_contemporary_memoirs.php.

Hamouda, Sandra. 2005. "Middle Eastern Women's Autobiography." In *Encyclopedia of Women's Autobiography*, edited by Victoria Boynton and Jo Malin, 386–95. Westport, CT: Greenwood Press.

Milani, Farzaneh. 1990. "Veiled Voices: Women's Autobiographies in Iran." In *Women's Autobiographies in Contemporary Iran*, edited by Afsaneh Najmabadi, 1–16. Cambridge, MA: Harvard University Press.

Chapter 12

Life at War

Description

The place of war memoirs in the canon of autobiographical literature is quite high in terms of sheer quantity written over a very long period of time and in terms of respect received in the public eye. One can distinguish between historical military writing and military memoirs, but often a reader can find both in a memoir.

Perhaps the earliest-known example of military writing is Homer's epic poem, ***Iliad***, believed to have been written in the middle of the ninth century, BCE. Not a memoir, it is the story of the last few days of the Trojan War. ***The Art of War*** by Sunzi (Sun Tzu), born in 500 BCE is the earliest-known treatise on war. It is a discourse on strategy and on management, however, and includes neither history nor biography. Later came writings that provided both: ***Anabasis***, the story of Xenophon's life as a soldier marching with Cyrus the Younger against Cyrus's brother King Artaxerxes II, and ***"De Bello Gallico" & Other Commentaries of Caius Julius Caesar***. By giving the history of the Gallic Wars, Caesar also provided his own story, as he was the one who led the battles he described. Both his memoir and Xenophon's were written in the third person for greater effect when being read in public by others, and both were dated in the last few centuries BCE. Flavius Josephus (37–100 CE) also included his own story in ***The Jewish War***, his account of the revolt of the Jews against the Roman government.

Military writing has been strong throughout written history, but the writing of autobiographical works did not really flourish until the middle of the eighteenth century, when junior officers and foot soldiers added their voices to those of the commanders. With the increase in literacy among fighters, particularly in the American Civil War, memoirs abounded, although not all were published. Descendants are still finding manuscripts in trunks and working to have them published.

The nature of military writing has changed as well. The military historian Yuval Noah Harari (2007) distinguishes between the bird's-eye view and the worm's-eye view of war. The bird's-eye view is often provided by commanders or historians, describing the overall strategies, the planning, and the command. With hindsight they can lay out the fields of battle and the wars waged on them, who did what to whom, who came up on whose flank, etc. The worm's-eye view is that of the grunt, the foot soldier, the one who is carrying out the orders. The worm's-eye view is immediate and close and usually doesn't have the same perspective as the bird's eye. Because of this difference in who was writing the memoir, the tenor of the memoir changed. The foot soldier provides a close-at-hand experience, often including the emotions (fear, disgust, exhilaration) that accompany the action.

The focus on war writing was traditionally a reflection of the honor involved and the behavior required to reflect that honor. There were some anomalous writings to counteract that, but the change in focus has been gradually increasing since World War I, so that now most of the military memoirs we see concentrate on the soldier's personal experience in a particular war or even one specific firefight. Another aspect of the war memoir that is seen increasingly is the homecoming. Hundreds of thousands of words have been written about the way the Vietnam veterans were treated on their homecoming, but relatively few were written by the vets themselves. Many of the current memoirs coming out of Iraq and Afghanistan, however, talk quite openly not only about how veterans are treated back home but also about their own reactions to what had been their normal lives prior to going to war. Post-traumatic stress disorder (PTSD) has played a major role in this; it took a long time before it was even acknowledged by the military brass and the government. It was only in 2010 that the law was changed so that veterans would not have to pinpoint the specific incident that sparked the disorder, thus recognizing the true nature of the disorder and paving the way for more accessible care.

One of the reasons that the focus in war writing has changed is that wars themselves have changed. Vietnam was the start of what could be referred to as "disorganized" war, wherein the traditionally trained American soldiers were fighting guerrilla tactics and an enemy that wasn't always obvious. Children and women were used to carry grenades, so that ultimately the uniformed American soldiers couldn't always discern whether or not they should be shooting at the people approaching them. In the current battlefields the situation is similar. Very little of what has been written about the Iraq War, for example, is useful for the overall bird's-eye view of the military historian "because it has largely lacked confrontational combat" (Martinez, 2009), with one side "facing" the other in pitched battle.

Since the American Civil War there have been countless wars—two global wars, some within one nation, and some between two nations. There have been countries invaded first by one country and then another, and perhaps even another. There have been wars in a country on one continent that citizens on other continents may not even know about. There is endless fodder for military history and memoirs. This chapter has winnowed it down to books centering on wars of the twentieth and twenty-first centuries, with one exception: General William T. Sherman's Civil War memoir.

> War memoirs offer a wide gamut of experiences, emotions, and perspectives to readers who want to make sense of what they hear on the news or read in their history books. But it is not just soldiers who write of war; those living in the war-torn countries and those reporting on the wars also tell their stories of what life at war has meant to them.

Appeal

It might be difficult to say which has the greater appeal in war memoirs—character or story. People are always looking for heroes to admire, to emulate, and to restore their faith in humanity, and they often turn to war stories to find such heroes. In these memoirs we see the characters "confront fundamentally human challenges like death, loss and survival as a matter of routine" (Martinez, 2009). Not all the heroes are soldiers, however. In this chapter we see the heroic lives of those whose homes are in the war zones, of those writing or photographing the war stories, or of those waiting back home. Heroism wears many outfits, and readers have a wide choice here. We also see the humanity of the people living through these experiences. Readers who have been through similar experiences can compare themselves to the memoirists, achieving catharsis and perhaps relief. Others who have never experienced war can be horrified or excited, but in a vicarious way without being shot at or suffering from extreme weather, or eating questionable food. Another value to some readers of the war memoir is to gain an understanding of what a friend or loved one has suffered. When Catherine Phillips, the sister of a man portrayed in the miniseries ***The Pacific,*** saw some footage of the film, she said, "'Oh my god, I wish that we had seen this footage back then because we probably would have been better wives had we known what our husbands had gone through'" ("*The Pacific*," 2010). The men usually didn't talk about their experiences.

The story is usually full of action, excitement, adrenaline, horror, and sometimes humor. Despite those attributes, however, the story can also depict utter boredom, the phenomenon of hurrying up to wait. It can also be about relationships, good or bad. The term "brotherhood of man" is often used in reference to wartime friendships. Accompanying the story is usually much detail, providing great opportunities for learning. The detail could be in the country where the war takes place, in the culture shock, in the clothing and armaments, in the daily routine, or in the types of battle.

Learning can also come in the form of history lessons, which readers often prefer in narrative format. They want "the highest quality information packed with 'value and credibility' " (Martinez, 2009). Through reading war memoirs, readers can learn "the history of humanity [that] can be traced from conflict to conflict and loss to loss; wars define eras and the humans who live in them"

(Carr, 2004). Coupled with the events of history, however, is the understanding of it. Many have trouble understanding war—why we go to war, what the thrill of it is for some, and how people can live with the horror of it. Reading these stories and listening to the perspectives of those engaged in war often helps readers come to a better understanding of their own views.

Sometimes readers will pick up a war memoir to have their beliefs validated, so the tone of the book and the author's perspective will make a difference. People who believe in the righteousness of war will not want to read a memoir by someone who has become disillusioned and rails against that war. By the same token, those who believe in the evils of war will not want to read a memoirist's story of how the war was a good and necessary event. There are enough books out there to satisfy and confirm most readers' views.

Organization of This Chapter

The classics section that begins the chapter includes wars from the Civil War to Vietnam. Following that are stories of soldiers in combat or at least in war zones in the twentieth and twenty-first centuries. "Victims of War" follows the actual war stories, and these include a wide assortment of situations. The section ends with the media that report on the wars.

Classics

In this section of war classics, dating from the Civil War to the war in Vietnam, are representations from generals to noncommissioned officers. Although only five, the differences among these memoirs reflect the changes in war memoirs through the ages, from Sherman's "triumphant" march to Caputo's disillusionment with the brutality of war, although we see that same horror of war in Robert Graves's memoir, coming out of World War I. The general who is represented here offers the wider view of war, with the planning, the strategies, and the execution of those strategies. The lower ranks offer a closer, more personal view, including their own emotions.

> Classic war memoirs reflect a historical culture. In these stories the rank of the writer can make a noticeable difference in the perspective offered on a war; generals provide strategy and foot soldiers provide the gritty detail. The journalists who report on the war are also usually free to write what they want.

Caputo, Philip (1941–)

A Rumor of War. Henry Holt and Co., 1996, 1977. With a Postscript by the author on the 20th-anniversary edition. 356pp. 9780805046953. 959.70438

As Caputo himself says, his memoir of sixteen months fighting in Vietnam is meant to illustrate "the things men do in war and the things war does to them." His was the first ground combat unit to land in Vietnam, the soldiers naïve and innocent about what was to come. They expected to defeat both the Communists and communism in one easy effort. Instead they encountered a brand-new kind of war, wherein the weapons were land mines, booby traps, and jungle foliage for the enemy to hide in, foliage that the soldiers had to spend tedious hours and days cutting back, surrounded by insects, humidity, heat, mud, and the ever-present fear of being ambushed. Without judging, Caputo reveals what can happen to the soldier's moral compass in such an environment, where events like the My Lai Massacre become an understood outcome instead of a horrible aberration.

A Rumor of War was selected as a Notable Book by the American Library Association.

Subjects: ALA Notable Books; Classics; Human Behavior; Journalists; Marines; Novelists; United States Marine Corps; Vietnam War (1961–1975); War

Now Try: Caputo has since written several novels, one in particular about the war in the Sudan, ***Acts of Faith,*** and a quasi-autobiography, ***Means of Escape,*** about his work as a war correspondent. Tim O'Brien's classic novel, ***The Things They Carried,*** speaks to the same psychological profile of the soldier in Vietnam as does Caputo's memoir. The novel by James H. Webb about Marines in Vietnam, ***Fields of Fire,*** has been recommended for readers by another Marine, Nathaniel Fick. David Halberstam's classic, ***The Best and the Brightest,*** discusses the unexpected effect of the Vietnam War on the men who were politically involved it, men like John F. Kennedy, Robert McNamara, and Dean Rusk.

Graves, Robert (1895–1985)

Good-Bye to All That: An Autobiography. Introduction by Paul Fussell. Doubleday. 1998, 1929. 9780385093309. 347pp. Also available in audiobook and e-book. 940.48141

The poet Robert Graves illustrates the societal changes that can take place because of a war, in this case, the First World War. Graves begins his autobiography with his early life as a member of the upper classes. When he enlists in the army, patriotic and ready to fight for the honor of the world he knows, he finds the class system alive and well among the ranks of the fighting men. As the war proceeds, however, things change: attitudes to war and attitudes to class. Graves discusses how seriously the First World War changed the army, the nation, and the world. Despite the horrors of this war—horrors that made him want to get wounded, in order to get out honorably—he still fights to go back after he is seriously wounded. Along with his depictions of the fighting and the conditions in which they were fighting, Graves also draws portraits of the men he was fighting with, including his poet friend Siegfried Sassoon. This friendship ended, however, after the publication of Graves's book, as Sassoon (and many others as well) felt that it was dishonorable to the fallen.

Good-Bye to All That was one of the Modern Library Top 100 Nonfiction Books of the 20th Century.

Subjects: Cairo, Egypt; Classics; Egypt; Family Relationships; Lawrence, T. E.; Mothers and Sons; Nonagenarians; Poets, England; Royal Welch Fusiliers; Sassoon, Siegfried; Soldiers; World War I (1914–1918)

Now Try: Paul Fussell, who wrote the introduction to this edition, has written a classic of his own, ***The Great War and Modern Memory***, a critical review of the First World War from a social and literary perspective. Siegfried Sassoon, erstwhile friend of Robert Graves, has penned his own classic view of the war in which he fought alongside Graves, ***Memoirs of an Infantry Officer***. Timothy Findley's novel, for which he won a Governor General's Literary Award for Fiction, ***The Wars***, is a vivid depiction of the horrors of World War I.

Herr, Michael (1940–)

Dispatches. Introduction by Robert Stone. Everyman/Knopf, 2009, 1977. 247pp. 9780307270801. Also available in audiobook and e-audiobook. 959.70433.

Michael Herr was on assignment in Vietnam for *Esquire* magazine as a roving reporter of sorts, one who could roam the country with his press credentials, talk to the people actually fighting the war instead of having to rely on press releases from the brass, and write the war as he saw it. He wasn't bothered by deadlines and could fashion the story the way he wanted. The stories in his war memoir are unfiled dispatches, published two years after the war's end, and the result is a highly acclaimed classic, considered to be one of the best war books written. Along with reported conversations with foot soldiers, reflections on the absurdity of it all, and descriptions of other correspondents, Herr also looked at himself in light of the war. He candidly proffered the opinion that many who were there, including himself, actually enjoyed the adrenaline, the excitement, and the opportunity of a lifetime for adventure that the war offered. Herr discovered that he had a serious responsibility to these soldiers, to tell the real story, as they didn't believe it was being done by mainstream journalism. Herr was a narrator for the movie, ***Apocalypse Now***; the chaos in that movie reflects the level of chaos that Herr so accurately depicts in his memoir.

Dispatches was a finalist for the National Book Critics Circle Award in General Nonfiction.

Subjects: Classics; *Esquire* (Magazine); Journalists; Vietnam War (1961–1975); War Correspondents

Now Try: John Sack was also commissioned by *Esquire*, in his case to follow a U.S. Infantry Brigade, M Company, from Fort Dix to Vietnam, where he stayed with them.

From that experience he published a book, ***M.*** General Howard G. Moore and journalist Joseph L. Galloway collaborated to tell the dreadful story of their experience in the Ia Drang Valley, ***We Were Soldiers Once—and Young: Ia Drang, the Battle That Changed the War in Vietnam.*** Frances FitzGerald was a freelance journalist who spent sixteen months in Vietnam; after her time there and her studies of Vietnamese and Chinese history and culture, she wrote an award-winning analysis of the war, ***Fire in the Lake; The Vietnamese and the Americans in Vietnam.***

9 10 11 12 13

Manchester, William Raymond (1922–2004)

Goodbye, Darkness: A Memoir of the Pacific War. Back Bay Books, 2002, 1980. 401pp. ill. 9780316501118. Also available in audiobook, e-audiobook, and e-book. 940.548373

Considered one of the best World War II memoirs written, this is William Manchester's narrative of his war in the Pacific with the U.S. Marine Corps. But it is not just his war he describes; his memoir is considered to be a no-holds-barred look at the lives of soldiers in combat and what they experience physically and mentally in general, as well as an illustration of their lives as soldiers in the Pacific in particular. It is also a philosophical inquiry of sorts. In his memoir Manchester writes about survivor's guilt—particularly his own after being the only one of his unit to survive a mortar attack. He also raises the question of how one side (one's own) can be considered heroic while the other side is considered fanatic. Manchester begins his memoir with his early life, paying homage to his father, William, a Marine in the First World War who suffered the effects of chemical warfare. After the war Manchester went on to become a well-respected biographer, one of his books being ***American Caesar, Douglas MacArthur, 1880–1964,*** portraying the life of General MacArthur, who fought in the Pacific as well.

Goodbye, Darkness was selected as a Notable Book by the American Library Association.

Subjects: ALA Notable Books; Biographers; Classics; Fathers and Sons; Marines; Octogenarians; United States Marine Corps; World War II (1939–1945)

Now Try: E. B. Sledge, not nearly so well-known as William Manchester, has also written what is considered a masterpiece on the war in the Pacific, ***With the Old Breed, at Peleliu and Okinawa.*** His memoir, along with Robert Leckie's ***Helmet for My Pillow: From Parris Island to the Pacific: A Young Marine's Stirring Account of Combat in World War II*** are the sources for the Steven Spielberg/Tom Hanks collaboration on a television miniseries entitled ***The Pacific.*** Hugh Ambrose, the son of the historian Stephen E. Ambrose, has written the book from the miniseries, with the same title. Another brutal aspect of the war in the Pacific was the treatment of prisoners, particularly the Bataan Death March. Hampton Sides recounts the story of those who fought to free prisoners of war, including some survivors of the Bataan Death March, in ***Ghost Soldiers: The Forgotten Epic Story of World War II's Most Dramatic Mission.***

Sherman, William T. (1820–1891)

Memoirs of General W. T. Sherman. Introduction and notes by Michael Fellman. Penguin, 2000, 1875. 855pp. ill. maps. 9780140437980. Also available in e-book. 973.7092

This Penguin Classics edition of Sherman's memoirs is the reprint of Sherman's second edition, in which he added two more chapters and an appendix. Considered a literary feat, Sherman's memoirs remain controversial, with readers trying to decide if he was a brilliant commander or a bloodthirsty one. He begins his memoir with his early childhood, his time in California, and the beginnings of his unremarkable military career. Having become good friends with Ulysses S. Grant, Sherman was in a good position to be given a role in the Civil War. Sherman wrote his memoirs in part to provide a history for generations to come and accordingly included much detail about the campaigns—how they were planned and executed—as well as the people involved in carrying them out. The tenor of his memoirs changes at the point where he begins to describe the Civil War and his role in it, since he includes documents and letters, breaking up the narrative tone as he does so. The result, however, is a very useful tool for historians and yet a very readable work for the general public.

Subjects: American South; Civil War, United States (1861–1865); Classics; Generals; Grant, Ulysses S.; United States Army

Now Try: Chief Historian for the National Park Service Edwin C. Bearss has personally explored and researched Civil War sites and has led countless tours of them. He has gathered his knowledge along with photographs in a book published by the National Geographic Society, ***Fields of Honor***. One of the war's pivotal battles was at Shenandoah, and the historian Peter Cozzens offers a rounded view of the battle from both the Confederate and the Union viewpoints. His dynamic account is entitled ***Shenandoah 1862: Stonewall Jackson's Valley Campaign***. A lesser-known Civil War general was Nathan Bedford Forrest, a man who fought for Lee and the Confederates. Madison Smartt Bell has written a lively fictional biography of him, ***Devil's Dream***.

Military Life

This section demonstrates the wide scope available in war memoirs. Represented here are a number of wars, from World War II through the Korean War, the war in Vietnam, and the various wars in the broad area of the Middle East and vicinity. But they are not all stories of military battle. Again the range is wide: soldiers in battle; soldiers imprisoned; soldiers severely wounded; soldiers dealing with Jim Crow laws; noncombatants, fighting the war from a desk; even soldiers and their relationships with animals. There are women and there are men; there are generals and there are enlisted soldiers and reservists. Given the wealth of material available, this is a microcosm of the war memoir, but it is telling nonetheless.

Memoirs of military life are told by those who have donned the uniform and used the weapons. They are gritty and often difficult to read because of the details that nonmilitary readers have not experienced. The tone will change depending on the writers' views about war, views that might have changed after the war experience; the tones might be proud, or they might be bitter. The memoirists may write to celebrate a war or a victory, or they may write to say there should never be another war.

Brady, James (1928–2009)

The Coldest War: A Memoir of Korea. Thomas Dunne, 2000, 1990. 248pp. ill. 9pp. of plates. 9780312265113. Also available in e-book. 951.9042

James Brady deliberately had his book published on the fortieth anniversary of a war that relatively little has been written about, particularly in comparison to other twentieth-century wars involving the United States. He relates in his memoir how he had attended a military camp in the summer while in college, hoping to avoid the draft. Coming out of school with a commission in the U.S. Marine Corps reserve, he was soon called up to fight in Korea. Although he was there for not even a year, his term bracketed by American Thanksgiving at the beginning and July 4 at the end, he still experienced war in its horror, its boredom, its camaraderie, and its revelations to him as a human. He describes the euphoria of being able to walk away from a firefight; the tedium of being on the frontlines for weeks at a time; and the most difficult enemy, the cold in the winter and the heat in the summer. He also points out that almost as many Americans were killed in the Korean War in its three years as in the Vietnam War in its more than ten years. Brady had said at the end of his memoir that he would never go back to Korea, but in fact he did, returning there with a fellow Marine, Eddie Adams, a combat photographer. The result is ***The Scariest Place in the World***. Brady also wrote a novel about the war, ***The Marines of Autumn: A Novel of the Korean War***.

James Brady was awarded the Presidential Medal of Freedom in 1996 by President Clinton.

Subjects: Cold War; Journalists; Korean War (1950–1953); Marines; Military Reserves; Octogenarians; United States Marine Corps

Now Try: A classic memoir of the Korean War was written not long after the war's end by Martin Russ, ***The Last Parallel; A Marine's War Journal***. Explaining the causes of the war and laying the main cause at the feet of the Cold War is Richard Whelan's ***Drawing the Line: The Korean War, 1950–1953***. David Halberstam provides an overview of the war in his award-winning book, ***The Coldest Winter: America and the Korean War***.

Crawford, John

The Last True Story I'll Ever Tell: An Accidental Soldier's Account of the War in Iraq. Riverhead, 2006, 2005. 220pp. 9781594482014. Also available in large print, audiobook, e-audiobook, and e-book. 956.7044342092

John Crawford was writing anecdotes of various aspects of the war in Iraq as he encountered them, when a journalist who was embedded with Crawford's unit not only encouraged him to publish them but also told others in the print world about them after he had left the unit. The result is this memoir by Crawford, which tells how he'd spent three years with the 101st Army Airborne Division and then signed up with the Florida National Guard as a way of acquiring a college education. Recently married, with one semester to go before getting his degree in anthropology, Crawford was called to active service and sent to Iraq. He illustrates very clearly what life was like there, in the dust storms, with inadequate weapons, rare opportunities for showers, and MREs (meals ready-to-eat) for their daily fare. The political situation proved to be difficult as well, as the troops were not there for a well-defined, defensible reason. The one good thing that came out of Iraq for Crawford was the realization of his purpose in writing these stories: to let others know what such a war is really like.

Subjects: 21st Century; Iraq War (2003–); Military Reserves; National Guard; Personal Essays; Soldiers; War on Terrorism (2001–)

Now Try: Crawford's book has been referred to as haunting and powerful, as has Adam Hochschild's book on another horrific "war"—Stalin's reign of terror. After interviewing people who still remembered Stalin, Hochschild then wrote ***The Unquiet Ghost: Russians Remember Stalin***. Having joined a battalion involved in the "surge," in the Iraq War, David Finkel offers an observer's view of the type of daily grind that Crawford and his fellow soldiers experienced, in ***The Good Soldiers***. In ***The Long Road Home: A Story of War and Family***, Martha Raddatz uses the disastrous firefight in Sadr City (Baghdad) to illustrate what the war is really like, for both the combatants and the people back home waiting to hear officially about their loved ones as they follow the news in local media.

Dole, Robert J. (1923–)

One Soldier's Story: A Memoir. Collins, 2006, 2005. 287pp. ill. 8pp. of plates. maps. 9780060763428. Also available in large print, audiobook, e-audiobook, and e-book. 940.548173092

Bob Dole begins this memoir with stories of his childhood, growing up in the small town of Russell, Kansas, during the Great Depression. His idyllic childhood and youth did little to prepare him for the difficulties of war, but he enlisted after Pearl Harbor, and at the level of second lieutenant was in charge of a group in the 10th Mountain Division in Italy. His memoir doesn't focus so much on the fighting conditions—difficult as they were—as on his almost-fatal wounding by a German shell. Two weeks before the war's end, he suffered a severely wounded shoulder and was almost paralyzed with spinal-cord damage. What his memoir really centers on is his three-year effort to recuperate—the many surgeries, the close calls with deadly infections, the love and support he received, and the faith that sustained him.

Dole was given the Presidential Medal of Freedom by President Clinton in 1997 and his book, ***One Soldier's Story***, was the winner of a Christopher Award.

Subjects: 10th Mountain Division; Christopher Awards; Courage; Faith; Octogenarians; Russell, KS; Senators; Soldiers; United States Army; War Wounded; World War II (1939–1945)

Now Try: Max Cleland is another ex-soldier (a Vietnam vet) who was sorely wounded in the war, required much rehabilitation, and became a U.S. senator. He recounts his story, with the help of Ben Raines, in ***Heart of a Patriot: How I Found the Courage to Survive Vietnam, Walter Reed and Karl Rove***. Walter Reed was a U.S. Army physician whose work in ending the threat of yellow fever was acknowledged by giving his name to the Walter Reed Army Medical Center in Washington, where most wounded vets go. Michael Weisskopf, although not a war veteran but a war-wounded journalist, was given special permission to be attended to at Walter Reed. Along with his own story, he includes the stories of three others being treated there in ***Blood Brothers: Among the Soldiers of Ward 57***. Dole's unit in Italy was a rather unusual one, an Alpine unit that was instrumental in successfully defeating Italy in the mountains. One of their stories (including Bob Dole's participation) has been told by McKay Jenkins in ***The Last Ridge: The Epic Story of the U.S. Army's 10th Mountain Division and the Assault on Hitler's Europe***.

Dryden, Charles W. (1920–2008)

A-Train: Memoirs of a Tuskegee Airman. Foreword by Benjamin O. Davis. University of Alabama Press, 2002, 1997. 421pp. ill. 9780807312664. Also available in e-book. 940.544973

Dryden's memoir opens an important window into the issue of segregation in the military service. Wanting to fly from the time he was a child, Dryden tried to enlist in the U.S. Army Air Corps but was told they didn't accept people of his race; no one thought Black men would be able to pilot an airplane. However, an "experiment" was underway at the Tuskegee Institute in Alabama to see if this were actually true, to see if perhaps African-Americans could be trained to fly and to maintain their aircraft. Dryden signed up and joined hundreds of others who successfully flew thousands of sorties and combat missions. He describes life in the military for the Black airman, the Jim Crow laws, the discrimination, and the closing of an Officers' Club in order not to have to integrate it. In 1948, when the U.S. armed forces were finally integrated, Dryden stayed on with the Air Corps and flew in the Korean War as well. By the time he retired in 1962 he had reached the level of command pilot, the highest level for a flier.

Charles Dryden was awarded the Congressional Gold Medal by President George W. Bush in 2007.

Subjects: 1940s; 99th Pursuit Squadron; African-American Men; African-Americans in the Military; Army Air Corps; Fighter Pilots; Integration in the Military; Octogenarians; Racism; Tuskegee Airmen

Now Try: Benjamin O. Davis, the man who wrote the foreword to Dryden's memoir, was the first Black man to graduate from West Point and the first Black general; he has written his own story, ***Benjamin O. Davis, Jr., American: An Autobiography***. Frank E. Petersen also broke the color line when he applied to fly for the Marines. In his memoir, written with J. Alfred Phelps, ***Into the Tiger's Jaw: America's First Black Marine Aviator/The Autobiography of Lt. Gen. Frank E. Petersen***, he tells how he succeeded, not just in getting in, but in excelling. David Colley interviewed various members of the first integrated combat unit in U.S. history. When the 5th Platoon of K Company fought alongside their White colleagues, they made history and paved the way for further integration, as recounted in ***Blood for Dignity: The Story of the First Integrated Combat Unit in the U.S. Army***.

Durant, Michael J. (1961–)
Hartov, Steven (1951–), coauthor

In the Company of Heroes. Introduction by Mark Bowden. NAL Calibar, 2006, 2003. 387pp. ill. 16pp.of plates. map. 9780451219930. Also available in large print, audiobook (read by the author), e-audiobook, and e-book. 967.73053

Michael Durant and his crew had just dropped off some men into Mogadishu, Somalia, for a "snatch and grab" operation when Durant's Black Hawk helicopter was shot down by a rocket grenade. His pilot and copilot were killed, and he was severely wounded, with a broken back and broken leg. Two men from another helicopter volunteered to be dropped down to keep the mob away from Durant but were killed trying to save him. This memoir recounts Durant's subsequent capture and captivity, visits by the Red Cross that did so much for his morale, the diplomatic efforts that were made for his release, and his eventual release and rehabilitation. He describes his captors—some harsh, some compassionate—and pays tribute to all the men who died in that operation, particularly Gary Gordon and Randy Shugart, who gave their lives for him. Throughout the narrative he weaves his life story, his yen for flying helicopters from the time he was a youth, his training, and his other missions in other countries. His title reflects his regard for those who fought with him.

Subjects: Black Hawk (Helicopter); Captivity; Hostages, Somalia; Mogadishu, Somalia; Operation Restore Hope (1992–1993); Pilots; Prisoners of War, Somalia; Somalia Civil War (1991–); War Wounded

Now Try: The man who wrote the introduction to Durant's book, Mark Bowden, is the author of the very popular ***Black Hawk Down: A Story of Modern War*** (made into a movie of the same name), based on Durant's story. In ***Mogadishu! Heroism and Tragedy***, Kent DeLong and Steven Tuckey provide a look at the entire battle of Mogadishu, which was largely responsible for the United States pulling out of Somalia. Another story of a Black Hawk down concerns the friendly-fire shooting of two helicopters carrying more than two dozen peacekeepers. Joan L. Piper, the mother of one of the victims and the wife of an officer in the Air Force, investigated the story herself and made it public in ***A Chain of Events: The Government Cover-Up of the Black Hawk Incident***

and the Friendly Fire Death of Lt. Laura Piper. The helicopter has been in use as a military weapon for decades; James R. Chiles recounts its history in ***The God Machine: From Boomerangs to Black Hawks, the Story of the Helicopter.***

Exum, Andrew

This Man's Army: A Soldier's Story from the Front Lines of the War on Terrorism. Gotham Books, 2005, 2004. 249pp. 9781592401376. Also available in e-book. 973.931

Attending an Ivy League college, studying English literature and the classics, Exum joined the ROTC (Reserve Officers' Training Corps) to help pay for his tuition. He enlisted in the army after graduating, entering training with the army's Ranger School. Not long after, the events of September 11, 2001 took place, completely altering what Exum had assumed would be his career with a peacekeeping force. As a member of the army's 10th Mountain Division, he was sent to Afghanistan, where he participated in Operation Anaconda in the Shah-i-Kot Valley. He injects his literary and classic studies into his reporting, narrating how he prepared himself to kill people, knowing that would be a reality of his job there. His life in Afghanistan was full of contradictions: fighting warlords while dealing with correspondents from cable news; fighting guerrilla warfare while laden with the trappings of modern technology. Two of his greatest difficulties were coming back home and hearing the media stories he knew were inaccurate and comparing his difficult, treacherous life in the mountains of Afghanistan to his academic life back home as he pursued further studies.

Subjects: 10th Mountain Division; Afghan War (2001–); Operation Anaconda; Soldiers; United States Army; War on Terrorism (2001–)

Now Try: Perhaps because of its literary bent, Exum's book has been compared to Tim O'Brien's classic memoir about fighting in Vietnam, ***If I Die in a Combat Zone: Box Me Up and Ship Me Home.*** Sean Naylor has investigated and written about the operation in which Exum participated, ***Not a Good Day to Die: The Untold Story of Operation Anaconda.*** A counterinsurgency advisor to General Petraeus in Iraq, David Kilcullen has written his own view of the way current wars need to be fought, ***The Accidental Guerrilla: Fighting Small Wars in the Midst of a Big One.***

Fick, Nathaniel (1977–)

One Bullet Away: The Making of a Marine Officer. Houghton Mifflin, 2006, 2005. 369pp. ill. 16pp. of plates. 9780618556137. Also available in audiobook, e-audiobook, and e-book. 359.96092

A student of the classics at Dartmouth, Nathaniel Fick wanted something more to challenge him than either academia or athletics. He applied to the Marines, training to be admitted to the First Reconnaissance Battalion (the First Recon), the elite unit of the already-tough Marines. Fick describes his training—as grueling as anything one can imagine—in great detail, bringing it right into the room for the reader. Sent first to Afghanistan, he and his unit didn't see much action, but then they became part of Operation Iraqi Freedom and were deployed in the invasion of Iraq in 2003. It was there that he found himself comparing his training with the reality of his situation. He is honest in describing the brutality of battle, but he takes pride in his goal to bring all his men home. The leadership training that he puts into effect and his relationship with his men both offer principles that would be relevant out of combat as well. After his return, recognizing that he was suffering from post-traumatic stress disorder (PTSD), Fick became an advocate for returning soldiers to receive psychological screening and professional help.

Subjects: Afghan War (2001–); First Recon Battalion; Iraq War (2003–); Marines; Military Training; Post-Traumatic Stress Disorder; United States Marine Corps; War on Terrorism (2001–)

Now Try: Evan Wright, a writer for *Rolling Stone*, accompanied Fick's platoon during the invasion of Iraq and, after writing some articles for the magazine, published the complete story in ***Generation Kill: Devil Dogs, Iceman, Captain America, and the New Face of American War***. In his book Fick recommends several books about the Marines to the reader, one of which is Thomas E. Ricks's ***Making the Corps***. James Brady interviewed a number of Marines for a new book, ***Why Marines Fight***, providing a bit of an oral history of the Marine Corps in the twentieth century. The issue of PTSD for those returning from war is a serious one. Clint Van Winkle is honest and open in his memoir, ***Soft Spots: A Marine's Memoir of Combat and Post-Traumatic Stress Disorder***, discussing his problem and what kind of response he received back home when looking for help.

Johnson, Shoshana (1973–)
Doyle, M. L., coauthor

I'm Still Standing: From Captive U.S. Soldier to Free Citizen—My Journey Home. Simon & Schuster, 2010. 9781416567486. Also available in audiobook, e-audiobook, and e-book. 956.7044

Shoshana Johnson, the daughter of an army veteran, signed up with the army in the hopes of getting a better education. Sent to Iraq as a Food Service Specialist, part of Operation Iraqi Freedom, she was in a convoy that was attacked; several were killed and several were taken prisoner—the first prisoners of war in Iraq. Wounded, Shoshana was one of those taken captive, the first African-American female ever to be a prisoner of war. Being wounded, a female, and an African-American only added to her fears in captivity. She describes the largely humane and compassionate treatment she received at the hands of the Iraqi doctors and her captors before being rescued by the Marines. Adding further to the post-traumatic stress disorder she suffered from her ordeal were the ungenerous reactions of some of the military, who said she should not have received a Bronze Star Medal because she was technically not a combatant. She now spends much of her time talking about her experiences and her PTSD.

Subjects: African-American Women; African-Americans in the Military; Captivity; Firsts; Iraq War (2003–); Operation Iraqi Freedom; Post-Traumatic Stress Disorder; Prisoners of War, Iraq; United States Army; War on Terrorism (2001–); War Wounded; Women in the Military

Now Try: One of the other captives taken that day was Jessica Lynch, whom the government tried to use as propaganda. She has told the truth of her story to Rick Bragg in ***I Am a Soldier, Too: The Jessica Lynch Story***. Helen Benedict is a journalism professor who collected stories from five military women in Iraq and distilled them into ***The Lonely Soldier: The Private War of Women Serving in Iraq***. Difficult as it is to be a woman in the military, being a woman who is different—a woman of color or a gay woman, for example—only adds to the stress. When Colonel Margarethe Cammermeyer said that she was a lesbian in response to a question about her sexual orientation, her life in the military changed: she was dismissed. Her story, ***Serving in Silence***, written with the help of Chris Fisher, has also been made into a movie with the same title.

Karpinski, Janis L. (1953–)
Strasser, Steven, coauthor

One Woman's Army: The Commanding General of Abu Ghraib Tells Her Story. Miramax, 2005. 242pp. ill. 8pp. of plates. 9781401352479. Also available in audiobook and e-book. 956.704437

Brigadier General Janis Karpinski, the head of the Military Police in Iraq, was charged with rebuilding the entire Iraqi prison system in 2003. Although she herself did not witness the abuse, the mistreatment and torture of prisoners at Abu Ghraib Prison did happen under her watch, and for that she accepts responsibility. And for that she was demoted to colonel, given a written reprimand, and relieved of her command. What she has a problem accepting, however, is that she believes (and backs up her belief in this memoir) that she was a scapegoat, that the men who should really be held responsible (Lieutenant General Ricardo Sanchez and Donald Rumsfeld specifically) will never be answerable for their roles in the cruelties perpetrated at Abu Ghraib. Karpinski's memoir is not just about Abu Ghraib, however. She also talks about her successes earlier in her career, including a Bronze Star Medal for her work in the earlier Iraq War. She moved into the Reserves and then headed the prison system in Iraq. Because she believes that the needs of reservists are not seen as a priority, she also believes that this attitude affected her ability to carry out her mandate. Ironically, her story as the first female general ever to be in command in a combat zone might never have been told but for the scandal surrounding her.

Subjects: Abu Ghraib Prison, Iraq; Firsts; Generals; Iraq War (2003–); Military Reserves; Prisoners of War, Iraq; Torture; War Atrocities, United States; War on Terrorism (2001–); Women in the Military

Now Try: Kirsten A. Holmstedt has created a creditable profile of military women, both officers and enlisted, by interviewing twelve and drawing their stories together in ***Band of Sisters: American Women at War in Iraq***. S. (Sara) A. Sheldon has done something similar with female Marines in Iraq, illustrating that they are Marines first; their gender is secondary. Her book is entitled ***The Few, the Proud: Women Marines in Harm's Way***. The situation surrounding Abu Ghraib has become very muddy with all the political obfuscations. Errol Morris interviewed many of the people involved and created a film from it; the journalist Philip Gourevitch used those interviews to create a book of the same name, ***Standard Operating Procedure***.

Key, Joshua (1978–)
Hill, Lawrence (1957–), coauthor

The Deserter's Tale: The Story of an Ordinary Soldier Who Walked Away from the War in Iraq. Atlantic Monthly Press, 2007. 237pp. ill. map. 9780871139542. Also available in e-book. 956.7044

As did so many soldiers, Joshua Key enlisted in the army after being approached by an army recruiter who promised he would be kept stateside. Key describes his life growing up in a poor, abusive household in Oklahoma and how he saw the army as a possible way out of a cycle of poverty for him, his wife, and their two young children. He was a willing trainee, and even when he arrived in Iraq, contrary to the promises made at recruitment, he was willing to follow orders. It was these orders, however, that Key eventually found problematic. He thought he was fighting terrorism, but in the raids on the houses they attacked, he saw no signs of terrorists, except the American soldiers who were destroying the lives of these Iraqi civilians. On leave stateside, he decided he could not go back, and after living underground for a while, found an organization in Canada to help him. He is still awaiting a decision there on his refugee status.

Subjects: Americans in Canada; Deserters; Iraq War (2003–); Refugees; Soldiers; United States Army; War on Terrorism (2001–); War Resisters

Now Try: Camilo Mejía came to the same conclusion as Key, but he decided to stay in the United States and fight his battle there, seeking conscientious objector status. He has told his story in ***Road from Ar Ramadi: The Private Rebellion of Staff Sergeant Camilo Mejía***. War resisters and Canada have a strong history that dates from the Vietnam War. John Hagan, one of these resisters, combed through documents and interviewed the now-Canadians to write ***Northern Passage: American Vietnam War Resisters in Canada***. The issue of who has done military service and who has managed to get out of it became political during the 2004 election. Kathy Roth-Douquet and Frank Schaeffer, both upper class themselves, address this issue in ***AWOL: The Unexcused Absence of America's Upper Classes from the Military—and How It Hurts Our Country***. One of their arguments is that those who make military policy have no military experience.

Kidder, Tracy (1945–)

My Detachment: A Memoir. Random House, 2006, 2005. 192pp. 9780812976168. Also available in large print, audiobook (read by the author), e-audiobook, and e-book. 959.70434092

This war memoir is not a combat narrative, as are so many of the others in this section. The title says it all: Kidder was responsible for a small detachment, but he was largely detached from them and from the war. He writes this book from the perspective of many years of experience following the Vietnam War, years spent learning and writing about other people's lives related to specific social issues. His memoir is a coming of age of sorts, reflecting on how unsuited was this young, antiwar Ivy League graduate, despite his being an ROTC intelligence officer, to working in intelligence at an infantry base camp, capturing and interpreting enemy conversations. The men in his detachment are enlisted and not too impressed with this callow, detached leader. Kidder writes countless letters, fictitiously putting himself in the thick of battle, letters he doesn't send. He also creates a Vietnamese girlfriend whom he writes about; most of these letters he doesn't send either, except for a few to his girlfriend, who is slowly breaking up with him via her correspondence. Kidder's memoir is droll, subtle, and honest, depicting the boredom that so many find in war.

Subjects: 1960s; Army Security Agency; Coming of Age; Ennui; Military Intelligence; Vietnam War (1961–1975); War Resisters; Writers

Now Try: *My Detachment* has been compared to Joseph Heller's ***Catch-22*** for its depiction of the absurdity of war as seen by some of the participants. James Crumley's first novel, ***One to Count Cadence,*** is a sardonic story about the Vietnam War, the action taking place on Clark Air Base in the Philippines. As a classic antiwar novel, it too may prove interesting for a reader who has enjoyed Kidder's memoir. His is a different war, but Jason Christopher Hartley shares some of Kidder's humor as he describes his war in ***Just Another Soldier: A Year on the Ground in Iraq***.

Kopelman, Jay
Roth, Melinda, coauthor

From Baghdad, with Love: A Marine, the War, and a Dog Named Lava. Lyons Press, 2008, 2006. 196pp. ill. 9781599211824. Also available in large print, audiobook, and e-audiobook. 956.70443092

Kopelman and other Marines in his unit came upon a tiny puppy when they were clearing a building in Iraq, and against all military orders decided to keep it. At some point early in the relationship between Lava, the dog, and the group, Kopelman realized he couldn't abandon the dog when it was time for their unit to move on. Garnering the help of several people, some American, some Iraqi, Kopelman was eventually successful in getting Lava out of Iraq to California. Throughout the book, Kopelman also talks about their situation in Iraq—the fear, the possibility of being blown up by any means (including stray dogs with explosives attached to them), and the corruption. Back in California Kopelman was able to adopt Lava and subsequently wrote a sequel to this book, entitled ***From Baghdad to America: Life Lessons from a Dog Named Lava***. Initially Kopelman wouldn't admit that he might be suffering from post-traumatic stress disorder (PTSD), but witnessing Lava's behavior finally made him recognize his own.

Subjects: Americans in Iraq; Animals in the Military; Baghdad, Iraq; Dogs; Iraq War (2003–); Marines; Post-Traumatic Stress Disorder; War on Terrorism (2001–)

Now Try: While dogs were not officially allowed in the Iraq War, they have been used in other wars. In Japan the Akita dogs served several purposes for war, including the use of their pelts to line the soldiers' coats. Morie Sawataishi defied all Japanese convention to bring back the Akita dog from near-extinction, a feat described by Martha Sherrill in ***Dog Man: An Uncommon Life on a Faraway Mountain.*** A much larger animal rescue operation that was effected at the beginning of the American invasion in Iraq was carried out by a South African conservationist, who went there to help rescue animals. Lawrence Anthony (the conservationist) and Graham Spence recount that story in ***Babylon's Ark: The Incredible Wartime Rescue of the Baghdad Zoo***. Kopelman wasn't the first Marine to have a dog; they were an official part of the action in Guam during World War II, as William W. Putney recounts in ***Always Faithful: A Memoir of the Marine Dogs of WWII.***

Marks, Leo (1920–2001)

Between Silk and Cyanide: A Codemaker's War, 1941–1945. Simon & Schuster, 2000, 1998. 613pp. ill. 8pp. of plates. 9780684867809. 940.548641

This memoir of Leo Marks is the stuff of espionage novels, as seen in John Le Carré's ***The Spy Who Came in from the Cold*** and continuing on for decades. It also reads like one. Initially working for his father, Ben, in the book shop made famous by Helene Hanff's ***84, Charing Cross Road,*** Marks headed out at the age of twenty-two to fight in the Second World War. There was some confusion about his name, suggesting that he might be related to the Marks of Marks & Spencer, and he was thus allowed to choose his post, which was with the cryptographers of the Special Operations Executive (SOE), working out of London. Although he acquired this position thanks to the class system, Marks proved to have a genius for cryptography and soon became head of communications. Not only did he break code, he also created it, developing a one-time code pad on silk that enabled SOE operatives to work more securely. In addition to relating his work as a cryptographer, Marks also provides new information on several other operations carried out in the field, as he was privy to most of the information going through their office. He also describes life in London at the time, particularly office life and its workers.

Subjects: Cryptographers; Espionage; London, England; Military Intelligence; Octogenarians; Special Operations Executive; World War II (1939–1945)

Now Try: Intelligence and espionage both proved to be essential to the winning of World War II. A classic true story of espionage is that written by William Stevenson about Sir William Stephenson, creator of a major spy network. The title reflects Stephenson's code name: ***A Man Called Intrepid: The Secret War.*** For a different perspective on cryptography work, readers can try Stephen Budiansky's ***Battle of Wits: The Complete Story of Codebreaking in World War II.*** Enigma was the name of the German code-creating machine. Hugh Sebag-Montefiore describes the efforts at breaking into its secrets in ***Enigma: The Battle for the Code.***

McCain, John (1936–)
Salter, Mark (1955–), coauthor

Faith of My Fathers. Harper, 2008, 1999. 349pp. ill. 9780061734953. Also available in large print, audiobook (read by the author), e-audiobook, and e-book. 973.90922

The fathers in the title are John McCain's father and grandfather. His grandfather was a naval commander, in charge of the Fast Carrier Task Force during World War II. McCain's father was also a naval commander, and by the time John McCain III was a POW in Vietnam, his father was Commander-in-Chief, Pacific Region. Both elder McCains became four-star admirals, the first time for such an achievement to occur in one family. The initial part of McCain's book is devoted to his grandfather and father, and then he moves to his own story: being shot down over Hanoi; breaking several bones in the crash; and being taken to the "Hanoi Hilton" (Hoa Lo Prison), the worst POW camp in North Vietnam. While in captivity, McCain was often tortured, and because he resisted his captors at every opportunity, he also spent much time in solitary confinement. Refusing special treatment because of his father's status, he used the faith and courage he had learned from his forebears to sustain him during his ordeal.

Subjects: Fathers and Sons; Grandfathers; Hanoi Hilton, Vietnam; McCain, John, Sr.; McCain, John Sidney; Pilots; Prisoners of War, Vietnam; Torture; United States Navy; Vietnam War (1961–1975); War Wounded

Now Try: Robert Timberg's ***The Nightingale's Song*** relates how the Vietnam War changed a number of graduates from the Naval Academy, including John McCain. Oliver L. North also graduated from the academy and has hosted several television programs subsequently published as books. One title that is particularly relevant here, written with Joe Musser, is ***War Stories II: Heroism in the Pacific***. Lewis B. Puller also had a father with large shoes to fill; his father, General "Chesty" Puller, had been a hero of five wars. Lewis went off to Vietnam, where he stepped on a land mine and was severely wounded. His memoir, ***Fortunate Son: The Autobiography of Lewis B. Puller, Jr.*** won a Pulitzer Prize for Biography or Autobiography.

Mullaney, Craig M.

The Unforgiving Minute: A Soldier's Education. Penguin, 2010, 2009. 386pp. ill. map. 9780143116875. Also available in audiobook, e-audiobook, and e-book. 958.1047

A literary war memoir in the same vein as Nathaniel Fick's ***One Bullet Away: The Making of a Marine Officer*** (see p. 485), Mullaney's book tries to answer the question, "What is a man?" To answer that question, he focuses on the various types of education he received. He divides his story into three parts, the first, "Student," being the longest. This first part deals with his formative years, growing up in a blue-collar family in Rhode Island and successfully gaining entrance to West Point. What he learned there was different in substance from what he learned at the army's Ranger School, where he was put through grueling paces. Winner of a Rhodes scholarship, he then went to Oxford to obtain master's degrees in diplomatic and economic history. The book then moves on to the second section, "Soldier," wherein, as a leader of a platoon in the 10th Mountain Division in Afghanistan, participating in Operation Enduring Freedom, he hopes that all of his education will stand him in good stead. When he loses one of his men in a bitter battle against al-Qaeda, he wonders how much good his education did him and if this fighting is worth it. The unforgiving minute comes time and again when he has to make immediate decisions under fire—Will they be the right ones? He finally returns stateside in the third section, "Veteran," which describes how he takes what he learns on the battlefield and tries to communicate it to the cadets he is now teaching at the Naval Academy in Annapolis. But he knows that they will really have to learn it for themselves.

Subjects: 10th Mountain Division; Afghan War (2001–); Army Ranger School, GA; Army Rangers; Military Training; Soldiers; University of Oxford, England; War on Terrorism (2001–); West Point Military Academy, NY

Now Try: Donovan Campbell is a Princeton and Harvard graduate who led a platoon in Iraq. As with most leaders, his concern was for his men. He writes about his time at war in ***Joker One: A Marine Platoon's Story of Courage, Sacrifice, and Brotherhood.*** Losing anyone in battle is devastating—for those on the battlefield and those at home. Rinker Buck wrote the story of the first Marine casualty in Iraq, Second Lieutenant Shane Childers: ***Shane Comes Home***. The class of 2002 at West Point was the first class to graduate in wartime in a generation. Tracing the life afterward of two graduates is Bill Murphy Jr.'s ***In a Time of War: The Proud and Perilous Journey of West Point's Class of 2002***.

Swofford, Anthony (1970–)

Jarhead: A Marine's Chronicle of the Gulf War and Other Battles. Scribner, 2005, 2003. 260pp. 9780743235358. Also available in large print, audiobook (read by the author), e-audiobook, e-book, and video. 956.7044245

This literary memoir tells of Swofford's nine months in the Persian Gulf War as a sniper with the U.S. Marine Corps. Literary it may be, but Swofford gets "down and dirty" and raw with his descriptions of Marine life. In trying to capture the moment for the reader—the absurdity, the insanity (almost literally meant here), the terror, and the exhilaration—Swofford's intent is to illustrate the realities of war, realities that are not witnessed in the television coverage that is often choreographed by the military brass back home. Swofford makes use of flashbacks to depict the youth he had been, son of a long line of veterans. He also describes the difficulties in coming home again; the disconnect between his life in the desert, always at the beck and call of a person in command; and his life in the United States, forced to make his own decisions.

Jarhead was a finalist for the *Los Angeles Times* Current Interest Book Prize and winner of the Pacific Northwest Booksellers Association Book Award and the PEN American Center Martha Albrand Award for the Art of the Memoir.

Subjects: Death; Marines; Operation Desert Shield; PEN American Center Martha Albrand Award for the Art of the Memoir; Persian Gulf War (1991); Snipers; United States Marine Corps; Writers

Now Try: The reservists are derisively referred to as "spare parts" by the enlisted men. Relating his own experiences in the Persian Gulf, Buzz Williams has written ***Spare Parts: A Marine Reservist's Journey from Campus to Combat in 38 Days***. Brandon Friedman was hawkish and a war junkie, happy to sign up with the army. After his stint in Afghanistan and Iraq, recognizing that those who set the policies and made the decisions actually had little or no military experience, he wrote his story, ***The War I Always Wanted: The Illusion of Glory and the Reality of War; A Screaming Eagle in Afghanistan and Iraq***. Michael Donnelly was afflicted with ALS (Lou Gehrig's disease) after his stint as a pilot in the Gulf War; with his sister Denise, he wrote ***Falcon's Cry: A Desert Storm Memoir***, a book that helped establish government recognition of the link between the Gulf War and the high incidence of ALS in its veterans.

Travers, Susan (1909–2003)
Holden, Wendy (1961–), coauthor

Tomorrow to Be Brave. Simon & Schuster, 2001. 304pp. 9780743200011. Also available in large print, audiobook, and e-book. 940.541244

Susan Travers was already in her nineties when she decided to make public her story, now that the main characters were no longer alive. As a child she regretted that she hadn't been born a boy (her father might have paid attention to her if she had been), and she grew up rebellious and in search of adventure. At the outset of World War II she decided to put aside her rebellions and seek her adventure. She joined the French Red Cross, although she hated the sight of blood, and soon realized her goal of becoming an ambulance driver. This skill, along with her courage, determination, and the love of her commanding officer in Algiers, are what enabled her to lead the escape of thousands of French soldiers—Free French and French Foreign Legion—out of a siege by Rommel. At the end of the war she decided to apply officially for the French Foreign Legion (omitting her gender from the application form). She was the only woman to be a member of that military group.

She resigned her commission in 1947 to be a wife and mother, but she had already been awarded the *Croix de Guerre* for her military service. In 1956 she received the *Médaille militaire* for her heroism in Algiers. In 1996 she was awarded the highest honor of the French Foreign Legion, the *Légion d'honneur*.

Subjects: Adventurers; Algiers, Algeria; Algeria; Ambulance Drivers; Bir Hakeim, Battle of (1942); English in France; Free French Commandos; French Foreign Legion; Red Cross; World War II (1939–1945)

Now Try: Readers may enjoy trying out a classic novel about the French Foreign Legion by Percival Christopher Wren, ***Beau Geste***. Ellen Hampton has brought to light the story of the women ambulance drivers who were "given" to a French general in World War II as a condition for a donation of nineteen ambulances. The women who defied the French general's expectations of their weaknesses became known as the "Rochambeau group," later termed the "Rochambelles"; Hampton's story is entitled ***Women of Valor: The Rochambelles on the WWII Front***. Another little-known war story has also come to light recently, that of Operation Halyard, in which the OSS organized the rescue of over 500 airmen from behind enemy Yugoslav lines. The story, ***The Forgotten 500: The Untold Story of the Men Who Risked All for the Greatest Rescue Mission of World War II***, is by Gregory A. Freeman.

Wolff, Tobias (1945–)

In Pharaoh's Army: Memories of the Lost War. Vintage Books, 1995, 1994. 221pp. 9780679760238. Also available in e-book. 959.70438

For those familiar with Wolff's ***This Boy's Life: A Memoir*** (see p. 271), this second memoir, set in Vietnam, may seem like a continuation, particularly in Wolff's use of language. In this book he goes back and forth from his childhood and youth to his current situation, but generally for the purpose of setting up a scene or to reflect his emotions. Able to speak Vietnamese after a year of studying it in Washington, DC, he is stationed with a South Vietnamese Army unit in the Mekong Delta as an advisor. He begins his war with enthusiasm and belief in its righteousness, but as happened to so many soldiers, that light gradually fades, and he becomes disillusioned with the futility and wrongness of it all. In many ways his war closely resembles Tracy Kidder's (see p. 488). One of the more interesting elements of this memoir, which undoubtedly heightens its quality, is that it is written from such a long vantage point, thirty years after the fact. We have, then, the older, more experienced, more mature writer and professor looking back at the poor sap who was so misguided, thus setting up a dual picture of the man, Tobias Wolff.

In Pharaoh's Army was a finalist for the *Los Angeles Times* Book Prize for Biography and for the National Book Award for Nonfiction. It was selected as a Notable Book by the American Library Association.

Subjects: 1960s; ALA Notable Books; College Professors; Fathers and Sons; Soldiers; United States Army; Vietnam War (1961–1975); Writers

Now Try: Although Jack Jacobs, also an advisor to a South Vietnamese unit, had a very different war from Wolff, he too describes it humorously in parts (with the help of Douglas Century) of ***If Not Now, When? Duty and Sacrifice in America's Time of Need***. Albert French is another novelist who fought in Vietnam, but he is African-American; as he describes in ***Patches of Fire: A Story of War and Redemption***, his return home was complicated not just by antiwar sentiment, but also by racial unrest. Much like Tobias

Wolff's, Nathaniel Tripp's father was absent in body but very much present in mind; Tripp too writes a literary memoir of his time in Vietnam, ***Father, Soldier, Son: Memoir of a Platoon Leader in Vietnam***.

Victims of War

"Collateral damage" is a term often used to describe the unknown civilians and homes destroyed in war. It has a less personal connotation, so that those hearing the news are not faced with the thought that someone's neighbors have just been killed by enemy (or friendly) fire. There is also little thought given to what life is like for those whose homes are in the middle of a war zone. In this section readers will find stories of those who have been wounded by war, physically or mentally, whether a civil war or a war of invasion. Many of these victims are children who found not just a way out but also a way to tell their stories. There are also those whose freedoms have been taken away; they too eventually managed to escape their war-torn countries. The downside to escaping, of course, is that now the writer is living in exile. What we see in many of these stories is the effects of fear, an offshoot of violence, and how this fear rules the lives of the writers and their families.

The group that is noticeably absent in this collection of memoirs is the family of the deployed. There are several children's books available and a few books on how the parent left at home can help children cope. For children, Deborah Ellis has written ***Off to War: Voices of Soldiers' Children***, and Allen Appel and Mike Rothmiller have also interviewed children to compile ***My Hero: Military Kids Write About Their Moms and Dads***. Andrew Carroll interviewed adults and edited their statements in ***Operation Homecoming: Iraq, Afghanistan, and the Home Front, in the Words of U.S. Troops and Their Families***, and Kristin Henderson has written ***While They're at War: The True Story of American Families on the Homefront***, but as yet there seem to be no individual memoirs for adults to read written from either the child's or the parent's perspective. The exception to this are the stories of losing a loved one to war, and two of those narratives are here (Sheehan and Tillman).

Memoirists who are victims of war can be those whose lives have been completely disrupted by war occurring in their country. They can also be those who have physically been caught up in their countries' wars, perhaps through brutal treatment from soldiers or as child soldiers. Victims of war are also the loved ones left behind, especially those who lose a friend or family member in the war.

Ahmedi, Farah
Ansary, Mir Tamim (1948–), coauthor

The Story of My Life: An Afghan Girl on the Other Side of the Sky. Simon Spotlight Entertainment. 2006, 2005. 249pp. 9781416918370. Also available in audiobook and e-audiobook. 305.23806

Farah Ahmedi was growing up in Afghanistan, a country at war, and for her education was very important. Afraid of being late for school one day, she took a shortcut through a field and stepped on a land mine. Only seven years old, she was shipped to Germany, where she stayed in the hospital for two years with no family or friends, dealing with the amputation of a leg; the other leg was made permanently rigid. Finally back at home, she and her mother went out shopping and returned home to find Ahmedi's father and sisters had been killed by a stray rocket hitting their house. She and her mother made the trek to a refugee camp in Pakistan and finally came to the attention of World Relief, which provided safe passage for them to Chicago. There they met a volunteer, Alyce Litz, who befriended them both. Alyce heard of a competition held by *Good Morning America,* asking for the story of one's life; she encouraged Ahmedi to submit what proved to be the winning entry; with the help of Mir Tamim Ansary, Ahmedi's story was published and has become required reading in high schools.

Subjects: Afghan-Americans; Afghanistan, Soviet Occupation (1979–1989); Amputees; Childhood and Youth; Children and War; Courage; Death of a Parent; Land Mine Victims; Refugees, Afghanistan; War; Women in Afghanistan

Now Try: Charles London interviewed scores of children growing up in war environments and includes their drawings as well in ***One Day the Soldiers Came: Voices of Children in War***. Without humanitarian aid, Farah Ahmedi would have been lost. Carol Bergman deliberately sought out humanitarian workers to tell their stories, not to spread more horror, but to bring hope and goodwill. She shares these stories in ***Another Day in Paradise: International Humanitarian Workers Tell Their Stories***. Although ostensibly used as a weapon of war against the military, land mines usually disable or kill civilians. Foreign correspondent Philip C. Winslow has seen the effects of land mines in the various theaters of war he has reported on and writes about his findings in ***Sowing the Dragon's Teeth: Land Mines and the Global Legacy of War***.

Bashir, Halima (1979–)
Lewis, Damien, coauthor

Tears of the Desert: A Memoir of Survival in Darfur. One World Ballantine Books, 2009, 2008. 335pp. 9780345510464. Also available in audiobook, e-audiobook, and e-book. 962.4043

This is a book of two parts, the first one a nostalgic description of life in a small village, living among Halima Bashir's Zaghawa people, secure in the love of her parents and her feisty grandmother, her father a progressive and successful cattle herder who saw to it that she had an education. Aside from the brutally clear picture of her circumcision at the age of eight, this is a lovely picture of life in

Western Sudan. The picture changed abruptly and horribly with the arrival at their village of the Janjaweed (Arab militia), who brutally raped a large group of schoolgirls and their teachers. Already a doctor, Bashir treated the rape survivors but could not keep silent. She told the newspapers and local NGOs what had happened. For this she was captured by forces of the government, tortured, and gang-raped, and her village was once again set upon. Finally able to leave Sudan, Bashir headed for England where her cousin lived, a cousin whom it had been arranged she would marry. By writing her book she hopes to bring the situation in Darfur to global attention, although she had to use a pseudonym to protect her family.

Subjects: Darfur Conflict (2003–); Fathers and Daughters; Female Circumcision; Genocide, Sudan; Grandmothers; Physicians; Rape; Refugees, Sudan; Sudan; Survivors of Rape; Victims of Violence

Now Try: Sam Childers does what he can to help the children of southern Sudan and northern Uganda. He hires Sudanese soldiers to go into the jungle and take the orphans and child soldiers away from their captors. His story is ***Another Man's War: The True Story of One Man's Battle to Save Children in the Sudan.*** Three independent filmmakers snuck into Darfur to interview scores of people about life there, and the resulting book is ***Darfur Diaries: Stories of Survival,*** edited by Jen Marlowe with Aisha Bain and Adam Shapiro. Martin Meredith has written a clear history of modern Africa, leading up to its current situation with so much unrest: ***The Fate of Africa: From the Hopes of Freedom to the Heart of Despair; A History of Fifty Years of Independence.***

Beah, Ishmael (1980–)

A Long Way Gone: Memoirs of a Boy Soldier. Farrar, Straus & Giroux, 2008, 2007. 229pp. map. 9780374531263. Also available in large print, Braille, audiobook (read by the author), and e-audiobook. 966.40492

Ishmael Beah was separated from his family when rebel soldiers attacked the villages around his home. Twelve years old at the time, he fled with other young boys and spent several months traveling the country, begging for food, trying to keep out of the hands of both the rebels and the government army. Eventually caught by a government soldier, he and other young boys were quickly indoctrinated into the life of war in Sierra Leone, helped by the hard drugs they were given to quash their conscience. Thanks to their training and the drugs, they committed unspeakable atrocities against the enemy, but Beah was fortunately rescued two years later by a UN worker before irreparable damage had been done. He spent a lot of time in rehabilitation at a center specifically set up for child soldiers; found to be an excellent spokesman against children in war, Beah was sent to New York to speak to the UN. He has set up the Ishmael Beah Foundation (http://www.beahfound.org/Beah_Foundation/Home.html) to help reintegrate child soldiers back into society.

A Long Way Gone was the winner of a Christopher Award.

Subjects: Child Soldiers; Children and War; Christopher Awards; Sierra Leone; Sierra Leone Civil War (1991–2002); Social Conditions, Sierra Leone; Violence; War Atrocities, Sierra Leone; West Africa

Now Try: Shocked as readers might be at the notion of boy soldiers, the existence of girl soldiers seems even more surprising, perhaps because there are not many stories told about them. Grace Akallo has told her story of being a child soldier, with the help of Faith J. H. McDonnell, ***Girl Soldier: A Story of Hope for Northern Uganda's Children***. David M. Rosen studied the phenomenon of child soldiers and in ***Armies of the Young: Child Soldiers in War and Terrorism*** offers a history, revealing that this theft of childhood is not new. Jimmie Briggs has been investigating child soldiers since the United Nations released its 1996 report by Graça Machel, ***Impact of Armed Conflict on Children***. He shares his findings in ***Innocents Lost: When Child Soldiers Go to War***.

Deng, Alephonsion (1982–), Benson Deng, and Benjamin Ajak (1982–) Bernstein, Judy A., coauthor

They Poured Fire on Us from the Sky: The True Story of Three Lost Boys from Sudan. Public Affairs, 2005. 311pp. map. 9781586482695. Also available in e-audiobook and e-book. 962.4043

The three young men (two brothers and a cousin) who have cowritten their refugee story were told by their parents that if the militia ever came to their village, they were to run. And one day there were marauding militia with their guns and their fire; in the midst of the horrific chaos the boys left, walking deeper and deeper into the forest. They walked for a thousand miles, first to a refugee camp in Ethiopia, where they were refused entry, and then back through Sudan for a bit to Kenya, to the Kakuma refugee camp. They were all six years old or younger. On their walk, aside from having to forage for food, avoid preying adults, and deal with separation from their families, they also encountered burnt-out villages, roads littered with land mines, and never-ending desert. The refugee camps were not much better except to prevent their being stolen to be child soldiers. Finally the International Rescue Committee discovered the three and arranged for their transfer to California, where they were at last able to get enough to eat and get an education, something that they greatly treasured.

They Poured Fire on Us was a Christopher Award winner. It also won the National Conflict Resolution Center Peacemaker Award.

Subjects: Childhood and Youth; Children and War; Christopher Awards; Courage; Kakuma Refugee Camp, Kenya; Lost Boys of Sudan; Personal Essays; Refugee Camps, Kenya; Refugees, Sudan; Sudan Civil War (1983–2005); War Atrocities, Sudan

Now Try: John Bul Dau's experience was similar to these boys', although he was a bit older, a teenager. His story, ***God Grew Tired of Us***, written with the help of Michael S. Sweeney, has also been made into a film. Dave Eggers's biographical novel, ***What Is the What: The Autobiography of Valentino Achak Deng: A Novel***, is about another lost boy, Valentino Deng, who wound up in Atlanta. For those who would like to see what happens to these boys once they arrive in the United States, Mark Bixler has written the story of four refugee boys, tracing their lives in the United States and portraying their helpers over here, the agencies, the professionals, the volunteers, and sometimes even celebrities. As he points out in ***The Lost Boys of Sudan: An American Story of the Refugee Experience,*** there have been at least 3,800 lost boys accepted into the United States.

Filipović, Zlata (1980–)

Zlata's Diary: A Child's Life in Sarajevo. New Preface by the author. Introduction by Janine Di Giovanni. Notes by Christina Pribichevich-Zorić. Penguin Books, 2006, 1994. 197pp. ill. 16pp. of plates. 9780143036876. Also available in large print, Braille, audiobook, e-audiobook, e-book, and video. 949.7024 [Trans. by Christina Pribichevich-Zorić]

Zlata started keeping her diary just before her eleventh birthday, filling her entries with talk of school, piano lessons, parties, friends, American television, and favorite pop stars. The tone and content of her diary gradually changed, however, as the siege of Sarajevo began. Her mother, a chemist, could no longer work, as her place of business was destroyed. The gas, water, and electricity were cut off. Food was hard to come by. School was no longer an option. Friends and family left in droves, and of those who didn't leave, several were killed. This became the stuff of her diary, along with her thoughts about it all. The efforts of her former English teacher and the International Center for Peace and Development resulted in Zlata's diary being published in part, which led to its being shown to a French publisher, who then pressured the government to let her and her family leave Sarajevo for France. Zlata and her diary have been used in school curricula to help American children understand current events and how difficult others' lives may be (see Erin Gruwell, p. 408).

Subjects: Adolescents, Yugoslavia; Children and War; Diaries; Refugees, Yugoslavia; Sarajevo, Siege (1992–1996); Translations; Yugoslav War (1991–1995)

Now Try: Filipović subsequently gathered diaries from children in several war zones, publishing the excerpts, with Melanie Challenger, as ***Stolen Voices: Young People's War Diaries, from World War I to Iraq***. Janine Di Giovanni, the journalist who wrote the introduction to this edition of ***Zlata's Diary***, has spent much of her professional life investigating and writing about the Balkan situation; one of these books is ***Madness Visible: A Memoir of War***. Lynne Jones offers a study of the children caught up in the violence in the Balkans in ***Then They Started Shooting: Growing Up in Wartime Bosnia***. In Saša Stanišić's novel, translated from the German by Anthea Bell, ***How the Soldier Repairs the Gramophone,*** the teenager Aleksandar leaves war-torn Bosnia with his family but can't forget a mysterious girl he had met there.

Him, Chanrithy (1965–)

When Broken Glass Floats: Growing Up Under the Khmer Rouge; a Memoir. W. W. Norton, 2001, 2000. 330pp. ill. maps. 9780393322101. Also available in e-book. 959.604092

From the age of three, Chanrithy Him lived in fear of the war in a neighboring country, Vietnam, and then she lived through the U.S. bombing of her own country, Cambodia. But her life changed horribly and dramatically when the Khmer Rouge took over in 1975; over the course of four years they killed almost two million people. Him and her family were sent off to labor camps, where her parents and some siblings died, but the remaining family encouraged each other with faith and hope and by sharing what meager food they could find. Finally the Khmer Rouge were overthrown and the remaining Hims were sent to a refugee camp in Thailand, eventually making their way to relatives in Oregon.

When Broken Glass Floats was a finalist for the Kiriyama Prize and the PEN USA West Literary Award and was winner of the Oregon Book Award for Literary Nonfiction.

Subjects: Cambodia; Children and War; Death of a Parent; Genocide, Cambodia; Khmer Rouge; Labor Camps; Political Atrocities; Refugees, Cambodia; War Atrocities, Cambodia

Now Try: Nic Dunlop, a photojournalist, was so horrified by the fact that the perpetrators of the Cambodian genocide had not even been captured that he went back to Cambodia to find out all he could about the man who headed the death camps, a former schoolteacher (Kech Ieu Kang) known in his notorious role as Comrade Duch. Dunlop's subsequent book, ***The Lost Executioner: A Journey to the Heart of the Killing Fields***, illuminates the man and the horrific activities he perpetrated over four years. The journalist François Bizot was captured by the Khmer Rouge and taken to a camp headed by Duch, who, ironically, was responsible for Bizot's being the only foreigner ever to be released. Bizot's story, ***The Gate***, translated from the French by Euan Cameron, provides a look at Cambodia before the Khmer Rouge and also offers a bit of a different perspective on Duch. (An interesting postscript is that thirty years after his war crimes, Duch finally came up for sentencing; victims of the Khmer Rouge are bitter that his sentence of thirty-five years has been reduced to nineteen for time served in prison in the countryside.) Dith Pran, featured as a main character in the movie ***The Killing Fields***, gathered eyewitness accounts of children who suffered through the atrocities of the Khmer Rouge and collected them in ***Children of Cambodia's Killing Fields: Memoirs by Survivors***; the collection was edited by Kim DePaul.

Jal, Emmanuel (c. 1980–)
Davies, Megan Lloyd, coauthor

War Child: A Child Soldier's Story. St. Martin's Press, 2010, 2009. 262pp. 9780312602970. Also available in audiobook, e-audiobook, and video. 962.4043092

Conscripted by soldiers for what he thought was a school for orphans, Jal willingly endured the forced march to Ethiopia, unprepared for what lay ahead of him for the next ten years. His father had left the family, joining the Sudanese People's Liberation Army, and in their travels from one burned-out village to another in search of food and shelter, Jal and his mother had become separated. Traveling with other lost boys, he was happy to be taken under the wing of the soldiers until he learned that his task was to wield the AK-47 that was taller than he and to kill as many Muslims as he could. Finding conditions more than intolerable, he and some other youth eventually defected, making their way to Kenya, where Jal was adopted by a British aid worker. Finding music therapeutic, Jal has since become a successful rap musician, using his music to help others in difficult circumstances and founding Gua Africa, an organization to help families overcome the effects of war (http://www.gua-africa.org/).

Subjects: Child Soldiers; Childhood and Youth; Children and War; Death of a Parent; Gua Africa; Humanitarians; Music as Therapy; Political Activists; Rap Musicians; Sudan Civil War (1983–2005); War Atrocities, Sudan

Now Try: Peter H. Eichstaedt looks at a specific region in Africa for his investigation into child soldiers: ***First Kill Your Family: Child Soldiers of Uganda and the Lord's Resistance Army***. Jal's searing prose is also a characteristic of Helon Habila's novel of a difficult life in Nigeria, ***Waiting for an Angel***. The story of Emma McCune, the British aid worker who married a Sudanese warlord, offers an unusual roadmap of the civil war in Sudan. Deborah Scroggins tells Emma's story in ***Emma's War***.

Nguyen, Kien (1967–)

The Unwanted: A Memoir. Little, Brown, 2001. 343pp. 9780316286640. Also available in e-book. 973.04959092

Kien Nguyen's memoir begins at the end of the war in Vietnam as he and his family wait in vain at the American Embassy to be airlifted out on the last day. His story, then, focuses not on the war itself but on the aftermath of war, with the Communists in power throughout the entire country. Making his life even more difficult is the fact that Nguyen's father was an American; Nguyen has blond, slightly curly hair and light eyes. He faces discrimination from his classmates, the Communists who tormented them, and even his family. When an attempt to escape fails, he winds up in a "reeducation camp." Nguyen says he wrote this memoir to encourage others who had difficult childhoods to look forward, not back. But he also wanted readers to have an understanding of Vietnam as it relates to the United States, and to share the story of many Amerasian children. Finally, he wants the reader to see what life under Communism looks like—Vietnam may be a beautiful country, but it was not a beautiful place to be after the war.

Subjects: Amerasians; Biracial Children; Childhood and Youth; Communism; Fatherless Children; Orderly Departure Program; Racism, Vietnam; Refugees, Vietnam; Vietnam War (1961–1975); Vietnamese-Americans

Now Try: Although he makes his living as a dentist now, Nguyen has also written fiction. One of his books, ***The Tapestries: A Novel,*** is grounded in the life of his grandfather, a tapestry-maker. Le Ly Hayslip's memoir, written with Jay Wurts, about living through the Vietnam War as a teenager, ***When Heaven and Earth Changed Places: A Vietnamese Woman's Journey from War to Peace,*** has become a classic. There was fear among many mothers about the treatment their Amerasian children might receive at the hands of the Communists; for that reason and others, many parents and orphanage directors gave up children to be taken away as part of Operation Babylift. Dana Sachs covered this large evacuation and has interviewed many of the people as adults, all of which she sets down in ***The Life We Were Given: Operation Babylift, International Adoption, and the Children of War in Vietnam***. Depicting life for the teenage Vietnamese refugee in the United States is Lan Cao's novel, ***Monkey Bridge***, a work that reflects her own experience.

Pazira, Nelofer (1973–)

A Bed of Red Flowers: In Search of My Afghanistan. Free Press, 2005. 408pp. ill. 9780743281331. Also available in e-book. 958.104092

The bed of red flowers refers to a springtime event when the tulips and poppies bloom and families head out of the city to see the fields of flowers. It is both a memory for Nelofer Pazira and a symbol of her life and her country before the Communists came in and arrested her father when she was five years old. The following year the Soviet army invaded and war began. War continued in Afghanistan even after the Soviets were defeated, but Pazira's family was able to leave, at first for Pakistan and then for Canada. When her good friend Dyana stopped returning her letters, Pazira returned to Afghanistan to find her. Learning the truth about her friend, she also learned more about her beloved country, now run by the Taliban. A journalist and filmmaker, Pazira subsequently made the award-winning documentary about this trip, ***Return to Kandahar***. She has also established a nonprofit to help develop literacy and other skills in young women in Afghanistan, the Dyana Afghan Women's Fund (http://www.dawf.ca/).

A Bed of Red Flowers won the Writers' Trust of Canada Drainie-Taylor Biography Prize.

Subjects: Afghanistan; Afghanistan, Soviet Occupation (1979–1989); Filmmakers, Canada; Female Friendships; Journalists, Canada; Taliban; War; Writers' Trust of Canada Drainie-Taylor Biography Prize; Women in Afghanistan

Now Try: One of the most lauded aspects of Pazira's memoir is her depiction of Afghanistan as a country in its own right. The story of Zubaida Hasan, told by Anthony Flacco in ***Tiny Dancer: The Incredible True Story of a Young Burn Survivor's Journey from Afghanistan***, accomplishes the same but highlights the stark differences between Afghanistan and the United States, as Hasan is taken to America for medical care. Women of Afghanistan seem to be depicted either as victims of the Taliban, as "Sulima" and "Hala" describe it to Batya Swift Yasgur in ***Behind the Burqa: Our Life in Afghanistan and How We Escaped to Freedom***, or as women fighting for their rights and the rights of other women, as in ***Women of Courage: Intimate Stories from Afghanistan***, profiles collected by Katherine Kiviat and Scott Heidler, with photographs by Katherine Kiviat.

Riverbend

Baghdad Burning: Girl Blog from Iraq. Foreword by Ahdaf Soueif. Introduction by James Ridgeway. Feminist Press, 2005. 286pp. ill. 9781558614895. Also available in e-book. 956.70443092

Riverbend, a twenty-four-year-old blogger from Baghdad, presents an insider's view of the American invasion and then occupation of Iraq in 2003. A computer programmer, she could no longer work after the fall of Saddam Hussein and the rise of Islamic fundamentalism, as no one was willing to guarantee her safety as a woman. It soon developed that women couldn't leave their homes without being veiled or accompanied by a male. When there was electricity in the house she was able to write her blog and answer e-mails from her wide group of readers. While her blog provides a look at daily life in Iraq during occupation, it also informs the Westerner of real life in Iraq, with or without a foreign presence—food, habits, and religion. Well-informed, she offers her opinion on much of what goes on about her, whether the source is the local "puppet" government, the local Muslim clergy, or the American politicos who have such an influence on her daily life. Riverbend continues her blog in ***Baghdad Burning II: More Girl Blog from Iraq***, up to her last blog from Syria, where she is in Damascus as a refugee. In his introduction, the journalist James Ridgeway provides historical background to the situation Riverbend writes about.

Subjects: Abu Ghraib Prison, Iraq; Arab Women; Baghdad, Iraq; Blogs; Diaries; Iraq; Iraq War (2003); Social History, Iraq; War on Terrorism (2001–)

Now Try: Before Riverbend's book came out, a male blogger, codename Salam Pax, had a book published, ***Salam Pax: The Clandestine Diary of an Ordinary Iraqi***. Zainab Salbi, with the help of Laurie Becklund, tells about her life literally living under Saddam Hussein's shadow, as her father was his personal pilot. Happy to be able to leave, she has written ***Between Two Worlds: Escape from Tyranny; Growing up in the Shadow of Saddam***. The lives of four women in Baghdad during the occupation—two Iraqi sisters and two Americans, one military and the other a Muslim social worker—are portrayed and joined together by Christina Asquith in ***Sisters in War: A Story of Love, Family, and Survival in the New Iraq***.

Sheehan, Cindy (1957–)

Peace Mom: A Mother's Journey Through Heartache to Activism. Atria Books, 2006. 242pp. 9780743297912. Also available in e-book. 956.70443

Cindy Sheehan describes herself as someone who had no real knowledge of or interest in history or politics; who trusted her political leaders; and who was proud of her son, Casey, for enlisting, even when he was sent to Iraq. That all changed the day she learned of his death in Sadr City. Crazed by grief, she decided she had to do something to make his death worthwhile. She began to fight, and she is still fighting. In her book she describes how she became a peace activist—a nonviolent activist, but a vocal, in-your-face activist. And the person whose face she tried the hardest to get into was that of George W. Bush, whose policies had sent her son to war and to his death. She camped out (setting up what the media dubbed "Camp Casey") near the Bush ranch in Crawford, Texas, while Bush was on vacation, wanting him to come speak to her. She has met with various lawmakers and policy makers, she has held demonstrations, she has an Internet radio show and a Web site (http://www.cindysheehanssoapbox.com/), and she is vilified by many. Her son died in 2004, and she has been campaigning ever since, often to no avail. One other loss Cindy Sheehan suffered through the death of her son was the loss of her husband through divorce.

Subjects: Bush, George W.; Death of a Child; Iraq War (2003–); Marines; Pacifists; Peace Activists; Sheehan, Casey; War Casualties

Now Try: Jim Sheeler writes about one of the men who comes to the door back home to deliver the horrible news. In ***Final Salute: A Story of Unfinished Lives*** Sheeler describes shadowing Major Steve Beck as he made his house calls; at the same time, Sheeler offers a tribute to all the fallen soldiers. Martin Schram wrote an exposé, ***Vets Under Siege: How America Deceives and Dishonors Those Who Fight Our Battles***, which backs up much of what Cindy Sheehan has been saying in her speeches. Many women have been recognized for their peace efforts; a specific group has been described in ***Champions for Peace: Women Winners of the Nobel Peace Prize*** by Judith Stiehm.

Thwe, Pascal Khoo (1967–)

From the Land of Green Ghosts: A Burmese Odyssey. Introduction by John Casey. Illustrated by the author. Perennial, 2003, 2002. 304pp. 8pp. of plates. 9780060505233. 959.105092

Pascal Thwe was a member of the Padaung tribe in Burma, a Catholic living in the mountains, but also formed by long-held animist beliefs. By the time he was at university in Mandalay, Thwe's once-prosperous country was changing, failing under the direction of a one-party dictator, General U Ne Win. While waiting on tables to help pay for university, Thwe met a Cambridge don, John Casey, with whom he corresponded after Casey returned to England. As the political situation in Burma worsened, Thwe became quite involved with rebel groups, until he was forced to flee to their camps, away from the city. With the help of John Casey, he then fled to England, burdened with guilt at leaving behind his people; he remains haunted by the "green ghosts" of those who have been killed.

From the Land of Green Ghosts was awarded the Kiriyama Prize.

Subjects: Burma; Burma Civil War (1948–); College Professors; English Literature; Guerrillas; Kiriyama Prize; Padaung Tribe, Burma; War

Now Try: One of Thwe's difficulties is that he cannot return to Burma; to visit his family he can see them for a few hours only on the Thai border. Because Aung San Suu Kyi chose to stay in Burma to fight for her people, she has never been able to leave the country. She is able to write, however, and has published a collection of letters written for a Japanese newspaper shortly after her release from one of her house arrests, ***Letters from Burma***, in which she describes her country, presenting it optimistically, always hopeful for positive change. As the grandson of U Thant, former Secretary-General of the United Nations, Thant Myint-U is well placed to provide an overview of his country, Burma, in ***The River of Lost Footsteps: Histories of Burma***. Following in George Orwell's footsteps and talking to people throughout Burma about him, Emma

Larkin presents a political travelogue of the country that had such an influence on the British writer, ***Finding George Orwell in Burma***.

Tillman, Mary
Zacchino, Narda, coauthor

Boots on the Ground by Dusk: My Tribute to Pat Tillman. Modern Times, 2008. 344pp. ill. map. 9781594868801. Also available in large print, audiobook (read by the author), e-audiobook, and e-book. 796.332092

Mary Tillman came from a long line of army people, so if she had been told her son was killed by friendly fire, she would have accepted that as a possible outcome of being at war. What she could not accept was the way the government handled her son's death, with lies, contradictions, obfuscations, and a total lack of respect. This is not to say that she accepted the tragedy of her son's death, or that she wasn't torn apart by grief. The first story Mary was told was that Pat had been shot getting out of a vehicle; then in a move toward creating propaganda, it was said that he was shot leading a charge up a hill. Describing her efforts to learn the truth of her son's death, Mary also weaves the story of her son's childhood and youth throughout her story, as she wanted to bring alive for the general public the man who was her son, who was more than a football celebrity or a victim of war.

Subjects: Afghan War (2001–); Army Rangers; Bureaucracy; Death of a Child; Football; Soldiers; Tillman, Pat; United States Government; War Casualties

Now Try: Pat and Mary Tillman's case was already well-known because of Pat's celebrity status as a football player who forsook his large salary to enlist. Gaining permission from Pat's wife, Marie, to go through his journals, Jon Krakauer wrote ***Where Men Win Glory: The Odyssey of Pat Tillman***. The documentary, ***The Tillman Story***, also came out in 2010. A similar situation had come into the news during the Vietnam War when Michael Mullen was killed by friendly fire. The government's efforts to cover up the real cause of his death turned Michael's mother, Peg, into a war resister and peace activist. She wrote her story in ***Unfriendly Fire: A Mother's Memoir***. Jason Dunham was a Marine who sacrificed his life for his men by putting his own helmet over a live grenade in Iraq. Michael M. Phillips recounts the life and death of this hero in ***The Gift of Valor: A War Story***. Spouses also suffer from their loved ones being in a war zone. Tanya Biank was both an army "brat" and an army wife, who interviewed four army wives for her book, ***Under the Sabers: The Unwritten Code of Army Wives***. They describe life back home, dealing with the normal stresses of raising children and running households with the added stress of missing and worrying about their husbands while trying to comfort the children.

Ung, Loung (1970–)

First They Killed My Father: A Daughter of Cambodia Remembers. Harper Perennial, 2006, 2000. 238pp. ill. 9780060856267. 959.6042

Loung Ung was five years old when her family was "evacuated" from their home in Phnom Penh by the Khmer Rouge. From the beginning of their exile, Ung's parents had understood that they should hide both their wealth and their literacy. Finally, Ung's father (to whom she had been very close) was taken away, never to be seen again. What sustained Ung through the four years of trying both to survive and to help her family despite her youth was that very family and the love and closeness she felt among them. But this same closeness nearly tore her apart as one sibling after another died, in addition to her parents. Remaining were her older brother, Meng, and an older sister, Chou. When her brother had the opportunity to flee to Thailand and from there to the United States, he took Ung with him, believing she would be better able to make a go of it. She subsequently wrote another memoir, recounting her reunion fifteen years later with her sister, ***Lucky Child: A Daughter of Cambodia Reunites with the Sister She Left Behind***.

Subjects: Cambodia; Children and War; Death of a Parent; Genocide, Cambodia; Khmer Rouge; Labor Camps; Political Atrocities; Refugees, Cambodia; War Atrocities, Cambodia

Now Try: Another very poignant story of a little girl caught in a war is that of the Vietnamese child burning with napalm whose picture was taken by Nick Ut, a photographer for the Associated Press. Kim Phuc eventually moved to Canada, where the Canadian writer Denise Chong was asked to write her story, ***The Girl in the Picture: The Story of Kim Phuc, the Photograph, and the Vietnam War***. Kim Phuc has founded an organization to help children of war: Kim Phuc Foundation International: Healing Children of War (http://www.kimfoundation.com). In ***Crossing Three Wildernesses: A Memoir***, the poet U Sam Oeur, helped by his translator, Ken McCullough, describes how he and his family had to feign illiteracy and poverty to survive the Pol Pot regime in Cambodia. Readers who are curious about how a little girl like Loung could assimilate in a country so different from her own might enjoy reading the assimilation story of Kao Kalia Yang, ***The Latehomecomer: A Hmong Family Memoir***.

War Correspondents

The greatest dignity and respect you can give [victims of war] is to show the horror they suffered, the absolute gruesome horror.—David Leeson (quoted in Weitzel, 2006)

The media play a large role in the reader's understanding of war, and that understanding can often depend on who owns a television station or newspaper. Conservatives will get one view of the war and progressives another, depending on which station they watch or which newspaper they read. Questions of a moral or ethical nature abound in war reporting. Should the reporter be objective or biased, reflect the emotions stirred up by what is being witnessed or be dry in the telling? Very often all that is offered to journalists are the daily press releases from the information distillers. Should this be what is reported back, or should the journalist risk life and limb to discern the truth? Aeschylus (525–456 BCE) said, "In war, truth is the first casualty." But the journalists in this section seem determined to dig out the truth and to tell it. Many of them have risked their lives to do so, whether the war took place in the 1940s or is still continuing.

Particularly in the latest rash of wars, there are distinctions being made between embedded and unembedded journalists. The former are with a specific unit and report on the war from that unit's perspective, providing a worm's-eye view of the war. The advantages are the immediacy and the reflection of the experience of the war. The journalist also has to agree to certain restrictions about what can and cannot be reported and when. The unembedded journalist has much more freedom of movement and can look at the war from a broader perspective but may not have the same access as the embedded journalist.

Memoirs by war correspondents do not have to maintain the level of objectivity that their reporting should have had. Correspondents describe their lives and what they have witnessed, recognizing that their participation in the war is quite different from that of those who are enlisted combatants. They may use their memoirs as vehicles they felt their reports could not be, so that they might be more impassioned in tone.

Garrels, Anne (1951–)

Naked in Baghdad. Letters by Vint Lawrence. Picador, 2004, 2003. 246pp. maps. 9780312424190. Also available in large print, Braille, and audiobook. 956.70443

Initially during the build-up to the Iraq War, Anne Garrels could go in only briefly, as visa extensions were not being granted to foreign correspondents. She still managed to capture the mood of Baghdad and its people—frightened, just waiting for the bombs to drop—and see the rampant corruption. But she found the Baghdadi people warm and friendly, even when they knew she was American. Once she was allowed in for a longer period of time, she stayed in the Al-Rashid Hotel, one of sixteen unembedded journalists covering Iraq at the time. Normally journalists were assigned a "minder" for the times that they were interviewing locals, as the locals would be too frightened to speak their minds in the front of the minder. Reports were given out by the Ministry of Information, which sometimes was all the information the reporters would have. Fortunately—or perhaps due to her experience and professionalism—Garrels acquired a minder who became her friend, confidant, and facilitator in meeting professionals and middle-class people who would speak openly to her. Her title comes from the fact that one night she did her reporting while naked in her hotel room, as the satellite phone she was using was illegal to have and she thought that using the guise of having to get dressed would give her time to hide the phone if anyone came to her room. Garrels's memoir is interspersed with copies of e-mails that her husband sent to friends and family, offering a personal look into the life of a correspondent. Garrels was in Iraq from October 2002 until April 2003.

Subjects: Diaries; Foreign Correspondents; Iraq War (2003–); Journalists; Letters; National Public Radio; Newswomen; War on Terrorism (2001–)

Now Try: Molly Moore was the Pentagon correspondent for *The Washington Post* who accompanied a commanding general into battle in Kuwait during the Persian Gulf War; she tells her story in ***A Woman at War: Storming Kuwait with the U.S. Marines***. Providing the perspectives of a number of journalists working in Baghdad is the collection by Bill Katovsky and Timothy Carlson, ***Embedded: The Media at War in Iraq***. Garrels provided more of the human and political interest of the war in her memoir. Colonel Peter R. Mansoor provides a commanding officer's view of it in ***Baghdad at Sunrise: A Brigade Commander's War in Iraq***.

Guibert, Emmanuel (1964–), Didier Lefèvre (1957–2007), and Frédéric Lemercier (1962–)

The Photographer. First Second, 2009. 267pp. chiefly ill. maps. 9781596433755. 070.49095 [Trans. by Alexis Siegel]

Didier Lefèvre was a photojournalist who accompanied a group from Doctors Without Borders (*Médecins sans Frontières*) through the mountains of Afghanistan to treat the wounded mujahideen during the Soviet invasion. The result is this collaboration. Lefèvre's photographs and narration are the primary source for this story of heroism amid the brutality of war. Emmanuel Guibert is a graphic illustrator who embeds Lefèvre's narration into his own illustrations. The graphic designer Frédéric Lemercier then put the work together, juxtaposing Guibert's illustrations with Lefèvre's photographs. The end product is a testament to the courage of Doctors Without Borders and to the woman (Juliette Fournot) who led them in Afghanistan. It is also a testament to the courage of Lefèvre, who thought he was going to die out there, abandoned by his guides on the way back, taking long-lens photographs so people would know where he had died, but ultimately rescued by a group of roving brigands.

The Photographer was selected as a Notable Book by the American Library Association.

Subjects: Afghanistan, Soviet Occupation (1979–1989); ALA Notable Books; Courage; Doctors Without Borders; Fournot, Juliette; Graphic Narratives; Humanitarians; Lefèvre, Didier; Medical Assistance; Photojournalists; Translations; War Photography

Now Try: Photojournalists often find themselves in a moral quagmire: their job is to photograph what is happening, without being able to do anything to stop it. (One notable exception is Nick Ut, who took Kim Phuc's photograph in Vietnam: before he filed his pictures, he took the burning child to the hospital.) This dilemma is vocalized by a number of photographers for the National Geographic Society in Cathy Newman's ***Women Photographers at National Geographic***. Deborah Copaken Kogan is a photojournalist who was always looking for adventure and asked to go to Afghanistan during the Soviet invasion. There she came of age, telling her story in ***Shutterbabe: Adventures in Love and War***. For readers who would like to know more about war photographers, Peter Howe has collected stories from a variety of them in ***Shooting Under Fire: The World of the War Photographer***.

Laurence, John (1939–)

The Cat from Hué: A Vietnam War Story. PublicAffairs, 2002. 850pp. map. 9781891620317. Also available in e-book. 959.7043092

John Laurence had three tours of duty in Vietnam for CBS news, getting up close to the fighting and the fighters. He was there at the beginning from 1965 to1966, then at its height in 1968, and finally at the Cambodian Incursion in 1970. He begins his reminiscences with the story of finding a kitten during the battle at Hué, a feisty kitten that didn't seem to like Americans and thus embodied for him the Viet Cong. He uses the kitten as a referral point throughout his memoir. Because he was in Vietnam with audio equipment and a cameraman, Laurence was able to re-create verbatim much of the conversation that he had witnessed then, giving his memoir a sense of immediacy and honesty. During his different tours he stayed with different groups—the U.S. Army, the Marines, and the South Vietnamese Army—providing a variety of personalities and experiences. He also has much to say about specific correspondents he encountered there. While there he was comfortably accommodated, supported by the military; he includes a portrait of his day-to-day life in Vietnam as well. One of his final conclusions about the war was that while he thoroughly disagreed with it in principle and in practice, he had a tremendous respect for the soldiers and Marines who put their lives on the line every day.

Subjects: Cats; CBS (Television Network); Foreign Correspondents; Journalists; Vietnam War (1961–1975)

Now Try: Ward S. Just was a correspondent for *The Washington Post* when he was sent to Vietnam. The book he wrote from his experiences there was initially written while the war was still going on, but has been reissued since: ***To What End: Report from Vietnam***. Much has been reported by male correspondents, but there were women in Vietnam as well, whom Joyce Hoffmann researched for her book, ***On Their Own: Women Journalists and the American Experience in Vietnam***. And if the reader would like to hear from the combatants themselves, Bernard Edelman and the New York Vietnam Veterans Memorial Commission have collected letters from many of them in ***Dear America: Letters Home from Vietnam***; at the end of each letter the compilers have described what happened to the letter writer.

Rooney, Andrew (Andy) (1920–)

My War. Foreword by Tom Brokaw. PublicAffairs, 2000, 1995. 333pp. ill. 9781586480103. Also available in large print, audiobook (read by the author), and e-book. 940.548173

When Andy Rooney was drafted as a junior in college during World War II, he was a joker who did not endear himself to his drill instructor, thus eliminating his candidacy for officer training. He includes in his memoir a picture of himself as a private when he started his war service as an artilleryman. It wasn't long before he answered a "Help Wanted" ad for the army newspaper, *The Stars and Stripes*, and changed his life by writing for the paper for the duration of the war. Because he was a member of the army, he had access to army equipment and personnel, and he saw warfare in several theaters. Notable (for him) among his experiences were the battle at Saint-Lô, for which he won a Bronze Medal; the liberation of Paris; and the opening of the gates of Buchenwald. Although his memoir is written from the vantage point of a man fifty years older, he still presents his youthful self in the book. Throughout his memoir he offers opinions on war itself and whether any peace was better than war. After he went through the gates at Buchenwald, however, he believed that there were some manifestations of "peace," or at least noncombat, that were worse than war, and he realized finally what everyone had been fighting for.

Subjects: Foreign Correspondents; Soldiers; *The Stars and Stripes* (Newspaper); Television Journalists; United States Army; World War II (1939–1945)

Now Try: Perhaps the best-known correspondent of World War II was Ernie Pyle, who wrote about the war from the soldier's point of view and was killed by machine-gun fire while traveling with a commanding officer and three other men. He published a number of collections of his articles, but the most interesting might be one that distills them all, edited by David Nichols: ***Ernie's War: The Best of Ernie Pyle's World War II Dispatches***. Eric Sevareid, a CBS television journalist like Rooney, wrote a memoir as soon as the world war was over, ***Not So Wild a Dream***, but also included his life up to that point. Michelle Ferrari compiled transcripts of interviews with a number of reporters who have covered various wars in the twentieth century, and James Tobin added his commentary, in ***Reporting America at War: An Oral History***.

Seierstad, Åsne (1970–)

The Angel of Grozny: Orphans of a Forgotten War. Basic Books, 2010, 2008. 340pp. 9780465019496. Also available in e-book. 974.52086 [Trans. by Nadia Christensen]

Seierstad was a foreign correspondent in Moscow in 1994 when the Russians invaded Chechnia, a war that Seierstad then reported on, going back and forth to Chechnia several times between 1994 and 1996. Returning ten years later, she found that although Vladimir Putin said the war was over, it in fact presented itself in another fashion. The lens through which she examines war is the victims, particularly the children, whom she highlights here in this story of a people dehumanized by the brutal treatment they have received. Forced to disguise herself, she often stayed with Hadijat and Malik Gataev, Hadijat being the angel in the title. Ramzan Kadyrov, Putin's chosen president of Chechnia, declared that his republic no longer had need of orphanages and closed all the state-run orphanages, leaving thousands of children with no place to go. Hadijat went out on the streets and brought home those who would come, trying to offer some succor, but Seierstad has no illusions about the long-lasting effects of the war on these children, particularly since the terrorizing of Chechen citizens is still a part of daily life.

Subjects: 21st Century; Abandonment; Chechnia (Russia); Chechnia (Russia), Civil War (1994–); Children and War; Fear; Foreign Correspondents, Norway; Gataev, Hadijat; Journalists; Orphans; Russia; Social Conditions, Chechnia (Russia); Totalitarianism; Translations

Now Try: Seierstad has lived in various trouble spots, writing about them afterward. One of her more recent books is ***With Their Backs to the World: Portraits from Serbia,*** translated from the Norwegian by Sindre Kartvedt, in which she sets out to discover how the people of Serbia are faring today. The journalist Anna Politkovskai'a' also reported from Russia and Chechnia and received many death threats for her work. Before the final threat was carried out in 2006, she published (among other titles) ***A Small Corner of Hell: Dispatches from Chechnya,*** translated from the Russian by Alexander Burry and Tatiana Tulchinsky. The Chechens have learned brutality from their masters, a fact that Timothy Phillips describes in his reportage of the attack on schoolchildren and their teachers in ***Beslan: The Tragedy of School No. 1.*** Scott Anderson is a war correspondent who became obsessed with the story of the intrepid aid worker who went missing in Chechnia. In his book, ***The Man Who Tried to Save the World: The Dangerous Life and Mysterious Disappearance of Fred Cuny,*** he describes how he traveled throughout Chechnyia interviewing people, getting nothing but lies.

Woodruff, Lee, and Bob Woodruff (1961–)

In an Instant: A Family's Journey of Love and Healing. With a new Afterword. Random House, 2008, 2007. 292pp. ill. 9780812978254. Also available in large print, audiobook (read by the authors), e-audiobook, and e-book. 070.4333092

A month after Bob Woodruff was promoted to the position of coanchor of ABC's *World News Tonight,* replacing Peter Jennings, he was embedded with American soldiers in Iraq. The armored vehicle he was in was hit by an improvised explosive device (IED), and Woodruff was seriously hurt. Part of his skull blew off, resulting in traumatic brain injury. He and his wife, Lee, both recognize his good fortune in the care he received from the military doctors right from the very beginning. In their memoir of his trauma and healing they go back and forth, recalling events and feelings from before the explosion as well as during and after. They are both honest in revealing the natural stresses one would find in a marriage, but Lee comments that she can't imagine what it would be like to go through what they'd been through—including her sitting vigil wondering if he would live and if he did, whether he would be a vegetable—if you didn't really love that person. Frightening for Bob was the fact that he had to relearn language, how to speak, and how to walk properly. For someone who makes his life writing and speaking, such a head trauma could be devastating.

Subjects: Family Relationships; Improvised Explosive Devices; Iraq War (2003–); Marriage; Television Journalists; Traumatic Brain Injury; War Wounded

Now Try: All those who care for a family member in need know how challenging it can be. Nell Casey asked a number of writers who have experienced this to send in essays, which she collected into ***An Uncertain Inheritance: Writers on Caring for Family***. Paula Butturini's husband, John Tagliabue, was shot by a sniper when he was reporting in Romania; her memoir, ***Keeping the Feast: One Couple's Story of Love, Food, and Healing in Italy***, describes their journey toward his healing and the restoration of their marriage to the way it was before this violence overtook them. C. E. Crimmins wasn't quite as lucky as Lee Woodward. As she relates in ***Where Is the Mango Princess?***, her husband did not come back the same person at all after his brain injury in a boating accident.

Consider Starting With . . .

Bashir, Halima. *Tears of the Desert: A Memoir of Survival in Darfur*

Brady, James. *The Coldest War: A Memoir of Korea*

Caputo, Philip. *A Rumor of War*

Dole, Robert J. *One Soldier's Story: A Memoir*

Dryden, Charles W. *A-Train: Memoirs of a Tuskegee Airman*

Fick, Nathaniel. *One Bullet Away: The Making of a Marine Officer*

Herr, Michael. *Dispatches*

Him, Chanrithy. *When Broken Glass Floats: Growing Up Under the Khmer Rouge; a Memoir*

Jal, Emmanuel. *War Child: A Child Soldier's Story*

Pazira, Nelofer. *A Bed of Red Flowers: In Search of My Afghanistan*

Fiction Read-Alikes

Abani, Christopher. *Song for Night: A Novella*. My Luck is a young teen, deliberately made mute and trained as a human mine detector for a rebel force in a West African country.

Barker, Pat. The Regeneration Trilogy, a series surrounding World War I, begins with *Regeneration*, in which the poet Siegfried Sassoon has been shipped off to a hospital for shell-shocked soldiers.

Charlesworth, Monique. *The Children's War* features a young half-Jewish girl, Ilse, sent to Morocco for safety, and Nicolai, a young German boy whose family hires Ilse's mother to work as a nanny for them.

Del Vecchio, John M. *Carry Me Home*. The dreams of home cherished while fighting in Vietnam prove to be bitter when some veterans actually do get home and try to create a new life for themselves.

Doctorow, E. L. *The March: A Novel*. General William T. Sherman wreaks havoc in his march through Georgia and the Carolinas during the Civil War.

Faulks, Sebastian. *Birdsong*. A clear-cut picture of fighting conditions in World War I is drawn in this story of a French woman and a British man fighting in France.

Harris, Robert. *Enigma*. Set in Bletchley Park, this thriller involves a mathematician who has been called back from medical leave to help break the German code, Enigma.

Iweala, Uzodinma. *Beasts of No Nation: A Novel*. In an unnamed African country, a young boy is forced to change from the gentle son of a schoolteacher into a brutal killer in his country's civil war.

MacFarquhar, Neil. *The Sand Café: A Novel*. A foreign correspondent himself, MacFarquhar has written a satire of journalistic life in Cairo during the build-up to the first Gulf War.

Marlantes, Karl A. *Matterhorn: A Novel of the Vietnam War*. A group of Marines come of age as they progress through the Vietnam War in a physical and mental environment unlike anything they'd ever experienced.

Works Cited

Carr, David. 2004. "Many Kinds of Crafted Truths: An Introduction to Nonfiction." In *Nonfiction Readers' Advisory*, edited by Robert Burgin, 47–65. Westport, CT: Libraries Unlimited.

Harari, Yuval Noah. 2007. "Military Memoirs: A Historical Overview of the Genre from the Middle Ages to the Late Modern Era." *War in History* 14 (3): 289–309. *Academic Search Premier*, EBSCO*host*. Accessed July 9, 2010.

Martinez, Juan. 2009. "Words of War: Military History and War Memoirs Hold Their Ground." *Publishers Weekly* 256 (4) (August 24): 29–35. *Academic OneFile*. Accessed July 8, 2010.

"*The Pacific*—In Their Own Words." 2010. *Sky Movies*. Accessed July 11, 2010. http://movies.sky.com/the-pacific-in-their-own-words.

Weitzel, Robert. 2006. "Victims of War Are Not to Be Seen or Heard or Mentioned." *CommonDreams.org*. Accessed July 10, 2010. http://www.commondreams.org/views06/0222-22.htm.

Chapter 13

Surviving Life

Description

All of the memoirists in this section have suffered a trauma or major hurt of some sort, and the number of categories in the chapter suggests the wide variety of ordeals that the writers have undergone. Some of the people suffered as children and may continue to suffer as adults; others have been taken by surprise as adults with unexpected and unwanted twists in life. Not being included in this chapter does not mean that the memoirists in other parts of the book have not suffered trauma. One need only look at some of the chapter titles ("Life on the Darker Side of History," "Life at War") to know that. Racism, for example, is seen in many other titles throughout this book, as is child abuse. Here, however, the focus is on how the protagonists at least survived, while some have even triumphed over their sufferings. "However different the nature of the trauma itself . . . what the writers share in common is an impulse to represent the overcoming of the wound, whether through repair, reconciliation, or redemption" (Birkerts, 2008). And what many of them want is for their struggle to mean something, for someone else to benefit from reading about it.

There continues to be a raging debate over the worthiness of these books. In Britain, books revealing trauma, particularly such events as child abuse, are referred to as "misery memoirs." The term is often used disdainfully, with an accusation of wallowing on the part of the memoirist and voyeurism on the part of the reader.

The dangers that people see in this outpouring of trauma memoirs are several. "These books give the impression that, far from being rare instances of individual tragedy, abuse, degradation and torture constitute real life these days. In essence, they help to normalise the abnormal" (Furedi, 2007). As an extension of that, if the trauma has been visited upon a child through sexual abuse, the frequent occurrence in these books normalizes pedophilia specifically so that pedophiles and their behavior seem no longer aberrations but fairly common. Another concern is that it may begin to appear that most childhoods are fraught with danger, that the home is no longer a sanctuary, and the feeling will grow that no one can be trusted. As children become adults, they may feel almost entitled to their adult misbehavior, blaming it on their difficult childhoods. And finally, there are those who are concerned with what is perceived as a major downslide into "mass narcissism and exhibitionism" (Jefferson, 1997).

For many, however, the writing and the publication of such memoirs are largely perceived to be a good thing, a sign of progress in our society. In Britain there is a suggestion of doing away with the "stiff upper lip" and breaking down the barriers of silence. In North America, too, particularly in terms of both race and gender violations, giving voice to the hurt is very positive, and perhaps a first step to lessening, if not eliminating, the commission of such violations.

One obvious benefit of these memoirs is that "the fact that the work exists argues that the writer attained some eventual reconciliation or mastery" (Birkerts, 2008). Unfortunately that is not true of all the memoirists here, but the fact of writing does reflect a modicum of coming to terms with the trauma. Giving voice to the event or even way of life is strengthening for the writer. "Survivor narratives have been seen as a necessary part of a therapeutic, healing process for the speaker, as well as an inspiration for others who may have had similar experiences. Though they are often silent or silenced, survivors may indeed be motivated to tell their stories and thereby bear witness to an unspeakable truth" (Potter, 2005).

Some therapists put a caveat on writing about trauma, however, for a few reasons. Their concern is that the reader may expect a happy ending, a recognition that all must be well now in all cases; if the writer cannot provide that happy ending, there may be an inclination to create one in response to a subtle pressure. There is also the notion that if the story is published, the familiar world surrounding the writer may be shattered, with isolation from family and/or friends who were featured in the book. And finally, there is doubt that the writer could even communicate the depth of his or her pain, as there may be no vocabulary adequate enough to translate the experience.

The actual writing of these memoirs proves interesting. The reader is often so caught up in the narrative, wanting so much for the writer to do this or that or say such and such as a natural outcome of the event, that it is difficult to remember that while the writer may have had no control over the actions or events that perpetrated the story, there is more control over the writing. If there is no obvious explosion of temper at a certain juncture, it may be that the explosion occurred in real life, but the effect of including it at that point in the narrative might have lessened the overall effect the writer was striving for. In other words, "the reading experience . . . is based on deliberate craft decisions made by the author" (Birkerts, 2008). Just as the writer may feel obliged to provide a happy ending, so too might there be a compulsion to hide details that could be perceived as invoking disapproval on the part of the reader.

The how of the writing can be difficult. Elie Wiesel found he could not write about his experiences during the Holocaust for ten years (see ***Night***, p. 443). As he wrote in ***A Jew Today*** (translated from the French by Marion Wiesel), "Should one say it all or hold it all back? Should one shout or whisper? . . . How does one describe the indescribable? . . . how can one be sure that the words, once uttered, will not betray, distort the message they bear?" (quoted in Yagoda, 2009).

Memory and truth always play an important role in memoirs, but here there is an interesting aspect to these elements. There may indeed be factual errors in the telling, but those errors could be a result of trying to mitigate the trauma for the writer. There may be omissions: Alice Sebold readily admits that she doesn't remember a specific detail here or there (making her story all the more realistic), but for what matters, she has court transcripts to provide her with necessary details. Tobias Wolff says it well at the beginning of his ***This Boy's Life: A Memoir*** (see p. 271): "I have been corrected on some points, mostly of chronology . . . I've allowed some of the points to stand, because this is a book of memory, and memory has its own story to tell. But I have done my best to make it tell a truthful story." Emotional truth may be what the narrator is striving for more than anything.

Memoirs written about the surviving life are stories of people whose lives have been very difficult, either as children (and continuing into adulthood) or as adults. In most cases the writers come out ahead, learning to put their past or their difficulties behind them, so that while the narrative may be harsh and sometimes difficult to read, the tone by the end may also be upbeat.

Appeal

Perhaps the greatest appeal factor in this chapter is the experiential one. If the narrator is accomplished enough as a writer to transcend the self and the specific travail and to connect to what is human in us all (Gutkind and Fletcher, 2008), the reader will then be able to make the connection, too. If the reader has suffered anything similar to the writer, there will be a feeling of companionship, that one is not alone, not the only one to have suffered such an event. There may also be a sense of self-congratulation, the reader saying to the writer, "we both came through this." The experience of sharing may be cathartic for the reader, suffering with the writer, feeling the emotions, recognizing those same emotions, seeing that there really is no need for shame or guilt (one of the predominant outcomes of trauma). The experience of reading can also put one's own situation into perspective, help one come to a greater understanding of what one is contending with.

Even if the reader has never gone through what the memoirist is describing, he or she can have empathy and derive a greater understanding of those who have walked in the writer's shoes. Again, there may be a new perspective for the reader, seeing that what might have appeared in his or her own life as difficult is not so bad after all. And despite the difficulty of the writer's life, there may still be an escape for the reader, engrossed in the story, in the characters, in what the outcome will be.

Then, of course, character is of major appeal. What did the character actually suffer through? How was it handled? Does the reader feel admiration? Pity? Disappointment? There is an intimacy here because the writer's story is of a real person who actually experienced such a life; the reader may feel as though a new friend has arrived. The kind of bonding that can happen can raise the emotional reaction of the reader—anger and outrage at the perpetrators or those who won't listen, sadness in the face of the character's own sorrow, hope for better days ahead, and satisfaction if the writer has a chance and the courage to confront the one responsible.

Depending on the story—who, what, where, when—details and more learning opportunities may abound. What exactly is Munchausen by Proxy syndrome? What does a sharecropper do? What is the caste system like? Even a question like: How does one survive? In the case of illness, there is much to be learned, not only from the specific and personal experiences of the writer, but also from the resources often offered throughout the book.

Organization of This Chapter

The chapter begins with five enduring classics dealing primarily with race, poverty, and blindness. The eight sections that follow reflect the very real traumas, heartaches, and difficulties that people have suffered, either as children or adults.

The first four of these sections, "Surviving Abuse," "Breaking the Cycle," "Discrimination," and "Living with a Difference," tell the stories primarily of those whose abuse or troubles began in childhood, although there are two in the "Discrimination" section who faced their major issues as adults. Here the reader will find stories of people who have survived abuse, who have been born into an often repeating cycle of unhappiness, who have suffered discrimination, and finally, who were born with or developed a physical ailment that has rendered them different.

The final four sections feature memoirists who have survived addiction, who have survived acts of violence, who have been seriously ill, and who have suffered the loss of a loved one.

Classics

Claude Brown and Anne Moody are perhaps not especially well-known apart from their books. And even those books may not be very well-known to the general public. They are, however, mainstays in the canon of autobiography; in the case of Brown, his is a classic in the literature of poor, urban Black youth, while Moody's is an enduring autobiography of growing up in the South on the cusp of the Civil Rights Movement. The other three authors are well-known apart from their books, but their books are an integral part of their history. Interestingly, all but one are stories of the

Black experience, which suggests that historically it is stories of race that have endured over other stories.

> Classic stories of the surviving life illustrate how important one's own efforts are in effecting a move from a difficult childhood to an adulthood of success and triumph. With one exception, the stories in this section demonstrate how difficult life can be if you are a Black person in a racist world. These narratives have the same kind of story to tell, but they all tell it differently.

Brown, Claude (1937–2002)

Manchild in the Promised Land. Touchstone, 2000, 1965. 415pp. 9780684864181. Also available in large print, Braille, and e-book. 309.17471

During his first year in college, Brown wrote an article about life in Harlem for *Dissent* magazine, which was seen by a publisher, who encouraged him to write his autobiography. Although that publisher was bought out by another, the manuscript still managed to make it through the pipelines and become a best seller. Claude Brown himself also managed to make it through the pipelines of a violent Harlem, where he was born. His parents had been sharecroppers in the South and came north to what they thought would be a land of opportunity. Instead, as we see through the young Claude's eyes and actions, they found a grim urban landscape, overcrowded, dirty, dangerous, and eventually given over to heroin. For the first decade and a half of his life Claude seemed destined to have a short life there, ending it in death by violence or long-term prison. He fortunately saw how destructive heroin was and managed to stay away from it; after being shot in the stomach as a young teen and spending several stints in juvenile hall, he decided that perhaps education was his way out. Because he's offering a realistic version of his coming of age, his young voice is proud of his role on the streets—the things he can accomplish and the way he can survive, including the beatings he received at his father's hands for his wayward life.

Manchild in the Promised Land won the Anisfield-Wolf Book Award and was selected as a Notable Book by the American Library Association.

Subjects: African-American Men; ALA Notable Books; Anisfield-Wolf Book Award; Classics; Coming of Age; Drugs; Harlem (New York, NY); Poverty; Race Relations; Urban Youth; Violence

Now Try: Stanley Tookie Williams finally saw the error of his ways, but not until he was on death row. The cofounder of a lethal gang, the Crips, he still managed to do what he could within the prison system as an antigang activist. His ***Blue Rage, Black Redemption: A Memoir*** was published after his execution.

R. Dwayne Betts is an example of how quickly a young boy can get himself into serious trouble, but he had enough wits about him to learn in prison how to stay out of trouble, as he describes in ***A Question of Freedom: A Memoir of Survival, Learning, and Coming of Age in Prison***. Dick Gregory, the popular African-American comedian and civil rights worker, wrote his seminal memoir at the same time as Brown, entitled ***Nigger; An Autobiography***, and written with Robert Lipsyte. He told his mother that the next time she heard the word it would be because people were talking about his book.

Keller, Helen (1880–1968)

The Story of My Life. Introduction by Jim Knipfel. Afterword by Marlee Matlin. Signet Classics, 2010, 1902. 232pp. ill. 9780451531568. Also available in large print, Braille, audiobook, e-audiobook, and video. 362.4109

Those who have seen the movie ***The Miracle Worker*** may feel they know the story of Helen Keller, and perhaps from that they would have a sense of the frustration both Helen and her parents felt before Anne Sullivan came on the scene. This classic memoir takes the reader up to the point where Helen is a young woman, making her own way in the world, but still with Anne Sullivan by her side. Anne had come to her when Helen was seven, a wild child with a temper and no manners to speak of; her parents had simply not known what to do with this child who could neither see nor hear and therefore could not talk. She would have known some language, as she was around nineteen months old when she became seriously ill. She survived her illness, but her parents were horrified to realize she was now deaf and blind. After doing some research, Helen's mother found and hired Anne Sullivan, a teacher who had been blind but who had had some sight restored through surgery. As a result of her association with Teacher (as Helen called Anne Sullivan), Helen was able to acquire a B.A. from Radcliffe and went on to become a lecturer and writer, focusing on blindness and deafness, as one might expect, but also on civil and women's rights, in addition to world peace.

Helen Keller was inducted into the National Women's Hall of Fame, was awarded the Presidential Medal of Freedom in 1964 by President Johnson, and was named one of *Time*'s People of the Century in the Heroes & Icons category.

Subjects: Blind; Childhood and Youth; Classics; Deafblind Women; Educators; Lecturers; Octogenarians; People with Disabilities; Sullivan, Anne; Writers

Now Try: Keller followed her early-years memoir with one a few decades later, ***Midstream; My Later Life***. Kim E. Nielsen has written a biography focusing on the woman Helen called "Teacher": ***Beyond the Miracle Worker: The Remarkable Life of Anne Sullivan Macy and Her Extraordinary Friendship with Helen Keller***. The woman whose story inspired Helen's mother to seek help for Helen was a sensation in her time, who then slipped into the background. Ernest Freeberg has brought her back into the light with ***The Education of Laura Bridgman: First Deaf and Blind Person to Learn Language***. Alexander Graham Bell's mother was deaf, and his father was a speech therapist, thus engendering in him a strong desire to teach deaf children. Charlotte Gray brings out this aspect of his interest in her biography, ***Reluctant Genius: Alexander Graham Bell and the Passion for Invention***. James Reston understands how a child with difficulties can change the family dynamic, as he describes in ***Fragile Innocence: A Father's Memoir of His Daughter's Courageous Journey***.

Moody, Anne (1940–)

Coming of Age in Mississippi. Delta Trade Paperbacks, 2004, 1968. 424pp. 9780385337816. Also available in e-book. 917.62250360924

Anne Moody's autobiography provides a bird's-eye view of what it was like to grow up poor and Black in Mississippi in the 1940s and 1950s. Her mother was maid to a White woman and would occasionally bring home leftover food from work. Moody marveled at such food, so different from bread and beans, their regular fare. As she passes through each phase in her childhood, her narrating voice changes so that the reader sees her coming of age quite clearly. This is especially evident when she starts to become aware, not just of such differences as White and Black lifestyles, but also of the differences enforced by the Jim Crow laws. She also recognizes that having her skin color can actually be a danger to her. She is shocked by the lynching of Emmett Till, which begins her activism. Moody is equally shocked by the passivity of her parents' generation, not even beginning to understand how they can stand by and do nothing. She is too young yet to understand the pervasive effects of being told all your life that you are no good. While getting a college degree, Moody becomes quite active in the Civil Rights Movement, describing in great detail, for example, the sit-in at Woolworth's in Jackson in 1963. After the bombing of the church in Birmingham, however, Moody becomes disenchanted with Martin Luther King Jr. and the nonviolent movement. The book ends before the Voting Rights Act of 1965, with her saying she has her doubts about whether or not Blacks will overcome.

Subjects: 1940s; 1950s; African-American Women; Childhood and Youth, African-American; Civil Rights Movement; Classics; Coming of Age; Mississippi; Race Relations; Racism; Till, Emmett

Now Try: Taylor Branch's Pulitzer-Prize winning social history, ***Parting the Waters: America in the King Years, 1954–63***, is a clear portrait of the time when Anne Moody herself was so active. The death of Emmett Till was not a catalyst just for Anne Moody: it provided a watershed for civil rights activists throughout the country. Mamie Till-Mobley (Emmett's mother, who hadn't wanted Emmett to go to Mississippi that summer), with the help of Christopher Benson, finally wrote her remembrance of Emmett: ***Death of Innocence: The Story of the Hate Crime That Changed America***. In his award-winning look at White sheriffs in Mississippi at the time, ***Sons of Mississippi: A Story of Race and Its Legacy***, Paul Hendrickson illuminates the racial intolerance of the time and the place.

Washington, Booker T. (1856–1915)

Up from Slavery; An Autobiography. Introduction by Ishmael Reed. Afterword by Robert J. Norrell. Signet Classics, 2010, 1901. 240pp. 9780451531476. Also available in large print, Braille, audiobook, e-audiobook, and e-book. 371.974

Washington was the son of a slave woman and a White man; because his mother was a slave, he was too until emancipation at the end of the Civil War. When he moved to West Virginia at the age of nine with his mother and siblings, he first worked in a mine but was then taken on as house boy for the owner of the mine. The woman of the house encouraged him to learn to read and write and to get an education, which he did, moving to Virginia to do so. After graduating from the Wayland Seminary in Washington, DC, he returned to his first school at the Hampton Normal and Agricultural Institute. It was there that he received the call to be the first teacher of the Tuskegee Institute—at that point the school for Black students was one room and he was the sole teacher. But he and the men who founded the school worked hard to build it up, and in 1892 the Tuskegee Normal and Industrial Institute became independent from the state of Alabama. Washington was its principal from its founding date, July 4, 1881, until his death in 1915. During this time he became well-known, not just as an educator, but also as an orator, and met with several prominent people, all the while working for the advancement of his people.

Subjects: African-American Men; Alabama; Biracial Children; Classics; College Presidents; Education; Educators; Orators; Slavery; Tuskegee Institute

Now Try: Washington followed his first memoir with a second: ***Working with the Hands: Being a Sequel to "Up from Slavery," Covering the Author's Experiences in Industrial Training at Tuskegee***. Robert J. Norrell, the man who wrote the afterword in this edition, has also written a biography of Washington, ***Up from History: The Life of Booker T. Washington***, which sets out to re-establish his reputation, as Washington was reviled by people from the North like W. E. B. Dubois. Norrell has also written a history of Black/White relations over the last century: ***The House I Live in: Race in the American Century***. George Washington Carver was one of the men whom Washington asked to come to Tuskegee; he eventually became the Director of Agriculture at Tuskegee. Linda McMurry Edwards tells Carver's story in ***George Washington Carver, Scientist and Symbol***. Slavery comes in many forms, and for some it could be the ghetto. Education was the way up from this slavery for Greg Mathis, as he recounts in ***Inner City Miracle***, with help from Blair S. Walker.

Wright, Richard (1908–1960)

Black Boy: (American Hunger); A Record of Childhood and Youth. Harper Perennial Modern Classics, 2006, 1945. 419pp. ill. 9780061130243. Also available in Braille, audiobook, and e-book. 813.52

By the time Richard Wright wrote this memoir, he had already successfully published ***Native Son***, a novel that established his reputation with both Black and White readers. So it was that when he wrote his memoir, Book-of-the-Month Club was interested in featuring it. But they wanted a more positive outlook than Wright had presented in his book. His childhood had been at times brutal, both in the racism he suffered and in the unloving, stultifying treatment he received from his family. His father had abandoned the family when Wright was five, and another man he became close to, his Uncle Silas, was murdered. The remainder of the family wanted only to keep the intelligent and verbal Richard quiet and subservient. When he finally got away and moved to Chicago, his life improved somewhat, but not significantly. Acknowledging that racism was a part of life in the North was more than the Book-of-the-Month Club was prepared to do. The editors at Book-of-the-Month asked him to delete his final six chapters on life in Chicago and instead insert a statement of hope about his move north to Chicago; the book, originally entitled ***American Hunger***, was renamed ***Black Boy***. In 1977 the expurgated chapters were published as ***American Hunger*** and then in 1991, with the editorial help of Arnold Rampersad, the Library of America published the entire work as ***Black Boy (American Hunger)***.

Black Boy was selected as a Notable Book by the American Library Association.

Subjects: African-American Men; ALA Notable Books; American South; Chicago, IL; Childhood and Youth, African-American; Classics; Coming of Age; Mississippi; Poverty; Racism; Writers

Now Try: Wright got his first big publishing break when he submitted four novellas to *Story* magazine, which had opened a competition to writers such as Wright, who were involved in the Federal Writers' Project. The publication that came out of that was ***Uncle Tom's Children, Four Novellas***. The Federal Writers' Project was instituted during the Great Depression to help unemployed people. Its history has been written by David A. Taylor: ***Soul of a People: The WPA Writers' Project Uncovers Depression America***. Racism and poverty formed Louis Armstrong's childhood, too, but he directed his development and talents into music, as recounted by Thomas David Brothers in ***Louis Armstrong's New Orleans***. Karl Fleming also used his pen to detail the facts of poverty and racism in the South, both as a journalist and in his memoir, ***Son of the Rough South: An Uncivil Memoir***.

Man hands on misery to man.
It deepens like a coastal shelf.
—Philip Larkin, "This Be the Verse," stanza 3

Surviving Abuse

Adults don't like to think of children suffering through their childhoods, yet many of the adult readers who will read these titles did just that themselves: suffered through their years growing up. There could be many reasons for that. The life may have been one of poverty, although there are many who will say that poverty does not necessitate an unhappy childhood. It could be poverty combined with other factors such as a parent not handling adversity well, or it could be extreme poverty so that all one remembers is being hungry all the time. The difficulty could come directly from one or both parents or even surrogate parents, as in foster care: a mentally ill adult, an adult who visits his or her own problems on the child, an adult who has no anger-management skills, or an adult who has no parenting skills. Examples of these different childhoods are to be found in this next section, offering readers an opportunity to see what some young children have suffered through and how they've survived as adults. It is primarily these stories that have earned the label "misery memoirs." As the quote from Philip Larkin suggests, a child's misery has often come down the generational line from the parent's own misery as a child.

Memoirs about surviving abuse cover a broad area of experience, as the writers tell of negligent or abusive parents or horrific foster-care systems. These narratives reveal the depths to which adults can descend in their treatment of children, and they also reveal the strength, optimism, and hope of the children themselves, now that the children as adults themselves relate their stories. In addition to their storytelling, however, many of these memoirists discuss the underlying issues in their problems and how they have made efforts to effect changes that will prevent similar tragedies occurring to other children.

Bridge, Andrew

Hope's Boy. Hyperion, 2008. 306pp. 9781401303228. Also available in audiobook and e-book. 362.733092

From the time he was born, Andrew Bridge had one thing going for him: his mother loved him and he loved her. But as she was unable to cope with the pressures of being a teen mom, life with her was not good. He lived with his grandmother in his very early years and then with his mother, who suffered from mental illness and a tendency toward petty crime. The state of California intervened and took Andrew from his mother, literally wrenching him from her arms, when he was seven. The institution they put him in was more like a prison than a refuge for young children, and in fact has since been shut down. His move to a foster home was little improvement: the foster mother had been a prisoner at Dachau and had no resources of her own to offer love and care to a child lonely and missing his mother. Andrew finally grew up, the only way for him to get out of the foster system, but throughout his tenure with his caretakers, he found solace in school, obtaining a scholarship to Wesleyan University. He is now at work on a book about former residents, now grown men, of the broken foster-care system in Alabama, specifically the Eufaula Adolescent Center, since closed due to the civil-rights lawsuit filed against it.

Subjects: Adult Child Abuse Victims; California; Childhood and Youth; Children's Rights Activists; Foster Care; Loneliness; Mothers and Sons; Single Mothers; Teenage Mothers

Now Try: The classic novel of unloving institutional care is Charles Dickens's ***Oliver Twist***, a story that Dickens had hoped would precipitate changes in attitudes toward foster care. Ashley Rhodes-Courter also spent much time in foster care and is now advocating for changes to the system. She narrates her foster-care life in ***Three Little***

Words: A Memoir. Illustrating the fact that not all foster situations are draconian is Kathy Harrison's memoir, ***Another Place at the Table: A Story of Shattered Childhoods Redeemed by Love.***

Burroughs, Augusten (1965–)

A Wolf at the Table: A Memoir of My Father. Picador/St. Martin's Press, 2009. 251pp. 9780312428723. Also available in audiobook (read by the author), e-audiobook, and e-book. 813.6

This memoir by Burroughs (né Christopher Robison) is considered to be a prequel of sorts. In ***Running with Scissors: A Memoir,*** he described his life with his mentally ill mother and with the family of a psychiatrist that he lived with after his mother dropped him off to stay with them. His memoir ***Dry*** follows the time period of his first memoir, recounting his experience with alcoholism and becoming sober (although the veracity of both those memoirs has been called into serious question). In ***A Wolf at the Table*** he goes back to his early childhood and youth, when his father, John Robison, was a big presence in his life. Or perhaps Burroughs would say his father's absence was a big presence in his life. His father, also abused as a child, was an alcoholic, who would either rage or sit in silence. Burroughs describes the various attempts he made at getting his father's attention and affection, none of them successful. Christopher's love for his father eventually turned to hate, and he even put a gun in his older brother John's hand, exhorting him to kill their father. The memoir takes us up to the age of twelve, when Christopher's mother finally leaves her husband for good, and then jumps over time to the point of his father's death, when nothing has been resolved. One element that is noticeably absent from this memoir is Burroughs's usual black humor; he has written a serious story with a serious tone.

Subjects: Absentee Fathers; Abuse (Parental); Amherst, MA: Childhood and Youth; Children of Alcoholics; College Professors; Family Relationships; Fathers and Sons; Loss; Neglect; Robison, John Sr; Triumph over Adversity; Writers

Now Try: By the time Lee Martin was aware of his surroundings, his father had changed from the man who would do anything for a neighbor to the man who would fly into violent rages, after losing both hands in a farming accident. Lee tells his story in ***From Our House: A Memoir***. Psychological abuse is often harder to deal with, as there are no obvious scars for others to see and sympathize with. Rachel Sontag's father was so controlling at home as to be pathological about it. She tries to come to terms with his autocracy in ***House Rules: A Memoir.*** Ianthe Brautigan's father, the poet and novelist Richard Brautigan, was also often distant, an alcoholic, troubled man. After his suicide she went in search of the man she hardly knew, writing their story in ***You Can't Catch Death: A Daughter's Memoir.***

Chen, Da (1962–)

Colors of the Mountain. Anchor Books, 2001. 310pp. 9780385720601. Also available in audiobook and e-book. 951.05092

Because Da Chen's family had been landlords when the Cultural Revolution began, by the time he was born, the family life had been reduced to one of poverty and abuse by the neighborhood and government. Chen did manage to gather friends around him, but they were not the acceptable kind. However, he also befriended an elderly woman who taught him English and showed him the doors that he could walk through if he worked hard enough at his studies. Chen was very bright and usually performed at the top of his class; despite this, however, he was often deprived of the opportunity even to attend school. In 1977 that all changed, when the country held its first nationwide education exams after the death of Mao. Chen took the exams and scored in the top 2 percent, thus enabling him to attend Beijing Language Institute. Even in Beijing he was poverty stricken, but at least he could work to provide for himself, so that economically his life wasn't as impoverished as it had been when he was a child. In ***Sounds of the River: A Memoir,*** Chen continues his story, taking the reader to the point where he moves to the United States.

Subjects: Childhood and Youth; China; Chinese-Americans; Cultural Revolution, China (1966–1976); Education; Poverty, China; Social History, China; Triumph over Adversity

Now Try: Guanlong Cao was also the son of a landlord, but his family lived in Shanghai, rather than in rural China as Da Chen's family did. Cao speaks of growing up in straitened circumstances in ***The Attic: Memoir of a Chinese Landlord's Son,*** translated by Cao and by Nancy Moskin, the attic being the small space where his family lived. The story of Zhengguo Kang's childhood and youth (translated by Susan Wilf) illustrates just how much worse Da Chen's life could have been, as we learn of Kang's life in the Chinese prison camp system in ***Confessions: An Innocent Life in Communist China.*** Born around the same time as Chen, Lijia Zhang doesn't mince words as she describes her feelings about China after Mao, in ***"Socialism Is Great!" A Worker's Memoir of the New China.***

Fox, Paula (1923–)

Borrowed Finery: A Memoir. Henry Holt, 2005, 2001. 210pp. ill. 9780312425197. Also available in Braille. 813.54

Paula Fox's chapter headings are places, indicating how much she was shunted about as a child. Her parents put her into an orphanage in Manhattan at birth, but she was rescued from there by a kindly minister, a man she called Uncle Elwood, who took her to a small New York town, Balmville. He might have raised her except for her parents' intrusive and demanding visits. They didn't want to keep her and raise her to be a loved and loving person, but they also didn't want her to forget that she had "parents." The kindness of strangers clothed her and sustained her throughout her childhood and youth (thus the title of her memoir); the cruelties of her parents taught her self-sufficiency and provided her with much fodder for the fiction that would make her famous. When she was a young adult, Fox gave birth to a girl whom she put up for adoption. That child, Linda Carroll, had difficulty with her own first-born daughter and then became a grandmother; she felt it was time to track down her biological mother, something she did successfully, as she recounts in ***Her Mother's Daughter: A Memoir of the Mother I Never Knew and of My Daughter, Courtney Love***.

Borrowed Finery was a finalist for the National Book Critics Circle Award in Biography/Autobiography and winner of the PEN American Center Martha Albrand Award for the Art of the Memoir.

Subjects: Abandonment; Abuse (Parental); Adoption; Books and Reading; Childhood and Youth; Children of Alcoholics; Children's Writers; Neglect; Octogenarians; Orphans; PEN American Center Martha Albrand Award for the Art of the Memoir

Now Try: In a noticeable departure from her fiction and her first memoir, Fox follows up her story of her childhood with one of a year in postwar Europe, reporting on the ruins of the cities and their people for a British news service, in ***The Coldest Winter: A Stringer in Liberated Europe***. Margo Perin has edited a collection of stories that are basically about bad mothers: ***How I Learned to Cook: And Other Writings on Complex Mother-Daughter Relationships***. Often it seems to make no difference if one is born into a poor family or into a rich family: dysfunction is dysfunction, as the great-great-great-granddaughter of Cornelius Vanderbilt, Wendy Burden, tells it in ***Dead End Gene Pool: A Memoir***. The fact that Paula Fox is a widely read author adds an interesting element to her life story. Elizabeth Berg offers advice to would-be writers in her own autobiographical venture, ***Escaping into the Open: The Art of Writing True***.

Gregory, Julie (1969–)

Sickened: The Memoir of a Munchausen by Proxy Childhood. Foreword by Dr. Marc Feldman. Bantam Books, 2003. 244pp. ill. 6 pp. of plates. 9780553803075. 616.85092

Munchausen by proxy syndrome (MbPS) is a parent's illness. The parent was usually abused as a child and now seeks attention from the medical community. The way to get that attention is to make the child sick so that the parent gets both attention and sympathy. That the child may suffer and perhaps even die from this is not relevant; it is all about the parent. This is what happened to Julie Gregory. Her childhood was a bit strange anyway; her father, Dan, a handyman and six years younger than her mother, was ostensibly schizophrenic (Gregory wrote a later memoir, ***My Father's Keeper***). Much of Julie's life was spent in doctors' offices and emergency and operating rooms. Her mother, Sandy, would withhold food, feed her prescription drugs inappropriately—drugs obtained from all these visits to the doctor—and otherwise make her sick, all the while reminding her how to behave sick in the doctor's office. Julie's belief was that if she didn't do as her mother said, she would lose her mother's approval and love. By the same token, her mother would also suggest to Julie that if only they could get her well, her mother wouldn't need to go to all this trouble. Until she was an adult Julie believed that she was a sickly person, and that all her mother's difficulties were her fault. In a psychology class one day this syndrome was being discussed, opening up a whole new world of possibility to Gregory, who now travels the country advising on MbPS and speaking as an expert witness at court trials.

Subjects: Abuse (Parental); Family Relationships; Gregory, Sandy; Mental Health; Mothers and Daughters; Munchausen by Proxy Syndrome; Ohio

Now Try: The term Munchausen syndrome was initially used for patients who made themselves sick in order to be able to go to the doctor. Marc D. Feldman, the doctor who wrote the foreword to Gregory's book, was an expert in Munchausen syndrome and was pulled into Munchausen by Proxy syndrome as it became an inevitable offshoot of his field. He has written a book on this and related disorders: ***Playing Sick? Untangling the Web of Munchausen Syndrome, Munchausen by Proxy, Malingering & Factitious Disorder***. T. Greenwood's ***Nearer Than the Sky: A Novel*** takes a daughter back to her childhood, where she begins to question the family dynamic, recognizing signs of Munchausen in both her mother and her sister. Laura Flynn's mother also suffered from a mental illness, in her case paranoid schizophrenia. Flynn describes what it was like growing up with her mother in ***Swallow the Ocean: A Memoir.***

Karr, Mary (1955–)

The Liars' Club: A Memoir. 10th anniversary ed. New Introduction by the author. Penguin, 2005, 1995. 320pp. 9780143035749. Also available in Braille, audiobook (read by the author), and e-book. 818.5403

Mary Karr was a poet before she was a memoirist, and her poet's ear for language is reflected throughout her poignant, often hilarious recounting of a highly dysfunctional childhood. She also studied with writers such as Tobias Wolff and Frank Conroy; it is little wonder that her memoir stands out as a piece of literature to be savored. As she explains in her introduction, however, it also stands out as an exemplar for many people who have suffered as children. While they may not have undergone the same frightful things that she did—her mother standing over her with a butcher knife, being raped by a teenager, being whipped by her grandmother with a horse quirt—the feelings are the same. They are all drifting in the same boat of dysfunctional family. It is this universality of emotional experience that makes Karr's book a classic. She also manages to get the voice right as well, the feisty little girl who will give as good as she gets. Throughout all of her experiences she retains an affection for both parents, which may be why she is able to inject such humor into the telling.

The Liars' Club was a finalist for the National Book Critics Circle Award in Biography/Autobiography and winner of the PEN American Center Martha Albrand Award for First Nonfiction. It was selected as a Notable Book by the American Library Association.

Subjects: Abuse (Parental); ALA Notable Books; Childhood and Youth; Children of Alcoholics; Dysfunctional Families; Family Relationships; Fathers and Daughters; Leechfield, TX; Mothers and Daughters; PEN American Center Martha Albrand Award for First Nonfiction; Poets

Now Try: One of the comments Mary Karr made in her new introduction was that since she has written her book, all those deep, dark family secrets that had been bottled up for so long are now common parlance at her table; since they were talked about so widely by all her readers they no longer have the power to hurt. Robert Goolrick found the same need to write his story, ***The End of the World as We Know It: Scenes from a Life,*** to tear open the façade of a perfect life and show it for the alcoholic mess it was. Readers of ***The Liars' Club*** may find some interesting similarities in the story of two sisters who move with their parents from Washington, DC, to Florida when the space program is active. Jesse Lee Kercheval explains in ***Space: A Memoir*** how her mother slips into a woeful depression at the change in her circumstances. Emily Dickinson's life apparently was also quite different on the inside from what is generally believed. Lyndall Gordon has unearthed some interesting information about her and her family, all laid out in ***Lives Like Loaded Guns: Emily Dickinson and Her Family's Feuds***. Mary Karr followed her first memoir with a second, ***Cherry: A Memoir,*** this one focused on her adolescence.

Mah, Adeline Yen (1937–)

Falling Leaves: The True Story of an Unwanted Chinese Daughter. Penguin, 1999, 1997. 278pp. ill. 9780767903578. Also available in large print, audiobook (read by the author), and e-book. 305.488951073092

Adeline Mah was considered an unlucky child because her mother died while giving birth to her. She was the youngest of five children, and then her father and stepmother had two more. Her greatest nemesis was her stepmother, a Eurasian woman who seemed to take sadistic delight in tormenting Adeline. She also encouraged the other children to be mean and harass Adeline. Her father was not much better: pleased with the fact of marrying a Eurasian woman, he had little time for his full-blooded Chinese children, the second-class citizens of the family. Mah fortunately had equally strong role models (in particular her father's sister and her grandaunt), who influenced her in a positive fashion so that she was able to withstand the cruelties of her childhood and make something of herself (a doctor and writer) as an adult. Throughout her memoir the reader is also offered a view of life in the East—first in Shanghai, including during World War II, and then in Hong Kong, where they escaped after the 1949 revolution. She also shares many Chinese proverbs, which help illuminate her response to the emotional abuse she suffered. She moved to the United States as an adult, accepting a job in obstetrics in New York City.

Subjects: Abuse (Parental); China; Chinese-Americans; Death of a Parent; Family Relationships; Physicians; Social History, China; Stepmothers; Women in China

Now Try: In ***China Boy: A Novel,*** Gus Lee tells the story of a young boy, new to the United States, who endures a new stepmother who wants to eradicate anything Chinese from his world. Veronica Chambers also gained a cruel stepmother after her parents' messy divorce; but life with any of her parents was difficult, as she describes in ***Mama's Girl.*** Mah's story has been called the Chinese ***Mommie Dearest,*** referring to Christina Crawford's book about her actress mother, Joan, perhaps the first notable childhood memoir blaming a parent for an unhappy childhood.

Pelzer, David J. (1960–)

A Child Called "It": An Abused Child's Journey from Victim to Victor. Health Communications, 1997, 1993. 184pp. 9781558743663. Also available in large print, Braille, audiobook, and e-audiobook. 362.76092

She called him "It"; she burned him; she stabbed him. Catherine Pelzer, abused herself as a child, initially loved her children and loved her life. An alcoholic husband, a firefighter who was often away from home, as well as her own alcoholism and increasing mental instability, all changed that and contributed to the severe abuse she visited upon her oldest child, David. Her husband finally left the family, and David bore the brunt of his mother's dysfunction. Apart from the physical abuse, she also abused him emotionally, not allowing him to change his clothes for more than two years, with the result that he was mocked at school for his raggedy clothes and his body odor. Although at the time in California there were no laws about child abuse, the book begins with the chapter called "The Rescue," when the school administration finally decided to take matters into their own hands and call the police. Pelzer then moves on to the good times in his early life, making the reader then wonder what could possibly have happened to change his life so drastically and bring about such bad times. The rest of the book explains that. Pelzer has kept his readers up-to-date with his progress, as he describes his life in and out of foster homes in ***The Lost Boy: A Foster Child's Search for the Love of a Family*** and then ***The Privilege of Youth: A Teenager's Story of Longing for Acceptance and Friendship***. We finally meet the adult in ***A Man Named Dave: A Story of Triumph and Forgiveness***.

Subjects: 1960s; Abuse (Parental); Bullying; California; Children of Alcoholics; Coping in Children; Domestic Violence; Mothers and Sons; Pelzer, Catherine

Now Try: After David was taken away, his brother Richard B. Pelzer became his mother's target. He too has written his story: ***A Brother's Journey: Surviving a Childhood of Abuse*** and then ***A Teenager's Journey: Overcoming a Childhood of Abuse***. Wayne Theodore also suffered horrible abuse from both parents; with the help of Leslie A. Horvitz he describes the life he lived with eleven siblings in ***Wayne: An Abused Child's Story of Courage, Survival, and Hope***. Torey L. Hayden is a special education teacher who has seen shocking examples of the effects of abuse on children. One of her titles, ***Murphy's Boy***, recently republished in England as ***The Silent Boy***, tells the story of a teenager who lived in a cage created by chairs and who wouldn't speak until Hayden was finally able to draw him out. Many children know what it is like to be laughed at by their schoolmates, and those who experience it regularly will say how scarring it can be. In ***Please Stop Laughing at Me: One Woman's Inspirational Story*** Jodee Blanco describes vividly what happened to her as the ongoing victim of school bullying, although ultimately it made her a stronger person, one who has become an activist against bullying, as demonstrated in her later book, ***Please Stop Laughing at Us—: One Survivor's Extraordinary Quest to Prevent School Bullying***.

Small, David (1945–)

***Stitches: A Memoir*—.** W. W. Norton & Co., 2009. 329pp. ill. 9780393068573. 818.54092

David Small grew up in a house of silence: his father was often absent, his older brother had no interest in him, his mother was cold and unloving, and his grandmother was cranky. Communication was more through gesture than word. Because his father, a radiologist, believed in the efficacy of X-rays, David was often x-rayed for sinus problems. When he developed a real problem as a result of all that radiation, his parents couldn't be bothered to deal with it initially; four years later David was operated on for a malignant tumor on his vocal cords. David's world was now very silent, as he was rendered mute for several years by this procedure. The pages that follow his surgery are wordless—full of illustrations only. The title refers to the clumsy stitching done on his throat, which he uses in his graphic narrative as a symbol of high-riser stairs for his mother to climb. Because of the nature of illustration, Small is doubly able to communicate both his situation and his emotions.

Small became an award-winning illustrator of children's books, and his memoir, ***Stitches,*** was nominated for the National Book Award Young Adult section and selected as a Notable Book by the American Library Association.

Subjects: Abuse (Parental); ALA Notable Books; Artists; Cancer; Childhood and Youth; Family Relationships; Fathers and Sons; Graphic Narratives; Illustrators; Mothers and Sons

Now Try: Another graphic narrative by an illustrator with cancer, albeit quite different from David Small's, is Marisa Acocella Marchetto's ***Cancer Vixen: A True Story***. Partly through therapy and partly through a friend's advice, David Small came to realize that art was his forte and a way out. Danny Gregory happened upon the same realization after his wife was seriously injured; he describes the transformation in his graphic narrative, ***Everyday Matters: A New York Diary***. Carolyn Rubenstein became aware of child cancer survivors when she was young herself; she has interviewed a number of young adult cancer survivors for a book, ***Perseverance: True Voices of Cancer Survivors***.

Walls, Jeannette (1960–)

The Glass Castle: A Memoir. Scribner, 2009, 2005. 288pp. 9781439156964. Also available in large print, audiobook, and e-audiobook. 362.82092

Many parents who neglect and abuse their children do so out of ignorance and a lack of feeling for their children. In the case of Walls's parents, however, the overall impression of their parenting is that it was a specific philosophy they fostered, particularly allowing the children utmost independence and the opportunity to learn for themselves. Jeannette's mother, Rosemary, didn't supervise the three-year-old who was standing on a chair cooking something on the gas stove, because if anything happened to her, well, that would teach her a lesson. And when Jeannette was burned so badly her parents had to take her to the hospital, that was her lesson. Fire burns. We travel with Jeannette around the United States along with her nomadic family and shudder with her when they finally land, destitute, back with her father's family in West Virginia. We now know why her father, Rex, goes on alcoholic binges. The poverty in which they live seems unspeakable as the children, growing older now, become more and more obliged to look after their parents as well as themselves. When the children finally escape, one by one, to New York City, their parents eventually follow them, squatting in abandoned tenements, happy to be homeless. Despite the horror of their childhood, there is a lingering affection for their parents that comes through in the memoir. The glass castle in the title refers to a dream that Jeannette's father holds out to her: he is going to build a glass castle in the desert as soon as he strikes gold and becomes rich with his inventions.

The Glass Castle was a winner of the Christopher Award and a Book Sense Book of the Year Honor Book. It was also selected as a Notable Book by the American Library Association.

Subjects: Abuse (Parental); ALA Notable Books; Childhood and Youth; Children of Alcoholics; Christopher Awards; Coming of Age; Dysfunctional Families; Homelessness; Poverty; West Virginia

Now Try: Walls has since published a biographical novel about her maternal grandmother, Lily Casey Smith, ***Half Broke Horses: A True-Life Novel,*** a story that sheds some light on her mother's behavior. A father's alcoholism is only one of the problems hidden under the façade of respectability in Catherine McCall's memoir, ***Lifeguarding: A Memoir of Secrets, Swimming, and the South.*** Another title that belongs in the same category of "unbelievable parenting" as Wall's is ***Jesus Land: A Memoir,*** a story by Julia Scheeres of what she and her adopted brother are forced to put up with by their violent father and religious mother. Barbara Robinette Moss's mother was not at all like Jeannette Walls's, but her father was an alcoholic, and they lived in poverty in the American South; she too rose above her troubles, to become an artist and to write her story, ***Change Me into Zeus's Daughter: A Memoir.***

Breaking the Cycle

Very often social ills such as poverty, child abuse, cult life, societal influences, etc., are generational. Poverty begets poverty. A child born into a cult is a prisoner to be brainwashed and therefore unlikely to leave. Societal attitudes and expectations of children from backgrounds of poverty and/or lower class become more deeply engendered in the community and therefore in individuals. Some people, however, manage to break the generational cycle and start a new, more positive one.

Living in a negative cycle is more than just the nuts and bolts of that life. In some cases, the poverty is also a class and race issue. The cycle also includes a mindset of low self-esteem, unworthiness, and lack of confidence. This sense of powerlessness and low self-esteem gets transferred from one generation to the next, sometimes by society and sometimes by the parents, so that the children are socialized to believe they are no good; they're simply low-class and worthless and have nothing to contribute.

Worldwide, it is commonly accepted that education is one of the best ways out of that vicious circle, but this can create its own conundrum. In the United States, generally the quality of education a child receives is predicated on the economic strength of the neighborhood the child's school is in. If a poor child lives in a poor neighborhood, that child will likely get a poor education, and so the cycle continues. This is why there are memoirs, not just in this chapter, but throughout this book, wherein poor parents make every effort to have their children educated outside their neighborhood. Once a child gets an education in which efforts are rewarded by positive reinforcement and the child's confidence grows, change is made possible. This is also fertile ground for a child to recognize innate talents, thereby also increasing a sense of self-worth.

Those who discuss microcredit in developing nations claim that there are two types of poverty: "poverty of the mind and poverty of material things." It is poverty of the mind that is so important to change, to help people recognize that each is "a human being with rights . . . a person who has something worthwhile to contribute to the family, community and nation" ("Women," 2008).

The stories in this section do not focus on child abuse. Breaking that cycle may be harder to document in memoir form. Are there many people who will write a book expressly to say, "I was abused. I do not abuse my children"? One can hope that those who have written about their own abuse have enough self-awareness and self-esteem to recognize the need to break the cycle; perhaps the act of writing a memoir about oneself is enough to say, "It ends with me."

Societal attitudes, originally engendered by unfairness and hard lives, can continue to influence people, particularly adolescents, creating gangs and angry young people, as we will see in the case of Nathan McCall. While prejudice and bigotry help form these cycles, the stories in this section do not focus on that negative influence; those memoirs are in the following section, "Discrimination."

Stories about breaking the cycle usually begin with the writers' childhoods as they describe a life that is not very different from their parents' lives. They reveal a determination to change the cycle of their parents and their forebears, often by getting an education, which will facilitate a complete shift in self-regard, with each individual recognizing his or her own worth. There might be some bitterness in some of these memoirs, but there is also relief in actually breaking the cycle.

Dickerson, Debra J. (1959–)

An American Story. Anchor Books, 2001, 2000. 285pp. 9780385720281. Also available in audiobook and e-book. 070.92

This memoir is Dickerson's story of how she finally recognized her own self-worth and was thus able to make something of her life. She was one of five children with a domineering father who was not happy with his lot in life. A sharecropper in the American South, he moved his family north to Missouri in the hopes of finding better work, but never really found it. Her mother was strong and finally moved out, but by then Dickerson's self-esteem was already very low. Her saving grace was her love of books and the library, enabling her to succeed at school and thus find a way out. She didn't take it when it came, though. She chose the Air Force instead. Her Air Force experience, largely spent in intelligence in Korea, was a coming of age for her. She survived not only rape there but also the offensive military attitude toward it, which was like a second rape. She was finally able to recognize that her disdain for nonachieving Black people came from her own still-low self-esteem. When she was discharged from the Air Force she decided to make use of her brains, getting not just her undergraduate degree, but also a law degree from Harvard. Still working out her own psychological needs, she decided to become a journalist rather than a practicing lawyer, and through her writing she has come to learn who she is and what her worth is.

Subjects: Abuse (Parental); African-American Women; African-Americans in the Military; American Midwest; Books and Reading; Journalists; Lawyers; Military Life; Racism; Rape; Survivors of Rape; United States Air Force

Now Try: Patricia Ann Schechter has brought to life the accomplishments of the nineteenth-century African-American journalist Ida B. Wells in her study, ***Ida B. Wells-Barnett and American Reform, 1880–1930***. A college professor, Janice Dean Willis, chose Buddhism to help her improve her self-esteem. She describes what that spiritual work did for her in ***Dreaming Me: An African-American Woman's Spiritual Journey***. Comparable to Dickerson, Marita Golden is very conscious of race. In her book, ***Don't Play in the Sun: One Woman's Journey Through the Color Complex***, she addresses her own feelings about skin color while looking at attitudes toward it over the years.

Elders, M. Joycelyn (1933–)
Chanoff, David (1943–), coauthor

Joycelyn Elders, M.D.: From Sharecropper's Daughter to Surgeon General of the United States of America. Avon Books, 1997, 1996. 355pp. ill. 16pp. of plates. 9780380786480. Also available in large print and e-book. 610.92

Joycelyn Elders was the oldest of eight children, and the entire family lived in a three-room house. The closeness within her family and the moral codes of her parents, along with their not fearing hard work, helped her to become the strong woman she is. Determined not to have the same life as her parents, Joycelyn saw education as her way out and was able to get a scholarship for college. She joined the U.S. Army so she could continue her studies in medical school and was the first in many areas: the first Black resident at the University of Arkansas Medical School, its first Black chief resident and its first Black professor. She was very successful as the Director of the State Department of Health under Governor Bill Clinton, but her outspoken and unpopular views about healthy sexuality made her unpopular with Washington politicos when she was Surgeon General of the United States (the first African-American woman to hold that position). Her tenure there lasted fifteen months only. Currently in her seventies, she continues to write and speak out about healthy sexuality and other important health care matters.

Subjects: African-American Women; Arkansas; Firsts; Health Officers; Physicians; Public Health; Sexuality, Healthy; Sharecropping; Surgeon General of the United States

Now Try: Yvonne S. Thornton was the daughter of a man and woman who believed in breaking the cycle of poverty, and each worked two or three jobs to ensure their five daughters' education. In telling her story to Jo Coudert, Thornton describes her parents' sacrifices and her own ultimate success in becoming a doctor in ***The Ditchdigger's Daughters: A Black Family's Astonishing Success Story***. Connie Mariano is another medical figure who made her way to Washington. As she relates in ***White House Doctor: A Memoir***, she was the doctor for both George H. W. and George W. Bush as well as Bill Clinton. Joycelyn Elders has had to deal with political roadblocks in her career; in the nineteenth century it was worse for women, as it was deemed they were too weak to pursue an education. Dr. Mary Putnam Jacobi fought that notion all her professional life. Carla Jean Bittel describes Jacobi's lifelong fight in ***Mary Putnam Jacobi & the Politics of Medicine in Nineteenth-Century America***.

Fisher, Antwone Quenton (1959–)
Rivas, Mim Eichler, coauthor

Finding Fish: A Memoir. HarperTorch, 2002, 2001. 369pp. 9780060539863. Also available in audiobook, e-book, and video (title: *Antwone Fisher*). 791.43092

Born in prison to a teenage mother who was in jail for murder, Antwone Fisher was immediately put into the foster-care system in Cleveland, Ohio, since his father had been murdered by a girlfriend just before Antwone's birth. He was put into the care of the Pickett family, longtime foster parents who always put on a good face for case workers. The reality for "Fish" was quite different. Mr. Pickett was a stern minister, and Mrs. Pickett felt that her wards were worthless people who would never amount to anything; she took every opportunity to tell them so. A gentle, intelligent boy, Fisher rapidly became an exceedingly shy underachiever at school. Some of his teachers and some of his caseworkers were kind to him, which had a lot to do with his ultimate success and happiness. After Mrs. Pickett did him the favor of giving him back to Child Services when he was fifteen, he found himself with new problems—homelessness and criminal friends. The U.S. Navy proved to be a good way out for him, an opportunity for him to discover who he really was and what he really could do. He discovered that he could write. In writing this memoir, Fisher provides the reader with close-up views, not only of his life in foster care, but also of the larger picture of the Black neighborhoods in Cleveland in the 1960s and 1970s during the Black Power Movement.

Subjects: 1960s; 1970s; Abuse (Parental); Childhood and Youth, African-American; Cleveland, OH; Foster Care; Homelessness; Screenwriters; United States Navy

Now Try: Regina Louise just wanted to find someone to love her and think she was special, but the foster-care system she was thrown into in Texas was not the place to find that person. She tells her story in ***Somebody's Someone: A Memoir***. Lest readers think that there are no good people in the foster-care system, Victoria Rowell has a different story to tell in ***The Women Who Raised Me: A Memoir***. Michael Rosen's seven-year-old son started the Rosen family and a group of young Black and Latino boys on a journey that none of them would have dreamed of earlier, as Michael describes in ***What Else but Home: Seven Boys and an American Journey Between the Projects and the Penthouse***.

hooks, bell (1952–)

Bone Black: Memories of Girlhood. Henry Holt and Co., 2007, 1996. 183pp. 9780805055122. 305.48896092

In her foreword, bell hooks states that hers is a memoir of perceptions and ideas. As an adult she is a strong-minded, strong-worded feminist, always working to give Black women a place in feminism. By choosing two- to three-page vignettes of events or impressions from her life growing up poor in Kentucky, she delineates how the young girl came to be the adult woman. For bell hooks, identity was an issue: Who was she? Where did she belong? She felt like an outsider—her older siblings and her mother scorned her. She was Black and had to go to school through a phalanx of National Guardsmen. She was female and therefore gendered, although not always aware of it. Despite her alliance with the women in her extended family, it is her grandfather who gives her both excellent and comforting advice, telling her that it is her job, her work, to find out where she belongs. It is from her matrilineal line that she takes her name, "bell hooks." (She was born Gloria Watkins.) Hers is not a memoir of shocking revelations or horrifying situations. It is a memoir of one person, a young, Black female in a poor household with a large family, coming of age and determined to change the expected trajectory of her future, as she becomes more confident as both a woman and an African-American. She wrote a subsequent memoir, ***Wounds of Passion: A Writing Life***.

Subjects: African-American Women; American South; Belonging; Childhood and Youth, African-American; College Professors; Coming of Age; Feminists; Kentucky; Racism; Writers

Now Try: The Kentucky that hooks grew up in was the South where the White civil rights activists Anne and Carl Braden bought a house in a White neighborhood for Black friends. Anne Braden describes in ***The Wall Between*** the shocking violence that occurred as a result of that purchase, including the imprisonment of Carl for sedition.

Sister Souljah's environment was different from that of bell hooks—much more raw—but she still managed to acquire a love of reading and a respect for self, a recognition that she tries to pass on to other young women in her memoir, ***No Disrespect***. Audre Lorde, known as a "warrior poet," manages to convey her Black feminist views and support to women everywhere even when she is suffering from breast cancer. ***The Cancer Journals*** concerns her struggles with the daily minutiae of cancer, but it is also an inspiration to women everywhere to continue to fight for themselves and to be strong.

Jessop, Carolyn (1968–)
Palmer, Laura (1950–), coauthor

Escape. With a new Epilogue by the author. Broadway Books, 2008, 2007. 426pp. ill. 8pp. of plates. 9780767927574. Also available in audiobook, e-audiobook, and e-book. 289.3092

Carolyn Jessop was a multigenerational child in the break-off sect Fundamentalist Church of Jesus Christ of Latter-Day Saints (FLDS). She had only two mothers, but she was raised in a tightly closed environment, isolated from the rest of the world, trained to believe only what the male leaders wanted her to believe. As each leader was replaced by the next, life became more and more difficult and restrictive. By the time Jessop was thirty-five and the fourth wife of Merril Jessop, a man who had been in his fifties when she married him at age eighteen, she had eight children, one of whom was severely disabled from spinal cancer. Her child's illness was laid at her feet: it was because there was a problem with her spirituality. Although they didn't live there, her husband was in charge of the YFZ Ranch compound in Texas that was raided in 2008. Fear that she and her family would be moved to the compound, along with fear that her fourteen-year-old daughter would soon be married off, provided the impetus for Jessop to take all eight children and escape one night. She had been to college and was a teacher by training, so she wasn't completely ignorant of the world outside the sect, but she still needed to learn life skills like paying bills, registering children in school, etc. She followed ***Escape*** with a sequel, also written with Laura Palmer, describing her life after her escape, ***Triumph: Life After the Cult—A Survivor's Lessons***.

Subjects: Abuse (Spousal); Cults; Forced Marriage; Fundamentalist Church of Jesus Christ of Latter-Day Saints; Illness in the Family; Jessop, Merril; Marriage; Mormon Women; Polygamy; Utah

Now Try: One of the stories that isn't told very often is that of the young boys who were expelled from the FLDS cult, sent out to live in a world they'd always been taught was evil, and told that they'd been rejected by the prophet, when the truth was that the older men wanted no competition for the young women. Brent W. Jeffs is one of these young men who has found the courage to tell his story, ***Lost Boy***, with the help of Maia Szalavitz. Jon Krakauer offers an explanation in ***Under the Banner of Heaven: A Story of Violent Faith*** of the

9 10 11 12 13

formation of the fundamentalist sect that broke away from its parent religion because of the question of polygamy. As were all the women in this cult, Irene Spencer was taught that the way to salvation was to enter into a polygamous relationship, which is why she agreed to marry her brother-in-law although her mother was against it. In ***Shattered Dreams: My Life as a Polygamist's Wife*** she describes how eventually she learned how misguided she'd been.

McCall, Nathan (1955–)

Makes Me Wanna Holler: A Young Black Man in America. Vintage, 1995. 416pp. 9780679740704. Also available in e-book. 305.38967073092

Even though he lived in a solid, working-class neighborhood in Virginia with steady parents, Nathan McCall still had to face the gangs on the streets. Frustrated as a young Black man, he got caught up with those gangs and went along with everything they did—robbery, gang rape, violent use of weapons, and drugs. He was even going to college when he stabbed someone in the chest and then was arrested and imprisoned for armed robbery. Oddly enough, it was in prison that he turned his life around; there were older inmates to act as role models and mentors. He also worked in the library and became exposed to such writers as Richard Wright. It was in the library that he decided he wanted to be a journalist, which became his career goal once he was released from prison. Apart from his own story in this memoir, McCall also addresses the issue of young, urban, Black men and why they may be angry.

Subjects: Adolescents, African-American; African-American Men; Anger; Gangs; Journalists; Prisons, United States; Self-Destructive Behavior; Urban Youth; Violence; *The Washington Post* (Newspaper)

Now Try: Nathan McCall felt himself low on the hierarchical rung at *The Washington Post*, but Jill Nelson, an African-American woman, would have been one rung lower. She describes her life at the *Post* in ***Volunteer Slavery: My Authentic Negro Experience.*** Wilbert Rideau also did a stint in prison—in Angola and for much longer than McCall—but he too came out changed for the better, as he relates in ***In the Place of Justice: A Story of Punishment and Deliverance.*** Hill Harper is an African-American motivational speaker who has written a book directed at Black youth, ***Letters to a Young Brother: Manifest Your Destiny.***

Wall, Elissa (1986–)
Pulitzer, Lisa, coauthor

Stolen Innocence: My Story of Growing Up in a Polygamous Sect, Becoming a Teenage Bride, and Breaking Free of Warren Jeffs. Harper, 2009, 2008. 445pp. ill. 16pp. of plates. 9780061734960. Also available in large print, audiobook, e-audiobook, and e-book. 289.3092

A member of the Fundamentalist Church of Jesus Christ of Latter-Day Saints (FLDS), Elissa Wall was fourteen when she was forced to marry her nineteen-year-old first cousin, whom she had met only recently and who had tormented her on the occasions when they did meet. She did everything in her power to prevent the wedding, but to no avail. By the time she was eighteen she had had three miscarriages and one stillbirth. Elissa finally managed to escape from the cult at this point, and then lodged a formal complaint against Warren Jeffs, the leader of the group who had forced her to marry. Jeffs was charged with being an accomplice to rape, and a subsequent charge of rape was levied against her husband. In her book Wall provides some background to the FLDS, and she also details what it is like to leave, how one has to deprogram oneself and change one's way of thinking, in addition to learning how to manage finances and get around in an alien world.

Subjects: Abuse (Spousal); Child Marriage; Cults; Forced Marriage; Fundamentalist Church of Jesus Christ of Latter-Day Saints; Jeffs, Warren; Marriage; Miscarriages; Mormon Women; Polygamy; Pregnancy; Utah

Now Try: Dorothy Allred Solomon offers a view into Mormon life in its earlier days when the leaders were not so megalomaniac. She has written several books on various aspects of the Mormon Church, but this one is interesting for its specific perspective on polygamy: ***Predators, Prey, and Other Kinfolk: Growing Up in Polygamy***. Jana Richman had eight great-great-grandmothers who had traveled from Illinois to Utah, seven of them on foot along the Mormon Trail. Having a bit of a spiritual crisis in her midlife, she decided to ride the trail. She shares her reflections in ***Riding in the Shadows of Saints: A Woman's Story of Motorcycling the Mormon Trail***. The life described in Wall's book bears many similarities to the fictional community created by Margaret Atwood in ***The Handmaid's Tale***.

Discrimination

When one thinks of the word "discrimination," one normally thinks in terms of race. Most of the titles in this section are about race, although one is about sexual orientation and one is about weight. People can be discriminated against for any number of reasons, however, and we have seen that throughout this entire book. Race, religion, gender, sexual orientation, age, ethnicity, personal appearance, and class are all reasons for one group to discriminate against another. In the chapter "The Working Life" (Chapter 4), we saw discrimination on the basis of gender, how women had to fight against the so-called glass ceiling to make their way; in Chapter 11 we saw discrimination based on religion (the Holocaust) or ethnicity (the Rwanda genocide). The issue seems to be that if one is Other than what is constructed as the norm, it is reason enough to be discriminated against. Usually memoirs that deal with the subject of discrimination come from the person being discriminated against; it is not usually something even in the purview of those who do the discriminating, as it is not part of their perspective. One of the notable elements of discrimination is that those who show their bias do so because they have objectified the group as a whole, depersonalizing the group's members and removing their individuality. The group is now an "amorphous 'they,' " and stereotyped; expectations of that group's behavior become rigid (Roney, 2005).

The memoirs about discrimination in this chapter are about bias because of skin color, bias because of gender, bias because of sexual orientation, bias because of class, and bias because of physical appearance. The writers tell their stories and reflect on the effects on them personally of real and imagined discrimination.

Conley, Dalton (1969–)

Honky. Vintage Books, 2001, 2000. 207pp. 9780375727757. Also available in e-book. 305.2309747

This memoir is an oblique look at the issues of class and race in the Lower East Side of New York City. Conley, a sociologist in his adult life, offers the reader the story of his somewhat unusual life as a child. He and his family were welfare recipients; his father was an artist and his mother a writer, neither making enough to support themselves and their two children. On the other hand, they had relatives who might have been able to help out if the Conleys' principles hadn't been against accepting that help. When Conley gets to school the first day, the principal tells his parents he can go into whichever first-grade classroom he wants, as the rooms are divided by race and he's the only White child. They choose the class with Black and Latino children, but the school eventually moves him to the class with Chinese children. The issue here is as much about class as it is about race. Given his parents' professions and their race, Conley goes into school with much more cultural capital than his friends of color. Yet he is the Other there and desperately wants to be accepted and to make friends. His best friend, a Black boy named Jerome, is a big part of Conley's development. Apart from issues of race and class, Conley's memoir is still a coming-of-age story of a young boy growing up poor in a big city, and he delights the reader with some of his anecdotes.

Subjects: Inner-City Life; New York, NY; Poverty; Privilege; Race Relations; Social Class; Sociologists

Now Try: Although his family was on welfare, Conley still came from a family of relative privilege and was thus able to get a better education than his neighbors. Because the quality of education is largely dependent on the income of the neighborhood in which the school is located, there are egregious inequities in educational opportunities for children. Jonathan Kozol addresses this and other issues in ***The Shame of the Nation: The Restoration of Apartheid Schooling in America***. Thomas L. Webber, like Dalton Conley, was a White boy growing up in a traditionally Black neighborhood; he describes his childhood in ***Flying over 96th Street: Memoir of an East Harlem White Boy***. The muckraking journalist Jack Newfield offers another view of growing up poor in New York City in ***Somebody's Gotta Tell It: The Upbeat Memoir of a Working-Class Journalist***.

Conley, Frances K. (1940–)

Walking Out on the Boys. Farrar, Straus & Giroux, 1999, 1998. 245pp. 9780374525958. 617.48092

When Conley started out in her medical career, she had no interest in being a pioneer or in bucking the establishment. She simply followed her heart, which told her first that she wanted to be a surgeon and then that she wanted to be a neurosurgeon. Because of these choices she was a pioneer: in 1966 the first woman surgical intern at Stanford; in 1977, the fifth woman to be certified as a neurosurgeon; and in 1988, the first woman to be given tenure in neurosurgery at a medical school (Stanford University). Three years after receiving tenure status, however, she resigned from Stanford. Always bearing the brunt of sexism and what she refers to as gender insensitivity, she finally balked when a man known for his demeaning behavior toward the women on staff at all levels was to be appointed head of the department. Apart from her dismay at his lack of sensitivity, she knew that his appointment would mean the end of any advances she might make personally. Her departure from the university was not for long, as Stanford acted quickly to institute changes in policy toward sexism, gender insensitivity, and sexual harassment.

Subjects: Empowerment of Women; Firsts; Medicine; Neurosurgeons; Sex Discrimination; Sexual Harassment; Stanford University, CA

Now Try: Readers may be interested in a historical perspective on the progress women have made in gaining access to the medical community, offered by Beatrice Levin in ***Women and Medicine***. While Conley refuses to call her situation sexual harassment, there are others who would use that label. The sexual harassment accusations levied against Clarence Thomas by Anita Hill resulted in a wave of more women running for political positions. In ***Women on the Hill: Challenging the Culture of Congress*** Clara Bingham describes that influx of women, the roles the congresswomen have chosen to take, and the results of their work. Kathy Magliato is a heart surgeon who describes her professional life in ***Healing Hearts: A Memoir of a Female Heart Surgeon***, including in her story the gender difficulties she faced.

Hill, Anita (1956–)

Speaking Truth to Power. Anchor Books, 1998. 374pp. ill. 9780385476270. Also available in audiobook (read by the author) and e-book. 340.092

In 1991 the Senate was holding nomination hearings for the appointment of Clarence Thomas to the Supreme Court when Anita Hill, a lawyer who had worked with Thomas, stepped up and accused him of sexual harassment in the workplace. As would be expected, this unleashed a fury of media attention on both Hill and the hearings. Hill was called to testify, an event she describes in great detail in her memoir. She realized as the day progressed that she was the one on trial, that she was being treated as a defendant rather than as a plaintiff. She was vilified in the press, and

Clarence Thomas was appointed to the United States Supreme Court. In her memoir Hill explains how the whole matter has affected her life and why she felt it was time to speak her piece. Hill's memoir is not just about that part of her life, however. She describes her upbringing on a farm in Oklahoma, life with a large family, and parents who instilled in her the courage and strength she exhibited in the Senate. She also talks about her life after the hearings. Because the Senate did appoint Thomas, it was obvious that the Senate was saying Hill had lied. Jane Mayer and Jill Abramson, two investigative journalists, took it upon themselves to find out who was lying; in their book, ***Strange Justice: The Selling of Clarence Thomas***, they reveal the corroborating evidence of Hill's experience from all the witnesses they interviewed, along with other women Thomas had worked with. Despite that book, Hill felt it was time for her to set the record straight herself—for herself and for all those sexually harassed in the workplace.

Subjects: African-American Women; Empowerment of Women; Lawyers; Oklahoma; Sex Discrimination; Sexual Harassment; Thomas, Clarence; United States Senate; United States Supreme Court

Now Try: In the nomination hearings Arlen Specter was particularly vile to Anita Hill, something for which he has apologized. He does so again in his memoir, written with Charles Robbins, ***Passion for Truth: From Finding JFK's Single Bullet to Questioning Anita Hill to Impeaching Clinton***. Barbara Lee is an African-American congresswoman who has made it her life's mission to speak up for what she believes in, as she describes in ***Renegade for Peace and Justice: Congresswoman Barbara Lee Speaks for Me***. In her memoir, ***The Girls Are Coming***, Peggie Carlson describes with humor what it was like to become a pipefitter for a natural gas company in Minnesota, not long after they started hiring women for nonsecretarial jobs.

Jadhav, Narendra (1953–)

Untouchables: My Family's Triumphant Journey out of the Caste System in Modern India. University of California Press, 2007, 2003. 307pp. 9780520252639. Also available in e-book. 305.5688

Although the caste system in India was officially abolished in 1950, it is not that easy to eradicate inborn discrimination. The term used to refer to the group at the lowest level of the caste system, "untouchables" or "pariahs," was changed to "Dalit," the downtrodden. Although the author was born after the abolition of the caste system, he still was part of it and had to fight his way up. In his memoir, he uses his parents' diaries and journals and their voices as well to tell the story of their experiences with the discrimination that was a part of the daily weave of their lives. His father, Damu, told him about the day he learned that because he was a Mahar he was not considered as good as anyone else: a young boy of five, he was not allowed to drink from a bowl of water under a tree that a dog was permitted to use. His father joined forces with B. R. Ambedkar to fight against the caste system, for his sake and for the sake of his children. The end result of Narendra's also joining the fight with his father is that he became a widely recognized economist, the former Chief Economist of the Reserve Bank of India, currently holding a government position equivalent to that of minister.

Subjects: Caste System, India; Dalits; Economists, India; Fathers and Sons; India; Jadhav, Damu; Race Relations, India; Social History, India

Now Try: Rohinton Mistry's ***A Fine Balance: A Novel*** illustrates the reality of being an untouchable in India. Two researchers in India, Josiane and Jean-Luc Racine, listened to a Dalit tell the story of her life, thus presenting the picture from one person's perspective, but a person who just accepted that that was her role to play. Her story, translated by Will Dobson, is entitled ***Viramma, Life of an Untouchable***. For local color in India, readers may enjoy reading Thrity N. Umrigar's ***The Weight of Heaven: A Novel***.

Jennings, Kevin (1963–)

Mama's Boy, Preacher's Son: A Memoir. Beacon Press, 2007, 2006. 267pp. 9780807071472. Also available in e-book. 306.7662092

Kevin Jennings grew up largely in North Carolina, poor, overweight, and gay. His father was an itinerant preacher, always moving the family to find work; his mother was a school dropout, but one who could make her own way in the world. Kevin knew he didn't live up to his father's expectations of what a real man was like, and he also knew he was a blight in God's eye. But he couldn't figure out why God wouldn't help him get over his homosexuality. When he moved to Massachusetts to go to Harvard and then to teach in high school, Jennings found that his peers' attitudes to his sexual orientation were a refreshing change from what he had found in North Carolina. The administrators, however, were another story. Remembering the discrimination he had faced as a boy in high school, afraid to admit his orientation, and recognizing how harmful discrimination from teachers can be, Jennings founded the Gay, Lesbian, and Straight Education Network (http://www.glsen.org/cgi-bin/iowa/all/home/index.html), whose goal is to create safe-school environments for teens throughout the country, regardless of their sexual orientation or gender.

Subjects: Death of a Parent; Educators; Gay, Lesbian, and Straight Education Network; Gay Men; Hawai'i; Homosexuality; Mothers and Sons; North Carolina; Religion

Now Try: When Jennings came out to his mother, Alice, she initially had difficulty accepting it, but eventually started a PFLAG (Parents, Families & Friends of Lesbians and Gays) group in Winston-Salem and then volunteered at a hospice for AIDS patients. Marlene Fanta Shyer and Christopher Shyer document their joint stories, she of learning about her son and coming to accept him for who he is and he of learning to accept himself for who he is in ***Not Like Other Boys: Growing Up Gay; A Mother and Son Look Back***. Elizabeth Stone discovers that even teachers have a lot to learn as she accepts the gift of a former student's diaries after he has died of AIDS; through his diaries, she and the reader together get to know Vincent, in ***A Boy I Once Knew: What a Teacher Learned***

from Her Student. One of the most blatant and shocking examples of discrimination against sexual orientation was the murder of Matthew Shepard in Wyoming. Matthew's mother, Judy, has finally written her story with the help of Jon Barrett, ***The Meaning of Matthew: My Son's Murder in Laramie, and a World Transformed***, describing the horror of Matthew's assault and murder and explaining why his mother, Judy, is now a gay rights activist, creating the Matthew Shepard Foundation to erase hate (http://www.matthewshepard.org/).

Massaquoi, Hans J. (1926–)

Destined to Witness: Growing Up Black in Nazi Germany. Perennial, 2001, 1999. 443pp. ill. 9780060959616. Also available in audiobook and e-book. 943.004960092

Hans Massaquoi's father was the son of the Liberian consul general to Germany; his mother was a White German woman. With the political situation in Germany heating up and their political fortunes on the wane in Liberia, Hans's father and grandfather had to return to Liberia, but his mother didn't want to take him, as his health was frail and she feared the tropical weather. The result was that they were forced to leave their privileged environment and move to a cold-water flat, his mother just managing to make ends meet for both of them. During this time Hitler's group was in evidence everywhere, marching with bands, putting on fireworks shows, and generally making themselves very appealing to the youth of Germany, including Hans. Imagine his bitterness when he enthusiastically prepares to join the *Hitlerjugend* and is rejected because of the color of his skin—he is not Aryan and is therefore not worthy. His distress continues in the schoolyard as his classmates pick up on the discrimination they learn in the Hitler Youth; he is mocked and tormented. By the time he arrives in the United States in the early 1950s, he feels he is facing the same discrimination there that he had encountered under the Nazis.

Subjects: Africans in Germany; Biracial Children; Coming of Age; Hitler Youth; National Socialism; Octogenarians; Owens, Jesse; Racism, Germany

Now Try: James Agee's son, Joel, spent time in Germany in his youth as well, but the Germany he went to was different for him. Because he went with his mother and his stepfather, a German Communist, East Germany was a welcoming place, as he relates in ***Twelve Years: An American Boyhood in East Germany***. The story of Jesse Owens dashing Hitler's hopes of Aryan victories in the Olympic field, has been told in the highly acclaimed ***Triumph: The Untold Story of Jesse Owens and Hitler's Olympics*** by Jeremy Schaap. While the story of the Hitler Youth is chilling, its ascendancy may not be so different from the stories of some of today's madrassas in parts of the Middle East. To understand how political youth movements are sown and nurtured, readers may find informative Michael Griffin's ***Reaping the Whirlwind: The Taliban Movement in Afghanistan***.

Moore, Judith (1940–2006)

Fat Girl: A True Story. Plume, 2006, 2005. 196pp. 9780452285859. Also available in audiobook, e-audiobook, and e-book. 362.1963980092

Judith Moore's story of growing up fat is, in a certain way, every fat person's story of growing up: the love of food and/or the use of food to fill an emotional hole. When that indulgence in food turns into obesity, with it often comes disdain from the family, although in Moore's case it was more than disdain: it was cruelty and abuse. School becomes a nightmare, with teasing from classmates and a lack of friendship, except perhaps from others who are also considered "rejects." Moore pulls no punches in her memoir: she is open and very direct; she is also very angry. She starts out by saying she will not try to win the reader over, nor will she provide a fairy-tale ending. Her goal, it would seem, is to let her readers who are not fat know what it is like to be fat and to be judged for it. By the same token, many of her readers find much that resonates. While Moore was never hugely obese as an adult and even fell often within her normal weight boundaries, she always thought of herself as fat, a conundrum that plagues many people who have been overweight.

Fat Girl was a finalist for the National Book Critics Circle Award in Autobiography/Memoir.

Subjects: Abuse (Parental); Bullying; Childhood and Youth; Dieting; Food Writing; Obesity

Now Try: Prior to this memoir Moore had written a book about food that included some details from her life, ***Never Eat Your Heart Out***. Barry M. Popkin offers a look at obesity around the world and how the food industry today is contributing to it in ***The World Is Fat: The Fads, Trends, Policies, and Products That Are Fattening the Human Race***. Addressing the issue of prejudicial behavior toward fat women in particular is W. Charisse Goodman's ***The Invisible Woman: Confronting Weight Prejudice in America***. Reality TV has joined the weight-loss bandwagon with several programs, including *The Biggest Loser*. Ali Vincent was the first woman to win her round of competitions and chose to write about it afterward, in ***Believe It, Be It: How Being the Biggest Loser Won Me Back My Life***.

Williams, Gregory Howard (1943–)

Life on the Color Line: The True Story of a White Boy Who Discovered He Was Black. Penguin, 1996, 1995. 289pp. ill. 9781440673337. Also available in e-book. 305.896092

Growing up in Virginia with a White mother and a father who was "passing" for Italian, Gregory Williams received the shock of his life when his mother left the family and his father's alcoholism forced the family of two boys and their father back to Muncie, Indiana, to the Black side of town, where Gregory's father was really from. His mother's family was nearby, on the White side of town, but Williams didn't see them. Because of his light skin he was mocked by his Black classmates; because he was Black, he had a mark against him in his school records and he was almost removed from his position as high-school quarterback. Dating was a problem, as no one wanted him to date either White or Black girls. Despite his father's failure to provide for him and his brother, leaving them to be taken in by a poor widow, Williams found that one thing he did get from his father was the interest in and will to become a professional. This memoir takes the reader to the point where he is about to go to college, having decided that he will embrace his Black heritage.

Life on the Color Line was a recipient of the *Los Angeles Times* Book Prize for Current Interest.

Subjects: African-American Men; Biracial Children; Children of Alcoholics; Family Relationships; Fathers and Sons; Indiana; Lawyers; *Los Angeles Times* Book Prize for Current Interest; Motherless Children; Passing (Identity); Racism

Now Try: Clarence King is noted for his geological and travel writing relating to the American West and the Sierra Nevada Mountains in the nineteenth century. The part of his life that was not known has been documented recently by the historian Martha Sandweiss. ***Passing Strange: A Gilded Age Tale of Love and Deception Across the Color Line*** reveals how King passed himself off as an African-American, James Todd, a Pullman conductor, so that he could be with the Black woman he loved and with whom he fathered five children. He finally told her the truth on his deathbed. June Cross was a biracial child whose White mother gave her to an African-American family. Cross explains why in ***Secret Daughter: A Mixed-Race Daughter and the Mother Who Gave Her Away***. Bliss Broyard, the daughter of the literary critic Anatole Broyard, discovered her father's racial secret shortly before his death, a secret she shares in ***One Drop: My Father's Hidden Life; A Story of Race and Family Secrets***.

Living with a Difference

The memoirs here deal with people who all had difficulties from the time they were children, although they didn't always know the cause. What they all have in common is that while most might be labeled as persons with disabilities of one sort or another, they are all really persons with wonderful abilities who happen to be different from what is constructed as the norm. To call them disabled would be to misname them. Lucy Grealy's difference is the only really physical, visual one, with a face scarred by cancer and multiple surgeries. Jennifer Finney Boylan's difference was internal: born on the outside like a boy, she was expected to grow up to be a man, although inside she was a girl. In the case of some memoirists, their socialization might suggest a difference, but they've risen above that as well to learn acceptable comportment and social mores. Most of them have made contributions to society that might not have been possible except for their differences.

Stories of living with a difference are the memoirs of people for whom their differences cause them to present themselves differently from what is perceived to be normal. While the autism spectrum is widely represented here, it is not the only source of difference. Gender identity, learning disabilities, and physical disfigurement also play a role in the memoirists' stories, narratives of life with their difference and offerings of resources to help others in similar situations. By telling their stories, the memoirists also reveal how much they have to offer.

Boylan, Jennifer Finney (1958–)

She's Not There: A Life in Two Genders. Afterword by Richard Russo. Broadway Books, 2004, 2003. 300pp. ill. 9780767914291. Also available in e-book. 813.54

All her life Jennifer Boylan (née James) felt at odds with who she was. As a child she would lock herself in her bedroom and put on girls' clothes. Optimist that she was, she thought she might get over this, particularly if she were to fall in love and get married. She discovered, however, that even while being the husband of a wonderful woman and the father of two young children, her feelings about being out of place, not being herself, continued. By now her wife knew about her feelings and the only limit she put on Boylan's wearing women's clothes was " 'no pearls before five.' " Boylan sought out information about sex-change procedures and made the decision to strive for the life that seemed more natural and normal to her. She was forty when she accomplished that. Her wife is now her very good friend, and her children call her "Maddy." They all live together in Maine, where Jennifer continues to teach at Colby College with her good friend Richard Russo. She writes her story in a humorous fashion, trying to make the reader understand her needs and her choices and at the same time, trying not to dramatize her situation.

She's Not There was nominated for the Lambda Literary Award for Autobiography/Memoir and won the Lambda Literary Award for Transgender/Genderqueer Writing.

Subjects: Boylan, James; College Professors; Friendships; Gender Identity; Lambda Literary Award for Transgender/Genderqueer; Married Couples; Queer Parents; Self-Acceptance; Transsexuals; Writers

Now Try: In her subsequent memoir, ***I'm Looking Through You: Growing Up Haunted,*** Boylan adds insights to her situation, but also describes growing up in the "Coffin House," thought to be a haunted house in Pennsylvania. Jan Morris (née James) was one of the first notable people to come out openly about being a transsexual. Already the author of several well-respected travel books, her personal story was entitled ***Conundrum.*** Abuse of a colossal nature took place when a baby boy's circumcision was botched and he was operated on to be given female genitalia. As John Colapinto explains in ***As Nature Made Him: The Boy Who Was Raised as a Girl,*** he always knew he was a boy and set about to change things when he learned as an adolescent what had been done to him. What causes the body to present physically as one gender while the individual strongly feels the other gender is still being studied; in the meantime, readers may find Deborah Rudacille's study very interesting and informative: ***The Riddle of Gender: Science, Activism, and Transgender Rights.***

Buchman, Dana, and Charlotte Farber

A Special Education: One Family's Journey Through the Maze of Learning Disabilities. Perseus, 2007. 196pp. 9780738210896. 306.8743087

A fashion designer with her own label, Dana Buchman was a high achiever, used to juggling her different roles, always being a "superwoman." But when her daughter was about a year old, Dana and her husband began to notice elements in Charlotte that didn't seem right. When all the medical consultations were over, they discovered that Charlotte had some neurological differences that resulted in her having attention deficit disorder and dyslexia, as well as gross-motor anomalies. Dana is very honest in her memoir about how she reacted to all of this and how long it took her to accept Charlotte for who she was and that not everything was perfect in their apparently perfect lives. She also talks about the difficulties involved in having a child whose needs are different—special caregivers, special schools. Yet she also needs to be treated normally at the same time, a fine line to draw. All of this is in this memoir, including lists of resources. At the end, Charlotte, now in college, gets to tell her story, "Charlotte in Her Own Words."

Subjects: Children with Differences; Fashion Designers; Learning Difficulties; Mothers and Daughters; Parents of Children with Learning Difficulties; Special Education

Now Try: Anne Ford (the great-granddaughter of Henry Ford), with the help of John-Richard Thompson, describes her own journey with a child with learning difficulties in ***Laughing Allegra: The Inspiring Story of a Mother's Struggle and Triumph Raising a Daughter with Learning Disabilities***. Abigail Marshall offers an explanation of dyslexia and many tips for parents in dealing with it in ***The Everything Parent's Guide to Children with Dyslexia: All You Need to Ensure Your Child's Success***. In ***Becoming Citizens: Family Life and the Politics of Disability*** Susan Schwartzenberg describes how differently children were treated only a few decades ago when their capabilities did not seem to fall into a normal range.

Grandin, Temple (1947–)

Thinking in Pictures: And Other Reports from My Life with Autism. "Expanded edition including the most recent research, therapy, and resources." Foreword by Oliver Sacks. Vintage Books, 2006. 270pp. 9780307275653. Also available in e-audiobook, e-book, and video (entitled *Temple Grandin*). 616.8982092

If Temple Grandin had not been autistic, she likely would not have contributed to the well-being of animals in the United States as much as she has. The nature of her autism is such that she cannot empathize with human emotion—her interactions with humans are learned patterns—but she can empathize with animal emotion. Thanks to this and other attributes of her brain, Grandin has developed a more humane system of treating livestock. Growing up autistic was not easy for her, as she presented as an odd child, afraid of socialization and given to temper and outbursts. Her mother, Eustacia, was loving and steadfast, as was her mother's sister, Ann, an aunt who had a cattle ranch in Arizona where Temple made her all-important connections. This memoir is of great interest to those with or without autism; it offers one understanding of autism, how it can present, and what works in helping mitigate it. It also offers hope to those who deal with autism on a daily basis.

Subjects: Animal Scientists; Arizona; Autism Spectrum; Cattle Industry; College Professors; Industrial Engineers; Scientists

Now Try: Temple Grandin told Oliver W. Sacks that she felt like an anthropologist on Mars, a phrase he used for his book, ***An Anthropologist on Mars: Seven Paradoxical Tales***, about various neurological disorders, relating how each person in the book developed skills from those disorders. Grandin's ideas for change in the livestock industry were initially resisted for a number of reasons. Mary Anning had a similar problem in the nineteenth century when, as a twelve-year-old, she discovered the first dinosaur skeleton, debunking the belief that animals did not become extinct. Although women were not allowed in the meetings of the Geological Society of London, Mary's find still changed the course of scientific thought, as illustrated by Shelley Emling in ***The Fossil Hunter: Dinosaurs, Evolution, and the Woman Whose Discoveries Changed the World***. (Tracy Chevalier's novel, ***Remarkable Creatures***, is also about Mary Anning.) For Dawn Prince-Hughes it was gorillas at Seattle's Woodland Park Zoo that were her touchstone for understanding herself and learning to cope. She describes her life with autism in ***Songs of the Gorilla Nation: My Journey Through Autism***.

Grealy, Lucy (1963–2002)

Autobiography of a Face. Afterword by Ann Patchett. Perennial, 2003, 1994. 226pp. 9781439562260. Also available in Braille. 362.1969947092

A schoolyard accident led to the discovery of a malignant tumor in Lucy Grealy's jaw and began her life of surgeries, pain, and self-discovery. In the course of treatment for the cancer, Grealy's face became gravely disfigured, and she suffered throughout her childhood and adolescence, through various attempts at reconstructive surgery. The great challenge for her, however, was less the physical pain of her ordeal and much more the psychological pain. The cruelty of children is such that she suffered much torment from her peers in school. But there is more to her than a face, although it is hard to disconnect her face from her life. With a master's in fine arts, she writes in her memoir about the notion of beauty—how it has been co-opted by the media making superficial beauty so important in the world. Through her writing she discovered another kind of beauty, a love of life, an inner beauty. What she aimed to do with her memoir was to raise her situation above the personal and make it universal for her readers; everyone suffers from the idea that something about his or her physical appearance is unwelcome. Grealy wants her readers to look more deeply. She triumphed in her memoir's success, in the recognition she received of its literary value. In the afterword, her good friend Ann Patchett exhorts readers to listen to the Lucy in the memoir, to heed her words, and to appreciate her writing.

Subjects: Bullying; Children with Differences; Drug Abuse; Ewing's Sarcoma; Facial Abnormalities; Female Friendships; Mental Health; Pain; Poets; Self-Acceptance; Self-Destructive Behavior; Sexuality

Now Try: The issue of bullying in the schoolyard is a serious one. Emily and Sarah Buder, hearing about Olivia Gardner, an epileptic child who was severely bullied for her illness at school, started a letter-writing campaign to support

Olivia and other bullied children. Gardner and the Buders have written a book compiling some of these letters, ***Letters to a Bullied Girl: Messages of Healing and Hope.*** Ewing's sarcoma is the disease that attacked Lucy Grealy; it also caused the amputation of Josh Sundquist's leg when he was a child. In his memoir, ***Just Don't Fall: How I Grew Up, Conquered Illness, and Made It Down the Mountain,*** he describes what he had to overcome in order to be able to enter the Paralympics ski events. Natalie Kusz also grew up with a disfigured face, although hers was the result of a vicious dog attack; ***Road Song,*** Kusz's tale of her life with her family in Alaska, is one of courage and inspiration.

Robison, John Elder (1957–)

Look Me in the Eye: My Life with Asperger's. Foreword by Augusten Burroughs. Postscript by the author. Three Rivers Press, 2008. 302pp. 9780307396181. Also available in large print, audiobook, e-audiobook, and e-book. 362.196092

When he was a child Robison and his family had no idea he had Asperger's syndrome. With an abusive father and a mentally ill mother, this may not have been too surprising. (See page 525 for ***A Wolf at the Table: A Memoir of My Father*** by Robison's brother, Augusten Burroughs.) Robison talks about his childhood and how difficult he found social interaction, wanting to connect but being unable to; he finally "learned" social patterns that allowed him to cope. He was much more comfortable working with machines and mechanics, easily seeing how everything fit together, a fact he recognized as a blessing since it provided him with interesting careers. He was grateful to meet a man, through his work of restoring and repairing high-end cars, who was a therapist and who, after several conversations, was able to tell John that he had Asperger's and to give him a book about it. This made John feel finally that he was differently wired but not necessarily weird, something he'd believed all his life. One interesting point he makes is that once he started to develop more relationships with people, his mechanical skills deteriorated; he had lost that special connection.

Subjects: Abuse (Parental); Asperger's Syndrome; Autism Spectrum; Children with Differences; Family Relationships; Inventors; KISS (Musical Group); Milton Bradley Company

Now Try: Liane Holliday Willey also did not know she had Asperger's until her daughter was diagnosed with it. In her memoir, ***Pretending to Be Normal: Living with Asperger's Syndrome,*** she offers very specific tips for coping and for talking to others about it. Tim Page is a music critic who found that Asperger's played a creative role in his life; he tells his story in ***Parallel Play: Growing Up with Undiagnosed Asperger's.*** Perhaps the first view that many readers had of Asperger's was Mark Haddon's award-winning novel, ***The Curious Incident of the Dog in the Night-Time.***

Tammet, Daniel (1979–)

Born on a Blue Day: Inside the Extraordinary Mind of an Autistic Savant; A Memoir. Free Press, 2007, 2006. 237pp. 9781416535072. Also available in audiobook and e-audiobook. 362.196092

Anyone reading Daniel Tammet's memoir would automatically think about the movie ***Rain Man,*** the story written by Barry Morrow and based on the life of Kim

Peek. A primary difference between Tammet and Peek is that Tammet has achieved much greater socialization skills than Peek was able to. Tammet lives in a cottage in a small town in Kent, England, which he set up with his partner—a man much shyer than Tammet—but he still uses coping techniques developed as a child for bouts of nervousness or to deal with unexpected events. He is a highly unusual man for a number of reasons: he is one of perhaps a hundred known savants, interacting with numbers in ways that other people have a hard time understanding, never mind being able to replicate. He also has synesthesia, which he believes was caused by his epileptic seizures as a child. Because of that he visualizes people and things—including numbers—as colors. In addition to his mathematical prowess, however, he also has creative skills, as evidenced by the beauty with which he writes. And the fact that he is able to live in a loving relationship with another person reflects an added advancement on his part. He believes that his family is responsible in part for that; he was one of nine children in a loving family who wouldn't allow him to withdraw totally into himself. Using his skill at remembering and learning languages, he has created a language-learning Web site, by which he earns his living (http://www.optimnem.co.uk/index.php).

Subjects: Autism Spectrum; Epilepsy; Family Relationships; Gay Men; Language Acquisition; Mathematics; Memory; Savants; Synesthesia

Now Try: Tammet has followed his memoir with ***Embracing the Wide Sky: A Tour Across the Horizons of the Mind,*** an insider's explanation for the layperson of how he perceives things and how the scientists who have studied his brain see it (see the documentary ***Brainman***). The award-winning novel by Jeffrey Moore, ***The Memory Artists,*** features a man with total recall and synesthesia whose mother is suffering from Alzheimer's disease. In ***A Healing Family,*** the Nobel laureate author, Kenzaburō Ōe, wrote about life with his brain-damaged son. Now Lindsley Cameron looks at the creative talent of the son, Hikari, a widely renowned Japanese classical-music composer, in ***The Music of Light: The Extraordinary Story of Hikari and Kenzaburo Oe.*** Tammet's ability to memorize and recite the number pi further than it had ever been counted before is reminiscent of John Nash's mathematical prowess; his story is told by Sylvia Nasar in ***A Beautiful Mind: The Life of Mathematical Genius and Nobel Laureate John Nash.***

Williams, Donna (1963–)

Somebody Somewhere: Breaking Free from the World of Autism. Jessica Kingsley Publishers, 1999, 1994. 208pp. 9781853027192. Also available in e-book. 616.8982092

In her first memoir, ***Nobody Nowhere: The Extraordinary Autobiography of an Autistic,*** Donna Williams described her quest to determine what was wrong with her. After writing her story, she gave it to a psychologist, planning to burn the document after he told her what was wrong with her. After reading it, he told her she couldn't burn it because it was as yet the first documented case of autism by one who had it. She has gone on to write this memoir, which details her journey out of the world she had inhabited for the first part of her life. In that world she had a triad of personalities to help her cope with various facets of her life—a violent boy to deal with the abuse she suffered from her mother and brother; a girl to deal with school; and herself, caught in the fears and isolation of the autistic. Now Williams is learning to cope without relying on her alter egos. She could never understand feelings and is learning to do that, expressing them in her art; she is a painter, a writer, and a musician. She also writes about autism and offers consultations to those on the spectrum and to professionals dealing with it. After she fell in love and got married, she wrote a book about that, learning to live with someone else and separating when it didn't work out: ***Like Color to the Blind***.

Subjects: Adult Child Abuse Victims; Artists; Australia; Autism Spectrum; Coping in Women; Musicians; Writers, Australia

Now Try: Tony DeBlois is considered a prodigious savant, a man who is autistic and blind, but whose musical talent surpasses that of most musicians in general. As Janice DeBlois and Antonia Felix describe in ***Some Kind of Genius: The Extraordinary Journey of Musical Savant Tony DeBlois***, his talent was innate, demonstrated as soon as he received a toy piano as a toddler. One of the difficulties that Williams always encountered mentally was her awareness that her world wasn't the same as other people's worlds. Jessy Park was also different in that regard, and her mother, Clara Claiborne Park, has written two books about her; the second one, ***Exiting Nirvana: A Daughter's Life with Autism***, describes how Jessy has become a successful artist. Autism is a painful disorder for all; the Barron family experienced years of suffering until finally the endless effort and love that Judy and her husband, Ron, provided their son, Sean, paid off and he achieved a release of sorts from the isolated and troubled world he lived in. One example Judy and Sean share in their book, ***There's a Boy in Here***, is the tantrums he threw in the car whenever the driver made a left turn.

Addictions

This section covers one form of illness: addiction. Whereas there are a variety of addictions, the titles here represent only drug addiction and alcoholism. The writers don't always explain how they came to be dependent on the substance they were abusing, but they do describe their downward spiral; their bad behavior in the midst of that spiral; and their ultimate recognition that what they were doing was not only self-destructive, but also harmful to others. Memoirs that concern the people to whom that harm has been done—parents, spouses, children—can be found in other sections in this chapter and throughout the other chapters. Readers should remember that each writer's experience is a personal one and therefore not necessarily to be taken as the right way or only way out of the addiction. Obvious by their exclusion here are James Frey's ***A Million Little Pieces*** and Augusten Burroughs's ***Dry***, both due to their fictional content (see Appendix B).

Memoirs of addictions are confessional stories of how the writers succumbed to the lure of alcohol and drugs, to the point of becoming addicted. Because these are survival stories, their narratives include the stories of how they became sober again, and in the spirit of many who have been in serious trouble, they frequently offer advice and resources in their memoirs to help others.

Aldrin, Buzz (1930–)
Abraham, Ken (1951–), coauthor

Magnificent Desolation: The Long Journey Home from the Moon. With a new Epilogue. Harmony Books, 2010, 2009. 336pp. ill. 9780307463463. Also available in large print, audiobook, e-audiobook, and e-book. 629.45009

When Buzz Aldrin came back to Earth from the moon, his life became anticlimactic. He had a PhD from MIT, he had landed on the moon, and there was nowhere for him to go. Because of the number of people in the NASA program, another journey to the moon was no longer an option for him, particularly once the shuttle program was introduced. He worked regularly on developing products and techniques for the space movement, but had little luck selling his work. He was genetically prone to depression, and the letdown after his moonwalk fed into that. Whenever he felt depressed, he would drink; thus began a long pattern of trying to make progress in his career, becoming discouraged and depressed, and drinking. The worst of it was in the 1970s, when he underwent two divorces. In and out of rehab, in and out of Alcoholics Anonymous meetings, he finally found the right sponsor, the right clinic, the right program, and the right woman. He begins his memoir by covering much of the same territory he had in his first memoir, ***Return to Earth*** (published under the name Edwin E. Aldrin, with Wayne Warga), tracing his life from childhood to the moonwalk. He continues then with life from that point on, including a chapter devoted to his new wife, Lois.

Buzz Aldrin was awarded the Presidential Medal of Freedom in 1969 by President Nixon.

Subjects: Alcoholics; Alcoholics Anonymous; Astronauts; *Apollo 11* (Spacecraft); Depression; Family Relationships; Lunar Landing; Marriage; National Aeronautics and Space Administration; Octogenarians; Rehabilitation; Scientists; Self-Destructive Behavior; Sobriety

Now Try: In ***Rocket Men: The Epic Story of the First Men on the Moon,*** Craig Nelson looks closely at the Apollo mission, including the personal cost to the families of the three men involved in the first moonwalk. In his memoir Aldrin describes an event billed as "Operation Understanding," wherein a number of noted celebrities were invited by the National Council on Alcoholism and Drug Dependency to a press conference held expressly to admit in public their status as recovering alcoholics. Christopher Kennedy Lawford does the same thing in book form, ***Moments of Clarity: Voices from the Front Lines of Addiction and Recovery,*** wherein celebrities submitted essays about the point at which they realized they needed to address their addictions. Jason Peter also got caught up in a postcareer addiction; following a neck injury when he could no longer play NFL football, Peter became a drug addict, as he and Tony O'Neill relate in ***Hero of the Underground: A Memoir.***

Carr, David

The Night of the Gun: A Reporter Investigates the Darkest Story of His Life, His Own. Simon & Schuster, 2009, 2008. 389pp. 9781416541530. Also available in audiobook and e-audiobook. 616.860092

Once the newspaper journalist (currently writing for *The New York Times*) got back on his feet after a deeply ingrained drug addiction, he began to investigate his earlier life. Did he wave the gun in front of his friend's face, or did his friend do that in self-defense? To answer these and other questions, to see how far down he had gone and how far he had come back, he interviewed friends, family, and coworkers in Minneapolis, the place where he was at his lowest. He also interviewed other drug users and his drug dealer. He describes how he had just handed his girlfriend a crack pipe when her waters broke; she gave birth prematurely to twin girls, each weighing three pounds. When the girls were seven months old, with their mother still using drugs, Carr put the children into foster care, entered rehabilitation, and gradually took back his life and his children. A diagnosis of cancer didn't help, but it also didn't send him back to the drug world. Carr's book is gritty and explicit in relating the degradations of his addiction.

Subjects: Cocaine Abuse; Drug Abuse; Fathers and Daughters; Journalists; Minneapolis, MN; Rehabilitation; Self-Destructive Behavior; Single Fathers

Now Try: Oran Canfield, the son of the motivational writer Jack Canfield, describes his unusual childhood, which included drinking at the age of seven, his subsequent addiction problems, and his own views of the world, in ***Long Past Stopping: A Memoir.*** People often forget about the commercial side of illicit drugs. With the help of David Fisher, Roberto Escobar Gaviria writes about his brother Pablo's multi-billion-dollar cocaine industry in Colombia: ***The Accountant's Story: Inside the Violent World of the Medellín Cartel.*** Once he got his life back together, Carr moved on in his journalism career, so that now he is quite successful; another successful journalist, who covered the administrations of twelve presidents, was Daniel Schorr, whose memoir is entitled ***Staying Tuned: A Life in Journalism.***

Cheever, Susan (1943–)

Note Found in a Bottle: My Life as a Drinker. Simon & Schuster, 1999. 192pp. 9780684804323. 362.292092

Susan Cheever has written several memoirs, including ***Home Before Dark,*** about her father, John Cheever, and ***Treetops: A Family Memoir,*** about her family. But it was her children that finally induced her to take control of a problem that had been as much a part of her life as writing. Alcohol was always with her, from the time that her grandmother taught her at six how to mix a martini, through growing up with her parents' house parties and regular drinking habits, including her father's alcoholism. She describes the culture of drinking in affluent houses in the 1950s and 1960s, when it was standard fare to have a cocktail before, drinks with, and drinks after dinner. Because of her drinking she had three failed marriages, but she finally pulled herself together when her second child, born when she was a little older, was a toddler.

Subjects: Alcoholics; Alcoholism in the Family; Cheever, John; Children of Alcoholics; Divorce; Family Relationships; Novelists; Promiscuity; Rehabilitation; Social History, United States; Women and Addiction; Writers in the Family

Now Try: After this book on her alcoholism, Cheever wrote one about being a mother, ***As Good as I Could Be: A Memoir About Raising Wonderful Children in Difficult Times***. The daughter of Bernard Malamud, Janna Malamud Smith, has written a memoir also revealing what life was like for her as a writer's daughter: ***My Father Is a Book: A Memoir of Bernard Malamud***. Susan Cheever was fortunately able to overcome her addiction; as the historian and politician George S. McGovern reveals in ***Terry: My Daughter's Life-and-Death Struggle with Alcoholism***, his daughter was not. Cheever discusses the culture of drinking in her book, a topic that Thomas M. Wilson takes further in his exposition of the attitudes toward both drinking and not drinking in various parts of the world: ***Drinking Cultures: Alcohol and Identity***.

Fisher, Carrie (1956–)

Wishful Drinking. Simon & Schuster, 2009, 2008. 163pp. ill. 9781439153710. Also available in audiobook (read by the author). 791.43028092

Carrie Fisher had it all: a broken family (her father, Eddie Fisher, left her mother, Debbie Reynolds, for Liz Taylor); early fame (she was Princess Leia in ***Star Wars***); bipolar disorder; alcoholism and drug addiction; a dead man in her bed; and broken marriages. She had written some autobiographical novels prior to this memoir (notably ***Postcards from the Edge***), but this rather short book presents the highlights of her life so far, dealing with all that life has thrown her. The memoir was originally written for a one-woman Broadway show of the same name. Rather than a tragic telling, however, Fisher has turned her life into a comedy routine, one at which the reader (or audience) can laugh, but can also empathize with the real emotion behind the laughter. Fisher says that while readers may find some of her stories unbelievable, they should see what she left out.

Subjects: Actors; Alcoholics; Bipolar Disorder; Drug Abuse; Family Relationships; Humor; Mothers and Daughters; Rehabilitation; Self-Destructive Behavior; *Star Wars* (Film); Women and Addiction; Women in Film

Now Try: The one-woman, humorous show that Fisher has created is reminiscent of Willy Russell's ***Shirley Valentine: A Play***, the funny yet poignant story of a woman who heads off to Greece to get away from her stultifying life. Deana Martin knows what it is like to grow up with famous parents, particularly one with a drinking problem, as her mother had. She tells her story, with Wendy Holden's help, about life with a celebrity in ***Memories Are Made of This: Dean Martin Through His Daughter's Eyes***. A "victim" of ***Star Trek*** (rather than ***Star Wars***) is Adam Nimoy, son of Leonard; Adam tells in his own funny way about his life of addiction and recovery in ***My Incredibly Wonderful, Miserable Life: An Anti-Memoir***.

Hamill, Pete (1935–)

A Drinking Life: A Memoir. Little, Brown, 1997, 1994. 280pp. 9780316341028. Also available in audiobook and e-book. 818.5409

Pete Hamill grew up with drinking in Brooklyn in the 1940s. His Irish father worked at a job during the day and drank in a bar at night. By the time Hamill got a permanent job and settled down as a reporter for the *New York Post,* he was well on his way to being controlled by drink. He was in his twenties at the time. He continued this slide downward until after his marriage broke up; two years later he finally woke up to what his life really was like and vowed never to drink again. He managed to gain and maintain sobriety without the help of Alcoholics Anonymous, because he told himself he had to give up one drink only: the next one. Twenty years later he sat down to revisit his childhood and his life with alcohol, mixing nostalgia with brutal honesty.

Subjects: Alcoholics; Alcoholism; Brooklyn (New York, NY); Classics; Drinking Customs; Irish-Americans; Journalists; Novelists; Rehabilitation; Self-Destructive Behavior; Sobriety

Now Try: Hamill includes in his memoir a discussion of the custom of drinking, particularly in the Irish community in which he grew up. Iain Gately offers a wider perspective on that topic in ***Drink: A Cultural History of Alcohol***. The Irish community, this time in Queens, is brought to life in ***Charming Billy,*** a novel by Alice McDermott, as her characters gather at a bar for the wake of Billy Lynch, a friend who died of alcoholism. Neil Steinberg was also a newspaper journalist, whose world came crashing in on him one day, forcing him into outpatient rehab. His wry account of his alcoholic journey is ***Drunkard: A Hard-Drinking Life***.

Knapp, Caroline (1959–2002)

Drinking: A Love Story. Bantam Dell, 2005, 1996. 286pp. 9780385315548. Also available in audiobook (read by the author) and e-book. 362.292092.

Drinking was a part of Caroline Knapp's culture growing up: "cocktails at 7" for her parents and for herself. She drank from the age of fourteen, when she discovered that alcohol seemed to do a good job of mitigating strong emotions. For most of her alcoholic life she was high functioning; her disease was not obvious to most people. She describes in her memoir how much she loved drinking and what it did for her. She also talks about the desolation of the thought that if she were to try to recover, she could never have another drink again, a thought that may keep many people from trying to rehabilitate themselves. In her memoir, she describes the effect of her parents' deaths on her and her recognition that her therapist father was likely also an alcoholic. She also talks a lot about Alcoholics Anonymous and the many meetings she attended. She delves into the issue of alcohol and women, too. Knapp had been anorexic when she was in her twenties and believes that all of these addictions are related for women. In fact, shortly before her death from lung cancer she had finished a book on that topic: ***Appetites: Why Women Want***. Knapp wrote this memoir not long after she went into rehabilitation, so that there is an immediacy here in her writing. Because of its honesty, it may also have been part of her recovery.

Subjects: Alcoholics Anonymous; Alcoholism; Death of a Parent; Eating Disorders; Journalists; Self-Destructive Behavior; Sobriety; Women and Addiction

Now Try: Susan Cheever wrote a biography of the man who started Alcoholics Anonymous (AA), ***My Name Is Bill: Bill Wilson; His Life and the Creation of Alcoholics Anonymous***. Anne M. Fletcher offers other alternatives besides AA to recovering alcoholics or those who would like to be: ***Sober for Good: New Solutions for Drinking Problems—Advice from Those Who Have Succeeded***. The combination of honesty and feminism in Knapp's writing is matched by Patricia Foster in her memoir, ***Just Beneath My Skin: Autobiography and Self-Discovery***, a work in which Foster seeks to establish her own sense of identity.

Lau, Evelyn (1971–)

Runaway: Diary of a Street Kid. Harper PerennialCanada, 2001, 1989. 295pp. 9780006485872. Also available in video. 362.74092

Evelyn Lau had a compulsion to write, which she did constantly in her journal. Her strict parents, however, had other ideas for her: to be a medical doctor and not to write, an activity she was forbidden. Evelyn finally ran away from home at the age of fourteen, living on the streets in Vancouver, British Columbia, taking her notebook with her. Her memoir is a sorry tale of prostitution to make money, drug addiction, and attempted suicide. But it is also a redemptive tale of a strong social-safety net, of social workers who helped her and put her into foster care, allowing her to go back to school, providing psychiatric care to help her recover. And it is also the tale of a young writer who is able to accomplish her goal of being a published author, evidenced by this memoir. She has become a prize-winning poet and short-story writer.

Subjects: Adolescents, Canada; Chinese-Canadians; Diaries; Drug Abuse; Foster Care, Canada; Poets, Canada; Runaways; Self-Destructive Behavior; Sex Workers; Street Life; Vancouver, BC; Women and Addiction; Writers, Canada

Now Try: Lau followed up her early diary with a memoir, ***Inside out: Reflections on a Life So Far***. Cupcake Brown's life shared some similarities with Lau's, as perhaps do the lives of many street kids. Brown has also written a memoir of her life on the street, making money from sex and taking drugs and alcohol, although her tone is more upbeat than Lau's. Her story is entitled ***A Piece of***

Cake: A Memoir. The story of a runaway adolescent is a hard one to read; also difficult is reading about the parents' anguish. In ***Live Through This: A Mother's Memoir of Runaway Daughters and Reclaimed Love***, Debra Gwartney is open about why two of her daughters ran away to live on the street after the breakup of their parents' marriage and what she herself went through in the years it took her to get them back. She also illustrates how other children in the family are affected. In the case of Mia Fontaine, who wrote her story along with her mother, Claire, the situation was quite different, with Mia going to a tough-love school in the Czech Republic while her mother and stepfather underwent counseling at home, all of which is described in ***Comeback: A Mother and Daughter's Journey Through Hell and Back***.

Lawford, Christopher Kennedy (1955–)

Symptoms of Withdrawal: A Memoir of Snapshots and Redemption. Harper, 2006, 2005. 389pp. ill. 32pp. of plates. 9780061131233. Also available in large print, audiobook (read by the author), e-audiobook, and e-book. 792.028092

Christopher Lawford was born in California, the son of Patricia Kennedy (daughter of Joseph and Rose) and the actor Peter Lawford. As he tells it, he was born with the American Dream already having been handed to him. Given Lawford's history of alcohol and drug addiction, the phrase "too much too soon" comes to mind. But he was also genetically disposed, at least to an alcohol addiction, as both his parents were alcoholics, along with numerous members of the Kennedy clan. Part of Lawford's problem, which he recognizes, is his sense of entitlement, an entitlement that was indulged to the point where he had no boundaries or limits. Even the death by overdose of his best friend, David Kennedy (Robert's son), was not enough to wake him up fully to the dangers he was flirting with. As he tells it, his Aunt Joan finally took him to an AA meeting, where he realized that it didn't matter if he was a Kennedy—his behavior and addiction were no different from those of anyone in that room, regardless of their lineage. When he writes his memoir, it is with pride that he can claim twenty years of sobriety.

Subjects: Actors; Alcoholics; Alcoholism; Drug Abuse; Family Relationships; Fathers and Sons; Kennedy Family; Privilege; Rehabilitation; Self-Destructive Behavior; Self-Discovery; Sobriety; Upper Class

Now Try: Christopher Lawford is obviously not the only well-known person to suffer from addiction; Gary Stromberg and Jane Merrill have collected addiction stories from celebrities in ***The Harder They Fall: Celebrities Tell Their Real-Life Stories of Addiction and Recovery***. The poets Lorna Crozier and Patrick Lane (himself a recovering alcoholic) gathered stories from writers about their various addictions, as they describe how their addictions and recoveries have affected their lives: ***Addicted: Notes from the Belly of the Beast***. Christopher Lawford's maternal grandfather, Joseph, was also involved in Hollywood life, buying several studios to form RKO. This is one side of his business dealings that was not well-known until Cari Beauchamp wrote the biography, ***Joseph P. Kennedy Presents: His Hollywood Years***.

McCourt, Malachy (1931–)

Singing My Him Song. Perennial, 2001. 242pp. 9780060955489. Also available in large print, audiobook (read by the author), and e-book.974.71043

This memoir is the sequel to McCourt's ***A Monk Swimming: A Memoir,*** the title of his first book playing on what a child hears or understands when adults say things. ("A Monk Swimming" is really "amongst women," a phrase in a Catholic prayer.) This memoir begins in 1963, after Malachy's first marriage has broken up. The focus in this second book is really how he gets his life in order. A serious alcoholic, the reason for his marriage breakup, he finally recognizes that he is not much better than his own father, a man who drank his wages before finally abandoning his family. Malachy describes the strength of the woman, Diana, who became his second wife; his own successful fight against his addiction; and his subsequent battle with cancer. He also recounts the various jobs he's had, many of them tending bar before he went straight or playing small bits on television, often a bartender. In fact, the tenor of his memoir is that of a bartender amusing his clientele with stories as they spend the afternoon in the pub. His greatest victory was in being in Ireland, filming on location, and not drinking, quite a feat.

Subjects: Actors; Alcoholics; Alcoholism; Bartenders; Cancer; Irish-Americans; Los Angeles, CA; Marriage; New York, NY; Radio Broadcasters; Rehabilitation; Self-Destructive Behavior; Sobriety; Writers

Now Try: Joe Queenan grew up in an Irish-Catholic environment in Philadelphia with an alcoholic father. His book, ***Closing Time: A Memoir,*** describes a father who doesn't seem all that different from McCourt's. Mitch Albom's first novel deals with a young man who uses alcohol to mitigate his emotions, but he has help from the ghost of his mother in ***For One More Day***. The bartender may tell stories, but he (or she) also hears a lot of them from people with varying relationships with alcohol. Toby Cecchini presents a bit of a day in the life in ***Cosmopolitan: A Bartender's Life***.

Zailckas, Koren (1980–)

Smashed: Story of a Drunken Girlhood. Penguin, 2006, 2005. 342pp. 9780143036470. Also available in large print, audiobook, e-audiobook, and e-book. 616.861092

One interesting tidbit about Zailckas is that she was a student in Mary Karr's class at Syracuse University. Mary's memoir about her alcoholism, ***Lit: A Memoir,*** is actually in the "Confession" section of Chapter 8, "The Inner Life" (p. 342). Zailckas admits that she liked the confidence she felt when she was drunk, so she drank for the purpose of getting drunk. She catalogs her firsts: her first drink (at fourteen), the first time she was caught by her parents (the following year), her first blackout, her first alcohol poisoning. Date rape was a part of her life as well as casual sex with anyone. Throughout her memoir she drops statistics gleaned from Harvard School of Public Health studies that tell how at-risk girls are. They drink as much as boys but have a lower tolerance for alcohol, which stays in their systems longer. Binge drinking is the norm—at least at Syracuse, according to Zailckas. After finishing college and moving to Manhattan, she woke up one day not knowing where she was or with whom; this started her on her road to recovery. Now she is writing a cautionary tale for others, particularly young girls.

Subjects: Adolescents; Alcohol Poisoning; Alcoholics; Date Rape; Promiscuity; Rehabilitation; Self-Destructive Behavior; Sexual Exploitation; Sobriety; Syracuse University, NY; Women and Addiction

Now Try: While doing research on the illegal use of prescription drugs, Joshua Lyon became addicted himself. Throughout his memoir of his addiction, ***Pill Head: The Secret Life of a Painkiller Addict***, the journalist in him offers statistical data on the growing addiction to prescription drugs. It wasn't until after he had graduated from college and was volunteering for the Peace Corps that Toren Volkmann recognized he was a full-blown alcoholic. He and his mother, Chris, together tell the story of their experience in ***From Binge to Blackout: A Mother and Son Struggle with Teen Drinking***. Roddy Doyle has written two novels about Paula Spencer, an abused and alcoholic woman in Dublin; the first is ***The Woman Who Walked into Doors***.

Survivors of Violence

It is certainly true that there is much violence throughout this book, but here the story is about very specific acts of violence. In many cases it is rape, although elsewhere in the book stories of sexual abuse and incest can also be stories of rape. Many of these stories focus on the recovery after the violence. Different from those with an illness, no one here says it's a good thing this violence happened because now the survivor is a stronger person, but they do see sometimes how they can take pride in their strength. Many have set out to help others who have suffered the same violence. Rape isn't the only form of violence represented here, however; there are also stories of murder and brutal physical attacks.

Stories from survivors of violence are narratives of the attacks that eventually led to the memoir. The survivors relate their emotional responses and coping techniques, revealing how they felt violated and vulnerable. But they also describe how they have managed to recover their lives despite the trauma, and they occasionally offer suggestions to help others in similar circumstances.

Doe, Jane

The Story of Jane Doe: A Book About Rape. Illustrated by Shary Boyle. Vintage Canada, 2004, 2003. 363pp. 9780679312758. Also available in e-book and video. 362.88309

In 1986 Jane Doe was the fifth woman to be raped by a serial rapist known by the police to go after women with a very specific profile. Because the police never alerted the women in the community, not wanting them to become "hysterical" and foil police efforts to nab the rapist, Jane Doe was unaware and unprepared.

She was raped. To make matters worse, her rape was not deemed violent because she wasn't badly hurt physically. This memoir is the story, not just of her rape by the serial rapist, but the subsequent rape by the justice system as she fought for her rights. Fighting for her rights included a civil trial after the criminal trial of the rapist (caught thanks to a poster campaign she had initiated), wherein Jane Doe sued the Metropolitan Toronto Police Force for violating her constitutional rights in not warning her and the others in her community about the danger they were in. She intersperses her narrative with excerpts from her medical assessment, newspaper reports, and trial transcripts.

The Story of Jane Doe was nominated for the Writers' Trust of Canada Shaughnessy Cohen Award for Political Writing and the Arthur Ellis Award for Best Non-Fiction.

Subjects: Civil Suits, Canada; Police Misconduct, Canada; Rape; Survivors of Rape; Toronto, ON; Trials (Rape), Canada; True Crime; Violent Crimes

Now Try: A visually impaired woman from Wisconsin was raped in her home and badly treated by the rookie detective who answered the call; as Bill Lueders relates in ***Cry Rape: The True Story of One Woman's Harrowing Quest for Justice,*** she too sued the criminal justice system. When Jane Doe was raped, the hospital did use a rape kit, although she comments on how rarely the evidence from it comes into the trial, but the process has since become much more streamlined and professional. Serita Stevens is a forensic nurse who provides details, with the assistance of members of the International Association of Forensic Nurses, on her work in the emergency room in ***Forensic Nurse: The New Role of the Nurse in Law Enforcement,*** as she is often the first contact the survivor has after the attack. Joanna Bourke examines the history of rape from the point of view of the perpetrator in ***Rape: Sex, Violence, History***.

Ellroy, James (1948–)

My Dark Places: An L.A. Crime Memoir. Vintage Books, 1997, 1996. 427pp. 9780679762058. Also available in e-book. 813.54

This memoir is novelist James Ellroy's story of how he attempted not only to come to grips with his mother's murder but also to solve the crime itself. His mother, Geneva, was found in a deserted schoolyard, strangled to death, when he was ten years old (he'd been living with his father at the time). Ellroy includes in this memoir his own coming of age and how he dealt with his mother's death, immersing himself in dark, negative worlds to the point of becoming an alcoholic and drug addict. Once he finally got himself cleaned up and began writing for a living, he decided to see what he could do about solving his mother's murder. The memoir then takes us through his actions in trying to accomplish that task.

Subjects: Alcoholics; Crime Novelists; Death of a Parent; Drug Abuse; Los Angeles, CA; Mothers and Sons; Murder; Rehabilitation; Self-Destructive Behavior; Sobriety; True Crime; Victims of Violence

Now Try: Ellroy was always fascinated by the unsolved murder of the woman dubbed "The Black Dahlia" and even wrote a novel with that title. Steve Hodel, a former Los Angeles Police officer, believes that his late father, a doctor, was the serial killer responsible for her death. He explains why in ***Black Dahlia Avenger: A Genius for Murder***. Joseph Wambaugh writes with the same gritty and dark language that Ellroy does; ***The Onion Field,*** one of his few nonfiction books, is about the murder of a Los Angeles policeman. Writing in the *noir* tradition of Ellroy's writing is Walter Mosley, whose ***Devil in a Blue Dress*** is also set in Los Angeles in the 1950s. Ellroy has recently written a book about his views on women, a tribute of sorts to his mother, ***The Hilliker Curse: My Pursuit of Women***.

Jentz, Terri (1957–)

Strange Piece of Paradise. Picador, 2007, 2006. 729pp. 9780312426699. Also available in audiobook. 364.1555092

Several years after being brutally attacked in a campground in Oregon, Terri Jentz went back to put her demons to rest and to try to determine just what was done to her and by whom. She had several factors going against her: the attitude that she and her traveling companion, Shayna Weiss, shouldn't have been there, as it was an unapproved campground, so the girls were just asking for it; the fact that three different policing agencies were fighting for jurisdiction; the notion that serial violence was not part of the culture, so no one would have been looking for similar violent attacks; and the three-year statute of limitations on attempted murder in Oregon. Jentz's story includes the initial attack and its effect on her and her roommate; the several trips she made back to Oregon; the interviews she conducted; the medical reports; newspaper clippings; and all the help she received from locals, many of whom had a pretty good idea of who the culprit was. Jentz even enlisted the help of former girlfriends of this man, women who might have been beaten by him. Readers should be aware that some of the descriptions, particularly the details of the assault itself, are quite graphic.

Strange Piece of Paradise was a finalist for the National Book Critics Circle Award in Autobiography.

Subjects: Attempted Murder; Criminal Investigation; Cyclists; Oregon; True Crime; Violent Crimes; Weiss, Shayna

Now Try: Another case of random violence in Oregon was the killing of three family members by a teenager, Billy Gilley. For some reason he didn't kill his teenage sister, Jody, who cooperated with Kathryn Harrison, as Harrison told the story in ***While They Slept: An Inquiry into the Murder of a Family***. The case of Natalee Holloway, the young woman gone missing on vacation in Aruba, is another situation wherein it is likely that the perpetrators are known, but nothing has been done to bring them to justice. Natalee's father has written about his investigation into her disappearance, finding that the initial police investigation was mishandled, probably because of corruption. With the help of R. Stephanie Good and Larry Garrison, Dave Holloway recounts his investigation in ***Aruba: The Tragic Untold Story of Natalee Holloway and Corruption in Paradise***. Terri Jentz's former roommate was very seriously hurt in the incident, as the culprit used an axe to hit her on the head; she has no memory of the attack and wants nothing to do with Jentz, a reminder of that trip and the attack. Roy Freirich has written an award-winning novel, ***Winged Creatures***, about the victims of a violent crime and how they process such a life-changing event.

Land, Brad (1976–)

Goat: A Memoir. Random House, 2005, 2004. 210pp. 9780812969689. Also available in large print, audiobook, and e-book. 305.235092

Violence struck Brad Land unexpectedly in the form of a carjacking and vicious beating by two men at a party who asked him for a ride. He had always been a nervous young man, not very self-confident, so when they asked, although he wanted to say no, he found himself nodding yes. After they left him beaten in an isolated area and he made his way to a stranger's house, he had to deal not only with his physical pain but also with his psychic pain, particularly when the police seemed to doubt his story and wanted to lay the blame on him. This is only part of the violence in this memoir, however. He had already decided to transfer to Clemson University in South Carolina, where his younger brother, Brett, was already enrolled. By the time he got there, pledging and rushing were taking place in the fraternity he had applied to, his brother's Kappa Sigma. Already vulnerable from one form of violence, Brad was not prepared for the violence of the fraternity system, rituals he describes in great detail. This memoir is noteworthy for being an honest and open narration of violence against a man.

Subjects: Adolescents; Carjacking; Clemson University, SC; College Life; Family Relationships; Fraternities; South Carolina; Victims of Violence; Violence

Now Try: Barry Raine was with other friends—a woman and two other young men—when a stranger appeared, raped the woman, and beat two of the men, Barry being one of them. Years later he is finally able to look closely at the violence against him and others and write about it in ***Where the River Bends: A Memoir***. Howard Zehr looks at victims and their responses to the crimes perpetrated against them in a collection of essays, ***Transcending: Reflections of Crime Victims; Portraits and Interviews***. For many, the life of a fraternity or sorority member is almost unknown. Shining a mirror on that aspect of college life is Hank Nuwer's ***Wrongs of Passage: Fraternities, Sororities, Hazing, and Binge Drinking***.

Meili, Trisha (1960–)

I Am the Central Park Jogger: A Story of Hope and Possibility. Scribner, 2004, 2003. 267pp. 9780743244381. Also available in large print, audiobook (read by the author), e-audiobook, and e-book. 364.1532092

Trisha Meili describes the brutal beating she suffered in Central Park in the third person, largely because she has no memory of it herself. Her last memory is of a conversation she had with someone at 5:00 that evening; her memory loss is due to the severe brain damage she incurred from the beating, an attack that included rape, sodomy, and being left for dead in the mud. Her memoir, though, really isn't about the trauma. She has chosen to focus on the new life that rose out of that trauma. She says that she had a life before the attack and now has a different life after the attack, but she is proud of both of them. The writing of her book was the first public unveiling of her identity as the survivor of that infamous attack. Until then she had chosen to remain private; however, talking to small groups of people in rehabilitation and seeing their reaction to her story and her own recovery was enough to make her feel it was important to share her recovery story, the help she received, and the hope she derived from others.

Subjects: Hope; New York, NY; Rape; Rehabilitation; Runners; Survivors of Rape; True Crime; Victims of Violence; Violent Crimes

Now Try: Nancy Ziegenmeyer also decided to go public with her rape, when *The Des Moines Register* put a call out to rape survivors to tell their stories. She then wrote a book, with Larkin Warren, about her recovery and her work with other rape survivors, ***Taking Back My Life***. Claudia L. Osborn, a physician, suffered a traumatic brain injury, but was healed enough to write about it for others, particularly for those who can't understand what a loved one suffering a similar injury might be feeling or even trying to say. Her book is ***Over My Head: A Doctor's Own Story of Head Injury from the Inside Looking Out***. One of the aspects of a violent attack that Meili addresses is the ripple effect on family and friends. Jamie Kalven, the husband of a woman severely attacked and raped in Chicago, has written a book about that very thing, ***Working with Available Light: A Family's World After Violence***.

Raine, Nancy Venable (1946–)

After Silence: Rape and My Journey Back. Virago, 1999, 1998. 278pp. 9781860496448. Also available in e-book. 362.883092

The theme of silence runs throughout this memoir: for three hours as her rapist was brutalizing her, he kept yelling at Raine to "shut up" whenever she screamed, said no, tried to bargain with him, or resisted. She also realized on the first anniversary of her rape that silence was still required, that she had to stop talking about it, as it was too disturbing for others to hear. Raine had been a poet and realized that she couldn't even speak through that medium. Thinking that perhaps she was "over it," she began working on a novel, but even that came to a halt around the anniversary of her rape. What came out instead was an essay, "Returns of the Day," which she wrote for herself but published the following year in *The New York Times Magazine*. She received so much positive feedback from readers on her essay that she decided it was time to break her silence: "'Writing this book renewed my faith in the redemptive power of language' " (*Nancy Venable Raine*, 2004). A woman named Vera was so inspired by Raine's memoir that she created a Web site for rape survivors to tell their stories and to find resources: *After Silence* (http://www.aftersilence.org/index.php).

Subjects: Coping in Women; Family Relationships; Poets; Post-Traumatic Stress Disorder; Rape; Survivors of Rape; True Crime; Victims of Violence; Violent Crimes

Now Try: One of the many values of women writing their rape-survivor stories is to help those who are family members understand what their loved one might still be suffering or thinking even years after the trauma. Patricia Weaver Francisco, also a writer, has accomplished this with her story, ***Telling: A Memoir of Rape and Recovery***. Charlotte Pierce-Baker, a rape survivor herself, collected stories from other African-American women to help break the silence and to discuss issues particularly germane to them. Her book is entitled ***Surviving the Silence: Black Women's Stories of Rape***. Jessica Stern is an expert in post-traumatic stress disorder (PTSD) who suffered a sexual assault in her early teens, which she repressed. In working with terrorists, she finally recognized that she herself was suffering from PTSD, a discovery she reveals in ***Denial: A Memoir of Terror***.

Sebold, Alice (1963–)

Lucky. Picador, 2002, 1999. 254pp. 9780330418362. Also available in large print, Braille, audiobook (read by the author), e-audiobook, and e-book. 364.1532092

Much like Nancy Venable Raine, Alice Sebold tried unsuccessfully to write a novel; she found that until she articulated on paper what had happened to her when she was eighteen, she wouldn't be able to do any creative writing. Once she decided to do that, she put her journalistic skills to work, going back to Syracuse to talk to people, to read court transcripts, and to relive the nightmare. Tobias Wolff had been her fiction professor at Syracuse and a mentor. When she was talking to him about her experience, he told her to try to remember everything. She starts her memoir with, "This is what I remember," and when there are parts she doesn't remember, she says so. Apart from the rape itself, the work she did to get her rapist to trial, and the trial, what she brings out in her story is how rape makes the survivor "Other." People don't know how to talk to the victim—even family—but she also recognizes how others are affected, too. She recalls her childhood—her life before, who she was before. She also talks about her subsequent heroin addiction, as she suffered from untreated post-traumatic stress disorder (PTSD).

Subjects: College Life; Drug Abuse; Post-Traumatic Stress Disorder; Rape; Self-Destructive Behavior; Survivors of Rape; Syracuse University, NY; Trials (Rape); True Crime; Victims of Violence; Violent Crimes; Writers

Now Try: Once Sebold had written her memoir, she was finally able to write her first novel, ***The Lovely Bones: A Novel***. Debra Puglisi Sharp also suffered from PTSD after her brutal rape and abduction, an incident that also resulted in the murder of her husband. With the help of Marjorie Preston, she describes her long road back to recovery in ***Shattered: Reclaiming a Life Torn Apart by Violence***. Elizabeth Cox's novel, ***The Slow Moon: A Novel***, concerns the rape of a young woman in a small town and the repercussions that spread throughout the town. Raped at the age of thirteen, Martha Ramsey looks back from the perspective of an adult in ***Where I Stopped: Remembering Rape at Thirteen***, remembering how her rape was treated by her family and considering how it may have affected her own major decisions about her life.

Life with an Illness

One of the elements that most of the memoirists in this section have in common is their keen interest in sharing their story for the benefit of others. Whether theirs is a physical or mental illness, many include tips, Internet resources, book resources, and organization names. The other goal they have in common is to raise awareness of their disease in the hopes of removing whatever stigma may be attached to that illness. Another point that several want to make is: don't do as they did, do as they say. They admit they were not sensible patients and made avoidable mistakes. The final common thread running through several of these stories is how the illness has enhanced the person's character and/or life.

One cautionary word here: while most of these memoirs were originally written in the twenty-first century, there still may be advances in medical technology and thought since the time of the writing, so it would behoove the reader not to accept any medical advice as current and cutting-edge.

Memoirs of illness are the stories of writers who have suffered either a sudden or a chronic illness. Often the writers felt compelled to tell their stories because they wanted the world to know more about the illness, in hopes of advocating for research into it, or with the intent of removing a stigma. The stories are generally tales of courage, upbeat and positive, although most of the writers suffered the usual responses on first hearing of their illnesses. The general attitude in the writing, however, is that the illness has been life-changing, usually in a positive way, for the memoirist.

Armstrong, Lance (1971–)
Jenkins, Sally, coauthor

It's Not About the Bike: My Journey Back to Life. Berkley Books, 2001, 2000. 289pp. ill. 16pp. of plates. 9780425179611. Also available in large print, Braille, audiobook, e-audiobook, and e-book. 796.62092

In a very frank and detailed memoir Lance Armstrong tells the world what it is really like to have cancer. He also talks about his life in Texas with Linda, his single mother, a woman of great determination who did everything she could to support her son and to see that he was able to achieve his athletic dreams. He had won a Tour de France stage by the time he was twenty-two and appeared to be on top of the world. That world came crashing down three years later when he was diagnosed with testicular cancer, a malignancy that was virulent, as he had initially ignored the pain in his groin, working through it. Before long the cancer had spread to other parts of his body, including his brain, and the doctors were not hopeful. The strength of this memoir is reflected in the strength of Armstrong himself—his determination not to be beaten by this cancer. He describes the various steps in his illness and recovery, making it quite plain for all who read it just how horrible chemotherapy is and how frightening cancer can be. But he also reveals how important the support of friends and family is and that he was very lucky in this regard. His book ends with various triumphs, including his getting married and their having a baby boy.

It's Not About the Bike was the winner of a Christopher Award.

Subjects: Athletes; Christopher Awards; Cyclists; Endurance Sports; Friendships; Mothers and Sons; Testicular Cancer; Tour de France

Now Try: Jami Goldman did not become a world-class athlete until after both legs were amputated, necessitated by a freak blizzard that she and a friend were caught in for eleven days. She recounts her tremendous struggles and victories, with Andrea Cagan, in ***Up and Running: The Jami Goldman Story***. Bill Strickland was the executive editor of *Bicycling Magazine* when his preschool-aged daughter challenged him to win ten points one season in bicycle competitions. This means coming within the top four ten times in the summer, competing against Olympians and professional athletes. As he explains in ***Ten Points***, he accepted her challenge in the hopes of defeating the demons that threatened to overtake him, demons engendered by the severe abuse he'd suffered as a child from his father. The bicycle is likely something most of us take for granted, but David V. Herlihy has written a fascinating history of it, ***Bicycle: The History***.

Bauby, Jean-Dominique (1952–1997)

The Diving Bell and the Butterfly. Vintage Books, 1998, 1997. 132pp. 9780307389251. Also available in large print, Braille, audiobook, e-book, and video. 362.19681 [Trans. by Jeremy Leggatt]

Thanks to Jean-Dominique Bauby's courage and resilience, "locked-in syndrome" has become much more widely known to the general public. Usually brought on by stroke, which is what happened to this man in his forties, the editor-in-chief of *Elle* magazine, it results in complete or nearly complete paralysis of the body. In Bauby's case he could blink his left eyelid. The title comes from his feeling that while his body kept him grounded as a diving bell would, his mind could soar like a butterfly. And so he soared to places he'd been or to places he'd never been. Some of these trips made their way into the essays in this book, along with anecdotes about his everyday life in the hospital, his memories of delicious meals, his wish to ruffle his son's hair or to climb into bed with his girlfriend. By blinking his left eyelid, he dictated these thoughts to his amanuensis, a speech therapist who devised an alphabet chart based on letter frequency. Bauby was able to see the publication of this book in its original French edition; he died of heart failure two days later.

Subjects: Cerebrovascular Disease; Courage; Editors, France; France; Journalists, France; Locked-in Syndrome; Personal Essays; Quadriplegics; Stroke; Translations

Now Try: Not everyone has the good fortune of having sensitive caregivers as Bauby did, but eventually Julia Tavalaro's life changed when a therapist realized she was not in a coma, as people had thought for six years, but was conscious. The therapist encouraged her to use her eyes to communicate, explaining the title of her memoir, ***Look Up for Yes***, written with the help of Richard Tayson. Robert McCrum was editor-in-chief of Faber & Faber publishers, married for only two months, and also in his forties when he suffered a stroke that paralyzed him on his left side. His story of this unexpected experience is entitled ***My Year Off***. Courage comes in all kinds of packages. Mike May lived his life to the fullest as a blind man, learning to downhill ski (where he met his wife, a guide, and where he broke world records), working for the CIA, and becoming an inventor and entrepreneur. The greatest challenge to his courage, however, was accepting a corneal transplant that might restore his sight. Robert Kurson tells his story in ***Crashing Through: A True Story of Risk, Adventure, and the Man Who Dared to See***.

Cohen, Richard M. (1948–)

Blindsided: Lifting a Life Above Illness; A Reluctant Memoir. Perennial, 2005, 2004. 242pp. 9780060014100. Also available in large print, audiobook, and e-audiobook. 362.1968340092

Richard Cohen at first denied his symptoms of multiple sclerosis (MS) as he continued to report for CBS from such war-torn places as Beirut. Whether or not that denial exacerbated his illness, he wouldn't particularly care, as he believes in living life to the fullest. This memoir about his life, which includes living with the degenerative disease of MS, focuses on the importance of moving on, of getting past the anger and the depression, for the sake of others as well as for one's own sake. Married to the television host Meredith Vieira, with three children, Cohen recognized he could lose the most important elements of his life if he didn't rise above his illness. In his memoir he deals with the increasing debilitation caused by MS (including a gradual loss of his sight) with humor and good grace. He admits nearly losing it all when he was first diagnosed with colon cancer in 1999, but he managed to come out of that as well. He looks beyond himself in his illness and his life and offers hope and inspiration to others while doing so.

Subjects: Blind; Chronic Illness; Colon Cancer; Family Relationships; Illness in the Family; Journalists; Multiple Sclerosis; Television Producers; Vieira, Meredith

Now Try: Montel Williams found himself faced with the same struggle as Cohen when he was diagnosed with multiple sclerosis in 1999. As he says in ***Climbing Higher***, written with Lawrence Grobel, it was necessary for him to get past the grief and anger too. Tom Watson's caddy, Bruce Edwards, was diagnosed with a degenerative disease as well, in his case ALS (Lou Gehrig's disease). John Feinstein tells how Bruce continued to caddy as long as he could in ***Caddy for Life: The Bruce Edwards Story***. Fighting a disease is one thing; knowing there is no fighting it is another. Ulla-Carin Lindquist knew that she was deteriorating too fast with ALS and set out to make the most of the end of her life by writing about it for her family and friends, the pleasures she took from little things and from big things like the support of that family and friends. Her memoir, translated from the Swedish by Margaret Myers, ***Rowing***

Without Oars, is for all, teaching us how to die once we know that living is coming to an end.

DeBaggio, Thomas (1942–2011)

Losing My Mind: An Intimate Look at Life with Alzheimer's. Free Press, 2003, 2002. 210pp. 9780743205665. Also available in large print and audiobook (read by the author). 616.831

When Thomas DeBaggio was diagnosed with early-onset Alzheimer's disease, he wanted the world to know it, not for himself but for everyone else. He wanted to bring this disease into the forefront, to document its progress as much as he could, and to share his empirical knowledge. Having been a journalist and freelance writer before starting his herb farm, he contacted National Public Radio; *All Things Considered* did a program on him and continued to do so every few years. He also wrote this memoir. He focuses on memory—the joy of it as he remembers his past life—and the pain of losing it. He expresses his concern that his son Francesco may have to face the same fate. He also describes what it's like to slowly lose the ability to remember, then to think, then to function. But he was still rather high functioning when he wrote his second book, ***When It Gets Dark: An Enlightened Reflection on Life with Alzheimer's***. Unlike most people with Alzheimer's disease, DeBaggio started writing about it the day he was diagnosed, thus providing for both the medical community and the general populace a personal insight into what this disease actually looks like.

Subjects: Alzheimer's Disease; Family Relationships; Fathers and Sons; Herbalists; Journalists; Memory; Mental Health; National Public Radio; Virginia

Now Try: David Shenk wrote a seminal book on Alzheimer's disease, ***The Forgetting: Alzheimer's, Portrait of an Epidemic,*** including its history and talks with people associated with it. Mary Ellen Geist was a CBS radio anchor who left her job to help her mother care for her father. As she writes in her memoir, ***Measure of the Heart: A Father's Alzheimer's, a Daughter's Return,*** this became an important life change for her as well as for her father. Despite all his years of reporting tragedies as a television journalist, Barry Petersen was not prepared to hear the diagnosis of early-onset Alzheimer's disease in his wife. In his memoir, ***Jan's Story: Love Lost to the Long Goodbye of Alzheimer's,*** Petersen writes honestly of the changing relationship between a couple when one of the partners ceases to be the person one married.

Douglas, Kirk (1916–)

My Stroke of Luck. W. Morrow, 2002. 196pp. ill. 9780060009268. Also available in large print, audiobook (read by the author), and e-audiobook. 362.19681

This veteran actor turned writer's memoir was written five years after Douglas suffered a stroke, an event that he found life-changing. Initially depressed and suicidal, wondering just how an actor was supposed to manage if he couldn't talk, Douglas decided—with the help of family and friends—that he needed to reassert himself and not let those who would coddle him enable him to become a victim and an invalid. He initially tries to draw himself out of his depression by remembering happier times and good friends. He has had a wonderfully long and loving relationship with his wife, Anne, which is also part of his healing. He discovers that by trying to help others a stroke victim helps himself. And he develops a better relationship with his God and with his religion. Douglas also includes an "Operator's Manual," a list of directions and/or aphorisms that he realized apply to life in general, not just to stroke victims. Five years after writing this stroke memoir, Douglas wrote another, a sort of summing up: ***Let's Face It: 90 Years of Living, Loving, and Learning***.

Douglas was awarded the Presidential Medal of Freedom by President Carter in 1981 and received both the Kennedy Center Honors and the National Medal of Arts.

Subjects: Actors; Cerebrovascular Disease; Family Relationships; Friendships; Jewish Men; Marriage; Nonagenarians; Stroke

Now Try: Douglas's most popular memoir was his first, ***The Ragman's Son: An Autobiography***. He also wrote a memoir about his increasing spiritualism following his stroke, ***Climbing the Mountain: My Search for Meaning***. A reflective collection of personal essays by a writer whose life took an unexpected turn is Andre Dubus's ***Meditations from a Movable Chair: Essays***. The actress Patricia Neal's experience with stroke and recovery was similar to Douglas's, in that her husband did not enable her, but it was also quite different, as she didn't seem to have the same level of love and support that Douglas did. She told her story, with Richard DeNeut, in ***As I Am: An Autobiography***. Because his symptoms of stroke were misdiagnosed at the outset, delaying important interventions, Mark McEwen nearly died. A television journalist and weather reporter, he initially lost his ability to speak, a vital asset to him in his career. His memoir, ***Change in the Weather: Life After Stroke***, written with the help of Daniel Paisner, is both a cautionary tale for people who might suspect they are having a stroke and an inspiration for those who have had one.

Engel, Howard (1931–)

The Man Who Forgot How to Read. Afterword by Oliver Sacks. Thomas Dunne Books/ St. Martin's Press, 2008, 2007. 157pp. 9780312382094. 362.196855

Howard Engel is the very successful writer of the long-standing **Benny Cooperman Mystery Series** featuring a Jewish private eye in a medium-sized town in Ontario. Engel obviously writes for a living, and as a writer he is also a voracious reader. When he went to pick up his daily newspaper one morning, he thought *The Globe and Mail* had become multilingual; the print looked like a Slavic language to him—totally unreadable and incomprehensible. Remembering a story by Oliver Sacks he'd read, about a man who had been struck by a car and couldn't read the police report because it literally looked like Greek to him, Engel took himself to the hospital in case he had had a stroke. That is exactly what had happened, and his particular stroke manifested itself as *alexia sine agraphia*, a "word-blindedness" that still allowed him to write. But what good would that do, if one couldn't read what one wrote? A highly literate man, Engel became like millions of people with functional illiteracy: he couldn't read street signs, directions, or food labels. He describes in his memoir how he became proactive in his own recovery, how he was determined to use his ability to write to learn to read again. He also mined the rehabilitation center for grist for his next novel, ***Memory Book***, in which Benny experiences what Engel himself had experienced. The mystery Benny needs to solve is who hit him and left him by a dumpster, resulting in his head injury.

Subjects: *Alexia Sine Agraphia*; Cerebrovascular Disease; Language Disorders; Mystery Writers, Canada; Reading Disabilities; Stroke

Now Try: Once we know how to read, we take it for granted until we try to teach someone else how to do it. Maryanne Wolf, with illustrations by Catherine Stoodley, has written a fascinating history of reading along with the physiological aspects of it, something that may help those struggling with reading: ***Proust and the Squid: The Story and Science of the Reading Brain***. Michael Paul Mason describes various head traumas and how they affect the lives of the victims and their families in ***Head Cases: Stories of Brain Injury and Its Aftermath***. Engel demonstrated a lot of courage in the way he dealt with his challenge. Richard M. Cohen, suffering himself from illness, nonetheless followed the lives of five people suffering with chronic illness and recounts their courage in ***Strong at the Broken Places: Voices of Illness, a Chorus of Hope***.

Fox, Michael J. (1961–)

Lucky Man: A Memoir. Hyperion, 2002. 260pp. ill. 9780786867646. Also available in large print, Braille, audiobook (read by the author), e-audiobook, and e-book. 791.43028092

Ten years after contracting early-onset Parkinson's disease, Michael J. Fox considers himself a lucky man because he says those last ten years have been the best of his life. In his memoir he talks about his easy childhood growing up in Canada and his desire to become an actor, which he does fairly handily, an unknown being cast in an important role in the television series *Family Ties*. He also talks about his party life, his drinking problem, and then his diagnosis of Parkinson's disease. When he left *Spin City* it was to spend more time with his family, a family that has largely contributed to his feeling of being a lucky man. After he went through the usual reactions to his diagnosis—disbelief, anger, "why me?"—he decided he could do something positive with this new aspect of his life and work toward bringing the disease more into the public eye and advocating for finding a cure for it. He brings that theme right to the fore in a subsequent book, ***Always Looking Up: The Adventures of an Incurable Optimist***. Fox and

Debi Brooks cofounded The Michael J. Fox Foundation for Parkinson's Research (http://www.michaeljfox.org/) to fund research for a cure more aggressively.

Michael J. Fox was inducted into the Broadcasting & Cable Hall of Fame and named an officer of the Order of Canada.

Subjects: Actors, Canada; Alcoholics; Disease Politics; Edmonton, AB; *Family Ties* (Television Program); Grandmothers; Married Couples; Michael J. Fox Foundation for Parkinson's Research; Parkinson's Disease; Sobriety; Young Onset Parkinson's Disease

Now Try: Fox has recently written a follow-up to his two earlier books, ***A Funny Thing Happened on the Way to the Future***. Thomas B. Graboys was a cardiologist who is now suffering from Parkinson's disease; such a change in his life's direction is made all the more difficult by his medical knowledge, as he knows what lies ahead. He and Peter Zheutlin have written Graboys's story in ***Life in the Balance: A Physician's Memoir of Life, Love, and Loss with Parkinson's Disease and Dementia***. Stem cell research is an important facet of research into Parkinson's; it is also important for studies of ALS (Lou Gehrig's disease). Jonathan Weiner narrates the story of a brother, Jamie Heywood, advocating for a resolution to ALS for his brother Stephen. Weiner stays in contact with the family throughout Stephen's illness, described in ***His Brother's Keeper: A Story from the Edge of Medicine***. One of the elements of illness that Fox covers in his book is the effects on the family. Three specialists in Parkinson's disease, William J. Weiner, Lisa M. Shulman, and Anthony E. Lang, all contributed to ***Parkinson's Disease: A Complete Guide for Patients and Families***.

Hornbacher, Marya (1974–)

Madness: A Bipolar Life. Mariner, 2009, 2008. 320pp. 9780547237800. Also available in audiobook, e-audiobook, and e-book. 616.895

Marya Hornbacher, a freelance journalist and writer, has already written one harrowing memoir, ***Wasted: A Memoir of Anorexia and Bulimia***, a confession of her eating disorders from a very early age and an elucidation for the general public about the place of eating disorders in North American culture. One of the interesting statements she makes in that book is that she suffered from a childhood anxiety disorder. After the publication of that book she actually received a true diagnosis of what has ailed her all her life: rapid-cycling type 1 bipolar disorder. She begins her later memoir in manic mode, going from one anecdote to another of all the self-destructive behaviors she indulged in: bulimia, anorexia, self-cutting, drug use, prostitution, and alcoholism. She had a doctor who was blunt with her: the abusive substances she was adding to her prescribed medications were not only not helping but were actively hindering any progress she could make; ultimately, her destiny was in her own hands. Once she finally accepted the truth of that, Hornbacher could then try to take control of her life and her health. What this memoir does for others is offer some insights into what bipolar disorder looks like from the point of view of the sufferer.

Subjects: Affective Disorders; Alcoholics; Alcoholism; Bipolar Disorder; Drug Abuse; Journalists; Rehabilitation; Self-Destructive Behavior; Women and Addiction; Writers

Now Try: In much the same way as Hornbacher does, Terri Cheney offers a firsthand account of how manic depression feels in ***Manic: A Memoir***. Patty Duke will be well-known to a certain generation, both for her portrayal of two young girls in *The Patty Duke Show* and for her award-winning performance as Helen Keller in ***The Miracle Worker***. Because she was out of the limelight as an adult, that same generation may not be aware of her battles with bipolar disorder, a struggle she describes with Gloria Hochman in ***A Brilliant Madness: Living with Manic-Depressive Illness***. For those whose family member(s) may suffer from this illness, Francis Mark Mondimore has written ***Bipolar Disorder: A Guide for Patients and Families***.

Jamison, Kay R. (1946–)

An Unquiet Mind. Knopf, 2004, 1995. 223pp. 9780679443742. Also available in audiobook (read by the author), e-audiobook, and e-book. 616.895

Kay Jamison is a clinical psychologist and professor of psychiatry at Johns Hopkins, specializing in mood disorders. This memoir reveals that she has personal experience with her topic, having been manic-depressive since adolescence. She believes hers is a genetic disposition, as her father began exhibiting signs of the disease after his retirement from the Air Force. She tried to live with her illness without intervention, despite her knowledge, until after she acquired her doctorate at UCLA. While describing the horrors of sinking into depression, easily becoming suicidal, she also recognizes what were for her the benefits of rising into the mania, the creativity and exhilaration she felt. She didn't want to be drug-dependent because she didn't want to have to give up the pleasure she derived from the mania, but the resulting lows cost her serious relationships. She finally recognized that she needed to be responsible for herself and others and take lithium for life in order to have a more balanced life. By writing so honestly about this, Jamison hopes to illustrate to others in a similar situation just how important it is to realize one cannot always control everything about one's life.

Kay Jamison was the recipient of a MacArthur Fellowship.

Subjects: Adolescents; Bipolar Disorder; Clinical Psychologists; College Professors; Depression in Women; Drug Therapy

Now Try: People who are in Jamison's situation find much comfort from reading such stories, as they feel they are not alone and they often get helpful tips and advice. Therese Johnson Borchard offers comfort in her humorous take on her own mental disorder, ***Beyond Blue: Surviving Depression & Anxiety and Making the Most of Bad Genes***. Elizabeth Wurtzel paints an honest, disquieting picture of her own bouts with depression, which she has dealt with using various means of therapy, some helpful (licit drugs), some not (illicit drugs). She is still at the stage in her life where she does not want to be permanently drug-dependent for her mental health, which she explains in ***Prozac Nation: Young and Depressed in America***. Martha Manning is also a psychotherapist dealing with depression. Her memoir, ***Undercurrents: A Therapist's Reckoning with Her Own Depression***, will provide solace to others who suffer from this illness.

Kaysen, Susanna (1948–)

Girl, Interrupted. Vintage Books, 1999, 1993. 168pp. ill. 9780679746041. Also available in large print and video. 616.89092

Susanna Kaysen had seen a Vermeer painting at the Frick Museum, *Girl Interrupted at Her Music,* a painting that resonated deeply within herself, creating a unifying feature of her story about her time at McLean Hospital in Boston, a psychiatric hospital in which she spent close to two years in the later 1960s. She wrote this memoir twenty-five years after being released and after requesting her file, documents from which she intersperses into her narration. The documents sometimes support her story, and they also sometimes contradict what she describes, reflecting perhaps her tendency at the time to distort the facts, one of the problems she had been experiencing back then. Kaysen had been diagnosed with borderline personality disorder, and she does admit that she was very unhappy, especially in her relationship with her family, her father in particular. But she wonders if her diagnosis was a convenient label to apply to women who acted out. Throughout her memoir she uses stories of the friends she made in the hospital as a filter for her own story. She refers to the parallel universe she and her friends inhabited and recounts specific events and anecdotes. She also admits elsewhere that of course she made up the dialogue: " 'My argument is that it's true even if it might not be the facts' " (Cheever, 1993).

Girl, Interrupted was selected as a Notable Book by the American Library Association.

Subjects: ALA Notable Books; Borderline Personality Disorder; Boston, MA; McLean Hospital, MA; Mental Health; Novelists; Psychiatric Patients

Now Try: There is no question that Brent Runyon was in a serious mental state when he set himself on fire in an attempt to commit suicide. In his memoir, ***The Burn Journals,*** he details the ensuing year in the Burn Unit and then in rehab, where he undergoes both physical and psychological rehabilitation. Norah Vincent had done some investigative journalism (***Self-Made Man: One Woman's Journey into Manhood and Back Again***) that put her into a fairly severe depression. On the advice of her psychologist she committed herself to a psychiatric hospital. Her time there led her to her next book, a look at whether or not seriously ill people benefit from the treatments they receive in psychiatric hospitals. After checking herself into three different hospitals she wrote ***Voluntary Madness: My Year Lost and Found in the Loony Bin.*** McLean Hospital boasts a who's who of former patients, including several well-known poets. Alex Beam offers a history of the hospital in ***Gracefully Insane: The Rise and Fall of America's Premier Mental Hospital.***

Moore, Mary Tyler (1936–)

Growing Up Again: Life, Loves, and Oh Yeah, Diabetes. St. Martin's Griffin, 2010, 2009. 216pp. ill. 8pp. of plates. 9780312612351. Also available in large print and e-book. 362.1964620092

Mary Tyler Moore confesses that she was not an ideal "patient" when she learned at the age of thirty-three that she had Type 1 (juvenile) diabetes. (Adding insult to the injury, she discovered this because of a miscarriage she had suffered.) She was in denial and she was rebellious. She continued to drink for several years until after she entered the Betty Ford Center, and only after that did she stop smoking. She still finds the restrictions imposed on those with diabetes onerous, but at the same time she is grateful for all the research done that enables a diabetic to have a much fuller life than previously. Throughout her story of diabetes she reflects on the joys and humor in other parts of her life as an actor, a businesswoman, and a wife. She has long been very active in the Juvenile Diabetes Research Foundation International (http://www.jdrf.org/), currently its international chairwoman. It was because of that role that she was asked to write her story by an editor at St. Martin's Press whose daughter also has Type 1 diabetes. The end of her memoir has several appendices with various types of information on diabetes, current research, and where to look further.

Moore has a star on the Hollywood Walk of Fame for her television work and has been inducted into the Broadcasting & Cable Hall of Fame.

Subjects: Actors; Alcoholics; Businesswomen; Diabetes; Disease Politics; Juvenile Diabetes Research Foundation International; Levine, Robert; Miscarriages; Sobriety; Television Actors; Women in Film

Now Try: Prior to writing this memoir, Moore had written an earlier one, ***After All***, focusing on her childhood, her television roles, and her business with her then-husband Grant Tinker. In her second major television role, Moore was seen as a feminist icon, as it was the first time a woman was portrayed on television as having an important job and no man in her life. Allison Klein looks at this show along with others, to see what influence they have had, in ***What Would Murphy Brown Do? How the Women of Prime Time Changed Our Lives***. The other cause that is close to Mary Tyler Moore's heart is animals; she is cofounder of a New York event, "Broadway Barks," which fosters awareness of the plight of homeless and orphaned pets. She has written the foreword to ***Best Friends: The True Story of the World's Most Beloved Animal Sanctuary*** by Samantha Glen. Zippora Karz is a ballerina with diabetes. In her memoir, ***The Sugarless Plum: A Ballerina's Triumph over Diabetes***, she reflects on her anger at how limiting she initially found her disease.

Oxnam, Robert B. (1942–)

A Fractured Mind: My Life with Multiple Personality Disorder. Hyperion, 2005. 285pp. 9781401302276. Also available in e-audiobook and e-book. 616.852360092

In his mind was a castle, and in the castle lived eleven personalities. This is the story of the man known publicly as Robert Oxnam, an Asian studies scholar who has provided guidance on Asia to such people as Bill Gates and Warren Buffett. After going for psychiatric help when his difficult and tumultuous life got too much for him (bulimia, rages, alcoholism) and finding the therapy not as effective as he had hoped, Oxnam decided to call it quits. During the appointment at which he meant to tell this to his psychiatrist, one of his alters emerged, precipitating a difficult but

9 10 11 12 13

ultimately satisfying journey. The work with his psychiatrist revealed his eleven alters, finally exposed the abuse that prompted the fracturing of the mind in order to cope, and merged all but three of the personalities. This memoir is almost a collective or family memoir, as it is told by the remaining three of Oxnam's personalities. Courageously frank about making his story public, he has also developed a sense of humor about this, signing his book for readers "Robert et al." One of his remaining alters is Bobby, a young man who wears Oxnam out by in-line skating for hours and embarrasses him by skating with bottles on his head—Bobby had become a well-known fixture in Central Park.

Subjects: Adult Child Abuse Victims; Alcoholics; Bulimia; College Professors; Coping in Men; Dissociative Identity Disorder

Now Try: A classic book on multiple personalities is ***The Three Faces of Eve***, written by Corbett H. Thigpen and Hervey M. Cleckley in 1957 and made into a movie of the same name. That book was based on the life of Chris Costner Sizemore, who subsequently wrote her own story, ***A Mind of My Own***. Richard K. Baer is a psychiatrist who spent several years working with a very troubled patient. As he explains in his memoir, ***Switching Time: A Doctor's Harrowing Story of Treating a Woman with 17 Personalities***, he felt he needed to garner the trust of each personality before he could successfully treat his patient. Cameron West explains in ***First Person Plural: My Life as a Multiple*** how as an adult he was unaware of the abuse he had suffered as a child because it was another of his alters who had suffered it.

Saks, Elyn R. (1955–)

The Center Cannot Hold: My Journey Through Madness. Hyperion, 2008, 2007. 351pp. 9781401309442. Also available in audiobook, e-audiobook, and e-book. 616.8980092

Elyn Saks, as a lawyer, professor of law, and adjunct professor of psychiatry, has brought not only her academic skills but also her personal experience to bear in advocating for the rights of mental health patients. Saks noticed when she was a young girl of eight that her behavior was starting to change in a strange way. As she grew older, the various presentations of her ill health continued to become more pronounced, but she tried to keep it all in the closet until she got tenure—she was well aware of the stigmatization of mental illness and did not want to fall victim to it herself. She has set up her memoir almost as a novel, building in intensity as her illness grows, portraying specific characters, some helpful and some not, and describing with real force some of her psychotic incidents. By writing clearly about her own mental problems, Saks is trying to bring mental illness out of the closet so that the person suffering from it can be treated like anyone with a physical illness.

Saks is the recipient of a MacArthur Fellowship, which she hopes to use to further her advocacy work and to interview a wide range of schizophrenics, particularly successful ones like herself, so that she can broadcast their stories to give hope to other schizophrenics.

Subjects: College Professors; Family Relationships; Human Rights Activists; Lawyers; Mental Health Activists; Psychiatric Patients; Schizophrenia

Now Try: Saks has already written one book on her thoughts about the kind of treatment and care America's mental health patients are receiving: ***Refusing Care: Forced Treatment and the Rights of the Mentally Ill.*** Lori Schiller, with the help of Amanda Bennett, tells a harrowing tale of schizophrenia and hearing voices in ***The Quiet Room: A Journey out of the Torment of Madness.*** Offering a contrary view to standard medical thought about mental illness is journalist Robert Whitaker's indictment, ***Anatomy of an Epidemic: Magic Bullets, Psychiatric Drugs, and the Astonishing Rise of Mental Illness in America.*** Kurt Snyder was a young college student when he began exhibiting signs of schizophrenia. Raquel E. Gur, a psychiatrist, and Linda Wasmer Andrews, a science writer, have joined him to write a book that is part memoir and part handbook for young people with the disease: ***Me, Myself, and Them: A Firsthand Account of One Young Person's Experience with Schizophrenia.***

Shields, Brooke (1965–)

Down Came the Rain. Hyperion. 2005. 226pp. 9781401301897. Also available in large print, audiobook (read by the author), and e-book. 618.76092

After suffering through fertility treatments and a difficult miscarriage, Brooke Shields and her husband finally had a baby girl. Shields had suffered from depression at various points in her life, and shortly before the birth of her daughter, her father died. When she went into hospital to give birth, after twenty-four hours of labor, she had to have a cesarean section. The end result of all this difficulty was shocking to her: she had no interest in bonding with her daughter, no eagerness to hold her, just a devastating depression. It was only after much urging from her husband, family, and friends that she finally sought help. After a combination of psychotherapy, medication, and talking with others in the same condition helped her come out of this serious depression, she felt it was important to share her story. She wanted to remove the silence and the stigma of postpartum depression, an illness that strikes one out of ten women. At the end of her book she includes lists of helpful resources.

Subjects: Actors; Family Relationships; In Vitro Fertilization; Infertility; Mental Health; Miscarriages; Postpartum Depression; Women in Film

Now Try: Marie Osmond also suffered from postpartum depression after her seventh child (four of her children are adopted), suggesting to readers that it doesn't necessarily happen with just the first. She and the doctor who helped her, Judith Moore, collaborated with the help of Marcia Wilkie to write ***Behind the Smile: My Journey out of Postpartum Depression.*** Natasha S. Mauthner interviewed thirty-five women who had suffered from postpartum depression; the stories they tell in ***The Darkest Days of My Life: Stories of Postpartum Depression*** will provide comfort to women suffering from the same illness, recognizing that they are not alone. ***Postpartum Depression Demystified: An Essential Guide to Understanding and Overcoming the Most Common Complication After Childbirth*** has been written by Joyce A. Venis (a mother who suffered through it and counsels other mothers) and Suzanne McCloskey (a health care professional).

Shreve, Susan Richards

Warm Springs: Traces of a Childhood at FDR's Polio Haven. Mariner Books, 2008, 2007. 215pp. ill. 9780547053837. 362.1968350092

Memoirs written about the 1950s have certain common threads running through them: fears of nuclear fallout, McCarthyism, and polio. Even if one didn't contract the polio virus, behaviors changed, often with children not allowed to play outside during the summer. Although Franklin Roosevelt was a wonderful example of how one could succeed even while having been seriously touched by the disease, he was also an example of how lives could be changed by the virus. The novelist Susan Shreve contracted polio when she was one year old, and her mother worked with her for years to try to restore life to the damaged muscles in her right leg. When Shreve was eleven she went to Warm Springs, Georgia, a rehabilitation center founded by Roosevelt. Shreve's story of her time there is as much a coming-of-age story as it is about having polio. It is also a clear portrayal of life in the 1950s, a way of life that Shreve confronted. One of the higher-functioning patients with greater mobility, even though she was in a wheelchair, she was asked to leave because of her high spirits and her lack of respect for conventional behavior.

Subjects: 1950s; Childhood and Youth; Coming of Age; Friendships; Georgia; Health Resorts; Novelists; Polio; Roosevelt, Franklin Delano; Warm Springs, GA

Now Try: The Salk vaccine to counteract polio was discovered during Shreve's stay at Warm Springs; Jeffrey Kluger writes of that discovery in ***Splendid Solution: Jonas Salk and the Conquest of Polio***. Martha Mason spent sixty-one of seventy-one years living in an iron lung, the terrifying symbol of this frightening disease. Using voice-technology software she has been able to write her memoir, ***Breath: Life in the Rhythm of an Iron Lung,*** of the full life she led, due in part to her mother's devotion. Stephanie Klein's coming of age away from home was at a camp for overweight children. She tells how formative that experience was in ***Moose: A Memoir of Fat Camp***.

Solomon, Andrew (1963–)

The Noonday Demon: An Atlas of Depression. Scribner, 2003. 571pp. 9780684854670. Also available in e-audiobook and e-book. 616.85270092

Andrew Solomon is a successful writer and journalist, economically comfortable and suffering so painfully from depression that he tried to contract HIV to give himself an excuse for suicide. His memoir is much more than that, however. While he describes honestly and very clearly the trajectory of his own illness, he includes with that trips he made elsewhere to determine the nature of depression in other cultures. In Senegal he underwent an animist ritual called *ndeup*, allowing others to cover him with blood from chickens and rams and to dance and sing around him; he believed it was as effective as much of the group therapy conducted in the United States. He also went to Cambodia, particularly to speak to people who had suffered the pain of living under the Khmer Rouge, and he went to talk to the Inuit in Greenland. He lets others tell their stories, many very painful.

Having studied depression at length, Solomon offers the results of studies and doesn't shy away from giving his opinion on some of the therapies and some of the attitudes toward depression. He feels it was necessary to write about his experiences because of the multitude of people who think that depression is of one's own making and that one can "snap out of it." He believes it should be regarded as any disease, like pneumonia, that can strike anyone regardless of race, class, gender, or socioeconomic status. Fortunately, his last chapter is entitled "Hope."

The Noonday Demon was the winner of the Lambda Literary Award for Autobiography/Memoir and the National Book Award for Nonfiction. It was selected as a Notable Book by the American Library Association.

Subjects: ALA Notable Books; Cambodia; Death of a Parent; Depression; Gay Men; Greenland; Lambda Literary Award for Autobiography/Memoir; Mental Health; National Book Award for Nonfiction; Senegal

Now Try: Offering comfort to others with depression by sharing a variety of experiences, David Allen Karp's book, ***Speaking of Sadness: Depression, Disconnection, and the Meanings of Illness*** manages to reflect the reality of the disease. A number of authors contributed essays on their experiences with depression; collected by Nell Casey, the stories in ***Unholy Ghost: Writers on Depression*** offer readers an opportunity to see the variety of forms depression can take and how individuals have coped with it. Abraham Lincoln had suffered from depression for a good part of his life and applied his coping strategies for his illness to other aspects of his life. Joshua Wolf Shenk spent seven years researching ***Lincoln's Melancholy: How Depression Challenged a President and Fueled His Greatness***.

Styron, William (1925–2006)

Darkness Visible: A Memoir of Madness. The Modern Library, 2007, 1990. 84pp. 9780679643524. Also available in large print and e-book. 616.85270092

Although he had suffered from depression off and on throughout the years, William Styron was struck down by it in his sixties to the point where he began to plan his suicide. The depression began to affect him noticeably when he went to Paris to receive a literary award and acted inappropriately toward his hosts in public. His depression imbued every aspect of his life. He could no longer write, he had no interest in anything that had formerly been significant in his life, and he saw everyday objects like the sharp knives in the kitchen or the car in the garage as instruments of suicide. He went for help but found it unhelpful. Having finally decided to end his life, he went to a lawyer to write his will. He tried, unsuccessfully, to write a testament. On what he thought would be his last night he watched a video that had a clip of a contralto singing the Brahms "Alto Rhapsody" and inexplicably he was reminded of all the good things in his life. He wakened his wife, and they made arrangements for the next day, when he went to the hospital to begin his recovery. Styron's is a short book but a candid look at how crippling depression can be, regardless of one's age and one's success. It was one of the first to make public the nature of depression in a personal way.

Styron is a recipient of the National Medal of Arts.

Subjects: Classics; Depression; Mental Health; Music as Therapy; Novelists; Octogenarians; Suicidal Behavior

Now Try: The difficult part of John Bentley Mays's story of his debilitating depression is that he still lives with it; the encouraging part of his memoir, ***In the Jaws of the Black Dogs: A Memoir of Depression***, is how he is able to manage it. John Falk offers a zany antidote to depression: war journalism. In his rather upbeat account of depression, ***Hello to All That: A Memoir of War, Zoloft, and Peace***, discovering Zoloft (a medication that actually helped) and heading off to Sarajevo to report on the war there, he brings a new perspective to the illness. Rosalynn Carter, an advocate for mental health patients for thirty-five years, has worked with Susan K. Golant and Kathryn E. Cade to write about the existing state of mental health care in the United States: ***Within Our Reach: Ending the Mental Health Crisis***.

Taylor, Jill Bolte (1959–)

My Stroke of Insight: A Brain Scientist's Personal Journey. Plume, 2009, 2006. 206pp. ill. 9780452295544. Also available in large print, audiobook (read by the author), e-audiobook, and e-book. 362.196810092

Jill Taylor is a neuroanatomist, specializing in the brain, who had a stroke at the age of thirty-seven. After the fact, she is able to recall what she went through the morning of her stroke, a frustrating exercise for the reader who simply wants her to dial 911, although she is incapable of reaching that solution for herself. That she does eventually manage to get help for herself despite the extent of the stroke is remarkable. Throughout her memoir she explains the physiology of the brain in general and stroke in particular. She also demonstrates very clearly what it is like to be a stroke victim on the receiving end of "help" from people (including medical people) who have no idea about how she is processing information and actions. Her mother, Gladys, seems to intuit better than anyone what to do for her daughter. Taylor provides a list at the end of the book for family members of stroke victims of things to be aware of, a list that makes the book worth keeping in any house, as stroke is not a disease just of the old.

Subjects: Brain; Cerebrovascular Disease; Mothers and Daughters; Neuroanatomists; Scientists; Stroke

Now Try: Usually the roles are reversed when stroke is involved: the child is taking care of the parent rather than the mother taking care of the child. Sybil Lockhart is a neurobiologist whose mother is stricken with Alzheimer's disease when Sybil has young children to care for. She uses her knowledge of the brain to understand both her children's development and the progression of her mother's disease; at the same time she shares her story of being part of the sandwich generation in ***Mother in the Middle: A Biologist's Story of Caring for Parent and Child***. In her memoir Taylor talks about the flexibility of the brain; this is the basis of Norman Doidge's ***The Brain That Changes Itself: Stories of Personal Triumph from the Frontiers of Brain Science***, a book written after Doidge had traveled the country talking to brain scientists and those people who benefited from their work. Again demonstrating how stroke can affect the young is Tedy Bruschi's story, ***Never Give Up: My Stroke, My Recovery, and My Return to the NFL***, told with the help of Michael Holley, about how this New England Patriot suffered from a debilitating stroke only to return to active play in the next season.

Loss

Loss in this section usually comes in the form of death, although not always. The death might be of a spouse or partner, a child, or a sibling, but the grief is similar, despite the relationship. Two women "lose" their husbands in other ways: one through divorce and one through a permanently altering brain injury. They all have different ways of telling their stories, and while one might say that grief is grief, we see that it isn't necessarily so. Most of these stories recount not only the event of the loss and the immediate reaction but also the days, weeks, and months that ensue. They are meant to be therapeutic for the writer (coincidentally most of these memoirists are professional writers) and a comfort to the reader.

Memoirs of loss are narratives by writers who have lost people very close to them, primarily through death, but also through divorce or traumatic brain injury. Because they often focus on the actual loss more than on what preceded it, these memoirs tend to be more reflective as the survivors contemplate their futures without their loved ones. They also believe that by writing about their loss, they can also bring back the people whose loss they are mourning.

Buckley, Christopher (1952–)

Losing Mum and Pup: A Memoir. Twelve, 2009. 251p. ill. 9780446540940. Also available in large print, audiobook (read by the author), and e-book. 813.54

Christopher Buckley is a satirical novelist, always finding a way to inject humor into his writing. He does the same here in a mixed bag of a memoir. The book is meant to be an elegy to his parents, William F. Buckley and Patricia Buckley, who died within a year of each other. With Christopher being the only child, the burden of their care and burial was left solely to him. Or one could also say he was the only person gifted with taking care of them in their final months. That is one part of the memoir. He also talks about them as individuals and as a couple, thus providing a family history of sorts. By inserting himself into stories about them and his memories of them, this is also autobiography. Despite his humor and his satirical renderings of various aspects of their physical conditions and requisite care, the love and the attendant grief at losing them come through quite clearly. (See p. 352 for the memoir of Christopher's father, William.)

Subjects: Buckley, Patricia Taylor; Buckley, William F.; Death of a Parent; Family Relationships; Married Couples; Parent and Child; Upper Class; Writers

Now Try: The circles that the Buckleys traveled in were not unlike the circles of the Astors, but the Buckleys seem to have had fewer skeletons in the closet. Meryl Gordon reveals the sad end to Brooke Astor's life as her son sets out to mistreat her and plunder her estate in ***Mrs. Astor Regrets: The Hidden Betrayals of a Family Beyond Reproach***. Chronicling a situation that more and more people find themselves in is Judy Kramer's ***Changing Places: A Journey with My Parents into Their Old Age***, in which she describes making her way through the maze of Medicare and assisted-living facilities. Meg Federico injects humor into her tale of parental caregiving, humor that is reflected even in her title: ***Welcome to the Departure Lounge: Adventures in Mothering Mother***.

Didion, Joan (1934–)

The Year of Magical Thinking. Knopf, 2007, 2005. 227pp. 9781400043149. Also available in large print, audiobook, e-audiobook, and e-book. 813.54

Joan Didion's book following the death of her husband of forty years will likely become a classic in thanatological literature. She made one note about his death in January and then wrote nothing more for months. As a writer, though, it would be only natural for her to want to try to make sense of the grieving process by writing. She and her husband, John Gregory Dunne, had never been apart; both writers, they each had an office in their home and would visit each other frequently throughout the day with a question or a comment. This they did for forty years. A week before Dunne's death, their only daughter, Quintana Roo, had been hospitalized for what first appeared to be flu, then pneumonia, then septic shock. They were not long home from visiting her in intensive care when John had his fatal coronary attack. In her memoir Didion retraces life with John and Quintana Roo and addresses face-on the question of grief, trying to define it. A final irony for Joan Didion is that only months before this book was published, her daughter died after two months in hospital, perhaps from residual sepsis from her first illness. Didion worked her memoir into a stage play and a one-woman show, a story of grief that would now include her daughter. Another of life's ironies is the fact that Vanessa Redgrave was chosen to enact the role and that Vanessa lost her own daughter, Natasha Richardson, two years after the show's premiere while she was still performing it.

The Year of Magical Thinking was a finalist for the National Book Critics Circle Award in Autobiography/Memoir and the Pulitzer Prize in Biography or Autobiography and won the National Book Award for Nonfiction. Joan Didion is also the recipient of the American Academy of Arts and Letters Gold Medal for Belles Lettres and has been inducted into the Academy of Achievement.

Subjects: Death of a Child; Death of a Spouse; Dunne, John Gregory; Grief; Married Couples; Michael, Quintana Roo Dunne; Mothers and Daughters; National Book Award for Nonfiction; Widows; Writers

Now Try: An earlier classic on grieving by a great writer is ***A Grief Observed,*** which C. S. Lewis wrote (under the pseudonym N. W. Clerk) after the death of his wife, Joy Davidman. The British actress Sheila Hancock, after writing about life with her husband (***The Two of Us: My Life with John Thaw***), has since written the story of her widowhood, ***Just Me***. In Rafael Yglesias's novel, ***A Happy Marriage: A Novel,*** Enrique looks back at a thirty-year marriage while his wife, Margaret, is on her deathbed.

Doty, Mark (1953–)

Heaven's Coast: A Memoir. Harper Perennial, 1997, 1996. 305pp. 9780060928056. Also available in e-book. 362.1969792

Mark Doty's partner of eight years contracted HIV during the period when it was a death sentence in the United States. Doty is an award-winning poet whose life was going along beautifully until the day he and Wally Roberts, his partner, received the deadly news. Doty's memoir is a remembrance of the time they had together before this final time, along the coast of Massachusetts in Provincetown. It is also a remembrance of Wally's dying and death, the ugliness and the pain of it. Doty describes the grief in his life following Wally's death. He offers an elegy to Wally and to all his friends who died of AIDS-related illnesses in those days.

Heaven's Coast was a finalist for the Lambda Literary Award for Gay Men's Biography/Autobiography, was an Honor Book for the Stonewall Book Award-Israel Fishman Non-Fiction Award, and won the PEN American Center Martha Albrand Award for First Nonfiction.

Subjects: Death of a Partner; Dying; Grief; HIV/AIDS; Loss; PEN American Center Martha Albrand Award for First Nonfiction; Poets; Provincetown, MA; Roberts, Wally

Now Try: Dale Peck's well-received debut novel, ***Martin and John: A Novel,*** treats the same theme as ***Heaven's Coast***. When they discover that Martin has AIDS, John and Martin move from New York to Kansas, where Martin later dies. Interwoven with his reminiscences of Martin are John's stories that he has started to write, developing a new career and life. Marion Winik is a contributor to NPR and a writer who knowingly married a gay man. They had a happy life together until he contracted AIDS. She has told their story in ***First Comes Love***. The psychologist Kay R. Jamison has written a memoir about the death of her husband, a reflection that tries to get at the very heart of grief in her own way, in ***Nothing Was the Same: A Memoir***.

Gillies, Isabel (1970–)

Happens Every Day: An All-Too-True Story. Scribner, 2010, 2009. 261pp. ill. 9781439126622. Also available in large print, audiobook (read by the author), and e-audiobook. 792.028092

Isabel Gillies had a good career with a regular spot on *Law & Order: Special Victims Unit,* a career she gave up when her husband landed a tenure-track position in Ohio at Oberlin College. She packed up the family—herself, her husband, and two toddlers—and moved to a new environment, where she looked after the family and taught drama part-time. They hadn't been there all that long when her husband announced that he didn't want to be married to her anymore and left. Her memoir deals with her reaction to such a stunning announcement and how she dealt with the loss. She also includes conversations and visits she had with the woman he eventually moved in with. Because Gillies has written this in such a conversational style, giving the reader the feeling that writer and reader are having coffee together, the book offers comfort to those who have been through similar losses and heartache as well as understanding to those who haven't, yet may know someone who has.

Subjects: Actors; Betrayal; College Professors; Divorce; Marriage; Oberlin, OH; Television Actors

Now Try: Julie Metz suffered both a loss and a betrayal when her husband of seventeen years died suddenly of a pulmonary embolism; six months later she discovered he'd been unfaithful to her several times. In ***Perfection: A Memoir of Betrayal and Renewal,*** she reveals how she suffered through all that and worked her way to recovery. Theo Pauline Nestor was the one who initiated the separation from her husband, a gambling addict. Compelled to write about it, she first wrote an essay and then a memoir, ***How to Sleep Alone in a King-Size Bed: A Memoir***. Suzanne Finnamore had some inkling that her marriage was not rock-solid, but that didn't lessen the devastation when her husband said he wanted a divorce, leaving her with a young child. She tells her story in ***Split: A Memoir of Divorce***.

Hood, Ann (1956–)

Comfort: A Journey Through Grief. W. W. Norton & Co., 2009, 2008. 192pp. 9780393336597. 155.937092

No one who is a parent can imagine anything worse than losing a child, regardless of the child's or parent's age. Ann Hood lost her five-year-old daughter, Grace, in the space of thirty-six hours, to a strep infection in 2005. Her grief was so unbearable she couldn't even write. One sleepless night she read a call to writers for essays on lying, and that was the hesitant beginning of her getting back to writing. She wrote about all the lies well-meaning people said to her in her grief. This is also how she starts her memoir. But she still wasn't able to write about her daughter and her grief. Her next step was to write a quasi-autobiographical novel, ***The Knitting Circle,*** wherein she could distance herself from her own tragedy yet still write something about the death of a child. She finally took tentative steps to write this memoir, tentative because then she had to relive everything. She takes us from Grace's death to a very positive outcome at the end, and in doing so, brings Grace to life again as she remembers her. She doesn't know how her book can comfort others; she doesn't believe there is comfort for bereaved parents, but in fact she does validate others' feelings and experiences.

Subjects: Bereavement; Coping in Women; Death of a Child; Family Relationships; Grief; Knitting; Mothers and Daughters; Writers

Now Try: P. F. Thomése is a Dutch writer who lost a child; in his grief he set out to find language that could describe what he was going through. The result is ***Shadowchild: A Meditation on Love and Loss***, translated by Sam Garrett. Elizabeth McCracken is also a writer, who lost her child in her ninth month of pregnancy, giving her the added grief of not even getting to know him, as her title so aptly states: ***An Exact Replica of a Figment of My Imagination: A Memoir***. When Pam Cope's son, Jantsen, died of an unknown heart ailment at fifteen, Pam found an unexpected outlet for her grief through a trip to Vietnam. Recognizing the plight of street children, she established the Touch a Life Foundation (http://www.touchalifekids.org/), which helps street children in Vietnam, Ghana, and Cambodia. She tells her story, with help from Aimee Molloy, in ***Jantsen's Gift: A True Story of Grief, Rescue, and Grace***.

Monette, Paul (1945–1995)

Borrowed Time: An AIDS Memoir. Harcourt Brace, 1998, 1988. 342pp. 9780156005814. Also available in audiobook (read by the author) and e-book. 362.1969792

Monette had already written a poetic elegy to his partner of ten years (***Love Alone: 18 Elegies for Rog***) shortly before Rog's death, but one of Rog's doctors asked Paul why he didn't write a book about their journey with AIDS, as no one else was writing about it at the time. Using his language skills as a poet, Monette writes about the medical side of AIDS in the late 1980s as well as the emotional torment for them both, as Rog suffered through the horrors of the disease, knowing all the while that death was the only end. This memoir is important for illustrating the fear and ignorance that were so much a part of the response to AIDS in the early days, but it is also important in reflecting the pain of witnessing a loved one's illness, dying, and death, a reflection that will resonate with anyone else who has suffered through this, regardless of the disease.

Borrowed Time was a finalist for the National Book Critics Circle Award in Biography/Autobiography and winner of both the Lambda Literary Award for AIDS and the Lambda Literary Award for Gay Nonfiction, as well as the PEN Center USA Literary Award for Nonfiction.

Subjects: 1980s; Death of a Partner; Dying; Gay Men; HIV/AIDS; Lambda Literary Award for AIDS; Lambda Literary Award for Gay Nonfiction; PEN Center USA Literary Award for Nonfiction

Now Try: After writing this memoir, Monette wrote an award-winning autobiography in which he recounted his childhood and youth along with the pain of being in the closet: ***Becoming a Man: Half a Life Story***. James T. Wooten is the author of ***We Are All the Same: A Story of a Boy's Courage and a Mother's Love***, an award-winning recounting of the story of Nkosi Johnson, a young South African who had AIDS from birth; his mother's courage before she died; and the efforts of the South African woman, Gail Johnson, who took Nkosi in and became his foster mother when he was orphaned. Together they worked to bring to the fore the issue of AIDS in South Africa. The author and memoirist Bernard Cooper tells a not-unusual story in ***Truth Serum: Memoirs***

of growing up Jewish in Los Angeles, trying to ignore or get rid of his homosexual feelings. He even underwent therapy with truth serum for it, but finally embraced his sexual orientation, although he did contract the AIDS virus as well. Dominique Lapierre has written an engrossing story, ***Beyond Love*** (translated from the French by Kathryn Spink) of the beginning of the AIDS epidemic and the scientists involved in—and competing for—the discovery of its source and a cure, or at least a vaccine.

Roiphe, Anne Richardson (1935–)

Epilogue: A Memoir. Harper, 2008. 214pp. 9780061254628. Also available in large print, audiobook, e-audiobook, and e-book. 813.54

Anne Roiphe's husband of thirty-nine years died suddenly, leaving her to try to make a new life for herself when she was seventy. Her memoir is more about that aspect of widowhood than about the grief and the loss, although they are there, too. She talks about the loneliness of her new life, how one is no longer a couple, how that constant companionship is gone. She also addresses the contradiction of wanting to be with others to combat the loneliness, yet also wanting to be at home to curl up in whatever comfort is available there and to be free to be oneself with one's own messy emotions. Her daughters place a personal ad in a literary magazine, giving Anne some amusing stories to tell. But this is something new for her to consider. At her age, does she want to be with someone else? She engages in e-mail correspondence with a number of men and in doing so learns more about herself. Her situation is not unusual, but of course it is her own personal situation. Yet she is able to write a memoir that will resonate with others who have had her experience; it may also provide understanding to the children of a widowed parent.

Subjects: Bereavement; Dating; Death of a Spouse; Journalists; Loneliness; New York, NY; Novelists

Now Try: Anne Roiphe had earlier written a memoir of her childhood, ***1185 Park Avenue: A Memoir***. An incident that Roiphe describes with her first "date" sounds just like something out of Jane Juska's memoir, ***A Round-Heeled Woman: My Late-Life Adventures in Sex and Romance***, following a personal ad she had placed in *The New York Review of Books*. Roiphe describes the fears and general anxieties she has suffered since the death of her husband. These fears are also a part of the memoir by Joyce Brothers, a psychiatrist, entitled ***Widowed***. Phyllis Greene expresses many of the same sentiments as Roiphe after she lost her husband of fifty-six years. She offers a collection of essays—almost like diary entries—in ***It Must Have Been Moonglow: Reflections on the First Years of Widowhood***.

Smith, Alison (1968–)

Name All the Animals: A Memoir. Scribner, 2005, 2004. 319pp. 9780743255233. Also available in large print, audiobook (read by the author), and e-audiobook. 155.937092

Alison Smith and her brother Roy were three years apart in age and so close that her mother created a name for them, Alroy. When Alison was fifteen she lost her brother to a car accident. Her memoir deals with her grief and the grief of her parents, the way each of them and the larger community to which they belonged handled the tragedy. Her reaction was to act out, to stop eating and give her food at night to her brother's ghost, and to embark on a lesbian love affair with a fellow student. Her memoir, looking back at a tragedy softened by time, is a loving portrait of not only her brother, but her family as well, growing up in a close-knit suburb of Rochester, NY.

Name All the Animals was a finalist for the Book Sense Book of the Year Award and winner of the Lambda Literary Award for Autobiography/Memoir.

Subjects: Adolescents; *Anorexia Nervosa*; Bereavement; Brothers; Catholics; Coming of Age; Death of a Sibling; Family Relationships; Lambda Literary Award for Autobiography/Memoir; Lesbians; Rochester, NY

Now Try: Alison Smith felt that with the death of her brother she had lost her own identity, an issue that the novelist Margaret Diehl addresses in her memoir, ***The Boy on the Green Bicycle: A Memoir***, a remembrance of her own brother, who had died. Elizabeth DeVita-Raeburn basically lost her brother when she was six, although it took him eight years in a plastic bubble in a hospital to die. Older than she, he was her hero. In her memoir, ***The Empty Room: Surviving the Loss of a Brother or Sister at Any Age***, she describes their life together and her grief at her loss, but she also looks at the larger issue of a sibling's grief. Francine Prose's ***Goldengrove: A Novel*** deals with a young teenager who loses a sibling and finds that she really has to come to terms with it herself, as her parents can't help her in their own grief.

Thomas, Abigail

A Three Dog Life. Harcourt, 2007, 2006. 190pp. 9780156033237. Also available in large print and e-book. 813.54

In this collection of essays Abigail, the daughter of the scientist Lewis Thomas, describes how drastically life changed in an instant for her and her husband, Rich. He suffered a traumatic brain injury (TBI) when he was hit by a car in New York City, an injury that was so severe Abigail had to put him into a long-term-care home in upstate New York. She moved there to be close to him and acquired two more dogs to add to the one Rich had been walking when he was hurt. Rich had no memory, so everything was immediate, in the present only, leaving the past and the future for Abigail. She describes their life prior to the accident, so that people can see that the man she visits is not the man she married, and she describes how she makes a new life for herself, learning to knit, learning to cope on her own. She can't imagine life without Rich, even as he is. But it is still a grievous loss.

Subjects: Accident Victims; Brain; Dogs; Human–Animal Relationships; Knitting; Long-Term Care; Married Couples; New York (State); Personal Essays; Rogin, Richard; Traumatic Brain Injury

Now Try: The comfort that animals provide has been well-documented, and examples abound in this book, particularly in the "Animal Friends" section of Chapter 7. Judith Summers relates how her new dog, a King Charles spaniel, helped her and her son get through the initial pain of her husband's and his father's death in ***My Life with George: What I Learned About Joy from One Neurotic (and Very Expensive) Dog***. The writer Alix Kates Shulman endured the same kind of loss as Thomas when her husband suffered a traumatic brain injury from a freak accident; her memoir, quite different in many respects from Thomas's, is ***To Love What Is: A Marriage Transformed***. Ruthann Knechel Johansen describes what it was like for her and her family when her son suffered a traumatic brain injury in ***Listening in the Silence, Seeing in the Dark: Reconstructing Life After Brain Injury***.

Walsh, John (1945–)
Schindehette, Susan, coauthor

Tears of Rage: From Grieving Father to Crusader for Justice; The Untold Story of the Adam Walsh Case. Pocket Books, 2008, 1997. 404pp. ill. 16pp. of plates. 9781439136348. Also available in large print and e-book. 364.1523092

John Walsh's title reflects in part what his memoir is about. The six-year-old son of John and Revé Walsh was kidnapped from a Sears store in Hollywood, Florida, and his head was found in a canal two weeks later. Walsh's memoir details those horrible days when Adam first went missing and then moves on to the criminal investigation, or lack of it. Walsh was so frustrated by what he perceived as an indifferent police department and criminal justice system that he began to lobby for change. Walsh was responsible for the practice of putting missing children's faces on milk cartons. He also started the television program, *America's Most Wanted* (http://www.amw.com/), a show that featured specific crimes, their victims, and as much information about the case and suspect as they had. Through this program over 1, 100 criminals have been captured. The Walshes have also brought about several legislative changes, determined that Adam's death would not be in vain. After the writing and reprinting of this book, the Hollywood Police Department, apologizing to the Walshes for the unacceptably long delay in identifying the perpetrator, finally announced in December 2008 who was responsible for Adam's death. The culprit, a serial killer, had already died in prison, where he was serving five life sentences (Almanzar, 2008).

Subjects: *America's Most Wanted* (Television Program); Criminal Investigation; Criminal Law; Death of a Child; Florida; Grief; Hollywood, FL; Homicide Investigations; Kidnapping; Murder; True Crime; Violent Crimes

Now Try: John E. Douglas, the FBI profiler, and Mark Olshaker have written a book about the unsolved murders still in the FBI files, ***The Cases That Haunt Us: From Jack the Ripper to JonBenet Ramsey, the FBI's Legendary Mindhunter Sheds Light on the Mysteries That Won't Go Away***. The parents of JonBenét Ramsey doubly suffered in the loss of their daughter: the case has never been solved, and they were caught up in a media circus over it. John and Patricia Ann Ramsey wrote their story in ***The Death of Innocence: The Untold Story of JonBenét's Murder and How Its Exploitation Compromised the Pursuit of Truth***. Judith R. Bernstein is a psychologist and a grieving parent who spoke to others in the same situation, gathered their stories, and added her own professional expertise, in ***When the Bough Breaks: Forever After the Death of a Son or Daughter***.

Wickersham, Joan

The Suicide Index: Putting My Father's Death in Order. Mariner Books, 2009, 2008. 316pp. 9780151014903. Also available in e-book. 155.93709

In Wickersham's memoir, her index is at the front of the book; it is her table of contents. An index is both a searching tool and a way of ordering things; it was the only way Wickersham could grapple with the life-changing fact of her father's suicide. Suicide is the main entry, and the subentries represent the vignettes she shares in an effort to understand. He committed suicide in a shocking manner when he was sixty-one and his daughters had already moved away, living adult lives. For years after his death Wickersham sought answers to why, visiting psychiatrists, trying to write a novel about it, talking to family members. It was such a contradictory act on his part, not anything one would have expected from this man. As Wickersham delves into his past, looks at family relationships, and remembers her father as she thought he was, she starts to get an added perspective on him, but only time and the effort to write this book have muted the pain.

The Suicide Index was a finalist for the National Book Award and was selected as a Notable Book by the American Library Association.

Subjects: Adult Children; ALA Notable Books; Bereavement; Death of a Parent; Family Relationships; Fathers and Daughters; Suicide; Writers

Now Try: Suicide can strike a family at any age. The survivor in Marya Hornbacher's novel, ***The Center of Winter***, is a young wife with two small children. The psychologist Thomas E. Joiner offers insights and comfort to survivors in ***Why People Die by Suicide***. And for the children of suicides, there is a work by Judy Zionts Fox and Mia Roldan detailing their interviews with suicide survivors, ***Voices of Strength: Sons and Daughters of Suicide Speak Out***.

Consider Starting With . . .

Armstrong, Lance. *It's Not About the Bike: My Journey Back to Life*

Didion, Joan. *The Year of Magical Thinking*

Fisher, Antwone Quenton. *Finding Fish: A Memoir*

Grandin, Temple. *Thinking in Pictures: And Other Reports from My Life with Autism*

Hamill, Pete. *A Drinking Life: A Memoir*

Karr, Mary. *The Liars' Club: A Memoir*

Keller, Helen. *The Story of My Life*

Meili, Trisha. *I Am the Central Park Jogger: A Story of Hope and Possibility*

Taylor, Jill Bolte. *My Stroke of Insight: A Brain Scientist's Personal Journey*

Williams, Gregory Howard. *Life on the Color Line: The True Story of a White Boy Who Discovered He Was Black*

Fiction Read-Alikes

Berg, Elizabeth. *We Are All Welcome Here: A Novel.* Although strapped inside an iron lung because of polio, Paige Dunn is determined to raise her daughter, Diana, with the help of their Black caregiver in 1960s Tupelo, Mississippi.

Doyle, Malachy. *Georgie.* Georgie's early childhood has been so traumatic that he is rendered mute and has become incorrigible.

Eugenides, Jeffrey. *Middlesex.* Calliope Stephanides is a hermaphrodite raised as a girl, but Cal really sensed he was a boy.

Hoffman, Alice. *At Risk.* The Farrells are heartsick at their young daughter's diagnosis of AIDS from a blood transfusion and then face prejudice against her from the town.

Lee, Harper. *To Kill a Mockingbird.* In this classic novel racism becomes a reality for young Scout when her father defends a Black man falsely accused of rape.

Leimbach, Marti. *Daniel Isn't Talking.* When Melanie and Stephen Marsh cannot agree on the proper care and treatment for their autistic son, their marriage starts to unwind.

Oates, Joyce Carol. *Rape: A Love Story.* When Teena is brutally gang-raped, her daughter, a witness to the crime, identifies the culprits, but the town rallies around the culprits rather than the victims.

Scott, Joanna. *Make Believe: A Novel.* The custody battle between two sets of grandparents is seen through the eyes of their biracial, four-year-old orphaned grandchild.

Shreve, Anita. *The Pilot's Wife: A Novel.* Kathryn Lyons loses her husband to an airplane crash; the resultant media furor aggravates her discovery of his betrayal of her.

Woodward, Gerard. *I'll Go to Bed at Noon.* Alcoholism tears apart a family living in suburban London, in this novel short-listed for the Man Booker Prize.

Works Cited

Almanzar, Yolanne. 2008. "27 Years Later, Case Is Closed in Slaying of Abducted Child." *The New York Times*, December 16. Accessed August 4, 2010. http://www.nytimes.com/2008/12/17/us/17adam.html?scp=1&sq=john+walsh+ottis+toole&st=nyt.

Birkerts, Sven. 2008. *The Art of Time in Memoir: Then, Again.* Saint Paul, MN: Graywolf Press.

Cheever, Susan. 1993. "A Designated Crazy." Review of *Girl, Interrupted,* by Susanna Kaysen. *The New York Times,* June 20. Accessed July 22, 2010. http://www.nytimes.com/1993/06/20/books/a-designated-crazy.html?scp=9&sq=susanna+kaysen&st=nyt.

Furedi, Frank. 2007. "An Emotional Striptease." *The Spiked Review of Books* (May). Accessed July 12, 2010. http://www.spiked-online.com/index.php?/site/reviewofbooks_article/3353.

Gutkind, Lee, and Hattie Fletcher, eds. 2008. *Keep It Real: Everything You Need to Know about Researching and Writing Creative Nonfiction.* New York: W. W. Norton & Company.

Jefferson, Margo. 1997. "Facing Truth About Incest, in Memoir and Novel." Critic's Notebook, *The New York Times,* May 29. Accessed July 12, 2010. http://www.nytimes.com/1997/05/29/books/facing-truth-about-incest-in-memoir-and-novel.html.

Nancy Venable Raine: Biography. 2004, December 13. Accessed March 15, 2008. http://www.aftersilence-bynvraine.net/author/profile.htm.

Potter, Rebecca C. 2005. "Survivor Narrative." In *Encyclopedia of Women's Autobiography,* edited by Victoria Boynton and Jo Malin, 544–46. Westport, CT: Greenwood Press.

Roney, Kristen Simmons. 2005. "Race." In *Encyclopedia of Women's Autobiography,* edited by Victoria Boynton and Jo Malin, 475–78. Westport, CT: Greenwood Press.

"Women Breaking the Cycle of Poverty: Women's Organisations in Africa Are Taking the Issue of Income Generation Through Microcredit by Its Horns: As *New African Woman*'s Zarina Geloo Reports from Zambia, Economically Empowering Women Could Not Have Come at a Better Time and Is Long Overdue." 2008. *New African* 477 (October): S26(4). *General OneFile.* Accessed July 17, 2010.

Yagoda, Ben. 2009. *Memoir: A History.* New York: Riverhead Books.

Appendix A

Classics

The term "classics" can spark a debate anytime, particularly in defining it and in applying it to books, songs, movies, and other cultural activities and arts. I have taken its meaning at its broadest in order to include as many titles in this section as possible. The books in this section are those that have endured over decades and in some cases over centuries. They are still being sought and read and are of great interest to a wide variety of people, each found in more than 1,200 libraries throughout North America. In many cases their authors have been trailblazers in their fields, so that a record of their accomplishments should be readily available to readers. In order to populate the main section of the book with more current titles, it was necessary to set these classics aside, but I still wanted to make sure they are mentioned and brought to the attention of the reader. However, each chapter in the book begins with a sampling of five classics in that topic, and the remainder have been included here. (Please note that the bibliographic information given here does not include editors, coauthors, etc.)

Chapter 1: Travel and Adventure

Abagnale, Frank W. (1948–). *Catch Me If You Can*. Broadway Books, 2002, 1980.

Byrd, Richard Evelyn (1888–1957). *Alone*. Kodansha International, 1995, 1938.

Chatwin, Bruce (1940–1989). *What Am I Doing Here*. Penguin Books, 1990, 1989.

Chichester, Sir Francis (1901–1972). *Gipsy Moth Circles the World*. International Marine/McGraw-Hill, 2001, 1968.

Columbus, Christopher (ca. 1451–1506). *The Log of Christopher Columbus*. International Marine Publishing Co., 1987.

Doughty, Charles Montagu (1843–1926). *Travels in Arabia Deserta*. Bloomsbury Publishing, 1989, 1888.

Earhart, Amelia (1897–1937). *Last Flight*. Crown Trade Paperbacks, 1997,1937.

Halliburton, Richard (1900–1939). *The Royal Road to Romance*. Travelers' Tales, 2000, 1925.

Harrer, Heinrich (1912–2006). *Seven Years in Tibet*. Jeremy P. Tarcher/Penguin, 2009, 1953.

King, Clarence (1842–1901). *Mountaineering in the Sierra Nevada*. University of Nebraska Press, 1997, 1872.

Lewis, Meriwether (1774–1809); Clark, William (1770–1838). *The Lewis and Clark Journals: An American Epic of Discovery; The Abridgment of the Definitive Nebraska Edition*. University of Nebraska Press, 2003.

Markham, Beryl (1902–1986). *West with the Night*. North Point Press, 1983, 1942.

Parkman, Francis (1823–1893). *The Oregon Trail*. National Geographic Society, 2002, 1847.

Polo, Marco (1254–1323?). *The Travels of Marco Polo*. Liveright, 2003, 1926.

Slocum, Joshua (1844–ca. 1910). *Sailing Alone Around the World*. Naval Institute Press, 1985, 1899.

West, Rebecca (1892–1983). *Black Lamb and Grey Falcon; A Journey Through Yugoslavia*. Penguin Books, 2007, 1941.

Yeager, Chuck (1923–). *Yeager, an Autobiography*. Bantam, 1985.

Chapter 2: Celebrities

Basie, Count (1904–1984). *Good Morning Blues: The Autobiography of Count Basie*. Da Capo Press, 2002, 1985.

Brando, Marlon (1924–2004). *Brando: Songs My Mother Taught Me*. Random House, 1994.

Capra, Frank (1897–1991). *The Name Above the Title; An Autobiography*. Da Capo Press, 1997, 1971.

Chaplin, Charlie (1889–1977). *My Autobiography*. Plume, 1992, 1964.

Flynn, Errol (1909–1959). *My Wicked, Wicked Ways*. Cooper Square Press, 2003, 1959.

Guinness, Alec (1914–2000). *Blessings in Disguise*. Akadine Press, 2001, 1986.

Kazan, Elia (1909–2003). *Elia Kazan: A Life*. Da Capo Press, 1997, 1988.

Mays, Willie (1931–). *Say Hey: The Autobiography of Willie Mays*. Pocket Books, 1989, 1988.

Olivier, Laurence (1907–1989). *Confessions of an Actor: An Autobiography*. Simon & Schuster, 1992, 1982.

Vanderbilt, Gloria (1924–). *Once upon a Time: A True Story*. Fawcett/Ballantine, 1986, 1985.

Waters, Ethel (1896–1977). *His Eye Is on the Sparrow; An Autobiography*. Jove Publications, 1982, 1951.

Winters, Shelley (1920–2006). *Shelley: Also Known as Shirley*. Ballantine, 1981, 1980.

Chapter 3: The Creative Life

Alcott, Louisa May (1832–1888). *Louisa May Alcott; Her Life, Letters, and Journals*. Gramercy Books, 1995, 1889.

Beauvoir, Simone de (1908–1986). *Memoirs of a Dutiful Daughter*. Harper-Perennial, 2005, 1959.

Bombeck, Erma (1927–1996). *A Marriage Made in Heaven—Or, Too Tired for an Affair*. HarperPaperbacks, 1994, 1993.

Carr, Emily (1871–1945). *Klee Wyck*. Douglas & McIntyre, 2004, 1941.

Christie, Agatha (1890–1976). *An Autobiography*. Berkley Books, 1996, 1977.

Colette (1873–1954). *Earthly Paradise; An Autobiography*. Farrar, Straus & Giroux, 1966.

Copland, Aaron (1900–1990). *Copland, 1900 Through 1942*. St. Martin's Griffin, 1999, 1984.

De Mille, Agnes (1905–1993). *Dance to the Piper*. Da Capo Press, 1980, 1952.

Ellison, Ralph (1914–1994). *Going to the Territory*. Vintage International, 1995, 1986.

Emerson, Ralph Waldo (1803–1882). *Emerson in His Journals*. Belknap Press of Harvard University Press, 1982, 1909.

Fonteyn, Margot (1919–1991). *Margot Fonteyn: Autobiography*. Knopf, 1976.

Hart, Moss (1904–1961). *Act One, an Autobiography*. Random House, 2002, 1953.

Hayes, Helen (1900–1993). *My Life in Three Acts*. Simon & Schuster, 1991, 1990.

Hughes, Langston (1902–1967). *The Big Sea: An Autobiography*. Hill and Wang, 1998, 1940.

Kaplan, Alice Yaeger (1954–). *French Lessons: A Memoir*. University of Chicago Press, 1994, 1993.

Kazin, Alfred (1915–1998). *A Walker in the City*. Harcourt Brace, 1979, 1951.

Kerr, Jean (1922–2003). *Please Don't Eat the Daisies*. Doubleday, 1957.

Kipling, Rudyard (1865–1936). *Something of Myself: For My Friends Known and Unknown*. Cambridge University Press, 1990, 1937.

Laurence, Margaret (1926–1987). *Dance on the Earth: A Memoir*. McClelland & Stewart, 1998, 1989.

Lee, Laurie (1914–1997). *Cider with Rosie*. Penguin, 1998, 1959.

MacDonald, Betty Bard (1908–1958). *The Egg and I*. Perennial Library, 1987, 1945.

Maugham, W. Somerset (1874–1965). *A Writer's Notebook*. Vintage International, 2009, 1949.

Maynard, Fredelle Bruser (1922–1989). *Raisins and Almonds*. Paperjacks, 1978, 1972.

McCarthy, Mary (1912–1989). *Memories of a Catholic Girlhood*. Harcourt Brace Jovanovich, 2009, 1957.

Michener, James A. (1907–1997). *The World Is My Home: A Memoir*. Random House, 2007, 1992.

Montgomery, L. M. (1874–1942). *The Selected Journals of L. M. Montgomery*. Oxford University Press, 1985–2004.

Moses, Grandma (1860–1961). *Grandma Moses: My Life's History*. Harper, 1952, 1948.

Nin, Anaïs (1903–1977). *The Diary of Anaïs Nin*. Swallow Press, 1966–1980.

O'Connor, Frank (1903–1966). *An Only Child*. Syracuse University Press, 1997, 1961.

Pasternak, Boris Leonidovich (1890–1960). *I Remember; Sketch for an Autobiography*. Harvard University Press, 1983, 1959.

Paton, Alan (1903–1988). *Towards the Mountain: An Autobiography*. Scribner, 1987, 1977.

Plath, Sylvia (1932–1980). *The Unabridged Journals of Sylvia Plath, 1950–1962*. Anchor Books, 2000.

Sand, George (1804–1876). *My Life*. State University Press of New York, 1991, 1979.

Sarton, May (1912–1995). *Journal of a Solitude*. Norton, 1977, 1973.

Sartre, Jean-Paul (1905–1980). *The Words*. Vintage Books, 1981, 1964.

Sills, Beverly (1929–2007). *Beverly: An Autobiography*. Bantam Books, 1988, 1987.

Singer, Isaac Bashevis (1904–1991). *In My Father's Court*. Noonday Press, 1996, 1966.

Sitwell, Edith (1887–1964). *Taken Care of; The Autobiography of Edith Sitwell*. Atheneum, 1965.

Sparks, Muriel (1918–2006). *Curriculum Vitae: Autobiography*. Houghton Mifflin, 1993.

Thurber, James (1894–1961). *My Life and Hard Times*. Perennial Classics, 1999, 1933.

Walker, Alice (1944–). *In Search of Our Mothers' Gardens: Womanist Prose.* Harcourt, 2004, 1983.

Waugh, Evelyn (1903–1966). *The Diaries of Evelyn Waugh.* Little, Brown, 1977.

Welty, Eudora (1909–2001). *One Writer's Beginnings.* Harvard University Press, 2001, 1983.

West, Jessamyn (1902–1984). *The Woman Said Yes: Encounters with Life and Death; Memoirs.* Harcourt Brace Jovanovich, 1986, 1976.

White, Theodore H. (1915–1986). *In Search of History: A Personal Adventure.* Warner Books, 1981, 1978.

Williams, Tennessee (1911–1983). *Memoirs.* New Directions, 2006, 1975.

Wolfe, Thomas (1900–1938). *Look Homeward, Angel: A Story of the Buried Life.* Scribner, 2006, 1929.

Woolf, Virginia (1882–1941). *The Diary of Virginia Woolf.* Harcourt Brace Jovanovich, 1984, 1920.

Wordsworth, William (1770–1850). *The Fourteen-Book Prelude.* Cornell University Press, 1985, 1798–1805.

Wright, Frank Lloyd (1867–1959). *An Autobiography.* Horizon Press, 1977, 1932.

Chapter 4: The Working Life

Ashton-Warner, Sylvia (1908–1984). *Teacher.* Simon & Schuster, 1986, 1963.

Ballard, Martha (1735–1812), and Laurel Ulrich. *A Midwife's Tale: The Life of Martha Ballard, Based on Her Diary, 1785–1812.* Vintage Books, 1999, 1990.

Carnegie, Andrew (1835–1919). *Autobiography of Andrew Carnegie.* Cosimo Classics, 2005, 1920.

Darrow, Clarence (1857–1938). *The Story of My Life.* Da Capo Press, 1996, 1932.

Feynman, Richard P. (1918–1988). *"Surely You're Joking, Mr. Feynman!" Adventures of a Curious Character.* Norton, 1997, 1985.

Hurston, Zora Neale (1891?–1960). *Dust Tracks on a Road, an Autobiography.* University of Illinois Press, 1984, 1970, 2d ed.

Jung, C. G. (1875–1961). *Memories, Dreams, Reflections.* Vintage Books, 1989, 1963.

Lévi-Strauss, Claude (1908–2009). *Tristes Tropiques.* Atheneum, 1974, 1955.

MacNeil, Robert (1931–). *Wordstruck: A Memoir.* Penguin, 1990, 1989.

Mead, Margaret (1901–1978). *Blackberry Winter; My Earlier Years.* Peter Smith, 1989, 1972.

Ogilvy, David (1911–1999). *Confessions of an Advertising Man*. Scribner, 2002, 1963.

Turow, Scott (1949-). *One L*. Warner Time Company, 1998, 1977.

Chapter 5: Place and Time

Baker, Russell (1925–). *Growing Up*. New American Library, 1984, 1981.

Catton, Bruce (1899–1978). *Waiting for the Morning Train; An American Boyhood*. Wayne State University Press, 1987, 1972.

Dillard, Annie (1945–). *An American Childhood*. Harper Perennial, 1995, 1987.

Huxley, Elspeth Joscelin Grant (1907–1997). *The Flame Trees of Thika; Memories of an African Childhood*. Penguin Books, 2000, 1959.

Lord, Bette (1938–). *Legacies: A Chinese Mosaic*. Knopf, 1990.

Milne, Christopher (1920–1996). *The Enchanted Places*. Dutton, 1975, 1974.

Rawlings, Marjorie Kinnan (1896–1953). *Cross Creek*. Simon & Schuster, 1996, 1942.

Sei Shōnagon (b. ca. 967–1017?). *The Pillow-Book of Sei Shōnagon*. Columbia University Press, 1992.

Teale, Edwin Way (1899–1980). *Wandering Through Winter; A Naturalist's Record of a 20,000–Mile Journey Through the North American Winter*. St. Martin's Press, 1990, 1965.

Chapter 6: Life Away from Home

Moodie, Susanna (1803–1885). *Roughing It in the Bush*. W. W. Norton & Co, 2007, 1852.

Riis, Jacob A. (1849–1914). *The Making of an American*. University Press of the Pacific, 2003, 1901.

Rodriguez, Richard (1944–). *Hunger of Memory: The Education of Richard Rodriguez;An Autobiography*. Dell Publishing, 2004, 1982.

Seagrave, Gordon Stifler (1897–1956). *Burma Surgeon*. Transworld, 1958, 1943.

Traill, Catherine Parr Strickland (1802–1899). *The Backwoods of Canada: Being Letters from the Wife of an Emigrant Officer, Illustrative of the Domestic Economy of British America*. Carleton University Press, 1997, 1836.

Chapter 7: Life with Others

Buscaglia, Leo F. (1924–1998). *Papa, My Father: A Celebration of Dads*. Slack, 1993, 1989.

Gage, Nicholas (1939–). *Eleni*. Ballantine, 1996, 1983.

Gosse, Edmund (1849–1928). *Father and Son; A Study of Two Temperaments*. Penguin, 1986, 1907.

Korda, Michael (1933–). *Charmed Lives: A Family Romance*. Perennial, 2002, 1979.

Levi, Carlo (1902–1975). *Christ Stopped at Eboli; The Story of a Year*. Farrar, Straus & Giroux, 2006, 1947.

Villaseñor, Victor (1940–). *Rain of Gold*. Delta Trade Paperbacks, 1992, 1991.

Chapter 8: The Inner Life

Bunyan, John (1628–1688). *Grace Abounding to the Chief of Sinners*. Hendrickson, 2007, 1666.

Dante Alighieri (1265–1321). *Vita Nuova*. Oxford University Press, 2008, 1861.

De Quincey, Thomas (1785–1859). *Confessions of an English Opium-Eater*. Broadview Press, 2009, 1822.

Fire, John/Lame Deer (1903–1976). *Lame Deer, Seeker of Visions*. Simon & Schuster, 2009, 1972.

Hammarskjöld, Dag (1905–1961). *Markings*. Vintage, 2006, 1964.

Ignatius of Loyola, Saint (1491–1556). *A Pilgrim's Journey: The Autobiography of Ignatius of Loyola*. Ignatius Press, 2001, 1731.

John XXIII, Pope (1881–1963). *Journal of a Soul*. McGraw-Hill, 1965.

Lewis, C. S. (1898–1963). *Surprised by Joy; The Shape of My Early Life*. Barnes & Noble Books, 2002, 1955.

Newman, John Henry (1801–1890). *Apologia pro Vita Sua*. Dover Publications, 2005, 1864.

Peale, Norman Vincent (1898–1993). *The True Joy of Positive Living: An Autobiography*. Morrow, 1988, 1984.

Saint-Exupéry, Antoine de (1900–1944). *Wind, Sand and Stars*. Harcourt, 2002, 1939.

Thomas, Piri (1928–). *Down These Mean Streets*. Vintage Books, 1997, 1967.

Wilkerson, David R. (1931–). *The Cross and the Switchblade*. Chosen Books, 2008, 1962.

Chapter 9: The Political Life

Acheson, Dean (1893–1971). *Present at the Creation; My Years in the State Department*. Norton, 1987, 1969.

Chambers, Whittaker (1901–1961). *Witness*. Regnery Pub, 2001, 1952.

Eban, Abba Solomon (1915–2002). *Abba Eban: An Autobiography*. Random House, 1977.

Ford, Betty (1918–). *The Times of My Life*. Harper & Row, 1978.

Haldeman, H. R. (1926–1993). *The Ends of Power*. Times Books, 1978.

Hull, Cordell (1871–1955). *The Memoirs of Cordell Hull*. Macmillan, 1979, 1948.

Jefferson, Thomas (1743–1826). *The Life and Selected Writings of Thomas Jefferson*. Modern Library, 2004, 1853.

Kennan, George F. (1904–2005). *Memoirs*. Pantheon, 1983, 1967.

Kissinger, Henry (1923–). *White House Years*. Little, Brown, 1979.

Kravchenko, Victor (1905–1966). *I Chose Freedom, the Personal and Political Life of a Soviet Official*. Transaction, 1989, 1946.

Meir, Golda (1898–1978). *My Life*. Putnam, 1975.

Nixon, Richard M. (1913–1994). *RN: The Memoirs of Richard Nixon*. Simon & Schuster, 1990, 1978.

Norris, George W. (1861–1944). *Fighting Liberal*. University of Nebraska Press, 2009, 1945.

Ostrovsky, Victor (1949–). *By Way of Deception*. St. Martin's Press, 1991, 1990.

Sadat, Anwar (1918–1981). *In Search of Identity: An Autobiography*. The Easton Press, 1989, 1977.

Thatcher, Margaret (1925–). *The Downing Street Years*. HarperCollins, 1993.

Trotsky, Leon (1879–1940). *My Life; An Attempt at an Autobiography*. Dover, 2007, 1930.

Truman, Harry S. (1884–1972). *The Autobiography of Harry S. Truman*. University of Missouri Press, 2002, 1980.

Weizmann, Chaim (1874–1952). *Trial and Error; The Autobiography of Chaim Weizmann*. Greenwood Press, 1972, 1949.

Yeltsin, Boris Nikolayevich (1931–2007). *Against the Grain: An Autobiography*. Summit Books, 1990.

Chapter 10: Changing Lives in History

Abernathy, Ralph (1926–1990). *And the Walls Came Tumbling Down*. Lawrence Hill Books, 2010, 1989.

Addams, Jane (1860–1935). *Twenty Years at Hull-House, with Autobiographical Notes*. University of Illinois Press, 2008, 1910.

Drucker, Peter F. (1909–2005). *Adventures of a Bystander*. John Wiley, 1998, 1978.

Durant, Will (1885–1981) and Ariel (1898–1981). *A Dual Autobiography*. Simon & Schuster, 1977.

Einstein, Albert (1879–1955). *The World as I See It*. Citadel Press, 2006, 1934.

Galbraith, John Kenneth (1908–2006). *A Life in Our Times: Memoirs*. Ballantine, 1982, 1981.

Gandhi, Mahatma (1869–1948). *An Autobiography; The Story of My Experiments with Truth*. Beacon Press, 1993, 1957.

McClung, Nellie L. (1873–1951). *Nellie McClung, the Complete Autobiography*. Broadview Press, 2003, 1935, 1945.

Mill, John Stuart (1806–1873). *Autobiography of John Stuart Mill*. Columbia University Press, 1969, 1873.

Parker, John P. (1827–1900). *His Promised Land: The Autobiography of John P. Parker, Former Slave and Conductor on the Underground Railroad*. W. W. Norton, 1998, 1996.

Russell, Bertrand (1872–1970). *The Autobiography of Bertrand Russell*. Simon & Schuster, 1967–1969.

Saint-Simon, Louis de Rouvroy, duc de (1675–1755). *Historical Memoirs of the Duc de Saint-Simon*. McGraw-Hill, 1968–1972. 3 v.

Schweitzer, Albert (1875–1965). *Out of My Life and Thought, an Autobiography*. Johns Hopkins Paperbacks, 1998, 1933.

Shaw, Nate (1885–1973). *All God's Dangers; The Life of Nate Shaw*. University of Chicago Press, 2000, 1974.

Watson, James D. (1928–). *The Double Helix; A Personal Account of the Discovery of the Structure of DNA*. Simon & Schuster, 2001, 1968.

Wilkins, Roy (1901–1981). *Standing Fast: The Autobiography of Roy Wilkins*. Da Capo, 1994, 1982.

Chapter 11: Life on The Dark Side of History

Cheng, Nien (1915–). *Life and Death in Shanghai*. Penguin Books, 1988, 1986.

Hearst, Patricia (1954–). *Every Secret Thing*. Doubleday, 1982.

Hillesum, Etty (1914–1943). *An Interrupted Life: The Diaries of Etty Hillesum, 1941–1943*. Henry Holt, 1996, 1983.

Robinson, Jackie (1919–1972). *I Never Had It Made*. Harper Collins, 1995.

Rowlandson, Mary White (ca, 1635–1711). *The Sovereignty and Goodness of God: Together with the Faithfulness of His Promises Displayed; Being a Narrative of the Captivity and Restoration of Mrs. Mary Rowlandson and Related Documents*. Bedford/St. Martin's, 1997, 1682.

Salisbury, Harrison E. (1908–1993). *Tiananmen Diary: Thirteen Days in June*. Little, Brown, 1989.

Shcharansky, Anatoly (1948–). *Fear No Evil: The Classic Memoir of One Man's Triumph over a Police State*. PublicAffairs, 1998, 1988.

Ten Boom, Corrie (1892–1983). *The Hiding Place*. Hendrickson Publishers, 2010, 1971.

Timerman, Jacobo (1923–1999). *Prisoner Without a Name, Cell Without a Number*. University of Wisconsin Press, 2002, 1981.

Truth, Sojourner (1797–1883). *The Narrative of Sojourner Truth*. Dover Publications, 1997, 1850.

Valladares, Armando (1937–). *Against All Hope: A Memoir of Life in Castro's Gulag*. Heritage Foundation, 2002, 1986.

Chapter 12: Life at War

Bradley, Omar Nelson (1893–1981). *A Soldier's Story*. Modern Library, 1999, 1951

Brittain, Vera (1893–1970). *Testament of Youth; An Autobiographical Study of the Years 1900–1925*. Penguin, 2005, 1933.

Butcher, Harry C. (1901–1985). *My Three Years with Eisenhower; The Personal Diary of Captain Harry C. Butcher, USNR, Naval Aide to General Eisenhower, 1942 to 1945*. Simon & Schuster, 1946.

Dawson, Sarah Morgan (1842–1909). *The Civil War Diary of Sarah Morgan*. Simon & Schuster, 1992, 1991.

Duras, Marguerite (1914–1996). *The War: A Memoir*. New Press, 1994, 1986.

Eisenhower, Dwight D. (1890–1969). *Crusade in Europe*. Johns Hopkins University Press, 1997, 1948.

Gooding, James Henry (1837–1864). *On the Altar of Freedom: A Black Soldier's Civil War Letters from the Front*. University of Massachusetts Press, 1999, 1991.

Keith, Agnes (1901–1982). *Three Came Home*. Bantam, 1983, 1947.

Kovic, Ron (1946–). *Born on the Fourth of July*. Akashic Books, 2005, 1976.

Lawrence, T. E. (1888–1935). *Seven Pillars of Wisdom; A Triumph*. Penguin Books, 2000, 1935.

Montgomery of Alamein, Bernard Law Montgomery, Viscount (1887–1976). *The Memoirs of Field-Marshal the Viscount Montgomery of Alamein*. Da Capo, 1982, 1958.

Murphy, Audie (1924–1971). *To Hell and Back*. Henry Holt and Co, 2002, 1949.

Orwell, George (1903–1950). *Homage to Catalonia*. Harcourt Brace & Co, 1980, 1952.

Patton, George S. (1885–1945). *War as I Knew It*. Presidio, 2003, 1947.

Pershing, John J. (1860–1948). *My Experiences in the World War*. Da Capo, 1995, 1921.

Schwarzkopf, H. Norman (1934–). *It Doesn't Take a Hero: General H. Norman Schwarzkopf, the Autobiography*. Bantam, 1992.

Sheean, Vincent (1899–1975). *Personal History*. Citadel Press, 1986, 1935.

Taylor, Susie King (b. 1848). *A Black Woman's Civil War Memoirs: Reminiscences of My Life in Camp with the 33rd U. S. Colored Troops, Late 1st South Carolina Volunteers*. M. Wiener Pub, 1995, 1902.

Chapter 13: Surviving Life

Behan, Brendan (1923–1964). *Borstal Boy*. D. R. Godine, 2000, 1959.

Campbell, Maria (1940–). *Halfbreed*. Goodread Biographies, 1983, 1973.

Ford, Betty (1918–). *Betty, a Glad Awakening*. Doubleday, 1987.

Gordon, Barbara (1935–). *I'm Dancing as Fast as I Can*. Perennial Library, 1989, 1979.

Griffin, John Howard (1920–1980). *Black like Me*. Wings Press, 2006, 1961.

Gunther, John (1901–1970). *Death Be Not Proud: A Memoir*. HarperPerennial Modern Classics, 2007, 1949.

Hockenberry, John (1956–). *Moving Violations: War Zones, Wheelchairs, and Declarations of Independence*. Hyperion, 1996, 1995.

London, Jack (1876–1916). *John Barleycorn*. Modern Library, 2001, 1913.

Lund, Doris Herold (1919–2003). *Eric*. Perennial, 2000, 1974.

Price, Reynolds (1933–). *A Whole New Life*. Scribner, 2000, 1994.

Rodriguez, Luis J. (1954–). *Always Running: La Vida Loca, Gang Days in L.A.* Touchstone, 2005, 1993.

Vonnegut, Mark (1947–). *The Eden Express*. Dell, 1988, 1975.

Wilde, Oscar (1854–1900). *De Profundis*. Modern Library, 2000, 1964.

Appendix B

Controversial Titles

The titles listed below have all been considered by reviewers, friends, or family members to be either outright hoaxes, or so laden with untruths, exaggerations, or fiction as to have rendered them inappropriate for inclusion in the main body of this book on memoirs. Some of the writers have even created completely new personas for themselves, changing their names, their heritage and background, and, of course, the events in their lives, claiming to be someone they are not. The purpose in listing these books here is twofold: a) to indicate why readers who have heard of some of the more notorious titles would not have found them among the main entries in the book; b) to alert potential readers to the fact that while they may enjoy reading the story, they should be aware that the stories cannot actually be believed in full or in part. In some cases, the author has even acknowledged that part or all of the book written was a fabrication. For more on the topic, readers may want to check out the Web site, 100 Memoirs—Wordpress.com (http://100memoirs.com/) and click on "Memoir Controversies."

The debate continues to rage over certain titles, however, titles such as Guy Sajer's ***The Forgotten Soldier*** and ***Testimony: The Memoirs of Dmitri Shostakovich***. The arguments on both sides are convincing, so that the titles remain controversial, but as it doesn't seem fair to include them with such fabrications as those by Nasdijj, they will remain off the list. There are other authors, such as Lee Israel, who made her living by lying, by forging literary letters; should one believe her memoir, ***Can You Ever Forgive Me? Memoirs of a Literary Forger***. I have deliberately not added commentary to these titles, as the comments would have become too repetitive: basically, the author lied enough throughout the book to lose credibility.

Anderson, Sherwood (1876–1941). *A Story Teller's Story; The Tale of an American Writer's Journey Through His Own Imaginative World and Through the World of Facts, with Many of His Experiences and Impressions Among Other Writers—Told in Many Notes—in Four Books—and an Epilogue*. University of Michigan Press, 2005, 1924.

Bernall, M. (1961–). *She Said Yes: The Unlikely Martyrdom of Cassie Bernall*. Pocket Books, 2000, 1999.

Blair, Jayson (1976–). *Burning Down My Masters' House: My Life at The "New York Times."* New Millennium Press, 2004.

Burroughs, Augusten (1965–). *Running with Scissors: A Memoir*. St. Martin's Press, 2006, 2002.

Carcaterra, Lorenzo (1954–). *Sleepers*. Ballantine Books, 1996, 1995.

Carew, Tom (real name Philip Sessarego, 1952–2008). *Jihad! The Secret War in Afghanistan*. Mainstream, 2000.

Carter, Forrest (real name Asa Earl Carter, 1925–1979). *The Education of Little Tree*. University of New Mexico Press, 2004, 1976. [currently referred to as fiction; originally referred to as nonfiction]

Castaneda, Carlos (1931–1998). *Journey to Ixtlan: The Lessons of Don Juan*. Washington Square Press, 1991, 1972.

Charrière, Henri (1906–1973). *Papillon*. HarperPerennial, 2006, 1970.

Defonseca, Misha (1934–). *Misha: A Mémoire of the Holocaust Years*. Mt. Ivy Press, 1997.

Douglas, William O. (1898–1980). *Go East, Young Man: The Early Years; The Autobiography of William O. Douglas*. Random House, 1974.

Frey, James (1969–). *A Million Little Pieces*. Doubleday, 2005, 2003.

Glassco, John (1909–1981). *Memoirs of Montparnasse*. New York Review Books, 2007, 1970.

Go Ask Alice [original author Anonymous, now credited to Beatrice Sparks; currently referred to as fiction] Simon Pulse, 2006, 1971.

Gornick, Vivian (1935–). *Fierce Attachments: A Memoir*. Farrar, Straus & Giroux, 2005, 1987.

Hellman, Lillian (1906–1984). *An Unfinished Woman; A Memoir*. Barnes & Noble, 2001, 1969.

Hirsi Ali, Ayaan (1969–). *Infidel*. Free Press, 2008, 2007.

Johnson, Anthony Godby (suspected not to exist). *A Rock and a Hard Place: One Boy's Triumphant Story*. Signet Books, 1994, 1993.

Jones, Margaret B. (1875–) (real name Margaret Seltzer). *Love and Consequences: A Memoir of Hope and Survival*. Riverhead Books, 2008.

Judd, Naomi (1946–). *Love Can Build a Bridge*. Fawcett Crest, 1994, 1992.

Khouri, Norma (1970–) (real name Norma Bagain Toliopoulos). *Honor Lost: Love and Death in Modern-Day Jordan*. Washington Square Press, 2004, 2003.

Kosinski, Jerzy (1933–1991). *The Painted Bird*. Grove Press, 1995, 1965.

Lauck, Jennifer (1964–). *Blackbird: A Childhood Lost and Found*. Washington Square Press, 2001, 2000.

L'Engle, Madeleine (1918–2007). *A Circle of Quiet*. HarperSanFrancisco, 1997, 1972.

Lerner, Jimmy (1951–). *You Got Nothing Coming: Notes from a Prison Fish*. Broadway Books, 2003, 2002.

Morgan, Marlo (1937–). *Mutant Message down Under*. Perennial, 2004, 1991. [currently referred to as fiction; originally referred to as nonfiction]

Nasdijj (real name Timothy Patrick Barrus, 1950–). *The Blood Runs like a River Through My Dreams: A Memoir*. Houghton Mifflin, 2001, 2000.

O'Beirne, Kathy. *Kathy's Story: The True Story of a Childhood Hell Inside Ireland's Magdalen Laundries*. Greystone Books, 2006.

Rawicz, Slavomir (1915–2004). *The Long Walk*. Lyons Press, 1997, 1956.

Rodriguez, Deborah. *Kabul Beauty School: An American Woman Goes Behind the Veil*. Random House, 2007.

Slater, Lauren (1963–). *Lying: A Metaphorical Memoir*. Penguin Books, 2001, 2000.

Souad. *Burned Alive: A Victim of the Law of Men*. Grand Central Publishing, 2005.

Wilkomirski, Binjamin (real name Bruno Grosjean). *Fragments: Memories of a Wartime Childhood*. Schocken Books, 1997, 1996. [currently referred to as fiction; originally referred to as nonfiction]

Appendix C

Awards

The awards listed below are the ones that have been included in the subject headings of memoirs that actually won the award. The text describing the award is taken from the award Web site.

American Book Awards/Before Columbus Foundation (http://www.bookweb.org/btw/awards/The-American-Book-Awards—Before-Columbus-Foundation.html)

The American Book Awards recognize literary excellence from the entire spectrum of America's diverse literary community.

American Booksellers Book of the Year (ABBY) Award (http://www.bookweb.org/btw/awards/ABBY.html) SEE ALSO The Book Sense Book of the Year (BSBY) Award

The American Booksellers Book of the Year Award was presented from 1991 through 1999 to those books that booksellers most enjoyed recommending to their customers. It then became known as The Book Sense Book of the Year (BSBY) Award.

American Library Association Awards:

- **BCALA Literary Awards** (http://www.bcala.org/awards/literary.htm). The Black Caucus of the American Library Association Award recognizes excellence in adult fiction and nonfiction by African-American authors.
- **Notable Books for Adults** (http://www.ala.org/ala/mgrps/divs/rusa/awards/notablebooks/index.cfm). The Notable Books Council of the American Library Association compiles an annual list of twenty-five very good, very readable, and at times very important fiction, nonfiction, and poetry for the adult reader.
- **Stonewall Book Award-Israel Fishman Non-Fiction Award** (http://www.ala.org/ala/mgrps/rts/glbtrt/stonewall/index.cfm). The Stonewall Book Award-Israel Fishman Non-Fiction Award honors books for their exceptional merit relating to the gay/lesbian/bisexual/transgendered experience.

Anisfield-Wolf Book Awards (http://www.anisfield-wolf.org/)

The Anisfield-Wolf Book Award recognizes books that make important contributions to our understanding of racism and our appreciation of the rich diversity of human cultures.

BCALA Literary Awards. *See* American Library Association Awards

The Book Sense Book of the Year (BSBY) Award (http://www.bookweb.org/btw/awards/BSBY.html) SEE ALSO American Booksellers Book of the Year

The Book Sense Book of the Year Award, presented from 2000 to 2008 and before that known as the ABBY, featured books that booksellers most enjoyed handselling to their customers. It has been replaced by the Indies Choice Book Awards.

Canadian Authors Association Literary Awards (http://www.canauthors.org/awards/index.html)

The Canadian Authors Association Literary Awards honor writing that achieves excellence without sacrificing popular appeal and are bestowed on works, written by Canadian authors, which fall into a number of categories. The award for general nonfiction is no longer being offered.

Canadian Booksellers Association Libris Award for Non-Fiction Book of the Year (http://www.cbabook.org/libris-criteria.html)

The Canadian Booksellers Association offers a number of literary awards; the award for a Canadian work of nonfiction honors a title published in the previous year that had an outstanding impact on the Canadian bookselling industry, created wide media attention, brought people into bookstores, and had strong sales.

Charles Taylor Prize for Literary Non-Fiction (http://www.thecharlestaylorprize.ca/)

The Charles Taylor Prize for Literary Non-Fiction is awarded to the author whose book best combines a superb command of the English language, an elegance of style, and a subtlety of thought and perception.

Christopher Awards (http://www.christophers.org/Page.aspx?pid=217)

The Christopher Awards salute media that "affirm the highest values of the human spirit." Their goal is to encourage men, women and children to pursue excellence in creative arenas that have the potential to influence a mass audience positively. Award-winners encourage audiences to see the better side of human nature and motivate artists and the general public to use their best instincts on behalf of others.

Costa Book Awards. *See* Whitbread Literary Award

Edna Staebler Award for Creative Non-Fiction (http://libserve.wlu.ca/internet/prizes/staebler.html)

The Edna Staebler Award for Creative Non-Fiction was endowed to encourage and recognize the Canadian writer of a first or second published book. The book must have a Canadian locale or a particular Canadian significance and reflect the characteristics of creative nonfiction, combining original research with well-crafted interpretive writing.

Governor General's Literary Awards (http://www.canadacouncil.ca/prizes/ggla)

The Governor General's Literary Awards honor the finest in Canadian literature in seven categories, including nonfiction. They seek to recognize literary and artistic excellence.

Hurston/Wright Legacy Book Award (http://www.hurstonwright.org/ProgramsAwards/legacy.html)

The Hurston/Wright Legacy Book Award, named for Zora Neale Hurston and Richard Wright, is presented to published writers of African descent by the national community of Black writers for the highest quality of writing in Fiction, Debut Fiction, Nonfiction, and Poetry.

The James Beard Foundation Writing on Food Book Award (http://www.jamesbeard.org/index.php?q=about_awards)

The James Beard Foundation Writing on Food Book Award recognizes writers who contribute to the growing canon of information and knowledge about food and beverage.

The James Tait Black Memorial Prize (http://www.englit.ed.ac.uk/jtbinf.htm)

The James Tait Black Memorial Prizes for Biography and Fiction are Scotland's most prestigious literary award, recognizing literary excellence in biography and in fiction.

The Kiriyama Prize (http://www.kiriyamaprize.org/)

The Kiriyama Prize recognizes outstanding books about the Pacific Rim and South Asia that encourage greater mutual understanding of and among the peoples and nations of this vast and culturally diverse region.

Lambda Literary Awards (http://www.lambdaliterary.org/awards/)

The Lambda Literary Awards bring attention to and honor exceptional writing about queer lives across multiple genres published by large and small presses. If a book has a gold sticker saying 'Winner of the Lambda Literary Award' on its cover, you know it is both brilliantly written and a meaningful examination of the LGBTQ experience. As with many awards, the categories for the Lambdas have evolved. The specific Lambda Awards found in this book are for AIDS, Autobiography/Memoir, Gay Nonfiction, Humor, Lesbian Memoir/Biography, and Transgender/Genderqueer.

Lillian Smith Book Award (http://www.libs.uga.edu/hargrett/lilliansmith/lsmith.html)

The Lillian Smith Book Awards have as their mission the enhancement of racial awareness through literature. They honor Lillian Smith, an advocate for improved human relations and social justice.

***Los Angeles Times* Book Prizes** (http://events.latimes.com/bookprizes/)

The *Los Angeles Times* Book Prizes offer as their mission a commitment to literary excellence, to intelligence and engagement, to the writer of brilliance and the career of importance, to the most enduring aesthetic and cultural values. For nonfiction the prizes awarded are in Biography, Current Interest, History, and Science & Technology.

National Book Award (http://www.nationalbook.org/nba.html)

The National Book Awards aim to enhance the public's awareness of exceptional books written by fellow Americans, and to increase the popularity of reading in general. They offer a generous number of awards; the three represented in this book are those in Autobiography, Contemporary Thought, and Nonfiction.

National Book Critics Circle Award (http://bookcritics.org/awards)

The National Book Critics Circle Award is given in six categories, originally nominated by committee members and by publishers, discussed by the committee members, and then voted on by the Board of Directors. The specific subjects found in this book are Autobiography, Biography, and General Nonfiction. However, the names themselves have gone through various changes, as the import of the memoir genre has grown. Thus the reader will see references in this book to awards in Biography/Autobiography, Autobiography, and Autobiography/Memoir.

National Jewish Book Awards (http://www.jewishbookcouncil.org/page.php?7)

The National Jewish Book Awards are designed to give recognition to outstanding books, to stimulate writers to further literary creativity and to encourage the reading of worthwhile titles that reflect the rich variety of the Jewish experience.

Notable Books for Adults. *See* American Library Association Awards

PEN American Center / Martha Albrand Awards

The PEN American Center / Martha Albrand Awards are no longer being conferred. Their purpose, based on a bequest by Martha Albrand, was to call attention to the first works of authors in the genres of literary nonfiction and memoir, works that were distinguished by literary and stylistic excellence.

PEN Center USA Literary Awards (http://www.penusa.org/awards)

The PEN Center USA Literary Awards recognize literary excellence in ten categories, including Creative Nonfiction, originally referred to as simply Nonfiction, with no distinction made between Creative and Research writing. They are regional prizes, awarded to writers who live west of the Mississippi River.

The Pulitzer Prize (http://www.pulitzer.org/)

Pulitzer Prizes are awarded for excellence in a distinguished and appropriately documented work in one of twenty-one categories, including Biography or Autobiography and General Nonfiction.

Stonewall Book Award-Israel Fishman Non-Fiction Award. *See* American Library Association Awards

The Thomas Cook Travel Book Award (http://www.thomascookpublishing.com/travelbookawards.htm)

The Thomas Cook Travel Book Award, no longer being offered, was established to encourage and reward the art of literary travel writing.

Whitbread Literary Awards (http://www.costabookawards.com/index.aspx)

The Whitbread Literary Awards, now the Costa Book Awards, are offered in five categories, including Biography; the jury members who select the titles look for books that are well-written, enjoyable books they would recommend to anyone to read.

Writers' Trust of Canada Awards (http://www.writerstrust.com/Awards.aspx)

The Writers' Trust of Canada Awards are given to writers at various stages of their writing careers.

- **Writers' Trust of Canada Drainie-Taylor Biography Prize.** *See* Writers' Trust of Canada Non-Fiction Prize
- **Writers' Trust of Canada Non-Fiction Prize** (http://www.writerstrust.com/Awards/Writers--Trust-Non-Fiction-Prize.aspx)

The Non-Fiction Prize, earlier called the Pearson Writers' Trust Non-Fiction Prize, recognizes Canadian writers of exceptional talent for the year's best work of literary nonfiction. An earlier award, the Writers' Trust of Canada Drainie-Taylor Biography Prize, has also been incorporated into the Non-Fiction Prize.

- **Writers' Trust of Canada Shaughnessy Cohen Prize for Political Writing** (http://www.writerstrust.com/Awards/Shaughnessy-Cohen-Prize-for-Political-Writing.aspx)

The Shaughnessy Cohen Prize for Political Writing is presented to an author of a nonfiction book that captures a subject of political interest to the

Canadian reader and enhances our understanding of the issue. The winning work will combine compelling new insights with depth of research and be of significant literary merit. Strong consideration will be given to books that have the potential to shape or influence Canadian political life.

Appendix D

Resources

The titles listed below are a sampling for readers who are interested in an in-depth study of the genre of memoir and autobiography. The list also includes titles for those who think they might like to try writing their own life stories. As we have seen throughout this book, and as readers will see in the following titles, memoirists do not need to be famous to write their own stories and to have them published.

Barrington, Judith. 2002. *Writing the Memoir: From Truth to Art*. Portland, OR: The Eighth Mountain Press.

Baxter, Charles, ed. 1999. *The Business of Memory: The Art of Remembering in an Age of Forgetting*. St. Paul, MN: Graywolf Press.

Birkerts, Sven. 2008. *The Art of Time in Memoir: Then, Again*. St. Paul, MN: Graywolf Press.

Buss, Helen M. 1994. *Mapping Our Selves: Canadian Women's Autobiography in English*. Montreal, QC: McGill-Queen's University Press.

Conway, Jill Ker. 1999. *When Memory Speaks: Reflections on Autobiography*. New York: Vintage Books.

Eakin, Paul John. 2004. *The Ethics of Life Writing*. Ithaca, NY: Cornell University Press.

Hampl, Patricia, and Elaine Tyler May, eds. 2008. *Tell Me True: Memoir, History, and Writing a Life*. St. Paul, MN: Borealis Books.

Kappel, Lawrence, ed. 2001. *Autobiography*. San Diego, CA: Greenhaven Press.

Larson, Thomas. 2007. *The Memoir and the Memoirist: Reading and Writing Personal Narrative*. Athens: Swallow Press/Ohio University Press.

Ledoux, Denis. 2006. *Turning Memories into Memoirs: A Handbook for Writing Lifestories*. Lisbon Falls, ME: Soleil Press.

McDonnell, Jane Taylor. 1998. *Living to Tell the Tale: A Guide to Writing Memoir*. New York: Penguin Books.

Olney, James. 1998. *Memory & Narrative: The Weave of Life-writing*. Chicago: University of Chicago Press.

Silverman, Sue William. 2009. *Fearless Confessions: A Writer's Guide to Memoir*. Athens: University of Georgia Press.

Zinsser, William Knowlton, ed. 1998. *Inventing the Truth: The Art and Craft of Memoir*. Boston: Houghton Mifflin.

Author/Title Index

Page numbers in boldface type indicate the location of the main entry for that author or title. Series titles are underscored. The designation (ed.) following a page number indicates that the person served as the editor of the book cited on that page rather than as the author.

Subject Index

Some of the personal names in this index refer to people discussed in the main entry titles. However, many refer to people written about in the read-alikes section of the entry, to provide access to more life stories.

About the Author

After thirty-five years as a public librarian specializing in reference and readers' advisory, Maureen O'Connor chose to retire early. She now spends her time freelancing, still focused on her interests in books and reading, editing, and writing. In addition she is the English-language chair of the Canadian Culinary Cookbook Awards, sponsored by Cuisine Canada and the University of Guelph. Maureen is also the coauthor of *Canadian Fiction: A Guide to Reading Interests* (Libraries Unlimited, 2005).